The Law
of
Obscenity

The Law
of
Obscenity

Frederick F. Schauer

Associate Professor
West Virginia University College of Law

The Bureau of National Affairs, Inc.
Washington, D.C.
1976

Library of Congress Cataloging in Publication Data

Schauer, Frederick F.
    The law of obscenity.

    Includes index.
    1. Obscenity (Law)—United States. I. Title.
KF9444.S3   345'.73'0274   76-20445
ISBN 0-87179-254-0

Printed in the United States of America

To
M A R J I
who has triumphed over the "jealous mistress."

Preface

While this is by no means the first book ever written on obscenity law, it is the first one designed primarily for lawyers. Most books in this area are primarily historical or sociological, and attempt to analyze obscenity laws and cases in the context of their historical or societal impact. While such books may be of some use to lawyers, lawyers are not their primary audience. In that respect, this book is something new. It is designed for judges, prosecuting attorneys, members of the private bar, legal scholars, legislators, and others whose interest is in obscenity conceived as a relatively discrete area of the law, with the same questions of statutory interpretation, case analysis, constitutional interpretation, and practical application as many other legal subjects. This book is a treatise on the law of obscenity, designed to meet the same kinds of needs as a treatise in any other legal area.

Many books and articles on obscenity law have primarily been arguments as to why there should or should not be obscenity laws in this country. Whatever may be the merits of such arguments, the taking of either position is not the purpose of this treatise. Here the existence of obscenity laws is treated as a given, and the book discusses and analyzes the application of this body of law. The complete elimination of obscenity laws seems as remote a possibility as the complete elimination of the law of contracts, or of torts, and little purpose would be served by still another book advocating it, or by one supporting their retention. A brief summary of some of the arguments that have been made on both sides is to be found in Chapter 3, since the issue is certain to recur, but the remainder of the volume is directed toward treatment of obscenity law as an established body of legal precedent and legal problems. Where the law is unclear, or the authorities are divided, I have tried to suggest appropriate methods of analysis or to make predictions as to the future directions of judicial thinking, but this is always in the context of relatively narrow legal problems. This book is not an appropriate vehicle for suggesting entirely new directions in obscenity law.

It should be clear that I believe obscenity law to be fundamentally no different from many other legal areas. There are cases to analyze, statutes to interpret, and constitutional provisions to apply. Many of these processes create special problems in obscenity law, but this need not cause us to ignore them. By dealing with such problems, I hope to provide assistance to those who must interpret our obscenity laws, as well as to those who make and enforce them, or whose legal practice involves them. Thus far, obscenity is a confused, vague, and difficult area of the law. If this book serves to eliminate some of the legal uncertainty generated by the obscenity laws, then I shall consider it a success.

The structure of the book reflects my view of obscenity law as a discrete body of law. The first three chapters provide some historical background, but the remainder of the book is organized by functional areas rather than by chronology. Chapters 4 through 8 deal with the main substantive concepts of obscenity law. Although many of these concepts have been changed or elaborated upon in recent cases, particularly in the Supreme Court's cases in 1973, many other concepts have much earlier roots, and many of these earlier principles still retain considerable vitality. Discussion of these areas functionally rather than chronologically is helpful, I believe, in showing where obscenity law stands today. In Chapters 9 and 10 I describe state and federal obscenity regulation, so that the substantive principles can be applied in the presently existing regulatory scheme.

Obscenity cases do not exist, nor are they tried, in a vacuum. They arise in particular procedural contexts. Chapters 11 through 17 describe the procedural considerations relevant to obscenity litigation and discuss those practical problems of litigation that are peculiar to obscenity cases. As with any other area of law, the substantive law governs the procedure to be applied and the litigation techniques applicable, and these chapters discuss those problems in obscenity litigation which are founded in the particular nature of obscenity law. They are oriented toward neither the prosecution nor the defense, but rather include the practical problems of which each should be aware.

As a student, practitioner, and teacher of obscenity law, I have been exposed to the full range of practical and theoretical problems, and this background is, I hope, reflected in the book. Where possible, I have made specific suggestions for dealing with the actual trial of an obscenity case. The appendix of forms should also be of some assistance in this regard.

Naturally, no treatise will be the *only* source used by an attorney who desires to do a complete job in dealing with a legal problem. The book is heavily referenced for easy access to relevant cases, law review articles, statutes, and other materials. As much as this book is an exposition of the law, it is also a reference tool. It would be a logical starting place for research in obscenity law, and for those who wish to go further, the method is available.

While the writing of this book is entirely my own work, and I take responsibility for any errors it may contain, it would not have been possible without the inspiration and assistance of many other people. I would like to express my appreciation to them here.

I owe my interest and any abilities in constitutional law, the legal area of which obscenity law is but a portion, to Professor Vincent Starzinger of Dartmouth College and Professor Archibald Cox of the Harvard Law School. Without their guidance, I would have been ill equipped to write this book.

I believe that ideas are refined through discussion with others, and the ideas in this book are no exception. I have profited immeasurably from discussions with my students at the West Virginia University College of Law, as well as my colleagues on the faculty, in particular Professors James McLaughlin, Thomas Hindes, and Robert Batey. Without their advice and challenge to my ideas, I would have been unable to refine my views in this area so as to be able to write this book. I must also thank Dean Willard Lorensen for the support and encouragement necessary to convert the idea for this treatise into reality, and Professor William Johnson for invaluable assistance in providing the scholarly resources necessary to produce a work of this type. In addition, Michael Pezzulli and James Withrow, my research assistants, have enabled me to complete the formidable research work which a book of this type requires, and Mrs. Debbie Trushel has very ably converted a large pile of often illegible writing into a clear and finished manuscript.

Much of the book is based upon the knowledge and experience I gained while a private practitioner in obscenity law before entering the field of teaching. Had it not been for the confidence placed in me and the training I was given by Phil David Fine, Robert Sylvia, and Robert Caporale, of the Boston law firm of Fine and Ambrogne, to whom I remain indebted, I would have lacked the background necessary to commence, much less to complete, this project.

It is one thing to write a book and quite another to convert it into a publication that its audience can effectively use. I appreciate the efforts of my editor, Frances Reed, in helping to bring the project to completion.

Finally, I must thank my parents, Mr. and Mrs. John Schauer, who taught me that average wasn't good enough, and my wife, Margery Schauer, who knows more than anyone what writing this book has meant, and whose support has been unwavering, even when I have not deserved it.

December 1975   FREDERICK F. SCHAUER

Contents

1

The Historical Origins of American Obscenity Law

1.1 The Religious Origins of Obscenity Regulation

The legal regulation of obscenity [1] as we now know it of course concerns those works that are thought to be offensive because of their portrayal of sexual matters, and this is the focus of this treatise. Like many other areas of law,[2] the origins of obscenity regulation are religious. In ancient times, sexual explicitness in the drama or in written works was fully tolerated, in large part because such forms of entertainment were limited only to the most elite classes of the population. The works of Aristophanes, Plautus, Terence, and Juvenal are perhaps the best examples. However, blasphemy and heresy were both strongly condemned. In Athens during the reign of Pericles, Anaxagoras was fined for impiety, and Protagoras, charged with blasphemy, fled and his books were burned. Euripides was also prosecuted for impiety, and

---

[1] A few words about terminology are appropriate at this point. "Obscene" refers to that which is repugnant or disgusting to the senses, or offensive, filthy, foul, repulsive, or loathsome. Except as used in the law, it does not necessarily have any sexual connotations. "Pornography," on the other hand, derived from the Greek words for harlot and writing, is limited to depictions of sexual lewdness or erotic behavior. Definitionally, obscenity may or may not be pornographic, and pornography may or may not be obscene. "Censorship" refers to any prohibition or suppression of words, pictures, publications, or ideas, whether on sexual, religious, or political grounds. *See* Webster's Third New International Dictionary (unabridged, 1969); Oxford English Dictionary (1933 ed.); D. Tribe, Questions of Censorship 17–21 (1973); *Miller v. California,* 413 U.S. 15 n. 2 (1973); *Roth v. United States,* 354 U.S. 476, 487 n. 20 (1957).

[2] For example, the law of domestic relations and the Sunday closing laws have religious origins but have now been accepted as secular law. *See McGowan v. Maryland,* 366 U.S. 420 (1961).

Socrates was put to death in large part for "worshiping strange gods."[3] In the *Republic,* Plato advocated the censorship of plays which tell untruths about the gods.

In ancient China, the Analects of Confucius were destroyed by the Emperor Chi Huang Ti on religious grounds. In Rome, as in Greece, there was virtually unlimited freedom in dealing with sexual matters, but there was censorship on religious grounds. Although Rome heard Tiberius say that "if the gods are insulted, let them see to it themselves," it also saw Ovid banished for writing *Ars Amatori,* and witnessed the frequent punishment of Jews and Christians for blasphemous and heretical utterances.[4] When Christianity came to Rome as the predominant religious belief, censorship on religious grounds became more prevalent. In 325 A.D. the Council of Nicaea declared a book by Arius to be heretical, and in 333 A.D. all of his books were ordered burned by Constantine. Religious censorship was taken over more and more by the church and continued to increase in the next thousand years, reaching a peak under Popes Innocent III, Gregory IX, and Innocent IV.[5] During this time, however, secular censorship remained nonexistent. Bawdy ballads were fully accepted in medieval times, even though in 1120 Peter Abelard's *Introdutio ad Theologium* was ordered burned by the Synod of Soissons.[6]

The true turning point came with the invention of the printing press by Gutenberg in 1428. Purely secular bawdiness was still tolerated, as when Caxton published Malory's *Morte d'Arthur* and Chaucer's *Canterbury Tales.* But since printing made it possible for all classes to have access to written works, the Church began to feel

---

[3] The main purpose of this treatise is, of course, to provide a description and analysis of modern obscenity law, and not a complete history of obscenity regulation. But some history is necessary here in order to set the background for the current law. Among the better histories, and the sources for much of this chapter, are the following: D. TRIBE, QUESTIONS OF CENSORSHIP (1973); A. GERBER, SEX, PORNOGRAPHY, AND JUSTICE (1965); A. CRAIG, SUPPRESSED BOOKS, A HISTORY OF THE CONCEPTION OF LITERARY OBSCENITY (1963); C. ROLPH, BOOKS IN THE DOCK (1969); T. MURPHY, CENSORSHIP, GOVERNMENT AND OBSCENITY (1963); R. FINDLATER, BANNED! A REVIEW OF THEATRICAL CENSORSHIP IN BRITAIN (1967); H. CLOR, OBSCENITY AND PUBLIC MORALITY: CENSORSHIP IN A LIBERAL SOCIETY (1969); T SCHROEDER, "OBSCENE" LITERATURE AND CONSTITUTIONAL LAW (1972); M. ERNST, THE FIRST FREEDOM (1946); N. ST. JOHN-STEVAS, OBSCENITY AND THE LAW (1956); M. ERNST AND A. SCHWARTZ, CENSORSHIP: THE SEARCH FOR THE OBSCENE (1964); J. PAUL AND M. SCHWARTZ, FEDERAL CENSORSHIP: OBSCENITY IN THE MAIL (1961); Alpert, *Judicial Censorship of Obscene Literature,* 52 HARV. L. REV. 40 (1938); *Censorship,* 5 ENCYCLOPEDIA BRITANNICA 161 (1970 ed.).

[4] *Censorship,* 5 ENCYCLOPEDIA BRITANNICA 161–162 (1970 ed).

[5] *Id.*

[6] D. TRIBE, QUESTIONS OF CENSORSHIP (1973).

the need for increased control over blasphemous and heretical books. Paul IV introduced the *Index Librorum Prohibitorum,* which had substantial legal force until the Reformation. The focus, however, was still religious rather than sexual. The *Decameron* of Boccaccio was on the list, and thus subject to prior restraint, but an edition in which sinning priests and nuns were converted into sinning laymen was allowed by the Council of Trent in 1573.[7] While the *Index* has survived to modern times, the decline of the church as a factor in secular law has decreased the legal effect of this religious censorship.[8] It was not until the 16th century in England that anything resembling modern obscenity regulation by the state began to appear.

1.2   The Development of Modern Obscenity Law

The development of obscenity law to its current state started in England in the early part of the 18th century, but the foundations were laid some 200 years earlier, during the reign of Henry VIII. Control over literature was delegated to the infamous Court of Star Chamber, which through licensing and other means exercised strict censorship over books and the theater. The focus still, however, was on religious and political heresy and sedition, and matters of sexual explicitness, bad taste, or foul language were of little importance. Censorship increased through the Elizabethan era, when a charter was given to the Stationers' Company. This company received a monopoly on all printing in exchange for searching out undesirable or illegal books. In addition, no book could be published unless it was first licensed by royal authority, by the Archbishops of Canterbury or York, or by other designated censors. There also was vigorous control over the theater, through the office of the Master of Revels, including the requirement that all plays be sent or exhibited in advance, along with payment of a fee. Prohibitions and required modifications were common, but the standards for censorship were based on political and religious factors. That which was merely bawdy, without offending the church or the state, was tolerated.[9]

---

[7] A. CRAIG, SUPPRESSED BOOKS 19 (1963); C. ROLPH, BOOKS IN THE DOCK 28–32 (1969).

[8] *Id.*

[9] THE REPORT OF THE COMMISSION ON OBSCENITY AND PORNOGRAPHY 349 (New York Times ed. 1970); R. FINDLATER, BANNED! A REVIEW OF THEATRICAL CENSORSHIP IN BRITAIN 10–35 (1967).

With the abolition of the Star Chamber in 1640, literary freedom increased, but only briefly. Licensing returned in 1643, and in 1662 the Licensing Act was passed. As with previous systems of literary regulation, this act was limited to works which would offend the church or the state, not those which might offend secular morality.[10] Immediately thereafter, in 1663, came what is generally thought to be the first pure obscenity case, *King* v. *Sedley*,[11] although its facts are clearly distinguishable from any form of control over literary obscenity. The facts in the case were that Sir Charles Sedley became drunk, and removed his clothes on the balcony of a tavern in London, gave a speech which included profanity, and poured bottles filled with urine upon the audience below, causing a riot. Sedley was fined and jailed for a week for breach of the peace. Although the situation is markedly different from any traditional obscenity case, its significance lies in the fact that this was the first time that offensiveness to decency, apart from religious or political heresy, was an element of an offense against the state.[12]

England in the latter part of the 17th century saw the beginnings of a public demand for control over "pure" obscenity, that is, works which were offensive without regard to their religious or political content. English theater and literature had become increasingly frank in dealing with sexual matters, in part as a reaction to many years of Puritanism, and many began to take notice. By 1696, the Lord Chamberlain instructed the censors to be "very careful in correcting all obscenities and other scandalous matters and such as any ways offend against ye laws of God and good manners or the known statutes of the kingdom." And a year later the Reverend Jeremy Collier, who was also a lecturer in constitutional law at Gray's Inn, published a treatise entitled *A Short View of the Profaneness and Immorality of the English Stage*.[13] The public at large took up his plea and several

---

[10] D. Tribe, Questions of Censorship 51–55 (1973).

[11] There are two different reports of the case, at 1 Keble 620 (K.B.), 83 Eng. Rep. 1146 (1663), and at 1 Sid. 168, 82 Eng. Rep. 1036 (1663). This and many of the other early cases are reprinted in E. De Grazia, Censorship Landmarks (1969). Factual descriptions of the backgrounds of these cases are contained in the sources cited in note 3 *supra*, as well as Reynolds, *Our Misplaced Reliance on Early Obscenity Cases*, 61 A.B.A.J. 220 (1975). The actual works at issue are reprinted in A. Gerber, Sex, Pornography, and Justice (1965). Some of the cases report the name of the defendant as Sidley rather than Sedley.

[12] *See* Alpert, *Judicial Censorship of Obscene Literature*, 52 Harv. L. Rev. 40 (1938).

[13] R. Findlater, Banned! A Review of Theatrical Censorship in Britain 33–34 (1967).

societies for the censorship of immorality were formed. Official censorship, at the instance of both the Lord Chamberlain and Queen Anne herself, was extended to include bad manners and immorality, and the move to separate obscenity regulation from its religious and political origins had begun.

The courts, however, were not so quick to follow the lead. In 1708 James Read was indicted for publishing a book called *The Fifteen Plagues of a Maidenhead,* a work which might draw some public indignation even today. The Queen's Bench court, however, dismissed the indictment, saying that "[a] crime that shakes religion, as profaneness on the stage, &c. is indictable; but writing an obscene book, as that intitled, *The Fifteen Plagues of a Maidenhead,* is not indictable, but punishable only in the Spiritual Court."[14] The indictment had been for obscene libel, marking the first emergence of this form of action, which was to be the procedural basis of English obscenity law for many years. In this case, however, Justice Powell rejected the concept that a libel could encompass obscenity per se.

> This is for printing bawdy stuff but reflects on no person, and a libel must be against some particular person or persons, or against the Government. It is stuff not fit to be mentioned publicly; if there should be no remedy in the Spiritual Court, it does not follow there must be a remedy here. There is no law to punish it, I wish there were, but we cannot make law; it indeed tends to the corruption of good manners, but that is not sufficient for us to punish.[15]

Although there were occasional obscenity convictions in the lower courts,[16] the *Read* case essentially put an end to obscenity prosecutions for 20 years. But in 1727 Edmund Curll, a London book publisher, was tried and convicted for publishing a book called *Venus in the Cloister, or the Nun in Her Smock.*[17] The book was a rather intemperate dialogue about lesbian love in a convent, and thus the conviction may be argued to have had religious overtones. But since the religious elements were primarily anti-Catholic, rather than against the Church of England, this aspect seems insignificant. In fact, Sir

---

[14] *Queen* v. *Read,* 11 Mod. Rep. 142, 88 Eng. Rep. 953 (1708).

[15] *Queen* v. *Read,* Fortescue's Reports 98, 92 Eng. Rep. 777 (1708). This is a different report of the same case.

[16] Reynolds, *Our Misplaced Reliance on Early Obscenity Cases,* 61 A.B.A.J. 220, 221 (1975).

[17] *Dominus Rex* v. *Curll,* 2 Str. 789, 93 Eng. Rep. 849 (1727). Edmund Curll was an interesting historical figure. A rather complete account of his escapades is contained in Chapter II of A. CRAIG, SUPPRESSED BOOKS (1963).

John Fortescue, one of the judges to sit on the case, thought the book acceptable because it exposed "the Romish priests, the father confessors and Popish religion."[18] Curll was also a constant source of political irritation, and his prosecution and conviction had obvious political motives. Still, the case is of great significance because it marks the emergence of obscene libel as a common-law crime. The Court was troubled by *Queen* v. *Read,* but finally rejected it as precedent, relying more heavily on certain aspects of *Sedley's Case.* The Attorney-General had argued that the corruption of morals was an offense at common law and a breach of the King's Peace.[19] The court accepted the argument, fined Curll, and established that obscenity was now an independent crime.

Obscenity prosecutions remained rare throughout the 18th century, despite the favorable precedent of *Curll's Case.* In 1763, John Wilkes was convicted for publication of *Essay on Woman,* which was easily as obscene as Curll's book, but Wilkes's offenses and his prosecution were primarily political.[20] Obscenity was still not a matter of great public concern, as is evidenced by the fact that John Cleland's *Memoirs of a Woman of Pleasure (Fanny Hill),* when it first appeared in England in 1748, was not prosecuted.[21]

By the beginning of the 19th century, however, the common-law crime of obscene libel had matured and was used against works which were purely sexual in content, without the necessity of political or religious implications. There were about three obscenity prosecutions a year in England in the first half of the 19th century. Byron's *Don Juan* was deemed obscene by the Vice-Chancellor in 1823, and Shelley's *Queen Mab* was found obscene by a jury in 1841.[22] In 1802, the Society for the Suppression of Vice was founded, an offshoot of the earlier Organization for the Reformation of Manners. The society actively campaigned against the proliferation of obscene publications and, over the course of 50 years from its creation, started 159 criminal obscenity prosecutions resulting in 154 convictions. The society was also active in the legislative area. Its efforts resulted in the Vagrancy Act of 1824, which provided for imprisonment for publication of any indecent picture, and in 1857 Lord Campbell's Act was passed, empowering magistrates to order the destruction of any obscene material,

---

[18] Reynolds, *supra* note 16, at 221.
[19] 2 Str. at 789, 93 Eng. Rep. at 850.
[20] *The King* v. *John Wilkes,* 2 Wils. K.B. 151, 95 Eng. Rep. 737 (1764), 4 Burr. 2527, 98 Eng. Rep. 327 (1770).
[21] Craig, *supra* note 17, at 33-34.
[22] *Id.* at 22; Gerber, *supra* note 11, at 79, 2 Townsend's Mod. St. Trials 356.

as well as issue warrants to search any premises suspected of containing obscene material. Also, the importation of obscene materials was prohibited by an 1853 statute primarily directed towards the influx into England of French postcards.[23]

While the period from 1800 to 1860 thus witnessed the development of a great deal of obscenity law, there remained no definition of what obscenity was. Works were prosecuted and convicted on the basis of whether or not they were immoral, with little if any concern for precise definition of terms or application of the statutes, or for what constituted the common-law crime of obscene libel. Obscenity was something that all people felt they could recognize instantly, and there seemed no need for elaborate judicial definitions.

In 1868 a definition finally emerged. Henry Scott was a metal broker in the town of Wolverhampton who, pursuant to his Anglican beliefs, had distributed an anti-Catholic pamphlet entitled *The Confessional Unmasked; Shewing the Depravity of the Romish Priesthood, the Iniquity of the Confessional, and the Questions Put to Females in Confession.* Pursuant to Lord Campbell's Act, the Wolverhampton magistrates ordered the destruction of 252 copies of the pamphlet on the grounds that it was obscene, since it was rather explicit in its recitation of events in the confessional. Scott appealed to Wolverhampton Quarter Sessions, where the recorder, Benjamin Hicklin, reversed the decision on the grounds that although the work was obscene, its publication was an innocent one, in that Scott only desired to promote the objectives of the Protestant Electoral Union. This decision was then appealed to the Queen's Bench. In *Regina* v. *Hicklin,*[24] as the case was then designated, the court discussed the question of intent and motive at great length, finally deciding that the intent was irrelevant as long as the work itself was obscene. Since obscenity per se had been decided in the earlier proceedings, this disposed of the case, but Lord Chief Justice Cockburn, in dicta, went on to provide a definition of obscenity. Obscenity could be decided on the basis of certain passages, not necessarily the entire work, and he said further that "the test of obscenity is this, whether the tendency of the matter charged as obscenity is to deprave and corrupt those whose minds are open to such immoral influences and into whose hands a publication of this sort may fall."[25] Thus, the test was based

---

[23] Craig, *supra* note 17, at 36–37; Tribe, *supra* note 10, at 60–65; OBSCENITY COMMISSION REPORT, supra note 9, at 351.
[24] [1868] L.R. 3 Q. B. 360.
[25] *Id.* at 371.

upon the effect of certain passages on particularly susceptible individuals, and not on the public as a whole.

The *Hicklin* definition survived in England for approximately 100 years,[26] and had a significant effect on the development of American obscenity law. By the time *Hicklin* was decided, however, there was already a body of obscenity law in the United States capable of being developed on its own, and the effect of English law on American obscenity law after *Hicklin* was insignificant. It is therefore appropriate at this time to leave this discussion of English precedents and go back in time to the roots of American regulation of obscenity.[27]

1.3   Obscenity Regulation in the United States—History

The early history of obscenity regulation in the American colonies tends to parallel its development in England. All of the colonies made blasphemy or heresy a crime, by statute,[28] but sexual materials not having an antireligious aspect were left generally untouched. As might be expected because of its Puritan heritage, Massachusetts was the earliest of the colonies to recognize that obscenity per se could be a criminal act. Blasphemy was punishable by death until 1697, and by boring through the tongue with a hot iron thereafter, and censorship of antireligious materials was in existence from 1662.[29] By the early part of the 18th century, however, the influx of "bawdy" materials had increased and the antiobscenity movement which had begun in England spread to Massachusetts. Therefore, in 1711 a statute was passed which, although it was primarily religious in effect, could also be applicable to secular materials. Its statement of purpose observed that "evil communication, wicked, profane, impure, filthy and obscene songs, composures, writings or print do corrupt

---

[26] *See Regina* v. *Martin Secker Warburg* [1954], 2 All Eng. 683 (CCC).

[27] For those readers wishing to study modern English obscenity law, the following works are suggested. Craig, *supra* note 17; Tribe, *supra* note 10; Findlater, *supra* note 13; St. John-Stevas, *supra* note 3; Rolph, *supra* note 3; N. HUNNINGS, FILM CENSORS AND THE LAW (1967). This last work is a rather interesting comparative law study including India, Canada, Australia, Denmark, France, and the Soviet Union, as well as Great Britain and the United States. A similar comparative study, although less detailed, is to be found in the OBSCENITY COMMISSION REPORT, *supra* note 9, at 394-410.

[28] The statutes are all cited in *Roth* v. *United States,* 354 U.S. 476, 483 n. 12 (1957).

[29] OBSCENITY COMMISSION REPORT, *supra* note 9, at 352.

the mind and are incentive to all manner of impurities and debaucheries, more especially when digested, composed or uttered in imitation, or in mimicking of preaching, or any other part of divine worship." As a result of this, the statute prohibited the "composing, writing, printing or publishing of any filthy, obscene or profane song, pamphlet, libel or mock-sermon, in imitation of preaching, or any other part of divine worship."[30] However, there are no recorded prosecutions under this statute until 1821. Although most of the colonies had profanity statutes, thees too were religious in purpose, leaving true obscenity largely unregulated and not a matter of great concern.[31]

Obscenity regulation in the United States began to develop slowly in the early 1800s. The first reported conviction is the Pennsylvania case of *Commonwealth* v. *Sharpless*,[32] decided in 1815. Jesse Sharpless had profanity statutes, these too were religious in purpose, leaving ing and showing for money "a certain lewd, wicked, scandalous, infamous and obscene painting, representing a man in an obscene, impudent, and indecent posture with a woman, to the manifest corruption and subversion of youth, and other citizens of this commonwealth, to the evil example of all others in like case offending, and against the peace and dignity of the commonwealth of Pennsylvania." He consented to a verdict in the Mayor's Court and moved to arrest the judgment on several grounds, the most significant of which, for this discussion, was that the "indictment did not charge a crime at the common law." The opinion in the Supreme Court of Pennsylvania discussed the various English authorities, including *Sedley's Case, Queen* v. *Read, King* v. *Curll,* and *King* v. *Wilkes,* and concluded that obscene libel was a crime at common law and therefore a crime in Pennsylvania. In addition, the defense contended that even if the crime existed, a public exhibition was necessary to support a conviction. The court dismissed this contention, equating the showing of a picture with the publication of a book, and holding that charging a price for seeing the picture was enough to make it a public act. "If the privacy of the room was a protection, all the youth of the city might be corrupted by taking them one by one into the chamber, and there inflaming their passions by the exhibition of lascivious pictures. In the eye of the law, this would be a publication, and a most pernicious one."[33]

---

[30] Province Laws, 1711-1712, ch. 6 § 19.
[31] Obscenity Commission Report, *supra* note 9, at 352.
[32] 2 Serg. & R. 91 (1815).
[33] *Id.* at 104.

The other significant common-law obscenity case in the United States is *Commonwealth* v. *Holmes*,[34] a case decided by the Supreme Judicial Court of Massachusetts in 1821. Peter Holmes had been indicted, tried, and convicted for publishing *Memoirs of a Woman of Pleasure*. The indictment also charged him with publishing a lewd and obscene print, which was contained in this edition of the book. The conviction was upheld by the Supreme Judicial Court, which essentially assumed that obscene libel was a common-law misdemeanor and devoted most of the opinion to a discussion of jurisdictional issues involving the particular court in which the indictment was brought.

By this time the effect of the church on secular life had decreased, literacy and public education had increased, and the influx of sexually oriented materials continued to grow. All of these factors led to sentiments in the state legislatures for more rigorous control over this kind of material. Vermont passed the first obscenity statute in 1821,[35] providing "that if any persons shall hereafter print, publish or vend any lewd or obscene book, picture or print, on conviction . . . [they] shall be sentenced to pay a fine not exceeding two hundred dollars." Connecticut enacted a similar statute in 1834,[36] and Massachusetts followed in 1835 with a statute significantly expanding on its 1711 colonial statute.[37] Paralleling a similar English concern,[38] the first federal law dealing with obscenity was enacted in 1842 to deal with the influx of French postcards and similar materials.[39] The statute prohibited the admission into the United States of "all indecent and obscene prints, paintings, lithographs, engravings and transparencies" and provided for their destruction by customs authorities.[40] Later amendments to the statute included first, indecent and obscene articles, and then photographs and other forms of printed materials.

The years prior to the Civil War witnessed a proliferation of obscenity and lewdness statutes, but there were still few prosecutions. Many of these cases evidenced further attempts to define the scope of the common law in this area. It was established that the common law prohibited "whatever outrages decency and is injurious to public

---

34 17 Mass. 336 (1821).
35 Laws of Vermont, 1824, ch. XXIII, no. 1, § 23.
36 Stats. of Conn. (1830) 182–184.
37 Mass. Rev. Stat. Ch. 310 § 10.
38 *See* text accompanying note 23 *supra*.
39 5 Stat. 566 § 28.
40 The current version of this statute is to be found at 19 U.S.C. § 1305 (1970).

morals,"[41] and the cases interpreted this to include indecent exposure,[42] the use of profane, obscene, and indecent language,[43] and, in a smaller number of cases, obscene publications.[44] In addition, some cases dealt with the application of the recently enacted obscenity and lewdness statutes to these forms of behavior.[45] Interestingly, the largest number of cases dealt with an issue that exemplifies the prevailing moral climate of the day, namely, the necessity of including the allegedly obscene words or publications within the indictment itself. While some courts held that it was necessary to do so in order that the defendant could fully defend the charge, the majority of opinions concluded that this was not necessary, since "courts will never allow its [sic] records to be polluted by bawdy and obscene matters."[46] It is hard to discover the kind of language that so offended the judiciary, since the appellate opinion rarely discussed the substance of the offensive words with any detail.

> Our respect for the chastity of the records of our court will not suffer the outrageously vulgar words that were spoken and sung by the defendant in this case, in the hearing of both males and females, to be put on the records. But we have never had to examine the records of our inferior tribunals to find words more shocking to one's sense of decency than those charged and proved in this case.[47]

[41] *State* v. *Rose*, 32 Mo. 560 (1862); *State* v. *Gardner*, 28 Mo. 90 (1859).

[42] *State* v. *Rose*, 32 Mo. 560 (1862); *State* v. *Hazle*, 20 Ark. 156 (1859); *Commonwealth* v. *Haynes*, 68 Mass. (2 Gray) 72 (1854); *State* v. *Roper*, 18 N.C. 208 (1835); *Miller* v. *People*, 5 Barb. 203 (N.Y. Sup. Ct. 1849). In *Britain* v. *State*, 22 Tenn. (3 Humph.) 203 (1842), it was held that an owner of slaves committed a crime by permitting a slave to be seen in public without clothes.

[43] *State* v. *Appling*, 25 Mo. 315 (1857); *McJunkins* v. *State*, 10 Ind. 140 (1858) (indecent and vulgar songs and language not included in lewdness statute); *Bell* v. *State*, 31 Tenn. (1 Swan.) 42 (1851); *Barker* v. *Commonwealth*, 19 Pa. 412 (1852).

[44] *Commonwealth* v. *Tarbox*, 55 Mass. (1 Cush.) 66 (1848) (advertisement of "instrument for the prevention of conception"); *People* v. *Girardin*, 1 Mich. (Mann.) 90 (1848) (obscene newspaper); *Willis* v. *Warren*, 1 Hilt. 590 (N.Y. Ct. of Comm. Pleas 1859) (public exhibition of obscene pictures is both a nuisance and an offense against common law).

[45] *McJunkins* v. *State*, *supra* note 43; *State* v. *Hazle*, *supra* note 42.

[46] *People* v. *Girardin*, 1 Mich. (Mann.) 90, 91 (1848). *See also Commonwealth* v. *Tarbox*, 55 Mass. (1 Cush.) 66 (1848); *Barker* v. *Commonwealth*, 19 Pa. 412 (1852); *State* v. *Brown*, 27 Vt. (1 Williams) 619 (1855). Perhaps the leading case on this issue is *Commonwealth* v. *Holmes*, 17 Mass. 336 (1821), holding that the indictment must contain the exact words unless the indictment alleged that the words were too indecent to be reproduced. This case was the basis for most of the later decisions on this issue.

[47] *State* v. *Appling*, 25 Mo. 315, 317 (1857).

Those cases that have a more detailed discussion indicate that most of the prosecutions were for the publication of words dealing with sexual intercourse, or venereal disease, or related subjects. And the words themselves need not have been of the type now considered profane, as long as the subject matter was of the type not appropriate for public discussion.[48]

Throughout the pre-Civil War period, obscenity was still a crime that aroused little public concern and relatively few prosecutions. The postwar period, however, irreversibly changed this lack of concern and the man behind this change was Anthony Comstock,[49] a man about whom it has been said that he "had more effect on English literature than any writer, publisher, or critic."[50] Comstock was born in New Canaan, Conn., and his strict New England Congregationalist upbringing had a great effect upon his adult activities. After service in the Civil War, he moved to New York and spent several years as a clerk in a dry goods store. During this time, he became increasingly alarmed about the shocking books and pictures he saw in the hands of the public and in the hands of his fellow employees. In 1872, he helped bring about the arrest of a seller of bawdy books, and his new career had begun. He had always felt that art, literature, magazines, and newspapers were bad influences on people, and upon the young in particular,[51] and there were many who shared his view. He worked originally through the New York Y.M.C.A., campaigning for stricter obscenity laws and more vigorous prosecution of offenders. In 1872, Comstock created a committee for the suppression of vice, as part of the Y.M.C.A., and in 1873 this committee became an independently chartered organization, the New York Society for the Suppression of Vice. Until 1915, when he died, Comstock was the executive secretary of this organization, and through it he exercised his singular influence. Its supporters included J. P. Morgan and many other prominent New

[48] *See, e.g., Commonwealth* v. *Tarbox, supra note* 44.

[49] Excellent discussions of the life and work of this man and the vice-society movement are contained in P. BOYER, PURITY IN PRINT: THE VICE-SOCIETY MOVEMENT AND BOOK CENSORSHIP IN AMERICA (1968); H. BROWN and M. LEECH, ANTHONY COMSTOCK, ROUNDSMAN OF THE LORD (1927); C. TRUMBULL, ANTHONY COMSTOCK, FIGHTER (1913); J. KILPATRICK, THE SMUT PEDDLERS 35–44 (1960).

[50] A. GERBER, SEX, PORNOGRAPHY, AND JUSTICE 90–91 (1965).

[51] *See* A. COMSTOCK, TRAPS FOR THE YOUNG (1883); A. COMSTOCK, FRAUDS EXPOSED; HOW THE PEOPLE ARE DECEIVED AND ROBBED, AND YOUTH CORRUPTED (1880). Among the objects of Comstock's scorn were light literature, pool halls, lotteries, gambling dens, popular magazines, and weekly newspapers. Artistic motive was irrelevant. "No embellishment of art can rob lust of its power for evil upon the human nature," he wrote. See Kilpatrick, *supra* note 49, at 36–37.

Yorkers of the day. Similar vice societies emerged at about the same time in many other parts of the country, perhaps the most famous of which was Boston's Watch and Ward Society, an organization composed of members of most of Boston's finest families. Its activities gave rise to the catchphrase popular in the 1920s, "banned in Boston."[52]

The activities of Anthony Comstock and the New York Society for the Suppression of Vice centered around the strengthening of antiobscenity legislation and the initiation of prosecutions. Through the activities of Comstock and the various vice societies throughout the country, prosecutions increased greatly, and the relatively dormant case law of obscenity became a major area of judicial concern. Perhaps of greatest importance, however, was Comstock's almost singlehanded effort to secure stronger federal obscenity legislation. He went to Washington on February 6, 1873, to secure new federal legislation, and immediately attracted major support. Justice Strong of the United States Supreme Court assisted him and drafted a bill for Comstock to propose. Comstock also had significant help in both the executive and legislative branches, and on March 3, 1873, a new law prohibiting the mailing of obscene publications was enacted.[53] This law, which survives today in modified form,[54] was passed with less than an hour of Congressional debate, and there was no objection to its enactment in either the House or the Senate. Reflecting its origin, the law is still known as the Comstock Act.

Comstock saw to it that the new laws would be vigorously enforced. He was appointed a special agent of the Post Office Department to enforce the law, and a portion of the fines collected as a result of successful prosecutions went either to himself or to the New York Society for the Suppression of Vice. In the first year after the law's passage, Comstock claimed to have seized 200,000 pictures and photographs; 100,000 books; 5,000 packs of playing cards; and numerous contraceptive devices and allegedly aphrodisiac medicines. Forty years later, he noted that he had "convicted persons enough to fill a passenger train of sixty-one coaches, sixty coaches containing sixty passengers each and the sixty-first almost full. I have destroyed 160 tons of obscene literature."[55] From this description of Comstock's activities, one can see the extent of obscenity enforcement in the latter

[52] See Boyer, *supra* note 49, at 167–206.
[53] The first statute relating to the mailing of obscenity was passed by Congress in 1865. 13 Stat. 509. The 1873 amendment is found at 17 Stat. 598.
[54] 18 U.S.C. § 1461 (1970).
[55] Kilpatrick, *supra* note 49, at 35.

part of the 19th century. And the case law developed in this period was to be the basis for state and federal obscenity law until 1957.

The cases that arose following the Comstock Act were concerned primarily with the scope of the prohibition and various procedural issues, and the constitutional arguments that mark most modern obscenity cases were for the most part absent. Those cases that did deal with constitutional issues were concerned not so much with the First Amendment aspects of the statute as with the general powers of Congress to legislate in this area. The first of these was *United States v. Bott,*[56] decided by the Circuit Court for the Southern District of New York. Bott was charged with mailing a powder for the prevention of conception or the procuring of an abortion, both of which were prohibited, along with obscene publications, in the statute.[57] In defense, he claimed he had no intent to cause contraception or abortion, but the court held that this specific type of intent was unnecessary under the statute. In addition, the court ruled that Congress had the power to regulate the mails, and that therefore the statute was constitutional. There was no discussion of the obscenity aspects of the statute.

Four years later, a similar issue reached the Supreme Court. In *Ex parte Jackson,*[58] the issue was the power of Congress to exclude from the mails materials relating to lotteries.[59] Since this was also included in the Comstock Act, the Court dealt in general terms with the power of Congress to keep harmful matter, including obscenity, from the mails. Justice Field dealt first with the issue of the privacy of the mails. Although newspapers, magazines, and similar mailings might properly be examined by postal authorities, first class mail, whether letters or packages, was completely immune from examination.[60] This did not mean, however, that Congress might not prohibit the mailing, by first class mail or otherwise, of harmful materials. But enforcement, for first class mail, would have to be by way of criminal prosecution rather than by inspection and seizure of the mail itself.[61] Justice Field said that there was "no doubt" that the act was constitutional, and that it did not interfere with freedom of the press, but there was no extended discussion of this issue. Freedom of the press

---

[56] 24 F. Cas. 1204 (No. 14,626) (C.C.S.D.N.Y. 1873).

[57] These prohibitions have only recently been removed from the coverage of the statute. *See* Chapter 9 *infra.*

[58] 96 U.S. 727 (1877).

[59] This was in fact the main purpose of the 1865 statute, cited in note 53 *supra.*

[60] 96 U.S. at 733. This principle remains to the present day.

[61] *Id.*

was related to political commentary and criticism, and since prohibition of material relating to lotteries and obscenity did not come within the definition of "press," there was no constitutional problem.[62] Again, the constitutional aspects of the case appear more related to congressional powers and less to fundamental First Amendment issues.

With the constitutionality of the act thus established, cases began to involve issues relating to its scope and the definition of obscenity. Perhaps the most significant was *United States* v. *Bennett,*[63] a federal court of appeals decision arising out of the Southern District of New York, in which the opinion was written by Judge Blatchford. The defendant was charged with having mailed a copy of a book entitled *Cupid's Yokes, or the Binding Forces of Conjugal Life.* Only certain parts of the book had been read to the jury, and the defense objected to this "selective" prosecution. The court of appeals, however, approved the concept that it was unnecessary to present the entire work to the jury, relying substantially on *Regina* v. *Hicklin.*[64] Although the *Hicklin* case dealt mainly with the test for determination of obscenity, and only peripherally with the issue of whether all or part of a work should be the basis for such a finding, it is in fact the latter aspect of the case that has been most significant in American obscenity law.[65] In addition to adopting *Hicklin* for the proposition that selected parts of a book can be the foundation for a determination of obscenity, the *Bennett* case also approved a charge to the jury, based on *Hicklin,* that a work is obscene if it would tend to "deprave and corrupt" those who would in fact have access to it.[66] *Bennett* is merely one example showing the source of the standards used during this time, for in fact virtually every obscenity case of the time adopted the *Hicklin* definition of obscenity.[67]

One of the significant aspects of the *Hicklin* test, as adopted in the American cases, is that the obscenity *vel non* of a book, pamphlet, magazine, or picture was to be evaluated not in terms of its effect on the hypothetical "average man," but by its effect on anyone who

---

[62] *Id.* at 737. *See also In re Rapier,* 143 U.S. 110 (1892); *Hoke* v. *United States,* 227 U.S. 308, 321 (1913); *Caminetti* v. *United States,* 242 U.S. 470 (1917); *Brooks* v. *United States,* 267 U.S. 432, 437 (1925).

[63] 24 F. Cas. 1093 (No. 14, 571) (C.C.S.D.N.Y. 1879).

[64] [1868] L.R. 3 Q. B. 360. *See* text accompanying notes 24–26 *supra.*

[65] *See also United States* v. *Clarke,* 38 F. 732, 736 (E. D. Mo. 1889), and text accompanying notes 119, 135–137, and 147–150, *infra.*

[66] 24 F. Cas. at 1103.

[67] *See, e.g., United States* v. *Clarke,* 38 F. 500, 502 (E.D. Mo. 1889); *Commonwealth* v. *Havens,* 6 Pa. County Ct. Rep. 545 (1888); *United States* v. *Bebout,* 28 F. 522 (N.D. Ohio 1886).

might in fact conceivably read it.[68] The main effect of this distinction was to permit the evaluation of obscenity to be made in terms of a work's supposed effect on children, the mentally weak or immature, or, as it was later described, "a particularly susceptible" subclass of the community.[69] This issue often arose in the context of books or pamphlets of a "medical" nature that were made available to children or to the general public. For example, in *United States* v. *Chesman*,[70] the defendant was charged with mailing an obscene pamphlet containing extracts from certain medical books concerning impotency and related subjects. The court held that the fact that the statements may have had medical origins, or be medically correct, was irrelevant because the pamphlet was designed to be distributed to the general public and must therefore be evaluated in light of its effect on those members of the public who would be immorally influenced by a publication of this sort. Similarly, in the *Bennett* case, Judge Blatchford said that a publication is included within the scope of the obscenity statute if it would incite immoral thoughts and desires "in the young and inexperienced,"[71] and this evaluation of obscenity in terms of its potential effect on a minority of the community was followed in many other cases of the period.[72]

We have seen that *Hicklin* was adopted by most American courts in that it allowed only parts of a publication to be the basis for a finding of obscenity, and in terms of the "audience" by which that obscenity is to be evaluated. The third major aspect of *Hicklin* which found its way into American jurisprudence was related to the concept of intent. In *Hicklin*, the defendant contended that the pamphlet he was charged with publishing was not obscene because the author intended to educate, politically and religiously, rather than suggest impure thoughts. But Justice Cockburn's opinion indicates that the finder of fact is to look to the tendency of the words themselves, and not to the intent of the writer.[73] The intent issue was frequently liti-

[68] The expression used in *Hicklin* was "into whose hands a publication of this sort may fall."

[69] *Roth* v. *United States,* 354 U.S. 476, 489 (1957).

[70] 19 F. 497 (C.C.E.D. Mo. 1881).

[71] 24 F. Cas. at 1104–1105.

[72] *See, e.g., United States* v. *Britton,* 17 F. 731 (S.D. Ohio 1883); *In re Banks,* 56 Kan. 242, 42 P. 693 (1895).

[73] Justice Cockburn stated: "The question then presents itself in this simple form: May you commit an offense against the law in order that thereby you may effect some ulterior object which you have in view, which may be an honest and even laudable one? My answer is emphatically, no." This statement, of course, assumes that the work is obscene and thus does not answer the real question: Is intent relevant in determining whether, a priori, the work *is* obscene?

gated in cases arising in the latter half of the 19th century. Although some courts refused to follow this aspect of *Hicklin* and therefore looked to the author's purpose, the majority of decisions held that the intent of the author was irrelevant and that it is the effect or import of the words themselves that is determinative on the issue of obscenity.[74]

There were at this time many questions relating to the scope of the Comstock Act and to the scope of the definition of legal obscenity. The 1873 version of the act did not include letters, and thus there was a question whether or not obscene letters were included in the phrase "writings" found in the statute.[75] In 1895, however, the Supreme Court, in *United States* v. *Chase*,[76] held that letters were not included.[77] As a result of this ambiguity, however, the statute had been amended to include obscene letters, which presumably had been the intent of Congress all along.[78] In 1896, in *Andrews* v. *United States*,[79] the Supreme Court finally stated that obscene letters were clearly forbidden by the amended statute.[80]

Of more significance were those cases analyzing just what kinds of words, writings, or pictures were in fact encompassed by the definition of obscenity. Although obscenity law had been around for several hundred years, the number of cases had been so small that there was no reasoned discussion of just what was or was not obscene. It is perhaps natural that when there is a large amount of legal activity

[74] *United States* v. *Bennett*, 24 F. Cas. 1093, 1104-1105 (No. 14,571) (C.C.S.D.N.Y. 1879); *United States* v. *Bott*, 24 F. Cas. 1204 (No. 14,626) (C.C.S.D.N.Y. 1873); *United States* v. *Clarke*, 38 F. 500, 502 (E.D. Mo. 1889); *United States* v. *Britton*, 17 F. 731 (S.D. Ohio 1883).

[75] The statute enumerated certain types of prohibited forms of publication of obscenity, such as books, papers, pictures, and prints.

The lower courts were divided as to whether letters were included. Those decisions holding that letters were included are exemplified by *United States* v. *Gaylord*, 17 F. 438 (C.C. Ill. 1883); *United States* v. *Hanover*, 17 F. 444 (S.D. Ohio 1883); *United States* v. *Britton*, 17 F. 731 (S.D. Ohio 1883). Among those excluding letters from coverage were *United States* v. *Comerford*, 25 F. 902 (W.D. Tex. 1885) and *United States* v. *Mathias*, 36 F. 892 (C.C.S.C. 1888).

[76] 135 U.S. 255 (1890).

[77] The lower court case is *United States* v. *Chase*, 27 F. 807 (C.C. Mass. 1886).

[78] The speed with which the statute was enacted, and the source of its draftmanship and introduction, certainly support the inference that the statute was intended to be as broad as possible.

[79] 162 U.S. 420 (1896).

[80] The Court's decision was made necessary by several lower court decisions that still had difficulty with the word "letter." *United States* v. *Warner*, 59 F. 355 (N.D. Wash. 1894); *United States* v. *Wilson*, 58 F. 768 (N.D. Cal. 1893). The outsides of envelopes and postcards had always been covered by an 1872 statute. 17 Stat. 302 § 148.

in an area with so little theoretical background, there will be a period during which there are widely divergent views as to what the very purpose of the law is. This phenomenon seems to have existed in obscenity law in the late 1800s. Did obscenity include blasphemy, or coarse libel, or vulgar language, or insulting words? All of these were issues during this period. In 1882, a shopkeeper sent a postcard to a customer which read as follows: "Dear Sir, you are a damned scoundrel and a rascal. Respectfully, F. A. Smith." The shopkeeper was charged with mailing obscene matter, but the indictment was dismissed by a Kentucky federal judge as not being within the scope of the obscenity laws.[81] Ten years later, a federal court in Indiana concluded that a valentine was not obscene despite the fact that its inscription read "You can keep this to wipe your dirty arse on."[82] Similar cases excluded from the definition of obscenity such epithets as "deadbeat,"[83] "lying son of a bitch,"[84] and other coarse statements.[85]

In like fashion, most courts held that blasphemy was not within the ambit of the obscenity laws. In *United States* v. *Moore*,[86] an indictment for mailing an antireligious pamphlet ridiculing the Virgin Mary was dismissed because, although coarse and vulgar, the pamphlet was not openly lewd or lascivious. Several other cases also refused to expand the concept of obscenity to include the crudely antireligious, despite the fact that publications of this sort actually constituted the matter of most of the early English obscenity cases.[87] As befits an era of legal development, the cases were by no means entirely consistent. A federal court in Tennessee convicted a man for mailing a postcard in which he referred to someone as a radical,[88] and that same court was the forum for a conviction for sending a postcard to a newspaper which read: "You can take your paper and Democracy and go to hell with it."[89] Letters which suggested sexual relations were found obscene in some courts and not obscene in others, often depending upon how explicit the letters were.[90]

---

[81] *United States* v. *Smith*, 11 F. 663 (C.C. Ky. 1882).

[82] *United States* v. *Males*, 51 F. 41 (D. Ind. 1892).

[83] *Ex parte Doran*, 32 F. 76 (D. Minn. 1887).

[84] *United States* v. *Durant*, 46 F. 753 (E.D.S.C. 1891).

[85] *See, e.g., Shields* v. *State*, 89 Ga. 549, 16 S.E. 66 (1892); *United States* v. *Wightman.* 29 F. 636 (D. Pa. 1886); *Roberts* v. *State*, 120 Ga. 177, 47 S.E. 511 (1904).

[86] 104 F. 78 (D. Ky. 1900).

[87] *See* text accompanying notes 14–26 *supra*.

[88] *United States* v. *Davis*, 38 F. 326 (W.D. Tenn. 1889).

[89] *United States* v. *Olney*, 38 F. 328 (W.D. Tenn. 1889).

[90] Compare *Kinaird* v. *Commonwealth*, 134 Ky. 575, 121 S.W. 489 (1909) and *United States* v. *Lamkin*, 73 F. 459 (C.C.E.D. Va. 1896), with *United States* v.

This muddied area finally reached the Supreme Court in the mid-1890s. In *Grimm* v. *United States*,[91] the Court held that the Comstock Act included letters advertising objectionable matter, even if the letters themselves might not meet the prevailing test for obscenity. And in *Swearingen* v. *United States*[92] a year later, the Court dealt with a newspaper article which was characterized as coarse, vulgar, and libelous. This, however, was not enough to have it deemed obscene. "[B]ut we cannot perceive in it anything of a lewd, lascivious, and obscene tendency, calculated to corrupt and debauch the mind and morals of those into whose hands it might fall."[93] Thus it became clear that obscenity included only matters of a sexual nature, but if the materials were of such a nature, it then became a question for the jury whether the materials were in fact obscene.[94]

Throughout this period, only one case squarely faced the possible conflict between obscenity laws and First Amendment principles. In *United States* v. *Harmon*,[95] the Comstock Act was directly attacked on First Amendment grounds. Although a Kansas district court discussed the issue at some length, it never reached the full depth of constitutional analysis found in more modern cases. The court merely concluded that it was of course obvious that the First Amendment does not protect that which "outrages the common sense of decency, or endangers the public safety,"[96] and the statute was left intact.

Concurrent with these substantive developments, many procedural issues began to arise in obscenity law. As in many of the earlier cases,[97] a major issue was whether or not the exact and full language alleged to be obscene must be included in the indictment. Many cases discussed this in considerable detail, analyzing all of the earlier precedents, and most followed the rule of *Commonwealth* v. *Holmes*,[98]

Martin, 50 F. 918 (W.D. Va. 1892) and *United States* v. *Moore,* 129 F. 159 (W.D. Mo. 1904).

[91] 156 U.S. 604 (1895).

[92] 161 U.S. 446 (1896). *See also United States* v. *Wightman,* 29 F. 636 (W.D. Pa. 1886).

[93] *Id.* at 451.

[94] *United States* v. *Clarke,* 38 F. 500, 501 (E.D. Mo. 1889) (the actual instructions given in this case are reported at 38 F. 733); *Rosen* v. *United States,* 161 U.S. 29, 42 (1896).

[95] 45 F. 414 (D. Kan. 1891), *rev'd on other grounds,* 50 F. 921 (1892).

[96] *Id.* at 416.

[97] *See* cases cited in notes 46 and 47 *supra.*

[98] 17 Mass. 336 (1821).

a Massachusetts case holding that the indictment did not have to include the obscene language if it alleged specifically that the words were too indecent to be included.[99] Finally the Supreme Court, in *Rosen* v. *United States*,[100] also adopted this rule, and the issue has rarely been litigated since. This is partially because of the *Rosen* precedent, but perhaps more because of relaxed modern requirements in criminal pleading that require far less specificity than was customary in the 19th century.[101]

The *Rosen*[102] case may be of even more current significance for its discussion of the defendant's knowledge. Lew Rosen was the publisher of a magazine known as *Broadway*, of which one particular issue, known as the "Tenderloin Number," contained a number of rather suggestive pictures of nude females. The pictures were covered with lamp black but it was intended that this could easily be removed by the reader. Rosen was convicted at trial of mailing obscene materials, and sentenced to 13 months at hard labor. On appeal to the U. S. Supreme Court, he argued that he did not know the contents of the publication were legally obscene, and was therefore lacking in any criminal intent. Justice Harlan, writing for a 7-2 majority, held that although a defendant in an obscenity case could not be convicted unless he knew what the contents of the package were, this did not require specific knowledge that the materials were in fact legally obscene. All that was necessary was a showing that the defendant knew the "character" of the materials involved.[103] At trial, the jury had been instructed to determine obscenity on the basis of whether or not the material "would suggest or convey lewd and lascivious thoughts to the young and inexperienced," yet another modification of the basic *Hicklin* test. In affirming this test, Justice Harlan observed that "in view of the character of the paper, the test prescribed was quite as liberal as the defendant had any right to demand."[104] The court

---

[99] *See, e.g., United States* v. *Bennett,* 24 F. Cas. 1093 (No. 14, 571) (C.C.S.D.N.Y. 1879); *Bates* v. *United States,* 10 F. 92 (C.C.N.D. Ill. 1881); *United States* v. *Foote,* 25 F. Cas. 1140 (No. 15, 128) (C.C.S.D.N.Y. 1876); *United States* v. *Kaltmeyer,* 16 F. 760 (C.C.E.D. Mo 1883).

[100] 161 U.S. 29 (1896).

[101] *See Flying Eagle Publications, Inc.* v. *United States,* 273 F.2d 799 (1st Cir. 1960); *United States* v. *Rebhuhn,* 109 F.2d 512 (2d Cir. 1940), *cert. denied,* 310 U.S. 629; *United States* v. *Wells,* 262 F. 833 (D. Wash. 1917); *Coomer* v. *United States,* 213 F. 1 (8th Cir. 1914); *Rinker* v. *United States,* 151 F. 755 (8th Cir. 1907).

[102] *Rosen* v. *United States,* 161 U.S. 29 (1896).

[103] *Id.* at 41. This case is still of significant importance on this issue. See chapter 11 *infra*.

[104] *Id.* at 43.

thereby approved the view that obscenity was a question of fact, for determination by the jury, affirming the position that had consistently been taken by lower courts when called upon to decide whether obscenity was a question for the jury or for the court.[105]

Finally, a number of cases dealt with an issue that would now be referred to as entrapment. The standard method of enforcement of the Comstock Act was for postal officials, acting as "decoys," to send requests for materials to suspected mailers of obscene matter. When the matter was received, a prosecution based on that mailing was commenced. A number of defendants challenged this practice, although the law of entrapment was yet to be fully developed. The main contention was that since the transaction was to a federal official, albeit unknown, and not to a private individual, no crime had been committed. But a long line of cases,[106] culminating in two Supreme Court cases in 1895 and 1896,[107] approved the use of such decoy letters as an acceptable, and perhaps the only, method of enforcement of the statute.

By the beginning of the 20th century the Comstock Act had been amended to include letters that were "filthy" as well as those that were obscene,[108] and a new statute prohibited the transportation of obscene matter in interstate commerce by common carrier.[109] This statute, when coupled with the already existing statutes prohibiting the mailing or importation of obscene materials, thus rendered complete the exercise of federal power in the obscenity area.[110]

The emphasis on federal cases under the Comstock Act in the foregoing discussion should not be taken to mean that state obscenity enforcement was at a standstill. Most states were expanding their obscenity statutes, and many of the substantive and procedural issues arising in federal cases were simultaneously being litigated in state courts. Just as in the federal cases there was little attention to what was or was not obscene as long as the material dealt with sexual matters, so also in state cases almost anything that concerned sexual rela-

---

[105] *See* note 94 *supra. See also Dunlap* v. *United States,* 165 U.S. 486 (1897).

[106] *See, e.g., Bates* v. *United States,* 10 F. 92 (C.C.N.D. Ill. 1881). (Most of the cases up to this time are collected in the editor's notes, 10 F. at 97–100).

[107] *Grimm* v. *United States,* 156 U.S. 604 (1895); *Andrews* v. *United States,* 162 U.S. 420 (1896); *see also Goode* v. *United States,* 159 U.S. 663 (1895).

[108] *See United States* v. *Limehouse,* 285 U.S. 424 (1932); *United States* v. *Davidson,* 244 F. 523 (N.D.N.Y. 1917).

[109] 29 Stat. 512 (1897). The current version is 18 U.S.C. § 1462 (Supp. 1975).

[110] It must be remembered that the scope of Congressional power over interstate commerce was thought to be more limited before 1900 than it is now. *See Champion* v. *Ames,* 188 U.S. 321 (1903) (also called the "Lottery Case").

tionships in any way was presumed to be obscene. Many states by now had statutes prohibiting the selling, publication, or distribution of obscene, immoral, or indecent newspapers and magazines, and a large number of prosecutions dealt with "scandal sheet" publications such as *The National Police Gazette, The Illustrated Police News*,[111] and similar publications. In none of these cases was there any consideration of whether such publications were in fact legally obscene or whether their prohibition involved constitutional problems.

In an 1895 Kansas case, the publisher of the Kansas City *Sunday Sun* was prosecuted for publishing a newspaper "devoted largely to the publication of scandals, lechery, assignations, intrigues between men and women, and immoral conduct of persons."[112] The court found that publications of this sort corrupt the morals of the young and lead them to "vicious paths and immoral acts," and therefore the suppression of such publications did not in any way violate the freedom of the press.

Perhaps the most interesting example is the Massachusetts case of *Commonwealth* v. *Dejardin*.[113] The statute made illegal the importation, printing, publishing, selling, or distribution of obscene, indecent, or impure ballads, papers, pictures, or figures, or publications with obscene, indecent, or impure language in them. The indictment charged the defendant with selling pictures of "naked girls." In fact, the pictures showed the women as being unclothed only above the waist. Since they were not entirely naked, the proof did not conform to the indictment and the conviction was reversed. The court observed that the pictures might very well be obscene and illegal, but the inaccuracy in the indictment prevented a conviction.[114]

As with the federal cases, many state obscenity cases centered on procedural issues. Most of the cases held that determination of the issue of obscenity was for the jury,[115] which led to the exclusion of any expert testimony. "The character of the book was a question purely for the jury, in which they could not be aided by the testimony of experts. Obscenity is determined by the common sense and feelings of mankind, and not by the skill of the learned."[116] Similarly, the fact

---

[111] *See, e.g., Commonwealth* v. *Havens*, 6 Pa. Co. Ct. Rep. 545 (1888); *People* v. *Danahy*, 63 Hun. 579, 18 N.Y.S. 467 (Sup. Ct. 1892).

[112] *In re Banks*, 56 Kan. 242, 42 P. 693 (1895).

[113] 126 Mass. 46 (1878).

[114] *Id.* at 48.

[115] *People* v. *Muller*, 32 Hun. 209, 96 N.Y. 408 (1884); *cf. Carter* v. *State*, 107 Ala. 146, 18 So. 232 (1894); *Collins* v. *State*, 78 Ga. 87 (1886); *contra, Smith* v. *State*, 24 Tex App. 1, 5 S.W. 510 (1887).

[116] *Commonwealth* v. *Landis*, 8 Phila. 453 (1870).

that the picture involved in a case may have been exhibited in a respectable art gallery,[117] or that similar materials were accepted and available in the community,[118] was likewise irrelevant. The cases tended to adopt the *Hicklin* test for obscenity,[119] and therefore selected excerpts could be the foundation for a finding of obscenity. There were still many cases dealing with the necessity of having the exact words or publications in the indictment, and most of these held that this was unnecessary.[120] The intent of the defendant was not an element of obscenity[121], and, in a case that preceded *Rosen* by seven years, it was held that specific knowledge of obscenity on the part of the defendant was not an element of the offense.[122] Thus, the state cases tended to parallel the federal decisions, both as to the issues raised and as to the courts' resolution of those issues.

One of the most frequent criticisms of literary censorship is that works of substantial literary merit may be suppressed by overzealous censors. However, most of the objects of obscenity prosecutions prior to 1900 were books, magazines, newspapers, and pictures, which although probably not legally obscene today, were of little literary value. Those who were prosecuted in the 19th century were for the most part the commercial pornographers of the day, and few works of established literary value wound up in court.[123] The first half of the

---

[117] *People* v. *Muller*, 32 Hun. 209, 96 N.Y. 408 (1884).

[118] *State* v. *Ulsemer*, 24 Wash. 657, 64 P. 800 (1901); *Montross* v. *State*, 72 Ga. 261 (1884).

[119] *Commonwealth* v. *Havens*, *supra* note 111; *In re Banks*, 56 Kan. 242, 42 P. 693 (1895); *People* v. *Muller*, *supra* note 115.

[120] *McNair* v. *People*, 80 Ill. 441 (1878); *Fuller* v. *People*, 92 Ill. 182 (1879); *Commonwealth* v. *Wright*, 139 Mass. 382, 1 N.E. 411 (1885); *State* v. *Smith*, 17 R.I. 371, 22 A. 282 (1891); *State* v. *Van Wye*, 136 Mo. 227, 37 S.W. 938 (1896); *People* v. *Kaufman*, 14 App. Div. 305, 43 N.Y.S. 1046 (1897). *Contra*, *Reyes* v. *State*, 34 Fla. 181, 15 So. 875 (1894); *State* v. *Hayward*, 83 Mo. 299 (1884).

[121] *People* v. *Muller*, 32 Hun. 209, 96 N.Y. 408 (1884); *Commonwealth* v. *Havens*, 6 Pa. Co. Ct. Rep. 545 (1888). But *cf. Commonwealth* v. *Landis*, 8 Phila. 453 (1870).

[122] *Commonwealth* v. *Havens*, 6 Pa. Co. Ct. Rep. at 548.

[123] A rather interesting exception is *In re Worthington Co.*, 30 N.Y.S. 361 (Sup. Ct. 1894). The company had become insolvent, and a receiver was appointed to sell its assets. Among those assets were books, including *The Arabian Nights*, *Tom Jones*, Ovid's *Art of Love*, Boccaccio's *Decameron*, the works of Rabelais, *The Heptameron* by Queen Margaret of Navarre, and Rousseau's *Confessions*. When the receiver petitioned for instructions as to the sale, Anthony Comstock appeared in opposition on the grounds that the court should not sanction the sale of "immoral literature." Comparing this literature to that of Shakespeare and Chaucer, the court refused to condemn such "standard literary works." "A seeker after the sensual and degrading parts of narrative may find in all these works, as in those of other great authors, something to satisfy his pruriency. But to condemn a standard

20th century, however, is marked by heated litigation over books which are now generally regarded as classics.

Perhaps the most famous of these cases was *United States* v. *One Book Called "Ulysses,"*[124] a case in the Southern District of New York involving the issue of whether or not *Ulysses,* by James Joyce, could be imported into the United States.[125] Judge Woolsey, sitting without a jury by agreement of the parties, observed that the first inquiry must be whether or not there was "pornographic intent"—the purpose of exploiting obscenity—on behalf of the author. If this existed, then forfeiture was required. If this intent did not exist, then the court must look further to the actual effect of the book upon the average member of the community. If it would tend "to stir the sex impulses or to lead to sexually impure and lustful thoughts," then the book would be obscene. Upon reading and studying the book, however, the judge determined that it was a sincere and honest book, and that the very explicit descriptions of sexual acts and rather coarse language were a serious and necessary part of it.[126] Since the book was a serious literary effort, and a successful one in the judge's eye, it was not an obscene publication and would be admitted into the United States. The government appealed, and the Second Circuit, in an opinion by Judge Augustus Hand, affirmed the decision below.[127] Taking the work as a whole, the court held, its literary value was apparent and it was thus not obscene. In a departure, then, from the *Hicklin* guideline, selected excerpts were no longer the basis for the determination, and the literary value of the work was to be considered as well as the mere existence of specific words or descriptions.

A similar result had been reached several years earlier in the case of *United States* v. *Dennett.*[128] Mary Ware Dennett had desired

---

literary work, because of a few of its episodes, would compel the exclusion from circulation of a very large proportion of the works of fiction of the most famous writers of the English language." *See also St. Hubert Guild* v. *Quinn,* 64 Misc. 336, 118 N.Y.S. 582 (Sup. Ct. 1909).

[124] 5 F. Supp. 182 (S.D.N.Y. 1933).

[125] This was a forfeiture case under 19 U.S.C. § 1305.

[126] There are several interesting factual accounts of the background of this case. T. Murphy, Censorship: Government and Obscenity 3–5 (1963); J. Kilpatrick, The Smut Peddlers 119–125 (1960); A. Gerber, Sex, Pornography, and Justice 99–104 (1965).

[127] *United States* v. *One Book Called "Ulysses,"* 72 F.2d 705 (2d Cir. 1934).

[128] 39 F.2d 564 (2d Cir. 1930). After her conviction, but prior to her successful appeal, Mrs. Dennett described the entire litigation. M. Dennett, What's Obscene (1930). Mrs. Dennett was defended by Morris L. Ernst and Alexander Lindey, who represented books or defendants in many of the most prominent cases of this period.

to give her two sons some basic sex education, and discovered that none of the publications then available for this purpose satisfied her. She then wrote a pamphlet entitled *The Sex Side of Life,* which she sent to her sons. The pamphlet was eventually published and thereupon Mrs. Dennett was prosecuted for mailing an obscene publication. She was found guilty by the jury and fined $300. The conviction, however, was reversed by the Second Circuit Court of Appeals, with Judge Augustus Hand writing the opinion. Although the intent of the author was not relevant in the determination of obscenity, the identity of the reading audience was, he said, and this was not a publication that would be expected to be read by those whose desires might be inflamed by it. The main effect of the book was educational, and in this respect it was held to be a valuable publication, despite the occasional overly explicit description.[129] It is important to note, however, that this determination on the basis of educational value was not in any way a constitutional decision, but rather was merely a question of application of the statutory language, as it was in all of the obscenity cases of this time. Although obscenity statutes were on occasion challenged on First Amendment grounds, these challenges were all unsuccessful.[130] And once the validity of the statute was established, its application to particular publications was not at the time thought to involve any First Amendment considerations.

Other books were less fortunate. Lower court cases in New York, abiding by the *Hicklin* rule and 19th century American precedents, found obscene *Casanova's Homecoming,* by Arthur Schnitzler;[131] *The Well of Loneliness,* by Radclyffe Hall;[132] and *Lady Chatterley's Lover,* by D. H. Lawrence.[133] Many of the most significant cases arose in Massachusetts.[134] In *Commonwealth* v. *Friede,*[135] the Supreme Judicial Court of Massachusetts affirmed the conviction of a bookseller for selling copies of *An American Tragedy,* by Theo-

---

[129] 39 F.2d at 569.

[130] *Commonwealth* v. *Isenstadt,* 318 Mass. 543, 63 N.E.2d 840 (1945); *Tyomies Pub. Co.* v. *United States,* 211 F. 385 (6th Cir 1914); *Knowles* v. *United States,* 170 F. 409 (8th Cir. 1919); *United States* v. *One Book Entitled "Contraception," by Marie C. Stopes,* 51 F.2d 525 (S.D.N.Y. 1931); *Williams* v. *State,* 130 Miss. 827, 94 So. 882 (1923).

[131] *People* v. *Seltzer,* 122 Misc. 329, 203 N.Y.S. 809 (Sup. Ct. 1924).

[132] *People* v. *Friede,* 133 Misc. 611, 233 N.Y.S. 565 (Magis. Ct. 1929).

[133] *People* v. *Dial Press,* 182 Misc. 416 (Magis. Ct. 1944).

[134] *See* P. BOYER, PURITY IN PRINT: THE VICE-SOCIETY MOVEMENT AND BOOK CENSORSHIP IN AMERICA (1968), for a factual account of the "banned in Boston" phenomenon. *See also* Grant and Angoff, *Massachusetts and Censorship,* 10 BOSTON UNIV. L. REV. 36, 147 (1930).

[135] 271 Mass. 318, 171 N.E. 472 (1930).

dore Dreiser.[136] The trial judge had refused to allow the defendant to give or read the entire book to the jury. Only those chapters in which the allegedly obscene sections appeared (dealing in subdued language with an illicit sexual relationship) were read to the jury. In affirming the conviction based on the "selected passages" approach, the Court noted that "the seller of a book which contains passages offensive to the statute has no right to assume that children to whom the book might come would not read the obscene passages, or having read them, would continue to read on until the evil effects of the obscene passages were weakened or dissipated with the tragic denouement of the tale."[137]

This approach was changed by the Supreme Judicial Court 15 years later in the case of *Commonwealth* v. *Isenstadt*.[138] In this case the court affirmed a conviction based upon the selling of a book entitled *Strange Fruit*. Rejecting the selected-passages approach of its earlier cases, the court held that the work must be looked at as a whole. The total impression was to be the deciding factor. "It is not to be [considered obscene] merely because it may contain somewhere between its covers some expressions which, taken by themselves alone, might be obnoxious to the statute."[139] The court also required that obscenity be determined in light of the book's effect on the average person or the reasonable man. Furthermore, this effect was to be measured in light of the customs and habits of thought at the time and place of the allegedly illegal publication. However, the sincerity or artistic nature of the author was irrelevant, as was the actual literary merit of the work. Based on all of these factors, the conviction was affirmed.

Several other cases followed shortly thereafter. In 1948 the court, in a civil action for the adjudication of obscenity,[140] determined that *Forever Amber* was not obscene. Although it contained references to sexual acts "almost to the point of tedium," there was no great detail and the book had considerable historical value. Based on its effect on the "average adult reader," and considering "current sex mores,"

---

[136] Dreiser's works were no strangers to the courts. Both *The Genius* and *Sister Carrie* (183 App. Div. 773) had substantial encounters with the obscenity laws, and *An American Tragedy* itself was based upon the case of *People* v. *Gillette,* 191 N.Y. 107, 83 N.E. 680 (1908).

[137] 271 Mass. at 322–323.

[138] 318 Mass. 543, 62 N.E.2d 840 (1945).

[139] 62 N.E.2d at 843–844.

[140] Unlike the New York cases, which are mostly criminal proceedings, most Massachusetts obscenity cases have arisen in these civil proceedings.

as interpreted by testimony of psychiatrists and literary scholars, the book was held not to be obscene.[141] Similarly, a book entitled *Serenade* was held nonobscene. Mere sexual episodes were insufficient; they must dominate, and have a "substantial tendency to deprave or corrupt its readers by inciting lascivious thoughts or arousing lustful desire."[142] But in the same year the court found Erskine Caldwell's *God's Little Acre* to be obscene.[143] The court found that the book "abounds in sexual episodes," had an "abundance of realistic detail," and "descends to outright pornography." This finding was based on the court's own evaluation of the book, substantially disregarding the imposing array of expert testimony in support of the literary value of the book, as well as the considerable critical acclaim which the book drew.

The *Hicklin* test had by no means been completely abandoned by this time. In *United States* v. *Two Obscene Books*,[144] the subjects of the forfeiture proceedings were *Tropic of Cancer* and *Tropic of Capricorn*, both by Henry Miller. Looking at particular passages only, and holding that expert testimony was immaterial, the United States District Court in San Francisco held both books to be obscene. The decision was affirmed by the Court of Appeals for the Ninth Circuit.[145]

The attention given to books whose literary merit was at the very least arguable was one of two noteworthy aspects of obscenity law from 1900 to 1950. The other was the gradual adoption of certain more sophisticated concepts that were to culminate with *Roth* v. *United States*.[146] As has been seen from a number of the cases just described, perhaps the most significant of these conceptual changes was the general adoption of the view that the work must be evaluated in its entirety, not merely by the use of selected excerpts. In the 1922 case of *Halsey* v. *New York Society for Suppression of Vice*,[147] the Court of Appeals of New York held that the work

---

[141] *Attorney General* v. *Book Named "Forever Amber,"* 323 Mass. 302, 81 N.E.2d 663 (1948).

[142] *Attorney General* v. *Book Named "Serenade,"* 326 Mass. 324, 94 N.E.2d 259 (1950).

[143] *Attorney General* v. *Book Named "God's Little Acre,"* 326 Mass. 281, 93 N.E.2d 819 (1950). Efforts against this book were less successful in New York. *People* v. *Viking Press, Inc.,* 147 Misc. 813, 264 N.Y.S. 534 (Magis. Ct. 1933).

[144] 99 F. Supp. 760 (N.D. Cal. 1951), *aff'd sub nom. Besig* v. *United States,* 208 F.2d 142 (9th Cir. 1953).

[145] *Id.*

[146] 354 U.S. 476 (1957).

[147] 234 N.Y. 1, 136 N.E. 219 (1922).

must be looked at "as a whole"; that separate paragraphs might seem obscene out of context even if the entire work were not, as for example "selections from Aristophanes or Chaucer or Boccaccio or even from the Bible." This approach led to the finding in 1933 by a lower New York court that *God's Little Acre* was not obscene.[148] The view that the work must be looked at as a whole was also adopted by the Second Circuit in a decision by Judge Learned Hand,[149] and in general accepted by most courts by 1950.[150] It was by then the "dominant theme" that was determinative.

This period also saw the erosion of the *Hicklin* concept that the work was to be judged according to its effect on particularly susceptible individuals, such as children or "weak-willed" adults. Most of the 20th century cases rejected this view in favor of looking either to the average or reasonable person[151] or to the actual intended audience for the work,[152] reasoning that to hold otherwise would subject society to a "least common denominator" approach to reading matter.

Somewhat related to the acceptance of the "taken as a whole" and "average person" concepts was the acceptance of the idea that it was now permissible to look to the literary value of the work in making the determination of obscenity. Works of clear literary intent and value could "get away" with more sexual explicitness than could those lacking that value.[153] And since literary value was now a factor, expert testimony was commonly received on this and other issues,[154] despite earlier authority to the contrary.

Finally, there is the emergence of the community-standards concept. Although it appears in one earlier case,[155] the concept was first clearly elucidated in *United States* v. *Kennerley*,[156] where Learned Hand, then a U. S. District Judge, ruled that obscenity must be

---

[148] *See* note 143 *supra*.

[149] *United States* v. *Levine*, 83 F.2d 156 (2d Cir. 1936).

[150] Many of these cases are contained in the very thorough analysis in *American Civil Liberties Union* v. *The City of Chicago*, 3 Ill. 2d 334, 121 N.E.2d 585 (1954). *See also* the Massachusetts cases cited in notes 138–143 *supra;* the *Ulysses* cases, notes 124–127 *supra; Parmelee* v. *United States*, 113 F.2d 729 (D.C. Cir. 1940).

[151] *See, e.g., Commonwealth* v. *Isenstadt*, 318 Mass. 543, 62 N.E.2d 840 (1945); *United States* v. *One Book Called "Ulysses,"* 5 F. Supp. 182 (S.D.N.Y. 1933).

[152] *United States* v. *Dennett*, 39 F.2d 564 (2d Cir. 1930).

[153] *See People* v. *Berg*, 241 App. Div. 543, 272 N.Y.S. 586 (1934), *aff'd*, 269 N.Y. 514, 199 N.E. 513 (1935), finding no literary value.

[154] Virtually every case cited in notes 124–152 *supra* involved an evaluation of literary merit and the considerable use of expert testimony.

[155] *McJunkins* v. *State*, 10 Ind. 140 (1858).

[156] 209 F. 119 (S.D.N.Y. 1913).

determined in accordance with the "present critical point in the compromise between candor and shame at which the community may have arrived here and now." In this and in many other cases that followed,[157] it was recognized that societal tolerance of sexual matters varies over time, and that this must of necessity be a component in the determination of whether or not a given publication is in fact obscene. This concept and the other changes during the first half of the 20th century are still major factors in obscenity law, and there will be more complete discussions of them in later chapters of this book. It is significant to note here that most of the standards that appeared in *Roth* v. *United States* [158] had their origin in the developing case law of the previous 50 years.

During this time there were several Supreme Court decisions on obscenity, but all of them dealt with regulatory and licensing schemes and the First Amendment problems related thereto, and not with the actual development of substantive obscenity law. Discussion of these cases will therefore be reserved for a later chapter. But in none of these cases did any court deal with the fundamental relationship between obscenity and the First Amendment, an issue that now dominates the field of obscenity law.

[157] A fairly complete list is contained in *Roth* v. *United States*, 354 U.S. 476, 489 n. 26 (1957).

[158] 354 U.S. 476 (1957).

2

The Emerging
Constitutional Standards:
From *Roth* to *Miller*

2.1 The Supreme Court Enters the Scene—Roth v. United States

Although the purpose of this section is to describe the entry of the U.S. Supreme Court into the field of defining obscenity and analyzing the constitutional limitations of obscenity laws, a discussion of the precursors of this entry is appropriate. For this we must first look to 1948 and the Supreme Court case of *Winters* v. *New York*.[1] *Winters* involved a New York statute prohibiting publication of materials "devoted to the publication, and principally made up, of criminal news, police reports, or accounts of criminal deeds, or pictures, or stories of deeds of bloodshed, lust or crime."[2] The defendant had been convicted under this statute, and the New York courts had upheld both the conviction and the validity of the statute.[3] On appeal to the U.S. Supreme Court the case was argued three separate times before the Court finally handed down its decision in 1948.

The primary issue in the case was that which is now called overbreadth: the inclusion within the potential coverage of the statute of that which cannot be made criminal. Justice Reed wrote the opinion of the Court and concluded that the statute could not stand because it did indeed include publications other than the "'indecent and

---

[1] 333 U.S. 507 (1948).
[2] New York Penal Law § 1141, subsection 2 (1945).
[3] *People* v. *Winters*, 268 App. Div 30, 48 N.Y.S.2d 230, *aff'd*, 294 N.Y. 545, 63 N.E.2d 98, *modified*, 294 N.Y. 979, 63 N.E.2d 713 (1945).

30

obscene."[4] In effect, the legislature had created a new crime and had attempted to enforce it by an overly vague statute. But the true significance of the case, for the present purpose, lies in the Court's disclaimer at the end of the opinion. "To say that a state may not punish by such a vague statute carries no implication that it may not punish circulation of objectionable printed matter, assuming that it is not protected by the principles of the First Amendment, by the use of apt words to describe the prohibited publications."[5] What is important here is the specific recognition for the first time by the Supreme Court that laws making criminal the distribution of "harmful" material involve substantial First Amendment considerations and, even more significantly, that even objectionable materials may in some instances be protected by the First Amendment.

At about the same time, the Court did in fact consider the full impact of the constitutional considerations, but no decision resulted. Edmund Wilson was at the time perhaps the most distinguished literary critic in the country. In 1946, Doubleday and Company had published a collection of his stories entitled *Memoirs of Hecate County.* One of those stories, "The Princess With the Golden Hair," contained a rather detailed description of a sexual episode, but the general reaction to the book was nonetheless enthusiastic. Among those who objected, however, was the New York Society for the Improvement of Morals, the successor to the New York Society for the Suppression of Vice. Doubleday was charged in New York with the publication and sale of an obscene book, and convicted by a Court of Special Sessions. The conviction was affirmed without opinion,[6] and eventually reached the U.S. Supreme Court.[7] Here, for the first time, there was a full airing of all of the constitutional considerations relating to obscenity laws.[8] Both Doubleday and the American Civil Liberties Union, as amicus curiae, argued only the First Amendment issues, claiming that suppression of literary works is permitted only in cases of a "clear and present danger" to a significant state interest.[9] The Court was concerned about the First Amendment considerations but was also troubled at the prospect of having to review the merits of

[4] 333 U.S. at 519.

[5] *Id.* at 520.

[6] *People* v. *Doubleday and Co.,* 297 N.Y. 687 (1947).

[7] A full account of the entire litigation appears in Lockhart and McClure, *Literature, The Law of Obscenity, and the Constitution,* 38 MINN. L. REV. 295–301 (1954).

[8] The argument is reported at 17 U.S.L.W. 3117–3119 (1948).

[9] *See, e.g., Schenk* v. *United States,* 249 U.S. 47 (1919); *Stromberg* v. *California,* 283 U.S. 359 (1931); *Herndon* v. *Lowry,* 301 U.S. 242 (1937).

every literary work charged with obscenity.[10] The briefs and arguments produced no opinion, however. As a personal friend of the author, Justice Frankfurter had disqualified himself, and the remaining eight members of the Court divided equally, thereby producing no opinion and affirming the decision below.[11] The first major shot at a full consideration of the constitutional issues had misfired.

The significance of the constitutional issues was not lost, however. Several lower courts began to deal with this problem,[12] the most noteworthy decision being the opinion of Judge Curtis Bok in *Commonwealth* v. *Gordon.*[13] This case involved an indictment for selling a large number of books, including the *Studs Lonigan* trilogy, by James T. Farrell; *Sanctuary,* by William Faulkner; *God's Little Acre,* by Erskine Caldwell; and other works by these authors as well as works by Calder Willingham and Harold Robbins. Judge Bok analyzed the case law, both English and American, in considerable detail and then turned to the constitutional considerations. He concluded that the only way to avoid restricting freedom of speech with the obscenity laws was to limit the applications of those laws to the "sexually impure and pornographic," and even then only if there is a clear and present danger that a crime has been or is about to be committed as a result of the publication. This causal connection between the book and the harmful effects must, he said, appear beyond a reasonable doubt. "The opinion of anyone that a tendency thereto exists or that such a result is self-evident is insufficient and irrelevant." Finding no such proof in the case before him, he found the books not obscene and sustained the defendants' demurrers.

These developments in the case law caused a proliferation of legal material regarding obscenity and constitutional law.[14] It was

---

[10] 17 U.S.L.W. at 3119.

[11] *Doubleday and Co.* v. *New York,* 335 U.S. 848 (1948).

[12] *State of Ohio* v. *Lerner,* 51 Ohio L. Abs. 321, 81 N.E.2d 282 (Ct. Comm. Pl. 1948); *Esquire* v. *Walker,* 151 F.2d (D.C. Cir. 1945), *aff'd sub nom. Hannegan* v. *Esquire,* 327 U.S. 146 (1946); *Bantam Books, Inc.,* v. *Melko,* 25 N.J. Sup. 292, 96 A.2d 47 (1953) (this opinion contains a remarkably complete history of the case law from English origins to 1953); *Commercial Pictures Corp.* v. *Regents,* 305 N.Y. 336, 113 N.E.2d 502 (1953); *New American Library of World Literature, Inc.* v. *Allen,* 114 F. Supp. 823 (N.D. Ohio 1953); *cf. Adams Theatre Co.* v. *Keenan,* 12 N.J. 267, 91 A.2d 519 (Brennan, J.).

[13] 66 Pa. D. and C. 101 (Phila. 1949), *aff'd sub nom. Commonwealth* v. *Feiginbaum,* 166 Pa. Super. 120, 70 A.2d 389.

[14] *See, e.g.,* Lockhart and McClure, *Literature, the Law of Obscenity, and the Constitution,* 38 MINN. L. REV. 295 (1954); Symposium, *Obscenity and the Arts,* 20 L. AND CONTEMP. PROB. 531 (1955); Note, *Construction and Constitutionality of Statutes Regulating Obscene Literature,* 28 N.Y.U.L. REV. 877 (1953); Note, *Obscene Literature,* 34 MARQ. L. REV. 301 (1951).

thus against a background of 10 years of attention to the constitutional implications of obscenity law, in the cases and in the legal literature, that the Supreme Court first dealt with the issue. It is important to recognize that this period marked the height of obscenity prosecution of respected literary works, as opposed to commercial pornography. Had this not been the case, the Supreme Court's opinion may very well have been rather different.

Finally the issue reached the Supreme Court. Samuel Roth had been convicted on four counts of a 26-count indictment for violating 18 U.S.C. § 1461 by mailing obscene books, periodicals, and photographs, as well as advertisements of these materials. The publications involved were not the literary classics at issue in many of the cases of the time. Roth's publications were such as *Wild Passion, Wanton by Night,* and *Sexual Conduct of Men and Women.* In fact, Roth was at the time a leading distributor of sexually oriented materials and this was hardly his first brush with the law.[15] At trial, his main contention was that 18 U.S.C. § 1461 was an unconstitutional restriction on the freedom of speech and the press.

On appeal to the Court of Appeals for the Second Circuit, he made the same argument, again unsuccessfully.[16] Judge Clark, writing for the court, considered that obscenity was not within the scope of First Amendment protection and that the evidence seemed to support the need for obscenity control. Acknowledging that "a serious problem does arise when real literature is censored," he found that Roth was hardly the person to raise that objection in light of the particular materials at issue. Judge Frank and Judge Waterman concurred on the grounds that the Supreme Court had implicitly upheld the statute so many times that it was not their province to declare it unconstitutional. Since the statute was deemed to be valid, therefore, and since the works involved were clearly within its coverage, the conviction was affirmed. Judge Frank, however, in an appendix to his opinion, dealt with the competing philosophical and legal considerations, concluding that in his view obscenity prosecutions should only be allowed where there was a clear and present danger shown that works of the type on trial would induce serious antisocial conduct.[17]

---

[15] *See Roth* v. *Goldman,* 172 F.2d 788 (2d Cir. 1948), *cert. denied,* 337 U.S. 938. He was also involved with the first importation, ultimately unsuccessful, of *Ulysses.* For descriptions of Roth's business and the factual background of the *Roth* case, see J. Kilpatrick, THE SMUT PEDDLERS 81–85 (1960); T. Murphy, CENSORSHIP: GOVERNMENT AND OBSCENITY 21–24 (1963).

[16] *United States* v. *Roth,* 237 F.2d 796 (2d Cir. 1956).

[17] *Id.* at 806, 826. Judge Frank's opinion is one of the few judicial opinions to merit a book review. Kalven, Book Review, 24 CHI. L. REV. 769 (1957).

At about the same time, David Alberts was convicted in California under a state law prohibiting the sale of obscene or indecent material. His products were little different from Roth's and included such works as *The Prostitute and Her Lover, The Love Affair of a Priest and a Nun,* and *Male Homosexuals Tell Their Stories.* Alberts, too, challenged the constitutionality of the statute under which he was prosecuted, both on First Amendment grounds and on the grounds that the Federal Government had preempted the field of obscenity regulation, rendering state statutes invalid as violative of the federal postal powers. Like Roth's, his appeal was unsuccessful.[18] He then appealed to the Supreme Court where the case was consolidated with Roth's, in which certiorari had been granted. The decision in these cases remains the cornerstone of American obscenity law.[19]

The briefs and arguments presented to the Supreme Court essentially gave two drastically different theories of the relationship of obscenity to the protections of the First Amendment. Counsel for Roth and most of the amicus curiae briefs[20] argued for the clear-and-present-danger test, saying that no speech of any kind, including obscenity, could be prohibited unless there were a clear and present danger that the material would cause a "substantive evil" such as Congress had the authority to prevent. Essentially, their position was that the clear-and-present-danger test required the government to prove that "gravity of the 'evil,' discounted by its improbability, justifies such invasion of free speech as is necessary to avoid the danger."[21] Since the government could not make this showing, it was argued, the statute must fall.

---

[18] *People* v. *Alberts,* 138 Cal. App. 2d Supp. 909, 292 P.2d 90 (1955).

[19] *Roth* v. *United States; Alberts* v. *California,* 354 U.S. 476 (1957) (hereinafter referred to as *Roth* or *Roth* v. *United States*). There has, of course, been an enormous amount of legal commentary on this case, some very good, some very bad, and most in between. Among the best are Kalven, *The Metaphysics of the Law of Obscenity,* 1960 SUP. CT. REV. 1 (1960); Lockhart and McClure, *Censorship of Obscenity: The Developing Constitutional Standards,* 45 MINN. L. REV. 1 (1960); *The Supreme Court, 1956 Term,* 71 HARV. L. REV. 94, 146 (1957); Henkin, *Morals and the Constitution: The Sin of Obscenity,* 63 COLUM. L. REV. 391 (1963); Note, *Obscenity and the Supreme Court: Nine Years of Confusion,* 19 STAN. L. REV. 167 (1966).

[20] Amicus curiae briefs were submitted on behalf of the American Civil Liberties Union, several publishing groups, the Authors League of America, Inc., and Morris Ernst.

[21] *Dennis* v. *United States,* 341 U.S. 494, 510 (1951). This was the Supreme Court's most current exposition of the clear-and-present-danger test at the time of *Roth.*

The question then arises as to what is the "substantive evil" that is the aim of the obscenity laws. There seem to be two possibilities. One is the danger of inciting lustful desires and ideas, and the other is the danger of inciting specific criminal and antisocial conduct. It was argued that the former is not an evil that governmental power can properly regulate, and that the latter has yet to be proved to be the result of obscene literature.[22]

As might be expected, the government did not accept this formulation of the issues. It was argued by the United States that the Court must adopt a balancing test, and weigh "these basic factors: the value of the kind of speech involved, the public interest served by the restriction, and the extent and form of the restriction imposed."[23] The government suggested a continuum of First Amendment values, based upon the original history and purposes of the amendment and on the case law interpreting it. At the top of the continuum was political speech, which could be restricted only under the most extreme circumstances. The scale continued with religious, economic, and scientific speech down through current commentary, literature, and various forms of entertainment, and concluded with obscenity, profanity, and commercial pornography. For these latter items, the governmental interests could be less imminent, and the probability of their occurrence slighter. Therefore, general interests in morality would justify an antiobscenity statute, although not a statute which affected political or religious speech.

The government was also prepared for the argument that the history of the obscenity laws is a history of suppression of literature now considered great. Representing to the court that 90 percent of the postal seizures and prosecutions involved "hard-core pornography," the Solicitor General's office delivered to the Court a large package of samples of hard-core pornography so the Court could see just what the statute was designed to prevent. The effect of this submission remains unknown.

On June 24, 1957, Justice Brennan delivered the opinion of the Court. That opinion accepted neither the views of the defendants nor the views of the government. Instead, the Court ruled that obscenity was not speech at all, so that if material were in fact obscene, the First Amendment was no longer involved and a dispute as to which test to use was unnecessary. Justice Brennan reasoned that speech does not mean *any* utterance, and not *all* utterances are protected by

[22] *See* Brief of the American Book Publishers Council, amicus curiae, in *Roth*.
[23] Brief of the United States at 40.

the First Amendment. In support of this proposition, he cited statutes against libel, blasphemy, and profanity to show that these utterances were not thought to be protected at the time of the adoption of the First Amendment. In *Beauharnais* v. *Illinois*,[24] the Court had recently held that libelous utterances were not within the area of protected speech. The Court was now taking the same approach with obscenity, and on much the same type of authority. Of course, the historical argument is one that is rarely the basis of a decision but is often used to support one made on other grounds. It is highly questionable whether a blasphemy statute could pass constitutional muster today, despite the existence of such statutes when the First Amendment was adopted. And the existence of profanity statutes in 1797 did not seem to affect the Supreme Court's decision in *Cohen* v. *California*.[25] In any event, the opinion of Justice Brennan reserved for First Amendment protection only those utterances relating to ideas.

> All ideas having even the slightest redeeming social importance—unorthodox ideas, controversial ideas, even ideas hateful to the prevailing climate of opinion—have the full protection of the guaranties, unless excludable because they encroach upon the limited area of more important interests. But implicit in the history of the First Amendment is the rejection of obscenity as utterly without redeeming social importance.[26]

Since obscenity was thus held to be outside the range of First Amendment protection, it was unnecessary for there to be any specific showing of the harmful effects of obscenity, whether by a clear-and-present-danger standard or any other. Since neither *Roth* nor *Alberts* had argued that the specific materials at issue were not obscene, this holding thus disposed of the case and was sufficient to affirm the convictions.[27] Justice Brennan's opinion, however, went on to define obscenity, and that definition has been the basis of all of the Court's subsequent efforts to define this extremely elusive term.

At the outset, it appeared necessary to define obscenity in such a manner as to exclude from its scope many of the classic works of literature which contained descriptions of or references to sex or sexual activities. The Court could hardly have been unmindful of the

[24] 343 U.S. 250 (1952).

[25] 403 U.S. 15 (1971) (wearing of a jacket bearing the words "Fuck the Draft" in a corridor of a courthouse was constitutionally protected speech).

[26] 354 U.S. at 484 (footnote omitted).

[27] The contention that the concept of obscenity was so vague as to invalidate the statutes was dismissed in a brief discussion. 354 U.S. at 491–492.

types of books which were then being prosecuted around the country, and thus we have the first hint of the Court's desire to limit the reach of the obscenity statutes to commercial pornography.

> However, sex and obscenity are not synonymous. Obscene material is material which deals with sex in a manner appealing to prurient interest. The portrayal of sex, *e.g.,* in art, literature and scientific works, is not itself sufficient reason to deny material the constitutional protection of freedom of speech and press. Sex, a great and mysterious motive force in human life, has indisputably been a subject of absorbing interest to mankind through the ages; it is one of the vital problems of human interest and public concern.[28]

Thus there is seen the emergence of the requirement that material is obscene only if it appeals to the prurient interest. And lest that term be misunderstood, a lengthy footnote attempted to collect the various definitions of "prurient," showing that prurient material was that which had "a tendency to excite lustful thoughts." [29]

But merely excluding the artistic or the literary is not a complete definition of obscenity. Justice Brennan went on to discuss the specific tests in light of the traditional reliance on *Regina* v. *Hicklin.*[30] He rejected the view that isolated passages could be the basis of a finding of obscenity, as this view might involve a substantial risk of restriction of material which was in fact protected by the constitutional guarantees of freedom of speech and freedom of the press. Similarly, the material could not be judged on the basis of its effect upon "particularly susceptible persons," as to do so might, again, prevent the distribution of constitutionally protected materials. Thus, to the extent it was still viable, *Hicklin* was rejected and a new test substituted. Material is obscene if ". . . to the average person, applying contemporary community standards, the dominant theme of the material taken as a whole appeals to prurient interest."[31] There was little new in this test. Justice Brennan acknowledged that it was based on a number of American decisions over a period of 40 years, and it is substantially similar to the test that was at that time proposed in the Model Penal Code of the American Law Institute. But for the first time a definition of obscenity had received the endorsement of the Supreme Court, and the complete exclusion of obscenity from the

[28] *Id*. at 487.
[29] *Id*. at 487 n. 20.
[30] [1868] L.R. 3 Q.B. 360. This case and its adoption by most American courts in the 19th century are discussed at length in the previous chapter.
[31] 354 U.S. at 489.

definition of speech provided a theoretical basis for all of the Court's subsequent decisions in this area.

Chief Justice Warren concurred in the result but felt the opinion of the Court went unnecessarily far.[32] Since the material involved in these cases was clearly commercial pornography and since some degree of willfulness had been found by the courts below, that was sufficient, in his view, to sustain the convictions. The Chief Justice seemed inclined to look more at the conduct of the defendants than at the literary merit of any particular work, and since the conduct of these defendants was so extreme, the statutes involved would, at the very least, include such behavior.

> They were plainly engaged in the commercial exploitation of the morbid and shameful craving for materials with prurient effect. I believe that the State and Federal Governments can constitutionally punish such conduct. That is all that these cases present to us, and that is all we need decide.[33]

Justice Harlan's opinion, concurring in *Alberts* but dissenting in *Roth*,[34] stated a position that he held to in many subsequent cases, namely, that there is a difference in state as opposed to federal power in the regulation of obscenity. Since protection of the morality of the public was primarily the responsibility of the states, the states are to be free to make judgments as to what types of publications may be prohibited, and experiment with various types of obscenity laws. These judgments could not, of course, be completely uncontrolled, for it was still the duty of the Supreme Court to evaluate the materials suppressed to see if that suppression so interfered with the communication of ideas as to offend the Due Process Clause of the Fourteenth Amendment. But, he argued, much different principles applied to federal obscenity regulation. It is not the primary function of the Federal Government to regulate public morality, and the dangers of federal censorship, being nationwide, are much greater.

> The danger is perhaps not great if the people of one State, through their legislature, decide that *Lady Chatterley's Lover* goes so far beyond acceptable standards of candor that it will be deemed offensive and non-sellable, for the State next door is still free to make its own choice. At least we do not have one uniform standard. But the dangers to free thought and expression are truly great if the

[32] 354 U.S. at 494–496 (Warren, C. J., concurring).
[33] *Id.* at 496.
[34] 354 U.S. at 496 (Harlan, J.).

Federal Government imposes a blanket ban over the nation on such a book . . . . The fact that the people of one state cannot read some of the works of D. H. Lawrence seems to me, if not wise or desirable, at least acceptable. But that no person in the United States should be allowed to do so seems to be to be intolerable, and violative of both the letter and spirit of the First Amendment.[35]

Therefore, he argued that Federal obscenity laws could include only hard-core pornography.

Justice Douglas, joined by Justice Black, dissented on the grounds that the First Amendment permits no suppression whatsoever of "utterances," either by the states or the Federal Government, no matter how offensive those utterances may be, unless those utterances are "so closely brigaded with illegal action as to be an inseparable part of it."[36] To try to decide which publications had value and which did not, as the Court was doing, he argued, was to exalt the role of the censor and sacrifice the values of literary freedom. "I have the same confidence in the ability of our people to reject noxious literature as I have in their capacity to sort out the true from the false in theology, economics, politics, or any other field."[37] Both Justice Douglas and Justice Black remained aligned to this position throughout the remainder of their careers on the Court.[38]

Although the scope of obscenity regulation has changed a number of times since *Roth,* and although the definition of obscenity has also been modified, the *Roth* case remains the cornerstone of American obscenity law. By excluding obscenity, however defined, from the definition of speech, the Supreme Court established the theoretical basis for the continuing validity of obscenity laws without the necessity of entering the debate as to the effects of obscenity and without the necessity of modifying obscenity law to meet other changes in First Amendment theory.[39] But although *Roth* was seem-

[35] *Id.* at 506.

[36] *Id.* at 508–514 (Douglas, J., dissenting).

[37] *Id.* at 514.

[38] *See, e.g., Pryba* v. *United States,* 95 S. Ct. 815, 816 (1975) (Douglas, J., dissenting); *Jenkins* v. *Georgia,* 418 U.S. 153, 162 (1974) (Douglas J., concurring).

[39] This "two-level" theory of the First Amendment, excluding certain utterances entirely from First Amendment considerations, has its basis in *Beauharnais* v. *Illinois,* 343 U.S. 250 (1952), and *Chaplinsky* v. *New Hampshire,* 315 U.S. 568 (1942), excluding libel and "fighting words," respectively, from the scope of First Amendment protection. Perhaps the best discussion of this theory as applied to the obscenity area is in Kalven, *The Metaphysics of the Law of Obscenity,* 1960 SUP. CT. REV. 1 (1960). *See also* Lockhart and McClure, *Censorship of Obscenity: The Developing Constitutional Standards,* 45 MINN. L. REV. 5, 19–29 (1960).

ingly intended to be a definitive pronouncement by the Supreme Court, it created far more issues than it solved, and was merely the beginning of a long line of Supreme Court obscenity cases.

2.2   The Minimal Regulation of the Memoirs Test

Although there were several per curiam reversals of obscenity convictions after *Roth,*[40] the Court's next full substantive treatment of an obscenity case revealed a significant division of opinion. The case was *Kingsley International Pictures Corp.* v. *Regents,*[41] arising out of the New York State courts. New York had prohibited the exhibition of the movie version of *Lady Chatterley's Lover* by denying a license for exhibition under a statute permitting the denial of such license to a motion picture that was "obscene, indecent, immoral, inhuman, sacrilegious, or . . . of such character that its exhibition would tend to corrupt morals or incite to crime."[42] These terms were defined to include motion pictures which were "erotic or pornographic; or which portray acts of sexual immorality, perversion, or lewdness, or which expressly or impliedly present such acts as desirable, acceptable or proper patterns of behavior."[43] Reversing the New York Court of Appeals, Justice Stewart wrote the opinion of the Supreme Court. A motion picture, he wrote, could not be suppressed merely because it advocated an idea, even if that idea was that adultery might be proper behavior. Mere immorality was insufficient. Unless the movie was in fact obscene, it could not be suppressed.[44] Therefore, the statute was declared unconstitutional.

The other opinions show a significant divergence as to approach. Justices Black[45] and Douglas[46] reiterated their views that no such licensing system was permissible, while Justice Frankfurter would have evaluated each motion picture on a case-by-case basis to determine

---

[40] *See, e.g., One, Inc.* v. *Oleson,* 355 U.S. 371 (1958) (determination of non-mailability in lower court pursuant to 18 U.S.C. § 1461); *Sunshine Book Co.* v. *Summerfield,* 355 U.S. 372 (1958) (same); *Times Film Corp.* v. *City of Chicago,* 355 U.S. 35 (1957); *Mounce* v. *United States,* 355 U.S. 180 (1957).

[41] 360 U.S. 684 (1959). *See The Supreme Court, 1958 Term,* 73 Harv. L. Rev. 84, 164 (1959); 58 Mich. L. Rev. 134 (1959); 13 Vand. L. Rev. 541 (1960).

[42] McKinney's N.Y. Laws, 1953, Education Law, § 122.

[43] McKinney's N.Y. Laws, 1953 (Cum. Supp. 1958), Education Law, § 122–a.

[44] 360 U.S. at 688.

[45] *Id.* at 690 (Black, J., concurring).

[46] *Id.* at 697 (Douglas, J., concurring).

whether or not it could be censored.[47] Justice Clark's opinion also found the prohibition of ideas impermissible.[48] Justice Harlan found the statute's application to this film, but not the statute itself, unconstitutional.[49]

This decision is significant for two reasons. First, it demonstrates the divergence in approaches on the Court that continues to be a major characteristic of obscenity cases. And it also marks the beginning of a process narrowing the scope of obscenity regulation, leading to the ultimate result of limiting obscenity regulation only to hard-core pornography.[50]

This trend[51] toward the hard-core requirement was continued in 1962 when the Court handed down its decision in *Manual Enterprises* v. *Day*.[52] The Post Office Department had declared three homosexual magazines to be nonmailable matter and the publishers appealed. The Supreme Court reversed the ban. Again there were multiple opinions, with Justice Harlan announcing the judgment of the Court and writing an opinion in which Justice Stewart joined. In this opinion, the "patent offensiveness" standard emerged. Although *Roth* required an appeal to prurient interest, Justice Harlan said that this must be present in a patently offensive way for the material to be obscene under federal obscenity statutes. It is interesting to note that Justice Harlan focused on the words of the statute, 18 U.S.C. § 1461, to conclude that offensive portrayal was required. "The words of § 1461, 'obscene, lewd, lascivious, indecent, filthy or vile,' connote something that is portrayed in a manner so offensive as to make it unacceptable under current community mores."[53] Thus, in characteristic fashion, Justice Harlan avoided the constitutional ideas while

[47] *Id.* at 691 (Frankfurter, J., concurring).

[48] *Id.* at 699 (Clark, J., concurring).

[49] *Id.* at 702 (Harlan, J., concurring).

[50] This result was predicted by Professor Kalven in 1960. Kalven, *The Metaphysics of the Law of Obscenity*, 1960 SUP. CT. REV. 1, 43 (1960). New York courts adopted the "hard-core" requirement in 1961. *People* v. *Richmond County News, Inc.*, 9 N.Y.2d 578, 175 N.E. 2d (1961).

[51] For a detailed analysis of all of the opinions in the post-*Roth* era, see Magrath, *The Obscenity Cases: Grapes of Roth*, 1966 SUP. CT. REV. 7 (1966); Note, *More Ado About Dirty Books*, 75 YALE L. J. 1364 (1966); Note, *Obscenity in the Supreme Court; Nine Years of Confusion*, 19 STAN L. REV. 167 (1966); Survey Note, *Church-State: Religious Institutions and Values*, 41 NOTRE DAME LAW, 681, 753 (1966).

[52] 370 U.S. 478 (1962). *See The Supreme Court, 1961 Term*, 76 HARV. L. REV. 54, 125 (1962); 31 FORD. L. REV. 570 (1963); 29 BROOK. L. REV. 325 (1963); 27 ALB. L. REV. 127 (1963); 17 RUT. L. REV. 213 (1962); 30 TENN. L. REV. 291 (1963).

[53] *Id.* at 482.

being consistent with the view he expressed in *Roth* that the First Amendment permitted federal suppression only of hard-core pornography. Although the decision was based on statutory interpretation, however, the requirement of patent offensiveness became a permanent part of the definition of obscenity.

In *Jacobellis* v. *Ohio*,[54] decided two years later, the permissible scope of obscenity regulation was again narrowed.[55] Justice Brennan, writing for himself and Justice Goldberg, observed that obscenity was outside the range of First Amendment protection because it was "utterly without redeeming social importance . . . [M]aterial dealing with sex in a manner that advocates ideas, or that has literary or scientific value or any other form of social importance, may not be branded as obscenity and denied the constitutional protection."[56] And the opinion also adopted, as a matter of constitutional law, Justice Harlan's patent-offensiveness requirement. As a result, the conviction of an Ohio theater owner for exhibiting the French motion picture *Les Amants* ("The Lovers") was reversed. *Jacobellis* is perhaps most well known for the concurring opinion of Justice Stewart. He felt, quite correctly, that the Court's actions from 1957 to 1964 were leading, or had led, to a "hard-core only" policy. But like any other term in this area, hard-core pornography is not especially easy to define. Recognizing this, Justice Stewart declined to even attempt any such definitions.

> I shall not today attempt to define the kinds of material I understand to be embraced within that short-hand definition; and perhaps I could never succeed in intelligibly doing so. But I know it when I see it and the motion picture involved in this case is not that.[57]

The trend towards minimal regulation culminated with the 1966 Supreme Court case of *Memoirs* v. *Massachusetts*.[58] The work at issue was John Cleland's *Memoirs of a Woman of Pleasure*, more popularly known as *Fanny Hill*. The book had been adjudged obscene in an in rem proceeding against the book itself. The publisher had intervened and brought the appeal to the Supreme Court. Justice

---

[54] 378 U.S. 184 (1964). *See* O'Meara and Shaffer, *Obscenity in the Supreme Court: A Note on Jacobellis v. Ohio*, 40 NOTRE DAME LAW 1 (1964); 16 WEST. RES. L. REV. 780 (1965).

[55] *Jacobellis* is also significant for its treatment of the issue of contemporary community standards. See Chapter 6.2 *infra*.

[56] 378 U.S. at 191.

[57] *Id.* at 197 (Stewart, J., concurring).

[58] 383 U.S. 413 (1966). *See* Monaghan, *Obscenity, 1966: The Marriage of Obscenity Per Se and Obscenity Per Quod*, 76 YALE L. J. 127 (1966).

Brennan, writing as well for Chief Justice Warren and Justice Fortas, attempted to restate the *Roth* definition of obscenity as elaborated by the cases since *Roth*. "Three elements must coalesce," he said, those being that "(a) the dominant theme of the material taken as a whole appeals to a prurient interest in sex; (b) the material is patently offensive because it affronts contemporary community standards relating to the description or representation of sexual matters; and (c) the material is utterly without redeeming social value."[59]

Important in this new formulation were a number of factors. First, *all* of these elements must be established before there could be a finding of obscenity and thus a lack of First Amendment protection. Second, the "patently offensive" standard was now a formal requirement. A third factor was the emergence of the "utterly without redeeming social value" standard. In *Roth* it was observed that obscenity is utterly without redeeming social value, but this factor had not been treated as a test for obscenity.[60] In *Jacobellis*, however, Mr. Justice Brennan had made this complete lack of value a test.[61] This, of course, is eminently logical. If obscenity is utterly without redeeming social value, then material that is not lacking in such value cannot be obscene, and it is this observation that reached fruition in *Memoirs*.

By requiring that material be utterly without redeeming social value in order to escape constitutional protection, the *Memoirs* decision in fact embodied the "hard-core only" trend that had been growing since *Roth*, and paved the way for seven years of extremely minimal regulation of obscenity. Chief Justice Burger accurately observed that the "utterly without redeeming social value" standard was a "burden virtually impossible to discharge under our criminal standards of proof."[62] In the years following the *Memoirs* decision, obscenity convictions were few and many of those were reversed because the material had some modicum of arguable social value.[63]

---

[59] *Id.* at 418.

[60] *Roth* v. *United States*, 354 U.S. 476, 484 (1957).

[61] *Jacobellis* v. *Ohio*, 378 U.S. 184, 191 (1964).

[62] *Miller* v. *California*, 413 U.S. 15, 22 (1973).

[63] *See, e.g., United States* v. *One Carton Positive Motion Picture Film Entitled "491"*, 367 F.2d 889 (2d Cir. 1966); *United States* v. *A Motion Picture Film Entitled "I Am Curious-Yellow,"* 404 F.2d 196, 200 (2d Cir. 1968); *Commonwealth* v. *Baer*, 209 Pa. Super. 349, 227 A.2d 915 (1967); *Attorney General* v. *A Book Named "Naked Lunch,"* 351 Mass. 298, 218 N.E.2d 571 (1966); *Commonwealth* v. *Dell Publications, Inc.*, 427 Pa. 189, 233 A.2d 840 (1967). At least one court reasoned that the *Memoirs* decision *broadened* the definition of obscenity. *People* v. *Weingarten*, 50 Misc. 2d 635, 271 N.Y.S.2d 158 (Crim. Ct. 1966).

One year after *Memoirs,* the Supreme Court agreed to review three state cases dealing with magazines of predominantly sexual content such as *Lust Pool, Shame Agent, Gent, Modern Man, High Heels,* and *Spree.* In a short per curiam opinion, the Court noted the differences in views among its members as to the proper test for obscenity or scope of obscenity regulation, but the conclusion of the Court was merely an acknowledgment of their divergence. "Whichever of these constitutional views is brought to bear upon the cases before us, it is clear that the judgments cannot stand. Accordingly, the judgment in each case is reversed."[64] As a result, the Court embarked upon a six-year policy of issuing what came to be called "*Redrup* reversals." These were summary reversals, without opinion, of any conviction relating to materials that at least five Justices, each applying his own test, found to be protected by the First Amendment. From 1967 until 1973, the Court decided 31 cases in this fashion, writing opinions in only those obscenity cases which raised significant procedural issues. The *Redrup* reversals included materials which, although perhaps not strictly "hard-core," were for the most part sexually explicit and had little "redeeming social value." As a result, the lower courts throughout the country followed the Supreme Court's lead in refusing to convict except in the most "extreme" cases.[65] Thus, if not by words then by results, the Supreme Court adopted a policy of banning only hard-core pornography, a policy which, in connection with the Court's willingness to review each obscenity conviction, resulted in a lengthy period of minimal regulation of obscenity.[66]

2.3   Obscenity and the Burger Court—the Miller Cases

Although there were several Supreme Court cases dealing with the validity of various state laws and municipal ordinances, primarily

[64] *Redrup* v. *New York,* 386 U.S. 767, 771 (1967).

[65] *See, e.g., Hunt* v. *Keriakos,* 428 F.2d (1st Cir. 1970) ("Rather, we are obliged to conclude that no photograph of the female anatomy, no matter how posed if no sexual activity is being engaged in, or however lacking in social value, can be held obscene."); *United States* v. *35mm. Motion Picture Film Entitled "Language of Love,"* 432 F.2d 705 (2d Cir. 1970); *House* v. *Commonwealth,* 210 Va. 121, 169 S.E.2d 572 (1969); *People* v. *Billingsley,* 20 Mich. App. 10, 173 N.W.2d 785 (1969) (this case contains a very inclusive listing of the publications involved in the various *Redrup* reversals as well as those found not obscene by many lower courts in the wake of *Redrup*).

[66] *See Luros* v. *United States,* 389 F.2d 200, 205 (8th Cir. 1968).

on charges of undue breadth or vagueness,[67] and several other cases dealing with various procedural aspects of obscenity law,[68] there were no major developments in the substantive scope of obscenity regulation, or the tests for obscenity, until 1973.[69] By then the Court was significantly different than it had been at the time of the *Memoirs* decision in 1966. Warren Burger was now the Chief Justice, and Justices Black, Fortas, and Harlan had been replaced by Justices Blackmun, Powell, and Rehnquist. This new Court accepted for argument a large number of obscenity cases dealing with the whole range of procedural, substantive, and constitutional issues raised by the concept of obscenity regulation. It was therefore expected that a major reformulation of obscenity doctrine would occur, and some, optimistically or pessimistically depending upon their point of view, thought the Court would strike down any obscenity laws dealing with "consenting adults."[70]

The Court handed down eight decisions on obscenity in June of 1973.[71] They dealt with a variety of issues and all are dealt with further on in this treatise. For purposes of the current discussion, the most significant is *Miller* v. *California*,[72] which focused on the actual definition of obscenity, the first time the Court had done this since the *Memoirs* decision in 1966. In at least one way, *Miller* was factually distinguishable from almost all other obscenity cases. While most involve the selling of books or magazines to "willing" buyers, or the exhibition of a motion picture to "willing" patrons, Miller was

[67] *See generally* Chapters 8 and 12 *infra*.

[68] *See generally* Chapter 11 *infra*.

[69] Cases dealing with minors, and with the issue of "pandering," are discussed in Chapter 4 *infra*.

[70] *See* Chapter 3.5 *infra*.

[71] *Miller* v. *California,* 413 U.S. 15 (1973) (*see* Chapter 6.3 *infra*); *Paris Adult Theatre I* v. *Slaton,* 413 U.S. 49 (1973) (*see* Chapter 3.5 *infra*); *Kaplan* v. *California,* 413 U.S. 115 (1973) (*see* Chapter 5 *infra*); *United States* v. *12 200-Ft. Reels,* 413 U.S. 123 (1973) (*see* Chapters 9.5 and 12.2 *infra*); *United States* v. *Orito,* 413 U.S. 139 (1973) (*see* Chapter 9.3 *infra*); *Heller* v. *New York,* 413 U.S. 483 (1973) (*see* Chapter 11.1 *infra*); *Roaden* v. *Kentucky,* 413 U.S. 497 (1973) (*see* Chapter 11.2 *infra*); *Alexander* v. *Virginia,* 413 U.S. 836 (1973) (per curiam) (*see* Chapter 12.3 *infra*.).

[72] 413 U.S. 15 (1973). *See* Leventhal, *1973 Round of Obscenity–Pornography Decisions,* 59 A.B.A.J. 1261 (1973); Hunsaker, *1973 Obscenity–Pornography Decisions: Analysis, Impact, and Legislative Alternatives,* 11 S. Diego L. Rev. 906 (1974); Clor, *Obscenity and the First Amendment: Round Three,* 7 Loyola U. L. Rev. (L.A.) 207 (1974); Fahringer and Brown, *Rise and Fall of Roth—A Critique of the Recent Supreme Court Obscenity Decisions,* 10 Crim. L. Bull. 785 (1974) and 62 Ky. L. J. 731 (1974); Note, *Obscenity '73: Something Old, A Little Bit New, Quite a Bit Borrowed, But Nothing Blue,* 33 Md. L. Rev. 421 (1973); *The Supreme Court, 1972 Term,* 87 Harv. L. Rev. 1, 160 (1973).

tried and convicted in California for sending unsolicited advertising brochures, themselves sexually explicit, to comparatively "unwilling" recipients. "This case involves the application of a State's criminal obscenity statute to a situation in which sexually explicit materials have been thrust by aggressive sales action upon unwilling recipients who had in no way indicated any desire to receive such materials."[73] Thus the Court had an opportunity to deal with the case on these narrow grounds, but declined to do so. Chief Justice Burger wrote the opinion for a five-man majority, the first majority opinion dealing with the definition of obscenity since *Roth,* 16 years earlier. His opinion dissected each element of the *Memoirs* standards, and from this there emerged a new set of standards designed to balance the state's interest in obscenity regulation [74] with the demands of the First Amendment.

At the outset, the *Miller* majority reaffirmed the basic elements of the *Roth* test for obscenity. Thus, a work is obscene if "the average person, applying contemporary community standards, would find that the work, taken as a whole, appeals to the prurient interest."[75] Of significance here is the reaffirmation of the concept of the average person as the standard by which the material's effect is to be measured,[76] of "contemporary community standards" as the appropriate frame of reference,[77] of the necessity of evaluating the work "as a whole,"[78] and the requirements that the work appeal to the prurient interest.[79] The basis of this first part of the three-part *Miller* test was a reemphasis of the *Roth* doctrine that obscenity was not speech at all and thus not protected by the First Amendment, and a statement as to the continuing vitality of the basic *Roth* test for defining obscenity.

Having reaffirmed the *Roth* test, the *Miller* Court then went on to add two other requirements for a finding of obscenity. One was that material is obscene if, and only if, it "depicts or describes, in a patently offensive way, sexual conduct specifically defined by the applicable state law."[80] Thus the requirement that the material be patently offen-

---

[73] 413 U.S. at 18.

[74] Whether the state had such a valid interest was discussed and answered affirmatively in *Paris Adult Theatre I* v. *Slaton,* 413 U.S. 49 (1973), discussed in Chapter 3.5 *infra.*

[75] 413 U.S. at 24.

[76] *See* Chapter 4 *infra.*

[77] *Miller* is perhaps of greatest significance for its discussion of local community standards. The subject is discussed fully in Chapter 6.6 *infra.*

[78] *See* Chapter 5.5 *infra.*

[79] *See* Chapter 5.2 *infra.*

[80] 413 U.S. at 24.

sive, as first enunciated in *Manual Enterprises* and *Jacobellis*, was retained,[81] and the court added a due process standard, that the type of depiction that was unlawful was required to be specifically stated by the controlling statute.[82] The essence of this second test, however, is that only hard-core pornography may be the subject of obscenity laws or obscenity prosecutions. "As a result, we now confine the permissible scope of such regulation to works which depict or describe sexual conduct."[83] "Under the holdings announced today, no one will be subject to prosecution for the sale or exposure of obscene materials unless these materials depict or describe patently offensive 'hard-core' sexual conduct specifically defined by the regulating state law, as written or construed."[84]

The third element of the *Miller* test, and the one that represented the most significant departure from prior law, was that material is obscene if "the work, taken as a whole, lacks serious literary, artistic, political, or scientific value."[85] This test specifically replaced the standard found in *Memoirs*. "We do not adopt as a constitutional standard the 'utterly without redeeming social value' test of *Memoirs* v. *Massachusetts,* 383 U.S., at 419; that concept has never commanded the adherence of more than three Justices at one time."[86] By thus changing the test for the "value" of the work, the *Miller* majority made the most clear break with the standards of previous cases.[87]

[81] *See* Chapter 5.3 *infra*.
[82] *See* Chapter 8 *infra*.
[83] 413 U.S. at 24.
[84] *Id*. at 27.
[85] *Id*. at 24. See Chapter 7 *infra*.
[86] *Id*. at 24–25. In a footnote, the Court quoted from *Kois* v. *Wisconsin*, 408 U.S. 229, 231 (1972), saying that "[a] quotation from Voltaire in the fly-leaf of a book will not constitutionally redeem an otherwise obscene publication." And the Court also rejected "the ambiguous concept of 'social importance.'" 413 U.S. at 15 n. 7.
[87] The extent to which the *Miller* standards were or were not "new" generated a substantial amount of litigation concerned with whether or not the decision would have retroactive application or whether offenses committed prior to *Miller* could be prosecuted at all, since some of the language in *Miller* perhaps supports the view that prior to that decision the standards might have been unduly vague. But in *Hamling* v. *United States,* 418 U.S. 87 (1974), the Court held that the change was not so major as to constitute a lack of notice, for pre-*Miller* conduct, of what activities were proscribed. 418 U.S. at 115–117. And the *Hamling* decision seems to support the view, taken by a number of lower courts, that a defendant charged with pre-*Miller* conduct, while he may be validly prosecuted, is entitled to those elements of either the *Memoirs* or *Miller* tests most beneficial to his defense. *See United States* v. *Palladino,* 490 F.2d 499, 500–501 (1st Cir. 1974) (pre-*Miller* material must be obscene under *both Miller* and *Roth-Memoirs* standards); *United States* v. *Thevis,*

To recapitulate, the *Miller* majority set forth a tripartite test for the determination of obscenity:

> (a) whether "the average person, applying contemporary community standards" would find that the work, taken as a whole, appeals to the prurient interest, . . . (b) whether the work depicts or describes, in a patently offensive way, sexual conduct specifically defined by the applicable state law; and (c) whether the work, taken as a whole, lacks serious artistic, political, or scientific value.[88]

This test must be taken in the context of the Court's pronouncements that only hard-core pornography may be prosecuted,[89] and it must be remembered that only if material meets *all* of these tests may it be legally obscene. This test now remains as the Court's latest attempt to solve "the intractable obscenity problem."[90] The particulars of each element of this test, and the treatment of the test by lower courts in the wake of *Miller,* are discussed fully in Chapters 4 through 8 of this work.

---

484 F.2d 1149, 1155 (5th Cir. 1973), *cert. denied,* 94 S. Ct. 3222 (1974); *United States* v. *Millican,* 487 F.2d 311, 332 (5th Cir. 1973), *cert. denied,* 94 S. Ct. 3233 (1974); *United States* v. *Alexander,* 498 F.2d 934 (2d Cir. 1974); *United States* v. *Wasserman,* 504 F.2d 1012 (5th Cir. 1974). The most detailed discussion of the issue is Judge Doyle's opinion in *United States* v. *B & H Dist. Corp.,* 375 F. Supp. 136 (W.D. Wis. 1974). *See also Ballew* v. *State,* 292 Ala. 468, 296 So.2d 206, 212 (1974) (Heflin, C. J., concurring); *People* v. *Enskat,* 33 Cal. App. 3d 900, 109 Cal. Rptr. 433 (1973).

[88] 413 U.S. at 24.

[89] As to the meaning of this term, see Chapter 5.1 *infra.*

[90] *Interstate Circuit, Inc.* v. *Dallas,* 390 U.S. 676, 704 (1968) (opinion of Harlan, J.).

3

Political, Sociological, and Psychological Considerations

3.1 The Arguments For and Against Obscenity Regulation

It is not the purpose of this treatise to make an argument either for or against the legal regulation of obscene material. That has been the aim of numerous books, speeches, pamphlets, articles, and other materials, by both lawyers and laymen, and from legal, political, religious, psychological, sociological, and medical viewpoints. The present treatise is an analysis of a body of law, and whether or not that body of law should exist at all is beyond the scope of this book. But no discussion of the law of obscenity would be complete if it did not at least include a discussion of those arguments that have been made, along with some of their strengths and weaknesses. The very existence of obscenity law, more than that of virtually any other body of law, is constantly being either challenged or justified, and this theoretical debate is a "brooding omnipresence" over any obscenity litigation. A discussion of the debate is therefore a necessary part of this book.[1]

---

[1] Since this chapter is more of a philosophical discussion or analysis than a study of existing law, footnotes will be kept to a minimum. General references include the following: CLOR, OBSCENITY AND PUBLIC MORALITY: CENSORSHIP IN A LIBERAL SOCIETY (1969); THE REPORT OF THE COMMISSION ON OBSCENITY AND PORNOGRAPHY (1970); T. MURPHY, CENSORSHIP: GOVERNMENT AND OBSCENITY (1963); M. ERNST, THE FIRST FREEDOM (1946); N. ST. JOHN-STEVAS, OBSCENITY AND THE LAW (1956); H. GARDINER, CATHOLIC VIEWPOINT ON CENSORSHIP (1958); L. LEVY, LEGACY OF SUPPRESSION (1960); R. KUH, FOOLISH FIGLEAVES? PORNOGRAPHY IN AND OUT OF COURT (1967); M. ERNST AND A. LINDEY, THE CENSOR MARCHES ON (1940); M. ERNST AND A. SCHWARTZ, CENSORSHIP: THE SEARCH FOR THE OBSCENE (1964); J. CHANDOS, ed., "TO DEPRAVE AND CORRUPT" (1962); W. CELLHORN, INDIVIDUAL FREEDOM AND GOVERNMENTAL RESTRAINTS (1956); A. GERBER, SEX, PORNOGRAPHY, AND JUSTICE (1965); H.L.A. HART, LAW, LIBERTY AND MORALITY (1966); J. KILPATRICK, THE SMUT PED-

49

The focus of the debate has been the issue of whether or not obscenity is protected by the First Amendment. Despite the fact that the Supreme Court answered this question in the negative in 1957,[2] and has reaffirmed this position in every subsequent obscenity case, the issue is still discussed. The most straightforward argument is the one that has been made repeatedly by Mr. Justice Black and Mr. Justice Douglas,[3] that the First Amendment is written and should be read in terms absolute, and therefore no form of speech, including obscenity, may be regulated by the state. While both would acknowledge the power of the states or of the Federal Government to act against speech inevitably interwined with conduct, no power, it is said, exists when words or pictures stand alone, as in the area of obscenity.

No other Justice of the Court has adopted this view, and it contains several significant weaknesses. Foremost, it seems, is that the argument is based on the premise that the First Amendment speaks in absolute terms, yet in fact this is not the case. Although the First Amendment does say that "Congress shall make no law", it is not these words that seem operative in interpreting the First Amendment. The amendment mandates that Congress shall make no law "abridging the freedom of speech, or of the press." Whatever may be the clarity of *"no law,"* the terms "abridge" and "freedom of speech, or of the press," are much less precise. It is possible that "abridge" means any lessening whatsoever, however, de minimis, and it is possible it does not. One dictionary meaning is to "deprive," and another is to "lessen," [4] and certainly the former connotes more of a taking than does the latter. But which one do we use? Similarly, what is included within

---

DLERS (1960); D. H. LAWRENCE, SEX, LITERATURE AND CENSORSHIP (1912); A. MEI-KLEJOHN, POLITICAL FREEDOM: THE CONSTITUTIONAL POWERS OF THE PEOPLE (1965); J. PAUL and M. SCHWARTZ, FEDERAL CENSORSHIP: OBSCENITY IN THE MAIL (1961); Henkin, *Morals and the Constitution,* 63 COLUM. L. REV. 391 (1963); Meiklejohn, *The First Amendment is an Absolute,* 1961 SUP. CT. REV. 245 (1961); Kristol, *Pornography, Obscenity and the Case for Censorship,* N.Y. TIMES MAG., March 28, 1971, pp. 24 ff; Richards, *Free Speech and Obscenity Law: Toward a Moral Theory of the First Amendment,* 123 U. PA. L. REV. 45 (1974); T. SCHROEDER, "OBSCENE" LITERATURE AND CONSTITUTIONAL LAW (1911).

[2] *Roth* v. *United States,* 354 U.S. 476 (1957).

[3] *See, e.g., Roth* v. *United States,* 354 U.S. 476, 508 (1957) (Douglas, J., dissenting); *Jacobellis* v. *Ohio,* 378 U.S. 184, 196 (1964) (Black, J.); *Kingsley Pictures Corp.* v. *Regents,* 360 U.S. 684, 690 (1959) (Black, J., concurring); *Memoirs* v. *Massachusetts,* 383 U.S. 413, 424 (1966) (Douglas, J., concurring); *Ginzburg* v. *United States,* 383 U.S. 463, 476 (1966) (Black, J., dissenting); *Miller* v. *California,* 413 U.S. 15, 37 (1973) (Douglas, J., dissenting); Black, *The Bill of Rights,* 35 N.Y.U. L. REV. 865 (1960).

[4] WEBSTER'S THIRD NEW INTERNATIONAL DICTIONARY 6 (1961).

"freedom of speech, or of the press"? If speech means *any* words, then shouting "fire" in a crowded theater is as much included by the literal words of the amendment as are the works of Shakespeare. But if some words are excluded, or some are intertwined with conduct, then we leave the realm of literal definitions for the complexities of constitutional theory. Similarly, even those constitutional provisions which are more explicit are not necessarily read literally. Although the Eleventh Amendment precludes suits in federal courts only by citizens of one state against *another* state, it has been interpreted, with virtually no objection, to preclude suits by a citizen against his own state, despite the complete absence of a way of interpreting the words of the amendment to support this result.[5] While it may be said that the First Amendment embodies principles more important than those embodied in the Eleventh, this again is a departure from the literal words into the spectrum of theory and analysis. The theory and analysis may lead to the position advocated by Mr. Justice Black and Mr. Justice Douglas, but it is a gross oversimplification to say that the result follows naturally from the words of the First Amendment.

It has been argued that the First Amendment speaks in absolute terms, and prohibits any obscenity regulation, on the basis of a closer analysis of First Amendment theory and principles. Perhaps the most persuasive of these arguments is that the First Amendment embodies a principle of diversity and toleration in the area of utterances, and, as a matter of policy, prohibits the government from deciding which utterances are acceptable and which are unacceptable, no matter how offensive the utterances may be. This is, of course, the classic libertarian[6] argument, most often associated with John Stuart Mill.[7] The premise of the argument is twofold. First of all, it is said that to allow the government the power to decide that some speech is bad or offensive is to allow the potential for suppression of political or religious ideas that are offensive to some. At the heart of every act of censorship, whether literary or political, it is argued, is the fact that someone is offended. Therefore, to remove an utterance from the area of

---

[5] *Hans* v. *Louisiana*, 134 U.S. 1 (1890).

[6] In this discussion, "libertarian" is used in a reasonably precise way, to denote those views, best exemplified by John Stuart Mill and to some extent John Locke (albeit in the context of religious toleration), which emphasize governmental tolerance of opposing views and deny the power of the government to decide that some speech is good and some is bad. While others may advocate the abolition of obscenity laws for other reasons, such as some argued value for obscenity, or the inability to define the term, or the inappropriateness of the judicial function in obscenity law, none of these are, in the strict sense, libertarian arguments.

[7] JOHN STUART MILL, ON LIBERTY (1859).

protected speech because it is offensive is to give the state a power it was not intended to have and should not have, since suppression of obscenity and suppression of opposing political views or criticisms of the government are merely different degrees or different applications of the same evil. Second, to assume that some expressions are better than others, or that some are worthless, is to assume infallibility, because no matter how offensive a statement may seem to some, it may be proved to be true in the future.[8] Thus, we should not suppress any utterance, because we may in fact be suppressing the truth, even though it may not appear so at the time.

The difficulty with the "fallibilist" argument is that it seems to prove too much. Virtually any political, social, legislative, or executive decision may be wrong, but we are forced to make decisions based on our best judgment at the moment. Carried too far, the fallibilist notion would deny to society the right to take any action that would have the effect of stifling any other approach. We should not, it could be said, zone our cities in such a way as to keep steel mills out of public parks because, no matter how unlikely it may seem to us now, future values may look upon steel mills as artistic masterpieces. The difference, of course, is that we are talking not of construction but of words and pictures, of speech, and speech is different from other things. Stifling speech is not the same as stifling actual embodiment of the views expressed by that speech. We are, then, back to a consideration of the theory of the First Amendment. What is it, exactly, that the concept of freedom of speech is designed to protect, and is the control of obscenity consistent or inconsistent with those values?

Similarly, the "foot in the door" argument that censorship of obscenity may lead to censorship of other things of more value may also be an overgeneralization, since the process of line-drawing is essential to both the legislative and the judicial process. That there is potential for abuse does not render an entire legal concept void, as long as there are appropriate safeguards. One is reminded of Mr. Justice Holmes's response to this argument in another context: "The power to tax is not the power to destroy while this Court sits."[9] Of course it can be argued that, unlike other areas, there is hard evidence here of potential abuse, given the history of suppression of serious literary works by Shelley, Theodore Dreiser, D. H. Lawrence, James

---

[8] Mill, *Id.*, and John Locke's *Letter Concerning Human Toleration* are considered the leading expositions of fallibilist theory.

[9] *Panhandle Oil Co.* v. *Knox*, 277 U.S. 218, 223 (1928) (Holmes, J., dissenting).

Joyce, and many others. It is true that many tales of horror about censorship include works which were not ultimately banned,[10] but an atmosphere in which the potential exists does have a "chilling effect" on artistic and literary freedom generally. Furthermore, how can we measure the effect of one month of suppression, even if not permanent? In the final analysis, it must be acknowledged that in the 18 years since *Roth* the Supreme Court has not, with the possible exception of the *Ginzburg* case,[11] affirmed or approved the censorship of any publication or motion picture of real literary merit. Arguments based on the abuses of the first half of the 20th century seem to lose their vitality as they pass more and more into the background.

Much of the foregoing discussion, of course, is based upon the view that there can be some agreement among learned people that certain books or movies have literary merit and others do not. But at least some part of the theory of the First Amendment is based on no such congruence of views. The essence of our society and of the First Amendment, it is said, is diversity, and government has no business deciding among these different views. Even if the views of "others" are not correct, society is still better off by letting all views flourish and not becoming involved in their evaluation. Whatever danger there might be in certain views is, first of all, best combatted in the "marketplace of ideas," and, second, is still less than the danger of a government which has the power to decide which views and tastes shall be allowed and which shall not. Thus, much of the support for abolition of obscenity regulation comes from the idea that, in the broadest view, the government has no business making moral, private, or personal decisions for individuals. In the narrower sense, government may at least not decide what people may say, see, print, or read.[12] People, it is said, have vastly different interests and tastes, and "one man's vulgarity is another's lyric."[13] This, the argument goes, is natural and the government should not force all of society into the majority's view of what seems best.

However, say the main proponents of obscenity regulation, what is so wrong with the government making laws based on moral judgments? Virtually all laws incorporate some moral values, especially

---

[10] *See* H. Clor, Obscenity and Public Morality 289 n. 53 (1969).

[11] *Ginzburg* v. *United States,* 383 U.S. 463 (1966). *See* Chapter 2.5 *supra.*

[12] There is also an argument that obscenity or pornography is actually good for people in that it provides a safe outlet for sexual desires, or that it breaks down taboos about sex. These arguments are discussed in more detail in the next section of this chapter.

[13] *Cohen* v. *California,* 403 U.S. 15, 25 (1971).

those dealing with adultery, Sunday closing, indecent exposure, and the like, or those having something of a paternalistic nature. Why then, they ask, are the opponents of obscenity regulation so appalled by the idea of the government's making moral decisions, especially in a society where those decisions are in fact being made by the majority of the population through their elected representatives? Furthermore, it is argued, obscenity degrades society, and makes it a less pleasant place in which to live. We have zoning ordinances, and spend an immense amount of public funds to improve the quality of life. Why is it so unthinkable to do the same thing by eliminating offensive, distasteful, and unpleasant literature or movies which pollute the environment no less than the fumes of automobiles or the discharge of chemicals into our rivers? It is true, they say, that this involves making a judgment, but if we cannot decide that explicit motion pictures or books showing human beings having sexual relations with animals are unacceptable, how can we presume to make any other decisions? While censorship has weaknesses and dangers, so does the flow of pornography, and the absence of censorship is not the *only* value our society should adopt.

The difficulty with this approach is that it seems to neglect the fact that speech is different from other forms of human activity. While it is true that governmental decisions are often based upon moral premises, and often deal directly with issues of individual morality, there is no constitutional provision prohibiting such concerns, but there is one setting up a general policy against interference with freedom of speech and of the press. Speech is "special" in our system of government, and we have made a specific decision to treat it as such by way of the First Amendment. Those who argue for the existence of obscenity laws often base their arguments upon the concept of majority rule. But this ignores the concept of the First Amendment and of the Bill of Rights generally. Certain rights are to be protected *from* majority rule. If this were not so we would need no Bill of Rights at all. Forms of governmental action to restrict or restrain conduct are not acceptable when it comes to restricting or restraining speech. So the question again arises as to whether or not obscenity is in that area of speech which is or should be protected. Like many of the other arguments for or against obscenity regulation, this one, too, seems to lead to a consideration of the theoretical basis of the First Admendment.[14]

[14] The essential work on the theory of the First Amendment is still T. Emerson, Toward a General Theory of the First Amendment (1963).

In the area of First Amendment theory, there are no easy answers. A complete discussion of First Amendment theory as it relates to obscenity law would, of course, begin with a study of constitutional history in an attempt to determine the intentions, if any, on this point of the framers of the Constitution. Many of the sources referred to in the first footnote of this chapter contain extensive discussions of the intentions of the founding fathers, and many come to drastically different conclusions from the same evidence. At best, the evidence is inconclusive. In fact, it is impossible to use effectively any constitutional history written in the 18th century in this regard because it is clear that at the time the First Amendment was drafted and adopted, it was to be solely a restriction on the Federal Government in an era when the states had considerably more autonomy than they now do. Thus, it is weak logic to use the intentions of the founding fathers regarding a Constitution which was intended to govern only a small segment of public and governmental activity to interpret a provision which now is a control over the activities of all the states as well as the Federal Government.[15]

Underlying the debate over the scope of the First Amendment is the issue of whether the First Amendment protects all utterances, or only those relating to "ideas." Morris Ernst would restrict the protections to ideas, excluding sedition and commercial speech, but includes obscenity in the concept of ideas.[16] Alexander Meiklejohn, on the other hand, would give the greatest protection to public speech, that dealing with political and governmental subjects and criticism, but a more qualified protection to private speech. But although obscenity may be thought of as private speech, he concludes that literature and the arts are essential to preparing the people to exercise political judgment, and thus sees no place for any censorship on obscenity grounds.[17] Mr. Justice Douglas would not enter into the debate at all as to what is or is not an idea, and would include any utterance whatsoever within the protection of the First Amendment, unless the danger was unequivocal, clear, present, and potentially disastrous, as

---

[15] It was not until the 20th century that First Amendment principles were thought to apply to the states by virtue of the Fourteenth Amendment. *Compare Gitlow* v. *New York,* 268 U.S. 652 (1925) with *Barron* v. *Baltimore,* 32 U.S. (7 Pet.) 243 (1833).

[16] *See* Brief of Morris L. Ernst, amicus curiae, *Roth* v. *United States,* 354 U.S. 476 (1957).

[17] A. MEIKLEJOHN, POLITICAL FREEDOM: THE CONSTITUTIONAL POWERS OF THE PEOPLE (1965); Meiklejohn, *The First Amendment is an Absolute,* 1961 SUP. CT. REV. 245 (1961).

in shouting "fire" in a theater.[18] Most commentators on the First
Amendment, however, take a less extreme position, and limit the
protection of the First Amendment to anything that looks like an
intellectual idea, as opposed to slander, commercial speech, or hard-
core pornography. Freedom of speech is designed to protect thought
and discussion and expression, they say, and certain classes of utterance bear no relation whatsoever to these goals. Others say the problems become greater when certain classes of speech are completely
excluded from First Amendment protection, as in the "two-level"
theory of *Roth,* and as to all speech the advantages of the speech
should be weighed against the disadvantages or the dangers, giving
speech either no presumption, a preferred position, or a rebuttable
presumption, depending upon the particular point of view which is
espoused. It is for this reason that most commentators who have
studied the issue would exclude hard-core pornography, and only that,
from First Amendment protection, since it is clearly worthless, while
other arguably obscene materials have some value. But this approach,
too, depends upon the ability to brand somethings as without value,
or as expressing no ideas, or the like. The fundamental issue, it seems
to this author, is still the concept of fallibilism. Are we willing to
decide, for present purposes, that some utterances have no value, and
are not entitled to protection, bearing in mind that equally condemned
speech in the past is now considered politically correct or artistically
important? Or are we going to allow all utterances to flourish on the
slight possibility that they may be proved valuable, or correct, if not
to all then to some, even though our current judgment tells us otherwise? This is a question I do not presume to answer, but one which
seems to lie at the heart of the theoretical debate on the legitimacy
of the obscenity laws.

There are, of course, arguments that are made on a more practical level. First among these is that obscenity is dangerous because
it either directly causes or slowly contributes to antisocial behavior,
such as rape, child molesting, adultery, and the like. Whether this is
or is not the case is discussed in the next section of this chapter. This
argument, too, is interrelated with the theoretical argument, for if obscenity is protected speech, then this showing must be made in such
a way as to meet the "clear and present danger" standard. If it is not
within the area of protected speech, or is less protected than other

---

[18] *See Beauharnais* v. *Illinois,* 343 U.S. 250, 384 (1952) (Douglas, J., dissenting);
Pittsburgh Press Co. v. *Human Relations Commission,* 413 U.S. 376, 397 (1973)
(Douglas, J., dissenting).

forms of speech, then a much less rigorous standard of proof is required. There is no argument that if the danger were both immediate and definite, obscenity laws would be justified. The argument comes in considering whether this degree of proof is necessary or not.

It is often argued that even though the exclusion of obscenity may be justified, the concept is so vague as to encroach inevitably upon protected speech, either directly by misapplication of uncertain standards, or indirectly by virtue of a chilling effect on political, literary, and artistic freedom. Alternatively, it is argued that since the standards are so uncertain, people are forced to make difficult literary and legal distinctions at the risk of criminal penalties for the wrong decision. It is this view that led Mr. Justice Brennan to change the position he took in *Roth* in favor of eliminating any restrictions on material available to "consenting adults."

> Our experience with the *Roth* approach has certainly taught us that outright suppression of obscenity cannot be reconciled with the fundamental principles of the First and Fourteenth Amendments. For we have failed to formulate a standard that sharply distinguishes protected from unprotected speech, . . .
>
> . . .
>
> But after 16 years of experimentation and debate I am reluctantly forced to the conclusion that none of the available formulas, including the one announced today, can reduce the vagueness to a tolerable level while at the same time striking an acceptable balance between the protections of the First and Fourteenth Amendments, on the one hand, and on the other the asserted state interest in regulating the dissemination of certain sexually oriented materials.[19]

Whether this argument is correct depends on two factors. First of all, should an otherwise valid concept be rejected in constitutional terms because of unworkability, or should the courts keep trying to make it workable? Second, is the factual premise correct? Are the obscenity laws suppressing materials of any value which are or should be protected? As to the latter, while it is true that there are instances like *Jenkins* v. *Georgia*,[20] where the obscenity laws have had a clearly unintended effect and were not rectified until the case reached the Supreme Court of the United States, the great bulk of obscenity findings since *Roth* have involved clearly commercial pornography.

[19] *Paris Adult Theatre I* v. *Slaton*, 413 U.S. 49, 83–84 (1973) (Brennan, J., dissenting).
[20] 418 U.S. 153 (1974).

Whether the amount of "leakage" is acceptable or unacceptable, how-ever, must remain essentially a subjective or individual judgment.

Somewhat related to this is the argument that the courts of the country, and in particular the Supreme Court, have better things to do than read dirty magazines or watch movies and make a large num-ber of obscenity decisions on a case-by-case basis, and that, in any event, the courts are not especially equipped to make essentially literary judgments. Those who are most ardent in their support of the obscenity laws have argued that the "solution" is to withdraw much of the appellate jurisdiction from appellate courts, or from the Su-preme Court only, in obscenity cases, leaving the determination as one of fact only to be made by the jury.[21] But to single out one area of substantive law for this treatment, or to remove from the Supreme Court a significant area of conflict regarding First Amendment prin-ciples, allows an extremely dangerous precedent. Conversely, the burdens on the courts have led some to suggest that if there were no obscenity laws, or more limited ones, the burden would be lessened.[22] But again, the making of constitutional decisions on this basis also seems to create a dangerous precedent in constitutional adjudication.

This section has not been a complete list of all of the arguments relating to the existence vel non of the obscenity laws, nor has it attempted to provide an exhaustive discussion of each one mentioned. To do this would require a separate volume at least as long as this treatise. This is merely a brief overview of some of the major argu-ments and positions, and the interested reader is referred to footnote 1 of this section if deeper study or analysis is desired.

3.2   The Psychological and Behavioral Effects of Obscenity

This section is not an attempt, any more than was the last, at a complete discussion of the relationship between sexually oriented literature or motion pictures and human behavior. But such considera-tions, and the empirical and other studies supporting them, are an essential part of the broader discussion of the necessity for or de-sirability of obscenity laws in general which is the subject of this

---

[21] This issue is discussed fully in Note, *Removal of Supreme Court Appellate Jurisdiction: A Weapon Against Obscenity,* 1969 DUKE L.J. 291 (1969). *See also* Chapters 7.3 and 7.4 *infra.*

[22] *Paris Adult Theatre I* v. *Slaton,* 413 U.S. 49, 92–93 (1973) (Brennan, J., dis-senting).

chapter. Therefore, this section will present a cursory look at the main behavioral connections between obscenity and conduct which have been hypothesized, the types of studies which have been done, and the current status of scientific knowledge in this area.[23]

One of the difficulties in trying to analyze the "state of the art" of research on the effects of obscenity is that few of the available studies have been able to dissociate themselves from a particular political or legal viewpoint. This is not to imply bias, but only to suggest that the answers depend on what questions are asked, and the formulation of the questions may involve the making of a priori legal or political judgments. For example, one work defined its task, in part, by asking if "the use of pornography is injurious to society. Does it present some clear and present danger that should be averted?"[24] Naturally, the formulation of the issues in terms of "clear and present danger" may lead to a different conclusion than if formulated, for instance, in terms of "an arguable correlation" or "unprovable assumption," the standards used most recently by the Supreme Court in upholding the validity of obscenity regulation.[25] And, of course, similar assumptions are made in much of the other psychological literature, resulting in a substantial body of literature which is of limited usefulness.

Any analysis of the effects of pornography on human behavior must be divided into short-term and long-term components. In the short term, does exposure to pornography cause readers or viewers to experience sexual stimulation, to commit antisocial acts, or to increase or decrease their sexual activity? In the long term, does expo-

---

[23] For those readers seeking to do further research or study in this area, the best starting place would be one of the more comprehensive literature reviews in the area, which attempt to summarize all of the published research available. *See, e.g.,* M. GOLDSTEIN and H. KANT, PORNOGRAPHY AND SEXUAL DEVIANCE 12–33 (1973); THE REPORT OF THE COMMISSION ON OBSCENITY AND PORNOGRAPHY 173–187, 287–308, 463, 614–624, 632–670 (N.Y. Times ed. 1970); H. CLOR, OBSCENITY AND PUBLIC MORALITY: CENSORSHIP IN A LIBERAL SOCIETY 136–174 (1969); Cairns, Paul, and Wishner, *Sex Censorship: The Assumptions of Anti-Obscenity Laws and the Empirical Evidence,* 46 MINN. L. REV. 1009 (1962).

In addition to the above, the following general works on the subject are recommended: E. KRONHAUSEN and P. KRONHAUSEN, PORNOGRAPHY AND THE LAW (1964); M. JAHODA, THE IMPACT OF LITERATURE: A PSYCHOLOGICAL DISCUSSION OF SOME ASSUMPTIONS IN THE CENSORSHIP DEBATE (1954); F. WERTHAM, SEDUCTION OF THE INNOCENT (1953); Symposium, *Obscenity and the Arts,* 20 L. & CONTEMP. PROB. 531 (1955); Kutchinsky, *The Effect of Easy Availability of Pornography on the Incidence of Sex Crimes: The Danish Experience,* 29 J. OF SOC. ISSUES 163 (1973).

See also the works cited in note 1 of this chapter.

[24] M. GOLDSTEIN and H. KANT, PORNOGRAPHY AND SEXUAL DEVIANCE 3 (1973).

[25] *Paris Adult Theatre I* v. *Slaton,* 413 U.S. 49, 58–61 (1973).

sure to pornography, or lack of such exposure, make it more or less likely that the subject will become a sexual "deviant," or be prone to commit antisocial acts such as rape or child molesting, or have normal or abnormal sexual desires? Or, in the long run, does a *general* proliferation of pornography increase or decrease the incidence of sexual aberration in society at large?

As to short-term effects, there is fairly universal agreement among the studies done that exposure to erotica results in immediate sexual stimulation. Thus, at the very least, there is a scientific basis for the concept of prurient interest. Reading or viewing sexually explicit materials can, and does in the large majority of cases, produce some degree of physical stimulation, as opposed to a purely intellectual or cognitive response. This does not, however, deal directly with the real problem, that of whether there is a relationship between erotic literature and some actual behavior which society desires to minimize.

Much of the evidence in support of a positive correlation between pornography and short-term or immediate antisocial conduct has come from law enforcement officers or police records. Much of it is in the form of case histories of sex offenders who, shortly before the crime occurred, have been found to have been reading or viewing pornographic material or who were found to have been frequent users of pornography.[26] However, although there may very well be a cause-and-effect relationship, the case histories do not present strong evidence of this. It may just as well be that the same mental or social aberrations which lead people to commit sex offenses also lead them to pornography. This does not bear on the issue of whether the pornography contributes to the aberration or to the sex offenses, or whether a reduction in the availability of pornography will reduce the number of sex offenses. There is some case-history evidence that indicates a causal relationship, but this is clearly in the minority.

There has also been considerable expert testimony and opinion on the causative relationship from law enforcement officials, psychiatrists, psychologists, and others.[27] Certainly there is no reason to discount expert testimony in this area any more than in any other, but for every expert opinion on the existence of a short-run causal relationship, there is an expert opinion reaching just the opposite conclusion. Thus the nonempirical evidence seems inconclusive at this

[26] *See, e.g.,* REPORT OF THE COMMISSION ON OBSCENITY AND PORNOGRAPHY 640–654 (N.Y. Times ed. 1970) (Minority Report of Charles H. Keating, Jr.).

[27] *See, e.g.,* Hoover, *Combating Merchants of Filth: The Role of the FBI,* 25 U. PITT. L. REV. 469 (1964).

point and, given the nature of such evidence, may be destined to remain so.

As to the empirical evidence, the research to date has been similarly inconclusive. Most of the studies indicate that there is some increase in sexual behavior shortly after exposure to erotic materials for a substantial number of subjects, at least for more than the number who exhibit a decreased amount of sexual activity. The increase is generally, on the average, no more for sex offenders than for the population at large, and most of the evidence supports the proposition that sex offenders are, in general, no more stimulated by erotica than the population at large. This does not end the inquiry, however, since the danger of stimulating someone who is predisposed toward rape is of course far more than the danger of stimulating someone not so disposed. While it seems clear that pornography cannot be shown to be the major cause of sexual antisocial acts, neither can it be completely excluded as a cause, at least among those who might otherwise be so disposed.

Perhaps the strongest evidence in support of the lack of a causal relationship is the Danish experience. After the abolition of all restrictions on the sale or exhibition of obscene or pornographic material, the evidence indicates that there was a decrease in the amount of sexual crime, supporting the hypothesis that pornography may constitute a safe outlet for sexual urges that might, in certain people, otherwise result in criminal activity. This hypothesis has also received the support of a number of psychologists and psychiatrists. But counterbalancing the Danish evidence is the fact that in the United States in the last 10 years there has been reasonably free access to pornography, despite the lack of decriminalization, and yet there has been no decrease, and in fact there has been an increase, in the rate of sexual crimes. Somewhat related is the theory that one of the appeals of pornography is its very illegality, and if it were legal it would have less appeal. Both the Danish experience and other evidence have tended to disprove this theory, however.

As to longer term effects, most of the studies have attempted to focus on the adolescent and preadolescent exposure to erotic material of adult and juvenile sex offenders.[28] While some studies show that certain groups of sex offenders have had significantly less exposure to erotic materials in adolescent years than control groups (which is consistent with the theory that some types of sexual maladjustments

---

[28] The amount of research on long-term effects of pornography is much less than the amount dealing with the short-term effects.

are caused by sexually repressed adolescence), there are others which show a somewhat greater exposure during preadolescent years for the sex offenders. To date the evidence as to long-term effects remains inconclusive.

Somewhat related is the hypothesis that exposure to erotica causes a long-run deterioration in moral values, resulting in long-term changes in sexual conduct which society finds unacceptable, including extramarital relations, premarital sex, divorce, and the like. There is, of course, substantial disagreement as to the harm of these types of conduct, and there have been no significant empirical studies in this area. In addition, there are some who hypothesize a long-run gain for society from sexual openness and the breaking down of many of society's taboos regarding sex. Thus, even if empirical evidence were available in this area, there is much less of a consensus that this is a societal problem than for more obvious dangers such as an increase in the number of rapes or similar crimes.

The best summary of the research to date seems to indicate that exposure to pornographic materials tends to reinforce, in the short run, preexisting patterns of sexual behavior. The research does not seem to indicate a *primary* causal relationship, but a significant proportion indicates some relationship between pornography and antisocial conduct for those who, on account of other factors, would be so disposed in any event.

3.3   The Commission on Obscenity and Pornography

Obscenity law and the obscenity "market" in the United States have been a matter of significant public concern and comment for many years. It is not surprising, therefore, that it has also been a matter of legislative, and in particular congressional, concern for some time. Congressional committees have been looking into obscenity and pornography since 1952.[29] The most well known and most recent congressional inquiry was that leading to the creation of the Com-

---

[29] *See* U.S. Congress, House Select Committee on Current Pornographic Materials, *Hearings before Select Committee and Report of Select Committee to the House,* 83d Cong., 2d sess., 1952, H. Rep. 2510 (Gathings committee); U.S. Congress, Senate, Committee on the Judiciary, Subcommittee to Investigate, 83d Cong., 2d sess., 1954; 84th Cong., 1st sess., 1955 (*Obscene and Pornographic Materials*); 84th Cong., 2d sess., 1956 (Kefauver committee); U.S. Congress, House, Committee on Post Office and Civil Service, Subcommittee on Postal Operations, *Hearings before Subcommittee and Report of Subcommittee to Committee,* 86th Cong., 1st sess., 1959, 86th Cong., 2d sess., 1960, 87th Cong., 1st sess., 1961 (Granahan committee).

mission on Obscenity and Pornography, which completed its work and presented its findings in 1970.[30] Authorized by Congress, with its members appointed by the President, under the chairmanship of Dean William B. Lockhart of the University of Minnesota Law School, the Commission studied obscenity from political, psychological, sociological, and legal viewpoints for three years before making its recommendations. For research purposes, the Commission was divided into four panels, each of which prepared a final report. The panels were Traffic and Distribution, Effects, Positive Approaches, and Legal. Although its recommendations or research methodology may be criticized by some, there is little dispute that the Commission, by extensive research, added a great deal to the knowledge and literature of the law and science of obscenity control.[31]

The Commission authorized and supervised a large number of legal and empirical studies, conducted hearings, and emerged with recommendations based on those findings. The majority of the Commission found the evidence to support the *lack* of a significant causal relationship between pornography and antisocial conduct, a reasonably minor degree of public concern about sexually explicit materials and their growing availability, a possibly beneficial effect of pornography in its function of providing an outlet for those with potential antisocial tendencies, and the significant possibility that the courts would, on the basis of *Stanley* v. *Georgia*,[32] significantly limit or eliminate the regulation of obscenity as to "consenting adults." On the basis of these findings, the Commission recommended that society be more "open and direct in dealing with sexual matters" and that this be fostered by a "massive sex education effort," by continued discussion of the issues raised by obscenity and pornography, and similar approaches. These efforts, the Commission felt, might very well decrease the need for pornographic materials in society. But the most noteworthy of the Commission's recommendations was that recom-

---

[30] The authorization for the commission came in 1967. P.L. 90–100. In addition to the report itself (REPORT OF THE COMMISSION ON OBSCENITY AND PORNOGRAPHY (1970)), *see* Lockhart, *The Findings and Recommendations of the Commission on Obscenity and Pornography: A Case Study of the Role of Social Science in Formulating Public Policy*, 24 OKLA. L. REV. 209 (1971); Clor, *Science, Eros and the Law: A Critique of the Obscenity Commission Report*, 10 DUQUESNE L. REV. 63 (1971); Johnson, *The Pornography Report: Epistemology, Methodology and Ideology*, 10 DU-QUESNE L. REV. 190 (1971); Barnett, *Corruption of Morals—The Underlying Issue of the Pornography Commission Report*, 1971 L. & SOC. ORDER 189 (1971).

[31] The compilation of all of the Commission's research is in the 10-volume series of TECHNICAL REPORTS OF THE COMMISSION ON OBSCENITY AND PORNOGRAPHY (1970–1971).

[32] 394 U.S. 557 (1969).

mending that all "federal, state, and local legislation prohibiting the sale, exhibition, or distribution of sexual material to consenting adults be repealed." The Commission recommended controls as to minors and public displays, but suggested complete decontrol as to consenting adults, based on the lack of a proven relationship between erotica and crime, on the lack of clear legal standards, on the lack of strong public opinion in favor of control, and on some positive advantages of erotica.

Needless to say, these recommendations were both surprising and a source of much public controversy. The findings, recommendations, and research methodology were criticized by Commissioners Hill and Link in the Hill-Link Minority Report, and by Commissioner Keating, who would not participate in the meetings of the Commission for reasons most clearly stated in his report. Both minority reports were strongly critical of the ideological makeup of the Commission as well as of its entire method of operation. The President of the United States declared the report to be "morally bankrupt" and Congress rejected the recommendations and the report by a vote of 96–3. Furthermore, the legal premise upon which many of the Commission's recommendations were based was rejected by the Supreme Court three years later, as is discussed in the next section of this chapter.

But although the Report of the Commission on Obscenity and Pornography has had little effect, and many of the criticisms of its research methods have some validity, it remains the most comprehensive collection of study and research on all aspects of obscenity to this date, and presents, by virtue of its majority and minority reports, a clear exposition of the most significant arguments for and against governmental control of obscenity.

3.4 *"Consenting Adults"—The Limited Scope of* Stanley v. Georgia

While material which is legally obscene is outside the scope of First Amendment protection of speech, controls on obscenity are not completely outside the range of constitutional protection. One of the major exceptions and its implications are discussed in this section. The exception arose in *Stanley* v. *Georgia,*[33] in which the Supreme

[33] 394 U.S. 557 (1969). *See* Note, *Obscenity from Stanley to Karalexis: A Back Door Approach to First Amendment Protection,* 23 VAND. L. REV. 369 (1970); Katz, *Privacy and Pornography,* 1969 SUP. CT. REV. 203 (1969); Note, *Private Morality*

Court held that private possession of obscene material in the home was protected by the constitutional right of privacy. Stanley's home was the subject of a police search as a result of his alleged bookmaking activities. In the process of conducting the search, the officers found three reels of 8-millimeter film which, upon viewing, appeared to the officers to be obscene. Stanley was arrested, tried, and convicted under Georgia law for possession of obscene matter. Although his conviction was upheld by the Supreme Court of Georgia, the U.S. Supreme Court reversed, in an opinion written by Mr. Justice Marshall, on the grounds that "mere private possession of obscene matter cannot constitutionally be made a crime." [34] Asserting the constitutional protection of privacy and of "the right to receive information and ideas," the opinion distinguished this type of obscenity regulation from the type permitted by *Roth* and its progeny.

> Whatever may be the justifications for other statutes regulating obscenity, we do not think they reach into the privacy of one's own house. If the First Amendment means anything, it means that a State has no business telling a man, sitting alone in his own house, what books he may read or what films he may watch. Our whole constitutional heritage rebels at the thought of giving government the power to control men's minds. [35]
>
> . . .
>
> Whatever the power of the state to control public dissemination of ideas inimical to the public morality, it cannot constitutionally premise legislation on the desirability of controlling a person's private thoughts. [36]
>
> . . .
>
> We hold that the First and Fourteenth Amendments prohibit making mere private possession of obscene material a crime. *Roth* and the cases following that decision are not impaired by today's holding. As

---

and the Right to be Free: The Thrust of Stanley v. Georgia, 11 ARIZ. L. REV. 792 (1969); Note, *Stanley* v. *Georgia: A First Amendment Approach to Obscenity Control,* 31 OHIO ST. L.J. 364 (1970); Comment, *Stanley* v. *Georgia: New Directions in Obscenity Regulation,* 48 TEXAS L. REV. 646 (1970); *The Supreme Court, 1968 Term,* 83 HARV. L. REV. 7, 147 (1969); 57 CAL. L. REV. 660 (1970); 43 TEMP. L.Q. 89 (1969)

[34] 394 U.S. at 559. Mr. Justice Black concurred on the grounds of the total invalidity of any obscenity laws (394 U.S. at 568) and Justices Stewart, Brennan, and White concurred on the grounds that there had been an illegal search and seizure, declining to reach the constitutional issue dealt with by Mr. Justice Marshall. There was no dissent.

[35] 394 U.S. at 565.

[36] *Id.* at 566.

we have said, the States retain broad power to regulate obscenity; that power simply does not extend to mere possession by the individual in the privacy of his own home.[37]

Neither the facts nor the narrow holding of *Stanley* were of any great practical importance. Most states with possession-of-obscenity statutes required that the possession be with intent to sell, distribute, or the like.[38] And mere possession was certainly a very rarely prosecuted crime, even in those states which did make it a criminal act. The importance of *Stanley* lay with its possible extension. Mr. Justice Marshall's opinion, while referring to the right of privacy, was specifically based upon the First Amendment and referred many times to the impropriety of governmental control over minds, even as to obscene material. This, in the opinion of many,[39] signalled the demise of any obscenity law, or at least a substantial chance for the extension of the principles of *Stanley* beyond the physical confines of the home. For example, a Massachusetts federal court reasoned that the principles of *Stanley* extended to theaters, open to the public but controlled so as to allow entrance only to "consenting adults."[40] "If a rich Stanley can view a film, or read a book, in his own home, a poorer Stanley should be free to visit a protected theatre or library. We see no reason for saying he must go alone."[41] Another court reasoned that the right to own in *Stanley* implied the right to receive, and thus invalidated the federal prohibition on importation of obscene material.[42] Similar cases invalidated prohibitions on mailing obscene matter,[43] or transporting it across state lines.[44]

But the Supreme Court shortly made it clear that such broad readings of *Stanley* were unjustified. The principles of *Stanley* did not apply to materials in the channels of commerce, and they cer-

---

[37] *Id.* at 568.

[38] *See e.g.,* Mass. G. L. ch. 272 § 29 (Supp. 1974); N.Y. Penal Law § 1141 (Supp. 1974)

[39] *See* authorities cited in note 33 *supra.*

[40] *Karalexis* v. *Byrne,* 306 F. Supp. 1363 (D. Mass. 1969) (three-judge court), *vacated and remanded,* 401 U.S. 216 (1971).

[41] *Id.* at 1367.

[42] *United States* v. *Thirty-Seven (37) Photographs,* 309 F. Supp. 36 (C.D. Cal. 1970) (three-judge court), *reversed,* 402 U.S. 363 (1971).

[43] *United States* v. *Reidel* (unreported, C.D. Cal. 1970), *reversed,* 402 U.S. 351 (1971). *Compare Miller* v. *United States,* 431 F.2d 655 (9th Cir. 1970), *vacated,* 413 U.S. 913 (1973), *reaffirmed,* 507 F.2d 1100 (9th Cir. 1974).

[44] *United States* v. *B & H Dist. Corp.,* 319 F. Supp. 1231 (W.D. Wis. 1970), *vacated and remanded,* 403 U.S. 927 (1971), *reaffirmed,* 347 F. Supp. 905 (W.D. Wis. 1972), *vacated,* 413 U.S. 909 (1973).

tainly did not apply to commercial distributors.[45] Stanley applied to the home and little else.

The final narrowing of *Stanley* (or at least the narrowing of popular opinion regarding the effect of *Stanley*) came in 1973 when, on the day the Supreme Court handed down its decision in *Miller,* it decided *Paris Adult Theatre I* v. *Slaton.*[46] *Paris* represented a broad attack on the entire concept of obscenity laws for consenting adults, based on First Amendment rights and the right of privacy. But the attack was rejected by the Supreme Court. The Court's opinion is based on a geographical or locational view of the right of privacy, despite some of the broad language in *Stanley* about thought control, and thus the principles of *Stanley* are applicable only to the private home, and not to sale, distribution, or exhibition in motion picture theaters. Unlike marital privacy, which the Court said was based on an intimate relationship, and not on a particular place, the privacy right to read material which by definition does not involve the true thought process relates only to the home.[47] "The idea of a privacy right and a place of public accommodation are, in this context, mutually exclusive."[48] Although the Court could have called the privacy right involved one dealing with the intimacy of the mind of man and equated that with the marital relationship of other privacy cases,[49] this approach would logically have required the extension of *Stanley* to other areas, in much the same way as *Griswold* led to *Eisenstadt* and *Roe.*[50] But it is certain that the Court had no such intention, and thus made it clear that *Stanley* was limited to private possession in the home, any broader language in that opinion notwithstanding.

Since, therefore, the exhibition of obscenity did not involve protected speech (*Roth* and *Miller*), it was unnecessary for a state to show a clear and present danger, or equivalent quantum of proof, that

---

[45] *United States* v. *Reidel,* 402 U.S. 351 (1971); *United States* v. *Thirty-Seven Photographs,* 402 U.S. 363 (1971). See Comments, 24 ALA. L. REV. 120 (1971); 23 ALA. L. REV. 135 (1970); 49 TEXAS L. REV. 575 (1971); 33 U. PITT. L. REV. 367 (1971); 25 VAND. L. REV. 196 (1972); 6 U. SAN. FRAN. L. REV. 399 (1972); 25 SW. L.J. 819 (1971); Note, *Still More Ado About Dirty Books,* 81 YALE L.J. 309 (1971).

[46] 413 U.S. 49 (1973). See Note, *Roe and Paris: Does Privacy Have a Principle?,* 26 STAN. L. REV. 1161 (1974), and materials cited in Chapter 2, note 72 *supra.*

[47] 413 U.S. at 66–67.

[48] *Id.*

[49] *See, e.g., Roe* v. *Wade,* 410 U.S. 113 (1973); *Griswold* v. *Connecticut,* 381 U.S. 479 (1965); *Eisenstadt* v. *Baird,* 405 U.S. 438 (1972).

[50] *Id.*

obscenity would cause antisocial conduct or other harm that a legislature could properly prevent. Similarly, since the right of privacy or an equivalent right was not involved (*Paris*), the state need not even show a compelling interest. All the state needed, therefore, was to show a "rational basis" for the legislation, which Chief Justice Burger said could be done by showing an arguable correlation between obscene material and crime, even if this is categorized as an "unprovable assumption." [51] Since there is no strict standard of review, a state's finding that the obscenity control would have moral or social benefits would not be challenged since these hypotheses, while not necessarily correct, were reasonable and rational, and certainly not proved to be incorrect. Thus, while no state is required to have obscenity laws, *Paris,* for the time being, seems to settle the question that they may do so if they wish.

[51] 413 U.S. at 57–62.

4

Who Sets the Standard?
Defining the "Average Person"

4.1   Development of the "Average Person" Test

As we have seen, the original *Roth* test, as reaffirmed by *Miller,* provides that material is obscene if, and only if, "the average person, applying contemporary community standards, would find that the work, taken as a whole, appeals to the prurient interest." [1] Virtually every clause of this test involves legal and definitional problems of major importance, all of which are treated at some point in this work. But central to all of these issues is the problem of defining the "average person." Clearly what is prurient to one may not be prurient to another. Some are more susceptible to sexually oriented materials than others, children may find things "prurient" that adults do not, and so on. The concept of the average man is a concept designed to provide some sort of measuring rod, in the hope that, by referring to such an external standard, determination of obscenity may be marked by some degree of consistency. That this objective has not been achieved is fairly apparent, but the notion of the average person is still central to a full understanding of obscenity law, and of crucial significance in most obscenity litigation. [2]

Even before the "average person" concept was conceived, it was recognized that there must be some frame of reference by which to

[1] *Miller* v. *California,* 413 U.S. 15, 24 (1973); *Roth* v. *United States,* 354 U.S. 476, 489 (1957); *see generally* Chapter 2 *supra* for a description of these cases and the development of the basic test for obscenity.

[2] *See generally* Lockhart and McClure, *Literature, the Law of Obscenity, and the Constitution,* 38 MINN. L. REV. 295, 338–342 (1954); Lockhart and McClure, *Censorship of Obscenity: The Developing Constitutional Standards,* 45 MINN. L. REV. 5, 70–78 (1960); Note, *The Law of Obscenity: New Significance of the Receiving Group,* 34 IND. L. J. 426 (1959).

determine whether the effects of allegedly obscene materials were such as to come within the range of legal prohibitions. The germinal case is of course the 1868 English decision of *Regina* v. *Hicklin*,[3] in which Lord Chief Justice Cockburn defined obscenity as the tendency of the material "to deprave and corrupt those whose minds are open to such immoral influences and into whose hands a publication of this sort may fall." [4] Thus the focus of the test was not the *probable* effect on the public at large, but the *possible* effect on those most likely to be influenced by sexually oriented materials: children, immature adults, and the like. Since the protection of children and "weak" adults has long been considered a major justification for obscenity laws, this test had considerable appeal and was adopted by most American courts.[5] But by directing attention to the effect on those who were especially susceptible, the *Hicklin* test tended toward a "lowest common denominator" approach to the availability of reading matter, in that only those words which would be safe for the entire population, young and old, normal and abnormal, could be distributed. This difficulty was noted by then District Judge Learned Hand in *United States* v. *Kennerley* [6] in 1913. Although he felt compelled by precedent to follow the *Hicklin* test, he observed that to continue to follow it would "reduce our treatment of sex to the standard of a child's library in the supposed interest of a salacious few. . . . To put thought in leash to the average conscience of the time is perhaps tolerable, but to fetter it by the necessities of the lowest and least capable seems a fatal policy." [7]

Judge Hand's observations soon began to develop in the case law. The focal point of the shift from the "most susceptible" to the "average man" is Judge Woolsey's decision in *United States* v. *One Book Called "Ulysses."* [8] Without citing any authority, Judge Woolsey rejected the *Hicklin* test and substituted the concept of the average man.

> Whether a particular book would tend to excite such impulses and thoughts must be tested by the Court's opinion as to its effect on a person with average sex instincts—what the French would call

[3] [1868] L. R. 3 Q.B. 360.

[4] *Id.* at 372.

[5] *See, e.g., United States* v. *Bennett*, 24 F. Cas. 1093 (No. 14,571) (C.C.S.D.N.Y. 1879); *United States* v. *Clarke*, 38 F. 500 (E.D. Mo. 1889); *In re Banks*, 56 Kan. 242, 42 P. 693 (1895); *Commonwealth* v. *New*, 142 Pa. Super. 358, 16 A.2d 437 (1940); *Commonwealth* v. *Friede*, 271 Mass. 318, 171 N.E. 472 (1930); *People* v. *Seltzer*, 122 Misc. 329, 203 N.Y.S. 809 (Sup. Ct. 1924).

[6] 209 F. 119 (S.D.N.Y. 1913).

[7] *Id.* at 121.

[8] 5 F. Supp. 182 (S.D.N.Y. 1933), *aff'd*, 72 F.2d 705 (2d Cir. 1934).

l'homme moyen sensuel—who plays, in this branch of legal inquiry, the same role of hypothetical reagent as does the "reasonable man" in the law of torts and "the man learned in the art" on questions of invention in patent law.[9]

Three years later, Judge Learned Hand finally was able to give legal effect to the opinion he had expressed 23 years earlier in *Kennerley*. In *United States* v. *Levine*,[10] the trial judge had instructed the jury that there was a class of people in every community of "the young and immature, the ignorant and those who are sensually inclined" and that the books at issue must be measured in terms of their likely effect on those people rather than on "people of a high order of intelligence and those who have reached mature years." This instruction, Hand wrote, was reversible error, as it unduly sacrificed the interests in "art, letters or science" to the "mere possibility that some prurient person may get a sensual gratification from reading or seeing what to most people is innocent and may be delightful or enlightening." [11] Following the action of the Second Circuit, most other American jurisdictions adopted the "average person" test or some modification thereof, and by the time *Roth* was decided, the *Hicklin* rule was clearly on the way out in American jurisprudence.[12]

In fact, the final demise of the *Hicklin* rule regarding a book's effect on the particularly susceptible came several months before *Roth*, in the case of *Butler* v. *Michigan*.[13] Butler had been convicted under a section of the Michigan Penal Code which in effect enacted the *Hicklin* rule. It made unlawful the selling of any material "tending to incite minors to violent or depraved or immoral acts," or "manifestly tending to the corruption of the morals of youth." Material which would have this tendency was unlawful even if sold to the

---

[9] 5 F. Supp. at 184.

[10] 83 F.2d 156 (2d Cir. 1936).

[11] Id. at 157. *See also United States* v. *Dennett*, 39 F.2d 564 (2nd Cir. 1930).

[12] *See, e.g., Walker* v. *Popenoe*, 149 F.2d 511, 512 (D.C. Cir. 1945); *People* v. *Viking Press*, 147 Misc. 813, 264 N.Y.S. 534 (Magis. Ct. 1933); *People* v. *Pesky*, 230 App. Div. 200, 204, 243 N.Y.S. 193, 197 (1930), *aff'd* 254 N.Y. 373, 173 N.E. 227 (1930); *State* v. *Lerner*, 81 N.E.2d 282, 289 (Ohio Ct. Comm. Pl. 1948). *But see United States* v. *Two Obscene Books*, 99 F. Supp. 760 (N.D. Cal. 1951), *aff'd sub nom. Besig* v. *United States*, 208 F.2d 142 (9th Cir. 1953).

Hicklin seems to retain some vitality in England. Obscene Publications Act, 1959, 7 & 8 Eliz, II ch. 66 § 1; *Regina* v. *Reiter* [1954] 1 All Eng. 741. *But see Regina* v. *Martin Secker Warburg, Inc.* [1954] 2 All Eng. 683.

[13] 353 U.S. 380 (1957). This case was decided during the same term of court as *Roth*, but the decision was announced two months before the *Roth* argument and four months before the *Roth* opinion. *See* Case Comment, 11 MIAMI L. Q. 523 (1957).

general public and, in fact, Butler had been charged with selling the allegedly obscene book to a police officer. On appeal to the Supreme Court, he charged that the statute unduly restricted freedom of speech by prohibiting "distribution of a book to the general public on the basis of the undesirable influence it may have upon youth." Writing for a unanimous Supreme Court, Mr. Justice Frankfurter agreed, holding that the legislation was "not reasonably restricted to the evil with which it is said to deal. The incidence of this enactment is to reduce the adult population of Michigan to reading only what is fit for children." [14] "Surely, this is to burn the house to roast the pig." [15] Thus the court made clear that if children were to be protected, it was not to be done by depriving the entire population of any material dealing with sex, a holding clearly at variance with the *Hicklin* rationale and thus a clear signal of what was to come in *Roth*.

If any doubt remained after *Butler,* there could be none after *Roth*. "The *Hicklin* test, judging obscenity by the effect of isolated passages upon the most susceptible persons, might well encompass material legitimately dealing with sex, and so it must be rejected as unconstitutionally restrictive of the freedoms of speech and press." [16] Thus *Roth* substituted the "average person" standard for that of the most vulnerable, not from any expressed desire to set a specific guideline, but rather from a desire to elaborate on the constitutional dimensions of obscenity regulation. And although there have been many legal issues arising out of the concept of the average person, the *Roth* statement of it remains the standard in force to the present day.[17]

4.2   Who is the Average Person?

It has been shown in the previous section of this chapter that one purpose of the average-person standard is to require the trier of fact to evaluate the effect of the material at issue on the population as a whole, rather than upon the most susceptible segments of that population. Of equal importance is the goal of applying some external standard other than the internal standards of the trier of fact. In other words, the judge or jury is not to determine whether the material

---

[14] 353 U.S. at 383.
[15] *Id.*
[16] *Roth* v. *United States,* 354 U.S. 476, 489 (1957).
[17] The statement in *Roth* referring to the "average person" was repeated and reaffirmed verbatim in *Miller* v. *California,* 413 U.S. 15, 24 (1973).

appeals to their prurient interest, but to the prurient interest of the hypothetical average man. It is not the personal standards of the judge or jury that are relevant, but the standards of the population as a whole, as interpreted or applied by the judge or jury.[18] It is questionable, however, whether this goal has been or can possibly be achieved. As Judge Woolsey pointed out in the *Ulysses* case, the "average person" may be compared with the hypothetical "reasonable man" in tort law. But although the words are similar and the comparison has a certain amount of surface appeal, a closer analysis causes the comparison to suffer. The reasonable man in tort law is not an average person, but an "ideal" person.[19] He is "a model of all proper qualities with only those human shortcomings and weaknesses which the community will tolerate." [20] "Nor is it proper to identify him even with any member of the very jury who are to apply the standard; he is rather a personification of a community ideal of reasonable behavior, determined by the jury's social judgment." [21] As can be seen, then, the emphasis of the reasonable-man concept in tort law is on the identification of the best human qualities of judgment, caution, and the like. The average-man concept in obscenity law, however, is aimed not at human strengths, but at human weaknesses. If the sexual sophistication of the reasonable man were as finely tuned as his judgment and caution, then the major justification for obscenity laws would disappear, since this "ideal" would not be aroused by *Ulysses* or *God's Little Acre,* and would be merely bored by commercial pornography. Thus, it must be recognized that the concept of the average man in obscenity law is most likely sui generis, and comparisons with the "reasonable man" of tort law, the "average prudent man" of trust law, or similar formulations are not likely to be helpful.

There is, also, a serious doubt as to whether the jury, especially in an obscenity case, despite instructions on the average man, can apply any evaluation of pruriency other than its own personal standard. It is no easy task to decide what may appeal to someone else's prurient interest. Most people probably assume themselves of "average sex instincts" [22] and thus, for purposes of an obscenity case,

---

[18] *See Smith* v. *California,* 361 U.S. 147, 172 n.3 (Harlan, J., concurring in part and dissenting in part); *United States* v. *One Book Called "Ulysses,"* 5 F. Supp. 182, 184 (S.D.N.Y. 1933); E. DEVITT and G. BLACKMAR, FEDERAL JURY PRACTICE AND INSTRUCTIONS § 41.10 (1970).

[19] W. PROSSER, HANDBOOK OF THE LAW OF TORTS § 32 at 150 (4th Ed. 1971).

[20] *Id.*

[21] *Id.* at 151.

[22] *See City of Cincinnati* v. *Walton,* 145 N.E.2d 407, 413 (Ohio Mun. Ct. 1957).

are inclined to align their own reactions with the reactions of the average man. If they themselves are offended, they are likely to find the work offensive, and if they are not offended, they are likely to find the work not offensive. This is not to say that a jury may not be appropriately guided by proper instructions, but in this area, more than most, the identification of an external standard seems especially difficult. Faced with a "reasonable man" instruction in a tort case, it is likely that many jurors would say "What would I have done?," or at least "What do I like to think I would have done?" It is likely that this same personalization exists, consciously or not, in applying the average-man standard in obscenity law. Of course, identifying the problem is far easier than solving it, and it may very well be that encouraging the trier of fact to apply this external standard is the best we can do.

In applying the average-man standard, courts have tended to distinguish the average man from either the very susceptible or the most immune. The average man has been said not to be the "highly sensitive or the callous, the educated or the uneducated." [23] He is not a "puritanical prude," [24] but is an "average, normal, adult person." [25] He is not an "abnormal adult of noxious tendencies or the person of defective or subnormal mentality." [26] The test cannot include "possible effects on the young and very susceptible or on the other hand, on the sensualists and libertines, . . ." [27] While of course the original purpose of the "average person" test was to remove from consideration the effect on the most susceptible segments of the population, it also removes from consideration the lack of effect on those unusually sophisticated, worldly, or educated.

> [T]he courts are concerned with the dominant theme as it appears to the *average* person—not as it may be considered by the small segment of the population represented by the "experts" who testified for appellant—sophisticated, cultured, highly educated, widely travelled and worldly-wise members of the intelligentsia whose judgment as to the reactions of the *average* person who reads *Candy* is of questionable, if any, value. The book may appeal to the intellectual elite on

[23] *State* v. *Miller,* 145 W. Va. 59, 112 S.E.2d 472, 478 (1960).
[24] *State* v. *Shapiro,* 122 N.H. Super. 409, 300 A.2d 595, 609 (1973).
[25] *In re Louisiana News Company,* 187 F. Supp. 241 (E.D. La. 1969).
[26] *State* v. *Mahoning Valley Distributing Agency, Inc.,* 169 N.E.2d 48, 59 (Ct. Comm. Pl. Ohio 1960).
[27] *People* v. *Bunis,* 23 Misc. 2d 156, 198 N.Y.S.2d 568, 571 (Buff. City Ct. 1960). *See also People* v. *Brooklyn News Co.,* 12 Misc. 2d 768, 174 N.Y.S.2d 813 (County Ct. 1958).

an intellectual plane. The erudite and sophisticated may be cultivated to the point where they are not affected by erotica or may be impervious to the storms of aroused passion. We are confident, however, that the *average* person is not so finely tuned or so smugly insulated.[28]

In the face of these varying definitions, at least one court has held that since the words "average person" are words of common meaning, no jury instruction as to their definition was necessary.[29] But the better practice would seem to be to include some definition in the instructions to the jury. Although the words themselves may be of common meaning, the use of the average-person concept is far less common to the jury. An instruction explaining the purpose of the average-person test, and explaining the exclusion of the especially susceptible and the especially sophisticated should help in the jury's understanding of exactly what it is they are being called upon to decide.

Of significant importance in this context is the issue of whether or not minors are to be included within that amalgam that comprises the average person. Taken by itself, the holding in *Butler* v. *Michigan*[30] would indicate that the average person must be the average adult, and any inclusion of minors within the definition of the average person would be reversible error.[31] While of course some books, magazines, and motion pictures that may be arguably obscene would be available to both adults and minors, the offense, in order to avoid the mandate of *Butler,* would have to be the actual distribution to minors, and of course in that prosecution the effect on minors would be for determination by the jury.[32] But in a prosecution under a general obscenity statute, it would appear from *Butler* that only the effect on the average adult would be relevant and constitutionally permissible. This interpretation seems to have been followed by the drafters of the Model Penal Code, which provides that "predominant appeal shall be judged with reference to ordinary adults unless it appears from the character of the material or the circumstances of its

[28] *State* v. *Smith*, 422 S.W.2d 50, 58–59 (Mo. 1967), *cert. denied*, 393 U.S. 895 (1968). *See also Raphart* v. *Hogan*, 305 F. Supp. 749, 754 (S.D.N.Y. 1969). Of course, serious literary or similar appeal to this "erudite" minority would be of considerable relevance in determining whether the work satisfied the third element of the *Miller* test by being without serious literary, artistic, scientific, or political value. See Chapter 7 *infra*.

[29] *State* v. *Jungclaus*, 176 Neb. 641, 126 N.W.2d 858, 863 (1964).

[30] 352 U.S. 380 (157). *See* text accompanying notes 13–15, *supra*.

[31] *See People* v. *Bunis*, 23 Misc. 2d 156, 198 N.Y.S.2d 568, 571 (Buff. City Ct. 1960).

[32] *See* Chapters 4.5 and 4.6 *infra*.

dissemination to be designed for children or other specially susceptible audience." [33] But on the other hand there is evidence that the Supreme Court may not object to the inclusion of the young within the "average person" formulation as long as the test or instructions do not particularly focus on youth or the very susceptible. In *Roth,* the Court approved the instructions of the trial judge which told the jury that "you are to consider the community as a whole, young and old, educated and uneducated, the religious and the irreligious—men, women and children." [34] And very recently the Supreme Court dismissed an appeal for want of a substantial federal question where the trial court judge had defined the average person to include children. [35] Thus it appears as if any formulation of the average-person standard not sounding overly much like *Hicklin* will be accepted by the Court. [36]

---

[33] Model Penal Code § 251.4 (1), 10 Uniform Laws Annotated 592 (1974). It must be remembered, however, that the Model Penal Code provisions regarding obscenity are not intended to include as much as is constitutionally permissible. *See* Schwartz, *Morals Offenses and the Model Penal Code,* 63 COLUM. L. REV. 669, 667–681 (1963).

[34] *Roth* v. *United States,* 354 U.S. 476, 490 (1957). But the trial judge's instructions, although including the young, did not place special emphasis on the appeal to the young. "The test is not whether it would arouse sexual desires or sexual impure thoughts in those comprising a particular segment of the community, the young, the immature or the highly prudish or would leave another segment, the scientific or highly educated or the so called wordly-wise and sophisticated indifferent and unmoved. . . . The test in each case is the effect of the book, picture or publication considered as a whole, not upon any particular class, but upon all those whom it is likely to reach. In other words you determine its impact upon the average person in the community." *Id.*

This formulation may be contrasted with that in *Commonwealth* v. *Isenstadt,* 318 Mass. 543, 62 N.E.2d 840 (1945), which also included children within the average-person formulation, but with a much greater emphasis. "The thing to be considered is whether the book will be appreciably injurious to society. . . . because of its effect upon those who read it, without segregating either the most susceptible, remembering that many persons who form part of the reading public and who cannot be called abnormal are highly susceptible to influences of the kind in question and that most persons are susceptible to some degree, and without forgetting youth as an important part of the mass, if the book is likely to be read by youth." 318 Mass. at 552, 62 N.E.2d at 845.

See also People v. *Vanguard Press,* 192 Misc. 127, 84 N.Y.S.2d 427, 430 (Magis. Ct. 1947) ("the effect of the whole book on reasonable normal readers both young and old").

[35] *Kensiger* v. *Ohio,* Hamilton Cty. Ct. App., Ohio (May 10, 1974), *appeal dismissed,* No. 74–226, 43 U.S.L.W. 3348 (December 17, 1974). Although four Justices dissented from the dismissal, none chose this as a stated ground for their view that the conviction should be reversed. *Id.* But the Court seems unwilling to *approve* the inclusion of children. *See Ginzburg* v. *United States,* 383 U.S. 463, 465 n.3 (1966).

[36] Lockhart and McClure argue that the "average person" formulation in *Roth* was nothing more than a rejection of the *Hicklin* rule, and was not intended itself

It should be obvious, however, that any mention of children or inclusion of children in a test is likely to have a disproportionate effect on a jury. Therefore, it would seem that such a standard, when there is no evidence of distribution to children, should be proscribed.[37] When there is evidence of distribution to minors, then this should be treated by separate statutes designed to prohibit the distribution of obscene material to minors.

4.3 Materials Aimed at "Deviant" Groups

Even the briefest look at a representative sample of what can best be called commercial pornography will reveal that much of it caters to the tastes or desires of that segment of the population with "unconventional" sexual interests. There is a large amount of material aimed at those with homosexual, sadomasochistic, or other atypical sex habits or desires. Attempting to fit these materials into the *Roth-Miller* test for obscenity has resulted in the one significant exception to the "average person" rule. This exception derives from *Mishkin* v. *New York*,[38] decided by the Supreme Court in 1966 on the same day as *Memoirs* v. *Massachusetts*.[39] *Mishkin* involved a number of books depicting various deviant sexual practices, such as flagellation, fetishism, beating, lesbianism, and the like. It was argued that these materials "do not satisfy the prurient-appeal requirement because they do not appeal to prurient interest of the 'average person' in sex, that instead of

---

to create a new standard. Lockhart and McClure, *Censorship of Obscenity: The Developing Constitutional Standards*, 45 MINN. L. REV. 5, 73 (1960). *See also Mishkin* v. *New York*, 383 U.S. 502, 509 (1966). On the emphasis as being controlling, *see United States* v. *Manarite*, 448 F.2d 583, 592 (2d Cir. 1971), *cert. denied*, 404 U.S. 947.

[37] In *Books, Inc.* v. *United States*, 358 F.2d 935 (1st Cir. 1966), *reversed on other grounds*, 388 U.S. 449 (1967), the trial court judge had given an instruction substantially identical to that given in *Roth* and quoted in note 34 *supra*. The First Circuit upheld his refusal specifically to exclude children in a proposed instruction reading as follows: "The average person, as construed and applied, must be the adult within the community . . . and anyone other than an adult must be absolutely excluded from your consideration." 358 F.2d at 938.

[38] 383 U.S. 502 (1966). *See* Reiss, *The Supreme Court and Obscenity—Mishkin and Ginzburg—Expansion of Freedom of Expression and Improved Regulation Through Flexible Standards of Obscenity*, 21 RUTG. L. REV. 43 (1966); 44 TEXAS L. REV. 1382 (1966). *Mishkin* is of equal significance for its treatment of the issue of scienter. *See* Chapter 11.4 *infra*.

[39] 383 U.S. 413 (1966). *See* Chapter 2.2 *supra*.

stimulating the erotic, they disgust and sicken." [40] Mishkin's argument
was imaginative and, in fact, true. Materials of this type were neither
designed to nor would in fact appeal to the prurient interest of the
average person. But it was equally clear that they were designed to
appeal to someone's prurient interest. That being the case, the Court,
in an opinion written by Mr. Justice Brennan, held that for materials
of this type the *Roth* test was met if the books appealed to the prurient
interest of the members of the deviant group for whom the materials
were intended.

> Where the material is designed for and primarily disseminated to a
> clearly defined deviant sexual group, rather than the public at large,
> the prurient-appeal requirement of the *Roth* test is satisfied if the
> dominant theme of the material taken as a whole appeals to the
> prurient interest in sex of the members of that group. The reference
> to the "average" or "normal" person in *Roth* . . . does not foreclose
> this holding. . . . We adjust the prurient appeal requirement to social
> realities by permitting the appeal of this type of material to be assessed
> in terms of sexual interests of its intended and probable recipient
> group; and since our holding requires that the recipient group be de-
> fined with more specificity than in terms of sexually immature persons,
> it also avoids the inadequacies of the most-susceptible-person facet
> of the *Hicklin* test.[41]

In order to make it even more clear that the particular deviant groups
involved must be clearly delineated and specifically described, Mr.
Justice Brennan referred to a standard psychiatric sourcebook for
descriptions of types of deviant groups.[42]

The words of the Court in *Mishkin* seem fairly self-explanatory.
If the materials are designed for a deviant group, then prurient appeal
must be measured in terms of that group.[43] Nonetheless, a number of
substantive and procedural issues have arisen in the application of
this exception to the "average person" rule. Probably of foremost

[40] 383 U.S. at 508. The titles of the books at issue included such works as
*Mistress of Leather, Dance With the Dominant Whip, Cult of the Spankers, The
Hours of Torture, Bound in Rubber, The Violated Wrestler,* and *Sorority Girls
Stringent Initiation.*

[41] 383 U.S. at 508–509.

[42] *Id.* at 509 n.8. The reference is to 1 AMERICAN HANDBOOK OF PSYCHIATRY
593–604 (Arieti ed. 1959).

[43] *Mishkin* is still "good law," having been reaffirmed on this point in *Miller* v.
California, 413 U.S. 15, 33 (1973), and *Hamling* v. *United States,* 418 U.S. 87,
127–130 (1974). Certain material may, of course, appeal to the prurient interest of
both average people and members of a deviant group, and this may be considered
by the jury. *Id.*

significance is the definition of a deviant group. The *Mishkin* Court clearly intended that standard medical categories of deviance would be used, and the cases have involved bestiality,[44] material of the " 'bondage' genre," [45] homosexuality,[46] and sado-masochism.[47] And while it is clear that neither mere nudity nor publications appealing to nudists are necessarily obscene,[48] presumably a magazine, book, or movie alleged to appeal to the prurient interest of nudists would be evaluated in that context. In the most unusual application of the rule, one federal court determined that the people who go to X-rated movies are a deviant group and proceeded to rule based on the pre-sumed appeal to that group.[49] It seems clear that this is somewhat beyond the purpose of the *Mishkin* holding.

Of course, the understanding of different deviant groups and what would or would not appeal to their prurient interest is a subject not necessarily within the general knowledge of the average juror in an obscenity case. Therefore, there has been considerable litigation as to whether or not expert testimony is required in these cases. Better practice would seem to indicate that expert psychiatric or other testi-mony should be used by the prosecution in cases of this sort, to ex-plain the appeal to the jury, and a number of cases demonstrate the effective use of such testimony.[50] The Second Circuit, in a case decided before *Mishkin,* held that there must be some evidence as to the type of appeal, and to whom, that is claimed,[51] but has more recently held that no expert testimony, as such, is necessary.[52] Nor is it necessary that there be *independent* proof that the material was designed for and primarily disseminated to a clearly defined sexual group. It is suffi-

---

[44] *United States* v. *Gundlach,* 345 F. Supp. 701 (M.D. Pa. 1972).

[45] *United States* v. *Klaw,* 350 F.2d 155, 167–168 (2d Cir. 1965).

[46] *United States* v. *56 Cartons Containing 19,500 Copies of a Magazine Entitled "Hellenic Sun,"* 373 F.2d 635, 640 (4th Cir. 1967), *rev'd on other grounds sub nom. Potomac News Co.* v. *United States,* 389 U.S. 47 (1967). *Cf. Manual Enterprises* v. *Day,* 370 U.S. 478, 482 (1962).

[47] *United States* v. *Ewing,* 445 F.2d 945, 947–948 (10th Cir. 1971).

[48] *See Sunshine Book Co.* v. *Summerfield,* 355 U.S. 372 (1958).

[49] *United States* v. *One Reel of 35mm Color Motion Picture Film Entitled "Sinderella,"* 369 F. Supp. 1082, 1086 (E.D.N.Y. 1972), *aff'd,* 491 F.2d 956 (2d Cir. 1974).

[50] *See, e.g., United States* v. *Ewing,* 445 F.2d 945, 947–948 (10th Cir. 1971); *Klaw* v. *Schaffer,* 151 F. Supp. 534 (S.D.N.Y. 1957), *aff'd,* 251 F.2d 615 (2d Cir. 1958), *vacated on procedural grounds,* 357 U.S. 346 (1958). *Cf. United States* v. *Hamling,* 481 F.2d 307, 321–322 (9th Cir. 1973), *aff'd,* 418 U.S. 87 (1974).

[51] *United States* v. *Klaw,* 350 F.2d 155, 167–168 (2d Cir. 1965).

[52] *United States* v. *Wild,* 422 F.2d 34 (2d Cir. 1969), *cert. denied,* 402 U.S. 986 (1971).

cient that a certain group seems to be the probable recipient.[53] But it still appears as if some type of guidance to the jury should be required in a case of this type. There is no reason to believe that a jury can understand whether or not certain material would or would not appeal to the prurient interest of a group with sexual inclinations vastly different from their own. While it may be reasonable to assume an understanding of the "average person's" desires, the desires of the abnormal are most likely best left to expert analysis. It is not surprising, therefore, that the Supreme Court has left open the possibility that such testimony will be required in "deviant" cases, although it no longer is required in cases dealing with more conventional materials.

> We reserve judgment, however, on the extreme case, not presented here, where contested materials are directed at such a bizarre deviant group that the experience of the trier of fact would be plainly inadequate to judge whether the material appeals to the prurient interest.[54]

Since the issue thus remains open, a complete prosecution case dealing with "deviant" materials should include expert testimony as to which group the materials seem directed at, whether or not the materials would in fact appeal to the prurient interest of members of that group, and why.

4.4 Pandering—Ginzburg v. United States

Perhaps the most controversial case in all of obscenity law is *Ginzburg* v. *United States,*[55] decided by the Supreme Court in 1966 on the same day as both the *Memoirs* and *Mishkin* cases. Ralph Ginzburg was the publisher of a number of books on sexual topics, the most noteworthy being *Eros,* an expensively produced hardbound magazine dealing with sex and erotica. He was prosecuted under 18

[53] *United States* v. *Manarite,* 448 F.2d 583, 592 (2d Cir. 1971), *cert. denied,* 404 U.S. 947 (1971).

[54] *Paris Adult Theatre I* v. *Slaton,* 413 U.S. 49, 56 n.6 (1973).

[55] 383 U.S. 463 (1966). *See* Monaghan, *Obscenity, 1966: The Marriage of Obscenity Per Se and Obscenity Per Quod,* 76 YALE L. J. 127 (1966); Dyson, *Looking-Glass Law: An Analysis of the Ginzburg Case,* 28 U. PITT. L. REV. 1 (1966); Semonche, *Definitional and Contextual Obscenity: The Supreme Court's New and Disturbing Accommodation,* 13 U.C.L.A. L. REV. 1173 (1966); *The Supreme Court, 1965 Term,* 80 HARV. L. REV. 91, 186 (1966); Note, *More Ado About Dirty Books,* 75 YALE L. J. 1364 (1966); Note, *Obscenity and the Supreme Court: Nine Years of Confusion,* 19 STAN. L. REV. 167 (1966).

U.S.C. § 1461 for mailing *Eros,* as well as another periodical, *Liaison,* and a book, *The Housewife's Handbook of Selective Promiscuity.* Ginzburg was convicted by a judge, sitting without a jury, on all 22 counts of the indictment, although as to the particular edition of *Eros* at issue, which contained 15 articles, only four were claimed and found to be obscene, these being an excerpt from *My Life And Loves,* by Frank Harris, an article by Drs. Eberhard and Phyllis Kronhausen, authors of *Pornography and the Law,* a collection of "locker room" variety limericks, and a photographic essay dealing with interracial love. It is clear that the offending pieces were far from the commercial pornography distributed by such as Roth, Alberts, and Mishkin, and in fact there was considerable expert testimony at trial from leading literary figures as to the value and serious purpose of the works at issue. Nonetheless, the court found *Eros* and the other publications to be obscene, and the conviction was ultimately upheld by the Supreme Court.[56]

Three factors, combined to give this case major public and legal significance. First, some of the materials, especially the individual articles in *Eros,* seemed to be serious literary efforts. Second, Ginzburg was sentenced to five years imprisonment,[57] considerably longer than the sentence in most obscenity cases, where fines or shorter prison terms seem to be the rule. Finally, in upholding his conviction, the Supreme Court introduced the concept of "pandering," the main subject of this section.

In dealing with the obscenity of the materials at issue, the opinion of Mr. Justice Brennan, for the Court, admitted that the materials involved, standing alone, presented a very close case. Therefore, he said, it was necessary to look at the setting in which the materials were distributed, a setting he described as the "commercial exploitation of erotica solely for the sake of their prurient appeal."[58] Thus, although the materials, in and of themselves, may not have been obscene, they became so by the manner in which they were made available to the public. In language quoting from Chief Justice Warren's

[56] This marked the first time the Supreme Court had ever found a work to be obscene. The findings of the trial court are at 224 F. Supp. 129 (E.D. Pa. 1963), *aff'd,* 338 F.2d 12 (3d Cir. 1964).

[57] Although his sentence was ultimately reduced, he did serve a substantial portion of this sentence. *See United States* v. *Ginzburg,* 398 F.2d 52 (3d Cir. 1968) (granting a hearing on petition for reconsideration of sentence), and *United States* v. *Ginzburg,* 436 F.2d 1386 (3d Cir. 1971), *cert. denied,* 403 U.S. 931 (1971) (affirming modified sentence of three years).

[58] 383 U.S. at 465–466.

concurrence in *Roth*,[59] Justice Brennan characterized Ginzburg as being in the "sordid business of pandering," [60] and of using advertising materials displaying the "leer of the sensualist." [61] Two factors were most damning to Ginzburg in this finding of "pandering." First, there was evidence that mailing privileges had been sought in Intercourse and Blue Ball, Pennsylvania, because of the "appeal" of the postmark, and were finally obtained in Middlesex, New Jersey. Secondly, the advertising for the publications stressed the erotic rather than the serious or literary aspects of the publications.

> The deliberate representation of petitioners' publications as erotically arousing, for example, stimulated the reader to accept them as prurient; he looks for titillation; not for saving intellectual content.
>
> . . .
>
> Where the purveyor's sole emphasis is on the sexually provocative aspects of his publications, that fact may be decisive in the determination of obscenity.
>
> . . .
>
> *Eros* was created, represented and sold solely as a claimed instrument of the sexual stimulation it would bring.[62]

Thus the Supreme Court held that where the obscenity of a work, standing alone, would be a close question, evidence as to pandering would be relevant in determining whether the work was in fact legally obscene. And the essential holding of *Ginzburg* was recently reaffirmed by the Court in *Hamling* v. *United States*.[63] "The District Court's instruction was clearly consistent with our decision in *Ginzburg* . . ., which held that evidence of pandering could be relevant

---

[59] It is not the book that is on trial; it is a person. The conduct of the defendant is the central issue, not the obscenity of a book or picture. The nature of the materials is, of course, relevant as an attribute of the defendant's conduct, but the materials are thus placed in context from which they draw color and character. A wholly different result might be reached in a different setting.

. . .

The defendants in both these cases were engaged in the business of purveying textual or graphic matter openly advertised to appeal to the erotic interest of their customers. They were plainly engaged in the commercial exploitation of the morbid and shameful craving for materials with prurient effect.

Roth v. *United States,* 354 U.S. 476, 495–496 (Warren, C. J., concurring). *See also United States* v. *Rebhuhn,* 109 F.2d 512 (2d Cir. 1940) (L. Hand., J.), which the *Ginzburg* Court took as authority for the pandering concept. 383 U.S. at 472–474.

[60] 383 U.S. at 467.

[61] *Id.* at 468.

[62] *Id.* at 470–471.

[63] 418 U.S. 87 (1974).

in the determination of the obscenity of the materials at issue, as long as the proper constitutional definition of obscenity is applied." [64]

But what exactly is the meaning of *Ginzburg?* The dissenters argued that the Court had in fact created a new crime of "pandering," a crime Ginzburg could have had no knowledge of at the time he distributed the materials in question.[65] But the Court has emphasized that pandering is neither a separate crime nor an element of the offense under federal obscenity statutes. It is merely a guide for the jury or court in determining the obscenity of materials as they apply the appropriate test for obscenity.[66] Even functionally, as opposed to technically, pandering does not appear to be an independent crime, since no amount of pandering can cause a conviction unless the materials involved are at least arguably obscene.[67] Pandering has been described as an indicator, rather than a separate offense.[68] The pandering concept is also much less than a wholesale adoption of the idea that obscenity must of necessity be evaluated in context. Contextual analysis is not the rule, but only the general description for a small number of well-defined exceptions. If anything, pandering seems based more on a theory of either an admission or an estoppel against a particular defendant. In other words, having proclaimed his materials to be obscene, or pornographic, or appealing to the prurient interest, or whatever, the distributor is estopped from denying those conclusions in court, or, at the very least, they constitute evidentiary admissions against him. Some of the language in *Ginzburg* seems to support this conclusion. Ginzburg had claimed that much of his material was of scholarly or professional interest. But the Court was not persuaded. Petitioners (Ginzburg and his codefendants)

> . . . did not sell the book to such a limited audience, or focus their claims for it on its suppressed therapeutic or educational value; rather, they deliberately emphasized the sexually provocative aspects

[64] *Id.* at 130.

[65] "Ginzburg . . . is finally and authoritatively condemned to serve five years in prison for distributing printed matter about sex which neither Ginzburg nor anyone else could possibly have known to be criminal." 383 U.S. at 476 (Black J., dissenting).

[66] *Hamling* v. *United States,* 418 U.S. 87, 130 (1974). *See also Milky Way Productions Inc.,* v. *Leary,* 305 F. Supp. 288, 294 (S.D.N.Y. 1969) (three-judge court), *aff'd per curiam sub nom. New York Feed Co.* v. *Leary,* 397 U.S. 98 (1970); *United States* v. *Leary,* 331 F. Supp. 712, 713 (D. Conn. 1971).

[67] *Cf. Papish* v. *Board of Curators of University of Missouri,* 331 F. Supp. 1321, 1330–1331 (W.D. Mo. 1971), *aff'd,* 464 F.2d 136 (8th Cir. 1972), *reversed,* 410 U.S. 667 (1973) (pandering found in lower court, but Supreme Court held language to be clearly protected speech).

[68] *United States* v. *Thevis,* 484 F.2d 1149, 1152 (5th Cir. 1973), *cert. denied,* 94 S. Ct. 3222 (1974).

of the work, in order to catch the salaciously disposed. They proclaimed its obscenity; and *we cannot conclude that the court below erred in taking their own evaluation at its face value and declaring the book as a whole obscene despite the other evidence.*[69]

Similarly, in *Mishkin* v. *New York,*[70] decided the same day as *Ginzburg,* the Court observed that "appellant's own evaluation of his material confirms such a finding. See *Ginzburg* v. *United States,* ante, p. 463." [71] This was also clarified in the third case of that day, *Memoirs* v. *Massachusetts.*[72]

It is not that in such a setting the social value is relaxed so as to dispense with the requirement that a book be *utterly* devoid of social value, but rather that, as we elaborate in *Ginzburg* v. *United States, post, pp. 470–473, where the purveyor's sole emphasis is on the sexually provocative aspects of his publications, a court could accept his evaluation at its face value.*[73]

Thus it is not only the character of the advertisements and the like which can lead to a finding of pandering, but also the source of the statements. A distributor who describes his own materials in order to increase sales may very likely see his words come back to haunt him.[74]

It would seem to be appropriate at this point to describe some of the activities which have been held to constitute or not to constitute pandering. Obviously, this is a very subjective question, and determination may vary from jurisdiction to jurisdiction, but a relatively substantial body of case law is developing. It is clear that mere open display and sale is not pandering, nor are enticing or lurid pictures and text on the cover.[75] Of course, the fact that the materials

[69] 383 U.S. at 472 (emphasis added).

[70] 383 U.S. 502 (1966).

[71] *Id.* at 510. *See also People* v. *Burnstad,* 32 Cal. App. 3d 560, 108 Cal. Rptr. 247 (1973) (defendant held to his own description of materials as "hardcore"); *Childs* v. *State of Oregon,* 431 F.2d 272, 276 (9th Cir. 1970) (distributor referred to materials at issue as "dirty books" and "worst ones"). *Compare People* v. *Rosakos,* 268 Cal. App. 2d 497, 74 Cal. Rptr. 34 (1969).

[72] 383 U.S. 413 (1966).

[73] *Id.* at 420 (emphasis added).

[74] An interesting converse arose in a case where it was urged that the government had admitted that a film had social value and was thus estopped from claiming it was obscene. *United States* v. *A Motion Picture Film Entitled "I Am Curious— Yellow,"* 285 F. Supp. 465, 471 (S.D.N.Y. 1968), *rev'd on other grounds,* 404 F.2d 192 (2d Cir.).

[75] *Redrup* v. *New York,* 386 U.S. 767 (1967); *Books, Inc.* v. *United States,* 388 U.S. 449 (1967), *rev'g* 358 F.2d 935 (1st Cir. 1966); *United States* v. *Baranov,* 418 F.2d 1051 (9th Cir. 1969).

are sold commercially is not in and of itself relevant, so it is logical that references in one book to others available from the same publisher,[76] or a high price or high mark-up for the materials,[77] do not constitute pandering. In none of these instances were the activities involved inconsistent with the distribution of protected speech, and it seems as if this would be the appropriate way of viewing the issue. If the activities are completely inconsistent with the distribution of materials for other than prurient purpose, then pandering, in the legal sense, exists. For example, where a motion picture was exhibited in the "Por-No" Theater, the name of the theater was relevant to support a finding of pandering.[78] Similarly, previews of a motion picture isolating and emphasizing only its prurient aspects may be relevant, even though the entire motion picture would present a close case.[79] So also, a large, unselective, and indiscriminate mailing list would seem to indicate pandering.[80] Although advertising, in itself, is not pandering,[81] sensationalist advertising emphasizing the erotic or prurient aspects is the most common type of pandering evidence.[82] But if the advertising emphasizes the serious rather than the prurient,[83] or merely warns about the sexually explicit aspects of the material,[84] then this is not pandering.

What seems to follow from the cases is the inevitable conclusion that the evidence of pandering must be made on a case-by-case basis. It is a subjective evaluation, at best, and the cases do not display a great deal of consistency. But it still must be remembered that no amount of pandering can render a clearly nonobscene work obscene, and without some evidence of prurient appeal, patent offensiveness, and lack of value, the question of pandering is irrelevant.

[76] *Aday* v. *United States,* 388 U.S. 447 (1967), *rev'g sub nom. United States* v. *West Coast News Company,* 357 F.2d 855 (6th Cir. 1966). But types of books available at the same bookstore may be relevant. *Orito* v. *State,* 55 Wis. 2d 161, 191 N.W.2d 763 (1972). *See also Hewitt* v. *Maryland Board of Censors,* 254 Md. 179, 254 A.2d 203, 210 (1969).

[77] *Potomac News Co.* v. *United States,* 389 U.S. 47 (1967), *rev'g* 373 F.2d 635 (4th Cir. 1967); *Luros* v. *United States,* 389 F.2d 200 (8th Cir. 1968).

[78] *People* v. *Sarnblad,* 26 Cal. App. 3d 801, 103 Cal. Rptr. 211 (1972).

[79] *New Riviera Arts Theatre* v. *State,* 219 Tenn. 652, 412 S.W.2d 890, 894–895 (1967).

[80] *Miller* v. *United States,* 431 F.2d 655, 657, (9th Cir. 1970).

[81] *People* v. *Bloss,* 388 Mich. 792, 201 N.W.2d 806 (1972); *People* v. *Mature Enterprises, Inc.,* 73 Misc. 2d 749, 343 N.Y.S.2d 911, 916 (1973).

[82] *United States* v. *Ratner,* 502 F.2d 1300, 1301 (5th Cir. 1974); *Childs* v. *State of Oregon,* 431 F.2d 272, 276 (9th Cir. 1970).

[83] *United States* v. *Pellegrino,* 467 F.2d 41, 45 (9th Cir. 1972).

[84] *United States* v. *Stewart,* 337 F. Supp. 299 (E.D. Pa. 1971); *State* v. *Lebevitz,* 294 Minn. 424, 202 N.W.2d 648 (1972).

Several procedural issues remain. Most often litigated is the issue of whether or not pandering must be alleged in the indictment. Since pandering has been held repeatedly not to be an element of the offense, it follows that pandering need not be alleged as such in the indictment, and so the majority of the cases have held.[85] But the pandering element may be so significant as to justify the granting of a motion for a bill of particulars, specifications, or similar action. It is the pandering that may make otherwise nonobscene material obscene, and therefore the appropriate motion should be granted to give adequate notice of the theory of the case. Similarly, any discovery should pay special attention to advertising and related materials, either to be able to adequately prepare a complete defense or, in the appropriate proceeding, so the prosecution may know of all types of advertising that were used.

Pandering raises an interesting res judicata problem. If a book, or film, or magazine, has been determined, in and of itself, not to be obscene and is then "pandered," is a prosecution based on the pandering barred by the first adjudication? This problem was noted by Mr. Justice Harlan on the day *Ginzburg* was decided.[86] He seriously questioned whether a prior civil adjudication would be effective to defeat a subsequent criminal prosecution which included pandering. Others have raised the same issue, and have also questioned whether there could be any res judicata effect in such a case.[87] But since pandering is merely evidentiary, this seems an untenable position. If a prior decision would, in all other respects, be entitled to collateral estoppel or res judicata effect, then the addition of pandering in the second trial should not change the result.[88] The problem really is that if the first proceeding is civil and the second criminal, or vice versa, there would

----

[85] *United States* v. *Ratner,* 502 F.2d 1300, 1301 (5th Cir. 1974); *United States* v. *Palladino,* 475 F.2d 65, 70–71 (1st Cir. 1973); *United States* v. *Gundlach,* 345 F. Supp. 709, 713 (M.D. Pa. 1972); *Gordon* v. *Christenson,* 317 F. Supp. 146 (D. Utah 1970); *United States* v. *Levy,* 331 F. Supp. 712, 713 (D. Conn. 1970). *Contra, United States* v. *Pinkus,* 333 F. Supp. 928, 931 (D.D. Cal. 1971); *People* v. *Noroff,* 67 Cal.2d 791, 793, 63 Cal. Rptr. 575, 576, 433 P.2d 479, 480 (1967).

[86] *Memoirs* v. *Massachusetts,* 383 U.S. 413, 485 n.3 (1966) (Harlan, J., dissenting).

[87] *United States* v. *A Motion Picture Film Entitled "I Am Curious—Yellow,"* 404 F.2d 196, 202 (2d Cir. 1968) (Friendly, J., concurring); *Busch* v. *Projection Room Theatre,* 44 Cal. App. 3d 111, 118 Cal. Rptr. 428 (1974).

[88] *Cf. City of Rochester* v. *Carlson,* 294 Minn. 417, 202 N.W.2d 632 (1972) (error to submit issue of pandering to jury where court held material not obscene as a matter of law).

not normally be any collateral estoppel or res judicata effect.[89] The issue then is whether First Amendment considerations overshadow traditional prior adjudication theory. There may very well be a substantial chilling effect on protected speech if nonobscene materials, as adjudicated, remain uncertain in the eyes of potential distributors. The Supreme Court has specifically noted the issue, without deciding the point,[90] but in light of the Court's encouragement of civil proceedings,[91] it is hard to imagine the Court would deny res judicata effect in this situation unless at the time it provided some clear guidance or definition as to the meaning of "pandering ."

4.5 The Difficult Problem of Minors—Ginsberg v. New York

As the Supreme Court's test for the determination of obscenity developed toward allowing the prohibition of only hard-core pornography, the issue of obscenity and minors became more significant. As long as the *Hicklin* standard was in force, there was no problem. If it might be harmful to minors, then no one could read it. But with the rejection of *Hicklin* and the adoption of the *Roth* concept of the "average person," a new difficulty arose. What about those materials, which although not necessarily prurient or offensive to the average adult, are potentially harmful to minors, or do appeal to the prurient interest of minors?

In *Butler* v. *Michigan*,[92] the Supreme Court held that objectionable materials could not be kept from adults because of their potential or supposed effect on minors. In doing so, the Court noted in a very positive manner that Michigan in fact had a statute that was aimed particularly at distribution of harmful material to minors.[93] An even stronger urging from the Court came seven years later, in *Jacobellis* v. *Ohio*,[94] when Mr. Justice Brennan observed that:

> We recognize the legitimate and indeed exigent interest of States and localities throughout the Nation in preventing the dissemination of material deemed harmful to children. But that interest does not justify a total suppression of such material, the effect of which would be to

[89] Civil proceedings are generally "in rem," so the identity of the parties would be different, which normally precludes collateral estoppel.

[90] *Paris Adult Theatre I* v. *Slaton*, 413 U.S. 49, 55 n.4 (1973). *See also Miller* v. *California*, 413 U.S. 15, 34 n.14 (1973).

[91] *Paris Adult Theatre I* v. *Slaton*, 413 U.S. at 55.

[92] 352 U.S. 380 (1957).

[93] *Id.* at 383.

[94] 378 U.S. 184 (1964).

"reduce the adult population . . . to reading only what is fit for children" . . . . State and local authorities might well consider whether their objectives in this area would be better served by laws aimed specifically at preventing distribution of objectionable material to children, rather than at totally prohibiting its dissemination.[95]

In the light of this language, it was then no surprise when the Supreme Court formally held that certain materials which may not be obscene when distributed to adults may nonetheless be kept from children. The case was *Ginsberg* v. *New York*,[96] and it presented an almost perfect test of this issue. Sam Ginsberg had been convicted under a New York statute which prohibited the distribution, to minors under the age of 17, of material which was "harmful to minors." Since the very materials at issue, a number of "girlie" magazines, had been held to be nonobscene as to adults in other cases, the issue was perfectly formulated.[97] Mr. Justice Brennan, writing the opinion of the Court, held that New York's statute was constitutionally acceptable. Relying on the State's interest in the well-being of youth, the Court found that the New York legislature could find a rational relationship between the type of materials involved and harm to minors, and thus the statute was constitutionally valid.[98] This method of analysis, of course, is not sufficient if the materials involved are subject to First Amendment protection. But the Court avoided dealing with the issue of the extent of minors' First Amendment rights as compared to those of adults. Instead, the Court's analysis is based on the premise that the materials prohibited by the New York statute are legally obscene, and thus not entitled to any First Amendment protection. What the Court did was to hold that in determining what is or is not obscene, the state may "adjust the definition of obscenity to social realities by

[95] *Id.* at 195 (footnote omitted).

[96] 390 U.S. 629 (1968). *See generally* Krislov, *From Ginzburg to Ginsberg: The Unhurried Children's Hour in Obscenity Litigation,* 1968 SUP. CT. REV. 153 (1968). Note, *A Double Standard of Obscenity: The Ginsberg Decision,* 3 VALP. L. REV. 57 (1968); 21 VAND. L. REV. 844 (1968); 33 ALB. L. REV. 173 (1968); 18 AM. U. L. REV. 195 (1968); *The Supreme Court, 1967 Term,* 82 HARV. L. REV. 63, 124 (1968). Some of the best material on obscenity and minors was written prior to the *Ginsberg* decision. *See, e.g.,* Note, *"For Adults Only": The Constitutionality of Governmental Film Censorship by Age Classification,* 69 YALE L. J. 141 (1959); Dibble, *Obscenity: A State Quarantine to Protect Children,* 39 So. CAL. L. REV. 345 (1966); Note, *Constitutional Problems in Obscenity Legislation Protecting Children,* 54 GEO L. J. 1379 (1966); 55 CAL. REV. 926 (1967).

[97] 390 U.S. at 634. In *Gent* v. *Arkansas,* 386 U.S. 767 (1967), a companion case to *Redrup* v. *New York, Sir* magazine had been found not obscene, and *Sir* was one of the publications which Ginsberg had been convicted for selling.

[98] 390 U.S. at 642–643.

permitting the appeal of this type of material to be assessed in terms of the sexual interests . . . of such minors." [99] Thus, what had been done for "deviant" groups in *Mishkin* v. *New York*[100] was now done for minors. If materials were in fact sold to minors, then the "average person" aspect of the *Roth* test could be replaced by an assessment of the materials' prurient interest to minors.

It is important to understand that although *Ginsberg* allows the obscenity test to be so adjusted where the audience is not the general public, it still requires a finding of obscenity. The statute at issue in *Ginsberg* still required an appeal to prurient interest, still required patent offensiveness, and still required a lack of redeeming social importance.[101] The *Ginsberg* test is still a test for obscenity, albeit modified, and if material does not meet each of the three tests, it may not be prohibited, even for minors. Although the test for obscenity after *Miller* is now different, the same principles apply, and a modified form of the *Miller* standards must still be used.[102] Unless a film or publication has prurient interest to minors, is patently offensive when distributed to minors, and lacks serious literary, artistic, scientific, or political value for minors, it is still protected by the First Amendment. Thus, *Ginsberg* does not allow the definition of obscenity, even for minors, to include standard art objects, great literature, or mere nudity in any context.[103] Similarly, *Ginsberg* does not allow the suppression of brutality and violence, since they are outside of the concept of prurient interest.[104]

[99] *Id.* at 638.

[100] 383 U.S. 502 (1966). *See* Chapter 4.3, *supra.*

[101] 390 U.S. at 633.

[102] On the *Ginsberg* test as merely a modification of the obscenity test, *see Koppell* v. *Levine,* 347 F. Supp. 456, 459 (E.D.N.Y. 1972); *Sullivan* v. *Houston Independent School District,* 333 F. Supp. 1149, 1162–1163 (S.D. Tex. 1971); *Broadway Distributors, Inc.,* v. *White,* 307 F. Supp. 1180, 1183 (D. Mass. 1970) (*Ginsberg* allows greater latitude in defining obscenity). Some courts have said that *Ginsberg* allows the suppression of material that falls short of being obscene. *P.B.I.C., Inc.* v. *Byrne,* 313 F. Supp. 757, 762 n.7 (D. Mass. 1970) (three-judge court); *Cactus Corp.* v. *State ex rel. Murphy,* 14 Ariz. App. 38, 480 P.2d 375, 378 (1971). This formulation is clearly incorrect, although it is true that *Ginsberg* allows the suppression for minors of materials that may not be obscene when distributed only to adults.

[103] *Cinecom Theatres Midwest St., Inc.* v. *City of Fort Wayne,* 473 F.2d 1297 (7th Cir. 1973).

[104] *Interstate Circuit, Inc.,* v. *City of Dallas,* 366 F.2d 590, 598–599 (5th Cir. 1966). In *State* v. *Vachon,* 113 N.H. 239, 306 A.2d 781 (1973), *rev'd on other grounds,* 414 U.S. 478 (1974), the conviction was under a "contributing to the delinquency of a minor" statute for selling a button bearing the words "Copulation Not Masturbation" to a 14-year-old. Although the Supreme Court did not discuss this issue, it seems questionable whether this button satisfies the prurient-interest test for anyone, regardless of age.

On the same day that *Ginsberg* was decided, the Supreme Court also handed down its decision in *Interstate Circuit, Inc.* v. *City of Dallas*.[105] This case involved a Dallas city ordinance which involved special licensing procedures for motion pictures "not suitable for young persons." The definition of "not suitable for young persons" was held by the Court to be unconstitutional for overbreadth, citing a number of cases dealing with licensing schemes for motion pictures in general.[106] The significance of the case, for this discussion, is that although statutes dealing with minors may embody a modified test of obscenity based on harm to minors, the procedural safeguards attendant to obscenity regulation generally are equally applicable to legislation aimed solely at juveniles.[107] Thus, the giving of legal sanction to the X, R, PG, G system of motion picture rating, without any hearing or other procedural safeguards as to individual motion pictures, would seem to run afoul of *Interstate Circuit* and the other licensing cases.[108] No more than a motion picture can be entirely suppressed without appropriate procedural safeguards may minors be excluded without those same safeguards. And since the statute must define the objectionable material with sufficient specificity, then, a fortiori, it seems clear that prosecutions dealing with books, magazines, motion pictures, or other related communications may not be based on "contributing to the delinquency of a minor" statutes.[109]

It should be clear from the foregoing discussion that states which wish to deal directly with the sale or distribution of objectionable material to minors must have statutes or local regulations specifically referring to minors and making sale or distribution to minors a separate offense. The elements of the offense should be clearly spelled out, and the substance of the offense must incorporate all of the elements of obscenity found in *Miller* v. *California*.[110] These standards may, however, be modified so as to relate to minors below a given age. Given this fairly clear procedural mandate from the case law, it is likely impermissible to merely modify the jury instructions to relate to minors in a case under a general obscenity statute, even if the

---

[105] 390 U.S. 676 (1968). *See also Rabeck* v. *New York,* 391 U.S. 462 (1968).

[106] See Chapters 8 and 12 *infra.*

[107] *Accord, Sokolic* v. *Ryan,* 304 F. Supp. 213, 217–218 (S.D. Ga. 1969). Of course, the mere existence of a separate licensing scheme for materials available to minors is no bar as long as there are appropriate procedural safeguards. *Universal Film Exchanges, Inc.* v. *City of Chicago,* 288 F. Supp. 286 (N.D. Ill. 1968).

[108] *Engdahl* v. *City of Kenosha, Wisconsin,* 317 F. Supp. 1133 (E.D. Wis. 1970).

[109] *Hanby* v. *State,* 479 P.2d 486 (Alas. 1970).

[110] 413 U.S. 15, 24 (1973).

distribution has in fact been to minors. Unless a separate and appropriately specific statute or regulation relating to minors is available, then the "average adult" must remain the context in which obscenity is to be measured, regardless of the age of the recipients.[111]

A problem arises as to the age of the minors involved. If the statute makes it an offense to distribute obscene material, defined as to minors, to anyone under the age of 18, and a sale is in fact made to a 13-year-old, is the jury to measure obscenity in terms of its effect on the average 13-year-old, the average 18-year-old, or some amalgamation of all minors of all ages? If the test is 18-year-olds, then the statute will probably not effectively deal with the problem it is designed to address. If the test is the average 13-year-old, in this case, then the burden on the theater owner or bookseller becomes enormous, because he must judge the effect on a large gradation of sexual sophistication. And merely saying the "average minor" fails to recognize that there is of course no such thing, because of the very nature of development as age progresses. Is the average minor 9 years old, which is the median age from birth to 18, or 12 years old, which may be the median from reading age to age 18, or what? Just as Mr. Justice Frankfurter observed in *Butler* v. *Michigan* [112] that Michigan's statute would reduce the adult population to reading only what is fit for children, so the inappropriate standard in this situation may reduce the 16- and 17-year-old population to reading only what is fit for 8- and 9-year-olds. This may very well be even a greater evil. But certainly a legislature may think that making available to 8-year-olds what is accepted by the "wordly-wise" is equally dangerous. In light of these conflicting goals, it would seem that none of the approaches described herein would be constitutionally deficient, and the choice among them should be for the legislature. But the choice should be clearly spelled out in the governing statute. Thus, although *Ginsberg* allows the adult obscenity test to be modified by a legislature, the legislature should also make clear what it is being modified to. Anything less may still be attacked on vagueness grounds.

Many of the problems dealing with prosecution and defense of "juveniles" cases, or drafting "juveniles" statutes, are similar or

---

[111] *See United States* v. *Pellegrino,* 467 F.2d 41, 44 n.9 (9th Cir. 1972); *United States* v. *35 mm Motion Picture Film Entitled "Language of Love,"* 432 F.2d 705, 714 (2d Cir. 1970).

There is no federal obscenity statute relating to minors, and thus the average adult is the test for all federal prosecutions, except those dealing with "deviant" materials.

[112] 353 U.S. 380 (1957).

identical to those involved under general obscenity statutes, and are therefore discussed in detail in other chapters of this book.

Caveat: There is now some question as to the continuing validity of the entire concept described in this section. In *Miller* v. *California,*[113] Chief Justice Burger addressed himself to the dissenting opinion of Mr. Justice Brennan and said: "Nor does [Mr. Justice Brennan] indicate where in the Constitution he finds the authority to distinguish between a willing 'adult' one month past the state law age of majority and a willing 'juvenile' one month younger." [114] When this observation is coupled with formal acceptance of the "hard-core" requirement, it is possible that the *Ginsberg* approach may be attacked or eroded by future decisions in favor of one standard of obscenity for adults and minors alike. In *Erznoznik* v. *City of Jacksonville,*[115] Mr. Justice Powell, writing for the majority, observed that "we have not had occasion to decide what effect *Miller* will have on the *Ginsberg* formulation." [116] Thus the possibility of such effect remains open.

4.6   The Uncertain Future of Variable Obscenity

The thread that connects *Mishkin, Ginzburg,* and *Ginsberg,* discussed in the last three sections of this chapter, is the concept of variable obscenity. Variable obscenity is a principle which holds that the obscenity vel non of given material may be determined only in the context of the method of distribution and the intended and actual audience for the material. It is to be contrasted with constant obscenity, which requires looking at the materials involved to make the determination of obscenity regardless of the method or objects of distribution.

Variable obscenity actually had its origin with *Regina* v. *Hicklin,*[117] since it required that the determination of obscenity be based on an evaluation of "into whose hands a publication of this sort may fall." [118] But *Roth* rejected this concept as well as the rest of the *Hicklin* test. Obscenity was to be judged by the materials themselves, and not on

---

[113] 413 U.S. 15 (1973).
[114] *Id.* at 27.
[115] U.S. Sup. Ct., June 24, 1975. No. 73–1942.
[116] *Id.* at n.10.
[117] [1868] L.R.3 Q.B. 360. See Chapters 1 and 2 *supra.*
[118] *Id.* at 371.

any contextual factors, and thus *Roth* represents the high point of constant obscenity. But shortly after *Roth* a case arose which forced the first exception to be made. In connection with research originally begun by Dr. Alfred Kinsey, the Institute for Sex Research at Indiana University was the intended recipient of a package of materials that clearly qualified as hard-core pornography. Pursuant to § 305 of the Tariff Act of 1930,[119] the materials were seized and the government sought their forfeiture and destruction on the grounds that they were obscene. In *United States* v. *31 Photographs*,[120] however, Judge Palmieri held that the materials were not obscene because, in the context of importation for scientific research, they did not appeal to the prurient interest.[121] Rejecting the government's contention that materials could be obscene per se, he reviewed the Second Circuit's previous use of "into whose hands the publication may fall.[122] *Roth*, he said, was distinguishable, since the "average person" standard relates only to material which is available to the public at large. When distribution is limited, then the "appeal to the prurient interest" aspect of the *Roth* test must be appropriately modified.

While the result in *31 Photographs* was generally accepted as a necessary decision, the rationale employed by the Court was not the only road to the same destination. It is also possible to maintain that the material is in fact obscene per se, but that there is either a privilege or an affirmative defense in the case of material used solely for scientific or scholarly purposes. For example, the Model Penal Code of the American Law Institute, in its section on obscenity, provides for obscenity per se but provides affirmative defenses for dissemination restricted to:

(a) institutions or persons having scientific, educational, governmental or other similar justification for possessing obscene material; or
(b) non-commercial dissemination to personal associates of the actor.[123]

[119] 19 U.S.C. 1305. See Chapter 9.5 *infra* for a full discussion of the provisions and operation of this statute.

[120] 156 F. Supp. 350 (S.D.N.Y. 1957). *See* Note, *The Law of Obscenity: New Significance of the Receiving Group*, 34 Ind. L. J. 426 (1959); 7 Kans L. Rev. 216 (1958).

[121] 156 F. Supp. at 354–355.

[122] *United States* v. *Levine*, 83 F.2d 156, 157 (2d Cir. 1936); *United States* v. *Dennett*, 39 F.2d 564, 568 (2d Cir. 1930).

[123] Model Penal Code 251.4 (3), Uniform Laws Annotated 592 (1974). *See* Schwartz, *Morals Offenses and the Model Penal Code*, 63 Colum. L. Rev. 669, 677–681 (1963).

At about the same time as the Model Penal Code was under discussion, however, a number of distinguished scholars began to advocate the variable-obscenity approach, most significantly Professors Lockhart and McClure.[124] They argued that the concept of variable obscenity, adjusting the prurient-interest test to accord with the context and objects of the distribution, was most logically sound in the face of practical realities, and best able to handle potentially conflicting societal goals, such as freedom of access to literature for adults and a desire to protect children, or maximum freedom for willing readers or viewers with a desire to protect the sensibilities of those who wish to avoid objectionable materials or public displays.

A detailed discussion of the pros and cons of variable obscenity may not be appropriate at this point, and the interested reader is referred to Lockhart and McClure's works for the best discussion.[125] But what is significant is that this concept had a profound effect on the Supreme Court's obscenity decisions. The most obvious is *Ginsberg* v. *New York*,[126] where the Court specifically approved New York's use of variable obscenity and spoke of it as such.[127] Similarly, *Mishkin* v. *New York*[128] allowed the definition of obscenity to take into account the probable readers, if they were members of "deviant" groups, and *Ginzburg* v. *United States*[129] permitted the contextual concept of pandering to be determinative on the issue of obscenity.

But these cases represented the high-water mark for variable obscenity. Now that the "hard-core" requirement is part of the case law, variable obscenity becomes a more difficult concept. There may not be any room in *Miller* for suppression of anything other than hard-core pornography, regardless of context. This view seems supported by *Erznoznik* v. *City of Jacksonville*,[130] the Court's most recent obscenity case, where the Court refused to allow a requirement that drive-in theaters "shield" passersby from adult or X-rated movies but

---

[124] Lockhart and McClure, *Censorship of Obscenity: The Developing Constitutional Standards*, 45 MINN. L. REV. 5, 68–88 (1860). *See also* Emerson, *Toward a General Theory of the First Amendment*, 72 YALE L. J. 877, 938–939 (1963). Gerber, *A Suggested Solution to the Riddle of Obscenity*, 112 U. PA. L. REV. 834 (1964).

[125] *See also* Lockhart and McClure, *Obscenity Censorship: The Core Constitutional Issue—What is Obscene?*, 7 UTAH L. REV. 289 (1961); Lockhart and McClure, *Literature, the Law of Obscenity and the Constitution*, 38 MINN. L. REV. 295 (1954).

[126] 390 U.S. 629 (1968). *See* Chapter 4.5 *supra*.

[127] *Id*. 635 n.4.

[128] 383 U.S. 502 (1966). *See* Chapter 4.3 *supra*.

[129] 383 U.S. 463 (1966). *See* Chapter 4.4 *supra*.

[130] U.S. Sup. Ct., June 24, 1975. No. 73–1942.

not from others. A full adoption of the variable-obscenity concept would clearly allow the definition to take account of a relatively public showing rather than a closed theater, but the majority refused to take this approach. And, as explained in the "caveat" concluding the previous section of this book, the remaining vitality of modifying the obscenity tests for juveniles is in question. While it is highly unlikely that the court will reject all concepts of stricter standards for minors, or that all vestiges of variable obscenity will be erased immediately, it is clear that the concept no longer lies as favorably with the Supreme Court as it did in the late 1960s. Perhaps the reason for this is best explained by the fact that what the idea of variable obscenity adds in terms of realities and flexibility, it may subtract in terms of the best possible notice or warning of what is prohibited. As with any statutory or regulatory scheme, maximum predictability often provides less than optimum "fairness," and the converse is equally true. In *Miller*, the Supreme Court placed a heavy emphasis on predictability and prior specific notice of the conduct that is to be proscribed, and to meet this goal the variable-obscenity concept may very well be sacrificed.

5

The Subjective Standards:
Of "Prurient Interest" and
"Patently Offensive"

5.1   The Meaning of "Prurient Interest"

The first third of the current test for obscenity as set forth in *Miller* v. *California* [1] is "whether 'the average person, applying contemporary community standards' would find that the work, taken as a whole, appeals to the prurient interest." [2] This part of the *Miller* test is directly derived from the standards first set forth by the Supreme Court in *Roth* v. *United States*. [3] The goal of this section will be to try to analyze and define "prurient interest," because without an appeal to prurient interest there can be no finding of obscenity.

Perhaps the main purpose of the prurient-interest test is to separate legal obscenity from the dictionary definition of obscenity. "Obscene" refers to that which is disgusting or revolting but does not necessarily have sexual connotations. [4] But "obscene material" in the eyes of the law is obscene material which deals with sex. [5] Thus, violence, or crime, or war, regardless of whether they may be "obscene" in the eyes of some, are outside of the permissible scope of obscenity regulation. "As a result, we now confine the permissible scope of such regulation to works which depict or describe sexual conduct." [6]

[1] 413 U.S. 15 (1973).
[2] *Id.* at 24.
[3] 354 U.S. 476, 489 (1957).
[4] *See* Chapter 1, note 1, *supra; Miller* v. *California*, 413 U.S. at 18 n.2.
[5] *Id.*
[6] *Id.* at 24. *See also State* v. *Jackson*, 224 Ore. 337, 356 P.2d 495 (1960); *Interstate Circuit, Inc.* v. *City of Dallas*, 366 F.2d 590, 598–599 (5th Cir. 1966).

But it is clear that not every discussion, description, or depiction of sexual conduct can be suppressed. As Mr. Justice Brennan noted in *Roth,*

> However, sex and obscenity are not synonymous. . . . The portrayal of sex, *e.g.,* in art, literature and scientific works, is not itself sufficient reason to deny material the constitutional protection of freedom of speech and press. Sex, a great and mysterious force in human life, has indisputably been a subject of absorbing interest to mankind through the ages; it is one of the vital problems of human interest and public concern.[7]

In order to insure constitutional protection for this type of legitimate sexual discussion, obscenity in the legal sense was limited to "material which deals with sex in a manner appealing to prurient interest."[8] In order to understand what the Court meant by prurient, it set forth a number of definitions, and the relevant footnote, because of its importance, is quoted verbatim:

> *I.e.,* material having a tendency to excite lustful thoughts. Webster's New International Dictionary (Unabridged, 2d ed., 1949) defines prurient, in pertinent part, as follows: ". . . Itching; longing; uneasy with desire or longing; of persons, having itching, morbid, or lascivious longings; of desire, curiosity, or propensity, lewd. . . ." *Pruriency* is defined, in pertinent part, as follows: ". . . Quality of being prurient; lascivious desire or thought. . . ." See also *Mutual Film Corp.* v. *Industrial Comm'n,* 236 U.S. 230, 242, where this Court said as to motion pictures: ". . . They take their attraction from the general interest, eager and wholesome it may be, in their subjects, but a *prurient interest may be excited and appealed to. . . ."* (*Emphasis* added.) We perceive no significant difference between the meaning of obscenity developed in the case law and the definition of the A.L.I., Model Penal Code, § 207.10 (2) (Tent. Draft No. 6, 1957), viz.: ". . . A thing is obscene if, considered as a whole, its predominant appeal is to prurient interest, *i.e.,* shameful or morbid interest in nudity, sex, or excretion, and if it goes substantially beyond customary limits of candor in description or representation of such matters. . . ." See Comment, *id.,* at 10, and the discussion at page 29 et seq.[9]

Most cases that have attempted to define "prurient," "pruriency," or "prurient interest" have tended to adopt one of the definitions found

---

[7] *Roth* v. *United States,* 354 U.S. 476, 487 (1957).
[8] *Id.*
[9] *Id.* at 487 n.20.

in the *Roth* footnote.[10] Others have attempted modifications which have the same effect, such as that prurient relates to "lecherous thoughts or desires,"[11] or that it caters to or relates to "a loose-lipped sensual leer."[12] But despite attempts to restate or modify the *Roth* collection of authority on the definition of prurient, several problems remain. First, the various definitions in the *Roth* footnote are inconsistent. Some relate to morbidity, abnormality, or shame, while others relate to excitement and desire. Whatever may have been the views of the 19th century, it seems fair to assume that we no longer consider sexual excitement or desire necessarily morbid or shameful, and it certainly is not abnormal. Are the obscenity laws designed to prevent that which excites or stimulates in a sexual manner, or just that which excites in an abnormal way? Perhaps being excited by literature or pornography is in itself abnormal, or perhaps not, but in any event it seems clear that the laws are aimed at sexual excitement per se, and the fact that the materials may not be morbid or shameful is irrelevant. The shame or abnormality comes in the fact that the influence is by virtue of pictures or words, and not "normal" interpersonal relationships, and this is in part the basis of the obscenity laws. Thus, in this context, prurient appeal merely means sexually stimulating, and that seems to have been the purpose of the prurient-interest requirement. Not all discussions or pictures of sexual activity are necessarily stimulating sexually, so it is this narrowing that seems the purpose of the requirement. It is those materials that have potentially physical as opposed to intellectual effect that are to be within the ambit of the obscenity laws. This separation of the physical from the intellectual appears to explain the necessity of an appeal to the prurient interest.

In addition, the prurient-interest requirement can be an exercise in circularity. That which is prurient is obscene because it is shameful. But what is shameful? That which is prurient or obscene. The insertion of the prurient-interest standard may not add any new substantive

---

[10] *See, e.g., State* v. *LeWitt,* 3 Conn. Cir. 605, 222 A.2d 579, 581 (App. Div. 1966); *State ex rel. Dowd* v. *"Pay the Baby Sitter,"* 31 Ohio Misc. 208, 387 N.E.2d 650, 654 (Comm. Pl. 1972) ("[p]rurient means to excite lustful thought; a shameful or morbid interest in sex; arouse sexual desires or sexual impure thoughts; inclined or disposed to lewdness; having lustful ideas or desires"); *United States* v. *Keller,* 259 F.2d 54, 58 (3d Cir. 1958).

[11] *People* v. *Mishkin,* 26 Misc. 2d 152, 207 N.Y.S.2d 390, 394 (Ct. Sp. Sess. 1960).

[12] *Flying Eagle Publications, Inc.,* v. *United States,* 273 F.2d 799, 803 (1st Cir. 1960); *State* v. *Harding,* _____ N.H. _____, 320 A.2d 646, 650 (1974).

concept, but may instead merely add some new words to the formulation of the ultimate legal conclusion.

It appears as if part of the problem has been in attempting to define "prurient" by looking in the dictionary. One doesn't define the legal parameters of the "reasonable man" concept in tort law by looking up "reasonable" and "man" in Webster's Dictionary, any more than one would use a like process for "clear and present danger," "res judicata," or any other legal concept. Looking up "party" in the dictionary will give little insight into the operation of the Federal Rules of Civil Procedure. In similar fashion, "prurient interest" should be treated as a legal concept whose purpose is to help set the boundaries of permissible obscenity regulation so as to regulate that which the majority of society wishes to prohibit while permitting those depictions or discussions of sex which the First Amendment protects. Therefore, it is more useful to trace the legal application of the prurient-interest requirement as an aid to understanding it than it is to compile a catalog of dictionary definitions.

At the outset, it is crucial to separate prurience from discussions of sex per se. The prurient-appeal requirement ensures that not every discussion or depiction of sex may be characterized as obscene, and that the obscenity laws may not be used to foster certain *ideas* regarding sex at the expense of other ideas. For example, it may be argued that materials dealing with sexual immorality in an approving way would appeal to the prurient interest, but, if anything, the effect is long-run and of an intellectual nature, and thus the approval of adultery or other sexual practices not approved by the mores of society cannot result in a work's being declared obscene.[13] In striking down a New York motion picture licensing scheme, the Supreme Court noted that:

> What New York has done, therefore, is to prevent the exhibition of a motion picture because that picture advocates an idea—that adultery under certain circumstances may be proper behavior. Yet the First Amendment's basic guarantee is of freedom to advocate ideas. The state, quite simply, has thus struck at the very heart of constitutionally protected liberty.[14]

---

[13] *Kingsley International Pictures Corp.* v. *Regents,* 360 U.S. 684 (1959); *Grove Press, Inc.* v. *Christenberry,* 276 F.2d 433, 439 n.10 (2d Cir. 1960) *(Lady Chatterley's Lover); People* v. *Richmond County News,* 9 N.Y.2d 578, 175 N.E.2d 681, 216 N.Y.S.2d 369 (1961).

[14] *Kingsley International Pictures Corp.* v. *Regents,* 360 U.S. 684, 688 (1959).

Thus the idea of prurience excludes mere discussions of sex, or the espousal or advocacy of sexual immorality, or "deviant" practices. While these may very well have a long-term effect on sexual morality or conduct very similar, or perhaps even greater, than explicit depictions of sexual conduct, it is only the latter, standing by itself, that may accomplish the end without the intervention of anything we can call an "idea," and thus it is only that that lies outside the range of First Amendment protection and can be labelled as obscene.

Similarly, mere "obscene" words, without any description or depiction of sexual acts, are within the scope of First Amendment protection and may not properly be prosecuted absent any connection with conduct.[15] In *Cohen* v. *California* [16] the petitioners had been convicted under an "offensive words" statute for wearing, in a courthouse lobby, a jacket bearing the words "Fuck the Draft." In reversing the conviction, the Supreme Court made it clear that despite the sexual connotations of the word used, this in no way could be classified as obscenity:

> This is not, for example, an obscenity case. Whatever else may be necessary to give rise to the States' broader power to prohibit obscene expression, *such expression must be, in some significant way, erotic. Roth* v. *United States. . . .* It cannot plausibly be maintained that this vulgar allusion to the Selective Service System would conjure up such *psychic stimulation* in anyone likely to be confronted with Cohen's crudely defaced jacket.[17]

Although Mr. Justice Harlan's opinion could have been narrowed to the holding that such "obscene" words are protected only when, as here, they were uttered in connection with a political or other idea, the language of his opinion is expressly not so limited. Thus, to the extent they are still on the statute books,[18] statutes condemning public profanity or obscene words, or the use of such words in the presence of females, may well be unenforceable. While the words may indeed offend, they lack the stimulative effect or attempt of the obscene, and thus remain within the scope of protected speech.

---

[15] If the words are likely to provoke violent reaction, and are thus "fighting words," they may be the basis of valid regulation. *Chaplinsky* v. *New Hampshire,* 315 U.S. 568 (1942). Similarly, if the words are inseparable from conduct, such as flag-burning or draft-card burning, they may be regulated. *United States* v. *O'Brien,* 391 U.S. 367 (1968); *Street* v. *New York,* 394 U.S. 576 (1969).

[16] 403 U.S. 15 (1971).

[17] *Id.* at 20 (emphasis added).

[18] *See, e.g.,* Code of Ala., Tit. 14 § 11 (1959).

Finally, to complete this compendium of major exclusions, nudity per se is outside of the range of the legally prurient. In reversing a finding that the motion picture *Carnal Knowledge* was obscene, Mr. Justice Rehnquist, for a unanimous Supreme Court, noted that "[t]here are occasional scenes of nudity, but nudity alone is not enough to make material legally obscene under the *Miller* standards."[19] Thus publications displaying nudity which are designed for a nudist audience are constitutionally protected,[20] and the fact that nude models may be in "seductive" poses,[21] or have exposed genitals,[22] does not diminish the degree of constitutional protection. While such materials may have some degree of prurient interest in that they provide some degree of psychic or physical stimulation for some, they seem to have been excluded mainly because the prurient interest is not the dominant or principal appeal involved, and because they cater to what has been called a "healthy and normal" interest in sex as opposed to a "morbid" interest in sex.[23]

In *Miller* v. *California*[24] the Supreme Court gave, as examples, some subjects which could properly be regulated by state obscenity laws. These examples, which were not all-inclusive, are, however, designed to fix "substantive constitutional limitations" on the type of material which may be found obscene.[25] These examples are:

(a) Patently offensive representations or descriptions of ultimate sex acts, normal or perverted, actual or simulated.

(b) Patently offensive representations or descriptions of masturbation, excretory functions, and lewd exhibition of the genitals.[26]

When these examples are combined with the judicial interpretations given to the concept of "prurient," it is clear that the term refers to that which shows erotic sexuality in a manner designed to create some

---

[19] *Jenkins* v. *Georgia*, 418 U.S. 153, 181 (1974). See also *Erznoznik* v. *City of Jacksonville*, U.S. Sup. Ct., June 23, 1975, No. 73–1942, at n.10.

[20] *Sunshine Book Co.* v. *Summerfield*, 355 U.S. 372 (1958); *United States* v. *1,000 Copies of Magazine Entitled "Solis,"* 254 F. Supp. 595 (D. Md. 1966); *Donnenberg* v. *State*, 1 Md. App. 591, 232 A.2d 264 (1967).

[21] *Excellent Publications, Inc.* v. *United States,* 309 F.2d 362 (1st Cir. 1962).

[22] *People* v. *Stabile*, 58 Misc. 2d 905, 396 N.Y.S.2d 815, 818 (Crim. Ct. 1969); *United States* v. *Central Magazine Sales, Ltd.*, 381 F.2d 821 (4th Cir. 1967).

[23] *See United States* v. *1,000 Copies of Magazine Entitled "Solis,"* 254 F. Supp. 595, 599 (D. Md. 1966); 1 DEVITT and BLACKMAR, FEDERAL JURY PRACTICE AND INSTRUCTIONS § 41.06 (1970).

[24] 413 U.S. 15 (1973).

[25] *Jenkins* v. *Georgia*, 418 U.S. 153, 160 (1974).

[26] 413 U.S. at 25.

form of immediate stimulation. If this is the appeal, then the prurient-interest test is met.

There remain some problems as to the words surrounding the prurient-interest test. That is, the test is that "the average person, applying contemporary community standards" must find that the work *appeals* to the prurient interest. If "appeal" is used in the sense of "he has an appealing personality," then it is the *effect* that is determinative. Alternatively, "appeal" may refer merely to the intentions or focus of the publications. The latter is clearly what the *Roth* Court had in mind, and is the only one which is consistent with other concepts in obscenity law. The average person would probably find that most hard-core pornography has little effect on him, and it may well disgust him. Or he may find that it is so overdone as to have anything but a stimulative effect. It is apparent that neither the Supreme Court nor the legislatures intended that tasteful pornography be suppressed while distasteful pornography remains unregulated. Rather, the emphasis must be on the intent or aim of the publication as a whole.[27] If this aim is to produce psychic or physical stimulation, on a less than intellectual plane, and on a short-term basis, then the prurient-interest aspect of the test for obscenity has been met.

5.2   The Meaning of "Patently Offensive"

The second third of the test set forth in *Miller,* and the other "subjective" standard, along with prurient appeal, is the requirement that the material be "patently offensive." The characterization of these two tests as subjective is made solely because the determinations in this area are primarily for the jury and because any attempt at a truly useful definition is destined to be futile.

The requirement of patent offensiveness was not part of the original *Roth* definition of obscenity. However, the Model Penal Code of the American Law Institute defined "obscene" in the following way:

> Material is obscene if, considered as a whole, its predominant appeal is to prurient interest, that is, a shameful or morbid interest, in nudity, sex or erection, and if *in addition it goes substantially beyond customary limits of candor* in describing or representing such matters.[28]

---

[27] The best discussion of the "effect-interest" dichotomy is in *State* v. *Jackson,* 224 Ore. 337, 356 P.2d 495, 503–507 (1960).

[28] A.L.I. Model Penal Code, § 251.4 (1962), 10 Uniform Laws Annotated 591–592 (1974) (emphasis added).

Thus, the Model Penal Code added a second element. Not only must material appeal to the prurient interest to be obscene, it must also be well beyond the kind of sexual representations or descriptions that society tolerates. This test seemed of significant effect to Mr. Justice Harlan when, in *Manual Enterprises* v. *Day*,[29] he suggested that this second element, the "affront" to "current community standards of decency," or "patent offensiveness," be an element of the offense under 18 U.S.C. § 1461.[30] This was followed by Mr. Justice Brennan's opinion two years later in *Jacobellis* v. *Ohio*,[31] where his plurality opinion made the following point.

> It should also be recognized that the *Roth* standard requires in the first instance a finding that the material "goes substantially beyond customary limits of candor in description or representation of such matters." This was a requirement of the Model Penal Code test that we approved in *Roth*. . . . *In the absence of such a deviation from society's standards of decency,* we do not see how any official inquiry into the allegedly prurient appeal of a work can be squared with the guarantees of the First and Fourteenth Amendments.[32]

And in *Memoirs* v. *Massachusetts*,[33] the patent-offensiveness standard was the second of the three elements of obscenity. Thus, it was required to be established that "the material is patently offensive because it affronts contemporary community standards relating to the description or representation of sexual matters."[34] We have, therefore, the background from which emerges, in *Miller* v. *California*,[35] the second requirement, that "the work depicts or describes, in a patently offensive way, sexual conduct specifically defined by the applicable state law."[36]

The development of the "patently offensive" standard also explains its meaning, for in each of the uses of the term prior to *Miller* it was equated with an affront to or surpassing of the current level of society's acceptance of sexual depictions or descriptions. Nowhere in the Supreme Court cases is there any reference to dictionary definitions of patent offensiveness, and it seems clear that the intent was for the

---

[29] 370 U.S. 478, 482–486 (1962).
[30] *Id.* at 482.
[31] 378 U.S. 184 (1964).
[32] *Id.* at 191–192 (emphasis added).
[33] 383 U.S. 413 (1966).
[34] *Id.* at 418.
[35] 413 U.S. 15 (1973).
[36] *Id.* at 24.

trier of fact to gauge whether the material at issue exceeded that which society generally considers decent, or at least tolerates. It is a standard susceptible to, and perhaps designed for, subjectivity, on the theory that the jury represents society's interests in the proceedings, and can therefore best set or measure society's willingness to tolerate sexual explicitness. Therefore, the concept of patent offensiveness is inevitably intertwined with the concept of contemporary community standards, discussed in detail in the next chapter. Although the concept of contemporary community standards is associated with the prurient-interest test, it is much more applicable and related to the patent-offensiveness test.[37]

From the above discussion, it should be apparent that there are few judicial discussions or applications of the patent-offensiveness standard other than to equate it with an affront to community standards, or decency, or moral values.[38] While a number of cases have held that nudity alone may not be patently offensive,[39] there are few other guidelines available from the case law. And some cases have tended to combine or confuse the prurient-interest and patent-offensiveness tests.[40] Although "patently offensive" had been described as focusing "predominantly upon what is sexually morbid, grossly perverse and bizarre," and being "insulting to sex and the human spirit," [41] this seems to add little to what we already know. The patent-offensiveness standard is designed to ask the jury, "does this material go too far?"

[37] *See McCauley* v. *Tropic of Cancer,* 20 Wis. 2d 134, 121 N.W.2d 545, 553 (1963).

[38] *See, e.g., State* v. *Hudson County News Co.,* 41 N.J. 247, 196 A.2d 225, 229 (1963); ("Indeed, it is the characteristic of indecency which is the basis of society's objection to obscene material, and if the test did not include both elements, many worthwhile works in literature, science, or art would fall under the sole test of 'prurient interest' appeal."). In *City of Youngstown* v. *Deloreto,* 19 Ohio App. 2d 267, 251 N.E.2d 491 (1969), the appellate court looked to state statutes regarding adultery, fornication, prostitution, indecent exposure, and sodomy to determine that the material at issue was "offensive to the moral standards of the people of Ohio." 251 N.E.2d at 501.

[39] *United States* v. *392 Copies of Magazine Entitled "Exclusive,"* 253 F. Supp. 385, 497 (D. Md. 1966), *aff'd,* 373 F.2d 633 (4th Cir. 1967), *rev'd sub nom. Central Magazine Sales, Ltd.* v. *United States,* 389 U.S. 50 (1967); *Miller* v. *United States,* 431 F.2d 655, 658 (9th Cir. 1970), *vacated,* 413 U.S. 913 (1973), *reaffirmed,* 505 F.2d 1247 (9th Cir. 1974). Each of these cases also held that where the nude models display their genitals prominantly and in an exaggerated fashion, with the focus exclusively on the genital area, then nudity becomes patently offensive. *See also People* v. *Berger,* 521 P.2d 1244, 1246 (Colo. 1974).

[40] *See, e.g., Chemline, Inc.* v. *City of Grand Prairie,* 364 F.2d 721, 727 (5th Cir. 1966).

[41] *State ex rel. Dowd* v. *"Pay the Baby Sitter,"* 31 Ohio Misc. 208, 287 N.E.2d 650, 654–655 (Comm. Pl. 1972).

And the best way of asking still seems to be that of the Model Penal Code. Material is patently offensive if it "goes substantially beyond customary limits of candor in describing or representing [sexual] matter." [42]

5.3 *"Taken as a Whole"*

As has been discussed in Chapters 1 and 2, perhaps the most significant aspect of *Roth* v. *United States*[43] was its final rejection of the concept, stemming from *Regina* v. *Hicklin,*[44] that obscenity could be judged on the basis of an isolated excerpt from the material. Instead, *Roth* substituted the requirement that material could be obscene if, and only if, the "dominant theme of the material *taken as a whole"* would appeal to the prurient interest.[45] Although the test for obscenity set forth in *Miller* v. *California*[46] omits the phrase "dominant theme," the "as a whole" concept is retained and it is clear that the meaning remains the same. The concept of dominant theme is merely a redundancy, and thus its omission bears no substantive significance. At the very least, then, the material objectionable in a constitutional sense must predominate, at least in effect if not mathematically. If the sexual theme or orientation is minor or subordinate, then there can be no finding of obscenity.[47] This may require an examination of the setting in which the allegedly prurient material is published. If the entire setting is literary, or political, and the prurient or offensive portions are an integral and relevant part of that setting, then the work taken as a whole cannot be deemed to be obscene.[48]

Lower courts have consistently upheld the principle of *Roth* that isolated excerpts cannot in any way be a basis for a finding of obscenity. Thus, a pattern of seizures by police, admittedly based on "indicators" such as bare breasts or buttocks, has been held to be impermissible, since one objectionable picture cannot render an entire pub-

---

[42] A.L.I. Model Penal Code § 251.4 (1) (1962).

[43] 354 U.S. 476 (1957).

[44] [1868] L.R. 3 Q.B. 360.

[45] 354 U.S. at 489.

[46] 413 U.S. 15, 24 (1973).

[47] *United States* v. *A Motion Picture Film Entitled "I Am Curious—Yellow,"* 404 F.2d 196, 199 (2d Cir. 1968).

[48] *See United States* v. *One Book Called "Ulysses,"* 5 F. Supp. 182, 184 (S.D.N.Y. 1933), *aff'd,* 72 F.2d 705 (2d Cir. 1934); *Grove Press, Inc.* v. *Christenberry,* 175 F. Supp. 488, 496–497 (S.D.N.Y. 1959), *aff'd,* 276 F.2d 433 (2d Cir. 1960) *(Lady Chatterley's Lover); Ackerman* v. *United States,* 293 F.2d 449, 451–452 (9th Cir. 1961) (private letters).

lication obscene.[49] Similarly, it has been held that since isolated episodes are insufficient, an arrest made on the basis of an offense committed in the presence of an officer requires that the officer have seen the entire motion picture.[50] The principle applies to trials as well as preliminary proceedings, and thus since a finding of obscenity must be based on the work as a whole, the judge, or jury, or officer must see the entire motion picture or consider the entire book.[51] Of course, if only a particular extract of a work is sold or distributed, then it is completely proper to base a finding on just the effect of that excerpt.[52]

The most difficult cases in this area have come from magazines and "underground" newspapers. The question to be asked is whether the objectionable materials are related to text or other materials which are themselves constitutionally protected, or whether the text is merely inserted as a sham to attempt to shield commercial pornography in a cloak of legitimacy. The Supreme Court had occasion to deal with the issue in 1972, in the context of an underground newspaper with several pictures which would, by themselves, be objectionable.[53] The

[49] *In re Louisiana News Company,* 187 F. Supp. 241, 246 (E.D. La. 1960) (three-judge court).

[50] *Cambist Films, Inc.,* v. *Duggan,* 298 F. Supp. 1148, 1152 (W.D. Pa. 1969), *rev'd on other grounds,* 420 F.2d 687 (3d Cir. 1969); *Hosey* v. *City of Jackson,* 309 F. Supp. 527, 534 (S.D. Miss. 1970) (three-judge court), *vacated on other grounds,* 401 U.S. 987 (1971); *Hanby* v. *State,* 479 P.2d 486, 493 (Alaska 1970). But even seeing the entire motion picture does not justify the officer in seizing the film itself without a warrant. *Roaden* v. *Kentucky,* 413 U.S. 496 (1973). See Chapters 11.1 and 11.2 *infra.*

[51] *Zenith International Film Corp.* v. *City of Chicago,* 291 F.2d 785, 789 (7th Cir. 1961); *Haldeman* v. *United States,* 340 F.2d 59, 62 (10th Cir. 1965); *McKinney* v. *Tuscaloosa,* 49 Ala. App. 21, 268 So.2d 488, 492 (1972); *Bryers* v. *State,* 480 S.W.2d 712, 717–719 (Tex. Crim. App. 1972); *Bourland* v. *State,* 502 S.W.2d 8, 9 (Tex. Crim. App. 1973); *United States* v. *West Coast News Co.,* 228 F. Supp. 171, 178 (W.D. Mich. 1964), *aff'd,* 357 F.2d 855 (6th Cir. 1966), *rev'd on other grounds sub nom. Aday* v. *United States,* 388 U.S. 447 (1967). Although in this last case the jury was required to read the books at issue in open court, there is also authority for merely instructing the jury to consider the books as a whole during their deliberations. *Alexander* v. *United States,* 271 F.2d 140, 144–145 (8th Cir. 1959). Although the requirement in *West Coast News* seems a bit overdone, the jury should be instructed to read the material. Otherwise, there seems too strong a temptation to consider merely the most offensive parts. Use of less than an entire book or motion picture at trial may also create "best evidence" problems. *See People* v. *Enskat,* 20 Cal. App. 3d Supp. 1, 98 Cal. Rptr. 646 (1971).

[52] *Kahm* v. *United States,* 300 F.2d 78, 82 (5th Cir. 1962); *cert. denied,* 369 U.S. 859 (1962) (excerpt from *Peyton Place,* by itself, may be obscene even if the entire book would not be).

Similarly, it is of course possible to have an obscene advertisement for a film or publication that may itself not be obscene. *Hamling* v. *United States,* 418 U.S. 87, 100–101 (1974).

[53] *Kois* v. *Wisconsin,* 408 U.S. 229 (1972).

Court held that "dominance" was a question of constitutional fact, and thus the jury's verdict was not conclusive.[54] The Court proceeded to analyze the material itself, and found that, as a whole, it was not obscene. The question to be asked was whether the article or text is "a mere vehicle for the publication of the pictures. A quotation from Voltaire in the flyleaf of a book will not redeem an otherwise obscene publication . . ." [55] But if, as here, the pictures were "relevant to the theme of the article" and "rationally related" to the article, then the publication as a whole was entitled to constitutional protection.[56] Thus, offensive cartoons in an underground newspaper were held to be protected where they were "inextricably bound to the iconoclastic nature of the entire periodical." [57] But other courts have reached contrary results with similar publications when they found the "cover picture unrelated to the balance of the pamphlet" [58] or that the "redeeming matter" was unrelated "to that which is to be redeemed." [59]

To summarize, then, both the trier of fact and the reviewing court must determine whether textual or other material, unobjectionable in and of itself, is inserted merely as a "pretext" or "feint" to try to dignify what is clearly intended to be sold as hard-core pornography that has offensive portrayals of prurient material as its clear "theme." [60] If so, then the dominant theme of the work remains controlling, and the work may still be deemed obscene. If, however, the text or other pictures are inserted for a bona fide purpose, are substantial in amount, and form the core of the material, and if the prurient

---

[54] *Id.* at 232.

[55] *Id.* at 231.

[56] *Id. See also Grove Press, Inc.* v. *Christenberry,* 175 F. Supp. 488, 489 (S.D.N.Y. 1959), *aff'd,* 276 F.2d 433 (2d Cir. 1960).

[57] *Dillingham* v. *State,* 9 Md. App. 669, 267 A.2d 777, 782 (1970) (this case contains a very complete discussion of the entire problem).

[58] *People* v. *Quentin,* 58 Misc. 2d 601, 296 N.Y.S.2d 443, 445 (Dist. Ct. 1968) (indictment dismissed on procedural grounds).

[59] *Scherr* v. *Municipal Court for Berkeley-Albany Judicial District,* 15 Cal. App. 3d 930, 93 Cal. Rptr. 556, 559 (1971).

[60] *State* v. *Vollmar,* 389 S.W.2d 20, 28 (Mo. 1965); *Kahm* v. *United States,* 300 F.2d 78, 84 (5th Cir. 1962), *cert. denied,* 369 U.S. 859; *United States* v. *56 Cartons Containing 19,500 Copies of a Magazine Entitled "Hellenic Sun,"* 373 F.2d 635, 641 (4th Cir. 1967), *rev'd sub nom. Potomac News Co.* v. *United States,* 389 U.S. 47 ("fillers do not change the character of the publication"); *Flying Eagle Publications, Inc.* v. *United States,* 285 F.2d 307, 308 (1st Cir. 1961) ("An obscene picture of a Roman orgy would be no less so because accompanied by an account of a Sunday school picnic which omitted the offensive details"); *Dillingham* v. *State,* 9 Md. App. 669, 267 A.2d 777, 781 (1970) ("innocuous text" would not help an otherwise obscene collection of pictures).

and offensive material is illustrative of and relevant to that core, then there can be no finding of obscenity.[61]

A related problem arises where a magazine or newspaper contains one or more obscene articles or pieces, but other articles in the periodical are not obscene. Is the entire publication to be looked at "as a whole," or does the court or jury look at each article separately, with each article being the "whole?" In *Ginzburg* v. *United States*,[62] the lower court had found *Eros* to be obscene even though only four of its 15 articles were found to be obscene, with the other 11 being "admittedly non-offensive." It was argued that it was therefore improper to find the magazine obscene as a whole. The opinion of the Supreme Court did not deal directly with the issue. "However erroneous such a conclusion [of obscenity] might be if unsupported by the evidence of pandering, the record here supports it." [63] Thus there is an indication from the Supreme Court that intent is the relevant factor in determining whether separate articles should be "integrated" or looked at individually. The New York courts have followed the approach of evaluating each story or article separately. "If any single item [in a magazine] considered as a whole, were pornographic, the circumstances that it was included in a collection otherwise without taint would not save it from criminal prosecution." [64] But it has also been suggested that, in general, the entire "physical item," that is, book, magazine, or other item, be looked at as a unit.[65] If the "physical item" test were rigidly applied, however, it would be far too easy to include hard-core pornography as one article in a magazine also containing excerpts from the writings of D. H. Lawrence or James Joyce. It would be more appropriate for the court, and the trier of fact, to make an evaluation in every instance as to the intended or likely "unit of perception." A magazine article, or a single book, or a motion picture, are intended to be seen or read as a unit, and should therefore be evaluated as such. So also when articles or stories are clearly interrelated and it is

[61] *See United States* v. *25,000 Magazines Entitled "Revue,"* 254 F. Supp. 1014, 1016 (D. Md. 1966).

[62] 383 U.S. 463 (1966).

[63] *Id.* at 471.

[64] *People* v. *Richmond County News, Inc.,* 9 N.Y.2d 578, 175 N.E.2d 681, 216 N.Y.S.2d 369, 376 (1961). *See also People* v. *Kirkpatrick,* 316 N.Y.S.2d 37, 66 (Crim Ct. 1970). *Cf. Flying Eagle Publications Inc.* v. *United States,* 273 F.2d 799 (1st Cir. 1960).

[65] *Dillingham* v. *State,* 9 Md. App. 669, 267 A.2d 777, 780–781 (1970); *United States* v. *Head,* 317 F.Supp. 1138, 1142–1143 (E.D. La. 1970). *Cf. Books, Inc.* v. *United States,* 358 F.2d 935 (1st Cir. 1966).

intended and expected that they will be perceived as a unit. But magazine "articles" with no connection except that of dealing with the same general subject matter are not necessarily likely to be seen or read together, and should therefore be evaluated separately.

5.4 *"I Know It When I See It"—The Hard-Core Requirement*

Superimposed on the tripartite test for obscenity in *Miller* v. *California* [66] is the requirement that only hard-core pornography may be included within the regulation of obscenity. The meaning, if any, of the term "hard-core pornography" has been elusive for many years. Judicially, the term existed as long ago as the *Roth* case, since Mr. Justice Harlan was of the opinion that while the Federal Government could regulate only hard-core pornography, the states were free to have more exclusive definitions of obscenity. [67] Although he did not define the term, he admitted taking it from the government's presentation, which, in addition to providing samples, [68] described hard-core pornography in the following way:

> This is commercially-produced material in obvious violation of present law . . . . This material is manufactured clandestinely in this country or abroad and smuggled in. There is no desire to portray the material in pseudo-scientific or "arty" terms. The production is plainly "hard-core" pornography, of the most explicit variety, devoid of any disguise.

> Some of this pornography consists of erotic objects. There are also large numbers of black and white photographs, individually, in sets, and in booklet form, of men and women engaged in every conceivable form of normal and abnormal sexual relations and acts. There are small printed pamphlets and books, illustrated with such photographs, which consist of stories in simple, explicit words of sexual excesses of every kind, over and over again. No one would suggest that they had the slightest literary merit or were intended to have any. There are also large numbers of "comic books," specifically drawn for the pornographic trade, which are likewise devoted to explicitly illustrated incidents of sexual activity, normal or perverted . . . . It may safely be said that most, if not all, of this type of booklets

[66] 413 U.S. 15, 24 (1973).

[67] *Roth* v. *United States,* 354 U.S. 476, 496–508 (1957) (Harlan, J., concurring in *Alberts* and dissenting in *Roth*).

[68] The Solicitor General sent the Supreme Court a box of samples of hard-core pornography in connection with the *Roth* argument.

contain drawings not only of normal fornication but also of perversions of various kinds.

The worst of the "hard-core" pornographic materials now being circulated are the motion picture films. These films, sometimes of high technical quality, sometimes in color, show people of both sexes engaged in orgies which again include every form of sexual activity known, all of which are presented in a favorable light. The impact of these pictures on the viewer cannot easily be imagined. No form of incitement to action or to excitation could be more explicit or more effective.[69]

Mr. Justice Harlan reiterated his views in *Manual Enterprises* v. *Day,*[70] and by then had been joined by Mr. Justice Stewart. It was Stewart who, three years later, left an indelible mark on the jurisprudence of pornography.

It is possible to read the Court's opinion in [*Roth*] in a variety of ways. In saying this, I imply no criticism of the Court, which in those cases was faced with the task of trying to define what may be indefinable. I have reached the conclusion . . . that under the First and Fourteenth Amendments criminal laws in this area are constitutionally limited to hard-core pornography. I shall not today attempt further to define the kinds of material I understand to be embraced within that shorthand description; and perhaps I could never succeed in intelligibly doing so. But I know it when I see it, and the motion picture involved in this case is not that.[71]

Two years later, however, Mr. Justice Stewart did attempt a definition, by indicating agreement with the following definition set forth by the Solicitor General.

Such materials include photographs, both still and motion picture, with no pretense of artistic value, graphically depicting acts of sexual intercourse, including various acts of sodomy and sadism, and sometimes involving several participants in scenes of orgy-like character. They also include strips of drawings in comic-book format grossly depicting similar activities in an exaggerated fashion. There are, in addition, pamphlets and booklets, sometimes with photographic illustrations, verbally describing such activities in a bizarre manner with no attempt whatsoever to afford portrayals of character or situation and with no pretense to literary value. All of this material . . . cannot

[69] Brief for the United States 37–38, *Roth* v. *United States,* 354 U.S. 476 (1957).

[70] 370 U.S. 478 (1962).

[71] *Jacobellis* v. *Ohio,* 378 U.S. 184, 197 (1964) (Stewart, J., concurring).

conceivably be characterized as embodying communication of ideas or artistic values inviolate under the First Amendment. . . ." [72]

During this time, a number of state courts began to deal with the "hard-core" problem, some deciding that obscenity regulation was limited to hard-core pornography,[73] and others taking the opposite view.[74]

In 1973, however, the Supreme Court specifically stated that only the depiction of "hard-core" sexual conduct may be prohibited.[75] As examples of what might be included, the Court indicated the following:

> (a) Patently offensive representations or descriptions of ultimate sexual acts, normal or perverted, actual or simulated.
> (b) Patently offensive representations or descriptions of masturbation, excretory functions, and lewd exhibition of the genitals." [76]

This definition seems to make it clear that hard-core pornography may include things other than actual sexual congress or activity, contrary to the views of a number of other courts prior to *Miller*.[77] These views seemed based primarily on the *Redrup* reversals of the Supreme Court, since for a number of years after 1967 the Court reversed any obscenity conviction where the material did not display actual sexual activity, regardless of the lewd or suggestive poses of individual models. But now, after *Miller*, it is clear that hard-core pornography may include material which does not depict sexual acts, and "lewd exhibition of the genitals" is specifically included. This should be interpreted in the light of a number of lower court cases defining hard-core pornography to include photographs which focus on, exaggerate, or emphasize the

---

[72] *Ginzburg* v. *United States*, 383 U.S. 463, 499 n.3 (1966) (Stewart, J., dissenting).

[73] *People* v. *Richmond County News, Inc.*, 9 N.Y.2d 578, 175 N.E.2d 681, 216 N.Y.S.2d 369 (1961); *Zeithlin* v. *Arnebergh*, 59 Cal. 2d 901, 383 P.2d 152, 31 Cal. Rptr. 800 (1963), *cert. denied*, 375 U.S. 957; *State* v. *J. L. Marshall News Co.*, 13 Ohio Misc. 60, 42 Ohio Op. 2d, 232 N.E.2d 435 (1969); *Attorney General* v. *Book Named "Tropic of Cancer,"* 345 Mass. 11, 184 N.E.2d 328 (1962).

[74] *State* v. *Hudson County News Co.*, 41 N.J. 247, 196 A.2d 225 (1963); *Rachleff* v. *Mahon*, 124 So.2d 878 (Fla. App. 160).

[75] *Miller* v. *California*, 413 U.S. 15, 27 (1973).

[76] *Id.* at 25.

[77] *See, e.g., Village Books, Inc.* v. *State's Attorney, Prince Georges County*, 263 Md. 76, 282 A|2d 126 (1971); *State* v. *Carlson*, 294 Minn. 433, 202 N.W.2d 640, 646–647 (1972), *vacated*, 414 U.S. 953 (1973), *rev'd*, 298 Minn. 415, 216 N.W.2d 650 (1974); *Commonwealth* v. *Bitsocas*, _____ Mass. _____, 281 N.E.2d 227, 228 (1972); *People* v. *Noroff*, 67 Cal. 2d 791, 433 P.3d 479, 63 Cal. Rptr. 575, 577 (1967).

genitalia or "erogenous zones." [78] It is this exaggeration or "highlight" on the genitalia which often distinguishes hard-core pornography from mere nudity. Similarly, hard-core pornography often emphasizes suggestive poses or lewdly intertwined bodies, even in the absence of actual sexual activity.[79]

In fact, of course, most hard-core pornography will have depictions of actual sexual acts. Although the depiction of sexual activity is not per se hard-core pornography, what distinguishes the latter is often an excess of detail in depicting the sexual act,[80] or a repetitive depiction of sexual activity.[81] And while it is clear that a depiction of normal heterosexual intercourse may itself, if the other tests are met, be hard-core pornography,[82] most hard-core pornography emphasizes various other sexual practices, such as homosexuality, bestiality, flagellation, sado-masochism, fellatio, cunnilingus, and the like.[83]

Although most hard-core pornography is in fact pictorial in nature, the Supreme Court has made it clear that a book with no pictures at all may constitute a description of "hard-core" sexual conduct.[84] While it is clear that photographs, and especially motion pic-

---

[78] *State* v. *Bongiorno,* 103 N.J. Super. 515, 247 A.2d 893, 894 (1968); *People* v. *Heller,* 33 N.Y.2d 314, 307 N.E.2d 805, 816 (1973); *Donnenberg* v. *State,* 1 Md. App. 591, 232 A.2d 264, 270 (1967); *United States* v. *Young,* 465 F.2d 1096, 1098 (9th Cir. 1972); *Collins* v. *State Beverage Department,* 239 So.2d 613, 614 (Fla. 1970); *People* v. *Andrews,* 23 Cal. App. 3d Supp. 1, 100 Cal. Rptr. 276 (1972).

[79] *See, e.g., Collins* v. *State Beverage Dept.,* 239 So.2d 613, 614 (Fla. 1970); *State* v. *Andrews,* 150 Conn. 92, 186 A.2d 546, 551 (1962); *State* v. *Bongiorno,* 103 N.J. Super. 515, 247 A.2d 893, 894 (1968).

[80] *B & A Company* v. *State,* 24 Md. App. 367, 330 A.2d 701, 705 (1974); *Miller* v. *Reddin,* 293 F. Supp. 216, 225–229 (C.D. Cal. 1968); *People* v. *Mature Enterprises, Inc.,* 73 Misc. 2d 749, 343 N.Y.S.2d 911, 923 (1973).

[81] *Miller* v. *Reddin,* 293 F. Supp. 216, 225–229 (C.D. Cal. 1968); *United States* v. *One Reel of Film,* 481 F.2d 206, 209 (1st Cir. 1973).

[82] *People* v. *Stabile,* 58 Misc. 2d 905, 296 N.Y.S.2d 815, 823 (Crim. Ct. 1969); *Richard* v. *State,* 497 S.W.2d 770 (Tex. Crim. App. 1973).

[83] *Hewitt* v. *Maryland Board of Censors,* 253 Md. 277, 254 A.2d 203, 212 (1969); *Donnenberg* v. *State,* 1 Md. App. 591, 232 A.2d 264, 270 (1967); *B & A Company* v. *State,* 24 Md. App. 367, 330 A.2d 701, 705 (1974); *People* v. *White,* 56 Misc. 2d 900, 290 N.Y.S.2d 253, 254 (1968); *Bee See Books, Inc.,* v. *Leary,* 291 F. Supp. 622, 623 (S.D.N.Y. 1968); *Miller* v. *Redding,* 293 F. Supp. 216, 225–229 (C.D. Cal. 1968); *United States* v. *Berger,* 325 F. Supp. 249, 255 (W.D. Mo. 1970); *State* v. *J-R Distributors, Inc.,* 82 Wash. 2d 584, 512 P.2d 1049, 1077 (1973); *State* v. *Valchar,* 34 Ohio App. 2d 21, 295 N.E.2d 424 (1973).

[84] *Kaplan* v. *California,* 413 U.S. 115 (1973) ("It is made up entirely of repetitive descriptions of physical, sexual conduct, 'clinically' explicit and offensive to the point of being nauseous"). *See also Armijo* v. *United States,* 384 F.2d 694, 695 (9th Cir. 1967) (private letters as hard-core pornography).

tures,[85] may have the greatest impact, textual material and cartoons,[86] if sufficiently explicit, prurient, offensive, and singleminded, may also constitute hard-core pornography.

While examples such as the above may help the reader understand what hard-core pornography is, it is more of a conclusion than a test. Thus, definitions of hard-core pornography have been equated with or intertwined with other tests for obscenity, such as contemporary community standards,[87] lack of artistic, scientific, or literary value,[88] appeal to the prurient interest,[89] or patent offensiveness.[90] And, in fact, the hard-core pornography "test" is probably best described as a "check" on the applicability of the other elements of the test for obscenity. Hard-core pornography is, as Mr. Justice Stewart said, reasonably obvious.[91] If material which has "failed" the *Miller* tests for obscenity does not look like hard-core pornography, then there has been an error in the application of one or all of the tests. Used in this way, the "hard-core" concept seems to be most useful.

5.5   The Scope of Review—Jenkins v. Georgia

While a complete discussion of law and fact in obscenity cases and the respective roles of judge, jury, and appellate court is presented elsewhere in this treatise,[92] a brief discussion of appellate review of

[85] *See People* v. *Mature Enterprises, Inc.,* 73 Misc. 2d 749, 343 N.Y.S.2d 911, 917 (Crim. Ct. 1973).

[86] *United States* v. *One Reel of 35mm Color Motion Picture Film Entitled "Sinderella,"* 491 F.2d 956 (2d Cir. 1973).

[87] *People* v. *Birch,* 40 Misc. 2d 626, 243 N.Y.S.2d 525, 532 (Sup. Ct. 1963) (what is or is not hard-core pornography must be related to "mores of these days").

[88] *Morris* v. *United States,* 259 A.2d 337 (D.C. Ct. of App. 1969) (it is the "sexually morbid, grossly perverse, and bizarre, without any artistic or scientific purpose or justification"); *United States* v. *Berger,* 325 F. Supp. 249, 255 (W.D. Mo. 1970) (absence of plot); *State* v. *Cox,* 3 Wash. App. 700, 477 P.2d 198, 204 (1970).

[89] *In re Van Geldern,* 14 Cal. App. 3d 843, 92 Cal. Rptr. 592, 595 (1971) ("deliberately designed to stimulate sexual feelings and act as an aphrodisiac").

[90] *People* v. *Burkhardt,* 11 Ill. App. 3d 760, 297 N.E.2d 694, 698 (1973).

[91] *See also B & A Company* v. *State,* 24 Md. App. 367, 330 A.2d 701, 705 (1974) ("Appellant contends that the magazines and movie are not obscene in the constitutional sense as a matter of law. Either appellant reviewed different material than did we or it refers to a different constitution.")

One of the best discussions of the concept of hard-core pornography, with additional sources, is Lockhart and McClure, *Censorship of Obscenity: The Developing Constitutional Standards,* 45 MINN. L. REV. 5, 58–68 (1960). The view that hard-core pornography is self-evident is shared by D. H. Lawrence, Margaret Mead, and others, all of whom are quoted by Lockhart and McClure.

[92] *See Chapters* 7.3 and 7.4 *infra.*

prurient-interest and patent-offensiveness determinations is best included here.

The Supreme Court in *Miller* made it clear that the initial determination of all of the elements of obscenity, prurient interest, patent offensiveness, and lack of serious literary, artistic, political, or scientific value is for the "trier of fact." [93] Thus, determinations of obscenity were not to be treated in a drastically different manner from factual determinations in other criminal cases.[94] Since prurient interest and patent offensiveness, however, are those aspects of the test which must be measured in light of contemporary community standards,[95] it is these two in which the greatest deference must be given to the findings of the jury. But the Court did not intend these findings to be conclusive. It recognized that every obscenity case involves an exercise of constitutional judgment, and thus the scope of review must be broader than that of a more conventional factual determination.[96] In *Kois* v. *Wisconsin*,[97] the Supreme Court held that the "dominance" of the theme of allegedly obscene material is a "question of constitutional fact," requiring independent review of the materials at issue while giving "due weight and respect" to conclusions of the trial court and lower appellate courts.[98]

A year after *Miller,* the Supreme Court was called upon to exercise this reviewing function. In *Jenkins* v. *Georgia*,[99] the Court reversed the finding of the Georgia Supreme Court that the motion picture *Carnal Knowledge* was obscene. This movie was a "fully legitimate" Hollywood production which starred Ann-Margret, Jack Nicholson, Art Garfunkel, and Candice Bergen. It had received a reasonable measure of critical acclaim, and Ann-Margret had been nominated for an Academy Award on the basis of her performance. But the general subject of the movie, as the title indicates, is sex— there are some nude scenes, and there are scenes in which sexual acts are "understood to be taking place." Jenkins, the theater manager, was

[93] *Miller* v. *California,* 413 U.S. 15, 24 (1973).

[94] *Id.* at 26.

[95] *Id.* at 30. *See* Chapter 6 *infra.*

[96] 413 U.S. at 29–30; *Roth* v. *United States,* 354 U.S. 476, 498 (1957) (opinion of Harlan, J.); *Jacobellis* v. *Ohio,* 378 U.S. 184, 188–191 (1964); Lockhart and McClure, *Censorship of Obscenity: The Developing Constitutional Standards,* 45 MINN. L. REV. 5, 116–119 (1960). *See also Hudson* v. *United States,* 234 A.2d 903, 904 (D.C. Ct. of App. 1967); *Donnenberg* v. *State,* 1 Md. App. 264, 232 A.2d. 264, 268–269 (1967); *United States* v. *Kaehler,* 353 F. Supp. 476 (N.D. Iowa 1973).

[97] 408 U.S. 229 (1972).

[98] *Id.* at 232.

[99] 418 U.S. 153 (1974).

convicted by a jury of having distributed obscene material. On appeal, the Georgia Supreme Court agreed with the state's contention that as long as there was some evidence to support the jury's finding, this finding was virtually conclusive on appeal.

But a unanimous Supreme Court reversed the conviction. Reiterating that the scope of review is greater where constitutional rights are concerned, Mr. Justice Rehnquist noted that "even though questions of appeal to the prurient interest or of patent offensiveness are essentially questions of fact, it would be a serious misreading of *Miller* to conclude that juries have unbridled discretion in determining what is 'patently offensive.' " [100] As an example, "it would be wholly at odds with this aspect of *Miller* to uphold an obscenity conviction based upon a defendant's depiction of a woman with a bare midriff, even though a properly charged jury unanimously agreed on a verdict of guilty." [101] Thus the Court reversed the conviction because neither the conduct portrayed nor the manner of its portrayal fit the contour of permissible obscenity regulation set forth in *Miller*. It is clear, based upon the Court's own description of the motion picture, that it could have reversed on the basis of serious artistic or literary value. But it appears as if the Court was intent on reaffirming the position that as to *all* of the elements of obscenity, there are still constitutional limitations. Thus, although an appellate court can and should still give great weight to factual findings in all cases at all close which involve commercial pornography of some sort, it remains the function and obligation of the appellate court to restrict obscenity findings to the guidelines of the *Miller* case, both as to legal and factual determinations.

[100] *Id.* at 160.
[101] *Id.* at 161.

6

The Move to Local Standards

6.1 Origins of the Community-Standards Test—Roth v. United States

In Chapter 2, we saw that the obscenity vel non of a given work is to be measured in terms of "contemporary community standards." [1] This chapter is devoted to an analysis of how those community standards are measured and just what is the relevant community. This issue is among the most troublesome in obscenity law,[2] in part because of the inherent ambiguity of the terms, and in part because the Supreme Court has been far from precise in attempting to define them.

In *Roth* v. *United States*,[3] the Supreme Court set forth the test for obscenity as "whether to the average person, applying contemporary community standards, the dominant theme of the material taken as a whole appeals to prurient interest." [4] This was the first use of the term "contemporary community standards," although this, as well as all

---

[1] See pp. 36 to 40, *supra*.

[2] The leading articles prior to the *Miller* case are: Lockhart and McClure, *Censorship of Obscenity: The Developing Constitutional Standards*, 45 MINN. L. REV. 5, 108–112 (1960); O'Meara and Shaffer, *Obscenity in the Supreme Court: A Note On Jacobellis v. Ohio*, 40 NOTRE DAME LAWYER 1, 6–7 (1965); Note, *The Geography of Obscenity's Contemporary Community Standard*, 8 WAKE FOREST L. REV. 81 (1971); Comment, *Multi-Venue and the Obscenity Statutes*, 115 U. PA. L. REV. 399 (1967); Post, *Standards of Judging Obscenity—Who? What? Where?*, 46 CHI. B. REC. 405 (1965); Note, *Venue: Its Impact on Obscenity*, 11 S.D.L. REV. 363 (1966); 1971 WASH. U.L.Q. 691 (1971); 16 S. CAR. L. REV. 639 (1964).

Articles which postdate *Miller*, and therefore analyze the issue in terms of the local-standard formulation, include: Shugrue, *An Atlas for Obscenity: Exploring Community Standards*, 7 CREIGHTON L. REV. 157 (1974); Comment, *Obscenity: Determined By Whose Standards*, 26 U. FLA. L. REV. 324 (1974); Comment, *Pornography, the Local Option*, 26 BAYLOR L. REV. 97 (1974); 8 GEO. L. REV. 225 (1973); 8 VALPARAISO L. REV. 166 (1973); 23 EMORY L.J. 551 (1974).

[3] 354 U.S. 476 (1957).

[4] *Id.* at 489.

other elements of the *Roth* test, was merely a restatement of the test used in many lower court opinions prior to *Roth*.[5] While none of these opinions explicitly used the phrase "contemporary community standards," they all placed considerable emphasis on the idea that prevailing concepts of decency and morality change with time and that therefore what is obscene at one time and place may not be obscene at another.[6] Thus, the concept of contemporary community standards as an element of the obscenity test was hardly new with *Roth*, although it was not until *Roth* that it became a major factor in obscenity litigation.

The real purpose of this aspect of the *Roth* test seems to be the need for the finder of fact to apply an external standard, rather than his personal views of decency. It was also designed to prevent the evaluation of obscenity from being made on the basis of whether the material had an adverse effect on a "particularly susceptible subclass" of the community.[7] But there was no discussion of the definition of community in *Roth*, and the Court does not seem to have considered the issue. There is, however, an inference to be drawn that the *Roth* Court envisaged a rather local community. At trial, the judge had instructed the jury on the community-standards issue by telling the jurors to "determine the impact [of the material] upon the average person in the community," and to judge the material "by present-day standards of the community."[8] Since the Supreme Court approved these instructions verbatim, and since the jurors' perceptions of the community would of necessity be local, it can be argued that the Supreme Court had in mind a geographically limited community. This view is supported by the concurring opinion of Chief Justice Warren, who focused on the "part of the community" to which the material was directed.[9] Following this view, a number of lower federal courts

[5] The concept seems first to have been enunciated by Learned Hand, then a federal district judge, in *United States* v. *Kennerley,* 209 F. 119, 121 (S.D.N.Y. 1913). *See also Commonwealth* v. *Isenstadt,* 318 Mass. 543, 62 N.E.2d 840 (1945); *State* v. *Becker,* 364 Mo. 1079, 272 S.W.2d 283 (1954); *Bantam Books, Inc.* v. *Melko,* 25 N.J. Super. 292, 96 A.2d 47 (1953). *Cf. McJunkins* v. *State,* 10 Ind. 140 (1858).

[6] Although the word "community" was frequently used in the earlier cases, the emphasis of the concept was that standards change over time. *See, e.g., Parmelee* v. *United States,* 113 F.2d 729, 731 (D.C. Cir. 1940). The shift in focus to the idea of geographic variations is of more recent origin.

[7] 354 U.S. at 488–489.

[8] *Id.* at 490.

[9] *Id.* at 495 (Warren, C. J., concurring). But this apparently was not what Justice Brennan had in mind. See *Jacobellis* v. *Ohio,* 378 U.S. 184, 192 (1964).

adopted a localized view of community standards after *Roth*.[10] But whether this inference is properly made from the Court's opinion is no longer relevant, since subsequent cases have dealt specifically with this issue.

6.2   The National-Standards Test—Manual Enterprises v. Day and Jacobellis v. Ohio

The Supreme Court first faced the issue of the geographic contours of the community in *Manual Enterprises* v. *Day*,[11] an appeal from a ruling barring certain magazines from the mails pursuant to 18 U.S.C. § 1461. Justice Harlan, who announced the judgment of the Court and wrote an opinion in which Justice Stewart joined, said that a "national standard of decency" is appropriate in this federal action, since the federal statute reached the entire United States.[12] Thus, in the absence of congressional action setting a more local geographic standard, the relevant community for a federal prosecution would be the entire country.[13] Although several other opinions were written in this case, none of them addressed the issue of the geographic scope of the community whose standards were being applied.[14]

Two years later, the Court was faced with this issue in the context of a state obscenity prosecution. In *Jacobellis* v. *Ohio*,[15] Justice Brennan stated that *Roth* did not in any way mandate a standard to be drawn from the local community. Saying that "it is, after all, a national Constitution we are expounding," he stated that the scope of constitutional protection must be uniform throughout the country.[16] To hold otherwise, he reasoned, would have a deterrent effect on the

[10] *See, e.g., United States* v. *West Coast News Company*, 30 F.R.D. 13 (W.D. Mich. 1962); *United States* v. *Frew*, 187 F. Supp. 500, 506 (E.D. Mich. 1960). *Cf. Eastman Kodak Company* v. *Hendricks*, 262 F.2d 392, 397 (9th Cir. 1958); *Alexander* v. *United States*, 271 F.2d 140, 146 (8th Cir. 1959).

[11] 370 U.S. 478 (1962).

[12] *Id.* at 488.

[13] The opinion left open the question of whether Congress could constitutionally prescribe a more local standard. *Id.* Although Congress never attempted to take such action, the opinion in *Hamling* v. *United States*, 418 U.S. 87 (1974), seems to allow such action.

[14] Justice Black concurred in the result and Justices Frankfurter and White did not participate in the decision. 370 U.S. at 495. Justice Brennan, joined by Justice Douglas and Chief Justice Warren, concurred on the ground that the Postmaster General could not himself exercise the censorship function. *Id.* at 495–519. Justice Clark dissented without discussing the issue of geographic standards. *Id.* at 519–529.

[15] 378 U.S. 184 (1964).

[16] *Id.* at 193–195.

total distribution of material that might be considered offensive in only a small part of the country, since no distributor would risk the varying adjudications that would result from a variable standard.[17] This argument, however, addresses itself only to the effect *of* a community with stricter than average standards, and not to the effect *on* a community with standards more permissive than the national norm. As has subsequently been noted,[18] a national standard has the effect of prohibiting the distribution of material in a more permissive community that that community is willing to accept.

Justice Brennan's views relating to a national standard did not command a majority of the Court. Only Justice Goldberg joined in his opinion. Justice White concurred without opinion, and the concurring opinions of Justices Stewart, Black, and Douglas did not discuss the issue of community standards. Chief Justice Warren, in a dissenting opinion joined by Justice Clark, disagreed with the national-standards test, chiefly because he felt that there was and could be no one national standard. Justice Harlan's dissent reiterated his position that a national standard should apply to federal statutes and a more local standard to state obscenity regulation.

The purpose of the opinion analysis is to show that on this issue, those Justices who expressed an opinion divided 2-2, excluding Justice Harlan's variable standard. Neither in *Jacobellis,* nor in any other case, did the national-standards view command a majority of the Court. Despite this, the overwhelming majority of lower courts which faced the problem after *Jacobellis* employed a national definition of contemporary community standards.[19] While some recognized the lack of

---

[17] *Id.* at 194.

[18] *Miller* v. *California*, 413 U.S. 15, 32 n.13 (1973); see text accompanying note 25 *infra.*

[19] Every federal court which faced the issue after *Jacobellis* selected a national standard. *Chemline, Inc.* v. *City of Grand Prairie*, 364 F.2d 721 (5th Cir. 1966); *United States* v. *Davis*, 353 F.2d 614 (2d Cir. 1965); *Haldeman* v. *United States*, 340 F.2d 59 (10th Cir. 1965); *United States* v. *West Coast News Company*, 357 F.2d 855 (6th Cir. 1966), *rev'd on other grounds sub nom. Aday* v. *United States*, 388 U.S. 447 (1967); *United States* v. *Ginzburg*, 338 F.2d 12 (3d Cir. 1964), *aff'd*, 383 U.S. 463 (1966); *United States* v. *Austin*, 319 F. Supp. 457 (M.D. Fla. 1970); *Grove Press, Inc.,* v. *City of Philadelphia*, 300 F. Supp. 281 (E.D. Pa. 1969); *United States* v. *392 Copies of a Magazine Entitled "Exclusive,"* 253 F. Supp. 485 (D. Md. 1966), *aff'd*, 373 F.2d 633 (4th Cir. 1967), *rev'd on other grounds*, 389 U.S. 50; *United States* v. *One Carton Positive Motion Picture Film Entitled "491"*, 247 F. Supp. 450 (S.D.N.Y. 1965), *rev'd on other grounds*, 367 F.2d 889 (2d Cir. 1966).

The First Circuit chose a national standard prior to *Jacobellis. Excellent Publications, Inc.* v. *United States*, 309 F.2d 362 (1st Cir. 1962); *Flying Eagle Publications, Inc.* v. *United States*, 273 F.2d 799 (1st Cir. 1960).

The state courts were divided. Those employing a national standard include:

definitive authority and thus analyzed the competing constitutional considerations, most felt that *Jacobellis* mandated national standards, a view that is hardly justified by the opinions in that case.[20] As a result, national standards became, with few exceptions, the law of the land, and remained so until 1972.

6.3   *National Standards Rejected*—Miller *v.* California

Unlike the previous cases, where the issue of national versus local standards was, at best, a collateral matter, *Miller* v. *California* [21] specifically focused on the issue. Chief Justice Burger, writing for the majority, held that there was no error in instructing the jury to apply "contemporary community standards of the State of California."[22] His opinion is based primarily on the argument, first made by Chief Justice Warren in *Jacobellis,* that a national standard is nonexistent, or, at best, not capable of determination. Although the *Miller* majority accepted the view that "fundamental First Amendment limitations" must be uniform, it did not feel that this view required that the essentially factual determination of contemporary community standards also be uniform.

> These are essentially questions of fact, and our nation is simply too big and too diverse for this Court to reasonably expect that such standards could be articulated for all 50 States in a single formulation, even assuming the prerequisite consensus exists. When triers of fact are asked to decide whether "the average person, applying con-

---

State v. *Locks,* 97 Ariz. 148, 397 P.2d 949 (1964); *State* v. *Lewitt,* 3 Conn. Cir. 605, 222 A.2d 579 (1966); *State* v. *Smith,* 422 S.W.2d 50 (Mo. 1967); *State* v. *Hudson County News Co.,* 41 N.J. Super. 489, 268 A.2d 753 (1970); *People* v. *Stabile,* 58 Misc.2d 905, 296 N.Y.S.2d 815 (1969); *State* v. *Childs,* 252 Ore. 91, 447 P.2d 304 (1968); *Robert Arthur Management Corp.* v. *State,* 220 Tenn. 101, 414 S.W.2d 638 (1967). Those adopting a statewide or smaller community were: *In re Giannini,* 69 Cal. 2d 563, 446 P.2d 535, 72 Cal. Rptr. 655 (1968); *Carter* v. *State,* 388 S.W.2d. 191 (Tex. Crim. 1965); *McCauley* v. *Tropic of Cancer,* 20 Wis. 2d 134, 121 N.W.2d 545 (1963); *People* v. *Bloss,* 27 Mich. App. 687, 184 N.W.2d 299 (1970); *Gent* v. *State,* 239 Ark. 474, 393 S.W.2d 219 (1965); *Felton* v. *City of Pensacola,* 200 So.2d 842 (Fla. 1967). These latter cases, although they predate *Miller,* can still be considered valid authority in the states and should be consulted by practitioners in those states for the light they may shed on the definition or boundaries of the local community.

[20] Of the cases cited in note 19, it is generally the state cases that have the more reasoned opinions.

[21] 413 U.S. 15 (1973).

[22] *Id.* at 30–34.

temporary community standards" would consider certain materials "prurient," it would be unrealistic to require that the answer be based on some abstract formulation. The adversary system, with lay jurors as the usual ultimate factfinders in criminal prosecutions, has historically permitted triers-of-fact to draw on the standards of their community, guided always by limiting instructions on the law. To require a State to structure obscenity proceedings around evidence of a *national* "community standard" would be an exercise in futility.[23] [Emphasis original.]

And later,

It is neither realistic nor constitutionally sound to read the First Amendment as requiring that people of Maine or Mississippi accept public depiction of conduct found tolerable in Las Vegas, or New York City.[24]

In a footnote, the Court again discussed the effect of a national or local standard on the total distribution of material that would be questionable but not necessarily legally obscene. While acknowledging the argument that a local standard might inhibit total distribution because sellers would not risk the variability of different standards, the majority said that it is at least equally likely that a national standard would exclude materials from areas in which they are deemed acceptable.[25] As a question of logic, the two dangers are probably of equal significance. In practice, however, they may not be equivalent. The danger of the "chilling effect" of local standards is fairly obvious. The danger of keeping materials from a more permissive community, as theoretically could happen with a national standard, is probably illusory, since the material is unlikely to be prosecuted in that community, or the community itself may, by statute, relax its regulation of obscenity. But the heart of the issue still seems to be which standard can best be measured. The national standard, as the *Miller* Court noted, is probably incapable of identification. Litigation under the national standard tended to focus on the temporal, rather than the geographic, nature of the concept of contemporary community standards. The more localized standard set forth by the *Miller* Court provides a standard which is more ascertainable and thus gives vitality to the geographic aspects of the standard without detracting from the temporal aspects. What *Miller* really does, then, is add a test which did not in fact exist under the national-standards formulation. Al-

[23] *Id.* at 30.
[24] *Id.* at 32.
[25] *Id.* at 32 n.13.

though it is true that distributors of material which may run afoul of the obscenity laws have opposed the change to local standards,[26] this seems based more on a spontaneous reaction than on an analysis of what the change really does. If anything, the local standard creates new opportunities for proof [27] which may be as advantageous to the defense as to the prosecution.

Thus far we have treated the subject of community standards in the abstract. We must now turn to a discussion of just where this test fits into the total scheme of the standards for determining whether or not material is legally obscene. When the expression "contemporary community standards" first appeared in *Roth,* it was part of the test that material is to be judged obscene according to "whether to the average person, applying contemporary community standards, the dominant theme of the material taken as a whole appeals to prurient interest."[28] Thus the purpose of community standards was to provide a frame of reference by which the prurient interest of the material could be measured. What is prurient in one time and place may not be prurient in another, and the community-standards test was designed to add focus to this determination. As the test for obscenity has become more detailed, however, new factors have been added and the question naturally arises as to which of these new factors the community-standards frame of reference applies.[29]

The first section of the tripartite test in *Miller* is merely a restatement of the original *Roth* test, quoted above. Thus there is no question that contemporary community standards still provide the guideline for determining whether or not material appeals to the prurient interest. But the relevance of the community-standards formula is still open to question as to the other two parts of the *Miller* test. The second part is "whether the work depicts or describes, in a patently offensive way, sexual conduct specifically defined by the applicable state law." [30] Must, then, patent offensiveness be determined by reference

[26] The briefs of the defendants and amici in *Jenkins* v. *Georgia,* 418 U.S. 153 (1974), probably best demonstrate this opposition.

[27] See Chapter 6.7 *infra.*

[28] 354 U.S. at 489.

[29] Although only one reported case had specifically discussed the issue, the problem frequently appears at trial in connection with admissibility of evidence and instructions to the jury. The one case is *United States* v. *B & H Dist. Corp.,* 375 F. Supp. 136, 141 (W.D. Wis. 1974), holding that patent offensiveness must be measured in light of local community standards. *Cf. McCauley* v. *Tropic of Cancer,* 20 Wis. 2d 134, 121 N.W.2d 545 (1963).

[30] 413 U.S. at 24.

to local community standards? In *Memoirs* v. *Massachusetts*,[31] the Court's test included the standard that material is obscene if it "is patently offensive because it affronts contemporary community standards relating to the description or representation of sexual matters." [32] The *Memoirs* plurality, then, clearly intended that patent offensiveness, as much as prurient interest, must be evaluated in the context of contemporary community standards. There is no indication in *Miller* that this view is erroneous.[33] Furthermore, the *Miller* Court discussed the failings of the national-standards test in terms of *both* the prurient-interest and patent-offensiveness standards, and on several occasions talked of contemporary community standards in a more general context than would be expected if the standards were to be used in only one of the three tests.[34] The only logical argument to the contrary is that the Court did not include contemporary community standards in the test itself, and the tests obviously were drafted with some care. Still, the most reasonable reading of the entire opinion is that local community standards apply also to the patent-offensiveness requirement. Nor is there any logical reason to restrict the community-standards factor to prurient interest alone. If anything, patent offensiveness is more susceptible to temporal and geographic variations than is prurient interest. What is offensive to one may not be offensive to another, even more than what is prurient to one may vary with the context. What the concept of contemporary community standards embodies is the idea that a work is not obscene unless it *offends* those standards. Therefore, both because of the Supreme Court's opinion and because of the logical reasons behind the tests, patent offensiveness as well as prurient interest must be evaluated in light of redefined contemporary community standards.

The foregoing analysis does not necessarily apply to the third element of the *Miller* test, that "the work, taken as a whole, lacks serious literary, artistic, political, or scientific value." [35] There has never been any indication by the Court that the merit of the material

[31] 388 U.S. 413 (1966).

[32] Id. at 418. *See also* Chapter 4.2 *supra*.

[33] The *Memoirs* test is severely criticized in *Miller*, but the criticism and abandonment of the *Memoirs* test seems limited to the "utterly without redeeming social value" factor. 413 U.S. at 22–25.

[34] "Under a national Constitution, fundamental First Amendment limitations on the States do not vary from community to community, but this does not mean that there are, or should or can be, fixed, uniform national standards of precisely what appeals to the 'prurient interest' *or is 'patently offensive.'* " [Emphasis added.] 413 U.S. at 30.

[35] *Id.* at 24.

itself, as embodied in this part of the test, should or can vary from community to community. In fact, community standards are looked upon as a factual consideration, an aid to the jury in making its factual findings. But while prurient interest and patent offensiveness are thought to be primarily questions of fact, the literary-merit standard is much less a question of fact and more a matter of constitutional law.[36] Although the *Memoirs* test of "utterly without redeeming social value" has been rejected in favor of the new *Miller* standard for literary merit, this is still the part of the test that embodies the essentials of First Amendment theory, the principle that *any* expression of *ideas* is within the scope of First Amendment protection. If this test were subject to the inherent variations of local community standards, then First Amendment values would vary with time and place, a result which the courts have properly sought to avoid.[37] Whether a work has literary, artistic, political, or scientific value, then, unlike the prurient-interest and patent-offensiveness requirements, is not subject to the community-standards factor and not affected by the change to local standards.

6.4   How Large (or Small) is the Local Community and Who Defines It?

In *Miller,* the Supreme Court approved the instructions of the California trial judge who instructed the jury to apply the community standards of the State of California.[38] The Court did not indicate directly whether such a more local community was in fact required, nor did it give any indication of whether local standards drawn from a geographical area narrower than an entire state would also be acceptable. The opinion said nothing at all about the size or definition of the community that was to provide the basis for the local contemporary community standards.

Certainly the Court expressed enough negative views about national standards to indicate that such a standard in a particular case would be unacceptable. The issue arose a year later when, in *Hamling* v. *United States,*[39] the Court was faced with a pre-*Miller* conviction in which both the admission of evidence and the instructions to the jury were based on national community standards. While acknowledg-

---

[36] *See* Chapter 7.3 *infra.*
[37] *Miller,* 413 U.S. at 30.
[38] *Id.* at 31.
[39] 418 U.S. 87 (1974).

ing that national standards were *no longer permissible,* the Court said that the requirement was not such a fundamental principle of constitutional law as to require reversal of the conviction where no specific harm or prejudice could be shown.[40] While it is now true that national standards have specifically been rejected, it is also significant to note the further indication of this decision that although all of the elements of the Supreme Court's obscenity tests have a constitutional basis, only the literary-value standard is really a question of fundamental constitutional rights. The other tests are mainly questions of fact requiring a less rigid standard of review.

The question still persists as to the size of the local community. In trials under state law, the trial can be conducted under the community standards of the entire state, as was done in *Miller,* even in the absence of any state law defining community standards. Or, in the absence of state law, the jury could be instructed to apply the standards of the county, of the city, of the judicial district in which the trial occurs, or any other appropriate geographical area. The standard to be applied should be based upon a balancing of the competing factors of workability of the standard, on the one hand, and the overall effect on First Amendment values, on the other. The workability will most often militate in favor of a narrow area, especially where the entire state encompasses either a large or a diverse community. Certainly the community standards of a small town in upstate New York are no more similar to the standards of New York City than the standards of Maine are similar to the standards of Las Vegas, to use the Supreme Court's example.[41] For a state like New York, or California, or Texas, a statewide standard is little more ascertainable than a national standard. But while these considerations should lead to use of a more limited geographic standard, the area must not be too small. If it is, there is again the problem of the chilling effect on the distribution of generally acceptable materials if a distributor or seller must deal with too many different community standards.[42] These

[40] *Id.* at 2902–2903.

[41] *Miller,* 413 U.S. at 32. Similarly, there may be no reason to believe that the standards, for instance, of adjacent and similar areas such as Westchester County, N.Y., and Fairfield County, Conn., would be different merely because a state line intervenes.

[42] The effect noted by the Supreme Court in *Miller* at n.13 becomes greater when the number of possible communities increases, as would happen by choosing a county as the community rather than a state. In the first place, it becomes less likely that a distributor could know the standards in a large number of different communities, and therefore the risk increases. Furthermore, the larger number of communities increases the chances that the material will be available in an unforeseen community.

competing considerations indicate that the decision, at least as to state obscenity laws, should be a legislative determination. This would prevent varying definitions of "community" from case to case and would give better notice as to the potential risks. Certainly it is a determination which can be made by a legislature, both because the Supreme Court has specifically indicated its propriety, and because of the general advisability of leaving such policy matters, involving the actual substantive definition of a crime, to the legislative branch. In fact, a number of legislatures have done so in the wake of *Miller*.[43]

Another approach is to ignore any specific instructions to the jury as to how the community is defined or to instruct the jury to call upon its own experience and knowledge in assessing the standards of the community. Thus the size of the community is theoretically the area from which the jury is drawn, but there is nothing to prevent jurors with wider or narrower perceptions from adopting a different community. The Supreme Court specifically approved such instructions in *Hamling* v. *United States*,[44] a federal prosecution, and this approach will probably be followed in most federal cases, although some federal courts have still utilized a specific and narrow definition of the community.[45] The difficulties with such an approach, however, are twofold. There is still the problem of fair notice of the standards, and there is also the issue of what will be the test for admissibility of evidence of community standards. If the jury will not be instructed on any specific local standard, then the scope of the evidence which can be presented should not be limited, as it might be by considerations of relevancy if a specific local standard were used. Of course,

---

[43] North Carolina had adopted the national standard by statute prior to *Miller*. N.C. GEN. STAT. § 14–190.1(b)(2)(Supp. 1971). The statute was amended after *Miller* to provide for a statewide definition of community.

All of the other states that have defined community after *Miller* have also defined community as being the state. CONN. G.S.A. § 53a–193(a) (amended by P.A. 74–126); MASS. G.L. ch. 272 § 31 (amended by ch. 430, Acts of 1974); ORE. R.S. § 167.002 (Supp. 1974); So. DAK., Ch. 165, Acts of 1974 § 1; TENN. CODE § 39–3010-(G)(Supp. 1974); VT. STAT. ANN. T. 13 § 2801(B)(Supp. 1974).

Illinois and Montana do not define community but provide that acceptance of the material in the state is relevant evidence. ILL. STAT. ch. 38 § 11–20 (Supp. 1974); MONT. CODE § 94–8–110(3)(Supp. 1974).

Missouri's Proposed Criminal Code has a provision similar to those of Illinois and Montana but includes as relevant evidence acceptance in the state or local community. Proposed Criminal Code of Missouri § 18.050 (1973).

[44] 418 U.S. 87, 104 (1974). *Accord, Jenkins* v. *Georgia*, 418 U.S. 153, 157 (1974). *See United States* v. *Cangiano*, 491 F.2d 906, 914 (2d Cir. 1974).

[45] The only reported case is *United States* v. *One Reel of 35mm Color Motion Picture Film Entitled "Sinderella,"* 491 F.2d 956, 958 (2d Cir. 1974) (court, sitting without jury, applied standards of Eastern District of New York).

Congress could define contemporary community standards by statute for federal cases, but such action seems highly unlikely.

6.5 Which Community Is To Be Chosen Where Several Discrete Communities May Be Relevant?—Obscenity and the Conflict of Laws

Thus far this chapter has dealt with the issue of contemporary community standards as if the only issue were the size of the community. In the majority of cases this will be the only issue. However, when the acts upon which a prosecution is based overrun community boundaries, however the community is defined, then the problem of which community to choose becomes as significant as the problem of how to define that community. For example, a defendant is charged with distributing, from New York, obscene materials to Connecticut and Rhode Island. At trial in New York, which community is the relevant one in defining contemporary community standards? Or a defendant is charged with transporting obscene material from Florida to North Carolina, in the course of which the material passes through Georgia and South Carolina. If tried in South Carolina, what standards are used and how are they proved? Similar examples can also be imagined within one state if the community is defined as a county or a judicial district.

The simplest solution, and the one that has been followed by those lower courts that have faced the problem,[46] is to apply the community standards of the forum of the prosecution. It is reasonable to assume that regardless of the evidence presented, and regardless of the instructions, a jury will inevitably apply the community standards of the community with which it is most familiar.[47] Thus, applying the standards of the forum avoids the problem of having the evidence and the instructions ignored. There are also practical problems when evidence of a standard other than that of the forum is used. Witnesses must be brought from other areas, and the prosecution would obviously have to present evidence of these standards as part of its case-in-chief, despite the holding of the Supreme Court that prosecu-

[46] *Id. See also United States* v. *Friedman,* 488 F.2d 1141, 1143 (10th Cir. 1973), where the court assumed that the standards applied must be those of the forum. *See generally* Schauer, *Obscenity and the Conflict of Laws,* 77 W. VA. L. REV. 377 (1975).

[47] The Supreme Court has recognized that instructions to the jury cannot always correct previous impressions. *See Bruton* v. *United States,* 391 U.S. 123 (1968); *Jackson* v. *Denno,* 378 U.S. 368 (1964).

tion evidence of community standards is not normally required.[48] In fact, it can be said that the elimination of the requirement of prosecution evidence on this issue indicates the Court's belief that the standards of the forum will prevail in all prosecutions.[49]

The major difficulty with such an approach is that it can lead to the most extreme examples of forum-shopping by the prosecution. Guilt or innocence should not, and do not normally, turn on where the prosecution occurs, but this is the inevitable result when a major substantive element of the offense must, by definition, vary from place to place. The selection of the proper place then takes on greater importance. The dangers of selective prosecution become even greater in situations, such as this one, where the place of prosecution defines the offense charged. In a prosecution under 18 U.S.C. § 1461 for sending obscene matter through the mails, the prosecution could be at the place of mailing, the place of delivery, or any state through which the package passes. If the standards are different in each state, then a putative defendant may run the risk of prosecution under standards that he has no logical reason to believe will be employed, nor can he, with assurance, plan his activities to avoid those areas in which such activities are illegal. To the extent that the shift to local standards may involve the chilling effect on constitutionally protected material which has been discussed earlier,[50] the uncertainty as to which community's standards will be applied increases the danger.

Since the issue has yet to be squarely faced by any court, a suggested analysis seems appropriate. In actuality, this is a conflict-of-laws problem, because the effect of a geographic variation in the substantive standards for criminality is analytically identical to a choice between conflicting statutes. Traditionally, choice of law in criminal law has been more localized than it would be in civil litigation. In order for a crime to be prosecuted in a given jurisdiction, some part of the crime must have been committed in that jurisdiction, and, in that event, the law of the forum is almost universally applied.[51] This rule would seem to favor the community standards of the forum in obscenity litigation, and this may be the basis for those decisions that

[48] *Paris Adult Theatre I* v. *Slaton,* 413 U.S. 49, 56 (1973).

[49] But in *Hamling,* the Court did say that it might, under certain circumstances, be proper to "admit evidence of standards in some place outside of this particular district." 418 U.S. at 106. It is impossible to tell whether this was meant to mean a larger area which includes the district, or a different area entirely.

[50] See text accompanying notes 25–27 *supra.*

[51] *See* R. LEFLAR, AMERICAN CONFLICTS LAW, Ch. 12 (1968); Leflar, *Conflict of Laws: Choice of Law in Criminal Cases,* 25 CASE W. RES. L. REV. 44 (1974).

have used, without discussion, the standards of the forum. But this traditional rule inevitably ignores some of the First Amendment considerations, as well as due process factors, both of which are especially relevant to obscenity law.

A possible solution, or at least a preferable method of analysis, may lie with some of the more modern theories of choice of law. A feasible alternative would be the "center of contacts" theory of a number of recent cases, most notably *Babcock* v. *Jackson*,[52] which chooses the law of the jurisdiction having the most significant contacts with the act or the cause of action. This approach would certainly eliminate the application of the standards of a community only incidentally involved, such as one merely on a mail route or on a bus route, and therefore would be an improvement. Even better might be the application of a functional choice-of-law theory, which looks to the purpose of the law involved in making the decision as to which law applies.[53] The primary purpose of most obscenity laws is to protect the "target" community, the community where the material is actually available to the public, and the purpose of the community-standards test is to allow that community to govern what will or will not be available. This view indicates that the point of ultimate availability or exhibition of the material is the relevant community. In other words, the relevant community is the one in which the materials come in contact with the group that the statute is designed to protect from the materials. This approach also has the advantages of fair notice and predictability, since it can be presumed that a distributor or sender will generally know the object of his actions. If material is sent through the mail, the route of the package, and perhaps even the place of mailing, are somewhat fortuitous, but the package must always have an intended destination. More complex problems may exist if a conspiracy is alleged, but these are taken up in the general discussion of conspiracy prosecutions under the obscenity laws.[54] Of course, if the purpose of the statute is to keep material out of the "stream of commerce," then there would be ample justification for employing the community

---

[52] 12 N.Y.2d 473, 191 N.E.2d 279, 240 N.Y.S.2d 743 (1963).

[53] See generally D. TRAUTMAN and A. VON MEHREN, THE LAW OF MULTISTATE PROBLEMS (1965); RESTATEMENT OF THE LAW (2D) CONFLICT OF LAWS § 6 (1971); *Clark* v. *Clark*, 107 N.H. 351, 222 A.2d 205 (1961); *Brown* v. *Church of Holy Jesus*, 105 R.I. 322, 252 A.2d 176 (1969); *Hunker* v. *Royal Indemnity Co.*, 57 Wis. 2d 588, 204 N.W.2d 897 (1973). Cf. *Auten* v. *Auten*, 308 N.Y. 155, 124 N.E.2d 99 (1954); *Lauritzen* v. *Larsen*, 345 U.S. 571 (1953); *Romero* v. *International Terminal Operating Co.*, 358 U.S. 354 (1959); RESTATEMENT OF THE LAW (2D) CONFLICT OF LAWS §§ 145, 188 (1971).

[54] See Chapter 9.8 *infra*.

standards of some intermediate point. In any event, the principle of looking to the purpose of the legislation or rule should provide more guidance and generally better solutions than selection of the community not based on any rational analysis.

6.6 Community Standards in Federal Prosecutions—Hamling v. United States

Many of the issues which arise in applying the contemporary-community-standards test to federal prosecutions have already been discussed in this chapter. It is appropriate here, however, to trace the application of that test to federal prosecutions. In *Manual Enterprises* v. *Day*,[55] Justice Harlan expressed the view that national standards must apply to federal prosecutions under federal law, even though states might choose to apply different standards in the enforcement of their obscenity laws.[56] This opinion, coupled with *Jacobellis* v. *Ohio*,[57] led to general acceptance of the proposition that national standards were to be applied under federal law.[58] However, two companion cases to *Miller* signalled the demise of the national-standards concept in federal as well as state prosecutions. In *United States* v. *12 200-Ft. Reels*[59] and *United States* v. *Orito*,[60] the Court said that the *Miller* standards were applicable to federal prosecutions. Since the *Miller* standards embodied the local-standards concept, there seemed a fairly clear inference that local community standards were to be applied in federal prosecutions. Since the major justification for the change to local standards was the elusive nature of national standards, it seemed unlikely that standards which were unascertainable or unworkable in state prosecutions would magically become ascertainable and workable when the location of the trial shifted to the federal courthouse. Despite this, however, at least one federal court stuck to the national-standards concept after *Miller*, relying on *Manual Enterprises* and *Jacobellis* and saying that such a significant change in federal law would have to be more explicit before these cases could be ignored.[61]

[55] 370 U.S. 478 (1962).
[56] 370 U.S. at 488.
[57] 378 U.S. 184 (1964).
[58] See cases cited in note 19 *supra*.
[59] 413 U.S. 123, 130 (1973).
[60] 413 U.S. 139, 145 (1973).
[61] *United States* v. *One Reel of Film*, 481 F.2d 206, 210 (1st Cir. 1973) (Coffin, J., concurring); *United States* v. *Palladino*, 490 F.2d 499, 502–503 (1st Cir. 1974).

The issue was resolved a year later in *Hamling* v. *United States.*[62] Justice Rehnquist, writing for the same members of the Court who made up the majority in *Miller,* said that the concept of local community standards was equally applicable to federal prosecutions. When *Orito* and *12 200-Ft. Reels* said that the *Miller* standards were applicable to federal prosecutions, this included the *Miller* definition of contemporary community standards.[63] The argument seems less persuasive for customs violations under 19 U.S.C. § 1305, where the port of entry may have little, if any, relationship to the relevant community, but this argument is also foreclosed by *Hamling.* It is possible, however, that the standards of a community other than that of the forum would be applied, or would at least be relevant.

6.7 Proof of Community Standards—Expert Testimony, Surveys, Statutes, Comparable Materials, and So Forth

Although issues relating to evidence generally are covered in several other chapters of this book,[64] the community-standards problem involves a number of unique issues relating to proof that are best covered in this chapter. Perhaps the most important of these is the need for the parties to any obscenity litigation, civil or criminal, to know, prior to trial, which community standards will be considered relevant at trial. If a party presents evidence of statewide standards and the judge rules that the standards to be applied are those of a county, then some or all of the proposed evidence may be excluded as irrelevant,[65] or the instructions to the jury may effectively tell it to ignore that evidence. At that point, it is too late to locate evidence that will conform with the definition of community. Although this is of course a risk in any trial, it is a risk that should be lessened where, as here, the issue is of critical importance. Furthermore, in the vast majority of cases, the selection of the relevant community will be exclusively a matter of law which can conveniently be resolved prior to trial. Therefore, the trial judge should, on motion of any party, advise the parties as to the definition of "community" which will be

---

[62] 418 U.S. 87 (1974).

[63] *Id.* at 104–105.

[64] *See generally* Chapters 7.5, 9.2.1, 9.3.1, 15, and 16.

[65] A party challenging the judge's ruling should probably present evidence relevant to the standards being used and make offers of proof as to other standards.

used at trial.[66] If a party objects to that ruling, at the time, his appellate rights are preserved, and he still has time to prepare relevant evidence for trial. Prudence, however, would indicate that an appropriate offer of proof should still be made at the time of trial as to the evidence for trial. Prudence, however, would indicate that an appro-such a pretrial ruling, in the federal courts, would seem to exist under Rule 17.1 of the Federal Rules of Criminal Procedure, relating to pretrial conferences, or under Rules 12 and 47, dealing with motions. In the state courts, analogous rules, or the general powers of the judge relating to pretrial rulings, should supply the necessary authority.

In any obscenity case, the prosecutor will be faced with the problem of whether to present evidence of contemporary community standards. In *Paris Adult Theatre I* v. *Slaton,*[67] the Supreme Court held that expert testimony is not necessary in obscenity cases, although this rule might not include a situation where the jury would have to decide the issues according to the standards of a community other than its own.[68] A prosecutor who decides not to use evidence of community standards is relying on the theory, which should be explained in argument, that the jurors are members of the community and know that community's standards. Any testimony on the issue, it can be argued, is an attempt to confuse the jury and an attempt to persuade the jury against its accumulated experience and knowledge. If a prosecutor chooses not to rely on this theory, he should present evidence of community standards, by surveys, expert testimony, or otherwise, so as to rebut the natural inference that there is no evidence that these materials offend the community. A prosecutor who does not do so is likely to have the jury see an impressive array of evidence with nothing to rebut it.

Expert testimony is one way for any party to present evidence of community standards, although not necessarily the best one. The experts should be individuals whose occupation necessarily involves an assessment of community standards, such as police officers, ministers, journalists, and perhaps public officials. Many other possibilities can be imagined. If the occupation involves an assessment of community standards on morality, as does the ministry, the testimony is especially valuable. Since the area of community standards is not a

[66] The judge should also advise the parties if he is going to omit any definition of community in his instructions, as in *Hamling*. If this is the case, then the community is probably the judicial district, for purposes of determining the relevancy of evidence.

[67] 413 U.S. 49, 56 n.6 (1973).

[68] See Chapter 6.5 *supra*.

traditional one for expert testimony, particular attention should be paid to qualifying the expert, and it may often be that the expert's description of his qualifications is as important as his conclusion. It is also important to focus the attention of the expert properly on the exact application of community standards to the relevant issues. Most often, the issue will be whether or not these materials offend the community.[69] But this is really a problem capable of two interpretations. One interpretation asks whether the materials themselves would actually offend the average member of the community, or the majority of the community, or the community as a whole. And it is this interpretation that will generally be urged by the prosecution. In most obscenity cases, the materials would in fact offend most people. But there is another possible interpretation, that asks not whether the materials offend the community or the average person, but whether the community or the average person is offended by the materials being available to those who wish to see them. In other words, are the community standards tolerant, even though most members of the community might themselves be offended by the materials. If so, it can be argued that the materials are not offensive to the community because they are restricted only to those who choose to see them. The latter interpretation should be urged by the defense, since it may be easier to show that the community tolerates the materials even though the majority of the community might be personally offended. The latter interpretation requires a broader interpretation of the Supreme Court's tests than does the former, but it does not seem to have been specifically excluded by any case.[70]

One of the most often attempted, and most rarely successful, methods of presenting evidence of contemporary community standards is the use of materials comparable to those on trial. The goal of such a presentation is to show that the material on trial is not obscene because similar material does not offend contemporary community standards. The purpose is to show that the community finds the comparable materials acceptable. "Comparables" may be books, magazines, newspapers, or motion pictures. The cases have uniformly held that in order for such evidence to be admissible it first must be shown to be similar to the material which is the subject of the proceedings.[71]

---

[69] See text accompanying notes 32–34 *supra*.

[70] In *Hamling*, Justice Rehnquist indicates that such a theory, along with an unqualified expert, might render the evidence inadmissible. 418 U.S. at 108 n.10. It is hard to say which defect was determinative to his views.

[71] *United States* v. *Manarite*, 448 F.2d 583, 593 (2d Cir. 1971), *cert. denied*, 404 U.S. 947; *United States* v. *Jacobs*, 433 F.2d 932, 933 (9th Cir. 1970); *Womack* v.

While the exact format need not necessarily be similar (a magazine could have content similar to that of a motion picture), the explicitness and subject matter must be such as to resemble the subject material. This, of course, is a determination that will be made by the trial judge prior to the admission of the materials. In addition, the materials offered as comparables must be reasonably *accepted* by the community.[72] This requirement of acceptance cannot be met by a mere showing of availability or nonprosecution by local authorities,[73] although such factors may be relevant. Nor would "approval" of such materials in judicial proceedings be sufficient.[74] Rather, true acceptance must be shown, perhaps by the lack of any community objection, by numbers of people who have purchased or seen the materials, by knowledgeable acquiescence by local authorities, by surveys, or other such means. If true acceptance can be shown, as opposed to mere availability, then the materials should be admitted as evidence of the standards of the community. The argument can then be made that if the subject materials are no "worse" than the comparable materials, the subject materials are also acceptable and thus do not offend contemporary community standards.

In a federal prosecution under local standards, pursuant to *Hamling*,[75] state statutes may be relevant evidence of community standards. If the state law of the relevant community does not make "obscenity" a crime, or perhaps only includes minors, then the law, theoretically embodying the wishes of the community, should be probative as to the standards of the community.[76] If the community does not make the activity a crime, it can be said that it does not offend the community. Under the proper circumstances, legislative history may also be admissible on the relationship between the statute and the standards or wishes of the state. Municipal ordinances may also be relevant, as would evidence of a consistent and explicit policy of nonenforcement, even though the statutes nominally exist.

United States, 294 F.2d 204, 206 (D.C. Cir. 1961). Attempts to introduce such evidence are by no means new. *See, e.g., State* v. *Ulsemer*, 24 Wash. 657, 64 P.800 (1901).

[72] *See* cases cited in note 71 *supra*, as well as *Hamling* v. *United States*, 418 U.S. 87 (1974), and *United States* v. *One Reel of 35mm Color Motion Picture Film Entitled "Sinderella"*, 491 F.2d 956, 958–959 (2d Cir. 1974).

[73] *Id.*

[74] 491 F.2d at 958 n.4; *Huffman* v. *United States*, _____ F.2d _____ (D.C. Cir. No. 23, 781).

[75] See Chapter 6.6 *supra*.

[76] If the state has no obscenity laws, this fact should also be admissible.

A survey of community views, either as to the subject material itself, or as to material of that type generally, should be admissible on the issue of community standards, and in fact the Supreme Court on two occasions has indicated that such evidence would be proper.[77] The survey can be informal, perhaps taken by a witness who will otherwise be testifying, but such a nonscientific survey could, and perhaps should, be excluded as having so little probative value as to be legally irrelevant. A survey taken by professionals in a scientific manner is preferable. It is important, of course, that the questions in the survey be framed so as to be consistent with the legal theory which the survey is designed to support. Thus, the survey may ask the respondents whether *they* are offended by the material, or whether they are offended by its availability in the community to those who want it.[78] A prosecutor who uses a scientific survey, however, should bear in mind that the results of such a survey might be considered to be a scientific test under Rule 16(a)(2) of the Federal Rules of Criminal Procedure, or an equivalent state rule, and thus be available to the defendant. If the results of the survey are unfavorable, the effect could be very damaging to the prosecution case. Similarly, a survey taken on behalf of the defendant could be discovered by the prosecution pursuant to Federal Rule 16(c), which authorizes *mutual* discovery of scientific tests. In addition, if a survey indicated that the subject material did not offend community standards, this might be exculpatory evidence which the prosecution would have to disclose under *Brady* v. *Maryland*.[79]

Other forms of evidence of community standards may of course be thought of by imaginative counsel, and should be admitted or not depending on much the same factors that have been discussed in this chapter.

---

[77] *Miller* v. *California*, 413 U.S. 15, 31 n.12 (1973). In *Hamling*, the Court discussed survey evidence without indicating it is necessarily invalid. 418 U.S. at 108 n.10. *See generally* Lamont, *Public Opinion Polls and Survey Evidence in Obscenity Cases*, 15 CRIM. L. Q. 135 (1973).

[78] See text accompanying notes 69–70 *supra*.

[79] 373 U.S. 83 (1963).

7

The Value of the Work

7.1 The "Utterly Without Redeeming Social Value" Test

As has been discussed in Chapter 1, the first half of the 20th century saw considerable enforcement of obscenity regulation directed against works of acknowledged, or at least arguable, literary merit. Since then, any test for or approach to obscenity has tried to insure that this phenomenon would not recur. Of course, if standards and attitudes did not change, this would not be a great problem. Determining which are the serious or important or valuable works of today, while not easy in any context, would be a simpler task if we could be sure that citizens of the future would not look back and criticize the suppression of great literature in 1975 in the same way that we in 1975 look back at 1925. But standards and values do change, and one of the great difficulties with obscenity law lies in trying to locate and protect from regulation not only those works which are fully accepted by society today, but also those which might be fully accepted in 10 years. If the obscenity laws prevent the development of those styles or forms or portrayals which might be lauded as art or literature in 10 years, then the function of obscenity law will be indefinitely to freeze values in politics, art, literature, and science at present levels, and the worst fears of the critics of all obscenity law will be realized. Thus, to make a determination of the value of a work requires the ability both to understand the present and to see the future, no easy task for those responsible for the decision.

The merit, or value, of the material was not originally thought of as an independent element in the test for obscenity. The Model Penal Code of the American Law Institute, which provides a substantial basis for the test of obscenity in *Roth,*[1] defined obscenity in terms of appeal to prurient interest and a surpassing of "customary limits of candor" in description or depiction of sexual matters.[2] While not a part of the test, evidence as to the "artistic, literary, scientific, educational or other merits of the material"[3] was specifically made admissible. The implication, therefore, is that works possessing this kind of merit could not, by definition, be found to appeal predominantly to the prurient interest or to surpass customary limits of candor. Similarly, the *Roth* test for obscenity speaks solely in terms of prurient interest.[4] The *Roth* Court recognized the problem, however, and specifically said that "the portrayal of sex, *e.g.*, in art, literature and scientific works, is not itself sufficient reason to deny material the constitutional protection of freedom of speech and press."[5] Thus, like the drafters of the Model Penal Code, the *Roth* majority assumed that appeal to the prurient interest excluded and was excluded by serious literature of any kind. Obscenity, Mr. Justice Brennan noted, was "utterly without redeeming social importance,"[6] but this was not part of the test for obscenity, only a justification for the exclusion of obscenity from First Amendment protection. Seven years later, in *Jacobellis* v. *Ohio,*[7] this definition started to become a test for obscenity. Since obscenity is "utterly without redeeming social importance," wrote Mr. Justice Brennan, then it follows that "material dealing with sex in a manner that advocates ideas . . . or that has any literary or scientific or artistic value or any other form of social importance, may not be branded as obscenity and denied the constitutional protection. Nor may the constitutional status of the material be made to turn on a 'weighing' of its social importance against its prurient appeal, for a work cannot be proscribed unless it is 'utterly' without social importance."[8] The logic of this transformation seems clear. If, as was said by the majority in *Roth,* obscenity is utterly without redeeming social importance, then something that is *not*

---

[1] *Roth* v. *United States*, 354 U.S. 476, 487 n.20 (1957). For a discussion of the differences between the Model Penal Code test and the *Roth* test, see the opinion of Mr. Justice Harlan in *Roth*, 354 U.S. at 499–500, and Schwartz, *Morals Offenses and the Model Penal Code*, 63 Colum. L. Rev. 669, 677–681 (1963).

[2] A.L.I., Model Penal Code § 251.4(1) (1962), 10 Uniform Laws Annotated 591–592 (1974). The tentative draft of this provision that was available to the Supreme Court in 1957 was substantially similar but not identical.

[3] *Id.* at § 251.4 (4)(c).

[4] 354 U.S. at 489.

[5] *Id.* at 487.

[6] *Id.* at 484.

[7] 378 U.S. 184 (1964).

[8] *Id.* at 191.

utterly without redeeming social importance cannot be obscenity. While this transformation from characteristic or justification to standard has been severely criticized,[9] the criticism of the logic seems misplaced. If the reason for suppressing obscenity is that it is utterly without redeeming social importance, then the test should make sure that only those things which are so lacking are suppressed, because if material with some "social importance" is or can be suppressed, then the justification, in *Roth* terms, is lost. The real problem is that the "utterly without redeeming social value" formulation was probably ill-advised in the first place, and the phrase may not have gained the concurrence of the *Roth* majority if they had been aware of its potential use. But the phrase having been used, and in one of the rare majority opinions in obscenity law, its subsequent use is not illogical.

In any event, the standard was clarified two years later, when, in *Memoirs* v. *Massachusetts,*[10] Mr. Justice Brennan delivered a plurality opinion in which Chief Justice Warren and Mr. Justice Fortas joined. This opinion restated the test for obscenity for the first time since *Roth*.

> As elaborated in subsequent cases, three elements must coalesce: it must be established that (a) the dominant theme of the material taken as a whole appeals to a prurient interest in sex; (b) the material is patently offensive because it affronts contemporary community standards relating to the description or representation of sexual matters; and (c) *the material is utterly without redeeming social value.*[11]

And, by way of elaboration on the third part of the test, the following was added:

> The Supreme Judicial Court [of Massachusetts] erred in holding that a book need not be "unqualifiedly worthless before it can be deemed obscene." A book cannot be proscribed unless it is found to be *utterly* without redeeming social value.[12]

While it is true that this formulation was adopted by only three members of the Court, it must be remembered that at the time both Mr. Justice Douglas and Mr. Justice Black were sitting, neither of whom would affirm *any* obscenity conviction. Therefore, unless the "utterly without redeeming social value" test was utilized and met, any obscenity conviction was sure to have five votes against it in the

---

[9] *Miller* v. *California*, 413 U.S. 15, 21–22 (1973); *Memoirs* v. *Massachusetts*, 383 U.S. 413, 460–462 (1966) (White, J., dissenting).

[10] 383 U.S. 413 (1966).

[11] *Id.* at 418 (emphasis added).

[12] *Id.* at 419 (emphasis original).

Supreme Court, and would be overturned. As a result, the three-part test of *Memoirs,* while only a plurality opinion, became the acknowledged standard and remained so until 1973.

In *Miller* v. *California,*[13] Chief Justice Burger noted that the *"utterly* without redeeming social value" standard created a "burden virtually impossible to discharge under our criminal standards of proof." [14] A review of the case law from 1966 to 1973 indicates that this assessment was substantially correct. Since the *Memoirs* standard has been discarded and is no longer the applicable test, there seems little point in providing an exhaustive analysis or long list of cases under it. The formulation of the *Memoirs* standard in this respect is so different from that now set forth in *Miller* that, in general, the pre-1973 cases are of extremely limited utility. Many of those cases, of course, dealt with material of such "hard-core" character that there could be little question as to the lack of value regardless of which standard was in effect.[15] But in a number of other cases, considerable weight was given to expert testimony of questionable value or to hypotheses about value with little evidentiary support.[16] While in many of these latter cases the judgment may very well have been against a finding of obscenity even under the *Miller* standards, the characteristic of the pre-*Miller* cases is a less than searching or rigorous evaluation of claimed social value and a tendency to take any plausible contention of social importance at face value.

7.2   *The* Memoirs *Test Rejected—"Serious Literary, Artistic, Political, or Scientific Value"*

Miller v. *California* [17] made two major changes in the substantive law of obscenity. One was the rejection of the concept of national community standards, discussed at length in the previous chapter. The other was the rejection of that element of the *Memoirs* test requiring that material could be found to be obscene only if it was "utterly

---

[13] 413 U.S. 15 (1973).

[14] *Id.* at 22.

[15] *See, e.g., United States* v. *Manarite,* 448 F.2d 583 (2d Cir. 1971), *cert. denied,* 404 U.S. 947; *United States* v. *Gundlach,* 345 F.Supp. 709, 717 (M.D. Pa. 1972) ("In short, merely giving an intellectual gloss to literary trash cannot automatically render the courts powerless to act"); *Price* v. *Commonwealth,* 213 Va. 113, 189 S.E.2d 324 (1972).

[16] *See, e.g., United States* v. *Stewart,* 336 F. Supp. 299 (E.D. Pa. 1971); *United States* v. *Ten Erotic Paintings,* 432 F.2d 420 (4th Cir. 1970); *Commonwealth* v. *Dell Publications, Inc.,* 427 Pa. 189, 233 A.2d 840 (1967).

[17] 413 U.S. 15 (1973).

without redeeming social value." [18] Observing that this element of the test for obscenity was never part of a majority opinion of the Supreme Court, that it was based on a misreading of *Roth,* and that it created "a burden virtually impossible to discharge under our criminal standards of proof," the *Miller* majority substituted the requirement that material could be obscene only if "the work, taken as a whole, lacks serious literary, artistic, political, or scientific value." [19] This, of course, is not the only element of the test. It is one of three parts, the others being the prurient-interest and patent-offensiveness requirements, *all* of which must be satisfied in order that a work may be properly denominated as obscene. Therefore, regardless of anything else, if a work has serious literary, artistic, political, or scientific value, it cannot be obscene.

Three elements of this change are significant. First, and probably most important, is the rejection of such language as "utterly" or "unqualifiedly" worthless, or "modicum of social value" found in *Memoirs.*[20] The significance lies in the quantum of value required to redeem an otherwise obscene work. Under the *Memoirs* standard, some very slight degree of seemingly serious matter or intent would be sufficient. Under *Miller,* the value must be more predominant, more serious, and more pervasive throughout the entire work. It is, of course, difficult to describe in words an increase in amount or degree, but it is clear that some attempts at value which would have been sufficient under *Memoirs* will be rejected under *Miller.* The insertion of the requirement that the value be "serious" does not, of course, mean that humorous or irreverent vehicles for value are to be rejected. What the addition of the "serious" element does is to allow the jury and the court to look beneath the argued or claimed value of the material to the relationship between the nonpornographic and the pornographic, and to the *intent* upon which the insertion of literary, artistic, political, or scientific material is based. If that intent is to convey a literary, artistic, political, or scientific idea or message, or to impart information, or advocate a position, then the purpose or intent is "serious" as the word appears to be used in *Miller.* If, on the other hand, it appears or is found that the purpose is to "dress up" or try to "redeem" otherwise obscene matter, sold or distributed for its obscenity rather than for its ideas or message, then the value is not "serious." Thus, the requirement that the value be serious requires an evaluation of the

[18] *Memoirs* v. *Massachusetts,* 388 U.S. 413, 418 (1966).
[19] 413 U.S. at 22–25.
[20] 383 U.S. at 418–420.

intent of the publication as a whole. Furthermore, it allows an assessment of the claimed value. Not every purported "value" must be accepted either by the jury, as a matter of fact, or by the court, as a matter of law.[21]

The second notable change embodied in the *Miller* test for value is the rejection of "the ambiguous concept of 'social importance.' "[22] There seem to be several reasons for this rejection on the part of the *Miller* court. First of all, "social importance" can mean anything or everything, especially to a jury, and the indefiniteness of the term makes the presence or lack of social importance difficult or impossible to prove, with the inevitable result of extremely inconsistent verdicts. Secondly, it has been argued that obscene or pornographic material has a beneficial effect on some individuals, or that it is beneficial to society at large in that it encourages openness about sexual matters and an advantageous breakdown of archaic taboos and strictures about sex.[23] This very effect may be deemed to constitute social importance, at least by some, and the effect, if not the intent, of the *Miller* Court seems to be to prevent the anomaly of pornography's being nonobscene by virtue of its very obscenity.[24]

[21] *See People* v. *Heller*, 33 N.Y.2d 322, 307 N.E.2d 805, 352 N.Y.S.2d 601, 607 (1973), *cert. denied sub nom. Buckley* v. *New York*, 418 U.S. 944 (1974) ("effectuation of a pretense as a serious work" insufficient).

[22] 413 U.S. at 25 n.7. In *Memoirs* v. *Massachusetts*, Mr. Justice White, in dissent, felt that " 'social importance' is not an independent test of obscenity, but is relevant only to determining the predominant prurient interest of the material, a determination which the court or the jury will make based on the material itself and all the evidence in the case, expert or otherwise." 383 U.S. at 462 (White, J., dissenting).

[23] See generally Chapters 3.1 and 3.2 *supra,* and the authorities cited therein.

[24] In *United States* v. *One Reel of Film*, 481 F.2d 206 (1st Cir. 1973), it was claimed that the motion picture *Deep Throat* had value as defined in *Miller* because it encourages sexual liberation and may be instructive as to sex techniques. But the First Circuit held that "the argument proves too much. . . . We can only read the recent cases as an express rejection of any argument that pornography itself, because of its liberating impact, has for that reason alone, serious literary, artistic, political, or scientific value." 481 F.2d at 210. *See also People* v. *Birch*, 25 App. Div. 2d 854, 269 N.Y.S.2d 752 (1966), *appeal dismissed,* 220 N.E.2d 804, 18 N.Y.2d 724, 274 N.Y.S.2d 159 ("escape" literature not per se of redeeming social importance).

While it may be debated whether the change from national to local community standards results in a greater or lesser burden on defendants, it seems clear that the *Miller* standard as to value is considerably harder to satisfy than is the older *Memoirs* standard, or, conversely, that it is easier to show a lack of *Miller* value than it is to show a lack of *Memoirs* value. In *United States* v. *Harding*, 507 F.2d 294 (9th Cir. 1974), *cert. denied,* 95 S. Ct. 1437 (1975), the defendant had stipulated to the lack of redeeming social value before *Miller* was decided, and the court held that this necessarily implied a stipulation as to a lack of value as defined in *Miller*. 507 F.2d at 298.

Finally, *Miller* specifically enumerated the kinds of value which would save an otherwise prurient and patently offensive work. It is not *any* serious value that is relevant, but only serious literary, artistic, political, or scientific value. These are not listed as examples, but as a seemingly exclusive list of the kinds of value that are relevant. Yet the list does not include some arguable types of value that might have been added. For example, entertainment value might be argued, but this also seems to prove too much, since if obscenity had no entertainment value, then it would have no market. Similarly, humor has not been added, presumably on the assumption that good humor, parody, or satire would be found to have some serious literary value, and bad humor may be obscene. There is also no mention of educational value, and it appears that this is not included because it is potentially too broad. Any pornography may be educational as to sexual techniques, or just as to what pornography is,[25] and thus the term seems to include too much. Legitimate sex or marriage manuals can easily be found to have scientific value, and discussions of pornography can be deemed to have literary, political, or scientific value. The four categories enumerated in *Miller* should be read very broadly, but if the claimed value still does not fit within any of the broadly construed values, then it is insufficient to defeat a finding of obscenity.

There has been extremely little case law on what in fact constitutes serious literary, artistic, political, or scientific value, since most of the obscenity cases in the two years since *Miller* have dealt predominantly with broader issues created by the promulgation of the *Miller* standards, rather than with the application of those standards to particular works. But some principles which were enunciated in earlier cases still retain some validity after *Miller,* and some general observations regarding the application of the *Miller* standards seem appropriate, even in the context of a large body of case law. Therefore, the remainder of this section will be devoted to a discussion and analysis of the kinds of legal issues that are likely to arise in attempting to determine just what makes up serious literary, artistic, political, or scientific value.

Literary value is perhaps the oldest and most often litigated of the factors which weigh against a finding of obscenity. In most of the cases in Chapter 1 dealing with works of now-acknowledged literary merit, testimony as to the actual literary value of the work was a predominant part of the litigation. It was not until *Memoirs* v. *Massa-*

---

[25] *See United States* v. *One Reel of Film,* 481 F.2d 206, 210 (1st Cir. 1973).

chusetts,[26] however, that literary value was considered as a separate element of the test for obscenity. Prior to *Memoirs,* literary value was merely a factor to be considered in the determination of obscenity, and it was to be balanced against the objectionable elements of the material at issue.[27] Material could have some serious literary value and still be obscene. Now, however, this is not possible, at least if the Supreme Court's opinions are properly applied. If a work is found to have serious literary value, this absolutely precludes a finding of obscenity. Although *Miller* changed the formulation of the literary-value element, it did not weaken its significance as an independent element of the test for obscenity. It is clear that a determination as to literary value involves a subjective judgment necessarily requiring the weighing of many factors. Certainly, the mere existence of a "plot" or story line does not create literary value, nor does an isolated idea, as for example, the advocacy of incest and sexual intercourse coupled with graphic depictions of everything which is advocated.[28] While it is true that obscenity is defined in *Roth,* in part, as being an utterance that does not advocate ideas,[29] and the mere advocacy of sexually "immoral" ideas may not be proscribed,[30] the idea must be at least serious and not a mere pretext for the distribution of pictures or explicit text "illustrating" that idea. This is, of course, a difficult line to draw, but the absence of any line would make it too easy for "a quotation from Voltaire in the flyleaf of a book [to] constitutionally redeem an otherwise obscene publication."[31]

Similarly, the mere existence of critical acclaim, or the fact of large numbers of readers or viewers, or the reputation of the author, do not per se indicate literary value,[32] even though these and other

[26] 383 U.S. 413 (1966).

[27] *See, e.g., McCauley* v. *Tropic of Cancer,* 20 Wis.2d 134, 121 N.W.2d 545 (1963); *Commonwealth* v. *Isenstadt,* 318 Mass. 543, 62 N.E.2d 840 (1945); *Commonwealth* v. *New,* 142 Pa. Super. 358, 16 A.2d 437 (1940); *People* v. *Vanguard Press,* 192 Misc. 127, 84 N.Y.S. 2d 427 (Magis. Ct. 1947).

There also prevailed, prior to *Roth,* the view that literary merit was completely irrelevant, and no amount of literary merit could save an otherwise obscene work. *See, e.g., People* v. *Wepplo,* 78 Cal. App. 2d Supp. 959, 178 P.2d 853 (1947); *Commonwealth* v. *Buckley,* 200 Mass. 346, 86 N.E. 910 (1909).

[28] *United States* v. *Four (4) Books,* 289 F. Supp. 972 (C.D. Cal. 1968).

[29] *Roth* v. *United States,* 354 U.S. 476, 484 (1957).

[30] *Kingsley Pictures Corp.* v. *Regents,* 360 U.S. 684 (1959).

[31] *Kois* v. *Wisconsin,* 408 U.S. 229, 231 (1972).

[32] *State* v. *Smith,* 422 S.W.2d 50, 60–62 (Mo. 1967), *cert. denied,* 393 U.S. 895 (1968); *Larkin* v. *G. P. Putnam's Sons,* 40 Misc. 2d 25, 243 N.Y.S.2d 145, 148–149 (Sup. Ct. 1963) (the citation of these cases as authority for specific legal propositions does not, of course, indicate that the results would be the same under current law in those cases, even though the principles appear to remain valid).

factors may have some evidentiary weight. Although there is some contrary authority,[33] a finding of serious literary value should be made, or is at least open, where that serious literary value is only perceivable by a sophisticated (or perhaps unsophisticated) segment of the population. Unlike the prurient-interest or patent-offensiveness tests, the literary-value test embodies implicitly the concept that the purpose of the obscenity laws is not to "level" the available reading matter to the majority or lowest common denominator of the population.[34] While the courts have not expressly dealt with this issue in this way, it is apparent from the results reached. It is obvious that neither *Ulysses* nor *Lady Chatterley's Lover* would have literary appeal to the majority of the population. It is doubtful that a majority of the population could be considered "literary," or would care to be so designated. Yet this has not prevented the courts from finding literary merit in these and other works which clearly have an intellectual appeal to only a minority of the population. Obviously there is someone, and perhaps even some "expert," who will see literary merit in anything, and this principle cannot be extended too far. But if material has serious literary value for a significant portion of the population, then the fact that this portion is neither average nor in the majority is irrelevant.

There is a difference, however, between literature and good writing. Although most commercial pornography of the type allowed to be prohibited after *Miller* is poorly written, the fact that some may be well-written does not prevent a determination of obscenity.[35] Of course, writing in and of itself may be literature or have serious literary value, but the mere fact that obscenity is written in long words or grammatically correct language will be of little avail.

Ultimately the question of literary value will be decided in most cases by an evaluation of expert testimony. What would or would not have literary value in the opinion of experts is impossible to generalize in any way. But the crucial determination must be the even more subjective evaluation of intent. If a work is a serious literary endeavor, with the purpose of stimulating the mind, and if it has this

[33] *G. P. Putnam's Sons* v. *Calissi,* 86 N.J. Super. 82, 205 A.2d 913 (1964); *People* v. *Fritch,* 13 N.Y.2d 119, 192 N.E.2d 713, 243 N.Y.S.2d 1 (1963); *People* v. *Kirkpatrick,* 64 Misc. 2d 1055, 316 N.Y.S.2d 37, 62–63 (Crim. Ct. 1970), *aff'd,* 69 Misc. 2d 212, 329 N.Y.S.2d 769, *aff'd,* 32 N.Y.2d 17, 295 N.E.2d 753, 343 N.Y.S.2d 70 (1973), *appeal dismissed,* 414 U.S. 948 (1973).

[34] *See United States* v. *Kennerley,* 209 F. 119 (S.D.N.Y. 1913) (L. Hand., J.).

[35] *G. P. Putnam's Sons* v. *Calissi,* 86 N.J. Super. 82, 205 A.2d 913 (1964); *People* v. *Bookcase, Inc.,* 40 Misc. 2d 796, 244 N.Y.S.2d 297, 299–300 (Crim. Ct. 1963).

effect on a significant number of people,[36] then literary value exists and there can be no finding of obscenity.

While it is true that most people read (or see) literature for the purpose of entertainment, this does not indicate that anything that entertains is literature or has literary value. While literature need not necessarily be serious, or dry, entertainment value or humor cannot be equated with literary value.

> Presumably, the Romans of the First Century derived entertainment from witnessing Christians being devoured by lions. Given the right audience, the spectacle of a man committing an act of sodomy on another man would provide entertainment value. However, neither this spectacle nor the activities described in the instant case are invested with constitutionally protected values merely because they entertain viewers.[37]

The same kind of evaluation of seriousness of purpose and value that goes into the determination of literary merit is also applicable to assessments of artistic value. Given the divergence of views about artistic or musical [38] works, it is doubtful to expect judges or juries to be any more unanimous. Again, expert testimony will play a large role in most cases. It has been said that art can be distinguished from pornography because art embodies a thought, a perception, or a speculation.[39] Again, there must be the presence of an "idea" as a predominant part of the work, not necessarily in terms of underlying purpose. An idea may be the most difficult to define of all concepts, and artistic value one of the most difficult determinations to make. Art is, in part, designed to appeal to the senses, and thus "erotic art"

---

[36] If the intent was there, but no one found the intent successful, the work could not be said to have literary *value,* a word that must be contrasted with "appeal" and "intent." *But see United States Corporation* v. *Gladwell,* 373 F. Supp. 247, 249 (N.D. Ohio 1974).

[37] *People ex rel. Hicks* v. *"Sarong Gals,"* 27 Cal. App. 3d 46, 103 Cal. Rptr. 414, 417 (1972). *See also People* v. *Mature Enterprises, Inc.,* 73 Misc. 2d 749, 343 N.Y.S.2d 911, 913 (Crim. Ct. 1973), *supplemented,* 73 Misc. 2d 773, 343 N.Y.S.2d 934; *United States* v. *New Orleans Book Mart, Inc.,* 328 F. Supp. 136, 142–143 (E.D. La. 1971).

[38] It is irrelevant, for this discussion, whether music be deemed closer to literature or art. It is clear that serious and predominant musical value would "save" a work from being obscene. If *La Traviata* were performed in the nude, it is hard to see how it could be deemed obscene, even if a jury determined that it appealed to the prurient interest and was patently offensive. On the other hand, a "hard-core" motion picture of intercourse between humans and animals will not be "redeemed" if the activities are being performed to the strains of Beethoven's Fifth Symphony.

[39] *City of Youngstown* v. *DeLoreto,* 19 Ohio App. 2d 267, 251 N.E.2d 491, 498 (1969), quoting Dr. Natalie Shainness.

is almost by definition prurient. But whether there is also artistic value is a determination that can only be made by experts in art, and indirectly by juries evaluating those opinions.

Determinations of serious political value are likely to be the least troublesome for the courts, mainly because the courts have had much more extensive and varied experience in dealing with political speech than they have had with most other forms of expression. Assessments of claimed political value are perhaps the most crucial determinations to be made, as well, since if there is any agreement at all on what the First Amendment is designed to protect, it is that governmental power cannot be used to suppress criticisms of that government. Thus the Supreme Court has recognized, and found to be protected, criticisms of the government, or the country, or some aspect of governmental action, which are expressed in forms that most people would find vulgar and offensive.[40] Political commentary regarding the draft, the Vietnam War, race relations, and the like should not pose especially difficult problems. But advocacy of abolition of the obscenity laws would be a political view, as would advocacy of different standards of sexual conduct than those now in force.[41] If these ideas were the major theme of a work, then it would be protected, even if parts of it contained depictions or descriptions of sexual conduct.

Scientific value must be read to include more than the physical sciences. Serious discussions, whether in motion picture or book form, of sex, sexuality, sex education, or pornography can clearly have value

[40] *Kois* v. *Wisconsin,* 408 U.S. 229 (1972); *Cohen* v. *California,* 403 U.S. 15 (1971). *See also Rosenfeld* v. *New Jersey,* 408 U.S. 901 (1972); *Lewis* v. *New Orleans,* 408 U.S. 913 (1972); *Brown* v. *Oklahoma,* 415 U.S. 130 (1974); *Eaton* v. *City of Tulsa,* 415 U.S. 697 (1974); *Papish* v. *Board of Curators of University of Missouri,* 410 U.S. 667 (1973). *See* Rutzick, *Offensive Language and the Evolution of First Amendment Protection,* 9 HARV. CIV. RIGHTS L. REV. 1 (1974); Note, *"Offensive Speech" and the First Amendment,* 53 BOSTON UNIV. L. REV. 834 (1973); Note, *Violence and Obscenity—Chaplinsky Revisited,* 42 FORD. L. REV. 141 (1973); Note, *Cohen* v. *California: A New Approach to an Old Problem,* 9 CAL. WEST. L. REV. 171 (1972); Note, *Purging Unseemly Expletives From the Public Scene: A Constitutional Dilemma,* 47 IND. L. J. 142 (1971); Comments, 50 N.C. L. REV. 382 (1972); 21 DE PAUL L. REV. 546 (1971); 5 SETON HALL L. REV. 108 (1973); 22 DE PAUL L. REV. 725 (1973).

[41] *Kingsley International Pictures Corp.* v. *Regents,* 360 U.S. 684 (1959). "What New York has done, therefore, is to prevent the exhibition of a motion picture because that picture advocates an idea—that adultery under certain circumstances may be proper behavior. Yet the First Amendment's basic guarantee is of freedom to advocate ideas. The State, quite simply, has thus struck at the very heart of constitutionally protected liberty." 360 U.S. at 688.

While the advocacy of adultery may not be a "political" idea in the narrowest sense of that word, this and related expressions of opinion seem clearly to come within what the *Miller* Court meant by "serious political value."

as ideas, and all would probably come within the scope of scientific value.[42] Of course, if the claimed scientific value is for physicians, sociologists, psychiatrists, or psychologists, and there is no effort to limit distribution to those groups, a court may very well give little credence to the claim of scientific value.[43] But educational value seems included within scientific value, if there is a predominant and serious intent to educate. However, the education must be of a cognitive nature. The overall educational value, if any, of exposure to pornography does not create scientific value.[44]

As a practical matter, virtually all determinations of literary, artistic, political, or scientific value will involve an analysis of the relationship of some allegedly significant matter to the sexually explicit matter or to the theme or intent of the material as a whole. This has been discussed in detail elsewhere in this treatise,[45] and the same considerations that apply in determining whether the work as a whole appeals to the prurient interest will apply in determining whether the work as a whole has serious literary, artistic, political, or scientific value. The value, to be serious, must be in a significant amount.[46] It must also represent a major purpose of the material. "Merely giving an intellectual gloss to literary trash cannot automatically render the courts powerless to act." [47] Thus, what is required is not only a searching inquiry into the actual merit of the material, but an analysis of the relationship of the serious matter to the sexually explicit matter, which will inevitably involve a determination of intent as well as effect.

7.3 Who Makes the Determination?—Law, Fact, or Both?

Prior to the decision of the Supreme Court in *Roth*,[48] obscenity prosecutions were not generally considered to raise significant consti-

---

[42] *Compare United States* v. *35mm. Motion Picture Film Entitled "Language of Love,"* 432 F.2d 705, 712–713 (2d Cir. 1970), *with People* v. *Shiffrin*, 64 Misc. 2d 311, 314 N.Y.S.2d 745 (Crim. Ct. 1970). *See also United States* v. *Stewart*, 336 F. Supp. 229 (E.D. Pa. 1971).

[43] *Ginzburg* v. *United States*, 383 U.S. 463, 471–474 (1966), relying, in part, on *United States* v. *Rebhuhn*, 109 F.2d 512 (1940) (L. Hand, J.).

[44] *United States* v. *One Reel of Film*, 481 F.2d 206, 210 (1st Cir. 1973); *Books, Inc.* v. *United States*, 358 F.2d 935 (1st Cir. 1966), *rev'd*, 388 U.S. 449 (1967).

[45] See Chapter 5.3 *supra*.

[46] *State* v. *Shapiro*, 122 N.J. Super. 409, 300 A.2d 595, 604–606 (1973).

[47] *United States* v. *Gundlach*, 345 F. Supp. 709, 717 (M.D. Pa. 1972). *See also United States* v. *Four (4) Books*, 289 F. Supp. 972 (C.D. Cal. 1968). *Cf. United States* v. *Palladino*, 475 F.2d 65 (1st Cir. 1973), *vacated*, 413 U.S. 416, *after remand*, 490 F.2d 499 (1974).

[48] *Roth* v. *United States*, 354 U.S. 476 (1957).

tutional issues and were treated in much the same way as any other criminal prosecution.[49] It was only logical, therefore, that determination as to whether or not a given work was obscene was exclusively a question for the jury. The obscenity of the material was, of course, an essential element of the offense charged, and the jury would have to find that the work was obscene, just as it would have to find the existence of any other component of any other criminal charge. There being no constitutional issues involved, there was no reason why the jury's decision could not be final, exclusive, and controlling on the question of obscenity.[50]

Roth, however, made it clear that although the issue of the obscenity of the material on trial was an element of the criminal offense charged, it also was a question of constitutional law, since only those works which were obscene could constitutionally be proscribed without running into the limitations of the First Amendment.[51] If material was not obscene, then not only did this mean that an element of the offense was missing, it also meant that as a matter of law the material was constitutionally protected and, regardless of a jury verdict, could not be suppressed. This view, that obscenity determination involves the making of legal judgments of the material as well as factual judgments, has been reaffirmed repeatedly by the Supreme Court since *Roth.*[52] This, of course, is not peculiar to obscenity law, but is basic to any area where factual determinations, or the inferences to be drawn from facts, implicate questions of constitutional rights.[53] Thus,

---

[49] *See generally Chapters* 1.3 and 2.1 *supra.*

[50] *See, e.g., People* v. *Muller,* 32 Hun. 209, *aff'd,* 96 N.Y. 408 (1884); *Hadley* v. *State,* 205 Ark. 1027, 172 S.W.2d 237 (1943); *People* v. *Wepplo,* 78 Cal. App. 2d Supp. 959, 178 P.2d 853 (1947). In *Attorney General* v. *Book Named "Forever Amber,"* 323 Mass. 302, 81 N.E.2d 663 (1948), the Massachusetts Supreme Judicial Court made a de novo review of the findings of the trial judge, not because of the existence of constitutional issues, but because of the general rule, at least in Massachusetts, that where findings are made completely on documentary evidence, the appellate court is not bound by any findings below. 81 N.E.2d at 667.

[51] *See* especially the concurring opinion of Mr. Justice Harlan. Obscenity is "not really an issue of fact but a question of constitutional judgment of the most sensitive and delicate kind." *Roth* v. *United States,* 354 U.S. 476, 498 (1957) (Harlan, J., concurring in part and dissenting in part).

[52] *See Jenkins* v. *Georgia,* 418 U.S. 153, 160 (1974); *Miller* v. *California,* 413 U.S. 15, 29–30 (1973); *Jacobellis* v. *Ohio,* 378 U.S. 184, 188 (1964) ("Since it is only 'obscenity' that is excluded from the constitutional protection, the question whether a particular work is obscene necessarily implicates an issue of constitutional law") (opinion of Brennan, J.); *Manual Enterprises, Inc.* v. *Day,* 370 U.S. 478, 488 (1962) (opinion of Harlan, J.); *Kingsley International Pictures Corp.* v. *Regents,* 360 U.S. 684, 708 (1959) (opinion of Harlan, J.).

[53] *See* Lockhart and McClure, *Censorship of Obscenity: The Developing Constitutional Standards,* 45 MINN. L. REV. 5, 116 (1960) and cases cited by Mr. Justice Brennan in *Jacobellis* v. *Ohio,* 378 U.S. 184, 189 (1964).

it is now settled that the determination of obscenity is a mixed question of law and fact.[54] The issues involved in an obscenity determination have sometimes been called questions of "constitutional fact,"[55] thus requiring an independent judgment to be made by the court as a matter of law.[56]

Against this background of general principles, we must turn to how this theory affects the actual division of functions between judge and jury in an obscenity case. Since there must be an independent legal determination of the issue of obscenity, it is appropriate that the issue may be decided in the context of a motion to dismiss the indictment,[57] or similar motion, on the grounds that the material is not obscene as a matter of law. Since this process of independent legal review by the court must occur at some point, there is no logical reason why it cannot occur prior to trial, thus saving the time and expense of a trial if the material is clearly constitutionally protected as a matter of law.[58] The court could, of course, hold a full pretrial evidentiary hearing on the obscenity issue,[59] but this seems to create undue duplication of evidence. If it is clear that the material is not obscene as a matter of law, then the indictment should be dismissed without the necessity of hearing extensive evidence. If the issue is close enough that the judge, in making his independent legal determination, desires the assistance of evidence other than the material itself, this is available during the trial itself. If, at that point, the judge feels that the material is constitutionally protected, he can direct a verdict before the case is actually given to the jury. This is clearly the

---

[54] *United States* v. *A Motion Picture Entitled "I Am Curious—Yellow,"* 404 F.2d 196, 199 (2d Cir. 1968); *City of Chicago* v. *Geraci,* 46 Ill. 2d 576, 264 N.E.2d 153, 155 (1970); *People* v. *Richmond County News, Inc.,* 9 N.Y.2d 578, 175 N.E.2d 681, 216 N.Y.S.2d 369, 370 (1961).

[55] *Kois* v. *Wisconsin,* 408 U.S. 229, 232 (1972) (dominance of theme question of constitutional fact); *Zeitlin* v. *Arnebergh,* 59 Cal. 2d 901, 383 P.2d 152, 31 Cal. Rptr. 800, 806 (1963), *cert. denied,* 375 U.S. 957.

[56] *Donnenberg* v. *State,* 1 Md. App. 591, 232 A.2d 264, 268–269 (1967). *See also Excellent Publications, Inc.* v. *United States,* 309 F.2d 362 (1st Cir. 1962); *Commonwealth* v. *Moniz,* 338 Mass. 442, 155 N.E.2d 762 (1959); *State* v. *Locks,* 97 Ariz. 148, 397 P.2d 949 (1964); *Landau* v. *Fording,* 245 Cal. App. 2d 820, 54 Cal. Rptr. 177 (1966).

[57] *See* Federal Rules of Criminal Procedure, Rule 12, allowing the determination, before trial, of "any defense or objection which is capable of determination without the trial of the general issue . . . ." FED. R. CRIM. P. 12(b)(1).

[58] *See* A.L.I. Model Penal Code § 251.4 (4), 10 Uniform Laws Annotated 593 (1974), providing that "the Court shall dismiss a prosecution for obscenity if it is satisfied that the material is not obscene." *People* v. *Stabile,* 58 Misc. 2d 905, 296 N.Y.S.2d 815 (Crim. Ct. 1969).

[59] *See United States* v. *New Orleans Book Mart, Inc.,* 328 F. Supp. 136 (E.D. La. 1971).

judge's duty in any event, and if the material is determined by him not to be obscene, he must withdraw the case from the jury's consideration.[60]

Of course the jury must still decide the ultimate question of obscenity as it relates to whether a substantive criminal offense has been committed. Even if the judge determines the material to be unprotected, the jury may still find it not obscene, using the same tests on the factual issue that the court did on the legal issue. In this context, the jury should not be apprised of the fact that the judge has already made a determination as to obscenity.[61] Even the jury, of course, is not deciding a strictly nonlegal issue. As the Supreme Court pointed out in *Miller*, issues of prurient interest and patent offensiveness are "essentially questions of fact" for jury determination.[62] Thus, if the court feels that these issues are "close" enough to go to the jury, the jury is making the constitutional as well as the factual decision when it decides these issues. Only if the jury could not, as a matter of constitutional law, find the materials to be obscene should the case be withdrawn from their consideration.[63]

If the issue goes to the jury, then the burden of proof, if a criminal case, will be that of proof beyond a reasonable doubt as to every element of the offense, including that of obscenity. But as to the determination of obscenity as a matter of law, this should be treated in the same way as the jurisdiction treats any other legal decision in a criminal case. It has been noted in a civil case that the evidence should be viewed by the court in a light favorable to the material's circulation,[64] but this seems implicit in the very formulation of the legal tests to be applied, and need not be a separate factor. The very facts of independent review and the standards to be applied adequately protect the presumption in favor of First Amendment protection.

The division of function between court and jury, or between legal and factual determinations, does not remain constant with the legal issues involved. Determinations of prurient interest and patent offensiveness,[65] and also, therefore, of contemporary community stand-

---

[60] *See State* v. *Hudson County News Co.*, 41 N.J. 247, 196 A.2d 225 (1963).
[61] *Id.*
[62] *Miller* v. *California*, 413 U.S. 15, 30 (1973).
[63] *See Books, Inc.* v. *United States*, 358 F.2d 935, 937 (1966), *rev'd*, 388 U.S. 449 (1967).
[64] *Duggan* v. *Guild Theatre, Inc.*, 436 Pa. 191, 258 A.2d 858, 863 (1969).
[65] *Miller* v. *California*, 413 U.S. 15, 30 (1973).

ards,[66] are such as to indicate that the major determination should be made by the jury, except in the more extreme cases.[67] The Supreme Court has repeatedly said that there is nothing inherently wrong with different juries reaching different verdicts as to the same materials in an obscenity case, any more than in any other criminal case.[68] But determinations of literary, artistic, political, or scientific value seem less majoritarian in purpose, in that they do not embody the community's views as a whole so much as they do those aspects of the First Amendment designed to protect minority or unpopular views, tastes, opinions, ideas, or desires. Thus, in this area, less weight should be given to the jury's verdict and the court should be more willing to make the ultimate determination even in the closer cases. As was said at the beginning of this section, however, the dual responsibility of judge and jury arises because nonobscene materials are immune from prosecution as a matter of constitutional law. It should be obvious, then, that issues in obscenity cases not going to matters of constitutional law are not subject to the same strictures, and the normal deference and finality given to jury findings in criminal cases generally should be given to jury determinations of such matters as whether the materials were actually distributed, or shipped, or exhibited,[69] or whether the shipment was for a scientific purpose,[70] or any other factual issue arising in the course of trial. Similarly, findings with a constitutional basis but which are especially related to the jury's traditional functions, such as determinations of intent, or scienter, should, as a general matter, be primarily for jury determination.[71]

7.4   Reviewability

Most of the discussion in the previous section is equally applicable to the scope of appellate review. Thus, to the extent that the court, at trial, must make an independent constitutional judgment as to the materials at issue, so too must this independent scrutiny be

[66] *See Hamling* v. *United States,* 418 U.S. 87, 104–105 (1974); *City of Chicago* v. *Kimmel,* 31 Ill.2d 202, 201 N.E.2d 386, 388–389 (1964).

[67] *Jenkins* v. *Georgia,* 418 U.S. 153 (1974).

[68] *Roth* v. *United States,* 354 U.S. 476, 492, n.30 (1957); *Miller* v. *California,* 413 U.S. 15, 26 n.9 (1973); *Hamling* v. *United States,* 418 U.S. 87, 101 (1974).

[69] *Cf. Alexander* v. *United States,* 271 F.2d 140, 143 (8th Cir. 1959).

[70] *People* v. *Marler,* 199 Cal. App. 2d Supp. 889, 18 Cal. Rptr. 923 (1962).

[71] *See State* v. *Vollmar,* 389 S.W.2d 20, 29 (Mo. 1965).

made by an appellate court.[72] There is authority to the effect that the purpose of appellate review is not to make a completely de novo review, but rather to determine if there was sufficient evidence at trial to support the finding below.[73] To the extent that these cases hold that there is to be no independent scrutiny by the appellate court, they represent a view that is both a minority view and also inconsistent with the general theory of review where constitutional considerations turn on mixed questions of law and fact. However, to the extent that they represent the view that there is a *range* within which the jury's (or judge's) finding is final, then the principle seems sound. If the appellate court were not in any way influenced by the rulings or verdict below, then there would be no purpose in having trials at all in obscenity cases. What the scope of review involves is a determination of whether, as a matter of constitutional law, the materials are of such character as to be clearly outside the scope of First Amendment protection, or, if the issue is not clear, to contain arguably prurient, patently offensive, and valueless depictions or descriptions such that jury findings of pruriency, offensiveness, and lack of value would not offend the Constitution. In other words, the appellate court must make an independent review, but the question to be asked is not whether the materials are obscene, but whether the materials create a jury issue as to obscenity. Since this involves questions of constitutional law, more evidence is needed to create a jury issue than in other criminal cases, not by virtue of a different standard, but by virtue of the various elements of the *Roth-Miller* test. Thus, the independent review by an appellate court must deal with prurient interest, dominance of the theme, patent offensiveness, lack of value, and whether or not the materials depict or describe hard-core sexual conduct. If, as to each of these issues, a jury issue is created, then the verdict must be allowed to stand. But if, as to *any one* of these issues, the reviewing court finds that the material is not within the *Roth-Miller* definition of obscenity, then a verdict of obscenity must be reversed.

---

[72] In addition to the authorities cited in the previous section, *see Childs* v. *Oregon,* 431 F.2d 272 (9th Cir. 1970), *rev'd,* 401 U.S. 1006 (1971), *vacated,* 443 F.2d 1177 (1971); *State* v. *LeWitt,* 3 Conn. Cir. 605, 222 A.2d 579 (1966); *Blue Island* v. *DeVilbiss,* 41 Ill.2d 135, 242 N.E.2d 761 (1969); *State ex rel. Londerholm* v. *A Quantity of Copies of Books,* 197 Kan. 306, 416 P.2d 703 (1966), *rev'd,* 388 U.S. 452 (1967); *Wagonheim* v. *Maryland State Board of Censors,* 255 Md. 297, 258 A.2d 240 (1969).

[73] *See, e.g., Nissinoff* v. *Harper,* 212 So.2d 666 (Fla. App. 1968); *Cain* v. *Commonwealth,* 437 S.W.2d 769 (Ariz. 1969); *Court* v. *State,* 51 Wis. 2d 683, 188 N.W.2d 475 (1971).

The clearest exposition of all of the above came in *Jenkins* v. *Georgia*,[74] where the Supreme Court reversed the conviction of a theater manager for the exhibition of the motion picture *Carnal Knowledge*. The opinion of the Court was written by Mr. Justice Rehnquist, who made it clear that as to each element of the *Miller* standards for obscenity, it was the duty of the reviewing court to conduct an independent review to see if those standards were met. While it is true that this will continue to result in a considerable logistical burden on the appellate courts, it is a process that seems mandated by the principles involved.

---

[74] 418 U.S. 153 (1974). *See also* Chapter 5.4 *supra.*

8

The Requirement of a
Strictly Drawn Statute

8.1 The Concept of Overbreadth

It is fair to say that the history of the legal regulation of obscenity exhibits a significant amount of legislative and prosecutorial aggressiveness towards material dealing generally with sex, with an occasional result being suppression of materials of clear literary or other value. Moreover, the very existence of obscenity statutes, even in the absence of unconstitutionally broad prosecution, can be said to have somewhat of a chilling effect [1] on the freedom to exhibit, or publish, or write about sexual matters. For these reasons, the courts have been especially sensitive to the wording of obscenity statutes, and have attempted to ensure that they include only obscenity, in the strict legal sense, within their proscriptions.

The basis for this judicial scrutiny has, in many cases, been a doctrine known as "overbreadth."[2] Essentially, overbreadth is a statutory defect which occurs when the statute punishes not only that which can properly be made criminal or otherwise restricted, but also that which cannot, without violating the Constitution, be made criminal. Thus, a statute which prohibits both protected and unprotected speech is unconstitutionally overbroad, and will be struck down by the courts.[3]

[1] See generally Note, *The Chilling Effect in Constitutional Law*, 69 COLUM. L. REV. 808 (1969); this potential effect of the obscenity laws was noted in *Smith* v. *California*, 361 U.S. 147, 150–154 (1959).

[2] See generally Note, *The First Amendment Overbreadth Doctrine*, 83 HARV. L. REV. 844 (1970).

[3] The question of who can attack an overbroad statute is still open. Some authority supports the proposition that someone whose conduct could properly be proscribed by a narrowly drawn statute could not attack the overbreadth of a

In the context of obscenity, a statute is unconstitutionally overbroad if it punishes, in the same manner and statute as legal obscenity, that which cannot be properly designated as obscenity. For example, in *Winters* v. *New York*,[4] the statute at issue defined obscenity to include material "devoted to the publication, and principally made up of criminal news, police reports, or accounts of criminal deeds, or pictures, or stories of deeds of bloodshed, hurt, or crime." [5] Since this clearly would include virtually any material dealing with crime, whether obscene, violent, amusing, or scholarly, the Court noted that "the subsection involved violates the rule . . . that statutes which include prohibitions of acts fairly within the protection of a free press are void. It covers detective stories, treatises on crime, reports of battle carnage, et cetera." [6]

Several years later another New York statute was at issue in the case of *Joseph Burstyn, Inc.* v. *Wilson.*[7] The statute authorized the denial of a license to show a motion picture if the motion picture was deemed by the censor to be "sacrilegious." The Supreme Court struck down the statute, or at least that part of it,[8] ostensibly on vagueness grounds. But a close reading of the decision indicates that the real defect in this standard was not so much its vagueness as its allowance of censorship on religious grounds. "It is not the business of government in our nation to suppress real or imagined attacks upon a par-

---

statute, while other authority indicates that the interests of the First Amendment require that anyone included within the statute be allowed to attack it, regardless of whether they could also be prosecuted by a valid statute. *Compare United States* v. *Thirty-Seven (37) Photographs,* 402 U.S. 363, 377–378 (1971) (Harlan, J., concurring), with *Gooding* v. *Wilson,* 405 U.S. 518, 520–521 (1972).

[4] 333 U.S. 507 (1948). *See* Comments, 61 HARV. L. REV. 1208 (1948); 23 NOT. DAME LAW. 602 (1948); 9 OHIO STATE L.J. 346 (1948); 96 U. PA. L. REV. 889 (1948).

[5] 333 U.S. at 508, quoting from New York Penal Law § 1141, subsection 2.

[6] 333 U.S. at 512. Since the statute had been judicially narrowed by the New York Court of Appeals, the main *ratio decidendi* was not overbreadth, but vagueness, which is dealt with in the next section of this chapter. However, overbreadth and vagueness are generally related and often indistinguishable. *See* Note, *The First Amendment Overbreadth Doctrine,* 83 HARV. L. REV. 844, 845 n.5 (1970).

[7] 343 U.S. 495 (1952). *See* Comments, 32 BOS. U. L. REV. 451 (1952); 41 GEO. L. J. 94 (1952); 27 N.Y.U.L. REV. 699 (1952); 3 SYR. L. REV. 365 (1952); 1952 U. ILL. L. J. 493 (1952); *The Supreme Court, 1951 Term,* 66 HARV L. REV. 89, 115 (1952).

This case is generally cited for the proposition that motion pictures are covered by the protections of the First Amendment. 343 U.S. at 502. *Compare Mutual Film Corp.* v. *Industrial Commission,* 236 U.S. 230 (1915).

[8] This raises the very large issue of severability which, of course, is beyond the scope of this treatise. *See* Note, *The First Amendment Overbreadth Doctrine,* 83 HARV. L. REV. 844, 891–901 (1970).

ticular religious doctrine, whether they appear in publications, speeches, or motion pictures." [9] Thus the issue is not so much that the term "sacrilegious" is vague, but that regardless of its specificity it embodies a concept—governmental action on religious grounds— which is inherently impermissible. The statute was therefore unconstitutionally overbroad.

In *Butler* v. *Michigan*,[10] the defendant was convicted under a Michigan statute designed for the protection of minors.[11] The statute made it unlawful to distribute materials "tending to incite minors to violent or depraved or immoral acts, manifestly tending to the corruption of the morals of youth."[12] Materials of this type were unlawful, even when sold to an adult, and the conviction on appeal was based on the sale of such materials to an adult police officer. The Supreme Court, in an opinion written by Mr. Justice Frankfurter, unanimously reversed the conviction on the grounds that the statute, by prohibiting the sale to adults of material that might be harmful to minors, thus had too broad a sweep.

> We have before us legislation not reasonably restricted to the evil with which it is said to deal. The incidence of this enactment is to reduce the adult population of Michigan to reading only what is fit for children. It thereby arbitrarily curtails one of those liberties of the individual, now enshrined in the Due Process Clause of the Fourteenth Amendment, that history has attested as the indispensable conditions for the maintenance and progress of a free society.[13]

Thus the decision is based, fundamentally, on the overbreadth doctrine. The defect in that statute was that it prohibited the dissemination of materials that were not in fact harmful, that is, adult material in the hands of adults. Since it thus included more than could be constitutionally prohibited, it suffered from being overbroad and was struck down by the Supreme Court. In addition, the decision was based in part on a concept now known as the doctrine of the "least restrictive alternative." [14] Briefly, this doctrine requires that whenever a statute or other governmental action may potentially in-

---

[9] 343 U.S. at 495.

[10] 352 U.S. 380 (1957). See Chapter 4.5 *supra*.

[11] Michigan Penal Code § 343.

[12] *Id.* 352 U.S. at 381.

[13] 352 U.S. at 383–384.

[14] *See generally* Note, *Less Drastic Means and the First Amendment,* 78 YALE L.J. 464 (1969). Unlike some other doctrines discussed in this chapter, such as overbreadth and the concept of the "chilling effect," the least-restrictive-alternative principle is not restricted solely to First Amendment issues, and has been used in many instances where a statute interferes with some fundamental interest.

fringe on some fundamental right, such as the freedom of speech, then the valid governmental interest may be furthered only in the manner which represents the smallest encroachment on the rights involved. Thus, the question to be asked is not whether the legislation is reasonable, as would be done in cases not involving fundamental rights, but whether this is the best possible legislation under the circumstances, at least insofar as its incidental effect on protected rights. The use of this doctrine in *Butler* once again indicates that because of the potential effect on protected speech, obscenity statutes will and must be scrutinized with a greater degree of care than would be the case with other types of legislation.

The final Supreme Court case of this type is *Kingsley International Pictures Corp.* v. *Regents.*[15] The statute at issue provided for the licensing of motion pictures, and required the denial of such a license if the film or any part of it was "obscene, indecent, immoral, inhuman, sacrilegious, or is of such character that its exhibition would tend to corrupt morals or incite to crime . . ."[16] The terms "immoral" and "tend to corrupt morals" had been defined by an amendment to "denote a motion picture or part thereof, the dominant purpose or effect of which is erotic or pornographic; or which portrays acts of sexual immorality, perversion, or lewdness, or which expressly or impliedly presents such acts as desirable, acceptable or proper patterns of behavior."[17] The case arose when a motion picture version of *Lady Chatterley's Lover* was denied a license on the grounds that it offended the statute by presenting adultery as appropriate behavior. In an opinion written by Mr. Justice Stewart, the Supreme Court reversed the Court of Appeals of New York. The difficulty with the statute, as construed by the New York courts and applied in this case, was that it reached beyond obscenity and pornography to the advocacy of ideas.

> What New York has done, therefore, is to prevent the exhibition of a motion picture because that picture advocates an idea—that adultery under certain circumstances may be proper behavior. Yet the First Amendment's basic guarantee is of freedom to advocate ideas.

[15] 360 U.S. 684 (1959). *See* Comments, 48 ILL. B.J. 213 (1959); 20 OHIO ST. L.J. 161 (1959); 13 VAND. L. REV. 541 (1960); 59 COLUM. L. REV. 337 (1959); 44 CORNELL L. Q. 411 (1959); 37 TEX. L. REV. 339 (1959); 44 MINN. L. REV. 334 (1959); 58 MICH. L. REV. 134 (1959).

[16] McKinney's New York Laws, 1953, Education Law, § 122, quoted at 360 U.S. 685. As to that element of the statute dealing with "sacrilegious" materials, see text accompanying notes 7–9 *supra*.

[17] McKinney's New York Laws, 1953 (Cum. Supp. 1958), Education Law, § 122–a, quoted at 360 U.S. 685.

The State, quite simply, has thus struck at the very heart of constitutionally protected liberty.

It is contended that the State's action was justified because the motion picture attractively portrays a relationship which is contrary to the moral standards, the religious precepts, and the legal code of its citizenry. This argument misconceives what it is that the Constitution protects. Its guarantee is not confined to the expression of ideas that are conventional or shared by a majority. It protects advocacy of the opinion that adultery may sometimes be proper, no less than advocacy of socialism or the single tax. And in the realm of ideas it protects expression which is eloquent no less than that which is unconvincing.[18]

By reaching beyond the obscene into the area of ideas protected by the First Amendment, the statute, as applied, reached too far and, therefore, was unconstitutionally overbroad in its application. The Court did not expressly refer to overbreadth in this opinion, nor in any of the others described in this section. But the principle is that of overbreadth nonetheless. If a statute is not restricted in its application to the legally obscene, it then prohibits that which the First Amendment protects, and must, therefore, be stricken.[19]

8.2   The Vice of Vagueness

For every obscenity statute which is struck down on overbreadth grounds, there are probably 10 that are voided as being unconstitutionally vague. This concept is more of a due process concept than one based on the First Amendment, and the concept, on its face, is simple. If a statute is so vague that no one can be sure what it regulates or

---

[18] 360 U.S. at 688–689.

[19] For statutes struck down by lower courts on overbreadth grounds, *see, e.g., Stein* v. *Batchelor,* 300 F. Supp. 602 (N.D. Tex. 1969), *vacated on other grounds sub nom. Dyson* v. *Stein,* 401 U.S. 200 (1971); *United States* v. *Orito,* 338 F. Supp. 308 (E.D. Wis. 1907), *vacated and remanded,* 413 U.S. 139 (1973); *United States* v. *B & H Dist. Corp.,* 319 F. Supp. 1231 (W.D. Wis. 1970), *vacated and remanded,* 402 U.S. 351 (1971), *after remand,* 347 F. Supp. 905 (1972), *vacated,* 413 U.S. 909 (1973), *after remand,* 375 F. Supp. 136 (1974); *Entertainment Ventures, Inc.* v. *Brewer,* 306 F. Supp. 802, 813–815 (M.D. Ala. 1969) (three-judge court); *Delta Book Distributors, Inc.* v. *Cronvich,* 304 F. Supp. 662, 669 (E.D. La. 1969) (three-judge court), *modified on other grounds sub nom. Perez* v. *Ledesma,* 401 U.S. 82 (1971); *Hayse* v. *Van Hommissen,* 321 F. Supp. 642 (D. Ore. 1970), *vacated,* 403 U.S. 927 (1971); *Dunn* v. *Maryland State Board of Censors,* 240 Md. 249, 213 A.2d 751 (1965); *Adams* v. *Hinkle,* 51 Wash.2d 763, 322 P.2d 844 (1958).

There are, of course, many cases which overturn state statutes on the grounds that the statute does not embody the then proper test for obscenity. To the extent that these cases may be said to be based on the theory that an improper test may include nonobscene material, these cases too are in a sence overbreadth cases.

includes, then no one can be expected to base his or her conduct upon it, and it cannot be allowed to support a criminal conviction. A statute which does not give adequate notice of what it prohibits is void for vagueness.[20]

This doctrine is especially relevant to obscenity statutes. The line between protected and unprotected speech is not an easy line to draw, and thus it is difficult for a bookseller, author, distributor, or exhibitor to know whether given material is obscene until a court has decided the issue. Furthermore, the dangers of vagueness in the obscenity area are twofold. First, there is the general due process aspect of the impropriety of punishing someone for conduct that was not clearly prohibited in advance. In addition, a vague obscenity statute may cause people to err on the side of caution, not distributing materials that are in fact protected by the First Amendment. Thus a vague statute will have a chilling effect on the promulgation of constitutionally protected materials, expression, and ideas. In light of this chilling effect, the Supreme Court has been especially rigorous in requiring obscenity statutes to meet a high standard of specificity.

Many of the cases discussed in the previous section were based as much on vagueness as on overbreadth grounds. For example, in *Winters* v. *New York,*[21] the majority opinion of Mr. Justice Reed noted that a criminal statute must be more specific than a statute imposing a civil sanction, and that vagueness may take the form of lack of "ascertainable standards of guilt," or "uncertainty in regard to persons within the scope of the act," or uncertainty "in regard to the applicable tests to ascertain guilt." [22] In *Winters,* the Court of Appeals of New York had defined New York's statute relating to descriptions of crime and violence, discussed in the previous section of this chapter, so as to limit it to stories of violence or crime so "massed" as to "incite crime" or to become "vehicles for inciting violent and depraved crimes." [23] Even this, the Court said, was too vague, and did not sufficiently describe the kinds of publications to be prohibited. While words such as "obscene, lewd, lascivious, filthy, indecent or disgusting" were "well understood through long use in the criminal law," the concept of "massing stories to incite crime" had no such "settled meaning and was therefore impermissibly vague." [24]

[20] *See generally* Note, *The Void-for-Vagueness Doctrine in the Supreme Court,* 109 U. PA. L. REV. 67 (1960).

[21] 333 U.S. 507 (1948).

[22] *Id.* at 515–516.

[23] *Id.* at 518–520.

[24] *Id.* at 518. Much of the *Winters* opinion uses the word "vagueness" also to

Similarly, in *Joseph Burstyn, Inc.* v. *Wilson,*[25] the New York standard of "sacrilegious" was struck down as a permissible criterion for the licensing of motion pictures not only because it created an impermissible classification based on religious doctrine, but also because "this is far from the kind of *narrow* exception to freedom of expression which a state may carve out to satisfy the adverse demands of other interests of society."[26] The *Burstyn* case also makes a point that is valuable in understanding the dangers of vagueness. A vague statute is constitutionally defective not only because the public does not adequately know what is constrained, but also because the enforcing authorities are not sufficiently limited. "In seeking to apply the broad and all-inclusive definition of sacrilegious given by the New York Courts, the censor is set adrift upon a boundless sea amid a myriad of conflicting currents of religious views, with no charts but those provided by the most vocal and powerful orthodoxies. New York cannot rest such unlimited restraining control over motion pictures in a censor."[27] Thus, a vague statute gives too little guidance to a censor or other enforcing authority, with the result of a possible adverse effect on the distribution of protected material.

Shortly after *Burstyn,* other vague obscenity or licensing statutes were invalidated by the Supreme Court. In *Gelling* v. *Texas,*[28] the Court invalidated, in a per curiam judgment based on *Burstyn* and *Winters,* a Texas local ordinance dealing with motion picture licensing. The ordinance authorized the denial of a license if the Board of Censors was "of the opinion" that the motion picture was "of such character as to be prejudicial to the best interests of the people of [the] city." This, noted Mr. Justice Frankfurter, "offends the Due Process Clause of the Fourteenth Amendment on the score of indefiniteness."[29] Several other per curiam reversals of licensing schemes with broad standards followed, implicitly invalidating standards such as "harmful" or "immoral."[30]

---

describe what we would now call overbreadth. For example, the Court says that "a statute so vague and indefinite, in form and as interpreted, as to permit within the scope of its language the punishment of incidents fairly within the protection of the guarantee of free speech is void, on its face, as contrary to the Fourteenth Amendment." 333 U.S. at 509.

[25] 343 U.S. 495 (1952).

[26] *Id.* at 504 (emphasis added). This was in particular reference to the attempt by the New York Court of Appeals to define the statutory provision at issue.

[27] 343 U.S. at 504–505.

[28] 343 U.S. 960 (1952) (per curiam).

[29] *Id.* (Frankfurter, J., concurring).

[30] *Superior Films, Inc.* v. *Department of Education of Ohio,* 346 U.S. 587 (1954)

All of these previous cases dealt with standards that were somewhat broader than mere obscenity, and thus inevitably involved considerations both of overbreadth and vagueness. But in *Roth* v. *United States,*[31] it was argued that obscenity itself is too vague a concept to survive the restriction of the Due Process Clause. Thus, it was argued that 18 U.S.C. § 1461 was unconstitutionally indefinite because it prohibited the mailing of material which was "obscene, lewd, lascivious, or filthy . . . or other publication of an indecent character."[32] Simultaneously, it was argued in *Alberts* that the California standard of "obscene or indecent" suffered from a similar defect.[33] While the Supreme Court admitted that the words were not "precise," however, this did not make them unconstitutionally vague. As defined in *Roth,* the terms gave "adequate warning of the conduct proscribed."[34] The Court quoted from *United States* v. *Petrillo*[35] as to the lack of necessity of absolute precision. All that was necessary was that there be

> . . . boundaries sufficiently distinct for judges and juries fairly to administer the law. . . . That there may be marginal cases in which it is difficult to determine the side of the line on which a particular fact situation falls is no sufficient reason to hold the language too ambiguous to define a criminal offense. . . .[36]

And so the situation remained for 10 years, during which time the Supreme Court made no major additions or modifications to the vagueness doctrine as it applied to obscenity.[37] But in 1968 the Court

---

(per curiam), *reversing* 159 Ohio St. 315, 112 N.E.2d 311 (1953); *Commercial Pictures Corp.* v. *Regents,* 346 U.S. 587 (1954) (per curiam), *reversing* 305 N.Y. 336, 113 N.E.2d 502 (1953); *Holmby Productions, Inc.* v. *Vaughan,* 350 U.S. 870 (1955) (per curiam), *reversing* 177 Kan. 728, 282 P.2d 412 (1955).

[31] 354 U.S. 476 (1957).

[32] 18 U.S.C. § 1461, quoted at 354 U.S. 491.

[33] West's California Penal Code Ann., 1955, § 311, quoted at 354 U.S. 491.

[34] 354 U.S. at 491.

[35] 332 U.S. 1 (1947).

[36] *Id.* at 7, quoted in *Roth* at 354 U.S. 491–492.

[37] Vagueness was mentioned a number of times but was not the basis for any decision. *See Times Film Corp.* v. *City of Chicago,* 365 U.S. 43, 46 (1961); *Smith* v. *California,* 361 U.S. 147, 151 (1959) ("And this Court has intimated that stricter standards of permissible statutory vagueness may be applied to a statute having a potentially inhibiting effect on speech; a man may the less be required to act at his peril here, because the free dissemination of ideas may be the loser."); *Kingsley International Pictures Corp.* v. *Regents,* 360 U.S. 684, 699–702 (1959) (Clark, J., concurring in the result). *See also Bantam Books, Inc.* v. *Sullivan,* 372 U.S. 58, 71 (1963).

handed down its decision in *Interstate Circuit, Inc.* v. *City of Dallas*,[38] which is its most extensive treatment of the vagueness problem. At issue was a municipal classification scheme designating motion pictures either as "suitable for young persons" or "not suitable for young persons." The definition of "not suitable for young persons" was as follows:

> (1) Describing or portraying brutality, criminal violence or depravity in such a manner as to be, in the judgment of the Board, likely to incite or encourage crime or delinquency on the part of young persons; or
>
> (2) Describing or portraying nudity beyond the customary limits of candor in the community, or sexual promiscuity or extra-marital or abnormal sexual relations in such a manner as to be, in the judgment of the Board, likely to incite or encourage delinquency or sexual promiscuity on the part of young persons or to appeal to their prurient interest.
>
> A film shall be considered "likely to incite or encourage" crime, delinquency or sexual promiscuity on the part of young persons, if, in the judgment of the Board, there is a substantial probability that it will create the impression on young persons that such conduct is profitable, desirable, acceptable, respectable, praiseworthy or commonly accepted. A film shall be considered as appealing to "prurient interest" of young persons if, in the judgment of the Board, its calculated or dominant effect on young persons is substantially to arouse sexual desire. In determining whether a film is "not suitable for young persons," the Board shall consider the film as a whole, rather than isolated portions, and shall determine whether its harmful effects outweigh artistic or educational values such film may have for young persons.[39]

This standard was different from those in previous vagueness cases for a number of reasons. First of all, it related to minors, not adults, and the Court had, on the same day as it decided *Interstate Circuit*, decided *Ginsberg* v. *New York*,[40] holding that different standards for minors and adults were permissible. But this holding related only to substantive standards, and not to the degree of procedural protection. "The permissible extent of vagueness is not directly proportional to, or a function of, the extent of the power to regulate or control expression with respect to children."[41] Secondly, this was not,

[38] 390 U.S. 676 (1968). *See* Comments, 33 ALB. L. REV. 173 (1968); 37 U. Mo. K.C.L. REV. 127 (1969); 54 A.B.A.J. 702 (1968).

[39] 390 U.S. at 681–682.

[40] 390 U.S. 629 (1968). *See* Chapter 4.5 *supra.*

[41] 390 U.S. at 689. *See also Rabeck* v. *New York*, 391 U.S. 462 (1968) (per curiam).

strictly speaking, a criminal statute, although criminal penalties could follow for violations of the licensing procedure. This distinction was also rejected by Mr. Justice Marshall. In fact, vagueness is an even more serious problem where licensing is involved, since the potential chilling effect is greater and there is the additional danger of an unguided censor exercising preliminary control, with little statutory direction to aid him.[42] Finally, the standards are clearly more extensive than the broad, one-word standards dealt with in the earlier cases, such as "immoral," "harmful," or "sacrilegious." The Court's decision is not clear as to which elements of the standard were dispositive, except to criticize the vagueness of the concepts of "sexual promiscuity" and "desirable, acceptable or proper." The fact that a great deal of discretion was given to the Board in making these determinations also seemed of importance.[43] But what emerges from the decision is the principle that if obscenity statutes, of whatever form, are defined in terms other than legal obscenity, as defined by the Supreme Court, then they will be held to be unconstitutionally vague. If the statute spoke of "obscenity," or the legal equivalent, it was acceptable, but anything else would most likely be found vague.[44]

The appropriate definition, or precision, need not necessarily appear in the statute itself. If a statute, vague or overbroad on its face, has been authoritatively construed by the state courts, then the defect is cured. For example, in *Ginsberg* v. *New York*,[45] the New York statute was attacked on vagueness grounds in reference to material which was "harmful to minors." But the challenge was not seriously considered, since the New York Court of Appeals had defined the term as being "virtually identical to the Supreme Court's most recent statement of the elements of obscenity." [46] Thus, the New York courts

---

[42] *Id.* at 683–685. The Court also rejected as a relevant distinction the fact that classification rather than direct suppression was involved. *Id.* at 688–689. It should be clear that classification has the inevitable result of suppression of certain materials entirely and all materials as to some groups, depending on the classification scheme used.

[43] *Id.* at 687–688.

[44] For lower court cases holding other statutes to be impermissibly vague, *see, e.g., People* v. *Bookcase, Inc.,* 14 N.Y.2d 409, 201 N.E.2d 14 (1964); *Hallmark Productions, Inc.,* v. *Carroll,* 384 Pa. 348, 121 A.2d 584 (1956); *Paramount Film Distributing Corp.* v. *City of Chicago,* 172 F. Supp. 69 (N.D. Ill. 1959); *Police Commissioner* v. *Siegel Enterprises, Inc.,* 223 Md. 110, 162 A.2d 727 (1969), *cert. denied,* 364 U.S. 909; *Roberts* v. *Clement,* 252 F. Supp. 835 (E.D. Tenn. 1966); *Louisiana News Co.* v. *Dayries,* 187 F. Supp. 241 (E.D. La. 1960).

[45] 390 U.S. 629 (1968).

[46] *Id.* at 643, quoting from *Bookcase, Inc.* v. *Broderick,* 18 N.Y.2d 71, 218 N.E.2d 668 (1966), *appeal dismissed for want of a properly presented federal question sub nom. Bookcase, Inc.* v. *Leary,* 385 U.S. 12 (1967).

had made up for any legislative defect [47] by construing the statute in a sufficiently narrow and specific manner.

8.3   The Effect of Miller

The vagueness cases decided prior to 1973 were primarily devoted to limiting obscenity legislation to legal obscenity, as described in *Roth*, by eliminating prohibitions on the "harmful," "immoral," and the like. If a statute were so limited, no further detail was necessary. This approach came to an end with *Miller* v. *California*,[48] where the Supreme Court held that considerably more detail was now necessary than was the case in the past.

In *Paris Adult Theatre I* v. *Slaton,* [49] one of the companion cases to *Miller,* Mr. Justice Brennan's dissent had been based largely on the contention that the entire concept of obscenity was inherently and irredeemably vague, that the experience since *Roth* had shown that no adequate line could be drawn between protected and unprotected speech, and that the result was adverse to First Amendment values generally.[50] The specificity requirements in *Miller* seem to emerge as a response to this dissent. "We acknowledge, however, the inherent dangers of undertaking to regulate any form of expression. State statutes designed to regulate obscene materials must be carefully limited." [51] This, of course, was nothing new. But the Court's interpretation of what this goal required represented a significant change in obscenity law.

> As a result, we now confine the permissible scope of such regulation to works which depict or describe sexual conduct. That conduct must be specifically defined by the applicable state law, as written or authoritatively construed. A state offense must also be limited to works, which, taken as a whole, appeal to the prurient interest in sex, which portray sexual conduct in a patently offensive way, and which, taken as a whole, do not have serious literary, artistic, political, or scientific value.
>
> . . .

---

[47] It is doubtful that the statute would have been considered vague in any event, since the statutory definition of "harmful to minors" was the *Memoirs* test for obscenity adjusted to minors.

[48] 413 U.S. 15 (1973).

[49] 413 U.S. 49 (1973).

[50] *Id.* at 73–114 (Brennan, J., dissenting).

[51] *Miller* v. *California,* 413 U.S. at 23–24.

The basic guidelines for the trier of fact must be:...(b) whether the work depicts or describes, in a patently offensive way, sexual conduct specifically defined by the applicable state law.[52]

What do these pronouncements by the Supreme Court mean? At the very least they mean a recognition that merely prohibiting the obscene, despite 16 years of case law (since *Roth*) defining the term, did not provide sufficient notice of what could or could not be published, distributed, or exhibited. Not only are obscenity statutes limited to the description or depiction of sexual conduct, but the statutes, in themselves or as interpreted by the appropriate court, must describe just what sexual conduct cannot be described or depicted. To clarify its ruling, the Supreme Court cited two state statutes, those of Oregon and Hawaii, which defined depictions of sexual conduct, and thus did not unconstitutionally proscribe expression.[53] If one looks at the statutes which the Court "approved," [54] one sees the significant characteristic of detailed description of what cannot be shown. For example, the Hawaii statute contains the following definitions:

(7) "Sexual conduct" means acts of masturbation, homosexuality, lesbianism, bestiality, sexual intercourse or physical contact with a person's clothed or unclothed genitals, pubic area, buttocks, or the breast or breasts of a female for the purpose of sexual stimulation, gratification, or perversion.

(8) "Sexual excitment" means the condition of the human male or female genitals when in a state of sexual stimulation or arousal.

(9) "Sadomasochistic abuse" means flagellation or torture by or upon a person as an act of sexual stimulation or gratification.[55]

And the Oregon statute has similarly explicit definitions of "nudity," "obscene performance," "sadomasochistic abuse," "sexual conduct," and "sexual excitement." [56]

The court in *Miller* set down some guidelines as to what was meant by sexual conduct, guidelines which, although not an exhaustive list, are "intended to fix substantive constitutional limitations . . . on the type of material subject to such a determination." [57] These guidelines are:

[52] *Id.* at 24.

[53] *Id.* at 24 n.6, citing Oregon Laws 1971, C. 743, Art. 29, §§ 255–262 (ORE. REV. STAT. §§ 167.060–167.100 (1973)), and Hawaii Penal Code, Tit. 37, §§ 1210–1216, 1972 Hawaii Session Laws, Art. 9, C. 12, pt. II, pp. 126–129.

[54] The Court carefully limited its approval to the matter of depiction of sexual conduct, and not to the statutes generally. 413 U.S. at 24 n.6.

[55] Hawaii Penal Code § 1210(7)(8)(9), (1973).

[56] ORE. REV. STAT. § 167.060(5)(6)(9)(10)(11), (1973).

[57] *Jenkins* v. *Georgia*, 418 U.S. 153, 160–161 (1974).

(a) Patently offensive representations or descriptions of ultimate sexual acts, normal or perverted, actual or simulated.

(b) Patently offensive representations or descriptions of masturbation, excretory functions, and lewd exhibition of the genitals.[58]

Thus the Court set out the broad parameters of permissible regulation, and in addition required that whatever types of representation within these parameters the state wishes to regulate must be described with some degree of detail. For the first time, the Court said that the mere condemnation of obscene materials was not constitutionally sufficient. Without more notice and guidance as to the meaning of that term, a statute would be insufficient.

As the Court pointed out, this degree of detail could come from the words of the statute itself, or from an authoritative construction by the state courts. The statute at issue must be looked at together with those constructions to see if the regulatory scheme is unconstitutionally vague.[59] If, even with any judicial construction, it still does not specifically describe the type of sexual conduct that cannot be shown, the statute will not survive *Miller*.

8.4 How Much Detail is Required?

It remains to be seen just what kind of statutes can in fact exist in the wake of the new specificity standards set forth in *Miller*. There has been a great deal of litigation concerning the constitutionality of various statutes since *Miller*, and an analysis of some of these cases will be instructive.[60]

In *Miller*, the Supreme Court set forth examples of the kinds of conduct which could be included within valid obscenity statutes.[61] It has been held that when these very descriptions are embodied in a statute, the requisite specificity exists.[62] Other courts have judicially

[58] *Miller* v. *California*, 413 U.S. at 25.

[59] *See, e.g., Rhodes* v. *State*, 382 So.2d 351 (Fla. 1973); *State* v. *J-R Distributors*, 82 Wash.2d 584, 512 P.2d 1049 (1973).

[60] For discussions of legislation after *Miller, see, e.g.,* Note, *Oregon's Obscenity Bill: New Fig Leaves, Old Faux Pas,* 53 ORE. L. REV. 375 (1974); Comment, 9 SUFFOLK U. L. REV. 255 (1974); Hunsaker, *1973 Obscenity-Pornography Decisions: Analysis, Impact, and Legislative Alternatives,* 11 S. DIEGO L. REV. 906 (1974); Comment, 5 U. TOL. L. REV. 171 (1973); Comment, 51 DENVER L.J. 75 (1974); Comment, 49 IND. L.J. 320 (1974); Note, *Miller* v. *California, A Mandate For New Obscenity Legislation,* 45 MISS. L.J. 435 (1974); Comment, 4 MEMPHIS ST. U.L. REV. 619 (1974).

[61] 413 U.S. at 25.

[62] *De Salvo* v. *Codd,* 386 F. Supp. 1293, 1300, (S.D.N.Y. 1974) (three-judge court).

added these standards into existing statutes, thus adding the necessary specificity by interpretation.[63] In fact, this is what the Supreme Court has done in relation to the federal obscenity statutes. In *United States* v. *12 200-Ft. Reels of Film,*[64] the Court indicated that it was prepared to define "obscene," "lewd," "lascivious," "filthy," "indecent," and "immoral" as being limited to the *Miller* examples,[65] and has specifically reaffirmed the validity of 18 U.S.C. § 1461 against a vagueness challenge.[66]

But, of course, the *Miller* examples are not the only way a statute can be constitutionally specific. It is not necessary to use the exact examples from *Miller,* nor is it necessary that a statute contain the exact language of the Supreme Court's test for obscenity.[67] If there is adequate notice of the type of conduct proscribed, there is no need to restate the obscenity test in the statute, since a defendant can expect that this test will be used at trial, as a matter of constitutional law, whether or not it appears in the statute. Conversely, the presence of the three-part *Miller* test in the statute does not meet the constitutional requirements for specification of the type of sexual conduct that cannot be depicted. The specificity requirement and the proper substantive test for obscenity are separate and independent. The presence of the latter does not eliminate the need for the former.[68] It is therefore obvious that merely using the word "obscene" or its equivalent, without the benefit of any statutory or judicial definition, is insufficient,[69] although other courts have done little more than pay lip service to the specificity requirement in *Miller.*[70]

[63] *Gibbs* v. *State,* 504 S.W.2d 719 (Ark. 1974), *State* v. *J-R Distributors, Inc.,* 82 Wash.2d 584, 512 P.2d 1049 (1973), *cert. denied,* 418 U.S. 949 (1974); *State* v. *Wilke,* 216 N.W.2d 641 (Minn. 1974); *State* v. *Harding,* 320 A.2d 646 (N.H. 1974) (defining "nudity, sex or excretion" to include depiction of listed forms of sexual conduct).

[64] 413 U.S. 123 (1973).

[65] *Id.* at 130 n.7.

[66] *Hamling* v. *United States,* 418 U.S. 87, 110–116 (1974). In light of n.7 of *12 200-Ft. Reels,* this clearly applies also to 18 U.S.C. § 1462 and 19 U.S.C. § 1305(a), and would apply to other federal obscenity statutes. *See also United States* v. *Friedman,* 506 F.2d 511, 514–515 (8th Cir. 1974).

[67] *See, e.g., People* v. *O'Neil,* 25 Ill. App.2d 227, 323 N.E.2d 7 (1974); *Hollington* v. *Ricco,* 40 Ohio App. 2d 57, 318 N.E.2d 442 (1973).

[68] *Commonwealth* v. *Burak,* 335 A.2d 820, 822 (Pa. Super. 1975). But an incorrect definition renders the statute unconstitutional on other grounds. *Hamar Theatres, Inc.* v. *Cryan,* 365 F. Supp. 1312 (D.N.J. 1973) (three-judge court).

[69] *McCright* v. *Olson,* 367 F. Supp. 937 (D.N.D. 1973) (three-judge court); *Miranda* v. *Hicks,* 388 F. Supp. 350, 357–360 (C.D. Cal. 1974) (three-judge court) (judicial gloss of "hard-core pornography" and "graphic description of sexual activity" insufficient); *State* v. *Wedelstedt,* 213 N.W.2d 652 (Iowa 1973).

[70] *See, e.g., State ex rel. Keating* v. *"Vixen,"* 35 Ohio St. 2d 215, 301 N.E.2d

In summation, what now seems to be required is some description, in the statute or by judicial construction, of the actual types of sexual acts or depictions or conduct that may not be exhibited or distributed.[71] Adjectives such as "obscene" or "filthy" or "hard-core" do not meet this requirement, nor does a restatement of the prurient-interest, patent-offensiveness, and lack-of-value tests. It is neither legal standards nor legal conclusions that make a statute specific, but reasonably precise definitions of what types of conduct are prohibited.

---

880 (1973); *State* v. *Little Art Corporation*, 191 Neb. 448, 215 N.W.2d 853 (1974); *People* v. *Ridens*, 59 Ill.2d 362, 321 N.E.2d 264 (1974); *B & A Co.* v. *State*, 24 Md. App. 367, 330 A.2d 701, 704 (1975).

[71] For a fairly complete listing of the large number of cases dealing with the specificity requirement since *Miller,* see *Commonwealth* v. *Horton,* _____ Mass._____, 310 N.E.2d 316, 319 n.5–n.8 (1974).

9

The Federal Obscenity Laws

9.1 A History of Federal Obscenity Regulation

Although the history of federal regulation of obscenity is dealt with elsewhere in this book,[1] and more extensively in other works,[2] a brief overview of this history seems a fitting introduction for this chapter dealing with the various federal obscenity statutes.

The first federal concern with obscenity came as a result of the circulation of French postcards in the middle of the 19th century. As this material spread outside of France, other countries became concerned with keeping it outside their borders. Therefore, the Customs Law of 1842 included a provision barring the importation of "indecent and obscene prints, paintings, lithographs, engravings, and transparencies."[3] Although the statute was on the books, however, it was at best infrequently enforced. Nonetheless, Congress sought to expand the exercise of federal power in the obscenity area and, in 1865, enacted the first legislation relating to obscenity in the mails. This was also the first federal criminal obscenity statute, and it provided

[1] See Chapter 1.3 *supra*.

[2] J. PAUL AND M. SCHWARTZ, FEDERAL CENSORSHIP: OBSCENITY IN THE MAIL (1961); Paul, *The Post Office and Non-Mailability of Obscenity, An Historical Note*, 8 U.C.L.A.L. REV. 44 (1961); Paul and Schwartz, *Obscenity in the Mails: A Comment on Some Problems of Federal Censorship*, 106 U. PA. L. REV. 214 (1957). *See also* DeGrazia, *Obscenity and the Mail: A Study of Administrative Restraint*, 20 L. & CONTEMP. PROB. 608 (1955); Note, *Obscenity and the Post Office: Removal From the Mail Under Section 1461*, 27 U. CHI. L. REV. 354 (1960); Zuckman, *Obscenity in the Mails*, 33 SO. CAL. L. REV. 171 (1960); Note, *Obscenity Through the Mails*, 11 WEST. RES L. REV. 480 (1960); Note, *Obscenity in the Mails: Post Office Department Procedures and the First Amendment*, 58 Nw. U. L. REV. 664 (1963).

[3] 5 Stat. 566 § 28 (1842). The statute merely provided for forefeiture and destruction, and not for criminal penalties. For an English statute directed towards the same activity, see 16 & 17 Vict., Ch. 107 (1853).

that no obscene book, pamphlet, picture, print, or other publication of a vulgar and indecent character, shall be admitted into the mails of the United States; any person or persons who shall deposit or cause to be deposited, in any post-office or branch post-office of the United States, for mailing or for delivery, an obscene book, pamphlet, picture, print, or other publication, knowing the same to be of a vulgar and indecent character, shall be deemed guilty of a misdemeanor, and, being duly convicted thereof, shall for every such offense be fined not more than five hundred dollars, or imprisoned not more than one year, or both, according to the circumstances and aggravations of the offense.[4]

This statute, too, was rarely used, and it was not until the entry of Anthony Comstock that federal obscenity laws became fully developed. Comstock, whose activities are described in Chapter 1 and in other materials,[5] brought about both a major revision in the federal obscenity statutes [6] and the first concerted effort to enforce them. Comstock's efforts resulted in the enactment of the predecessor of 18 U.S.C. § 1461, still known as the "Comstock Act." This statute, passed in 1873, was entitled "An Act for the Suppression of Trade in, and Circulation of, obscene Literature and Articles of immoral Use."[7] It encompassed articles designed for preventing conception and procuring abortions, as well as obscene literature, and listed virtually every way in which immoral stories or pictures might reach the public. The penalty for mailing any such material became one to 10 years imprisonment, and a fine of from $100 to $5,000 for each such offense. The customs statute was broadened to include all materials within this expanded definition of contraband, and search-and-seizure powers for obscenity were broadened. And just to make sure that there was no doubt as to the material involved, the prohibition extended to that which was "obscene, lewd, or lascivious" or "of an

---

[4] 13 Stat. 507 § 16 (1865).

[5] H. BROWN and M. LEECH, ANTHONY COMSTOCK: ROUNDSMAN OF THE LORD (1927); C. TRUMBULL, ANTHONY COMSTOCK, FIGHTER (1913); J. KILPATRICK, THE SMUT PEDDLERS 35–44 (1960); P. BOYER, PURITY IN PRINT: THE VICE SOCIETY MOVEMENT AND BOOK CENSORSHIP IN AMERICA (1968). *See also* A. COMSTOCK, TRAPS FOR THE YOUNG (1883); A. COMSTOCK, FRAUDS EXPOSED—HOW THE PEOPLE ARE DECEIVED AND ROBBED, AND YOUTH CORRUPTED (1880).

[6] There had been one minor change in the 1865 statute, which prevented the carrying in the mail of any "letter upon the envelope of which, or postal card upon which scurrilous epithets have been written." 17 Stat. 302 § 148 (1872).

[7] 17 Stat. 598 (1873). For an interesting account of its passage, see Paul, *The Post Office and Non-Mailability of Obscenity: An Historical Note*, 8 U.C.L.A.L. REV. 44, 51–57 (1961).

indecent character." Three years later, the Act was rewritten specifically to authorize post office censorship of the mail by declaring all obscene matter to be "non-mailable matter" and prohibiting its delivery.[8]

Armed with the statutory tools, Comstock (as a special agent of the Post Office Department) and others began to enforce the new laws aggressively. Seizure and destruction of objectionable literature became commonplace, and criminal convictions under federal obscenity statutes were frequent. There was no direct First Amendment challenge, since no one seriously thought that the First Amendment protected objectionable material of this sort,[9] and the constitutionality of the statute was repeatedly upheld by the Supreme Court.[10] In the 19th century, enforcement was directed mainly at pulp magazines, sensationalist newspapers, and dirty pictures. By the beginning of the 20th century, however, enforcement was expanded to cover "immoral" literature of a broad variety. During this time, the Comstock Act was amended on several occasions. An 1888 enactment made it clear that "obscene or scurrilous" matter on the outside as well as on the inside of mail was prohibited.[11] In 1908, "indecent" was defined to include "matter of a character tending to incite arson, murder, or assassination."[12] Although the statute has been rewritten and modified a number of times since then,[13] it remains substantially similar to the act first introduced by Anthony Comstock in 1873.

As conceptions of the scope of federal power under the commerce clause were expanded, so also was the scope of federal power in the regulation of obscenity. In 1897, Congress prohibited, by a criminal statute, the transportation of obscene material across state lines by means of a common carrier or express company.[14] This statute has also been modified a number of times since then,[15] and now

---

[8] 19 Stat. 90 § 1 (1876).

[9] *See United States* v. *Harmon*, 45 F. 414 (D. Kan. 1891).

[10] *Ex parte Jackson*, 96 U.S. 727 (1877); *In re Rapier*, 143 U.S. 110 (1892); *Hoke* v. *United States*, 227 U.S. 308 (1913).

[11] 25 Stat. 188 (1888) and 25 Stat. 496 (1888). Now a separate statute deals with this, derived from the latter act. 18 U.S.C. § 1463 (1975 Supp.).

[12] 35 Stat. 416 (1908). See also 36 Stat. 1339 § 2 (1911).

[13] See 62 Stat. 768 (1948); 64 Stat. 194 § 2 (1950); 69 Stat. 183 (1955); 72 Stat. 962 § 1 (1958); 84 Stat. 1973–1974 (1971). This last amendment deleted the prohibition on mailing materials or articles relating to the prevention of conception, presumably as a result of *Griswold* v. *Connecticut*, 381 U.S. 479 (1965).

[14] 29 Stat. 512 (1897).

[15] 33 Stat. 705 (1905); 35 Stat. 1138 (1909); 41 Stat. 1060 (1920); 62 Stat. 768 (1948); 64 Stat. 194 (1950); 72 Stat. 962 § 2 (1958); 84 Stat. 1973 (1971). The last amendment deleted contraceptive materials from the purview of the statute.

exists as 18 U.S.C. § 1462. This power has expanded, and by virtue
of 18 U.S.C. § 1465, added in 1955,[16] interstate transportation of
obscene materials for the purpose of sale or distribution is prohibited
by both the criminal sanction and the power to confiscate and destroy
the materials involved. These latter sections have become increasingly
important in recent years. As the flow of sexually oriented materials
has increased, and as motion pictures have become increasingly the
focus of obscenity enforcement efforts, the relative role of the post
office has decreased, and most interstate shipment of sexually oriented
materials is by airplane, bus, or truck, thus resulting in increased use
of 18 U.S.C. § 1462 and 18 U.S.C. § 1465, as well as 19 U.S.C.
§ 1305.[17]

The focus of federal obscenity enforcement has also changed in
recent years. In the 19th century, the focus was on the "hard-core"
materials of the day, while in the first half of the 20th century a
number of federal prosecutions were directed at what are at least
arguably literary works.[18] In the last 15 years, however, the scope of
federal obscenity prosecutions has been limited to sexually explicit
materials, and books and motion pictures merely showing nudity or
dealing with sex have remained outside the scope of federal prosecutorial efforts. In other words, it seems that the focus of federal prosecution has been consistent in tracking the current constitutional
standards. Unlike some of the state cases, there have been few federal
prosecutions in recent years based on material which is not at least
arguably pornographic.

9.2 Use of the Mails—18 U.S.C. § 1461 and 39 U.S.C. §§ 3001-3011

The Comstock Act, 18 U.S.C. § 1461, is the second oldest of
the federal obscenity statutes and has been the basis of the largest

---

[16] 69 Stat. 183 § 3 (1955).

[17] Providing for seizure at customs of obscene material being imported into the
United States. This is the successor to the 1842 statute described in text accompanying note 3 *supra.* The current version derives from 38 Stat. 194 (1913), superseded
by 42 Stat. 937 (1922); and the Tariff Act of 1930 § 305, 46 Stat. 688 (1930), as
amended by 62 Stat. 862 (1948); 84 Stat. 287 (1970), and 84 Stat. 1973 (1971).

[18] *See, e.g. United States* v. *One Book Called "Ulysses,"* 5 F. Supp. 182
(S.D.N.Y. 1933), *aff'd,* 72 F.2d 705 (2d Cir. 1934); *United States* v. *Dennett,* 39
F.2d 564 (2d Cir. 1930); *United States* v. *Two Obscene Books,* 99 F. Supp. 760
(N.D. Cal. 1951), *aff'd sub nom. Besig* v. *United States,* 208 F.2d 142 (9th Cir.
1953) (*Tropic of Cancer* and *Tropic of Capricorn* by Henry Miller); *Grove Press
Inc.* v. *Christenberry,* 175 F. Supp. 488 (S.D.N.Y. 1959), *aff'd,* 276 F.2d 433 (2d
Cir. 1960).

number of obscenity prosecutions of any of them. Its focus is twofold, but only the aspect of obscenity is relevant today. The other aspect concerns materials, articles, literature, and anything else relating to abortion, but it is doubtful whether any of these prohibitions would survive *Roe* v. *Wade* [19] and, especially, *Bigelow* v. *Virginia*.[20] In any event, the statute has rarely been used for this purpose, all of the reported cases being at least 30 years old.[21] The rest of 18 U.S.C. § 1461 remains one of the major vehicles for federal obscenity regulation. The statute declares to be nonmailable matter "every obscene, lewd, lascivious, indecent, filthy or vile article, matter, thing, device, or substance." While the adjectives "lewd, lascivious, indecent, filthy or vile" may have added something [22] prior to the *Roth* [23] decision, it is clear that they are now mere surplusage. The statute reaches to obscenity, as defined by the Supreme Court, and the additional words neither add nor detract from that purpose. Furthermore, obscenity has been judicially construed by the Supreme Court to reach to

> (a) Patently offensive representations or descriptions of ultimate sexual acts, normal or perverted, actual or simulated.
> (b) Patently offensive representations or descriptions of masturbation, excretory functions, and lewd exhibition of genitals.[24]

As so construed, its constitutionality has been affirmed three times by the Supreme Court against challenges based on freedom of speech, the right of privacy, and vagueness.[25]

Having declared obscene matter to be nonmailable, the statute prohibits the mailing, or causing to be mailed, or taking from the mails for the purpose of circulating or disposing of, or aiding in the

---

[19] 410 U.S. 113 (1973).

[20] _____ U.S. _____, 95 S. Ct. 2222 (1975), invalidating a Virginia ban on abortion advertisements. As to advertisements for abortion in particular, 18 U.S.C. § 1461 has been declared invalid. *Associated Students, Univ. of Cal. at Riverside* v. *Attorney General,* 368 F. Supp. 11 (C.D. Cal. 1973) (three-judge court).

[21] *See, e.g., Bours* v. *United States,* 229 F. 960 (7th Cir. 1915); *United States* v. *Kelly,* 26 Fed. Cas. 695 (Case No. 15, 514) (D. Nev. 1876). *See also United States* v. *Nicholas,* 97 F.2d 510 (2d Cir. 1938) (contraceptive articles and publications); *Ackley* v. *United States,* 200 F. 217 (8th Cir. 1912) (same); *Bates* v. *United States,* 10 F. 92 (N.D. Ill. 1881) (same).

[22] *See, e.g., United States* v. *Limehouse,* 285 U.S. 424 (1932); *United States* v. *Clarke,* 38 F. 732 (D. Mo. 1889).

[23] *Roth* v. *United States,* 354 U.S. 476 (1957).

[24] *Hamling* v. *United States,* 418 U.S. 87, 110–116 (1974). *Cf. United States* v. *12 200-Ft. Reels of Film,* 413 U.S. 123, 130 n.7 (1973). The source of the specifics is *Miller* v. *California,* 413 U.S. 15, 25 (1973).

[25] *Hamling* v. *United States,* 418 U.S. 87 (1974); *United States* v. *Reidel,* 402 U.S. 351 (1971); *Roth* v. *United States,* 354 U.S. 476 (1957).

circulation or disposing of any such matter. The penalty is imprisonment for not more than five years or a fine of not more than $5,000,
or both, for the first offense, and a fine of not more than $10,000 and
not more than 10 years imprisonment for every subsequent offense.
In addition, nonmailable matter may be subject to civil sanctions, discussed later in this section.

In recent years, the civil aspects of federal postal power and the
obscenity laws have been of lesser importance, and 18 U.S.C. § 1461
has been enforced primarily as a criminal statute. Since the jurisdictional basis is the use of the mails, no interstate commerce need be
alleged or proved.[26] There is thus no issue as to the jurisdiction of the
federal district courts to try offenses charged under this statute, but
venue has been a more difficult problem. Prior to 1958, the statute
prohibited the *depositing* for mailing or delivery, and thus it had been
held that the offense was complete when the deposit into the mailbox
or at the post office was complete. Therefore, venue was proper only
in the district where the article was mailed, since the Sixth Amendment to the Constitution requires that the prosecution be in the district where the offense was committed and this was not a continuing
offense.[27] As a result, Congress amended the statute to make the
crime that of *use* of the mails to send obscene materials.[28] Since 18
U.S.C. § 3237 specifically designates use of the mails as a continuing
offense, which may therefore be prosecuted "in any district in which
such offense was begun, continued, or completed," it is now clear that
venue is proper in a prosecution under 18 U.S.C. § 1461 in any district in which the matter is mailed, received, or through which the
material passes.[29]

The elements of the offense can be divided into three categories.
First, the obscenity of the materials involved must be proved in
accordance with appropriate constitutional definitions. Second, the
element of scienter must be proved. That is, it must be proved that the
defendant knew the character of the materials involved, although the

[26] *Schindler* v. *United States,* 221 F.2d 743 (9th Cir. 1955), *cert. denied,* 350
U.S. 938 (1956).

[27] *United States* v. *Ross,* 205 F.2d 619 (10th Cir. 1953); *United States* v. *Comerford,* 25 F.902 (D. Tex. 1885).

[28] Pub. L. 85-796, § 1, 72 Stat. 962 (1958).

[29] *Reed Enterprises* v. *Clark,* 278 F. Supp. 372 (D.D.C. 1967) (three-judge
court), *aff'd,* 390 U.S. 457 (1968); *United States* v. *Luros,* 243 F. Supp. 160 (D.
Iowa 1965); *United States* v. *Levy,* 331 F. Supp. 712 (D. Conn. 1971); *United
States* v. *Sidelko,* 248 F. Supp. 813 (E.D.Pa. 1964). *See generally* Note, *Multi-
Venue and the Obscenity Statutes,* 115 U. PA. L. REV. 399 (1967).

defendant need not be shown to have known that the materials were legally obscene.[30]

> It is constitutionally sufficient that the prosecution show that a defendant had knowledge of the contents of the materials he distributed, and that he knew the character and nature of the materials. To require proof of a defendant's knowledge of the legal status of the materials would permit the defendant to avoid prosecution by simply claiming that he had not brushed up on the law. Such a formulation of the scienter requirement is required neither by the language of 18 U.S.C. § 1461 nor by the Constitution.[31]

Thus, proof that the defendant knew that the materials were sexually oriented, that the materials contained depictions or descriptions of sexual contact, is sufficient both to satisfy the constitutional requirement of scienter and the "knowingly" element of 18 U.S.C. § 1461.[32]

Finally, it must be shown that the defendant knowingly used the mails to deliver, or caused to be delivered by mail, or took from the mails for the purpose of circulation or disposition of, or aided in the circulation or disposition of, any obscene matter. The statutory language is considerably more intricate than this, but generally covers any use of the mails, in the broadest sense. This use must also be done "knowingly," but the standard of proof is that of any other criminal case requiring intent for conviction.[33]

It should be noted that, with the exception of the clause relating to *receipt* for the purpose of circulation or disposition, there is no requirement whatsoever in 18 U.S.C. § 1461 that the use of the mails be for any commercial purpose. Therefore, private letters and packages are included within the reach of the statute.[34] However, it is the

---

[30] *Hamling* v. *United States,* 418 U.S. 87, 119–124 (1974); *Rosen* v. *United States,* 161 U.S. 29 (1896); *Manual Enterprises, Inc.* v. *Day,* 370 U.S. 478 (1962); *United States* v. *Sulaiman,* 490 F.2d 78, 79 (5th Cir. 1974), *cert denied,* _____ U.S. _____, 95 S. Ct. 192 (1974); *United States* v. *Millican,* 487 F.2d 331 (5th Cir. 1973); *United States* v. *Gundlach,* 345 F. Supp. 709 (E.D. Pa. 1972). *See generally* Chapter 11.6, *infra.*

[31] *Hamling* v. *United States,* 418 U.S. at 123–124.

[32] *United States* v. *Sulaiman,* 490 F.2d 78, 79 (5th Cir. 1974), *cert. denied,* _____ U.S. _____, 95 S. Ct. 192 (1974).

[33] See *Spillman* v. *United States,* 413 F.2d 527, 531 (9th Cir. 1969), *cert. denied,* 396 U.S. 930.

[34] *See generally* Ludwig, *Private Correspondence Under the Mail Obscenity Law,* 41 DENVER L.C.J. 152 (1964); Note, *Obscenity in Private Communications,* 23 OHIO ST. L.J. 553 (1962); Note, *Private Correspondence and Federal Obscenity Prosecution,* 4 SAN DIEGO L. REV. 76 (1967); Case Note, 1966 UTAH L. REV. 717 (1966).

See Armijo v. *United States,* 384 F.2d 694 (9th Cir. 1967), *cert. denied,* 390 U.S. 974; *Heath* v. *United States,* 375 F.2d 521 (8th Cir. 1967); *United States* v.

policy of the Department of Justice to enforce 18 U.S.C. §1461 as to private letters only in cases of repeated offenders, sex offenders, previous involvement with obscene materials, or some relationship with minors.[35] On the basis of this, the Solicitor General has moved the Supreme Court to vacate a conviction based upon private letters not involving any of these exceptions, as being in violation of Justice Department policy.[36] But it has been held that a defendant may not enforce this policy, and if the Justice Department chooses to prosecute on the basis of private letters, even if there are no "aggravating circumstances," an otherwise valid conviction will be affirmed.[37]

Enforcement of criminal penalties is not the only power which the United States has exercised over obscenity pursuant to its power over the use of the mails in 18 U.S.C. § 1461. The statute also declares obscene matter to be nonmailable and prohibits the carriage in the mails of such matter. The statutory procedures for dealing with such nonmailable matter are set forth in that section of the U.S. Code dealing with the Postal Service, 39 U.S.C. § 3001,[38] which reaffirms that "matter the deposit of which in the mails is punishable under section . . . 1461 . . . of title 18 is non-mailable"[39] and that proceedings concerning the mailability of matter shall be conducted in accordance with the Administrative Procedure Act and the federal statute relating to judicial review of administrative action.[40] The procedures for detaining obscene mail are set forth in 39 U.S.C. §§ 3006 and 3007. However, in *Blount* v. *Rizzi*,[41] the Supreme Court affirmed

---

Chapman, 333 F.2d 969 (4th Cir. 1964); *United States* v. *Darnell,* 316 F.2d 813 (2d Cir. 1963), *cert denied,* 375 U.S. 916; *Ackerman* v. *United States,* 293 F.2d 449 (9th Cir. 1961).

[35] United States Department of Justice Memorandum dated August 31, 1964.

[36] *Redmond* v. *United States,* 384 U.S. 264 (1966) (per curiam). Mr. Justice Stewart, joined by Mr. Justice Black and Mr. Justice Douglas, concurred, saying that the conviction should be reversed "not because it violates the policy of the Department of Justice, but because it violates the Constitution." *Id.* at 265. *See also Cox* v. *United States,* 370 F.2d 563 (9th Cir. 1967).

[37] *Spillman* v. *United States,* 413 F.2d 527 (9th Cir. 1969), *cert. denied,* 396 U.S. 930 (1969). This result might be different if the government's motives in selective prosecution were constitutionally suspect. *See United States* v. *Oaks,* 508 F.2d 1403, 1404 (9th Cir. 1974).

[38] Prior to the Postal Reorganization Act, Pub. L. 91-375, 84 Stat. 719 (1970), this was 39 U.S.C. § 4001.

[39] 39 U.S.C. § 3001(a) (Supp. 1975).

[40] 39 U.S.C. § 3001(f), referring to 5 U.S.C. Chapters 5 and 7.

[41] 400 U.S. 410 (1971), *aff'g* 305 F. Supp. 634 (C.D. Cal. 1969) (three-judge court) and 206 F. Supp. 1023 (N.D. Ga. 1969) (three-judge court). *See* 57 A.B.A.J. 266 (1971).

the rulings of two three-judge federal courts holding both of these sections unconstitutional, since they did not provide sufficient protection against the dangers of prior restraint to meet the standards set forth in *Freedman* v. *Maryland*.[42] Neither of these statutes has been amended to conform with the Supreme Court's opinion in *Blount,* and therefore they are not currently capable of being used. As a result, there is not now any valid procedure for detention of nonmailable matter, and this power is unused.

There are, however, statutes relating to other forms of sexually explicit mail, such as 39 U.S.C. § 3008, which permits the Postal Service to allow an addressee to refuse any mail which he, "in his sole discretion believes to be erotically arousing or sexually provocative."[43] Upon receipt of the appropriate notice,[44] the Postal Service will order the sender to cease sending any more of such material to that particular addressee, and this order of the Postal Service may be enforced by the injunctive power of the federal district courts.[45]

This statute was originally passed in 1967 and is distinctive because it reaches not only the legally obscene but any material the addressee in his own discretion finds objectionable. It is not surprising, therefore, that the constitutionality of the statute was challenged shortly thereafter. In *Rowan* v. *United States Post Office Department,*[46] however, the Supreme Court, in an opinion written by Chief Justice Burger, unanimously upheld the constitutionality of the statute, holding that the sender's right to communicate must be allowed to be limited by the right of an individual to keep material objectionable to him out of his own home. The only burden put on the sender, the Court noted, was the requirement that the objecting addressee receive no more such literature and that his name be removed from

---

[42] 380 U.S. 51 (1965). For a full discussion of this case and the prior-restraint issue generally, *see* Chapter 12 *infra.*

[43] 39 U.S.C § 3008(A) (Supp. 1975).

[44] The procedures for operation of this statute are set forth in 39 C.F.R. § 916.1 et seq. (1975).

[45] As to the enforcement of the injunction, the statute specifically provides for use of the contempt power. 39 U.S.C. § 3009(e). For use of this power, *see United States* v. *Consolidated Productions, Inc.,* 326 F. Supp. 603 (C.D. Cal. 1971); *United States* v. *Lanze,* 466 F.2d 1021 (9th Cir. 1972). On this statute generally (called the Federal Pandering Advertisements Act), *see* Note, *Federal Pandering Advertisements Statute: The Right of Privacy Versus the First Amendment,* 32 Ohio St. L.J. 149 (1971).

[46] 397 U.S. 728 (1970). See Comment, 3 Rutg.-Cam. L.J. 144 (1971); Zellick, *Offensive Advertisements in the Mail,* 1972 Crim. L. Rev. 724 (1972) (parallel developments in England); Comment, 7 Willamette L.J. 330 (1971); Comment, 5 Suff. U.L. Rev. 302 (1970); Comment, 22 Baylor L. Rev. 442 (1970); *The Supreme Court, 1969 Term,* 84 Harv. L. Rev. 1, 177 (1970).

any mailing lists. This, said the Court, was only a minimal burden and the statute was also both specific and protected by ample procedural safeguards, so there was little risk that the sender could "accidentally" be held in contempt.

A somewhat related pair of statutes are 39 U.S.C. §§ 3010 and 3011. Section 3010 deals with the same problem of unsolicited mail as 39 U.S.C. § 3008, but in a more general way. It provides that any mailing of a sexually oriented advertisement must be so marked on the outside by the sender and, furthermore, that anyone not wishing to receive such advertising may have his name put on a list, available to senders. No one may send a sexually oriented advertisement to a person on the list after the name has been on the list for more than 30 days. Section 3011 provides for judicial enforcement of section 3010. The constitutionality of the statute has not been determined by the Supreme Court, but has been affirmed by two three-judge courts on the authority of *Rowan*.[47] In light of the similarity in operation and purpose of this statute to the one at issue in *Rowan,* it is unlikely any constitutional challenge in the Supreme Court would be successful.

As to the exact method of operation of this regulatory system, the Postal Service has adopted fairly comprehensive regulations.[48] They provide that the notice as to the character of the material may appear either on the outside of the envelope or on the outside of an interior envelope.[49] Thus, the purpose is to allow the recipient some advance notice before he actually sees the sexually oriented materials. As to those members of the public who wish to receive no such material, their names are placed on a master list which is available to any mailer of such materials at the allocated cost of preparing the list, not to exceed $10,000 per year. Five thousand dollars must be paid in advance, with any excess refunded when the allocated cost is computed.[50] If a mailer sends material of the kind dealt with in the statute only to people who have requested it, he need not obtain the list.[51] But if a sender is mailing his material on an unsolicited basis,

---

[47] *Pent-R-Books, Inc.* v. *United States Postal Service,* 328 F. Supp. 297 (S.D.N.Y. 1971) (three-judge court); *Universal Specialties, Inc.* v. *Blount,* 331 F. Supp. 52 (C.D. Cal. 1971) (three-judge court). *See* Day, *Mailing Lists and Pornography,* 52 A.B.A.J. 1103 (1966).

[48] 39 C.F.R. § 124.9 (1974). As to the validity of the regulations, see the cases cited in the previous footnote.

[49] 39 C.F.R. § 124.9 (e).

[50] 39 C.F.R. § 124.9 (d). As to the validity of this charge, see the cases cited in note 47.

[51] 39 C.F.R. § 124.9 (f).

he must purchase the list and ensure that he does not mail sexually oriented advertisements to anyone on the list.

9.2.1 Problems of Proof Under 18 U.S.C. § 1461

Due to the relatively impersonal nature of the mails, counsel at a criminal trial under 18 U.S.C. § 1461, both for the government and for the defense, must pay particular attention to the proof, or lack thereof, of the elements of the offense other than obscenity vel non of the material involved. Criminal prosecutions under the obscenity laws are still criminal prosecutions and this fact should not be ignored. Prosecuting attorneys must still prove *every* element of the offense, and defense attorneys must be aware of this fact. If this seems obvious, it is stated because all too often counsel for the prosecution and defense are so concerned with the obscenity issue that they do not pay sufficient attention to the other aspects of the case.

The most common vehicle for investigating cases of obscenity in the mail is the "test buy," where a government official, or other decoy, orders material from the sender being investigated. Although it has been argued that this procedure constitutes entrapment, the argument has been repeatedly rejected.[52] However, where the government "actively promotes the crime," as opposed to merely answering an advertisement or being on a mailing list, there may very well be an issue as to entrapment.[53]

Obviously, the major element of proof, other than obscenity and scienter, will be proving that the defendant used the mails. This does not require that the defendant actually be the one who put the materials into the mailbox,[54] as long as the defendant caused the mails to be used, or set in motion a course of events which could reasonably be expected to require the use of the mails. Furthermore, virtually all indictments will be brought not only under 18 U.S.C. § 1461, but also under 18 U.S.C. § 2, which provides that anyone who "aids,

[52] *Price* v. *United States*, 165 U.S. 311 (1897); *Andrews* v. *United States*, 162 U.S. 420 (1896); *Rosen* v. *United States*, 161 U.S. 29 (1896); *Grimm* v. *United States*, 156 U.S. 604 (1895). See Annotation, *Entrapment to Commit Offense Against Obscenity Laws*, 77 A.L.R. 2d 792 (1961).

[53] As, for example, in *United States* v. *Kros*, 296 F. Supp. 972 (E.D. Pa. 1969), where it was the federal agent who placed the initial advertisement.

[54] *Demolli* v. *United States*, 144 F. 363 (8th Cir. 1906). See *United States* v. *Rubin*, 312 F. Supp. 950 (C.D. Cal. 1970) (interpreting 18 U.S.C. § 1462 as defining "use" to mean exercise of dominion and control).

abets, counsels, commands, induces or procures" the commission of an offense is punishable as a principal,[55] as is one who "willfully causes an act to be done which if directly performed by him or another would be an offense against the United States."[56] Thus, if there is no direct evidence that the defendant actually did the mailing, proof of his involvement in a system necessarily involving the mails will be sufficient.

9.3 Use of a Common Carrier—18 U.S.C. § 1462

As sexually explicit materials have come increasingly to be shipped by truck, bus, or plane, increased use has been made of 18 U.S.C. § 1462, which prohibits not only the importation of obscene material,[57] but also the use of "any express company or other common carrier, for carriage in interstate or foreign commerce" or the taking "from such express company or other common carrier" any "obscene, lewd, lascivious, or filthy book, pamphlet, picture, motion-picture film, paper, letter, writing, print, or other matter of indecent character" or "any obscene, lewd, lascivious, or filthy phonograph recording, electrical transcription, or other article or thing capable of producing sound."[58] Many of the considerations discussed in the section on 18 U.S.C. § 1461 are equally applicable to this statute. Thus, the prohibition can be read to include obscene materials generally, as that term is currently defined. The insertion of the verb "uses" by a 1958 Amendment,[59] in place of "deposits," ensures that this offense is also defined as a continuing offense and may be prosecuted in any district where the material originates, is received, or through which it passes.[60] As with the other major federal obscenity statutes, the constitutionality of 18 U.S.C. § 1462 has been authoritatively established.[61] Since the Supreme Court has specifically defined

---

[55] 18 U.S.C. § 2 (a) (1969).

[56] 18 U.S.C. § 2 (b) (1969).

[57] See Section 9.5 of this chapter, *infra.*

[58] 18 U.S.C. § 1462 (1975 Supp.) There is also a prohibition on materials and articles related to abortion "or any indecent or immoral use." This entire provision is of highly questionable validity and, in any event, is no longer used by federal law enforcement authorities.

[59] Pub. L. 85-796 § 2, 72 Stat. 962 (1958).

[60] *Gold* v. *United States,* 378 F.2d 588 (9th Cir. 1967); *Reed Enterprises* v. *Clark,* 278 F. Supp. 372 (D.D.C. 1967) (three-judge court), *aff'd,* 390 U.S. 457 (1968) (per curiam).

[61] *United States* v. *Orito,* 413 U.S. 139 (1973). *See also United States* v. *B & H Dist. Corp.,* 403 U.S. 927 (1971) and 413 U.S. 909 (1973).

obscenity in 18 U.S.C. § 1462 as including the *Miller* definitions of prohibited depictions or descriptions,[62] challenges on vagueness grounds are no longer available.[63]

The jurisdictional basis of the statute is the use of an instrumentality of interstate commerce—the express company or common carrier—for the purpose of transportation in interstate commerce. Although it will be most often the case that there is evidence that the material actually crossed state lines,[64] this is not strictly necessary, and the deposit with the carrier for purpose of interstate shipment completes the offense even before state lines have been crossed.[65]

The elements of the offense are, of course, the obscenity of the materials, scienter, use of an express company or common carrier and the purpose of sending the material across state lines (or out of the country).[66] There must be proof of knowledge both as to the character of the materials and the method of shipment in order for the statute to be violated. It need not be shown that the defendant actually gave the material to the common carrier or took it from the carrier, but only that he exercised "dominion and control" over the shipment.[67]

The penalties are the same as for prohibition on mailing: a fine of not more than $5,000 or not more than five years imprisonment, or both, for the first offense, with these amounts increased to $10,000 or 10 years for each subsequent offense. There is no requirement that the shipment be for any commercial purpose, but in fact prosecutions under this section have been exclusively limited to commercial distributions.

9.3.1 Problems of Proof Under 18 U.S.C. § 1462

Although use of a common carrier or express company is one of the elements of the offense, these terms are not defined anywhere in

[62] *United States v. 12 200-Ft. Reels of Film*, 413 U.S. 123, 130 n. 7 (1973).

[63] *United States v. Groner*, 494 F.2d 499 (5th Cir. 1974), *cert. denied*, ⸻ U.S. ⸻, 95 S. Ct. 331 (1974); *United States v. Thevis*, 484 F.2d 1149 (5th Cir. 1973), *cert denied*, 418 U.S. 932 (1974); *United States v. B & H Dist. Corp.*, 375 F. Supp. 136 (W.D. Wis. 1974).

[64] *See*, e.g., *United States v. One Carton Containing A Quantity of Paperback Books*, 324 F. Supp. 957, 958 (N.D. Ga. 1971).

[65] *See Gold v. United States*, 378 F.2d 588 (9th Cir. 1967).

[66] The statute also makes unlawful the knowing taking of the material from the common carrier. Presumably, this would require knowledge of the interstate character of the shipment. *See United States v. Melvin*, 419 F.2d 136 (4th Cir. 1969).

[67] *United States v. Rubin*, 312 F. Supp. 950 (C.D. Cal. 1970). *Cf. United States v. Rich*, 407 F.2d 934 (5th Cir. 1969), *cert denied*, 395 U.S. 922. *See also United States v. Miller*, 379 F.2d 483, 485 (7th Cir. 1967) (gambling statute).

the statute. While there are administrative and regulatory provisions of the U.S. Code dealing with common carriers, it seems clear that the purpose of the statute is broader than merely to cover those carriers actually licensed or regulated by federal authority. Rather, the intent is to include, generally, the instrumentalities of interstate commerce. Thus, although a cautious prosecutor may be prepared with a certificate for the carrier in question from the Interstate Commerce Commission, Civil Aeronautics Board, or the like, it is the common-law definition of just what a common carrier is that should control.[68] If there is evidence as to the particular carrier used, there is no reason that the trial judge could not, if appropriate, take judicial notice of the fact that a certain carrier is a common carrier.[69] And proof of use of the carrier will most often come from airbills, waybills, bills of lading and the like.

9.4 *Interstate Transportation—18 U.S.C. § 1465*

Although 18 U.S.C. § 1465 also deals with the interstate transportation of obscene material, it is significantly different from 18 U.S.C. § 1462. It prohibits the knowing "transportation in interstate or foreign commerce for the purpose of sale or distribution" of any obscene material, and provides for a fine of no more than $5,000, or imprisonment of no more than five years, or both.

Although the Supreme Court has never dealt with a case under this statute, it seems clear from cases involving 18 U.S.C. §§ 1461 and 1462 that the Court would interpret the statute as incorporating the descriptions or depictions of sexual conduct found in *Miller*,[70] and therefore affirm its constitutionality against attacks on grounds of vagueness, overbreadth, or restriction of First Amendment rights. The constitutionality of the statute has been specifically upheld by a number of lower courts.[71]

Unlike 18 U.S.C. §§ 1461 and 1462, this statute, on its face, deals only with commercial shipment. If the shipment is not for "the

[68] *See United States* v. *Queen,* 445 F.2d 358 (10th Cir. 1971).

[69] *Gold* v. *United States,* 378 F.2d 588 (9th Cir. 1967) (United Airlines as a common carrier).

[70] *Miller* v. *United States,* 413 U.S. 15, 25 (1973). The cases incorporating these standards into other federal obscenity statutes are discussed in previous sections of this chapter.

[71] *United States* v. *New Orleans Book Mart, Inc.,* 490 F.2d 73(5th Cir. 1974), *cert. denied,* 419 U.S. 801; *United States* v. *Manarite,* 448 F.2d 583 (2d Cir. 1971), *cert. denied,* 404 U.S. 947; *United States* v. *Marks,* 364 F. Supp. 1022, 1026–1027 (E.D. Ky. 1973).

purpose of sale or distribution," then it is outside the coverage of the statute. In recent years, this statute has been used, along with 18 U.S.C. § 1462, to reach the interstate transportation of motion pictures from distributor to exhibitor. It may be argued in these cases that the shipment is for the purpose of exhibition, not sale and not distribution, and that this statute has traditionally been limited in use to magazines, 8-millimeter movies in large quantities, and the like. But it is more reasonable to interpret "sale or distribution" to mean any commercial purpose, and exhibition to the public of a motion picture will most likely be held to be included.

Proving that a transportation is for a particular purpose is of course rather difficult, and the statute makes this proof somewhat easier by providing a rebuttable presumption that

> the transportation as aforesaid of two or more copies of any publication or two or more of any article of the character described above, or a combined total of five such publications or articles are intended for sale or distribution.

The United States Court of Appeals for the Second Circuit has affirmed the validity of this presumption,[72] but there has yet to be any detailed examination of its constitutionality in light of recent decisions dealing with the validity of statutory presumptions in criminal laws.[73] It is not at all clear exactly what standard is now to be used in testing the validity of a constitutional presumption.[74] The validity of the presumption in this case may very well depend on which test is employed. Since it is generally unlikely that a reader (or "user") of pornographic material would have more than one of the same publication or film, the first presumption, relating to two or more of the same publication, is likely sufficient under the "rational connection" test of *Tot* v. *United States*,[75] or the "more likely than not" standard

---

[72] *United States* v. *Manarite,* 448 F.2d 583, 594 (2d Cir. 1971), *cert. denied,* 404 U.S. 947. But the discussion was very brief and the court's holding is confined to "this case where each delivery involved large numbers of magazines and/or films, usually in the thousands." *Id.* As so phrased, this is not so much a ruling on the constitutionality of the presumption as it is a statement that quantities of this size seem circumstantially to prove the purpose of sale or distribution, even absent any statutory presumption.

[73] *Leary* v. *United States,* 395 U.S. 6 (1969); *United States* v. *Gainey,* 380 U.S. 63 (1965). See also *Barnes* v. *United States,* 412 U.S. 837 (1973); *Turner* v. *United States,* 396 U.S. 398 (1970); *United States* v. *Romano,* 382 U.S. 136 (1965).

[74] See *Barnes* v. *United States,* 412 U.S. 837, 843 (1973); *The Supreme Court, 1968 Term,* 83 HARV. L. REV. 7, 103 (1969). *See generally* Comment, *The Constitutionality of Statutory Criminal Presumptions,* 34 U. CHI. L. REV. 141 (1966).

[75] 319 U.S. 463 (1943). See also the authorities cited in the previous two footnotes.

of *Leary* v. *United States*,[76] but probably not if the strictest "reasonable doubt" test is used,[77] since having more than one copy of the same publication for purposes other than sale or distribution is far from implausible. The second half of the presumption, however, presents a somewhat different situation. It is hard to see how possession of five *different* obscene magazines would indicate an intent to sell or distribute, and thus this particular presumption seems invalid regardless of which test is used.[78]

Unlike 18 U.S.C. § 1462, § 1465 does not require the use of a common carrier or express company. But the transportation must be *in* interstate or foreign commerce, and although this might be very broadly construed to include all of the instrumentalities of interstate commerce, there should be proof that the material crossed state lines or left the country.[79] There must, of course, be scienter as to the character of the materials and also intent and knowledge as to the use of interstate commerce.[80]

Finally, the statute authorizes the confiscation and destruction of any such materials found in the possession of or under the control of the defendant at the time of his arrest, but this has been held to authorize seizure and destruction only after a conviction.[81]

9.5 Importation of Obscene Matter—18 U.S.C. § 1462 and 19 U.S.C. § 1305

The current successor to the 1842 customs statute described in the first section of this chapter is 19 U.S.C. § 1305, which was first enacted in substantially its present form as § 305(a) of the Tariff Act of 1930.[82] In essence, the statute is a prohibition on the importation into the United States of any obscene material. It is solely a civil statute, providing for in rem proceedings against the material itself, with the ultimate goal of seizure and destruction of obscene materials

---

[76] 395 U.S. 6 (1969).

[77] *Barnes* v. *United States*, 412 U.S. 837 (1973).

[78] There have not been very many cases under 18 U.S.C. § 1465 where the presumption has been significant. *See, e.g., United States v. Knight*, 395 F.2d 971 (2d Cir. 1968), *cert. denied*, 395 U.S. 930 (1969); *United States v. Russo*, 284 F.2d 539 (2d Cir. 1960).

[79] *See United States v. Wells*, 180 F. Supp. 707 (D. Del. 1959).

[80] *United States v. Astore*, 288 F.2d 26 (5th Cir. 1961), *cert. denied*, 366 U.S. 925 (1962); *United States v. Russo*, 284 F.2d 539 (2d Cir. 1960).

[81] *United States v. 50 Magazines*, 323 F. Supp. 395 (D.R.I. 1971).

[82] 46 Stat. 688 (1930).

appearing at the borders of the United States. The statute also deals with materials "advocating or urging treason or insurrection against the United States, or forcible resistance to any law of the United States, or containing any threat to take the life of or inflict bodily harm upon any person in the United States," or which deal with abortions or lotteries, but none of these prohibitions are within the scope of this book. What we are concerned with here is the prohibition on the importation of "any obscene book, pamphlet, paper, writing, advertisement, circular, print, picture, drawing, or other representation, figure, or image on or of paper or other material, or any cast, instrument, or other article which is obscene or immoral."[83] The statute provides "that the Secretary of the Treasury may, in his discretion, admit the so-called classics or books of recognized and established literary or scientific merit, but may, in his discretion, admit such classics or books only when imported for noncommercial purposes." It is clear that this clause is of limited applicability. In light of *Roth* [84] and *Miller*,[85] it is clear that the classics or books of established literary or scientific merit cannot constitutionally be designated as or held to be obscene and are thus outside of the scope of the statute, whether the Secretary of the Treasury says so or not.[86]

Detention of obscene materials is done by the customs authorities, who then transmit information about the seizure to the appropriate United States Attorney, who institutes judicial proceedings for the determination, in rem, of the obscenity of the materials. Upon a judicial determination of obscenity, the materials are destroyed.

The constitutionality of this statute has twice been affirmed by the Supreme Court. In *United States* v. *Thirty-Seven (37) Photographs*,[87] the Supreme Court upheld the statute's constitutionality in the case of photographs imported for commercial purposes, and in *United States* v. *12 200-Ft. Reels of Film*,[88] the statute was sustained against a challenge by an importer who imported the material in question "for private, personal use and possession only."[89] In both of

---

[83] *See generally* Comment, *Government Seizures of Imported Obscene Matter: Section 305 of the Tariff Act of 1930 and the Recent Supreme Court Obscenity Decisions,* 13 Colum. J. Transnat'l L. 114 (1974).

[84] *Roth* v. *United States,* 354 U.S. 476 (1957).

[85] *Miller* v. *California,* 413 U.S. 15 (1973).

[86] It appears as if materials in these categories may be entitled to a more abbreviated procedure, however. See 19 C.F.R. § 12.41 (g).

[87] 402 U.S. 363 (1971).

[88] 413 U.S. 123 (1973).

[89] *Id.* at 125.

these cases, the challenges that were rejected were based on a broader reading of *Stanley* v. *Georgia* [90] than the Court was willing to accept.

The more serious question raised in *37 Photographs,* however, related to the procedures to be followed pursuant to the statute. The statute clearly authorizes a prior restraint, and thus must conform to the standards of *Freedman* v. *Maryland.*[91] Since a federal statute was involved, the Court felt obliged, in dealing with this challenge, to determine if the statute might be construed in such a way as to avoid constitutional attack. The Court determined that the sole problem with the statute was the absence of any time requirement for the conduct of a judicial determination of obscenity. Therefore, it interpreted the statute as requiring that forfeiture proceedings be commenced within 14 days of the seizure and concluded within 60 days thereafter, unless the claimant is responsible for any additional delay.[92]

Proceedings in the district court are in rem proceedings against the materials,[93] by way of a libel comparable to that in admiralty cases.[94] Although the definition of obscenity is the same as that of other federal statutes,[95] there are some significant procedural distinctions. By the terms of the statute, any party in interest may claim a jury trial. But since the proceeding is civil rather than criminal, obscenity need be proved only by a preponderance of the evidence, rather than beyond a reasonable doubt.[96] The burden of proof of obscenity, however, remains with the government.[97] Naturally, there need not be any scienter evidence.

In the wake of *Miller* v. *California,*[98] and its rejection of the concept of national community standards,[99] additional problems have

[90] 394 U.S. 557 (1969).

[91] 380 U.S. 51 (1965). *See generally* Chapter 12 *infra.*

[92] 402 U.S. at 367–375.

[93] The regulations concerning commencement of proceedings are found at 19 C.F.R. §§ 12.40–12.41.

[94] *United States* v. *One Carton Positive Motion Picture Film,* 247 F. Supp. 450, 453 (S.D.N.Y. 1965), *rev'd on other grounds,* 367 F.2d 889 (1966).

[95] *See United States* v. *12 200-Ft. Reels of Film,* 413 U.S. 123, 130 n.7 (1973).

[96] *United States* v. *One Reel of 35mm Color Motion Picture Film Entitled "Sinderella,"* 369 F. Supp. 1082 (1972), *aff'd,* 491 F.2d 956; *United States* v. *One Carton Positive Motion Picture Film Entitled "Technique of Physical Love,"* 312 F. Supp. 1334 (E.D. La. 1970); *United States* v. *One Carton Positive Motion Picture Film Entitled "491",* 247 F. Supp. 450 (S.D.N.Y. 1965), *rev'd on other grounds,* 367 F.2d 889 (2d Cir. 1966).

[97] *United States* v. *One Book Entitled "The Adventures of Father Silas,"* 249 F. Supp. 911 (S.D.N.Y. 1966).

[98] 413 U.S. 15 (1973).

[99] *Id.* at 30–34. *See generally* Chapter 6 *supra.*

been created in § 1305 litigation. Whether community standards are based on a specific geographical location such as a state,[100] or on the jurors' own perceptions of what the relevant community is,[101] the standards actually employed are geographically related to the place of trial. Therefore, if this concept is applied in customs seizure cases under 19 U.S.C. § 1305, material which is to be imported into the United States will be judged, in most cases, on the contemporary community standards of Boston, New York, New Orleans, San Francisco, or the other major ports of entry, regardless of the intended destination of the material. It has been suggested that in customs cases, for this reason, there is a special justification for retention of the concept of national standards.[102] It is hard, however, to square this with the Supreme Court's unequivocal rejection of national standards on the grounds of unworkability.[103] If the standards of the point of destination are stricter than the standards of the port of entry, there seems little problem, because there can still be a prosecution at the ultimate destination, either under 18 U.S.C. § 1462 or under a state statute. The problem comes with the opposite situation, where material which is shipped from, say, France to Chicago, and which may be fully acceptable by Chicago standards, is seized, found obscene, and destroyed in Boston according to Boston community standards. One possibility might be to try the case in Boston according to Chicago standards, or at least admit evidence of those standards.[104] Another might be to approve a change of venue to Chicago. But as between the local standards of Boston or either of these other two approaches, there seems to be no constitutional bar on any of them. If Congress may prohibit the transportation between two states of materials legal in both of them,[105] then there seems no reason why Congress may not designate as regulatory standards those of the ports of entry in customs cases.

[100] As the lower court so instructed the jury in *Miller.*

[101] *See Hamling* v. *United States,* 418 U.S. 87, 105–106 (1974).

[102] *See* Comment, *supra* note 83, at 131–142. *See also United States* v. *One Reel of Film,* 481 F.2d 206, 210–211 (1st Cir. 1973) (Coffin, C.J., concurring). For applications of local standards, see *United States* v. *Various Articles of Obscene Merchandise, Schedule No. 896,* 363 F. Supp. 165, 167 (S.D.N.Y. 1973); *United States* v. *One Reel of 35mm Color Motion Picture Film Entitled "Sinderella,"* 369 F. Supp. 1082 (E.D.N.Y. 1972), *aff'd,* 491 F.2d 956 (2d Cir. 1974).

[103] *Miller v. California,* 413 U.S. 15, 30 (1973).

[104] The possibility of trying an obscenity case in accordance with the standards of an "external" jurisdiction seems to be implicitly approved in *Hamling* v. *United States,* 418 U.S. 87, 106 (1974).

[105] *Cf. Champion* v. *Ames (Lottery Case),* 188 U.S. 321, 355–363 (1903).

As has been explained, 19 U.S.C. § 1305 is purely a civil statute. However, the importation of obscene materials is included within the criminal prohibitions of 18 U.S.C. § 1462, and under certain circumstances importation by mail may also violate 18 U.S.C. § 1461. Both of these sections have been discussed elsewhere in this chapter. Of course, in a criminal prosecution, the burden of proof of obscenity can no longer be the "preponderance of evidence" standard of § 1305 proceedings, and scienter must always be proved.[106]

9.6 Miscellaneous Federal Statutes

Several additional federal controls on obscenity should be mentioned at this point. One is 18 U.S.C. § 1463, which prohibits the mailing of "indecent matter" on the outsides of envelopes, or postcards, or the external surfaces of mail generally. The prohibition incorporates a $5,000 fine or five years imprisonment, or both, and is worded in substantially the same language as 18 U.S.C. § 1461. The prohibition extends to "any delineations, epithets, terms or language of an indecent, lewd, lascivious, or obscene character." Although it might be argued by some that different standards should apply to this "intrusive" form of objectionable material, the courts have consistently held that this section incorporates only obscenity as legally defined.[107] The statute, however, is sparingly used, and there has been no reported case under it since 1965.[108]

A part of the Internal Revenue Code, 26 U.S.C. § 5723(d) prohibits indecent or immoral pictures, prints, or representations in or on the packages of cigarettes or other tobacco products. There is no indication that this statute has ever been used.

In 47 U.S.C. § 223, enacted in 1968,[109] the making of harassing telephone calls is prohibited, as well as those which include any "comment, request, suggestion, or proposal which is obscene, lewd, lascivious, filthy, or indecent",[110] in interstate or foreign commerce or in the District of Columbia. The penalty is a fine of not more than $500, or imprisonment for not more than six months, or both. It has been suggested that the words uttered must meet the legal definition

---

[106] As to the procedure for commencing a criminal proceeding after customs seizure, see 19 C.F.R. § 12.40(d) (1974).

[107] *See, e.g., United States* v. *Keller,* 259 F.2d 54 (3d Cir. 1958); *United States* v. *Davis,* 353 F.2d 614, 615 (2d Cir. 1965), *cert. denied,* 384 U.S. 953 (1966).

[108] *United States* v. *Davis,* 353 F.2d 614 (2d Cir. 1965), *cert. denied,* 384 U.S. 953 (1966).

[109] 82 Stat. 112 § 1 (1968).

[110] 47 U.S.C. § 223 (1)(A) (1975 Supp.).

of obscenity derived from First Amendment considerations.[111] The intrusive nature of the telephone, however, indicates that this is not really an obscenity statute as such, but is closer to a statute dealing with public profanity and the like, and therefore should be evaluated and applied in accordance with those principles. In other words, at least as used against people who make anonymous phone calls or calls to unwilling listeners, this statute should be evaluated by first looking to *Kovacs* v. *Cooper* [112] rather than to the obscenity cases.

9.7 Obscenity and the Federal Communications Commission

In 18 U.S.C. § 1464, the broadcasting of "any obscene, indecent, or profane language by means of radio communication" is prohibited, and the statute provides for a fine of not more than $10,000, or imprisonment for not more than two years, or both. Its primary use is against those who use obscene language in citizen's band or "ham" radio communications. As a criminal statute, it has been defined to incorporate both the constitutional definition of obscenity [113] and the scienter requirement.[114] As thus limited, in light of the *Miller* requirement that "hard-core" sexual conduct be described, it is a statute of extremely limited application.

Under 47 U.S.C. § 503(b)(1)(B) and 47 U.S.C. § 510, the Federal Communications Commission is implicitly allowed to impose a fine of up to $1000 for various violations, including the use of improper language over the airwaves. This, too, has been restricted to citizen's band radio and is applied on only very rare occasions.

Of greatest significance, however, is the power of the Federal Communications Commission over licensing and license renewals, a power that is considerably stronger than any available criminal sanction against broadcasters. In determining questions relating to licensing, the use of offensive speech by radio or television broadcasters, or the use of "immoral programming," is relevant in the determination of whether the operation of the station is in the public interest. This is not, however, strictly an obscenity issue. Since obscenity, as such, is not speech, and is not protected by the First Amendment, consideration or regulation of legal obscenity by the FCC creates few consti-

---

[111] *United States* v. *Darsey*, 431 F.2d 963, 964 (5th Cir. 1970) (Wisdom, J., concurring).

[112] 336 U.S. 77 (1949) (regulation of sound trucks).

[113] *United States* v. *Gagliardo*, 336 F.2d 720 (9th Cir. 1966).

[114] *United States* v. *Smith*, 467 F.2d 1126 (7th Cir. 1972); *Tallman* v. *United States*, 465 F.2d 282 (7th Cir. 1972).

tutional problems. The issue really relates, however, to the FCC's power over vulgar, profane, or sexually explicit presentations which are not legally obscene. The enabling act for the commission specifically prohibits it from interfering with the right of free speech.[115] But the question is whether the right of free speech is somewhat different in the context of the broadcast media, since those media are both intrusive and of limited access. These considerations mean that the analysis of what can or cannot be permitted on the airwaves is wholly unlike that for determining obscenity in other contexts.[116] The analysis is much more closely related to fairness doctrine considerations than to obscenity law. No further effort to make such an analysis will be undertaken in this book, since to do so would require a thorough study of the entire concept behind broadcasting regulations.

9.8 *Conspiracy Prosecutions Under the Federal Obscenity Laws*

Many prosecutions under 18 U.S.C. §§ 1461, 1462, and 1465 are also brought as conspiracy prosecutions pursuant to 18 U.S.C. § 371, prohibiting conspiracy to commit any offense against the United States. The Supreme Court has never had occasion to deal with the effect of a conspiracy charge on obscenity law.[117] Other cases have made clear that both as to scienter and the substantive standards for proving obscenity, there is no difference between a conspiracy charge under the federal obscenity statutes and an indictment merely charging the substantive offense.[118] In general, the principles of conspiracy law will govern that aspect of the prosecution. The problem that arises, however, concerns the effect of the end of the "national" view of contemporary community standards.[119] If the alleged members of the conspiracy sold, or exhibited, or distributed materials in different areas, but the conspiracy is tried in only one (or none) of those localities, distributors of sexually explicit materials may become

---

[115] 47 U.S.C. § 326 (1962).

[116] *See generally* Note, *Morality and the Broadcast Media: A Constitutional Analysis of FCC Regulatory Standards,* 84 HARV. L. REV. 664 (1971); Note, *Offensive Speech and the FCC,* 79 YALE L.J. 1343 (1970); Note, *X-Rated Motion Pictures: From Restricted Theatres and Drive-Ins to the Television Screen,* 8 VALP. U.L. REV. 107 (1973).

[117] *Hamling* v. *United States,* 418 U.S. 87 (1973), did involve a conspiracy indictment but the effect of this was not a part of the issues before the Court.

[118] *See, e.g., United States* v. *Mishkin,* 317 F.2d 634 (2d Cir. 1963), *cert. denied,* 375 U.S. 827 (1964); *United States* v. *Cappello,* 327 F.2d 378 (2d Cir. 1964); *United States* v. *Russo,* 284 F.2d 539 (2d Cir. 1960).

[119] *See generally* Chapter 6 *supra.*

responsible for standards outside their own area of activity.[120] While it may be true that under traditional conspiracy law a conspirator is responsible for all acts of his co-conspirators within the scope of the conspiracy, the effect of this consideration on an obscenity prosecution may be to generate an overall chilling effect on the distribution of materials which are fully acceptable in certain localities. A possible solution might be to require proof of the community standards in each area of distribution, but this could make for a cumbersome trial. Since the very obscenity of the material at issue, both as a matter of statutory definition and constitutional law, turns on the standards of some locality, it may very well be that the concept of an obscenity conspiracy spanning more than one locality is a definitional impossibility.

---

[120] For a more detailed discussion of this issue, *see* Schauer, *Obscenity and the Conflict of Laws,* 77 W.Va. L. Rev. 377 (1975).

10

State Obscenity Laws

10.1 The Varieties of State Obscenity Legislation

When this book was originally in the planning stages, it was thought that it would be useful to include brief descriptions of the obscenity laws of each of the 50 states, not as an exhaustive analysis, but as a general guide and starting point for attorneys practicing in those states. Such a project, however, underestimated the effect of *Miller* v. *California*[1] on state obscenity laws. First of all, *Miller* added the requirement that state statutes must be specifically drafted, specifying exactly what could or could not be portrayed, in order to survive constitutional attack.[2] Secondly, those state statutes which incorporated the Supreme Court definition of obscenity became obsolete, since the requirement that the material be "utterly without redeeming social value" was rejected and replaced by the standard of lack of "serious literary, artistic, political, or scientific value."[3] The third major change was the shift from the concept of national community standards to local community standards.[4] Since many state statutes had incorporated the concept of national standards, this too rendered many statutes obsolete. Finally, a number of states had eliminated obscenity laws as to adults, or sharply narrowed them, on the assumption that *Stanley* v. *Georgia*[5] had rendered unconstitutional those laws proscribing distribution of obscene materials to consenting adults. As a result of *Paris Adult Theatre I* v. *Slaton*,[6] however, it is now clear that such a reading of *Stanley* was unfounded.[7]

[1] 413 U.S. 15 (1973).
[2] *See generally* Chapter 8.3 *supra.*
[3] *See generally* Chapter 7.2 *supra.*
[4] *See generally* Chapter 6.3 *supra.*
[5] 394 U.S. 557 (1969).
[6] 413 U.S. 15 (1973).
[7] *See generally* Chapter 3.4 *supra.*

Therefore, many states have sought to expand their obscenity laws to include all that is now allowed in the wake of *Paris*.

The result of all of the above is that state obscenity laws are now in a constant state of flux. Many state statutes are clearly unconstitutional, but have yet to be amended to conform to *Miller* and other recent cases. Others appear to be unconstitutional but might be saved by an authoritative limiting construction which has yet to occur. In many states, the statutes have been amended to conform to the *Miller* cases, but in other states the amendment machinery is now in process. A number of state obscenity statutes have been declared unconstitutional by state and federal courts. In some cases, the statutes have been replaced or amended to conform to those cases, but in other cases there remains a void yet to be filled by legislative enactment. And finally, in a number of states there is litigation now pending, or cases now on appeal, challenging the constitutionality of existing statutes. The conclusion must inevitably be that now, over two years after *Miller*, state obscenity laws are so unsettled that any attempt at a catalog of current law would soon be obsolete, and the chances of error so great that reliance on anything said here would be impossible. Therefore, I have chosen to abandon any attempt at such a catalog, and instead merely advise that great caution be used when relying on any current state statute. It is important both to ascertain if the statute's constitutionality has been determined, and to determine whether or not there are any recent or pending amendments to the relevant statute. As an aid to making such an analysis of the current status of any state obscenity statute, the remainder of this section will describe the types of state obscenity laws and the various provisions they may or may not include, so as to enable the attorney to intelligently understand and find all of the relevant portions of the obscenity laws of a given state.

At the outset, mention should be made of the obscenity provisions of the Model Penal Code.[8] The Model Penal Code was cited by the Supreme Court in *Roth* as an exemplar of the then-prevailing definition of obscenity,[9] and a number of states either have adopted its

[8] The Model Penal Code was approved by the American Law Institute on May 24, 1962. The provisions dealing with obscenity may now be found at 10 UNIFORM LAWS ANNOTATED, Model Penal Code § 251.4 (1974), reproduced in Appendix D of this book. For a thorough discussion of the obscenity provisions of the Model Penal Code, see Schwartz, *Morals Offenses and the Model Penal Code*, 63 COLUM. L. REV. 669, 677–681 (1963).

[9] *Roth* v. *United States*, 354 U.S. 476, 487 n. 20 (1957). Mr. Justice Harlan was of the view that the majority opinion was somewhat simplistic in its characteriza-

obscenity provisions in entirety or have at least adopted its definitions of obscenity.[10] The opening section of the Code defines obscenity in a manner that is constitutionally obsolete at the present time, since it contains neither a "literary value" standard [11] nor the specific description of sexual conduct required by *Miller*. The Code then defines obscenity offenses, including sale, delivery, provision, publication, or exhibition of obscene materials, presentation of obscene plays, possession of obscene material for the purpose of sale or commercial distribution, and selling or advertising material, "whether or not obscene, by representing or suggesting that it is obscene." [12] It incorporates a presumption that dissemination or possession in the course of business is done knowingly or recklessly, a presumption that seems inconsistent with the scienter requirements of *Smith* v. *California*.[13] The model statute then provides for affirmative defenses for scientific uses of obscene material [14] and for noncommercial dissemination to personal associates of the disseminator. Finally, the Code specifically allows for the admissibility of a large variety of types of evidence as to prurient interest, value, intent, and so forth. But now it seems as if the obscenity provisions of the Model Penal Code are hopelessly obsolete. While most of the statute can be saved by judicial or legislative modifications and interpretations, this negates much of the purpose of a model act. With but few changes, the provisions of the Model Penal Code on obscenity date to pre-*Roth* days. Now, approximately 20 years later, there has been just too much intervening law to give the Model Penal Code any significant degree of utility.

Most states, at the present time, have a prohibition on obscene material generally. There are a few that control obscenity only as to minors,[15] but the vast majority of states control obscenity when distributed to adults as well. The ways in which the various state statutes accomplish this may vary in minor details or language, but most

---

tion. 354 U.S. at 498–500 (Harlan, J., concurring in *Alberts* v. *California* and dissenting in *Roth*).

[10] *See, e.g.,* GA. CODE Title 21 §2101 (1971); ILL. STAT. Ch. 38 § 11–20(b) (Cum. Supp. 1975).

[11] Evidence of "artistic, literary, scientific, educational or other merits of the material" is admissible, pursuant to § 251.4 (4)(c).

[12] This last offense seems to predict the pandering concept of *Ginzburg* v. *United States,* 383 U.S. 463 (1966). *See generally* Chapter 4.4 *supra*.

[13] 361 U.S. 147 (1959). *See generally* Chapter 11.4 *infra*.

[14] This defense seems to evolve from the case of *United States* v. *31 Photographs,* 156 F.Supp. 350 (S.D.N.Y. 1957). *See* Chapter 4.6 *supra*.

[15] *See, e.g.,* S. DAK. COMP. LAWS ANN. § 22–24–36 (Supp. 1975); W. VA. CODE § 61–8A (Supp. 1975).

statutes prohibit the sale, distribution, dissemination, or publication of obscene materials. Many specifically prohibit the exhibition of obscene films, or the printing or manufacture of obscene books. But regardless of the exact language used, the general intent of all of these statutes is to prohibit any dealing whatsoever with obscene materials. The language of some of these laws is such as to include only commercial distribution of obscene materials, but quite a few include even noncommercial distribution or exhibition. Many of these laws also include the possession of obscene materials for the purpose of sale or distribution. Although prior to 1969 many statutes prohibited any possession of obscene matter, the clear language of *Stanley* v. *Georgia* [16] prohibits making criminal the mere private possession without such intent.[17] Some statutes also prohibit the advertising of obscene materials, but these statutes have rarely been used. While it is true that the advertisement itself might not be obscene, there is no reason why the advertising of illegal matter could not be validly prohibited, assuming that the material advertised were proved to be legally obscene. Any First Amendment objections to the fact that the advertisement itself is not obscene would seem to be unfounded in light of the Supreme Court's holding that advertisement of illegal activity may be prohibited under the commercial speech "exception" to First Amendment doctrines.[18]

Virtually every state statute provides some definition of obscenity. Assuming that there has been the requisite authoritative judicial construction, such a statutory definition would not be absolutely necessary, and those statutes that merely prohibit obscene materials, without further defining that term, are not necessarily invalid.[19] Nonetheless, the great majority of state laws do define obscenity. Virtually all of these provide a definition identical with the Supreme Court's constitutional test for obscenity, containing the exact words of the tests for prurient interest, patent offensiveness, and lack of serious literary, artistic, political, or scientific value. Some statutes, while incorporating such a tripartite definition, still use the "utterly without re-

[16] 394 U.S. 557 (1969).

[17] Although *Stanley* has been substantially held to its facts by more recent cases, this aspect of it still seems valid.

[18] *Pittsburgh Press Co.* v. *Pittsburgh Commission on Human Relations,* 413 U.S. 376 (1973).

[19] The best authority for this proposition is clearly the federal obscenity statutes, which although they do not contain definitions of obscenity, have been deemed to be valid because of authoritative constructions supplied by the Supreme Court. *United States* v. *12 200-Ft Reels,* 413 U.S. 123 (1973); *United States* v. *Orito,* 413 U.S. 139 (1973); *Hamling* v. *United States,* 418 U.S. 87 (1974).

deeming social value" standard of *Memoirs* v. *Massachusetts*[20] instead of the test of lack of serious literary, artistic, political, or scientific value.[21] Although the Supreme Court in *Miller* rejected the latter as a requirement for lack of constitutional protection, there is no reason why a state might not retain this standard in its statute, since it has the result only of prohibiting less than is constitutionally permissible.

In addition to incorporating the basic constitutional definition as a statutory definition, many statutes go even further in defining terms so as to define some or all of the elements of the test for obscenity. Thus, many statutes provide definitions of "appeal to the prurient interest," "patently offensive," and "contemporary community standards." As to the latter, statutes occasionally specify whether the relevant community is to be the state as a whole or some smaller geographical unit, with statewide standards being most common.[22] But the more significant aspect of specificity in state obscenity laws is that imposed by *Miller* v. *California*,[23] requiring that state obscenity laws be limited to materials which depict or describe sexual conduct, and that the "conduct must be specifically defined by the applicable state law, as written or authoritatively construed."[24] This requirement has been the cause of the greatest number of changes in state obscenity laws since *Miller,* and as a result there are now many state obscenity statutes which describe in considerable detail the types of sexual conduct which may not be depicted or described. Some of these follow the examples given in *Miller,*[25] while others use different, and in some cases broader or more explicit, descriptions of the relevant sexual conduct.[26]

In addition to these statutes controlling obscene material when distributed to adults, virtually every state has a statute dealing in particular with the sale, distribution, or exhibition of obscene materials to minors. The origin of all of these statutes is the Supreme Court's decision in *Ginsberg* v. *New York*,[27] which upheld a New York stat-

---

[20] 383 U.S. 413 (1966).

[21] *See, e.g.,* KANS. STAT. ANN. § 21–4301 (2)(a) (1974).

[22] *See, e.g.,* CONN. GEN. STAT. § 53a–193(a)(3) (Supp. 1975); 13 VT. STAT. ANN. § 2801 (6)(B) (Supp. 1975); N. CAR. GEN. STAT. § 14–190.1 (b)(2) (Supp. 1975).

[23] 413 U.S. 15 (1973).

[24] *Id.* at 24. *See generally* Chapter 8.3 *supra.*

[25] *See, e.g.,* 11 DEL. CODE ANN. § 1364(2) (Supp. 1974); N. CAR. GEN. STAT. § 14–190.1 (c)(Supp. 1975).

[26] *E.g.,* IDAHO CODE § 18–4105 (Supp. 1975); LA. REV. STAT. 14:106 (1974). *Cf.* ALAS. STAT. § 11.40.170(4) (1970).

[27] 390 U.S. 629 (1968). *See generally* Chapter 4.5 *supra.*

ute modifying the then-prevailing test for obscenity so as to relate the various aspects of that test to minors as opposed to adults, or the average person.[28] Thus, current statistics dealing with the dissemination of obscene matter to juveniles generally track the standards applicable to adults, but define "obscene for minors" or "harmful to minors" by modifying the prurient-interest, patent-offensiveness, and lack-of-value standards so that these standards are applied in terms of minors rather than adults. As has been discussed previously, statutes of this type are essential if any type of "special" standard for minors is to be used. In the absence of such a statute, obscenity must be determined in light of the "average person," in other words the average adult, even if the material is actually sold or distributed to juveniles.

As to remedies, the predominant method of enforcement is by criminal prosecution, and all of the statutes previously described provide for criminal penalties, either as a misdemeanor or as a felony, for the sale, distribution, or exhibition of obscene materials to adults or minors. While some statutes set the penalty as only a fine, the majority provide for a fine and/or imprisonment, with the maximum prison terms ranging from 30 days to five years. In practice, the most common penalties are fines or short prison terms, with longer terms (more than one year) generally applied only in the cases of repeated offenders who are large commercial vendors of commercial pornography. While some statutes clearly include bookstore employees, or theater ticket takers and projectionists, within the ranges of persons liable, enforcement is generally restricted to those with a significantly greater degree of responsibility and control over the operation.

One of the recurring objections to obscenity laws has been the alleged unfairness of subjecting individuals to criminal penalties in the obscenity area, since the concept of obscenity has proved to be so difficult to define, and perhaps even more difficult to apply in a consistent manner. This concern led to the *Miller* requirement of greater specificity in obscenity statutes, and also led Chief Justice Burger to express strong approval for the concept of civil proceedings prior to any exposure to criminal penalties.

This is not to be read as disapproval of the Georgia civil procedure employed in this case, assuming the use of a constitutionally acceptable standard for determining what is unprotected by the First Amendment. On the contrary, such a procedure provides an exhibitor or purveyor of materials the best possible notice, prior to any crimi-

[28] *Id.*

nal indictments, as to whether the materials are unprotected by the First Amendment and subject to state regulation.[29]

. . .

This procedure would have even more merit if the exhibitor or purveyor could also test the issue of obscenity in a similar civil action, prior to any exposure to criminal penalty.[30]

As a result of this type of concern, many states do now provide some form of declaratory judgment procedure so that the obscenity *vel non* of a book, magazine, or motion picture can be determined prior to actual distribution or prior to the application of criminal sanctions. Some of these statutes provide for proceedings *in rem* directly against the material, and the Massachusetts statute is clearly the most prominent of these because it has been with us for so many years and has been frequently used.[31] Most common is the specific authorization for a traditional declaratory judgment action. Some statutes provide that the procedure may be initiated by the attorney general or prosecuting attorney,[32] some provide that the procedure may be initiated by an owner, seller, distributor, or exhibitor of the material [33], and still others provide that the declaratory judgment may be rendered at the initiation of either the prosecutor or the distributor.[34] In some states, the existence of a civil determination that the material is obscene is a prerequisite to any criminal prosecution.[35] In these states, the criminal penalty is available only against a seller, distributor, or exhibitor who disseminates obscene matter after such a judicial determination of obscenity, and therefore it is not expected that criminal penalties will be frequently imposed in these states. But in most states, the civil determination is not a prerequisite to a criminal action, and it is therefore up to the discretion of the prosecutor whether to proceed civilly or criminally in the first instance.

[29] *Paris Adult Theatre I* v. *Slaton,* 413 U.S. 49, 55 (1973).
[30] *Id.* at 55 n. 4.
[31] MASS. GEN. LAWS Ch. 272 §§ 28C–28G (Supp. 1974). The statute was originally enacted in 1945. There is a statutory right to trial by jury on the obscenity issue at the instance of "any person interested in the dissemination of said book." § 28D.
[32] *See, e.g.,* ARK. STAT. § 41–3566 (Crim. Code Supp. 1976).
[33] *See, e.g.,* 14 ALA. CODE § 374(16d) (Supp. 1973).
[34] *See, e.g.,* MICH. STAT. ANN. § 27A.2938 (1962); NEB. REV. STAT. §§ 28–926.01, 28–926.05 (1964).
[35] *See, e.g.,* MASS. GEN. LAWS Ch. 272 § 28I (Supp. 1974) (civil proceeding only for prosecution relating to books); 13 VT. STAT. ANN. § 2809 (Supp. 1975) (only as to written matter). Under 14 ALA. CODE § 374 (Supp. 1973), advance official warning is required, but not a judicial determination of obscenity.

One of the problems of obscenity enforcement in many areas is that, especially for motion pictures, criminal penalties have little deterrent effect and therefore do little to reduce the availability of obscene materials. The penalties, when imposed, are most often fines, and the length of the trial and appellate process is such that the criminal sanction often loses its deterrence. Therefore, a number of state statutes provide for ways of directly dealing with the obscene material itself, rather than relying solely on the deterrent effect of the criminal sanction. In some states this is done by providing that material found to be obscene may be destroyed after an adjudication of obscenity,[36] but this too seems of limited effectiveness. More common are statutes providing for injunctions against the showing of particular motion pictures, or the sale of particular publications,[37] after the obscenity of the materials has been adjudicated in an adversary proceeding. Most of these statutes are jurisdictional as well as substantive, in order to anticipate the objection that equitable remedies may not ordinarily be used to enjoin the commission of a criminal act.[38] Also, several states provide by statute that obscene performances, or places where obscene materials are available, are nuisances, and that therefore a public or private action to abate or enjoin such a nuisance may be maintained.[39] The legal issues, including constitutional restrictions, which relate to these various civil remedies are discussed in more detail in Chapter 12 of this book.

Thus far, this section has dealt with state obscenity statutes. But more localized enforcement is also possible, in terms of local ordinances, local licensing provisions, and the like. Many of the recently enacted or recently amended state obscenity statutes deal particularly with this issue. Thus, some states specifically allow cities, towns, and counties to enact their own ordinances regarding obscenity.[40] But a greater number have specifically prohibited any local control,[41] presumably on the theory that a large number of different local ordinances and enforcement policies would make it impossible for any seller or distributor to be aware of them all, thus leading to an inevi-

---

[36] *E.g.*, IDAHO CODE § 18–4112 (Supp. 1975); NEB. REV. STAT. §§ 28–925, 28–926.03 (1964).

[37] *E.g.*, COLO. REV. STAT. Sec. 40–9–21 (1963); FLA. STAT. ANN. ch. 847.001 (8) (Supp. 1975).

[38] *See* DE FUNIAK, HANDBOOK OF MODERN EQUITY §§ 39, 42 (1956).

[39] *E.g.*, DEL. CODE ANN. Title 10 §§ 7201–7210 (Supp. 1975).

[40] *E.g.*, LA. REV. STAT. 14:106 (E) (1974); UTAH CODE ANN. § 76–10–1210 (Supp. 1975).

[41] *E.g.*, 13 VT. STAT. ANN. § 2808 (Supp. 1975); FLA. STAT. ANN. Ch. 847.09 (1) (Supp. 1975); IOWA CODE ANN. §725.9 (Supp. 1975).

table chilling effect on the availability of constitutionally protected material.

10.2   State Obscenity Laws and Live Performances

In addition to laws against books, magazines, and motion pictures, most states have statutes prohibiting obscene plays, productions, or other live performances. In addition, there are laws against obscene conduct in most states. Since it is conduct that is at issue here, rather than pure expression, there is some question as to what standards must be used in determining both the constitutionality and the application of such statutes. Such live performances have traditionally received a lesser degree of First Amendment protection than written or pictorial "speech." The Supreme Court alluded to this issue in *Miller* v. *California*,[42] although such live performances were not at issue in the case.

> Although we are not presented here with the problem of regulating lewd public conduct itself, the States have greater power to regulate nonverbal, physical conduct than to suppress depictions or descriptions of the same behavior. In *United States* v. *O'Brien*, 391 U.S. 367,377 (1968), a case not dealing with obscenity, the Court held a State regulation of conduct which itself embodied both speech and nonspeech elements to be "sufficiently justified if . . . it furthers an important or substantial governmental interest; if the governmental interest is unrelated to the suppression of free expression; and if the incidental restriction on alleged First Amendment freedoms is no greater than is essential to the furtherance of that interest. See *California* v. *LaRue,* 409 U.S. 109, 117–118 (1972).[43]

Thus the Court indicated the limitations of the *Miller* ruling as to the constitutionally required standards for the determination of obscenity. Perhaps fearful that the First Amendment considerations in *Miller* would be applied to indecent exposure and public lewdness statutes, the Court clearly indicated that there were limits to the application of *Miller.* But while it is clear that *Miller* has no application to indecent exposure and the like, the live play, or dance, creates a more difficult problem. The Court's reference to *California* v. *La Rue* [44] in-

[42] 413 U.S. 15 (1973).
[43] *Id.* at 26 n. 8.
[44] 409 U.S. 109 (1972). At issue was California's power to suspend liquor licenses as a result of "bottomless" dancing in bars and nightclubs. *See* Comment, *Demon Rum and the Dirty Dance: Reconsidering Government Regulation of Live Sex Entertainment After California v. La Rue,* 1975 Wis. L. Rev. 161 (1975); Comment, 1 Pepperdine L. Rev. 116, 129 (1973); Comment, 17 U. Miami L.

dicates that the principles of this latter case extend beyond the limited context of liquor licensing and the special Twenty-First Amendment considerations related thereto.

> But as the mode of expression moves from the printed page to the commission of public acts that may themselves violate valid penal statutes, the scope of permissible state regulations significantly increases. States may sometimes proscribe expression that is directed to the accomplishment of an end that the State has declared to be illegal when such expression consists, in part, of 'conduct' or 'action.' [45]

But the Court also made it clear that live performances are not devoid of First Amendment protection, agreeing that "at least some of the performances to which these regulations address themselves are within the limits of the constitutional protection of freedom of expression." [46] This position was reaffirmed more recently in *Southeastern Promotions, Ltd.* v. *Conrad,*[47] where the issue was the denial of permission to use municipal facilities for a production of the rock musical *Hair*. Although the case was decided on "prior restraint" grounds, the Court suggested that the obscenity cases provide the starting point for the inquiry as to ultimate First Amendment protection.[48]

> Only if we were to conclude that live drama was unprotected by the First Amendment—or subject to a totally different standard than that applied to other forms of expression—could we possibly find no prior restraint here. Each medium of expression, of course, must be assessed for First Amendment purposes by standards suited to it, for each may present its own problems. . . . By its nature, theater usually is the acting out—or singing out—of the written word, and frequently mixes speech with live action or conduct. But that is no reason to hold theater to a drastically different standard.[49]

Thus the Court has strongly indicated that a different standard is to be applied to live performances, and that the standard may vary

---

REV. 509 (1973); Comment, 12 DUQ. L. REV. 1008 (1974); Comment, *The First Amendment Onstage,* 53 BOSTON UNIV. L. REV. 1121 (1973); Comment, 61 GEO. L.J. 1577 (1973); *The Supreme Court, 1972 Term,* 87 HARV. L. REV. 1, 133 (1973); Note, *California v. La Rue: The Supreme Court's View of Wine, Women, and the First Amendment,* 68 NW. L. REV. 130 (1973); Comment, 24 SYR. L. REV. 1131 (1973).

[45] 409 U.S. at 117.
[46] *Id.* at 118.
[47] 420 U.S. 546, 95 S.Ct. 1239 (1975).
[48] 95 S.Ct. at 1248. The lower courts had treated the performance as pure conduct, without any First Amendment protection. 95 S.Ct. at 1243.
[49] 95 S.Ct. at 1246.

with the type of performance, but exactly what the standard is to be, or what considerations are relevant in determining how the obscenity standard is to be "adjusted," remains to be seen.[50] Some lower courts have applied strict obscenity standards, requiring that all of the elements of the *Miller* test must be satisfied before live performances may be regulated.[51] In light of the *Miller* footnote, *La Rue,* and *Conrad,* this strict standard is clearly unwarranted. On the other hand, to say simply that because live conduct is involved, there are no First Amendment considerations, is equally unjustified.[52]

It appears as if the initial inquiry must be as to whether or not the particular activity at issue has a significant speech component. It is true that obscenity law involves major First Amendment considerations, and it is also true that obscenity law involves issues as to sexual conduct. But it is spurious logic to say, therefore, that all laws as to sexual conduct involve First Amendment considerations. Unless there is some aspect of speech, then the state's power to regulate is not subject to First Amendment factors. Therefore, issues involving massage parlors and the regulation thereof are not speech cases, and should not be so analyzed.[53] But as to the less obvious situations, there seems little possibility of avoiding a case-by-case determination of whether

[50] *See generally* Comment, 4 SETON HALL L. REV. 379 (1972).

[51] This was the position of the lower court in *La Rue. La Rue* v. *California,* 326 F. Supp. 348 (C.D.Cal. 1972). *See also Wood* v. *Moore,* 350 F.Supp. 29 (W.D.N.C. 1972) (topless dancing); *Haines* v. *State,* 512 P.2d 820 (Okla. Crim. 1973); *In re Giannini,* 69 Cal.2d 563, 72 Cal. Rptr. 655,446 P.2d 535 (1968), overruled by *Crownover* v. *Musick,* 9 Cal. 3d 405, 107 Cal. Rptr. 681, 509 P.2d 497 (1973), *cert. denied,* 415 U.S. 931 (1974); *Jones* v. *City of Birmingham,* 45 Ala. App. 86, 224 So.2d 922 (1969), *cert. denied,* 396 U.S. 1011 (1970); *Hudson* v. *United States,* 234 A.2d 903 (D.C.App. 1967); *People* v. *Conrad,* 70 Misc. 2d 408, 334 N.Y.S.2d 180 (1972); *City of Seattle* v. *Marshall,* 83 Wash.2d 665, 521 P.2d 693 (1974), *cert. denied,* 419 U.S. 1023; *Wood* v. *Moore,* 350 F.Supp. 29 (W.D.N.C. 1972).

[52] This was the position of the lower court in *Conrad. Southeastern Promotions Ltd.* v. *Conrad,* 486 F.2d 894 (6th Cir. 1973). *See also Raphael* v. *Hogan,* 305 F.Supp. 749 (S.D.N.Y. 1969).

[53] There have been many recent cases in this area, but virtually all have been decided on vagueness or equal protection grounds. *See, e.g., Lancaster* v. *Municipal Court for Beverly Hills,* 6 Cal. 3d 805, 100 Cal. Rptr. 609, 494 P.2d 681 (1972); *Smith* v. *Keator,* 21 N.C. App. 102, 203 S.E.2d 411 (1968); *Kisley* v. *City of Falls Church,* 212 Va. 693, 187 S.E.2d 168 (1972), *app. dism.,* 409 U.S. 907; *J.S.K. Enterprises* v. *City of Lacey,* 6 Wash. App. 43, 492 P.2d 600 (1971), *on rehearing,* 6 Wash. App. 433, 493 P.2d 1015 (1972); *Ciancolo* v. *Members of City Council, Knoxville, Tenn.,* 376 F.Supp. 719 (E.D. Tenn. 1974); *Joseph* v. *House,* 353 F.Supp. 367 (E.D.Va. 1973), *aff'd sub nom. Joseph* v. *Blair,* 482 F.2d 575 (4th Cir. 1973); *Valley Health Systems, Inc.* v. *City of Racine,* 369 F.Supp. 97 (E.D. Wis. 1973); *Colorado Springs Amusements, Ltd.* v. *Rizzo,* 387 F.Supp. 690 (E.D. Pa. 1974).

or not the particular activity has sufficient speech components to call into play a First Amendment analysis, or whether the activity is so clearly conduct as to be outside the ambit of First Amendment protection. For example, there have been many cases involving topless and bottomless waitresses or nude dancing. It is clear, of course, that some forms of dance, such as the ballet, must be protected by the First Amendment.[54] And any form of dance or exhibition presents a harder problem than the massage parlor, since the display is by its nature visual and, in a sense, communicative. It is at this point that the court must analyze whether the activity is primarily conduct or primarily speech.[55] This inquiry, although not based on the *Roth-Miller* test for obscenity, may involve many similar elements, such as communicative intent as opposed to appeal to the prurient interest, literary or artistic value, and the like. If it is determined that the activity has so few communicative elements as to be primarily conduct, then a state regulation of that conduct is valid as long as any incidental restriction on the speech elements is by the "least restrictive alternative." [56] But if it is determined that the activity is not primarily conduct, then First Amendment considerations must be taken into account. If the activity is theater, or something very close to theater, then it is clear that the speech elements predominate over the conduct elements.[57] In a case involving theater, the Supreme Court in *Conrad* has indicated that the appropriate standard should not be "drastically different" from that applied in obscenity cases involving books or motion pictures.[58] The appropriate standard should be the *Miller* obscen-

---

[54] *Paladino* v. *City of Omaha*, 335 F.Supp. 897, 898 (D. Neb. 1972), *aff'd*, 471 F.2d 812 (8th Cir. 1972). *Cf. Wood* v. *Moore*, 350 F.Supp. 29, 31 (W.D. N.C. 1972); *Haines* v. *State*, 512 P.2d 820 (Okla. Crim. 1973).

[55] *Paladino* v. *City of Omaha*, 335 F.Supp. 897, 898 (D. Neb. 1972), *aff'd*, 471 F.2d 812 (8th Cir. 1972); *Hoffman* v. *Carson*, 250 So.2d 891 (Fla. 1971); *Major Liquors, Inc.* v. *City of Omaha*, 188 Neb. 628, 198 N.W.2d 483, 488 (1972); *State* v. *Ray*, 292 Minn. 104, 193 N.W.2d 315, 317 (1971); *Jones* v. *City of Birmingham*, 45 Ala. App. 86, 224 So.2d 922 (1969), *cert. denied*, 396 U.S. 1011 (1970); *City of Portland* v. *Derrington*, 253 Ore. 289, 451 P.2d 111 (1969), *cert. denied*, 396 U.S. 901; *Wayside Restaurant* v. *City of Virginia Beach*, 215 Va. 231, 208 S.E.2d 51 (1974).

[56] The relevant mode of analysis where it is determined that the activity is conduct is that of *United States* v. *O'Brien*, 391 U.S. 367 (1968).

[57] *See, e.g., Southeastern Promotions, Ltd.* v. *Conrad*, 420 U.S. 546, 95 S.Ct. 1239, 1246 (1975); *Southeastern Promotions, Ltd.* v. *City of Mobile, Ala.*, 457 F.2d 340 (5th Cir. 1972); *Southeastern Promotions, Ltd.* v. *City of West Palm Beach*, 457 F.2d 1016 (5th Cir. 1972); *Southeastern Promotions, Ltd.* v. *City of Atlanta*, 334 F.Supp. 634, 638 (N.D. Ga. 1971); Comment, 4 SETON HALL LAW REV. 379, 386 (1972). *Contra, Raphael* v. *Hogan*, 305 F.Supp. 749 (S.D.N.Y. 1969).

[58] 95 S.Ct. at 1246.

ity standard, with the modification that the trier of fact may take into account, in determining appeal to the prurient interest and patent offensiveness, the fact that the performance is live. This conforms to the Court's view that live conduct may receive a somewhat lower degree of protection,[59] while recognizing the same type of First Amendment considerations, embodied in *Miller,* that make it important to ensure that nonobscene performances are not proscribed. This approach also recognizes the practical reality that live conduct may have a very different effect on the viewer than depictions or descriptions of the same conduct.

If the initial determination is that the activity has or may have substantial speech elements, then the determination may also turn on whether or not the state's control over liquor and its licensing is at issue, in accordance with *California* v. *La Rue.*[60] If this is the case, then the relevant inquiry is whether or not the activity is the kind of "gross sexuality" which the state may validly regulate under *La Rue.*[61] The analysis in *Clark* v. *City of Fremont, Neb.*[62] is instructive.

> Topless dancing per se and body painting do not fall within the gross sexual entertainment subject to unrestricted regulation under *La Rue.* Thus, if the City of Fremont desires to proscribe performances where the human female breast is uncovered, such as topless dancing or body painting, it must, prior to revocation of the license for an alleged violation of the ordinance by reason of the performance, provide for prompt judicial review. First, the question of whether the performance depicts sexual conduct must be decided. If it is determined that the performance depicts sexual conduct, then, in view of the state's broad power over liquor establishments, the judicial fact finder must first determine whether the performance sought to be proscribed, considered in its entirety and in light of its effect on the patrons of the licensed premises, constitutes gross sexuality and thus falls within the permissible limits of regulation as set forth in *La Rue.* If the judicial fact finder determines that the performance does not constitute gross sexuality, the performance must be considered in light of First Amendment obscenity standards recently adopted in *Miller.*[63]

[59] *Miller* v. *California,* 413 U.S. 15, 26 n. 8 (1973); *Maita* v. *Whitmore,* 365 F.Supp. 1331,1336 (N.D.Cal. 1973), *rev'd on other grounds,* 508 F.2d 143 (9th Cir. 1974).

[60] 409 U.S. 109 (1972).

[61] *See, e.g., Escheat, Inc.* v. *Pierstorff,* 354 F.Supp. 1120, 1123 (W.D. Wis. 1973); *Clark* v. *City of Fremont, Neb.,* 377 F.Supp. 327 (D. Neb. 1974); *Wayside Restaurant* v. *City of Virginia Beach,* 215 Va. 231, 208 S.E.2d 51 (1974). *Cf. Salem* v. *Liquor Control Commission,* 34 Ohio St.2d 213, 63 Ohio Op.2d 357, 298 N.E.2d 138 (1973).

[62] 377 F.Supp. 327 (D.Neb. 1974).

[63] *Id.* at 342.

If the activity does not come within *La Rue,* either because no liquor control is involved, or because the activity cannot be characterized as gross sexuality, then the *Miller* standards, as modified to pertain to live conduct, should determine the issue of whether regulation is permitted.

To summarize the issues pertaining to live performances, the first question must be whether the activity is primarily speech or primarily conduct.[64] If it is primarily conduct, then it may be regulated in the same manner as other conduct which the state has a valid interest in proscribing. If it is primarily speech, that is, if it has substantial communicative aspects, then it is possible that the activity may be regulated pursuant to *California* v. *La Rue* if it is in connection with liquor control. If this is the case, then the test for obscenity is either not used, or is relaxed, with any exhibition of "gross sexuality" being within the state's power of control. If this exception does not apply, then live performances which are primarily speech are to be evaluated in accordance with the *Miller* standards for determining obscenity, and only if the *Miller* tests are met may the performance be prohibited. But in applying the *Miller* test, the trier of fact may make appropriate adjustments, in determining appeal to the prurient interest and patent offensiveness, for the fact that actual live conduct, as opposed to depiction or description, is involved.

---

[64] The presentation of the performance to the trier of fact may present evidentiary problems. However, since no writing is involved, there could be no "best evidence" objection to a description of the performance.

11

Procedural Aspects of
Obscenity Regulation

11.1 The Adversary Hearing—From Quantity of Books to Heller

In the preceding chapters of this book, much emphasis has been placed on the development of a test for the determination of which material is obscene and which is not. The reason for the care courts have given to the development of this test is, of course, that speech which is not obscene is protected by the First Amendment. It is therefore especially important that obscenity regulation be constrained so as to include within its scope only that which is outside the range of First Amendment protection.

For the same reason, the courts have been especially careful to ensure that the determination of obscenity is surrounded by adequate procedural safeguards. The most precise test imaginable is of little use if there is no assurance that the test will be fairly applied, and that the test will be applied in every instance where suppression of constitutionally protected material is possible. Therefore, the courts have imposed the idea of the adversary hearing over all of obscenity law in an effort to ensure that no actual suppression of speech occurs until after it has been fully determined that the speech to be suppressed is in fact not protected by the First Amendment.

The Supreme Court has consistently held that procedures that may in general meet due process requirements can still be defective where their effect is to suppress some form of utterance without a procedure designed to determine fully whether those utterances may constitutionally be suppressed.[1] This concern was first expressed in reference

[1] See, e.g., Carroll v. President and Commissioner of Princess Anne, 393 U.S.

to the obscenity laws in *Kingsley Books, Inc.* v. *Brown,*[2] decided by the Supreme Court on the same day as it handed down its decision in *Roth.*[3] *Kingsley Books* concerned the validity of New York's injunctive remedy against obscene publications, allowing an injunction against the sale or distribution of obscene material, as well as seizure of the material. The Supreme Court upheld the procedure against an allegation that it authorized a prior restraint,[4] but the decision was based in large part on the existence of fairly extensive procedural safeguards, ensuring a full hearing on the issue of obscenity promptly after the proceedings were initiated.[5]

The concept of special procedural protection in the obscenity area was more fully developed in 1961, when the Supreme Court decided *Marcus* v. *Search Warrant.*[6] Missouri at the time had a separate statutory scheme for the search and seizure of obscene publications, resulting in destruction "by burning or otherwise" if the publications were found by a court to be obscene. Upon receipt of a sworn complaint, a judge or magistrate could issue a warrant against any obscene material without notice to the owner of the property. The proceeding was wholly *ex parte*. Final destruction could only obtain after a hearing, but, unlike the statute in *Kingsley Books,* there was no time limit during which the court had to announce its decision. In the case that came up before the Supreme Court, the warrant covered any obscene publications on the premises named in the warrant and resulted in a massive seizure, *ex parte,* of approximately 11,000 copies of 280 different publications. The determination as to which magazines were seized was solely in the hands of the police officers executing the warrant. The case came to the Supreme Court on a review of a denial of a motion to quash the warrant, and, in an opinion written by Mr. Justice Brennan, the Court

---

175 (1968) (invalidating *ex parte* restraining order against conduct of rallies or meetings by National States Rights Party).

[2] 354 U.S. 436 (1957). *See* Note, *Constitutionality of Enjoining Publication of Obscene Literature,* 6 J. Pub. L. 548 (1957); *The Supreme Court, 1956 Term,* 71 Harv. L. Rev. 83, 148 (1957); Comments, 43 A.B.A.J. 932 (1957); 7 Am. U. L. Rev. 41 (1958); 42 Cornell L.Q. 256 (1957); 41 Minn. L. Rev. 222 (1956); 8 Syr. L. Rev. 106 (1956); 11 Okla. L. Rev. 435 (1958). *See* Chapter 12.3 *infra.*

[3] *Roth* v. *United States,* 354 U.S. 476 (1957).

[4] *See generally* Chapter 12.1 infra.

[5] There was no jury trial, however, which caused Mr. Justice Brennan to dissent from the opinion of the Court, written by Mr. Justice Frankfurter. 354 U.S. at 447 (Brennan, J., dissenting).

[6] 367 U.S. 717 (1961). *See* Comments, 26 Mo. L. Rev. 501 (1961); 48 A.B.A.J. 80 (1962); *The Supreme Court, 1960 Term,* 75 Harv. L. Rev. 40, 141 (1961); Note, *Non-Criminal Obscenity Regulation and Freedom of Expression,* 1962 Wash. U. L. Q. 474 (1962).

held the procedure to be unconstitutional. Relying in part on the Court's recent decision in *Smith* v. *California*,[7] the opinion made it clear that procedures that might be acceptable in dealing with other types of contraband were not appropriate in the obscenity area because of the special danger of infringing upon constitutionally protected speech. "It follows that, under the Fourteenth Amendment, a State is not free to adopt whatever procedures it pleases for dealing with obscenity as here involved without regard to the possible consequences for constitutionally protected speech." [8] Thus, a state's procedure must contain the "safeguards which due process demands to assure non-obscene material the constitutional protection to which it is entitled." [9]

The Court found a number of defects in the Missouri procedure. The warrants were issued, not on the basis of any detailed presentation to the judge, but "on the strength of the conclusory assertions of a single police officer." [10] Furthermore, there was no "scrutiny by the judge of any materials considered by the complainant to be obscene." [11] The determination as to which magazines to seize was made by the police officers themselves. But, most significantly, there was no adversary proceeding prior to the imposition of "extensive restraints." While there was an eventual hearing, there was a period of over two months while the effects of this massive seizure remained in force without any judicial hearing as to whether or not the materials were actually obscene. Thus, what emerges from the case is that *before* a seizure of this type, there must be a step in the procedure "designed to focus searchingly on the question of obscenity," [12] that is, a full adversary hearing on the obscenity issue.

In 1964, the Supreme Court again dealt with the issue of the massive seizure of allegedly obscene materials. The case was *A Quantity of Books* v. *Kansas*,[13] which dealt with a seizure statute similar to the Missouri statute in *Marcus*. The seizure in *Quantity of Books* involved 1715 copies of 31 different "novels." Although the statute authorized procedures very similar to those employed in *Marcus*, the proceedings

---

[7] 361 U.S. 147 (1959). *See* section 4 of this chapter, *infra*, for a full discussion of this case.

[8] 367 U.S. at 731.

[9] *Id.*

[10] *Id.* at 731-732.

[11] *Id.*

[12] *Id.* at 732.

[13] 378 U.S. 205 (1964). *See* Note, *Blueprint for Censorship of Obscene Material: Standards for Procedural Due Process*, 11 VILL. L. REV. 125 (1965); Comment, 51 A.B.A.J. 174 (1965); *The Supreme Court, 1963 Term*, 78 HARV. L. REV. 143, 207 (1964).

in this case, which were commenced by the Attorney General of Kansas, did not begin until shortly after the *Marcus* decision. In an effort to comply with that decision, the prosecution filed seven of the books alleged to be obscene and, in a 45-minute *ex parte* inquiry, the judge examined the seven books and held that they appeared to be obscene. But this too was constitutionally insufficient, the Supreme Court said in an opinion written by Mr. Justice Brennan. Since the seizure was of *all* copies of the books in question, and since no adversary hearing preceded that seizure, the entire proceedings were invalid and the ultimate finding of obscenity was overturned.[14] Thus, it is clear that a seizure, prior to an adversary hearing, of a "massive" number of the same publication is constitutionally deficient. But the Court did not decide what was required if the seizure was not "massive," or did not include all available copies of the same publication. This one issue remained open for nine years, during which there was extensive lower court litigation about the scope of the adversary hearing requirement.[15]

The real question was the effect of *Marcus* and *Quantity of Books* on the seizure of one copy of allegedly obscene materials for use as evidence in a criminal trial. This is to be distinguished from the Missouri and Kansas procedures which did not relate to criminal proceedings at all, but which had as their ultimate goal the destruction of all copies of material found to be obscene. The seizure of one copy for use as evidence has in general arisen only in connection with motion pictures. With books or magazines, an undercover officer can purchase a copy from the suspected seller, but an officer cannot purchase the suspected film from the theater where it is being shown. Thus, it becomes necessary for criminal proceedings relating to obscene motion pictures to be commenced by a seizure of at least one print of the film in question.

This was the procedure that had been followed in *Lee Art Theatre*

[14] The Court made it clear that its holding was based solely on First Amendment (as applied to the states by the Fourteenth Amendment) considerations and not in any way on the search-and-seizure provisions of the Constitution. 378 U.S. at 210 n.2. With its emphasis on "conclusory allegations," *Marcus* seems much more based on Fourth Amendment considerations.

[15] *See generally* Monaghan, *First Amendment "Due Process,"* 83 HARV. L. REV. 518 (1970); Note, *Procedural Problems in the Seizure of Obscenity,* 37 ALB. L. REV. 203 (1972); Note, *Motion Picture Seizures and the Adversary Hearing: Settled Law or Fertile Ground for Change,* 21 AM. U. L. REV. 444 (1972); Note, *Prior Adversary Hearings on the Question of Obscenity,* 70 COLUM. L. REV. 1403 (1970); Note, *The Prior Adversary Hearing: Solution to Procedural Due Process Problems in Obscenity Seizures?,* 46 N.Y.U. L. REV. 80 (1971); Case Comment, 32 OHIO ST. L. J. 668 (1971).

v. *Virginia*,[16] decided by the Supreme Court in 1968. Films were seized pursuant to a warrant issued by a justice of the peace on the basis of a police officer's affidavit. The affidavit listed the titles of the motion pictures to be seized and contained the officer's conclusion that the films were obscene. The seizure was overturned by the Supreme Court in a short per curiam opinion, on the basis of the fact that the affidavit was conclusory and that the justice of the peace had not made any inquiry into the factual basis for the police officer's conclusions.[17] Since this came within the scope of *Marcus*, the Court did not have to decide whether an adversary hearing was necessary, or even whether the justice of the peace would have to view the film before issuing the warrant. The Court treated the issue very much as a search-and-seizure problem, under Fourth Amendment considerations, and in fact did not even cite *Quantity of Books*, which was specifically based on First Amendment considerations.

Without any clear Supreme Court guidance in the area, most lower federal courts held that there must be an adversary hearing prior to any search and seizure of obscene material, whether that seizure be pursuant to a search warrant [18] or incident to an arrest.[19] Most of these cases involved seizures of one copy of a motion picture as a method of

[16] 392 U.S. 636 (1968) (per curiam).

[17] Id. at 637.

[18] See, e.g., *United States* v. *Alexander*, 428 F.2d 1169 (8th Cir. 1970); *Demich, Inc.* v. *Ferdon*, 426 F.2d 643 (9th Cir. 1970), *vacated on other grounds*, 401 U.S. 990 (1971); *Astro Cinema Corp.* v. *Mackell*, 422 F.2d 293 (2d Cir. 1970); *Bethview Amusement Corp.* v. *Cahn*, 416 F.2d 410 (2d Cir. 1969), *cert. denied*, 397 U.S. 920 (1970); *Tyrone, Inc.* v. *Wilkmion*, 410 F.2d 639 (4th Cir. 1969), *cert. denied*, 396 U.S. 985 (1969); *Bongiovanni* v. *Hogan*, 309 F.Supp. 1364 (S.D.N.Y. 1970); *Natali* v. *Municipal Court of San Francisco*, 309 F.Supp. 192 (N.D. Cal. 1969). *Contra, Bazzell* v. *Gibbens*, 306 F.Supp. 1057 (E.D. La. 1969); *Star-Satellite, Inc.* v. *Rossetti*, 317 F.Supp. 1399 (S.D. Miss. 1970); *Hosey* v. *City of Jackson*, 309 F.Supp. 527 (S.D. Miss. 1970), *vacated on other grounds*, 401 U.S. 987 (1971); *McGrew* v. *City of Jackson*, 307 F.Supp. 754 (S.D. Miss. 1969), *vacated on other grounds*, 401 U.S. 987 (1971); *People* v. *Marcus*, 69 Misc. 2d 600, 330 N.Y.S.2d 628 (County Ct. 1972); *State* v. *Rabe*, 79 Wash.2d 254, 484 P.2d 917 (1971), *rev'd on other grounds*, 405 U.S. 313 (1972).

[19] *Cambist Films, Inc.* v. *Duggan*, 420 F.2d 687 (3d Cir. 1969); *Metzger* v. *Pearcy*, 393 F.2d 202 (7th Cir. 1968); *Carroll* v. *City of Orlando*, 311 F.Supp. 967 (M.D. Fla. 1970); *City News Center, Inc.* v. *Carson*, 310 F.Supp. 1018 (M.D. Fla. 1970); *Gable* v. *Jenkins*, 309 F.Supp. 998 (N.D. Ga. 1969), *aff'd*, 397 U.S. 592 (1970) (per curiam); *Jodbor Cinema, Ltd.* v. *Sedita*, 309 *F.Supp.* 868 (W.D.N.Y. 1970); *Entertainment Ventures, Inc.* v. *Brewer*, 306 F.Supp. 802 (M.D. Ala. 1969); *Leslie Tobin Imports, Inc.* v. *Rizzo*, 305 F.Supp. 1135 (E.D. Pa. 1969); *Carter* v. *Gautier*, 305 F.Supp. 1098 (M.D. Ga. 1969); *United States* v. *Brown*, 274 F.Supp. 561 (S.D.N.Y. 1967). *Contra, United States* v. *Wild*, 422 F.2d 34 (2d Cir. 1969), *cert. denied*, 402 U.S. 986 (1971); *Platt Amusement Arcade, Inc.* v. *Joyce*, 316 F.Supp. 298 (W.D. Pa. 1970); *Rage Books, Inc.* v. *Leary*, 301 F.Supp. 546 (S.D.N.Y. 1969).

commencing a criminal prosecution.[20] Although both *Marcus* and *Quantity of Books* had involved massive seizures of books and magazines, the courts requiring an adversary hearing in the context of films equated one motion picture, which could be seen by thousands of people, with many copies of the same book.[21] Since this was the rationale by which the seizure of single copies of movies was made to come within the scope of *Marcus* and *Quantity of Books,* books and magazines in small quantities were not included. If a criminal prosecution involving books, magazines, slides, and the like were to be commenced by a search, and if the quantities seized were only so large as to be used as evidence in an impending criminal case, then there was no necessity for an adversary hearing on the issue of obscenity prior to the seizure.[22]

It is against this background that the Supreme Court finally dealt with the matter which had produced so much lower court litigation.[23] The state courts in New York had, in general, refused to follow the Second Circuit precedents regarding an adversary hearing, and finally the New York Court of Appeals had specifically noted that the adversary hearing requirement imposed by the Second Circuit went "beyond any requirement imposed on State Courts by the Supreme Court." [24] In *Heller* v. *New York*,[25] the Supreme Court agreed with the New York Court of Appeals that there was no necessity of holding an adversary hearing prior to the seizure of one copy of a film for use as evidence in a criminal trial. In this case, a judge had actually seen the entire film prior to issuing the search warrant,[26] so there was no issue as to

[20] *See* Comment, *The Requirement and Techniques for Holding an Adversary Hearing Prior to Seizure of Obscene Material,* 48 N.C. L. REV. 830 (1970).

[21] "We are told that the Bethview Theater has 300 seats. Assuming half of them to be occupied for four showings of a film each day for a week, over 4,000 individuals would see the film. Preventing so large a group in the community from access to a film is no different, in the light of First Amendment rights, from preventing a similarly large number of books from being circulated." *Bethview Amusement Corp.* v. *Cahn,* 416 F.2d 410, 412 (2d Cir. 1969).

[22] *See, e.g., Overstock Book Company* v. *Barry,* 436 F.2d 1289, 1295 (2d Cir. 1970); *Halstead, Fauss and Potter, Inc.* v. *Murphy,* 348 F.Supp. 379, 382 (S.D.N.Y. 1972).

[23] The Court had an opportunity to clarify or refine *Marcus* and *Quantity of Books* in *Mishkin* v. *New York,* 383 U.S. 502 (1966), but refused to deal with the issue because of an inadequate record as to the method and effects of the seizure. 383 U.S. at 512–514.

[24] *People* v. *Heller,* 29 N.Y.2d 319, 323, 327 N.Y.S.2d 628, 631, 277 N.E.2d 651, 653 (1971). The Second Circuit cases referred to in *Heller* had been injunctions against state prosecutions.

[25] 413 U.S. 483 (1973).

[26] After three police officers had seen part of the film, an assistant district attor-

the sufficiency of an affidavit or other evidence of probable cause. But the warrants for the seizure of the film and the arrest of various theater personnel were signed and issued without any notice to any of the defendants or any other person possibly interested in the film. Nonetheless, the Court approved of this procedure.

> This Court has never held, or even implied, that there is an absolute First or Fourteenth Amendment right to a prior adversary hearing applicable to all cases where allegedly obscene material is seized. . . . In particular, there is no such absolute right where allegedly obscene material is seized, pursuant to a warrant, to preserve the material as evidence in a criminal prosecution." [27]

In holding that a temporary detention of the film to preserve it as evidence was permissible, the Court was careful to distinguish cases such as *United States* v. *Thirty-Seven (37) Photographs* [28] and *Freedman* v. *Maryland*,[29] since they involved a *final* restraint rather than the preliminary restraint at issue in *Heller*. Thus, while no permanent restraint could be authorized without an adversary hearing, a temporary restraint was acceptable as long as the length of the temporary restraint did not have the effect of a de facto form of censorship. In order to prevent this, the Court in *Heller* set down several guidelines designed to ensure that the extent of suppression prior to a judicial determination of obscenity would be minimized. First, the seizure must be "pursuant to a warrant, issued after a determination of probable cause by a neutral magistrate." [30] Second, there must be available to any interested party, promptly after the seizure, an adversary hearing on the issue of obscenity.[31] What this means is that regardless of a jurisdiction's normal procedure regarding motions to suppress evidence, motions for the return of property, or motions to dismiss, some framework must be available so that there can be an adversary hearing on the obscenity issue shortly after the seizure.[32] Finally, if it can be

---

ney asked the judge to see the film, which the judge did, in the company of a police inspector, by going to the theater and buying a ticket. 413 U.S. at 485.

[27] 413 U.S. at 488–489.

[28] 402 U.S. 363 (1971).

[29] 380 U.S. 51 (1965).

[30] 413 U.S. at 492. Thus, exceptions to the warrant requirement which are accepted in other areas of criminal law are unacceptable where the materials seized are arguably within the scope of First Amendment protection. *See Roaden* v. *Kentucky*, 413 U.S. 496 (1973), and the next section of this chapter.

[31] 413 U.S. at 492.

[32] Assuming that the initial seizure was in accordance with general Fourth Amendment standards, and with the particularized standards set forth in *Marcus* v. *Search Warrant*, 367 U.S. 717 (1961), *Lee Art Theatre* v. *Virginia*, 392 U.S. 636

shown that no other copies of a film are available, the court must allow the seized film to be copied so it can be shown pending an adversary proceeding.[33] If these procedures are not followed, the film must be returned.[34]

Thus, if a seizure is of a large quantity of materials, for the purpose of destruction and not for use or evidence in a criminal trial, there must be an adversary hearing, prior to the seizure, in accordance with the dictates of *Marcus* v. *Search Warrant*[35] and *Quantity of Books* v. *Kansas*.[36] But if the seizure is not for the purpose of ultimate destruction, but only for use as evidence, then no prior adversary hearing is necessary. This is true even if the seizure can be deemed "massive.' If all of the materials seized, in no matter what quantity, are seized for bona fide evidentiary purposes, then there is no necessity for a prior adversary hearing.[37]

Several additional problems remain in regard to the concept of

---

(1968), and *Roaden* v. *Kentucky,* 413 U.S. 496 (1973), a failure to comply with the requirement of a prompt adversary hearing would violate only the First Amendment and they would not require the exclusion of the materials at trial. *Heller* v. *New York,* 413 U.S. 483, 493 n.11 (1973). *See also United States* v. *Cangiano,* 464 F.2d 320 (2d Cir. 1972), *vacated,* 413 U.S. 913 (1973), *reaff'd,* 491 F.2d 905 (2d Cir. 1974), *cert. denied,* 418 U.S. 934 (1974); *Huffman* v. *United States,* 152 U.S. App. D.C. 238, 244, 470 F.2d 386, 392 (D.C. Cir. 1972), *rev'd on other grounds on rehearing,* 502 F.2d 419 (D.C. Cir. 1974). *Cf. United States* v. *Pryba,* 502 F.2d 391, 404 n.97 (D.C. Cir. 1974).

[33] 413 U.S. at 492–493. If the relevant statute is solely criminal and does not provide for seizure or destruction, copying may perhaps be permitted even after a determination of obscenity at an adversary hearing.

[34] 413 U.S. at 493. Since the exclusionary rule does not provide a remedy (note 32 supra), mandamus seems the most appropriate remedy for a failure to permit copying or return of the film. An attempt to appeal from the seizure would create a conflict between the principles of *Heller* and those of *DiBella* v. *United States,* 369 U.S. 121 (1961). *See Art Theatre Guild, Inc.* v. *Parrish,* 503 F.2d 133 (6th Cir. 1974).

[35] 367 U.S. 717 (1961).

[36] 378 U.S. 205 (1964). *See United States* v. *Pryba,* 502 F.2d 391, 405 (D.C. Cir. 1974).

[37] *See United States* v. *Cangiano,* 491 F.2d 906, 912-913 (2d Cir. 1974); *G.I. Distributors, Inc.* v. *Murphy,* 490 F.2d 1167, 1169 (2d Cir. 1973), *cert. denied,* 94 S. Ct. 1941 (1974). Compare *Bradford* v. *Wade,* 376 F.Supp. 45, 47 (N.D. Tex. 1974), 386 F.Supp. 1156 (N.D. Tex. 1974) (no seizure of multiple copies of the *same film* without an adversary hearing). The issue of multiple seizures of the same film was before the Supreme Court in *Hicks* v. *Miranda,* 95 S. Ct. 2281 (1975), but the Court failed to reach the merits. It would appear that if a valid reason for the use of multiple seizures for a criminal prosecution can be shown, then no adversary hearing is necessary prior to the seizures. But if the real purpose of the seizures is suppression of the film, then there is no *"bona fide* purpose of preserving it as evidence in a criminal proceeding" (*Heller,* 413 U.S. at 492) and such a seizure without an adversary hearing in advance is impermissible.

an adversary hearing. One concerns the timing of the hearing. Although the adversary hearing need not precede the seizure, it must be available promptly thereafter, and the Supreme Court defines prompt as meaning "the shortest period 'compatible with sound judicial resolution.' " [38] In the context of customs seizures under 19 U.S.C. § 1305 (a), the Court has held that this standard is met by a proceeding commenced within 14 days of seizure and concluded within 60 days thereafter.[39] But these times are admittedly based in part on "the lengthy process of bringing goods into this country from abroad."[40] Furthermore, 19 U.S.C. § 1305 provides for a trial by jury, a time-consuming process which is clearly not required for an adversary hearing in the *Heller* context. In *Heller,* an adversary trial occurred 48 days after the seizure, and the Court made it clear that this was not a prompt adversary hearing, although declining to give the delay any significance since the claimant had failed to avail himself of earlier opportunities for an adversary determination of the obscenity of the film.[41] In light of the purposes of an adversary hearing in this context, where copying is required in any event, and where it may take some time to collect evidence to be used at the hearing, it would seem that a hearing which would commence no more than 10 days after it is requested would be constitutionally sufficient.[42]

Since in most adversary hearings the claimant, or "interested party," will be the defendant against whom the evidence is proposed to be used, there may be substantial self-incrimination problems surrounding the conduct of the adversary hearing. Thus, it seems clear that the purpose of the adversary hearing may only be served if a defendant who testifies at such a hearing retains his privilege against self-incrimination as to the subsequent criminal trial. If the defendant gives evidence at the adversary hearing, that evidence may not be used at the subsequent trial and, *a fortiori,* his testimony does not constitute a general waiver of the privilege for future proceedings.[43] Similarly, the prosecution may not use the adversary hearing as a

[38] *Heller* v. *New York*, 413 U.S. 483, 492 n.9 (1973).

[39] *United States* v. *Thirty-Seven (37) Photographs*, 402 U.S. 363, 373 (1971).

[40] *Id.*

[41] 413 U.S. at 490.

[42] Of course, unlike *Thirty-Seven Photographs*, a postseizure adversary hearing in this context must be requested by a claimant. *Heller*, 413 U.S. at 492. Otherwise, there is no necessity of holding the hearing at all. In *United States* v. *Pryba*, 502 F.2d 391, 404–406, (D.C. Cir. 1974), a hearing held five days after the seizure was deemed sufficient.

[43] *United States* v. *Sherpix*, 502 F.2d 1361, 1371 (D.C. Cir. 1975), relying on the reasoning of *Simmons* v. *United States*, 390 U.S. 377 (1968).

method of discovery not otherwise available in a criminal case. Thus, if evidence of any kind is subpoenaed by use of a subpoena duces tecum directed at the defendant, then this must be accompanied by, at the very least, use immunity as to the materials summoned.[44] It could be argued that the purposes of the adversary hearing, to protect First Amendment rights pending a final resolution of the obscenity issue, could best be fostered by holding all evidence presented by the defendant at that hearing inadmissible at trial, but this seems unduly restrictive of the prosecution, especially in light of the fact that the copying requirement of *Heller* leaves open avenues other than the adversary hearing for the interim protection of First Amendment rights. Exclusion only of the defendant's testimony [45] and anything subpoenaed from the defendant adequately strikes the balance between the needs of the prosecution and the purposes of the adversary hearing.

11.2 Search and Seizure

Of course, the mere elimination of the requirement of a prior adversary hearing where the evidence is to be used in a criminal prosecution does not mean that First Amendment considerations are excluded from search and seizure in the obscenity area. Recognition of these First Amendment issues has led the courts to engraft additional standards on the constitutional requirements normally incident to searches and seizures since, at the time of seizure, the material seized in an obscenity case is still arguably within the range of First Amendment protection.

Again, we must look back to *Marcus* v. *Search Warrant* [46] as the starting point for this discussion. Although *Marcus* involved a seizure for the purpose of ultimate destruction of the materials, rather than use at a forthcoming criminal trial, several principles are equally applicable to both situations. Thus, in order that the maximum protection be available for nonobscene material, the search-and-seizure procedures must be so structured as to ensure that nonobscene material is neither seized nor its distribution stifled because of threat of

[44] *See Smith* v. *Fair,* 363 F.Supp. 1021 (N.D. Ohio 1973).

[45] This should also include documentary and real evidence produced through the defendant's testimony, although not such evidence produced through other witnesses. Of course, if the claimant and defendant are corporations, and thus do not have a privilege against self-incrimination, then there is no basis for limiting the use of the corporation's evidence adduced at the adversary hearing.

[46] 367 U.S. 717 (1961).

seizure. Thus, the warrants in *Marcus* were defective because they were issued on "the conclusory assertions of a single police officer," because there was no "scrutiny by the judge of any materials considered by the complainant to be obscene," and because the broadness of the warrant as finally issued put the determination of obscenity not in the hands of the court, but in the hands of the officer executing the warrant.[47] While the Court did not make clear which of these factors was determinative, it did mandate that seizures of allegedly obscene material must be *preceded* by a "procedure . . . designed to focus searchingly on the question of obscenity." [48] Although in the case of seizure for evidence in a criminal prosecution this procedure need no longer be an adversary hearing,[49] the requirement of some detailed inquiry by the issuing magistrate has not been abrogated. Thus, in *Lee Art Theatre* v. *Virginia*,[50] the Supreme Court voided a seizure, related to a criminal prosecution, where the officer's affidavit was conclusory, and thus the justice of the peace could not (and did not) make inquiry into the factual basis for the affidavit. As such, the entire proceeding did not "focus searchingly on the question of obscenity" and was thus constitutionally defective.

From 1968 to 1973, the Supreme Court did not deal with the search-and-seizure issue in obscenity law, and virtually every lower court opinion was based primarily on issues relating to the necessity or conduct of a prior adversary hearing. But on the same day that the Supreme Court decided *Heller* v. *New York*,[51] it decided *Roaden* v. *Kentucky*,[52] which now gives substantial guidance in the search-and-seizure aspects of obscenity law.

Roaden involved, specifically, the application of the concept of a search incident to an arrest [53] to a search and seizure of allegedly obscene materials. The sheriff of Pulaski County, Kentucky, had purchased a ticket to see the film *Cindy and Donna,* which was playing at a local drive-in theater. After viewing the movie in its entirety, he

---

[47] *Id.* at 732.

[48] *Id.*

[49] *See* Chapter 11.1 *supra.*

[50] 392 U.S. 636 (1968) (per curiam).

[51] 413 U.S. 483 (1973). This case is discussed in detail in the previous section of this chapter.

[52] 413 U.S. 496 (1973).

[53] While it is possible that a search conducted at the same time as the arrest could be conducted pursuant to a search warrant, a "search incident to an arrest" is a term of art referring to a search without a warrant, but purportedly within an exception to the warrant requirement based on the relationship of the search to the arrest. *See* generally *Chimel* v. *California,* 395 U.S. 752 (1969).

determined that it was obscene and therefore violated state law. He then went to the projection room, arrested the theater manager, and seized a copy of the film without a warrant. There was no warrant, no prior judicial determination of obscenity, and no evidence of obscenity other than the sheriff's viewing of the film.[54] Despite a motion to suppress use of the film at trial, Roaden was convicted and his conviction affirmed on appeal, on the basis of the fact that the film was seized incident to a lawful arrest. The Supreme Court reversed, holding that the seizure of a film, shown at the time to the general public, without a warrant, is constitutionally impermissible. In evaluating a search and seizure of a theatre or bookstore, the determination of what is or is not an unreasonable search and seizure, in violation of the Fourth Amendment, must take into account First Amendment values.[55] Thus, the requirements for specificity in the affidavit and the warrant are greater where the items to be seized are books or other materials embodying speech.[56] *Roaden* extended this principle by holding that an otherwise valid exception to the warrant requirement may not be valid when the effect is a prior restraint on speech.

> Seizing a film then being presented to the general public presents essentially the same restraint on expression as the seizure of all the books in a bookstore. Such precipitate action by a police officer, without the authority of a constitutionally sufficient warrant, is plainly a form of prior restraint and is, in those circumstances, unreasonable under Fourth Amendment standards. The seizure is unreasonable, not simply because it would have been easy to secure a warrant, but rather because prior restraint of the right of expression, whether by books or films, calls for a higher hurdle in the evaluation of reasonableness.[57]

Since the rule set forth in *Roaden* was based on Fourth Amendment principles, albeit embodying, in this case, some First Amendment values, the illegal search triggered the operation of the exclusionary rule and Roaden's conviction was reversed. In this and other aspects, the case is intimately related to *Heller* v. *New York*,[58] discussed in the previous section of this chapter, and the two cases should be read *in pari materia*. Thus, the holding in *Roaden* seems implicitly based on the fact that the procedure approved in *Heller* could have

---

[54] 413 U.S. at 497–499.

[55] *Id.* at 504. *See Stanford* v. *Texas,* 379 U.S. 476, 485–486 (1965).

[56] *Marcus* v. *Search Warrant,* 367 U.S. 717 (1961); *Lee Art Theatre* v. *Virginia,* 392 U.S. 636 (1968).

[57] 413 U.S. at 504.

[58] 413 U.S. 483 (1973).

been used here and in similar cases.[59] The Court did indicate that in a true "now or never" situation, a warrantless search might be permitted,[60] but on any less of a showing, the requirement of a search warrant, based on a procedure allowing a "searching" focus on the issue of obscenity, will be strictly enforced.

Based on *Roaden* and its predecessors, it is now clear that an obscenity prosecution must be commenced in such a way that there will, at the very least, be an opportunity for some judicial intervention before public access to the materials in question may be curtailed. Thus, an application for a search warrant, although it may contain hearsay, must describe what the books or films contain in some detail.[61] The Supreme Court has never decided whether the issuing magistrate *must* see the film or read the book before issuing the warrant, but the implication of *Heller* and *Roaden* is that a detailed affidavit or testimony would be sufficient, and anything more is not constitutionally required.[62] But an affidavit in conclusory or statutory terms is constitutionally insufficient.[63] Similarly, the warrant itself must describe with particularity, presumably by title of each book, magazine, or film in most cases, each item to be seized. The warrant should be specific in order that only materials which have been found to be probably obscene may be seized, and in order that the determination of obscenity will remain with the issuing magistrate, and not be delegated to the officer executing the warrant.[64]

It is important to note that the Fourth Amendment (and the Fourteenth, through which the Fourth is applied to the states) is a restriction only on governmental action. Thus, a search and seizure conducted by private individuals is not subject to the restrictions described in this section. This issue arises most often in the context of searches by airlines or other carriers of packages deposited with them for shipment. Unless it can be shown that the carrier or its agents were acting specifically on behalf of, or in cooperation with, govern-

[59] See *Roaden*, 413 U.S. at 505 n.6.

[60] *Id.* at 505. See *Smith* v. *United States*, 505 F.2d 824 (6th Cir. 1974); *G.I. Distributors, Inc.* v. *Murphy*, 490 F.2d 1167, 1170 (2d Cir. 1973), *cert. denied*, 94 S. Ct. 1941 (1974).

[61] See *United States* v. *Pryba*, 502 F.2d 391, 402–404 (D.C. Cir. 1974) (for affidavit deemed sufficient by this court, see 502 F.2d at 410); *United States* v. *Sherpix*, 512 F.2d 1361, 1318–1369 (D.C. Cir. 1975).

[62] 502 F.2d at 402–404, 512 F.2d at 1368.

[63] *Lee Art Theatre* v. *Virginia*, 392 U.S. 636 (1968); *United States* v. *Cangianio*, 491 F.2d 906, 913 (2d Cir. 1974).

[64] *Marcus* v. *Search Warrant*, 367 U.S. 717 (1961); *United States* v. *Cangianio*, 464 F.2d 320, 326 (2d Cir. 1972), *vacated on other grounds*, 413 U.S. 913 (1973).

mental authorities, a warrantless search by such private parties, even if without probable cause, is subject to no constitutional restrictions, notwithstanding the fact that the material seized is subsequently turned over to governmental bodies and used in a criminal prosecution.[65]

11.3   Res Judicata and Collateral Estoppel

Since allegedly obscene books, magazines, or films are often distributed in multiple copies, to different locations, and over a relatively long period of time, problems may arise as to the effect of one proceeding on subsequent proceedings involving the same material. These may arise in a number of different contexts, but the most probable are the effect of a prior proceeding as legal precedent, as creating double jeopardy in a subsequent criminal prosecution, or as res judicata or collateral estoppel as to the issues decided in the first case.

The most common problem is the effect of a Supreme Court or other higher court authority dealing with the same materials as are currently on trial, or with substantially similar materials. Resolution of this problem must depend on the interrelationship between the language of the allegedly controlling decision and the substantive variability embodied in the application of the obscenity laws. Thus, if an appellate opinion makes it clear that a particular work cannot possibly be constitutionally prosecuted, this must be treated as a decision as a matter of law,[66] and thus controlling on the court below to the extent that the issue of obscenity should not even be given to the jury. For example, it should be clear, after *Jenkins* v. *Georgia*,[67] that the motion picture at issue in that case could not be prosecuted anywhere in the country. And even if a controlling court's opinion is less specific, as long as it deals with the issue of obscenity it must be followed by courts under it.[68] But where the materials are merely similar, the bind-

[65] *See United States* v. *Pryba*, 502 F.2d 391, 398–401 (D.C. Cir. 1974); *United States* v. *Cangianio*, 464 F.2d 320, 324–325 (2d Cir. 1972), *vacated on other grounds,* 413 U.S. 913 (1973); *United States* v. *Harding*, 475 F.2d 480, 483–484 (10th Cir. 1973), *vacated on other grounds,* 414 U.S. 964; *Gold* v. *United States*, 378 F.2d 588, 591 (9th Cir. 1967). *See generally* Note, *Mapp* v. *Ohio and Exclusion of Evidence Illegally Obtained by Private Parties,* 72 YALE L.J. 1062 (1963); Note, *Private Assumption of the Police Function Under the Fourth Amendment,* 51 BOSTON UNIV. L. REV. 464 (1971).

[66] *See* Chapter 7.3 *supra.*

[67] 418 U.S. 153 (1974).

[68] *See Commonwealth* v. *Robin*, 421 Pa. 70, 218 A.2d 546 (1966), in which the Supreme Court of Pennsylvania found to be controlling on all of the states the U.S. Supreme Court's ruling in *Grove Press, Inc.* v. *Gerstein*, 378 U.S. 577 (1964), reversing a finding that Tropic of Cancer was obscene. The Pennsylvania court felt bound

ing effect is of course less. In making its legal determination of whether or not the materials can be found obscene, a lower court should consider the findings of superior courts as to similar works.[69] But as to the factual determination to be made by the jury, there seems no reason why other court decisions, or the materials involved in them, would be relevant to anything the jury is called upon to decide.[70]

Obscenity prosecutions may also present double jeopardy problems.[71] It should be clear that an offense of sale, or exhibition, or distribution of obscene materials can be committed more than once. To the extent that such multiple offenses result in multiple prosecutions, there are no double jeopardy problems. There is no reason to assume, furthermore, that an acquittal of one offense, regardless of the "grounds" for the acquittal, would bar, as a matter of double jeopardy, a subsequent prosecution for a different offense, but based on the same material. However, the absence of double jeopardy problems does not mean that the prosecution is necessarily to be permitted, since there is nonetheless the problem of prior adjudication.

Prior adjudication, as a defense or bar to a subsequent litigation, may take the form of either a claim of res judicata or collateral estoppel. Res judicata refers to a previous decision of essentially the same lawsuit, while collateral estoppel relates to the finality of a particular finding of fact previously litigated between the parties. It is the latter that is most likely to appear in obscenity litigation. For example, the Supreme Court, in *Miller,* properly identified as a collateral estoppel claim the argument that "once material has been found not to be obscene in one proceeding," the State cannot prosecute the same material in a different proceeding, despite allegedly different exposures at different times in different settings.[72] But whether or not this argument would succeed depends upon whether or not the parties in the

---

despite the fact that there was no opinion in *Grove Press* v. *Gerstein.* The case is noted at 13 WAYNE L. REV. 410 (1967).

[69] *See Huffman* v. *United States,* 470 F.2d 386, 403–404 (D.C. Cir. 1971).

[70] The *Huffman* case, *id.,* suggests that such materials might be helpful to the jury in some cases, but that this must be a matter of relatively uncontrolled judicial discretion.

[71] The defendant in *Miller* v. *California,* 413 U.S. 15 (1973), made a double jeopardy argument but the Supreme Court did not reach the merits of that argument. 413 U.S. at 34 n.14.

As to the particular prior adjudication or double jeopardy problems that may be created by the concept of pandering, see Chapter 4.4 supra, and in particular the text accompanying notes 86–90 thereof.

[72] 413 U.S. at 34 n.14.

prior proceeding were the same and whether or not the factual issue actually decided was also the same. Thus, a defendant in an obscenity case may successfully claim collateral estoppel only if the adverse party is the same in the former and in the instant proceeding, in accordance with the general rule that only parties in the former action are bound by the results in that action.[73] For example, if a given motion picture is found not to be obscene in a *federal* prosecution against X, there is no reason why X may not be prosecuted by a *state* for showing the same motion picture, and the state may still be able to prove obscenity.[74] But if the parties are the same, the question becomes more difficult. It is then necessary to determine whether or not the issue actually litigated and the issue actually decided were the same in the former case as in the latter. If A is prosecuted by the state for exhibiting *Porno Delights* on March 15, and acquitted, may he be prosecuted for showing the same movie on March 16? Since there have clearly been two separate "violations," this is not a double jeopardy issue, as such. But whether the state is collaterally estopped from claiming the film is obscene in the second prosecution depends, first, on whether the determination of obscenity would be based on the same factors, and second, on whether the issue of obscenity was necessarily decided in the first acquittal.

As to the first factor, the most relevant concept is the idea of local community standards. In other words, the clear message of *Miller* is that a determination of obscenity in one locality may not be the same as the determination in another locality. Therefore, a determination of no obscenity in one locus would not be a finding such as to preclude a determination of obscenity in another locus. The collateral estoppel effect will depend upon whether the community was defined in the same way in both prosecutions. If a prosecution in Texas is based upon a statewide definition of community, then an acquittal forecloses any further prosecutions of the same defendant for showing the same film, or selling the same book, throughout the state. But if the first determination was based upon a community defined as the city of Dallas, then there is no bar to subsequent prosecutions in any other city. If the community is not specifically defined, a procedure authorized in *Hamling* v. *United States*,[75] then the collateral estoppel

---

[73] *See generally* F. JAMES, CIVIL PROCEDURE § 11.26 (1965); Restatement of Judgments § 95.

[74] *United States* v. *Luros*, 243 F.Supp. 160, 169 (N.D. Iowa 1965) (previous state proceedings not a bar to federal prosecution of same materials).

[75] 418 U.S. 87 (1974).

effect should extend to the limits of the area from which jurors are or would be drawn in the first trial.

All of the above presumes that the first trial resulted in a specific finding of no obscenity. Of course, in a criminal trial, there will only be a general verdict, which may or may not be based on the jury's judgment as to the obscenity of the materials at issue. In *Ashe* v. *Swenson*,[76] the Supreme Court for the first time concluded that collateral estoppel was a concept of constitutional dimensions and a defense available to a defendant in both state and federal prosecutions. In the course of the Court's discussion, it noted that a determination of whether a particular factual issue was decided in the first case will depend upon a practical evaluation of the record, pleadings, evidence, charge, and other circumstances in order to see whether the first verdict could have reasonably been based upon a factor other than that which the defendant seeks to foreclose.[77] Therefore, if the defendant in the first trial raises only the defense that the materials were not obscene, then, providing the other factors discussed previously are met, the obscenity issue has been foreclosed by a not-guilty finding in the first case. But if the defendant raises a number of other defenses, any of which could reasonably have been relied upon by the jury to support the not-guilty verdict, then the state is not collaterally estopped from alleging obscenity in a second prosecution.

11.4   Scienter

A recurring issue in criminal prosecutions for violations of the obscenity laws is that of scienter, or the defendant's intent.[78] The legal issues are not especially complex, but problems of proof of scienter have dominated obscenity litigation. As a general proposition, it is fair to say that intent, or *mens rea,* is a generally accepted element of Anglo-American criminal jurisprudence. But the courts have accepted the concept that in some instances criminal liability may be imposed without proof of the defendant's knowledge, thus creating a number of "strict liability" crimes.[79] Whether distribution or sale of obscene material could be one of those crimes was the main issue before the

---

[76] 397 U.S. 436 (1970).

[77] *Id.* at 444.

[78] *See generally* Note, *The Scienter Requirement in Criminal Obscenity Prosecutions,* 41 N.Y.U.L. REV. 791 (1966); Note, *The Scienter Element in California's Obscenity Laws: Is There a Way to Know?*, 24 HASTINGS L.J. 1303 (1973).

[79] See the general discussion in *Lambert* v. *California,* 355 U.S. 225 (1957).

Supreme Court in *Smith* v. *California.*[80] *Smith* dealt with a Los Angeles city ordinance which made it a crime for a bookseller to have obscene books on his premises. No proof of knowledge, or scienter, on the part of the bookseller was necessary, and thus this was a strict liability crime. Writing for the Court, Mr. Justice Brennan acknowledged the existence and validity of some strict liability crimes, but found that this concept was unacceptable where the crime had some relationship to freedom of speech.[81] If this were done, there would be a significant chilling effect [82] on the distribution and availability of materials that were in fact protected by the First Amendment. If the Los Angeles ordinance, or any other strict-liability obscenity offense, were upheld, said the Court, the bookseller or distributor would

> tend to restrict the books he sells to those he has inspected; and thus the State will have imposed a restriction upon the distribution of constitutionally protected as well as obscene literature.[83]

This, in turn, would restrict public access to constitutionally protected reading matter and thus go to the heart of the concepts underlying the First Amendment. Although the general purpose of strict liability is to promote caution, there are detrimental effects to promoting caution in the area of speech or literature, and the inevitable self-censorship caused by a strict-liability statute would have the result of suppressing the nonobscene as well as the obscene.

While the Court in *Smith* thus said that any criminal obscenity statute must incorporate at least some concept of scienter, it was careful to leave the exact boundaries and definition to legislatures and lower courts, except to reaffirm that proof of scienter may of course be given by circumstantial evidence.[84] In order to see what scienter actually means in the obscenity area, we must go back in time to 1896 and the case of *Rosen* v. *United States.*[85] Rosen was prosecuted for mailing obscene matter and claimed, in defense, that he didn't know the material was obscene. But the Supreme Court, in an opinion written by Mr. Justice Harlan, held that such knowledge was not necessary in order for the conviction to stand. It was enough that Rosen

---

[80] 361 U.S. 147 (1959). *See* Comments, 26 BROOK. L. REV. 289 (1960); 9 DE PAUL L. REV. 250 (1960); 35 N.Y.U.L. REV. 1086 (1960); 38 N. CAR. L. REV. 634 (1960); 21 OHIO ST. L.J. 242 (1960); 2 WM. AND MARY L. REV. 491 (1960).

[81] 361 U.S. at 151.

[82] *See generally* Note, *The Chilling Effect in Constitutional Law,* 69 COLUM L. REV. 808 (1969).

[83] 361 U.S. at 153.

[84] *Id.* at 154.

[85] 161 U.S. 29 (1896).

knew the general contents of the publications at issue, and the prosecution was not required to show that he knew they were legally obscene.[86] It is clear that the principles first enunciated in *Rosen* remain valid today. In *Hamling* v. *United States*,[87] the Supreme Court specifically reaffirmed *Rosen* to the effect that "knowledge of the character of the materials" is sufficient, and that it need not be shown that the defendant believed the material to be obscene.[88]

> It is constitutionally sufficient that the prosecution show that a defendant had knowledge of the contents of the materials he distributed, and that he knew the character and nature of the materials. To require proof of a defendant's knowledge of the legal status of the materials would permit the defendant to avoid prosecution by simply claiming that he had not brushed up on the law. Such a formulation of the scienter requirement is required neither by the language of 18 U.S.C. § 1461 nor by the Constitution.[89]

The guidelines set forth by the Supreme Court had a great effect on various obscenity laws, causing a number of state laws to be invalidated for lack of a scienter requirement.[90] But the more common result was for courts to construe obscenity laws as incorporating a scienter requirement.[91] The issue remains as to how scienter is to be shown, even given the holding of *Hamling* that actual knowledge of legal obscenity is not necessary.[92]

[86] *Id.* at 41.

[87] 418 U.S. 87 (1974). Scienter issues were also peripherally before the Supreme Court in *Manual Enterprises, Inc.* v. *Day*, 370 U.S. 478 (1962), *Mishkin* v. *New York*, 383 U.S. 502 (1966), and *Ginsberg* v. *New York*, 390 U.S. 629 (1968).

[88] 418 U.S. at 119–120.

[89] *Id.* at 123–124. To the extent that it ever accurately stated the law, the defense of "good faith belief as to obscenity," as set forth in E. DEVITT and W. BLACKMAR, FEDERAL JURY PRACTICE AND INSTRUCTIONS § 41.17 (1970), is now clearly unwarranted as a matter of constitutional law. But there is, of course, no reason why Congress or any state could not, if it so desires, create such a defense, or impose a stricter scienter requirement than that of the Supreme Court.

[90] *See, e.g., People* v. *Villano*, 369 Mich. 420, 120 N.W.2d 204 (1963); *State* v. *Kuebel*, 241 Ind. 268, 172 N.E.2d 45 (1961).

[91] *See, e.g., Hamling* v. *United States*, 418 U.S. 87 (1974) (18 U.S.C. § 1461); *United States* v. *Mishkin*, 317 F.2d 634 (2d Cir. 1963), *cert. denied*, 375 U.S. 827 (18 U.S.C. § 1461); *United States* v. *Smith*, 467 F.2d 1126 (7th Cir. 1972) (18 U.S.C. § 1463); *United States* v. *New Orleans Book Mart, Inc.*, 490 F.2d 73 (5th Cir. 1974) (18 U.S.C. § 1465); *People* v. *Finkelstein*, 9 N.Y.2d 342, 214 N.Y.S.2d 363, 174 N.E.2d 470 (1961); *State* v. *Hudson County News Co.*, 35 N.J. 284, 173 A.2d 20 (1961); *State* v. *Jackson*, 224 Ore. 337, 356 P.2d 495 (1960).

[92] To the same effect, see also *Kahm* v. *United States*, 300 F.2d 78, 86 (5th Cir. 1962), *cert. denied*, 369 U.S. 859; *Schindler* v. *United States*, 208 F.2d 289, 290 (9th Cir. 1953), *cert denied*, 347 U.S. 938; *United States* v. *Gundlach*, 345 F.Supp. 709 (E.D. Pa. 1972).

Under the provisions of a "normal" obscenity statute, scienter is an element of the offense, express or implied, which must be proved to the same extent as any other element of the offense.[93] But a New York statute incorporating a rebuttable presumption that possession presumes knowledge has been upheld by the New York courts, and without opinion, by the Supreme Court.[94] This should not be taken to undercut the holding of *Smith* v. *California,* however.[95] A statutory presumption of this type should be upheld only if the presumption is, at the very least, justified by normal experiences,[96] and if the burden it creates does not impose such a strict standard as to chill the distribution of constitutionally protected materials. In the absence of such a presumption, scienter will generally be proved by the use of circumstantial evidence,[97] such as evidence that a defendant talked or wrote about the contents of the material, that the defendant was shown or given promotional literature describing the material, that the defendant's business engaged primarily or exclusively in material of a sexually explicit character, or that a defendant dealt in, or was prosecuted for, materials of an arguably obscene nature.[98] Of course it is not necessary for the prosecution to prove that the defendant actually read or saw the very materials in question.[99] Such a requirement would, as a practical matter, make prosecution of a seller or distributor

---

An indictment charging that the act was done knowingly or willfully is sufficient to allege scienter. *See Kirby* v. *Municipal Court,* 237 Cal. App. 2d 335, 46 Cal. Rptr. 844 (1965); *People* v. *Shapiro,* 6 App. Div. 2d 271, 177 N.Y.S.2d 670 (1958).

[93] *See, e.g., People* v. *Harris,* 192 Cal. App.2d Supp. 887, 13 Cal. Rptr. 642 (1961); *State* v. *Sul,* 146 Conn. 78, 147 A.2d 686 (1958); *People* v. *Finkelstein,* 9 N.Y.2d 342, 214 N.Y.S. 2d 363, 174 N.E.2d 470 (1961); *State* v. *Oman,* 261 Minn. 10, 110 N.W.2d 514 (1961); *Tracey* v. *State,* 130 So.2d 605 (Fla. 1961).

[94] *People* v. *Kirkpatrick,* 32 N.Y.2d 17, 343 N.Y.S.2d 70, 295 N.E.2d 753, *app. dism.,* 414 U.S. 948 (1973). *Contra, Grove Press, Inc.* v. *Evans,* 306 F.Supp. 1084 (E.D. Va. 1969).

[95] 361 U.S. 147 (1959).

[96] We would not normally tend to assume that a bookstore owner has knowledge of the character of all the books in a bookstore, especially where the presumption is applied to textual, rather than pictorial, materials.

[97] *Smith* v. *California,* 361 U.S. 147, 154 (1959); *Mishkin* v. *New York,* 383 U.S. 502 (1966); *Great Speckled Bird of Atlanta Co-operative News Project* v. *Stynchcombe,* 298 F.Supp. 1291 (N.D. Ga. 1969); *State* v. *Childs,* 447 P.2d 304 (Ore. 1968), *Richards* v. *State,* 497 S.W.2d 770 (Tex. Civ. App. 1973); *Orito* v. *State,* 55 Wis. 2d 161, 197 N.W.2d 763 (1972).

[98] Evidence of prior similar acts is generally admissible to show intent. McCORMICK ON EVIDENCE § 190 at 450 (2d ed. 1972).

[99] *State* v. *J-R Distributors, Inc.,* 82 Wash.2d 584, 512 P.2d 1049 (1973); *People* v. *Weingarten,* 50 Misc.2d. 365, 271 N.Y.S.2d 158 (1966); *ABC Books, Inc.* v. *Benson,* 315 F.Supp. 695 (M.D. Tenn. 1970). *Compare People* v. *Andrews,* 23 Cal. App. 3d Supp. 1, 100 Cal. Rptr. 276 (1972).

impossible, since few sellers or distributors actually see or read any substantial amount of the material sold. At the other extreme, some courts have held that the scienter requirement is satisfied if it is proved that the defendant knew or *should have known* of the contents of the materials.[100] Since *Smith* merely invalidates the concept of strict liability, any "fault" standard, whether negligence, recklessness, or actual specific knowledge, is probably sufficient, as a matter of current constitutional interpretation, and each statute should be evaluated in the context of the actual burden placed upon the seller or distributor. If the burden is merely that which can be normally expected, there would be no constitutional problems. But if a significant burden in checking all materials is created, then the principles of *Smith* are violated and the statute is unconstitutional.

11.5   A Short Note on "Affirmative" Federal Litigation

Traditionally, many substantive issues in obscenity law have been raised in the context of "affirmative" litigation in the federal courts, that is, suits brought *by* sellers or distributors of sexually explicit materials to enjoin the enforcement of allegedly unconstitutional prosecution. These suits often take the form of actions for declaratory judgments as well as actions for injunctions. No exhaustive treatment of the procedural issues raised by this type of action will be attempted here, since these issues are more appropriately discussed in works dealing with federal jurisdiction than in a treatise on obscenity law. But it should be noted that the main issue in these cases is whether or not it is appropriate for the federal courts to intervene in issues dealing primarily with state law.[101] The leading cases [102] setting

---

[100] *Newman* v. *Conover,* 313 F.Supp. 623 (N.D. Tex. 1970) (negligence standard); *Movies, Inc.* v. *Conlisk,* 345 F.Supp. 780 (N.D. Ill. 1973) (recklessness standard).

[101] *See generally* Note, *Federal Relief Against Threatened State Prosecutions: The Implications of Younger, Lake Carriers, and Roe,* 48 N.Y.U. REV. 965 (1973); Spears, *Supreme Court February Sextet, Younger* v. *Harris Revisited,* 26 BAYLOR L. REV. 1 (1974); Field, *Abstention in Constitutional Cases: The Scope of the Pullman Abstention Doctrine,* 122 U. PA. L. REV. 1071 (1974); Note, *Federal Declaratory Relief and the Non-pending State Criminal Suit,* 34 MD. L. REV. 87 (1974); Note, *Steffel* v. *Thompson: Federal Declaratory Relief and the State Criminal Process—A Compromise of Comity and Primacy,* 9 U. SAN FRAN. L. REV. 87 (1974); Donahue, *Abstention Doctrine and Equitable Restraint: Old and New Perceptions of Federalism,* 9 SUFF. L. REV. 34 (1974); McCormack, *Developments in the Availability of Federal Remedies Against State Activities,* 16 WM. AND MARY L. REV. 1 (1974); Comment, 28 RUTG. L. REV. 720 (1975); Comment, 19 ST. LOUIS L. J. 419 (1975).

[102] Among the most significant are *Dombrowski* v. *Pfister,* 380 U.S. 479 (1965);

the boundaries of permissible federal intervention should be consulted before any affirmative federal litigation is attempted, since the Supreme Court is clearly narrowing the range of areas in which federal interference with state activities is permitted. Two very recent obscenity cases demonstrate this trend. In *Hicks* v. *Miranda*,[103] the Court held that a lower federal court committed error in reaching the merits of the claim that, *inter alia,* multiple seizures of the same film were unconstitutional. Absent a stronger showing of bad faith than the Court found to have been presented, resolution of the issues should have remained with the state courts. And in *Huffman* v. *Pursue, Ltd.*,[104] the Court held that federal courts should not interfere with state *civil* proceedings where those civil proceedings are substantially similar to criminal proceedings. In this case, the civil suit was an action to enjoin as a nuisance the operation of a theater which "specialized" in pornographic movies. In such a situation, said the Court, determination of the validity of the statute and the action of the state officials, as against a constitutional attack, was, in the first instance, for the state court where the proceeding was instituted and not for the federal courts.

Thus, the areas in which the federal courts may interfere with state proceedings are being narrowed, and the reliance which has historically been placed upon this type of litigation may have to be directed elsewhere.

Younger v. *Harris,* 401 U.S. 37 (1971); *Samuels* v. *Mackell,* 401 U.S. 66 (1971); *Perez* v. *Ledesma,* 401 U.S. 82 (1971); *Steffel* v. *Thompson,* 415 U.S. 452 (1974); *Mitchum* v. *Foster,* 407 U.S. 225 (1972).

[103] 422 U.S. 332, 95 S. Ct. 2281 (1975).

[104] 420 U.S. 920, 95 S. Ct. 1200 (1975).

12

Civil Obscenity Regulation

12.1   The Doctrine of Prior Restraint

The predominant method of obscenity control in the United States has traditionally been that of criminal prosecution for the sale, distribution, or exhibition of obscene materials. Yet criminal prosecutions are by no means the only method available, and various civil regulatory procedures have been and are now employed in most jurisdictions. The Supreme Court has recognized this range of enforcement mechanisms available to the state.

> We need not linger over the suggestion that something can be drawn out of the Due Process Clause of the Fourteenth Amendment that restricts New York to the criminal process in seeking to protect its people against the dissemination of pornography. It is not for this Court thus to limit the State in resorting to various weapons in the armory of the law. Whether proscribed conduct is to be visited by a criminal prosecution or by a *qui tam* action or by an injunction or by some or all of these remedies in combination, is a matter within the legislature's range of choice.[1]

If it was this simple, of course, there would be no need for this chapter. But virtually any noncriminal method of enforcement of the obscenity laws involves very significant issues of prior restraint.

The doctrine of prior restraint is that principle, dating back to Blackstone,[2] which says that no legal restraint may prevent publication or speech, although criminal or civil actions may result from that speech. The principle has been most often associated with injunctions against newspapers, or speeches, and it was such an injunction that

---

[1] *Kingsley Books, Inc.* v. *Brown*, 354 U.S. 436 (1957). This case was decided on the same day as *Roth* v. *United States*, 354 U.S. 476 (1957).
[2] 4 W. BLACKSTONE, COMMENTARIES *151–153. *See generally* Emerson, *The Doctrine of Prior Restraint*, 20 LAW & CONTEMP. PROB. 648 (1955).

led the Supreme Court, in *Near* v. *Minnesota*,[3] to declare that prior restraints, while not absolutely prohibited in all instances, require the most exigent circumstances for justification.[4] It is against this background of judicial antagonism to prior restraints that any civil regulation of obscenity must be studied, bearing in mind that until there has been a determination of obscenity, there is a presumption that words or speech are within the range of First Amendment protection.

The rationale for the presumption against prior restraint is at times questionable. If the evil to be prevented is the suppression of constitutionally protected speech, then it is certainly possible that the threat of heavy fines or prison terms may have more of a chilling effect, resulting in self-censorship, than the availability of some procedure whereby the legality of the words is determined without the necessity of exposure to criminal sanctions.[5] This consideration, that civil adjudication may in some instances be preferable, has appeared twice in Supreme Court obscenity cases.[6] In addition, *Near* itself, the landmark prior-restraint case, suggested that control over obscenity may constitute an exception to the principles enunciated therein.[7] Finally, there is the fact that obscenity is not speech at all, and thus somewhat different considerations are applicable, since once obscenity has been determined, there is no prior restraint issue because there is no speech involved.[8] For all these reasons, the Supreme Court has been inclined to permit, in the obscenity area, forms of control which would be impermissible in other areas. But in permitting this type of regulation, the Court has been careful to scrutinize the procedures involved to ensure that only that which has been determined to be obscene may be so regulated.[9]

[3] 283 U.S. 697 (1931). Contemporary comment on the case can be found at 31 COLUM. L. REV. 1148 (1931), 9 N.Y.U.L.Q. REV. 64 (1931), and 41 YALE L.J. 262 (1931).

[4] More recent prior-restraint cases include *New York Times Co.* v. *United States*, 403 U.S. 713 (1971) and *Organization for a Better Austin* v. *Keefe*, 402 U.S. 415 (1971).

[5] See O. FISS, INJUNCTIONS 154 (1972).

[6] *Paris Adult Theater I* v. *Slaton*, 413 U.S. 49, 55 (1973); *Kingsley Books, Inc.* v. *Brown*, 354 U. S. 436, 442 (1957).

[7] 283 U.S. at 716.

[8] *See New York Times Co.* v. *United States*, 403 U.S. 713, 726 (1971) (Brennan, J., concurring).

[9] *See generally* Monaghan. *First Amendment "Due Process,"* 83 HARV. L. REV. 518 (1970); Bertelsman, *Injunctions Against Speech and Writing: A Re-Evaluation*, 59 KY. L. J. 319 (1970); Note, *A Model Movie Censorship Ordinance*, 5 HARV. J. LEGIS. 395 (1968); Giglio, *Prior Restraint of Motion Pictures*, 69 DICK. L. REV. 379 (1965); Verani, *Motion Picture Censorship and the Doctrine of Prior Restraint*, 3 HOUSTON L. REV. 11 (1965); Note, *A Blueprint for Censorship of Obscene Mate-*

The Court's first decision in this area was *Kingsley Books, Inc.* v. *Brown*,[10] involving a New York statute providing for injunctions against the sale of certain publications found to be obscene, as well as the seizure and destruction of those materials. The Court approved of the New York statute, and distinguished *Near* on the grounds that it dealt with publications yet to be judicially determined to be undeserving of First Amendment protection, while the New York statute related only to materials actually found to be obscene.[11] Furthermore, *Near* concerned criticism of a public official and thus was much more concerned with protected speech.[12] Although *Kingsley* did not get into any detailed discussion of required procedures,[13] it did lay the basis for all further civil cases. If material has been determined to be obscene, it may be enjoined or otherwise restricted.

Kingsley did not present a classic prior-restraint case, since no restraint had been imposed prior to the determination by a court in an adversary proceeding that the material was obscene and therefore unprotected by the First Amendment. But a true prior restraint was at issue in *Times Film Corp.* v. *City of Chicago*,[14] involving a city ordinance which required that all motion pictures had to be submitted for approval prior to their showing. The exact procedures were not at issue, and the only issue before the court was the existence, under any circumstances, of such a system of prior approval. While admitting that this system constituted a prior restraint,[15] the Court held that such a system would not be per se unconstitutional if the procedures provided adequate safeguards and if the standards applied were legally correct.[16] Since the issue before the Court was so narrow, the

---

rial: Standards for Procedural Due Process, 11 VILL. L. REV. 125 (1965); 33 OHIO ST. L. J. 326 (1972); Annotation, *Validity of Procedures Designed to Protect the Public Against Obscenity,* 5 A.L.R. 3d 1214 (1966 and 1974 Supp.).

[10] 354 U.S. 436 (1957).

[11] *Id.* at 445.

[12] *Id.*

[13] Mr. Justice Brennan dissented on the grounds that a jury trial should be required in any obscenity case, whether civil or criminal. 354 U.S. at 447–448. But this view has now been specifically rejected by the Court in *Alexander* v. *Virginia,* 413 U.S. 836 (1973), holding that a jury trial is not necessary in civil proceedings. The Court's citation, in *Alexander,* to a case holding that a right to jury trial in civil cases is not a fundamental concept of due process, and thus not applicable to the states, shows that the right to jury trial determination in an obscenity case is not to be based on any special factors involving the type of litigation.

[14] 365 U.S. 43 (1961).

[15] *Id.* at 46.

[16] *Id.* at 50. Other licensing schemes had been before the Court before, but in each case the issue was whether the standards were legally correct, and not unconstitutionally vague or overbroad. *Kingsley International Pictures Corp.* v. *Regents,* 360

decision does not provide much guidance, except to indicate that there is no absolute privilege against prior restraint,[17] and thus that some sort of motion picture licensing system would be constitutional.

The Court clarified its *Times Film* holding four years later in *Freedman* v. *Maryland*,[18] which remains the Court's landmark ruling in the licensing and prior-restraint area. *Freedman* involved the procedures of the Maryland State Board of Censors, whose prior approval was required for all motion pictures shown in the state. For the first time, the Court made it clear that prompt *judicial* participation was required for the licensing procedure to be valid. The existence of an adversary proceeding before a licensing board was not, in and of itself, sufficient.

> Because the censor's business is to censor, there inheres the danger that he may well be less responsive than a court—part of an independent branch of government—to the constitutionally protected interests in free expression.[19]

What is most significant about *Freedman* is that the Court clearly specified exactly what was required for a censorship system to be constitutionally acceptable.

> Applying the settled rule of our cases, we hold that a noncriminal process which requires the prior submission of a film to a censor avoids constitutional infirmity only if it takes place under procedural safeguards designed to obviate the dangers of a censorship system. First, the burden of proving that the film is unprotected expression must rest on the censor. . . . Second, while the State may require advance submission of all films, in order to proceed effectively to bar all showings of unprotected films, the requirement cannot be administered in a manner which would lend an effect of finality to the censor's determination whether a film constitutes protected expression. The teaching of our cases is that, because only a judicial determination in an adversary proceeding ensures the necessary sensitivity to freedom of expression, only a procedure requiring a judicial determination suffices to impose a valid final restraint. . . . To this end, the exhibitor must be assured, by statute or authoritative judicial construction, that the censor will, within a specified brief period, either issue a license or go to court to restrain showing the film. Any restraint imposed in advance of a final judicial determination on the

---

U.S. 684 (1959); *Superior Films, Inc.* v. *Department of Education*, 346 U.S. 587 (1954); *Commercial Pictures Corp.* v. *Regents*, 346 U.S. 587 (1954); *Gelling* v. *Texas*, 343 U.S. 960 (1952); *Joseph Burstyn, Inc.* v. *Wilson*, 343 U.S. 495 (1952). Cf. *Hannegan* v. *Esquire, Inc.*, 327 U.S. 146 (1946).

[17] 365 U.S. at 49.

[18] 380 U.S. 51 (1965).

[19] 380 U.S. at 57–58 (footnote omitted).

merits must similarly be limited to preservation of the status quo for the shortest period of time compatible with sound judicial resolution. Moreover, we are well aware that, even after expiration of a temporary restraint, an administrative refusal to license, signifying the censor's view that the film is unprotected, may have a discouraging effect on the exhibitor. . . . Therefore, the procedure must also assure a prompt final judicial decision, to minimize the deterrent effect of an interim and possibly erroneous denial of a license.[20]

Thus, the burden of proof is on the licensing authority, and that authority also has the affirmative obligation to seek judicial enforcement. A system placing the burden of seeking judicial review on the exhibitor is constitutionally insufficient. Finally, the entire procedure must be established to minimize delay, and thus to minimize the period of restraint prior to final judicial determination. As to the exact details of such a procedure, the Court suggested that the New York procedure set forth in *Kingsley Books* might provide an appropriate model, since there was no restraint until after a judicial determination following an adversary proceeding.[21] It should be noted also that the *Freedman* guidelines relate to films, and any system of censorship for books or magazines would probably be impermissible even if it did comply with *Freedman*.[22]

In subsequent cases, the Court was called upon to apply the *Freedman* principles to a wide range of state and federal regulatory schemes. The first of these cases was *Teitel Films* v. *Cusack*,[23] which held that a 50- to 57-day period to complete the administrative process in a licensing situation was impermissibly long, and that the appropriate statute or ordinance must contain a provision for a prompt judicial *decision*. Merely providing for prompt resort to the courts was not enough, if there was no control over the amount of time the case was before the court awaiting decision. In *Blount* v. *Rizzi*,[24] the Supreme Court reviewed the statutory procedures established by Con-

---

[20] *Id.* at 58–59. Subsequent cases have made it clear that a prompt decision by the trial court satisfies the requirements of *Freedman*, and there is no obligation that prompt appellate review be provided. *Interstate Circuit* v. *Dallas*, 390 U.S. 676 (1968); *Ellwest Stereo Theatres, Inc.* v. *Nichols*, 403 F.Supp. 857, 862 (M.D. Fla. 1975).

[21] 380 U.S. at 60. It should be obvious that any *ex parte* restraint, however short, creates grave constitutional problems. See *Carroll* v. *President and Commissioners of Princess Anne*, 393 U.S. 175 (1968); *Marcus* v. *Search Warrant*, 367 U.S. 717, 731 (1961); *Tenney* v. *Liberty News Distributors, Inc.*, 13 App. Div. 2d 770, 215 N.Y.S. 2d 663 (1961).

[22] 380 U.S. at 60–61. *See also Bantam Books, Inc.* v. *Sullivan*, 372 U.S. 58, 70 n.10 (1963).

[23] 390 U.S. 139 (1968).

[24] 400 U.S. 410 (1971).

gress for the detention of obscene mail by the Post Office Department. These procedures were declared unconstitutional since the burden of initiating judicial review was with the owner of the materials, or claimant, and not with the censor, where it must be to comply with *Freedman*.[25] Furthermore, detention was permitted under a probable-cause standard, which the Court held to be insufficient, since full judicial review on the obscenity issue, not merely a probable-cause determination, must be provided as soon as possible.[26] Since a federal statute was at issue, it is possible that the Supreme Court could have construed the statute to cure these infirmities, but the Court determined that rewriting of the statute was necessary, and that "it is for Congress, not this Court, to rewrite the statute." [27]

However, in *United States* v. *Thirty-Seven Photographs*,[28] the Supreme Court did construe a federal statute in such a way as to preserve its constitutionality. The case concerned 19 U.S.C. § 1305, which provides for customs seizures of obscene materials at the port of entry.[29] Although the general statutory scheme for seizure and judicial review conformed to the *Freedman* guidelines, the statute contained no time limits to ensure that the proceedings would be commenced and completed in a period of time short enough to minimize the effect of the prior restraint. But since this was the only defect, the Court construed the statute to provide that judicial proceedings have to be commenced within 14 days from the original seizure, and completed (issuance of a final decree by the court) within 60 days thereafter. This case marks the Court's most explicit statement of the requirement that the time limits must be clearly provided for, but the Court was also careful to note that these particular time periods pertained only to importation proceedings, thus taking into account the overall length of the importation process. The time periods must vary with the context of the type of regulation involved,[30] and it is clear that much shorter periods are required in the context of motion picture licensing and other forms of regulation not involving importation.

Finally, in *Southeastern Promotions, Ltd.* v. *Conrad*,[31] the Supreme Court reaffirmed the vitality of the *Freedman* guidelines [32] and

[25] *Id.* at 417–418.
[26] *Id.* at 420.
[27] *Id.* at 419. As of this writing, Congress has yet to accept this invitation.
[28] 402 U.S. 363 (1971).
[29] *See generally* Chapter 9.5 *supra*.
[30] 402 U.S. at 374.
[31] 420 U.S. 546, 95 S.Ct. 1239 (1975).
[32] 95 S.Ct. at 1247.

applied them to denial of permission to use a municipal facility for a live production of *Hair*. As restated by the Court, therefore, any prior restraint is invalid unless

> *First,* the burden of instituting judicial proceedings, and of proving that the material is unprotected, must rest on the censor. *Second,* any restraint prior to judicial review can be imposed only for a specified brief period and only for the purpose of preserving the status quo. *Third,* a prompt final judicial determination must be assured.[33]

12.2   Seizures

Perhaps the most direct method of control of obscenity is by actual seizure and destruction of obscene materials. It is a procedure authorized by many state statutes,[34] but is not often used at the present time, perhaps due to the ease with which replacement copies of books or magazines or motion pictures can be made available. Nonetheless, it is a method of obscenity regulation that is available and one that has been before the Supreme Court on a number of occasions.

Seizure and destruction may be accomplished in two ways. One is by treating the material as contraband, incident to a criminal prosecution, and destroying it after the conclusion of criminal proceedings. Generally, there must be some statute which provides for such a procedure.[35] If such a statute exists, the courts have consistently held that material which has been found by a court to be obscene can properly be treated as contraband.[36] Therefore, seizure and destruction in this context does not, at the present time, create any significant problems, constitutional or otherwise.[37] There has already been

---

[33] *Id.*

[34] *See* Chapter 10.1 *supra.*

[35] *See United States* v. *50 Magazines,* 323 F.Supp. 395, 409 (D.R.I. 1971).

[36] *See, e.g., United States* v. *Wild,* 422 F.2d 34, 38 (2d Cir. 1969); *People* v. *Steskal,* 55 Ill.2d 157, 302 N.E.2d 321 (1973); *State* v. *Vashart,* 39 Wis.2d 419, 159 N.W.2d 1 (1968); *McKenzie* v. *Butler,* 398 F.Supp. 1319, 1321 (W.D. Tex. 1975). *Cf. Hicks* v. *Miranda,* 422 U.S. 332, 95 S.Ct. 2281, 2290 n.15, 2291 (1975). In *People* v. *Steskal, supra,* the court noted that obscene materials became contraband only if used or intended for use illegally, and could not be deemed contraband *per se* because of the Supreme Court's holding in *Stanley* v. *Georgia,* 394 U.S. 557 (1969).

[37] Generally, only the materials themselves may be considered contraband. In *Moody* v. *Thrush Corporation,* 33 Ohio Misc. 84, 291 N.E. 2d 922, 927 (1972), the court declined to hold that the proceeds of a sale or exhibition of obscene material were contraband, and in *McKenzie* v. *Butler,* 398 F.Supp. 1319 (W.D. Tex. 1975), projection equipment was not found to be contraband.

an adjudication of obscenity, in an adversary proceeding, and thus the type of prior-restraint objection made to other types of proceeding is of no merit.

The other type of seizure-and-destruction proceeding, which has created more difficult constitutional issues, is one unconnected with any criminal action, and solely aimed at destruction of the materials. The Supreme Court approved of this type of procedure in *Kingsley Books, Inc.* v. *Brown*,[38] but more detailed exposition of the constitutional impediments to this type of procedure is to be found in *Marcus* v. *Search Warrant*[39] and *A Quantity of Books* v. *Kansas*.[40] In *Marcus,* a Missouri statute authorized the seizure of allegedly obscene publications, after which they would be destroyed if found by a court to be obscene. The original warrant procedure was entirely *ex parte,* the warrant being issued by a judge or magistrate solely upon the sworn complaint of the complainant. A hearing was held no more than 20 days after the seizure, but there was no time limit within which the court had to announce its decision. In the particular case before the Supreme Court, the sworn complaint did not contain or describe any of the allegedly obscene publications upon which the complaint was based, but merely said that obscene publications were kept at a designated location. On the basis of this complaint, a warrant was issued for the seizure of any obscene publication found at the premises. Thereafter, pursuant to the warrant, 11,000 copies of 280 publications were seized from six different locations named in the warrant. The final decision of the trial court, finding that 100 of the 280 publications were obscene, was issued slightly over two months after the seizure.[41]

In its decision, the Supreme Court distinguished allegedly obscene materials from other forms of contraband, such as intoxicating liquors and gambling paraphernalia, since only with the former is there a danger of suppressing constitutionally protected speech.

> It follows that, under the Fourteenth Amendment, a State is not free to adopt whatever procedures it pleases for dealing with obscenity as

[38] 354 U.S. 436, 444 (1957). "Section 22-a's provision for the seizure and destruction of the instruments of ascertained wrongdoing expresses resort to a legal remedy sanctioned by the long history of Anglo-American law." *Id. See also Beil* v. *Mahoning Valley Distributing Agency, Inc.,* 84 Ohio L. Abs. 427, 169 N.E. 2d 48, *aff'd,* 116 Ohio App. 57, 21 Ohio Ops. 2d 299, 186 N.E.2d 631 (1960).

[39] 367 U.S. 717 (1961).

[40] 378 U.S. 205 (1964). Both of these cases are discussed, in a slightly different context, in Chapter 11.1 *supra.*

[41] 367 U.S. at 720–724.

here involved without regard to the possible consequences for constitutionally protected speech.[42]

As a result, the Court struck down the Missouri procedure since it did not provide any opportunity to contest, before the seizure, the complaining police officer's belief that the materials were obscene, since the warrants were issued on the conclusory allegations of a single police officer, and since too much discretion, in determining which publications were obscene, was given to the officer executing the warrant.[43] In distinguishing *Kingsley Books,* the Supreme Court made it clear that a seizure of this type could only be acceptable if the particular materials were before the court prior to the seizure, if the determination of obscenity was made by the court and not by a police officer, if there was an opportunity for a hearing on the issue of obscenity prior to seizure, and if there was some specified and brief time limit within which a decision on the merits must be issued.

The issues were similar in *A Quantity of Books* v. *Kansas,* except that the warrant was issued after examination of seven of 59 books which were allegedly obscene,[44] and the warrant specifically named the books to be seized. In all, 1715 books were seized as a result of the *ex parte* procedure, and were ultimately held to be obscene. Again, the Supreme Court held the procedure unconstitutional, ruling that a seizure of all copies of a publication was impermissible without a prior adversary hearing "designed to focus searchingly on the question of obscenity." [45]

> [I]f seizure of books precedes an adversary determination of their obscenity, there is danger of abridgment of the right of the public in a free society to unobstructed circulation of non-obscene books.[46]

Thus, the teaching of these cases, as further explained in *Heller* v. *New York,*[47] is that no "massive" seizure of materials is permitted without a prior determination of their obscenity in an adversary proceeding. It seems clear, although not so stated in *Heller,* that individual copies for use as evidence in such a proceeding may be seized upon *ex parte* application, but the multiple seizures must await final judicial determination of obscenity. If, however, the procedural guidelines of *Marcus, Quantity of Books, Freedman,* and *Heller* are

[42] *Id.* at 731.
[43] *Id.* at 731–732.
[44] All 59 of the books were of the same "series."
[45] 378 U.S. at 210–211. The quote is from *Marcus* at 367 U.S. 732.
[46] 378 U.S. at 213.
[47] 413 U.S. 483 (1973). *See* Chapter 11.1 *supra.*

followed, there is no reason why a separate seizure proceeding would not be acceptable.

12.3   Injunctions

In addition to proceedings for the seizure and destruction of obscene materials, another possible civil regulatory process is an injunction prohibiting the sale of particular books or the showing of particular films.[48] Again, the general validity of such an approach was established in *Kingsley Books, Inc.* v. *Brown,*[49] but subsequent cases [50] have made it clear that the constitutional validity of such a procedure depends upon the exact procedures employed. Although both *Marcus* v. *Search Warrant* [51] and *A Quantity of Books* v. *Kansas* [52] dealt with seizure-and-destruction proceedings, their teaching is equally applicable to injunction proceedings. No final restraint may be imposed absent a full adversary hearing on the issue of obscenity, and therefore it is clear that no permanent injunction may issue until there has been a similar full adversary hearing. But if there is such a full adversary hearing, there is no reason why the defendant may not be permanently enjoined from showing the motion picture or selling the publications which have been determined to be obscene.

The difficult issues in the area of injunctions against obscene materials revolve around the scope of temporary or preliminary relief pending the full adversary hearing. In *Freedman* v. *Maryland,*[53] the Supreme Court held, in the context of a licensing procedure, that "any restraint imposed in advance of a final judicial determination on the merits must similarly be limited to preservation of the status quo for the shortest period of time compatible with sound judicial resolution." [54] This should be read in connection with those cases disapproving of any type of *ex parte* restraint where First Amendment interests may be involved, such as *Carroll* v. *President and Commis-*

[48] Some statutes establish this remedy by declaring such publications or films, upon a determination of their obscenity, to be nuisances, while others just create the injunctive remedy apart from any nuisance theory. Legally, however, the issues are the same under either type of statute.

[49] 354 U.S. 436 (1957).

[50] *See* the first section of this chapter.

[51] 367 U.S. 717 (1961). *See also Julian* v. *Las Vegas,* 493 P.2d 1037 (Nev. 1971).

[52] 378 U.S. 205 (1965). *See generally* the second section of this chapter and also Chapter 11.1 *supra.*

[53] 380 U.S. 51 (1965).

[54] *Id.* at 59.

sioner of Princess Anne.[55] Despite these considerations, a number of
courts have permitted *ex parte* temporary restraining orders against
the sale or exhibition of the materials involved, as long as some adversary proceeding was available, at the instance of the defendant,
within a very few days thereafter.[56] These cases, however, do not
seem to comport with the concept that any restraint prior to a full adversary determination must be limited solely to the preservation of
the status quo, and are dealing with materials presumptively entitled
to First Amendment protection. Recognizing this, a number of decisions have limited such preliminary restraint to destruction, alteration, or removal of the materials, but not to exhibition of films and
the like,[57] and others have been even stronger in condemning any *ex
parte* restraint.[58] Some courts have established a probable-cause hearing, thus assuring the defendant of at least some opportunity to be
heard before any restraint is imposed.[59] In order to properly balance
all of the concerns involved, a preliminary proceeding should provide
the following: (1) No *ex parte* relief should be permitted absent an
affirmative showing as to unsuccessful efforts to secure the defendant's presence at the first hearing, or a showing that it is likely the defendant will remove, alter, or destroy the materials in question if notified of the proceeding.[60] (2) If *ex parte* relief is to be given, it must
be limited to restraint against removal, alteration, or destruction of
the materials in question so as to do nothing more than preserve the
status quo. (3) If at all possible, the preliminary restraint should
come only after an abbreviated adversary hearing, at which probable
cause must be shown. (4) If *ex parte* relief is given, the defendant
shall have a right to the hearing specified in (3) upon one day's notice. (5) In any event, the defendant shall have a right to a full ad-

---

[55] 393 U.S. 175 (1968).

[56] *Grove Press, Inc.* v. *Kansas,* 304 F.Supp. 383 (D.Kan. 1969), and 307
F.Supp. 711 (D.Kan. 1969); *ABC Books, Inc.* v. *Benson,* 315 F.Supp. 695 (M.D.
Tenn. 1970); *Braha* v. *Texas,* 319 F.Supp. 1331 (W.D. Tex. 1970); *Grove Press,
Inc.* v. *Flask,* 326 F.Supp. 574 (N.D. Ohio 1970); *South Florida Art Theaters, Inc.*
v. *State,* 224 So.2d 706 (Fla. App. 1969); *Art Theater Guild, Inc.* v. *State,* 469
S.W. 2d 669 (Tenn. 1971); *Dykema* v. *Bloss,* 17 Mich. App. 318, 169 N.W. 2d 367
(1969).

[57] *Go* v. *Peterson,* 14 Ariz. App. 12, 480 P.2d 35 (1971); *Walter* v. *Slaton,* 227
Ga. 676, 182 S.E. 2d 464 (1971), *cert. denied,* 404 U.S. 1003.

[58] *Tenney* v. *Liberty News Distributors, Inc.,* 13 App. Div. 2d 770, 215 N.Y.S.
2d 663 (1961); *Commonwealth* v. *Guild Theatre, Inc.,* 432 Pa. 378, 248 A.2d 45
(1968).

[59] *NGC Theatre Corp.* v. *Mummert,* 107 Ariz. 484, 489 P.2d 823 (1971); *Walter* v. *Slaton,* 227 Ga. 676, 182 S.E. 2d 464 (1971); *cert. denied,* 404 U.S. 1003.

[60] *Cf.* Rule 65(b), FED. R. CIV. PROC.

versary hearing on no more than four days notice after imposition of the preliminary restraint.

Several problems remain as to the scope of the injunction issued. In light of the rejection by *Miller* of the concept of national community standards, the geographical scope of the injunction cannot be broader than the geographic boundaries of the community whose standards are used in determining the obscenity of the materials. If obscenity is determined by resort to statewide standards, then a statewide injunction would be appropriate, but if more localized standards are used, a statewide injunction would be improper.[61]

Issues as to the scope of the injunction also arise in connection with the effect of an injunction on defendants. In other words, who is bound by the injunction? Obviously, any actual defendants in the litigation would be bound, as well as those in some way connected, by agency, succession, or otherwise, with the actual defendant.[62] But is an injunction also binding on anyone attempting to sell, distribute, or exhibit the same materials in the same area, whether or not the person(s) had any connection with or notice of the injunction? Obviously, significant due process problems arise in attempting to impose criminal [63] or contempt sanctions in this situation, but there seems no reason why other parties may not be foreclosed from relitigating the obscenity issue. For this to occur, however, it would be necessary to treat the proceeding as one in rem, a procedure followed in a number of states.[64] In light of the broad mandate given the states by *Kingsley Books, Inc.* v. *Brown* [65] to utilize the full range of common-law remedies in enforcement of their obscenity laws, there is no constitutional objection to such a procedure which would, theoretically, bind the whole world, as long as sufficient notice were given for all persons interested in the outcome to have an opportunity to join the proceedings and participate in the litigation to determine the obscen-

[61] *Cf. United Theaters of Florida, Inc.* v. *State,* 259 So.2d 210 (Fla. App. 1972).

[62] *See* Rule 65(d), FED. R. CIV. PROC.; *In re Lennon,* 166 U.S. 548 (1897); *United States Pipe and Foundry Company* v. *National Labor Relations Board,* 398 F.2d 544 (5th Cir. 1968).

[63] The issue of whether or not a criminal penalty for distribution of obscene material, previously so adjudged in a civil action, may be imposed without independent proof, at the criminal trial, of the material's obscenity, is, at this writing, currently pending before the United States Supreme Court. *McKinney* v. *State,* 296 So. 2d 228, 231 (Ala. 1974), *cert. granted* June 23, 1975 (No. 74–532), 43 U.S.L.W. 3674.

[64] *See* Chapter 9.1 *supra.*

[65] 354 U.S. 436 (1957).

ity of the materials.[66] As long as these due process concerns are satisfied, and as long as the geographic scope is specifically and properly delineated, an in rem procedure, binding everyone, would be permissible. Furthermore, since community standards do change over time, a fact acknowledged by the Supreme Court's use of the word "contemporary," any injunction should be open to relitigation after a statutorily specified period of time, or after a "reasonable" time.[67]

An issue that has come up fairly recently is whether or not a bookstore, theater, or publication may be enjoined as a nuisance on the basis of one or more findings of obscenity, thus preventing any future sales, exhibitions, or publications of any material at all, not only that specifically found to be obscene.[68] The issue was before the U.S. Supreme Court in *Huffman* v. *Pursue, Ltd.*,[69] where the federal district court for the Northern District of Ohio had held that such a procedure was unconstitutionally overbroad "insofar as it permanently or temporarily prevented the showing of films which had not been adjudged obscene in prior adversary hearings."[70] The Supreme Court, however, did not reach the merits, holding that the district court should have given greater consideration to deferring to the state courts in light of the principles of *Younger* v. *Harris*.[71] Most lower courts that have dealt with the issue on the merits, however, have properly recognized that an injunction including materials not yet found to be obscene is constitutionally impermissible.[72] The prevention of future undetermined publication or exhibition, based on past activities, is closest to the Supreme Court's holding in *Near* v. *Minnesota*,[73] and is a clear prior restraint. Nuisance proceedings, to be valid, must be restricted to materials already determined to be ob-

---

[66] *Cf. Mullane* v. *Central Hanover Bank & Trust Co.*, 339 U.S. 306 (1950).

[67] The time might vary depending on whether or not community standards have in fact changed with regard to the material at issue, but the range would probably be from one to three years.

[68] *See* Annotation, *Pornoshops or Similar Places Disseminating Obscene Materials as Nuisance*, 55 A.L.R. 3d 1134 (1974 and 1975 Supp.).

[69] 420 U.S. 592, 95 S.Ct. 1200 (1975). *Cf. MTM, Inc.* v. *Baxley*, 420 U.S. 799, 95 S.Ct. 1278 (1975).

[70] 95 S.Ct. at 1206.

[71] 401 U.S. 37 (1971).

[72] *Sanders* v. *State*, 231 Ga. 608, 203 S.E.2d 153 (1974); *Universal Amusement Co., Inc.* v. *Vance*, 404 F.Supp. 33, 43–44 (S.D. Texas 1975) (three-judge court). *See also Mitchem* v. *State*, 250 So.2d 883 (Fla. 1971); *State ex rel. Ewing* v. *A Motion Picture Film Entitled "Without a Stitch,"* 37 Ohio St. 2d 95, 307 N.E. 2d 911 (1974). *Cf. People* v. *Goldman*, 7 Ill. App. 3d 253, 287 N.E. 2d 177 (1972). Compare *Richards* v. *State*, 497 S.W. 2d 770 (Tex. Civ. App. 1973).

[73] 283 U.S. 697 (1931).

scene, and if those proceedings include any blanket ban on future sales, publications, or exhibitions, they are constitutionally impermissible.

12.4 Zoning Ordinances and Related Municipal Controls

Most local or municipal, as opposed to statewide, forms of obscenity control will be subject to the same considerations as statewide controls, and thus need no separate discussion at this point. There are, however, some restrictions which are peculiar to local regulation, and some mention of these seems justified here. These restrictions generally deal with materials not classified as legally obscene, such as ordinances restricting certain types of motion pictures from being shown in drive-in, or outdoor, theaters, or requiring that such theaters erect walls or fences to keep the screens from being visible to passersby. An ordinance of this type was at issue in *Rabe* v. *Washington*,[74] but the case was decided on other grounds. It arose again, however, in *Erznoznik* v. *City of Jacksonville*,[75] where a section of the Jacksonville municipal code prohibited the showing of any motion picture "in which the human male or female bare buttocks, human female bare breasts, or human bare pubic areas are shown, if such motion picture. . . . is visible from any public street or public place." [76] In an opinion by Mr. Justice Powell, the Supreme Court struck down the ordinance, since it singled out for special restriction certain forms of speech on the basis of content. Since the restriction included films which were not legally obscene, they were protected speech and thus entitled to First Amendment protection, including freedom from imposition of special controls because of the content of the speech. But the Court's opinion does not mean that no such restrictions are valid. Clearly, a requirement that *all* drive-in theaters be shielded would not have the impediment of discrimination on the basis of the type of speech involved, and thus, if properly drafted, should be valid.[77] Also, the restriction could be limited to those motion pictures which were legally obscene, either as to adults or as to

[74] 405 U.S. 313 (1972).

[75] —— U.S. ——, 95 S.Ct. 2268 (1975).

[76] 95 S.Ct. at 2271. Lower court cases, prior to *Erznoznik*, dealing with similar ordinances, include *Chemline, Inc.* v. *City of Grand Prairie*, 364 F.2d 721 (5th Cir. 1966); *Cinecom Theatres Midwest States, Inc.* v. *City of Fort Wayne*, 473 F.2d 1297 (7th Cir. 1973); *Olympic Drive-In Theatre, Inc.* v. *City of Pagedale*, 441 S.W.2d 5 (Mo. 1969); *Bloss* v. *Paris Township*, 380 Mich. 466, 157 N.W.2d 260 (1968). *See* Comment, 45 TEX. L. REV. 345 (1966).

[77] 95 S.Ct. at 2276 n.13.

children.[78] Finally, there is no reason that signs, posters, billboards, advertisements, or other such displays could not have a restriction on nudity, since these forms of speech are much more intrusive than the screen of an outdoor theater. If "the degree of captivity makes it impractical for the unwilling viewer or auditor to avoid exposure," [79] then restrictions based on the content of the speech may be valid, and thus controls on public advertising or signs displaying nudity might well be an exception to the *Erznoznik* holding. The Court did say that a person on the public streets "readily can avert his eyes," [80] so the validity of the restriction will depend on the captivity of the environment.

Somewhat related is the concept of a zoning ordinance restricting "adult" bookstores, or theaters showing "adult" films, to particular locations. There seems no reason why a zoning ordinance could not restrict *all* drive-in theaters, or all motion picture theaters generally, or *all* bookstores, to particular locations.[81] And, of course, if the restriction is only as to the legally obscene, then there is no problem, since these materials could be prohibited entirely. But the designation of "adult", or "X-rated" materials for special restrictions suffers from exactly the same vice as the ordinance at issue in *Erznoznik*. A case raising exactly this issue is currently before the Supreme Court.[82] If the Court follows its reasoning in *Erznoznik,* these zoning restrictions, discriminating among forms of constitutionally protected speech, cannot be sustained. But if the Court feels the presence of adult theaters or bookstores is itself intrusive, or weighs the community interest as being greater than that in *Erznoznik,* then such ordinances might be upheld.

12.5   Licensing

Issues as to the licensing of particular films or publications, substantive and procedural, have already been discussed in Section 12.1 of this chapter. And it is clear that the restrictions on the licensing of motion pictures apply equally to their official classification, as well as

[78] *Id.* at 2276 n.15.

[79] *Id.* at 2272–2273. *See Lehman* v. *City of Shaker Heights,* 418 U.S. 298 (1974).

[80] 95 S.Ct. at 2274.

[81] *Id.* at 2274 n.9.

[82] *Gribbs* v. *American Mini Theatres, Inc.,* No. 75–312, *cert. granted* October 20, 1975, argued March 23, 1976. The opinion below can be found at 518 F.2d 1014 (6th Cir. 1975). *See* 44 FORDHAM L. REV. 657 (1975).

outright prohibition, if this classification places restrictions on certain types of films not placed on other types.[83] But establishments as well as particular films may be subject to a licensing system. There is no reason why a city may not require a license to operate a bookstore or a motion picture theater. However, if the grant or denial of the license depends upon the type of materials sold or exhibited, then the licensing system suffers from the same constitutional infirmity as the ordinance in *Erznoznik* v. *City of Jacksonville.*[84] A license may not be conditioned on the sale or exhibition of only certain types of constitutionally protected materials, nor may it be revoked if the licensee sells constitutionally protected materials. However, if the license is given only to those without criminal convictions, then a criminal conviction for violation of the obscenity laws may justify denial or revocation.

There is an exception to the above discussion for liquor licensing, based upon the Supreme Court's opinion in *California* v. *La Rue.*[85] Since this exception, allowing revocation or denial of a license for speech-related activities otherwise protected by the First Amendment, arises almost universally in the context of live performances, a full discussion is presented in that section of this book.[86]

12.6   Censorship Boards

The remainder of this chapter is concerned with censorship or civil obscenity regulation that is clearly official in nature, and has the force of law behind it. But this section concerns activities that are less clearly the action of the state. If censorship, of any kind, is clearly private, then the First Amendment is inapplicable and there are no constitutional restrictions on the types of censorship imposed.[87] But other forms of private censorship may have official aspects, and thus

[83]*Interstate Circuit, Inc.* v. *Dallas,* 390 U.S. 676 (1968).

[84] 95 S.Ct. 2268 (1975). *See* Section 12.4 of this chapter. This is also subject to the outcome of the case now pending before the Court. *See* note 82 *supra.*

[85] 409 U.S. 109 (1972).

[86] *See* Chapter 9.2 *supra.*

Another form of licensing is the copyright laws, a discussion of which is beyond the scope of this book. *See* Forkosch, *Obscenity, Copyright, and the Arts,* 10 NEW ENG. L. REV. 1 (1974); Schneider, *Authority of the Register of Copyrights to Deny Registration of a Claim to Copyright on the Ground of Obscenity,* 51 CHI.-KENT L. REV. 691 (1975); Note, *Immorality, Obscenity and the Law of Copyright,* 60 SO. DAK. L. REV. 109 (1961); Comment, 31 SO. CAL. L. REV. 301 (1958).

[87] *See Miami Herald Publishing Co.* v. *Tornillo,* 418 U.S. 241 (1974).

come within the restrictions of the First Amendment.[88] In *Bantam Books* v. *Sullivan*,[89] at issue was the legislatively created Rhode Island Commission to Encourage Morality in Youth, which was charged with the duty of investigating, educating, and recommending prosecution as to undesirable publications. The Commission's activities were entirely *ex parte,* but their official creation and operation was enough to bring into play First Amendment limitations on their activities. The Court noted that informal censorship may unconstitutionally inhibit circulation of constitutionally protected materials, and thus the Commission's practice of notifying publishers that works were objectionable for youth, coupled with threats of institution of official action, and creation of blacklists, was impermissible, since this was a prior administrative restraint with no safeguards "against the suppression of nonobscene and therefore constitutionally protected matter." [90]

The issue of informal censorship has arisen most often in attempts to key legal restrictions into the G, PG, R, X rating system of the Motion Picture Association of America.[91] These restrictions may take the form of absolute prohibitions on the exhibition of films with certain ratings, or their restriction to certain areas, or legal enforcement of the age limitations associated with R- and X-rated motion pictures. But any of these schemes involve a prohibition or classification without a determination as to legal obscenity, and thus lack of First Amendment protection, and also fail to provide a prior adversary hearing on the issue of obscenity prior to the imposition of governmental controls. As a result, lower courts have uniformly struck down any attempts at governmental incorporation of these MPAA standards.[92] While such a rating system is by itself free from

[88] *See generally* Note, *Private Censorship of Movies,* 22 STAN. L. REV. 618 (1970); Ayer, Bates, and Herman, *Self-Censorship in the Movie Industry: An Historical Perspective on Law and Social Change,* 1970 WIS. L. REV. 791 (1970); Note, *Legal Responsibility for Extra-Legal Censure,* 62 COLUM. L. REV. 475 (1962); Note, *Film is a Four Letter Word,* 5 MEMPHIS ST. L. REV. 41 (1974); Lockhart and McClure, *Censorship of Obscenity: The Developing Constitutional Standards,* 45 MINN. L. REV. 5, 6–9 and n.7–22 (1960); Note, *Extralegal Censorship of Literature,* 33 N.Y.U. L. REV. 989 (1958).

[89] 372 U.S. 58 (1963). *See also Interstate Circuit, Inc.* v. *Dallas,* 390 U.S. 676 (1968).

[90] *Id.* at 70.

[91] *See generally* Friedman, *The Motion Picture Rating System of 1968: A Constitutional Analysis of Self-Regulation by the Film Industry,* 73 COLUM. L. REV. 185 (1973); Note, *Private Ratings of Motion Pictures as a Basis for State Regulation,* 59 GEO. L. J. 1205 (1971); *see also* authorities cited in note 88 *supra.*

[92] *Motion Picture Association of America* v. *Specter,* 315 F.Supp. 824 (E.D.

any constitutional restraints, it may not be used to place governmental restrictions of any kind on nonobscene material, nor to shortcut the constitutional requirements of *Freedman* v. *Maryland*.[93]

12.7 Declaratory Judgments

As has been mentioned previously,[94] many states have provided for declaratory judgment proceedings, so that the obscenity of given materials might be determined in advance of any criminal prosecution, thus minimizing or eliminating the potential exposure to criminal penalties in the application of the standards for determining obscenity. Depending on the relevant statute, such a declaratory judgment may be sought by the prosecutor, by a potential seller, distributor, or exhibitor of the materials in question, or by either party. Since the issuance of the judgment of obscenity, even if unaccompanied by any coercive relief, would have significant effects on the circulation of the materials in question,[95] the procedures followed must comport with the requirements of *Freedman* v. *Maryland*,[96] at least as to prompt hearings, prompt decisions, and, presumably, burden of proof. If the declaratory judgment is sought by the prosecutor, it would bind the defendant and all others with notice of the proceedings, if the statute so provided,[97] although the defendant in a subsequent criminal prosecution, although chargeable with notice, would still be entitled to have the prosecutor prove the obscenity of the materials beyond a reasonable doubt at the criminal trial.[98] Of course, the scope of the declaratory judgment can extend only to an area congruent with the definition of community applied in application of the contemporary community standards.[99] If the declaratory judgment

---

Pa. 1970); *Engdahl* v. *City of Kenosha, Wis.,* 317 F.Supp. 1133 (E.D. Wis. 1970); *Hooksett Drive-In Theatre, Inc.* v. *Hooksett,* 110 N.H. 287, 266 A.2d 124 (1970) ($500 tax on each showing of X-rated motion picture); *National Association of Theater Owners* v. *Motion Picture Commission of the City of Milwaukee,* 328 F.Supp. 6 (E.D. Wis. 1971). *See* Note, *X-Rated Motion Pictures: From Restricted Theatres and Drive-Ins to the Television Screen?,* 8 VALP. UNIV. L. REV. 107 (1973).

[93] 380 U.S. 51 (1965). *See generally* Section 12.1 of this chapter.

The MPAA itself has resisted all attempts at governmental adoption of its ratings.

[94] *See* Chapter 9.1 *supra.*

[95] *See Bantam Books, Inc.* v. *Sullivan,* 372 U.S. 58, 67 (1963).

[96] 380 U.S. 51 (1965).

[97] *See* text accompanying notes 62 to 67 *supra.*

[98] *Contra, McKinney* v. *State,* 296 So.2d 228, 231 (Ala. 1974), *cert. granted,* June 23, 1975 (No. 74–532), 43 U.S.L.W. 3674.

[99] *See* text accompanying note 61 *supra.*

is sought by a producer, publisher, seller, distributor, or exhibitor, then it would bind only the prosecutor in that locality. As a result, it has been suggested that a defendant class action against all prosecutors might be appropriate in order to get a national determination of acceptability,[100] especially where the "serious literary, artistic, political, or scientific value" standard, which should be measured in accordance with national standards,[101] is determinative.

[100] Note, *Community Standards, Class Actions, and Obscenity Under Miller v. California,* 88 HARV. L. REV. 1838 (1975).
[101] *See* Chapters 6.3, 7.2, and 7.3 *supra.*

13

Pretrial Procedures in
Obscenity Cases

13.1   Grand Jury Proceedings

In virtually every criminal obscenity case, formal proceedings will be commenced by the action of a grand jury. Although, as has been discussed previously, special care must be taken to ensure the validity of any search or seizure,[1] in general an obscenity case may be commenced in the same manner, and according to the same procedures, as any other criminal case.[2] This general rule is now applicable to grand jury proceedings. Thus, although it has been suggested that there be special requirements or controls on the evidence upon which a grand jury can return an indictment, it is now settled that the validity of grand jury proceedings in an obscenity case is to be tested by the same standards that would apply in a more conventional case. No particular evidence of any of the elements of obscenity must be before the grand jury, and the materials themselves are sufficient.[3] The general rule is that an indictment which has been returned by a validly constituted grand jury and which is regular on its face is prima facie sufficient, and some particularized showing of impropriety is necessary in order to look beyond the indictment of the actual proceedings before the grand jury.[4] It is now clear that this principle is as applicable to obscenity cases as to any other kind of case.[5] Thus,

[1] See Chapters 11.1 and 11.2 *supra.*
[2] *Cf. Miller* v. *United States,* 431 F.2d 655 (9th Cir. 1970).
[3] *United States* v. *Hamling,* 481 F.2d 307 (9th Cir. 1973), *aff'd,* 418 U.S. 87 (1974).
[4] *Costello* v. *United States,* 350 U.S. 359, 363 (1956).
[5] *United States* v. *Manarite,* 448 F.2d 583, 594 (2d Cir. 1971), *cert. denied,* 404 U.S. 947; *United States* v. *New Orleans Book Mart, Inc.,* 328 F. Supp. 136, 147 (E.D. La. 1971); *United States* v. *Thevis,* 320 F. Supp. 713, 715 (N.D. Ga. 1970).

the institution of grand jury proceedings, and the standards for examining their validity, are no different merely because the case at issue
involves obscenity.

13.2   Pretrial Motions

A criminal obscenity case is invariably marked by a large
number of pretrial motions, and this is not surprising. The number of
legal issues presented by obscenity litigation is considerable, and
many of these issues are susceptible to resolution by pretrial motion.[6]

The defense should seriously consider filing a motion for a bill
of particulars or its equivalent. Since particulars further limit the
scope of the proof available at trial, the defense will try for as many
particulars as possible, while the prosecution, desiring as much flexibility as possible, should oppose the normal motion for a bill of particulars. The most common reason for denying a motion for a bill of
particulars is that the defense is looking for evidence, rather than particulars, yet defense motions for particulars continue to request large
amounts of material entirely inappropriate for particulars. In general,
a motion for a bill of particulars is more likely to be successful if it
focuses on appropriate subject matter. Matters appropriate for a bill
of particulars would include the date and place of the alleged offense,
the name of any publications alleged to be obscene, and whether or
not it is charged that the material was "pandered," in the legal sense.
Since the purposes of particulars are to advise the defendant of the
substance of the charge and to protect him from double jeopardy, it
would be fitting for the actual materials at issue to be part of the particulars, but this procedure never appears to have been suggested. If
the indictment charges use of a common carrier, or transportation of
obscene materials, then the name of the carrier or method of transportation should be particularized.

Motions to dismiss the indictment are also very common in
obscenity cases. Defense counsel should first see if there is any attack
available on the constitutionality of the governing statute. If the statute is arguably overbroad, overly vague, or incorporates an incorrect
test for obscenity, then a motion to dismiss should be made on these
grounds. The motion to dismiss should also attempt to raise the issue

---

[6] Cases dealing extensively with pretrial motions include *United States* v. *New
Orleans Book Mart, Inc.*, 328 F. Supp. 136 (E.D. La. 1971), and *United States* v.
Luros, 243 F. Supp. 160 (N.D. Iowa 1965), *rev'd on other grounds*, 389 F.2d 200
(8th Cir. 1968).

of the obscenity of the materials whose obscenity is charged, if defense counsel feels that there is some chance that the particular materials at issue could be deemed nonobscene as a matter of law. Finally, a motion to dismiss should, if possible, address any defects in the indictment. In light of the emphasis on specificity in *Miller* v. *California*,[7] it can be argued that an indictment merely in statutory language is insufficient. But the purpose of the specificity requirement in *Miller* was to provide prior notice of what is proscribed, and thus seems to be irrelevant on the issue of the specificity of the indictment. The Supreme Court has held in the context of a federal prosecution that an indictment in statutory language is sufficient.[8] However, state rules of criminal pleading often require considerably more specificity, and an indictment in the state courts merely in statutory language may be insufficient as a matter of law.[9] Although the indictment must charge scienter in some form, an indictment which charges that the acts were done knowingly or willfully is sufficient.[10]

As it is virtually impossible to get a conviction at trial without the actual materials, defense counsel should carefully examine the procedures employed in the seizure of the movie, books, magazines, or pictures, in light of the principles discussed in Chapter 11 of this book. If there is any possible defect, then a motion to suppress should be made. Of course, the defendant must be able to show that he has standing to challenge the particular seizure. And the possibility of a motion to suppress is not limited solely to the allegedly obscene materials. There may be other evidence that was illegally seized and can possibly be excluded from the trial by means of a promptly and properly presented motion to suppress.

Finally, the defense should present as many motions as possible aimed at clarifying the issues at trial. Motions designed to ascertain which community standards will be employed,[11] or what the method of jury selection will be,[12] will make trial preparation more meaningful.

Of course, other motions may be relevant in a particular case.

[7] 413 U.S. 15 (1973).

[8] *Hamling* v. *United States,* 418 U.S. 87 (1974).

[9] See *Spears* v. *State,* 253 Miss. 108, 175 So.2d 158 (1965) (mere allegation of obscenity is insufficient). *Compare State* v. *Clein,* 93 So.2d 876 (Fla. 1957); *Ratner* v. *Municipal Court,* 256 Cal. App. 2d 925, 64 Cal. Rptr. 500 (1967).

[10] *United States* v. *Zacher,* 332 F. Supp. 883 (E.D. Wis. 1971); *People* v. *Shapiro,* 6 App. Div. 2d 271, 177 N.Y.S.2d 670 (1958).

[11] See Chapter 6.4 *supra.*

[12] See Chapter 14.2 *infra.*

Motions for a change of venue, to dismiss on jurisdictional grounds, and the like should not be neglected if they seem appropriate.

13.3   Discovery

In a civil obscenity case, whether for an injunction, or a declaratory judgment, or an in rem proceeding, the full range of discovery tools will generally be available. Interrogatories, depositions, requests for admissions of facts, and motions for the production of documents should be extensively employed by both sides in order to increase the level of preparation, to find out as much as possible about the opposing case, and to minimize the possibility of surprise at trial. But discovery should not be ignored in a criminal case as well. Under the federal rules,[13] and many state rules and statutes, the defendant will have a right to see the defendant's grand jury testimony and any statements made by the defendant, but these will rarely be material. More significant, however, is the defendant's virtually absolute right, at least in the federal courts,[14] to any scientific tests or experiments. A logical interpretation of "scientific tests or experiments" should allow the defendant access to any expert evaluation of the material in question, and any survey evidence that may be used by the government.

The defendant should also consider moving for the production of documentary evidence prior to trial if this is permitted by the rules or statutes of the jurisdiction.[15] This is especially important if pandering is alleged or expected to be raised as an issue, or if scienter is likely to be a material issue. Certainly in the case of pandering, documentary evidence will be the basis of the prosecution's argument, and the particular advertisements upon which the government relies should be available to the defense. Similarly, scienter is often proved by documentary evidence such as letters, shipping instructions, brochures, and the like, and the defendant's motion for discovery should include these items.

If the defendant does move for discovery of evidence of this type, the prosecution should consider moving for reciprocal

---

[13] FED. R. CRIM. P. 16(a).

[14] See 1 C. WRIGHT, FEDERAL PRACTICE AND PROCEDURE § 253 at 500 (1969 and 1973 Supp.) and cases cited therein, such as *United States* v. *White,* 50 F.R.D. 70, 72 (N.D. Ga. 1970), *aff'd,* 450 F.2d 264 (5th Cir. 1971), *cert. denied,* 405 U.S. 1072.

[15] *See, e.g.,* FED. R. CRIM. P. 16(b).

discovery.[16] While it is true that this requires a clear showing of need,[17] material discovery of expert opinion and documentary evidence should result in fewer delays and surprises at trial.

13.4   Joinder

Issues regarding the joinder of offenses, counts in an indictment, and joinder of parties are generally no different in an obscenity case than they are in any other type of criminal case, but a few considerations should be mentioned.

Although the existence of a corporate entity will not shield its officers or managers from criminal liability, if every element of the offense can be proved against the individuals, the prosecutor should still attempt to have the corporation joined in the indictment or, if a civil case, the complaint. It is clear that a corporation, as well as an individual, can violate the obscenity laws.[18] But only an individual, and not a corporation, has a Fifth or Fourteenth Amendment privilege against self-incrimination, and thus joinder of the corporation may broaden the available discovery and subpoena rights. Of course, a corporation and its records can be subpoenaed even if not joined, but other investigatory techniques, such as discovery, are broader if the corporation is actually a party.

The prosecutor should make sure that each separate offense charged is contained in a separate count. It is, of course, possible to have more than one violation of the same statute, and this can even occur within the same general pattern of conduct, as, for example, when one is both the sender and recipient of obscene material.[19] But just because more than one book or magazine is sent or distributed does not mean that each copy must be a separate offense, and a count or indictment charging the sender with sending more than one copy is not duplicative.[20] It is generally advisable for the prosecutor to charge a violation of every applicable statute,[21] so as to give him the greatest flexibility in proving his case. Of course, if two or more statutes essentially penalize the same offense, he may be compelled to

[16] *See, e.g.,* FED. R. CRIM. P. 16(c).

[17] 1 C. WRIGHT, FEDERAL PRACTICE AND PROCEDURE § 255 (1969 and 1973 Supp.) and cases cited therein.

[18] *See United States* v. *New York Herald Co.,* 159 F. 296 (2d Cir. 1907).

[19] *See Rodd* v. *United States,* 165 F.2d 54 (9th Cir. 1947), *cert. denied,* 334 U.S. 815 (1948).

[20] *See Clark* v. *United States,* 211 F. 916 (8th Cir. 1914).

[21] For example, many federal indictments charge violations of both 18 U.S.C. § 1462 and 18 U.S.C. § 1465 for the same conduct.

elect among them at some point in the proceedings. The prosecutor should also make sure that each count is directed to only one act or pattern of conduct. In *United States* v. *Wells*,[22] an indictment under 18 U.S.C. § 1465 was dismissed because it was stated in the disjunctive, alleging a purpose of sale *or* distribution for the interstate shipment.

13.5   Fair Trial–Free Press Issues

Obscenity litigation, especially in smaller communities, often attracts a great deal of public attention. Furthermore, the topic of obscenity is one that draws considerable public comment on television and radio, and in newspapers and magazines. Because of this, in an obscenity trial involving a jury, special care must be taken to ensure that the amount of publicity is not so extensive and prejudicial as to deny to the defendant the right to a fair trial. Since the application of the concept of local community standards [23] makes a change of venue especially difficult, more efforts must be made to control prejudicial publicity than might otherwise be the case. The general guidelines on the appropriate balance among the right to a fair trial, the right to know, and the freedom of the press are of course derived from the Supreme Court.[24] But the special undesirability of a change of venue distinguishes obscenity cases from all others. Therefore, it is important that pretrial orders regarding prejudicial publicity be given, especially to counsel and, if possible, to the press, to lessen the effect on the defendant of the highly emotional and political setting of an obscenity trial.

[22] 180 F. Supp. 707 (D. Del. 1959).
[23] *See generally* Chapter 6 *supra.*
[24] *See Estes* v. *Texas,* 381 U.S. 532 (1965); *Sheppard* v. *Maxwell,* 384 U.S. 333 (1966); *Irvin* v. *Dowd,* 366 U.S. 717 (1961).

14

Jury Selection in Obscenity Cases

14.1 Standards for Jury Selection

Even more than in most criminal cases, jury selection in an
obscenity case is of the utmost importance, and may well be the most
important part of the entire trial. Therefore, even prior to the beginning of the trial, prosecution and defense counsel should give careful
consideration to the standards they will adopt in jury selection. In
other words, just what type of juror does counsel want on the jury?
One of the reasons jury selection is so important is that virtually
every member of the public has preexisting views on sex, sexual
morality, and pornography, and these views are generally deep-seated
and fervently held. In determining tactics and procedures for selecting
the jury, counsel should try to focus not only on what these personal
views of individual jurors are, but also on whether or not the individual juror will be willing or able to put aside these views and decide
the case solely on the facts brought out at trial and the law as it is
explained by the court. It is probably safe to say that it will be more
difficult for a juror completely to put aside his personal views on sex
and obscenity in an obscenity case than it would be for that same
juror to put aside his personal feelings in a case touching less on
moral and religious beliefs.

In a number of recent criminal trials which have received
national publicity, experts in criminology, sociology, and psychology
have been employed by counsel to assist in jury selection. These
experts often help prepare the voir dire examination and then observe
the appearance, demeanor, and responses of the prospective jurors so
as to assist counsel in exercising peremptory challenges and making
challenges for cause. Given the significant moral, religious, and psychological considerations in an obscenity case, and the concomitant

pressures on the jurors, it seems clear that if the assistance of such experts is useful in any case, then an obscenity case should provide an excellent opportunity for their use. Of course, counsel may feel that experts are of little value in an obscenity case, or that views as to obscenity may be easier to identify without expert assistance than views in a murder or political corruption case. This decision, of course, must be made by counsel depending on his or her feelings about experts and confidence in the fine art of jury selection. But employment of expert assistance in jury selection should at least be considered when the resources are available.

The process of jury selection consists in large part of judgments, based on intuition and experience, of the correlation between causally unrelated factors. In other words, counsel must evaluate the correlation between age and views on pornography, or occupation and views about the prosecution or defense, or marital status and views on morality, and the like. Much of the remainder of this section is devoted to a discussion of characteristics which correlate with factors advantageous to the prosecution or the defense.[1]

It should be reasonably obvious that, all other things being equal, the prosecution should favor older jurors and the defense younger jurors. Older jurors have been brought up in an age of considerably less permissiveness both as to sexually explicit material and sexual mores generally.[2] Their values are, more often than not, in keeping with times when suppression of obscenity was stricter and not curtailed by so many constitutional roadblocks. If they have been brought up in an era when not even nudity or four-letter words appeared on the motion picture screen or in print, they may assume that material showing actual sexual conduct is of course obscene, and be prosecution-oriented in an obscenity case. Moreover, older people are likely to be more conservative and settled in their personal habits, more sympathetic to police and government generally, and therefore have a tendency to believe the prosecution over the defense in disputed issues.

---

[1] Whether it is proper to take those characteristics into consideration, particularly ones like minority status, religion, sex, and age, is beyond the scope of this discussion, and the author, by including them, does not mean to either approve or disapprove of their use in jury selection. See *Swaim* v. *Alabama,* 380 U.S. 202 (1965); *United States* v. *Pollard,* 483 F.2d 929 (8th Cir. 1973), *cert. denied,* 414 U.S. 1137.

[2] When one makes a decision to aim for jurors of a certain age, or sex, or background, this is, of course, based on certain generalities about people with those characteristics. To the extent that the generalities are not applicable to a given individual, then the choice must be modified accordingly.

One caveat should be noted, however. The defendant in obscenity cases is very often the head of a small- to middle-sized self-made business, whether he or she is a distributor, exhibitor, or bookstore owner. A juror who has also owned or run a business, perhaps having had to do personally distasteful things in order to succeed, may very well have sympathy for a defendant who is seen as "just someone trying to make a living."

Conversely, the defense will, absent more significant indicators, try to get jurors who are younger, preferably under thirty. They are more likely to have been brought up in sympathy with the sexual permissiveness of modern times, and are less likely to be surprised, shocked, or offended by the material at issue in the trial. Furthermore, younger people are generally more likely to have a "live and let live" political philosophy, sympathetic to the notion that if people want to see or read obscene material, the government ought not to stop them. Also, younger people are generally less sympathetic to the government, the police, prosecutors, and authority generally, and therefore would tend to be defense-oriented.

The spread of pornography and the perceived lowering of moral standards are often associated with the increase in crime and a general decrease in feelings of public or private security. People who live in high crime areas, or who for some other reason feel personally threatened by changes in society, might be inclined to favor stricter law enforcement and a "crackdown" on pornography, and thus would be likely to be sympathetic towards the prosecution and antagonistic towards the defense. Those who do not feel threatened by such changes, and who have a feeling of security, are likely to be less concerned about obscenity as a crime and less sympathetic to the prosecution. This group may very well include older people whose children are grown, but whether this factor will dominate over more prosecution-oriented factors in older people is extremely difficult to judge.

Most arguments in favor of strict obscenity regulation generally include a strong judgment of the effect of obscenity on juveniles, and most parents of young children will be sympathetic to this appeal. The prosecution should therefore look for jurors, especially women, with young children and a relatively conventional family life. Someone with a spouse, children, and a house in the suburbs will be much more likely to favor the prosecution, as a force trying to preserve the security of that lifestyle, than would someone single, or without children, or with a more unconventional or more transient mode of living.

Somewhat related to these factors is personal income. Those who feel most threatened by the increase in crime and the sensed lowering of moral standards are the middle-income segments of the population, and they are likely to be in sympathy with the "law and order" ideals exemplified by the prosecution. Those with high incomes may feel more secure, and may have had more exposure to people with varied or unconventional lifestyles, and thus would be hesitant to consider obscenity a serious crime. However, those with very high incomes may also feel a significant interest in stability and law and order, while middle-income people who feel threatened by violent crimes could very well feel that less government money should be spent on obscenity prosecutions and more on increased police protection or other more direct methods of reducing the incidence of violent crime. Lower income people are likely to be the most threatened by the increase in crime and most respectful of authority figures such as the police or the prosecution, but they may also be alienated from government and thus not especially sympathetic to the prosecution. In short, socioeconomic factors can be correlated in different ways in different individuals with feelings about obscenity, and income level should thus not be a major independent factor in counsel's jury selection decisions.

Other lifestyle factors, however, may be considerably more determinative. If an individual lives in an area containing a large number of adult bookstores, or theatres showing X-rated movies, or where the presence of such businesses is a matter of public concern, then that individual is much more likely to be oriented towards the prosecution in an obscenity case. However, and this may apply to factors other than residence, the more removed an individual is from any of the detrimental, unpleasant, or harmful aspects of sexually explicit materials, the less likely he or she will be to be favorably disposed toward the prosecution.

An individual's lifestyle as reflected in his or her employment may be especially significant. Someone with a type of occupation highly regimented as to hours, hierarchy, and working conditions will generally tend to be more prosecution-minded, regardless of where he or she is in the hierarchy of the business or office. Someone with a less structured, nonauthoritarian, more independent type of occupation will tend to be less favorably disposed toward the prosecution and more sympathetic to the defense.

As a general rule, jurors with more education will be preferable for the defense in an obscenity case, and those with only a high school education or less are preferable for the prosecution. However, education here is construed to mean mainly the liberal arts or other more academic disciplines. In the technical areas such as engineering or the computer sciences, or in business fields such as management or accounting, higher education rarely correlates with a more libertarian outlook, and thus does not indicate any particular predisposition toward the defense.

A prospective juror's personal views as to sex and morality are of course of crucial importance in evaluation. Often an insight into these views can be gained from other factors, with religion being perhaps the most important. Regardless of the particular faith or denomination, religious people—especially regular churchgoers—will likely be most offended by the material on trial in an obscenity case, and thus most sympathetic with obscenity laws in general and the particular prosecution before them. Individuals who do not consider themselves religious, who are not members of any church or organized religious group, or who are not church-goers are likely to be less concerned with obscenity as a substantive evil and thus less sympathetic to the prosecution. If an individual is religious, and his or her church is active in the antipornography movement, or has strong strictures against sexually explicit materials, such as do the Catholic Church and most of the fundamentalist churches, then this individual is likely to be extremely dangerous for the defense. If an individual is strongly religious, and his or her religion actively condemns pornography, a challenge for cause by the defense may very well have merit. Certainly, if an individual feels it would be a sin to vote to acquit that which his church condemns, he cannot be free from bias, and should be excused for cause. If the individual can demonstrate, however, that his or her decision will be solely a legal one, based on the evidence and on the law, regardless of the views of the church to which he or she belongs, then the person should not be excused for cause. Mere church membership cannot justify exclusion for cause, but rather the extent to which that church membership prevents a decision based solely on the law. There is nothing wrong with religious support of the obscenity laws, but if religious principles forbid that which the law allows, and an individual feels more bound by religious principles than by the instructions of the judge, he should be excused.

Personal views as to sexual morality may be as significant as membership in an organized church. Persons with more liberal views of sexual morality, personal freedom, or marriage and divorce are more advantageous for the defense and less so for the prosecution.

Clearly, people who are more puritanical in outlook are better for the prosecution, and, other things being equal, older people who have never been married are good prosecution jurors, while married, and more especially divorced, people are good defense jurors.

Determinations based on the sex of the prospective juror are fraught with uncertainty. Among parents with children of high school age or younger, women tend to be more sensitive to the effects of obscenity than men, and thus make better prosecution jurors. Among older people, however, women tend to be more liberal than men as far as issues of personal freedom or diverse lifestyles are concerned, and, statistically, would be better defense jurors. It must be remembered that most of the material at issue in modern obscenity cases is likely to be directed towards men, and rather offensive to women; thus women in general may be better for the prosecution. Furthermore, women who consider themselves part of the women's liberation movement will be especially disturbed by the portrayal of women in most sexually explicit materials, and thus may be more favorable to the prosecution than other aspects of their lifestyle would indicate.

In general, members of minority groups are somewhat hostile to the prosecution, especially younger members of those groups, and this may be a factor in jury selection. However, most often the defendant in a criminal obscenity case will be white, wealthy, and well-dressed, and thus provoke hostility from minority group members who see him profiting from an illegal act and able to afford the best defense, while the quality of defense available to poor nonwhites is significantly lower.

People with a literary or artistic background, occupation,[3] or lifestyle are apt to be especially concerned with the dangers of censorship, and opposed to the idea of obscenity laws. They will probably be familiar with the use of coarse language and sexual descriptions in literature, and with sex and nudity in the arts, and so will be somewhat sympathetic to the defense and to the concept of complete creative freedom. But if the material is clearly commercial pornography, not presented in anything resembling an artistic or literary manner, these individuals may be annoyed at attempts to justify such materials as artistic or literary.

The more a juror is shocked or offended by the material in question, the more likely it is that he or she will find the material to be

---

[3] It should be noted that professional associations of authors, publishers, and librarians have been extremely active in opposition to obscenity laws and obscenity prosecutions.

obscene. Therefore, it is to the prosecution's disadvantage, and the defense's advantage, to have jurors who have had previous experiences with sexually explicit material. Individuals who have seen stag films or X-rated movies, or who have read magazines which are sexually oriented, will be less shocked by the material they see at trial and therefore less likely to convict. They are also likely to have a different perception of contemporary community standards than people without such previous exposure, and therefore will be less likely to think that the material shown to them is patently offensive in terms of contemporary community standards. Access to pornography and discussions about sex are generally more prevalent in all-male environments, and thus it is reasonable to assume that men who have been in the military, or belonged to college fraternities, are more likely than others to have had some exposure to sexually explicit materials.

The discussion in this section has thus far been based primarily on attitudes towards pornography and censorship that are likely to have a significant effect on the disposition of an individual juror. Equally important are beliefs and attitudes which may govern jurors' perceptions of and reactions to the trial and the evidence. A person who works for a law enforcement agency, or who has close friends or relatives who do, is much more likely to be sympathetic toward the prosecutor and any law enforcement officials giving testimony at the trial. To some extent this effect may be noted in government employment generally. Depending on the degree of relationship and the type of employment, the juror may well be excused for cause, as in the case of a postal employee in a prosecution for use of the mails where other postal employees may very well be witnesses for the prosecution. Even in less extreme cases, anything that would indicate a partiality toward governmental or law enforcement agencies is a significant factor to be considered.

Both sides must also consider the relationship of the individual juror to the judge. Those with more authoritarian occupations or beliefs are much more likely to be responsive to any perceived (even if not actual) bias on the part of the judge. If the defense or prosecution anticipates making a large number of objections, most of which will be overruled, they should try to exclude those jurors likely to be most respectful of the judge.[4] These are also the jurors who will listen most carefully to the judge's instructions, and try to follow them to

---

[4] Thus, it may be helpful to notice, during voir dire examinations, whether the juror addresses the judge as "sir" or "your honor" or nothing at all, or if the juror seems especially frightened by talking to the judge.

the letter. Whether this is deemed good or bad for the prosecution or defense will depend on how each foresees the case, and on the attitudes of the judge, but it is an important factor to be considered.

Finally, counsel must try to evaluate how the jury will act as a group. Are certain people likely to be leaders in any discussion? An otherwise "harmful" juror may be less so if he is not likely to be forceful in the jury room. If there is a shortage of peremptory challenges, they should be used on those who seem antagonistic to counsel's position *and* who are likely to be able to persuade others of their views. If counsel feels he has a weak case, and would consider a hung jury a victory, he should look, among those who seem most sympathetic to his case, for those who are least likely to succumb to majority pressure. If more than one juror seems sympathetic, he should look for jurors who are similar in their personal characteristics of age, education, and so forth, as they may be more likely to "hold out" if they stand together.

These are, of course, not the only factors that should be considered, nor is any one likely to be determinative as to how a given juror will vote. Others have mentioned other considerations which may very well have merit.[5] This section has attempted to present an analysis of the kinds of factors that may influence the verdict of an individual juror. This should not be looked upon as a hard and fast guide, nor as a substitute for counsel's judgment, intuition, and experience. But some detailed thought in advance as to just what counsel is looking for will make jury selection a more effective process.

14.2   Voir Dire Examination of Prospective Jurors

The extent to which counsel will be able to base jury selection decisions on any or all of the factors discussed above will, of course, depend upon how much counsel knows about the potential jurors, and this will in turn depend upon the method of voir dire examination employed by the court and the extent to which counsel can most effectively use the method available. In many states, not only is voir dire examination conducted solely by the court but the questioning of panel members is rather cursory, primarily devoted to identifying obvious cases of personal relationships between jurors and the parties or attorneys, or prior exposure to the particular facts at issue in the

[5] *See, e.g.,* G. LEFCOURT, ET AL., OBSCENITY LAW 135–141 (Practicing Law Institute Outline, 1974); Rogge, *Obscenity Litigation,* 10 AM. JUR. TRIALS §§ 50–51 at 168–172 (1965).

trial. If this is the normal practice, and if counsel wishes a more detailed examination, an effort should be made in advance of the trial to persuade the judge to undertake a more extensive examination of prospective jurors. Whether the voir dire examination is conducted by the judge or by the attorneys, an examination more searching than that in a more conventional case seems justified. In an obscenity case, more so than in most other cases, the personal political, moral, religious, and sexual opinions of the jurors are likely to affect the verdict they render. Few people think there ought not to be laws against murder, burglary, or rape, but many think there ought not to be laws against obscenity, and this is the kind of personal bias of which the prosecutor should be aware. Similarly, in few other areas of the law are jurors likely to discover that acts personally abhorrent and shocking to them are nonetheless legally protected. The defense should be given an opportunity to know of any such personal views in advance.

Assuming that the court has agreed to a reasonably searching examination of potential jurors, the next issue to be faced is determining who is going to conduct the examination. In most state courts, the general rule is for the court to conduct the voir dire examination. In the federal courts, questioning by counsel is more common, but it is still a matter for the judge's discretion.[6] The opportunity to question the prospective jurors gives counsel considerably more flexibility in adapting questions to the individual jurors, to their responses to prior questions, and to questions asked by opposing counsel. In addition, it provides an excellent opportunity for counsel to introduce himself and, if defending, his client, as well as to inform and "condition" the jury, as is discussed in the next section of this chapter. These are factors which the court will obviously understand and toward which it will in most cases be sympathetic, but the court will also be aware of the fact that where voir dire examination is conducted by counsel, considerably more time is expended in the process. The court may consider allowing counsel to do the questioning subject to a time limit, or may do most of the questioning itself subject to some additional questions by counsel. One factor to be considered is that in an obscenity case the questions may very well deal with sexual matters, opinions, or experiences, and the judge may feel it more appropriate if these types of questions are not asked by the court.

Preparation for the voir dire phase of the trial will be very dif-

---

[6] Federal Rules of Criminal Procedure, Rule 24(a); *see Rodgers* v. *United States,* 402 F.2d 830 (10th Cir. 1968).

ferent depending on whether the court or counsel is asking the questions, and so the attorneys should request advance determination from the court as to which procedure will be followed. Of course, if the judge is unwilling to rule in advance,[7] then counsel must prepare fully for either type of examination. If the judge is conducting the voir dire, the attorneys should present to the judge, in advance of the examination, a list of questions which they desire to have asked. While the judge is given broad discretion as to whether or not to ask the specific questions suggested by counsel,[8] or whether to inquire into certain areas,[9] a failure to examine about a clearly relevant area may, at least in the federal courts, constitute reversible error.[10] Counsel should therefore present as complete a list of suggested questions as possible to the court, covering all areas of possible relevancy. A list of 100 questions or more would certainly not be unprecedented. If the court feels the list is too lengthy, it can make appropriate modifications, but it is important that a complete list be presented, both to give the court an opportunity to see all that counsel considers relevant and to preserve, on the part of the defense, the possibility of appellate review. If questions in a certain area are not suggested, counsel may not complain on appeal that they should have been asked.[11] Of course, the suggested questions should be proper questions for voir dire examination. Counsel cannot complain of a failure to examine in a certain area if the only questions suggested in that area were clearly improper.[12]

Assuming that counsel has reached this point, the next issue to be faced is where the prospective jurors will be questioned. There is authority for the proposition that jurors should be questioned individually, outside the presence of those already selected or remaining to be questioned, where the case is especially controversial, has attracted a great deal of publicity, or involves especially sensitive areas of

---

[7] The judge may request suggested questions from counsel and not make his decision as to who will ask them until he sees what they are and what areas counsel wish to be explored in voir dire examination.

[8] *See Hamling* v. *United States,* 418 U.S. 87 (1974); *Ross* v. *United States,* 374 F.2d 97 (8th Cir. 1967), *cert. denied,* 389 U.S. 882 (1968).

[9] *Hamling* v. *United States,* 418 U.S. 87 (1974); *United States* v. *Smaldone,* 485 F.2d 1333 (8th Cir. 1973), *cert. denied,* 417 U.S. 926, 94 S. Ct. 1934 (1974).

[10] *United States* v. *Dellinger,* 472 F.2d 340 (7th Cir. 1972), *cert. denied,* 410 U.S. 970 (1971).

[11] *Cf. United States* v. *Townsend,* 426 F.2d 811 (4th Cir. 1970).

[12] *Brundage* v. *United States,* 365 F.2d 616 (8th Cir. 1965).

questioning.[13] This would seem to be especially desirable in obscenity cases, where the jurors may find some of the questions particularly personal or embarrassing, and thus be reluctant to give complete and frank answers in open court. If they are questioned individually, only in the presence of the judge, counsel, and essential court personnel, some of this reluctance may be lessened.

If counsel is to question the prospective jurors, then even though formal written questions may not be used, considerable preparation is necessary to ensure that all relevant areas are covered. Some attorneys prefer to focus most of their questions on the entire jury, and some prefer to ask the jurors individual questions, but this is generally a matter of personal style. Of course, if particular jurors give certain responses to group questions, then more individual probing may be called for.

Regardless of whether counsel or the court conducts it, the examination or requested questions should cover a broad range. Specific questions are given in Appendix A of this book, but certain generalizations are possible here. Both prosecution and defense should try to find out as much as possible about the personal backgrounds of the potential jurors, by asking questions relating to occupation, residence, marital status, education, number of children, membership in religious and civic organizations, and the like. Questions should also relate to the most obvious sources of bias, such as knowledge of or relationship to the parties, the attorneys, or the particular facts of the case. Except in the most unusual cases, anyone who has actually read the material or seen the movie or performance at issue prior to the trial should be excluded for cause. If the trial or the work at issue has attracted a large amount of publicity, then questions should be aimed at determining the effect on the individual juror of this pretrial publicity. Questions should be asked as to relationships with persons in law enforcement, in the book or magazine business, or in the entertainment business, as well as questions aimed at determining if any of the jurors themselves have had experience with law enforcement or with the publishing or entertainment businesses. Also, there must be inquiry as to membership in organizations particularly interested in obscenity laws one way or another, such as the Legion of Decency or the American Civil Liberties Union.

Having dealt with these "preliminaries," the questioning should

---

[13] *See United States* v. *Callabella,* 448 F.2d 1299 (2d Cir. 1971); *United States* v. *Addonizio,* 451 F.2d 49 (2d Cir. 1971), *cert. denied,* 405 U.S. 936 (1972).

turn to particular attitudes and beliefs. Counsel should ask about beliefs as to the necessity or desirability of obscenity laws in general, or censorship, or changes in the sexual mores of society, or the existence of X-rated movies, adult bookstores, and the like. Potential jurors should be asked if they are offended by adult bookstores or sex in movies. More specifically, questions should focus on actual exposure to sexually explicit materials; thus the members of the jury panel should be asked if they have ever seen a stag movie or an X-rated movie, or been in an adult bookstore, or read "adult" magazines and, if applicable, the frequency of such exposure should be determined. In this context would also come one of the most important, but perhaps the most sensitive, areas for questioning. Many of the books and movies at issue in modern obscenity cases deal with sexual conduct other than "normal" heterosexual intercourse between married adults. Prospective jurors should, if feasible, be asked if they are offended by the idea of premarital or extramarital sex, masturbation, homosexuality, oral sex, sex between adults and children, sex between humans and animals, or sadomasochistic acts. Every prospective juror will probably respond affirmatively to at least one of the above, but the particular acts that offend may tell a great deal about the individual's moral values and tolerance. There should be questions as to the juror's moral and religious beliefs and whether those beliefs might interfere with the ability to deliver a fair verdict.

Finally, questions should be directed to the actual nature of the trial. Jurors should be asked if they could deliver a guilty verdict despite a lack of belief in obscenity laws, or deliver a not-guilty verdict despite being personally offended by the material at issue. If there is to be expert testimony, or survey evidence, they should be asked if they have any particular beliefs as to the value of such evidence. And, most important of all, jurors should be asked if they would rather not be a juror in an obscenity case. Neither side should want such a juror, nor should the court keep an individual who has strong personal feelings against being on the jury in an obscenity case.

The foregoing discussion has dealt mainly in generalities, and the reader is again referred to Appendix A for examples of actual questions that may be applicable.

14.3 "Conditioning" the Jury

In the previous two sections, the assumption has been that voir dire examination is for the purpose of learning as much as possible about prospective jurors so that challenges for cause and peremptory challenges can be made and exercised in an intelligent and fully informed manner. This is, of course, the "official" purpose of voir dire examination, but there are other incidental purposes and advantages. As much as voir dire is an opportunity for the attorney to learn about the members of the jury,[14] it is also a chance for the jury to learn about the attorneys, the parties, and the nature of the case. This educational function should not be neglected by counsel, especially in an obscenity case. The concepts the jury will have to understand and apply are extremely difficult to master, and the more the jurors hear the words and have the terms explained, the more likely it is that they will understand exactly what it is they are being called upon to decide.

Even more important, especially for the defense, is the use of voir dire examination for the purpose of "conditioning" or desensitizing the jury. In almost every obscenity case, the material at issue, whether book, magazine, or movie, is considerably more explicit in sexual detail than what the jury is accustomed to seeing. For most jurors, the material will probably be the most graphic portrayal of sex they have ever seen in print or on the screen. Most jurors will be exposed to sexual acts and practices they have never seen, never experienced, and perhaps never knew existed. Given these factors, the initial reaction of most jurors when first shown the material they will be called upon to evaluate is shock. Many will be extremely offended. And the more the jury is shocked or offended, the less likely it is that any other evidence will change their minds, or that they will consider and try to understand all of the intricacies of the legal test for obscenity. Therefore, it is to the defense's advantage to "condition" the jury to what is to come. The voir dire examination, with its questions about various sexual practices, habits, experiences, and beliefs, is also getting the jurors accustomed to thinking about sex practices other than the ones they may be most familiar with. They know they will be seeing something fairly shocking and they will be getting ready for it. All of this will lessen the shock factor and increase the chances of a verdict based solely on the law and the facts, and not on the emotions. Ideally, the jurors should even be let down or "disappointed" when they actually see the material. If, as a result of voir dire examination and the opening statements, the jurors expect something considerably more offensive than what actually

[14] And, of course, knowledge about the backgrounds and beliefs of members of the jury is as useful in actually trying the case as it is in picking the jury.

appears, they may very well have a "so what" attitude advantageous to the defense. They may also believe that there are much worse things around, things which are "really" obscene, and may not be overly troubled by the material at issue. Thus, if in voir dire examination counsel is asking about knowledge of or reactions to various sexual practices, he should include some that are not only not in the subject material, but also sound considerably more offensive to the average juror. If the jurors are expecting a movie of sex between humans and animals, or of sadomasochistic abuse, and know that there are such movies, they will be much less offended when the movie they see contains neither of these subjects.

Although conditioning the jury is primarily a goal of the defense, for the reasons explained above, it may also be effective for the prosecution. Most obscenity defenses have two main underlying "themes." The first is that there ought not to be any obscenity laws as to consenting adults, and that no one is hurt if someone has different tastes than the majority of people. The second is that this material is no worse than a lot of other books, magazines, or motion pictures. If the prosecution can anticipate these or other defense arguments, it can use the voir dire examination as a way of explaining to the jury its duty, preparing it to resist, and perhaps to resent, arguments of this sort. If, in voir dire examination and opening statement, the jurors are convinced that the validity of the obscenity laws is not in any way at issue in the trial, then they may feel the defense is trying to trick them if this kind of suggestion is made.

14.4   Jury or Judge?—Tactical Considerations

This chapter has, of course been based on the assumption that a jury will be deciding the factual issues at trial, but this will not always be the case. In a proceeding for injunctive relief, or in judicial review of a licensing determination, there may very well be no right to trial by jury.[15] But in other types of civil proceedings,[16] and at some point in virtually every criminal case, the defendant will have a right to trial by jury. This is a right that would normally be exercised in an ordinary criminal case, but in an obscenity case careful thought must be given to whether or not to waive the right to trial by jury. In the federal courts, this will not completely be the choice of the

[15] *See* Chapter 12.3 *supra*.
[16] *See, e.g.* 19 U.S.C. § 1305 (1975 Supp.).

defendant, since the prosecution must consent to any waiver of a jury trial.[17] But in most state courts, the defendant has the sole choice.

One of the major factors to be considered in deciding whether to claim or waive a trial by jury is the makeup of the jury. First of all, counsel should try to find out, based on other juries in the vicinity, just what the jury pool is like. If it appears that there is a good possibility of getting jurors sympathetic to the defense, then a jury trial may be advantageous. Even more important a consideration is how much say counsel will have in getting a reasonably "good" jury. A number of factors go into this determination. Will counsel be able to conduct the voir dire examination? If not, is the judge likely to conduct an extensive examination of prospective jurors in accordance with the questions requested by counsel? How many peremptory challenges are available? How likely is the judge to excuse jurors for cause? Considering all of these factors, if defense counsel thinks he or she will have some significant "say" in choosing the final jury, then a jury trial may be preferable. If the final makeup of the jury is out of counsel's hands, however, there is added reason for waiving a jury.

Perhaps the most significant factor in making this decision is knowledge about the trial judge. In some states, such as Massachusetts, judges are not assigned to particular cases from beginning to end, and thus there may be no way of knowing who the trial judge will be at the time when counsel and his client must decide to waive a jury or not. But in the federal courts, and in most states, counsel will know who the judge will be. One of the purposes of pretrial motions, conferences, and hearings may very well be to have the judge confront many of the issues of the trial before he views the case, and this is of course helpful in deciding who the trier of fact is going to be.

Finally, defense counsel must objectively evaluate his own case. If the book, magazine, or movie is clearly of the "hard-core" variety, and if the judge seems to understand obscenity law fully, then having the judge make the decision as to obscenity is almost like admitting defeat. It is better to hope that a jury will be persuaded by expert testimony or argument, or comparable materials. On the other hand, if the material seems likely to be well within the scope of constitutional protection, it would be better to waive a jury, since in this case the judge is more likely to appreciate the idea that material which is explicit and possibly offensive to some can still be protected by the

---

[17] Fed. R. Crim. Proc. 23(a). *Singer* v. *United States,* 380 U.S. 24 (1965).

First Amendment.[18] If the material seems, in the judgment of counsel, to be so close as to present an irreversible jury question on the issue of obscenity, then counsel must compare the likely makeup of the jury with the known inclination of the judge and make the final decision on this basis.

Other factors not peculiar to an obscenity case may also be relevant, such as the impression the defendant or counsel is likely to make on the jury, whether the defendant is local or from out of state, and similar considerations. But the decision on whether to elect a jury or not is not an easy one to make, and it is one that should be carefully considered.

---

[18] Of course, the judge still has the power to direct a verdict as a matter of law even if there is a jury, and the likelihood of this happening must also be evaluated. *See* Chapter 7.3 *supra*.

15

The Trial of an Obscenity Case

15.1 Introductory Note

This book is not a step-by-step manual on how to try an obscenity case. Such a work is probably not possible and, even if it were, this author would not choose to write it, for the simple reason that obscenity trials are still trials first and obscenity cases second. All too often counsel focus solely on the constitutional issues and ignore the substantive, procedural, and factual issues that relate to any trial. Thus, when counsel is handling an obscenity case, the first thing he should ask is: "What would I do now if this were not an obscenity case?" In other words, there may be many issues of proof, pretrial procedure, joinder and severance, search and seizure, and the like which have nothing to do with the substantive question of obscenity but which must be properly handled if the case is to be won.

Of course, obscenity is still one of the important aspects of the trial, and counsel should have a thorough understanding of the substantive law of obscenity as well as of those procedural characteristics of obscenity cases which are different from other cases. Fostering that understanding is one of the purposes of this book. Also, there are some matters of trial preparation and strategy which are peculiar to obscenity cases. Most of these are discussed elsewhere in this book, such as in the sections on proof of community standards, jury selection, scienter, and expert testimony.[1] The purpose of this chapter is to deal with lesser points of trial theory that may be somewhat different in an obscenity case than in other types of litigation.

[1] *See also* G. LEFCOURT, ET AL., OBSCENITY LAW 141–144 (Practicing Law Institute Outline, 1974), Rogge, *Obscenity Litigation*, 10 AM. JUR. TRIALS 1 (1965, with 1974 Cumulative Supplement); 18 AM. JUR. PROOF OF FACTS, *Obscenity— Motion Pictures* 465 (1971). Many issues relating to trial are dealt with in *Hamling v. United States*, 418 U.S. 87 (1974).

15.2   Stipulations

Before the trial commences, there may be discussions between prosecution and defense regarding possible stipulations. Most possible stipulations will be based on the same considerations that would be relevant in any other case. But, if the material at issue is extremely hard-core pornography, the defense may consider stipulating the obscenity of the material. This, of course, is only feasible if there is some likelihood of a possible defense as to the other elements of the offense. But if this is possible, then the advantage of stipulating the obscenity of the material is that it is then very likely that the jury will not actually see the material at issue, and the possible adverse effect on the defense of this "shock" to the jury may be avoided. However, the jury will still have some idea of what kind of material is involved, and the slight advantage to be gained does not seem worth the risk of stipulating away a major element of the prosecution case. It must be remembered, too, that if obscenity is stipulated at trial, the defendant cannot try to get an appellate court to examine the materials to see if they are obscene. If the defendant stipulates to obscenity as a question of fact, he has waived his right to argue obscenity as a matter of law.[2]

15.3   Opening Statements

Opening statements in an obscenity case will probably not differ substantially from those in other types of cases. The prosecution will outline the theory of the case and describe what the evidence will be. The prosecutor should also make a special effort to explain that it is not the jury's function to decide whether there should or should not be obscenity laws, or whether censorship is good or bad. And, rather than leaving it at that, he ought also to explain briefly why there are obscenity laws.[3] By raising this issue at the outset of the trial, the prosecution is attempting to counter the defense argument that obscenity is a victimless crime and that censorship is always harmful. It is true that all of this is legally irrelevant at an obscenity trial, in light of *Paris Adult Theatre I* v. *Slaton,* [4] but it is doubtful that there has ever been an obscenity trial in which the defense has not been able to raise this issue in some way. The prosecutor should expect that this will happen and plan his opening statement accordingly. He should also

[2] *See Spillman* v. *United States,* 413 F.2d 527 (9th Cir 1969).
[3] *See* Chapter 3 *supra.*
[4] 413 U.S. 49 (1973).

remember that there may very well be jurors who do not wish to see the material at issue, but will of course be forced to do so by virtue of their function as jurors. A carefully worded apology to these jurors, explaining that it is, after all, the defendant whose acts made it necessary, can be very effective.

Defendant's counsel must decide at the outset whether to open immediately after the prosecution or whether to reserve his opening until after the close of the prosecution's case. The making of this decision should depend, in fact, on the defense's knowledge of the prosecution case. If, as a result of statute, rule, local practice, or pretrial order, the defense knows what the prosecution's case is going to be, who the witnesses are, what the exhibits will be, and so forth, then the defense may choose to open at the beginning of the trial. However, it is possible that defense counsel may know very little about the prosecution's method of presenting its case, and in that case he should reserve his opening until after he sees how the prosecution evidence comes in. Also relevant to making this decision is the extent to which defense counsel has been able to present his theory of the case to the jury during voir dire examination. If counsel has already had a chance to talk to the jury, there is more reason to defer the opening statement. If the opening statement of the defense is made before the prosecution presents its case, defense counsel should, at that time, dissociate the defense from actually "liking" the allegedly obscene material. Counsel should make clear that his function is not to praise the material,[5] or to suggest that it be seen or read by the public, but only to show that it does not come within the legal definition of obscenity. With reasonably hard-core material, the first reaction of many jurors will be "How can anyone like that?" One of defense counsel's jobs is to make sure that the jury knows that neither he nor his client like it either. Of course, to the extent that the material at issue is not hard-core pornography, in its most unadulterated sense, then this approach may have to be modified.

15.4 The Prosecution Case

The most important decision the prosecutor must make is when to have the jury see the actual material at issue. If the prosecution's case is relatively short, it is probably best to introduce the material as early as possible. But if the trial is expected to be lengthy, the mate-

---

[5] In most instances, this will be true. The days of cases involving *Ulysses* or *An American Tragedy* have clearly ended.

rial should be introduced as late as possible so as to minimize the time between initial exposure and deliberation. Whenever it is introduced, it is important to establish that the material in the courtroom is the material bought from the defendant, or seized from the defendant's theater, or has other such connection with him. The arresting official should testify as to the circumstances of the seizure, and the complete chain of custody should be established. Furthermore, every element of the offense should be proved at the same time as the chain of custody is established, so that the "technical" evidence is relatively concentrated. If a motion picture is seized from a theater, ownership of the theater should be established. If the defendant is a producer or distributor, the link between the defendant and the material in the courtroom must be clearly proved. In his effort to prove obscenity, the prosecutor must not neglect to prove every other element of the offense.

The prosecution should also introduce evidence relating to the marketing or distribution of the material at issue. Whether or not evidence of pandering is an essential part of the prosecution's case,[6] as much evidence as possible should be introduced as to advertising, labelling, possible exposure to minors, and other factors demonstrating a clearly commercial, "pandering" purpose on the part of the defendant. Similarly, it is often helpful to try to introduce some financial evidence. While it is true that a commercial purpose does not diminish the extent of First Amendment protection,[7] evidence of the defendant's profits will diminish the credibility of any defense evidence as to some educational or other lofty purpose.

Scienter[8] will often be the hardest element for the prosecution to prove. Direct evidence is of course best, but this may require the use of relatively uncooperative "insiders." More likely, evidence of scienter will be circumstantial, as by showing that the defendant saw or read the advertising material for the movies or publications at issue, or by showing that the defendant deals only with sexually explicit material, or other such factors. Very careful investigation is the key to being able to prove scienter successfully.

As to proof of obscenity itself, it is true that many recent decisions have said that no expert testimony or evidence of community standards is necessary, as the material can be said to "speak for itself."[9] But the

---

[6] *See* Chapter 4.6 *supra.*

[7] *See, e.g., New York Times Co.* v. *Sullivan,* 376 U.S. 254 (1964).

[8] *See generally* Chapter 11.7 *supra.*

[9] *See Paris Adult Theatre I* v. *Slaton,* 413 U.S. 49, 56 n.6 (1973). A possible exception is material directed toward "deviant" sexual groups. *Id.* To the extent that this kind of material is at issue, the prosecution should definitely use expert testimony

defense can be expected to produce a great deal of evidence as to lack of appeal to the prurient interest, lack of offense to contemporary community standards, and the presence of literary, artistic, scientific, or political value. This puts the prosecutor in a dilemma. If he uses no evidence other than the material itself, the jury is likely to be impressed with the relative weight of expert and scientific evidence brought forth by the defendant. But if the prosecution puts on such evidence, it may be hard pressed to claim that such evidence is not worth much in obscenity cases.[10] The best strategy, according to local rules and practice, may be to save such supportive evidence for rebuttal.

15.5   The Defense Case

The defense case will, of course, be based somewhat on what the prosecution does, but certain "themes" of the defense are fairly recurrent. One of these goals is to minimize the effect of the jury's seeing of the material. This can be done in either of two very divergent ways. One is to present a lot of evidence not relating to obscenity, such as evidence as to the other elements of the offense, or the defendant's business practices, or the like. The aim is to deflect the attention of the jury from their emotional reaction to the material, and several days of reasonably complex testimonial and documentary evidence may serve this purpose. The other method is to make the jury somewhat "immune" to the effect of sexually explicit material by showing them a lot of it, in the form of "comparables," if admissible,[11] or by repeated showings of the material at issue in connection with the defense's expert testimony. While the first exposure to this kind of material may shock the jury, repeated showings may leave them more bored then offended, and this will normally work to the defendant's advantage.

More often than not, the defense will choose to present evidence on the obscenity issue by way of expert testimony.[12] As is discussed in detail in Chapter 16, expert testimony as to prurient appeal will most often be of a medical, psychological, or scientific nature. But it is in the area of contemporary community standards that expert testimony

---

to explain to the jury the prurient appeal of the material to members of the particular group that is relevant.

[10] The prosecutor's decision in this regard should be based in part on an evaluation of just how much the material actually does speak for itself. If the decision as to obscenity is likely to be close, then supportive evidence should be used.

[11] *See* Chapter 6.6 *supra.*

[12] *See* Chapter 16 *infra.*

and other evidence, such as comparable materials and surveys, are most likely to be helpful to the defense. This evidence is discussed in detail elsewhere in this book.[13] Traditionally, most defense evidence in obscenity cases has been oriented toward proving redeeming social importance, the standard that is now expressed as "serious literary, artistic, political, or scientific value." [14] Whether to use such evidence must depend on counsel's attempt at an objective evaluation of whether the material in part has any such value. It is tempting to try to present evidence as to every element of the case, but if counsel tries to get the jury to believe that an explicit scene of sexual relationships between humans and animals, or a description of sadomasochistic abuse, has serious literary, artistic, political, or scientific value, then the jury is likely not to believe *any* of the defense's contentions. Evidence of this sort should be presented only if there is a likelihood of making a believable case.

Normally, there is no harm in putting the defendant on the witness stand, if this seems to be helpful, but the one major exception is where scienter is a vigorously contested issue. The prosecution may have a hard time showing that the defendant had any knowledge of the contents of a movie, but if the defendant admits he has seen the movie on cross-examination, any doubt is then resolved. In connection with this and the other elements of the case, it must be remembered that defense evidence can cure any defects in the prosecution case.[15]

15.6   Closing Statements

There is nothing magical about closing statements in obscenity cases. The prosecution will stress the hard-core nature of the material, the fact that the validity of the obscenity laws is not at issue, and the fact that expert testimony should not substitute for the jurors' common sense. The prosecutor should emphasize the jurors' role in embodying the moral standards of the community, and their responsibility to that community.

The defense, on the other hand, will try to bring in the idea that there are no victims of obscenity, that the jurors' personal tastes are irrelevant, and that individual freedom is valuable, which is why many seemingly offensive pieces of material or motion pictures are none-

---

[13] *See* Chapter 6.6 *supra.*
[14] *Miller* v. *California,* 413 U.S. 15, 24 (1973). *See* Chapter 7 *supra.*
[15] *See, e.g., Cline* v. *United States,* 395 F.2d 138 (7th Cir. 1968); *United States* v. *Ambrose,* 483 F.2d 742 (6th Cir. 1973).

theless not legally obscene. It is of crucial importance that the defense emphasize that *all* of the elements of obscenity, as explained by the judge, must be proved beyond a reasonable doubt. The whole concept of legal obscenity is so complex and so amorphous that the "beyond a reasonable doubt" aspects should be heavily emphasized. If the jury has doubts about what the instructions mean, they will certainly have doubts about the defendant's guilt.[16]

[16] *See People* v. *Mature Enterprises,* 343 N.Y.S. 2d 911, 924 n.13 (Crim. Ct. 1973).

16

Use of Expert Testimony
In Obscenity Cases

16.1 The Function and Necessity of Expert Testimony

Expert testimony has long constituted a major factor in obscenity litigation,[1] in large part because of the relative difficulty of the concepts which the jury or judge is required to apply. As a matter of general evidence law, it has been said that the function of an expert is "to draw inferences from the facts which a jury would not be competent to draw."[2] Thus, "the subject of the inference must be so distinctively related to some science, profession, business or occupation as to be beyond the ken of the average layman."[3] It should be apparent from this that the use of expert testimony in obscenity cases is thus intimately related to the substantive standards that are to be applied by the trier of fact, and thus the use of expert testimony has changed as the appropriate test for obscenity has changed.

The earliest attempts to use expert testimony in obscenity cases were rebuffed by the courts, since it was thought that whether a work was obscene or not was almost a matter of common knowledge, and in any event was clearly determinable by the jury without any expert assistance.[4] This, of course, followed naturally from the position

---

[1] See generally Stern, Toward a Rationale for the Use of Expert Testimony in Obscenity Litigation, 20 CASE WEST. RES. L. REV. 527 (1969); Comment, Expert Testimony in Obscenity Cases, 18 HASTINGS L. J. 161 (1966); Frank, Obscenity: Some Problems of Values and the Use of Experts, 41 WASH. L. REV. 631 (1966); McGaffey, A Realistic Look at Expert Witnesses in Obscenity Cases, 69 Nw. U. L. REV. 218 (1974); Note, The Use of Expert Testimony in Obscenity Litigation, 1965 WIS. L. REV. 113 (1965). See also 123 NEW L. J. 1171 (1973).

[2] McCORMICK ON EVIDENCE § 13 at 29 (2nd ed. E. Cleary 1972).

[3] Id.

[4] See, e.g., People v. Muller, 32 Hun. 209, 96 N.Y. 408 (1884); Commonwealth v. Landis, 8 Phila. 453 (1870).

acknowledged at the time that the literary or other value of a work was legally irrelevant. If the work was determined to be obscene, then any literary merit was unavailing.[5] This exclusion of expert testimony, however, changed drastically with a number of cases in the first half of the 20th century. During this period, *Roth* had yet to be decided, but the *Hicklin* test was clearly on the way out.[6] Thus, in the absence of any definitive standard, and with the frequency of prosecution of works of arguable literary merit, expert testimony as to the presence or lack of literary value became a predominant feature of obscenity litigation.[7]

The use of expert testimony in obscenity litigation took on new meaning after the Supreme Court's *Roth* decision in 1957.[8] Whereas prior cases relied either on the *Hicklin* definition of obscenity or on some nonarticulated standard, *Roth* introduced as a uniform standard the definition of obscenity as "whether to the average person, applying contemporary community standards, the dominant theme of the material taken as a whole appeals to the prurient interest." [9] Subsequent cases added the concepts of patent offensiveness and lack of redeeming social value.[10] Many of these concepts became almost terms of art and were, in any event, not the types of concepts commonly dealt with by the jury. Therefore, the use of expert testimony increased, not so much in terms of general expert commentary on literary merit, as was the case prior to *Roth*, but in terms of relating the material to the particular standards to be applied, such as prurient interest, dominant theme, and lack of redeeming social value. In fact, since the separation of these legal criteria from the jurors' personal views as to the materials at issue was deemed to be so crucial in any obscenity case, it was the view of Mr. Justice Frankfurter that expert testimony as to contemporary community standards could not constitutionally be excluded at trial, regardless of whether the admission or exclusion of such evidence might, in other types of cases, not raise

[5] *People* v. *Muller,* 32 Hun. 209, 96 N.Y. 408 (1884); *United States* v. *Bennett,* 24 F. Cas. 1093, 1104–1105 (No. 15,571) (C.C. S.D.N.Y. 1879); *United States* v. *Clarke,* 38 F. 500 (E.D. No. 1889); *United States* v. *Grimm,* 50 F. 528 (E.D. Mo. 1892).

[6] *See generally* Chapter 1, text accompanying notes 123 to 158.

[7] *See, e.g., United States* v. *One Book Called "Ulysses,"* 5 F.Supp. 182 (S.D. N.Y. 1933), *aff'd,* 72 F.2d 705 (2d Cir. 1934); *United States* v. *Dennett,* 39 F.2d 564 (2d Cir. 1930); *Attorney General* v. *Book Named "God's Little Acre,"* 326 Mass. 281, 93 N.E.2d 819 (1950).

[8] *Roth* v. *United States,* 354 U.S. 476 (1957).

[9] *Id.* at 489.

[10] *See, e.g., Manual Enterprises* v. *Day,* 370 U.S. 478 (1962); *Memoirs* v. *Massachusetts,* 383 U.S. 413 (1966). *See generally* Chapter 2.2 *supra.*

issues of constitutional dimensions.[11] A number of federal and state courts extended this position even further, holding that in an obscenity case, due process *required* that there be expert testimony on each element of the test for obscenity.[12] Without presenting such expert testimony to explain and help apply the constitutional tests for obscenity, the prosecution could not meet its burden of proof. But in *Paris Adult Theatre I* v. *Slaton*,[13] the Supreme Court held that such a requirement was not constitutionally mandated.

> Nor was it error to fail to require "expert" affirmative evidence that the materials were obscene when the materials themselves were actually placed in evidence. . . . The films, obviously, are the best evidence of what they represent.[14]

Although affirmative expert testimony on any of the elements of obscenity is thus no longer a constitutional requirement, the Supreme Court has adopted Mr. Justice Frankfurter's view in *Smith* v. *California*[15] that "the defense should be free to introduce appropriate expert testimony." [16] Although the Court has therefore permitted, while not requiring, the use of expert testimony in obscenity cases, it is clear that the members of the majority were far from persuaded as to the utility of such evidence.

> This is not a subject that lends itself to the traditional use of expert testimony. Such testimony is usually admitted for the purpose of explaining to lay jurors what they otherwise could not understand. . . . No such assistance is needed by jurors in obscenity cases; indeed the "expert witness" practices employed in these cases have often made a

---

[11] "For the reasons I have indicated, I would make the right to introduce such evidence a requirement of due process in obscenity prosecutions." *Smith* v. *California*, 361 U.S. 147, 167 (1959) (Frankfurter, J., concurring). *See also* § 207.10 of the Model Penal Code of the American Law Institute, which expressly allows the admission of expert testimony in obscenity cases, and Lockhart and McClure, *Censorship of Obscenity: The Developing Constitutional Standards*, 45 MINN. L. REV. 5, 99 (1960).

[12] *See, e.g., United States* v. *Palladino*, 475 F.2d 65, 72 (1st Cir. 1973); *United States* v. *Grover*, 475 F.2d 550 (5th Cir. 1972), *rev'd en banc*, 479 F.2d 577 (5th Cir. 1973); *United States* v. *Klaw*, 350 F.2d 155 (2nd Cir. 1965); *In re Giannini*, 69 Cal. 2d 563, 446 P.2d 535, 72 Cal. Rptr. 655 (1968); *In re Harris*, 56 Cal. 2d 879, 366 P.2d 305, 16 Cal. Rptr. 889 (1961), *vacated on other grounds*, 374 U.S. 499 (1963); *Dunn* v. *State Board of Censors*, 240 Md. 249, 213 A.2d 751 (1965).

Several cases provided for an exception to this rule when the materials were clearly of the "hard core" variety. *United States* v. *Wild*, 422 F.2d 34 (2d Cir. 1971), *cert. denied*, 402 U.S. 986; *United States* v. *Manarite*, 448 F.2d 583, 593 (2d Cir. 1971), *cert. denied*, 404 U.S. 947.

[13] 413 U.S. 49 (1973).

[14] *Id.* at 56. *See also Kaplan* v. *California*, 413 U.S. 115, 121 (1973).

[15] 361 U.S. 147, 167 (1959) (Frankfurter, J., concurring).

[16] *Kaplan* v. *California*, 413 U.S. 115, 121 (1973).

mockery of the otherwise sound concept of expert testimony. . . . "Simply stated, hard core pornography . . . can and does speak for itself." [17]

Thus it can be seen that the Supreme Court's denial of any affirmative obligation upon the prosecution to present expert testimony as to the elements of obscenity is intimately related to the Court's holding in *Miller* limiting the scope of obscenity prosecutions to hard-core pornography.[18] Taken in this context, the Court's views of expert testimony do not represent a significant departure from the trend of the case law prior to the *Miller* decision, since hard-core material was often deemed an exception to any rule requiring affirmative expert testimony.[19]

The Court's discussion of the use of expert testimony in *Paris* makes it clear that, in the view of the Supreme Court, the use of expert testimony in obscenity cases is not conceptually different from the use of expert testimony in any other type of litigation. The key question is whether or not the assistance of the expert will explain "to lay jurors what they otherwise could not understand." [20] The Court then goes on to say that this does not appear relevant to obscenity cases, but this statement must be taken in the context of the Court's views as to how expert testimony has in fact been used historically in obscenity cases, and the Court's identification of abuses is far from unfounded. But this does not mean that there is no function for expert testimony. In fact, on the same day that the Court expressed its disapproval of expert testimony in obscenity cases in *Paris* it also looked somewhat favorably upon its use in *Miller*.[21] There are difficult concepts in obscenity law, and there are areas in which the jurors' own views can be helpfully supplemented by expert analysis. Therefore, it is appropriate at this point to discuss the potential use of expert testimony in terms of the actual substantive issues that the trier of fact is called upon to decide.

Perhaps the most obvious misuse of expert testimony in obscenity cases is where an expert testifies that in his or her opinion the

---

[17] *Paris Adult Theatre I* v. *Slaton,* 413 U.S. 49, 56 n.6 (1973) (citations omitted).

[18] *Miller* v. *California,* 413 U.S. 15, 27 (1973). *See generally* Chapters 2.3 and 5.4 *supra.*

[19] *See, e.g.,* cases cited in note 12 *supra.*

[20] *Paris Adult Theatre I* v. *Slaton,* 413 U.S. at 56 n.6.

[21] At issue was the allowance of the State's expert on the community standards of the State of California. The Supreme Court recited his qualifications and concluded that "allowing such expert testimony was certainly not constitutional error." 413 U.S. at 31 n.12.

material at issue either is or is not obscene. This, of course, runs head on into the common-law rule against expert testimony or opinion as to the ultimate issue in the lawsuit,[22] and also is contrary to the principle prohibiting testimony as to matters of law, or mixed questions of law and fact.[23] While it is true that the blanket prohibition as to testimony on the ultimate issue is on the decline,[24] it is nonetheless still true that the opinion must be helpful in some way to the trier of fact, and there seems no way that an opinion of an "expert" that the work is or is not obscene provides any assistance whatsoever. Despite this, some courts have admitted such testimony,[25] although the vast majority of courts have properly excluded it.[26] Similarly, asking for an opinion on whether the complete test for obscenity has or has not been met suffers from the same defect, as in *State* v. *Watson*,[27] where the Supreme Court of Oregon appropriately required the exclusion of testimony that the book at issue "taken as a whole has a predominant theme that appeals to prurient interests." This is no more than testimony that in the opinion of the witness the book was obscene, and this type of testimony both is a legal conclusion and provides no assistance for the trier of fact.

The use of this type of conclusory testimony has led some courts to give little if any credence to the use of experts in obscenity litigation.[28] But the misuses of expert testimony should not result in a

---

[22] *See, e.g., Smith Beverages, Inc.* v. *Metropolitan Cas. Ins. Co.*, 337 Mass. 270, 149 N.E.2d 146 (1958); *United States* v. *Spaulding*, 293 U.S. 498, 506 (1935); *State* v. *Carr*, 196 N.C. 129, 144 S.E. 698 (1928).

[23] *See, e.g., Birch* v. *Strout*, 303 Mass. 28, 20 N.E. 2d 429 (1939); *Federal Underwriters' Exchange* v. *Cost*, 132 Tex. 299, 123 S.W. 2d 332 (1938); *Briney* v. *Tri-State Mutual Grain Dealers Fire Ins. Co.*, 254 Iowa 673, 117 N.W. 2d 889 (1962).

[24] *See, e.g.,* FED. R. Ev. 704; *Grismore* v. *Consolidated Products*, 232 Iowa 328, 5 N.W. 2d 646 (1942); *Rabata* v. *Rohner*, 45 Wis. 2d 111, 172 N.W. 2d 409 (1969). *See generally* Stoebuck, *Opinions on Ultimate Facts: Status, Trends, and a Note of Caution*, 41 DENVER L.C.J. 226 (1964).

[25] *See, e.g.,* Record at 10, *Memoirs* v. *Massachusetts*, 383 U.S. 413 (1966); *McCauley* v. *Tropic of Cancer*, 20 Wis. 2d 134, 146, 121 N.W.2d 545, 551 (1963).

Of even less utility would be the admission of personal opinions of various members of the public. See *United States* v. *4200 Copies International Journal*, 134 F.Supp. 490, 493 (E.D. Wash. 1955).

[26] *See, e.g., United States* v. *West Coast News Co.*, 357 F.2d 855, 859 (6th Cir. 1966), *rev'd on other grounds*, 388 U.S. 447 (1967), and cases cited therein. *Cf. Cain* v. *Commonwealth*, 437 S.W.2d 769, 772–773 (Ky. 1969), *rev'd on other grounds*, 397 U.S. 319 (1970).

[27] 243 Ore. 454, 414 P.2d 337 (1966). *See also* Gertz, *The "Tropic of Cancer" Litigation in Illinois*, 51 KY. L.J. 595, 601 (1963).

[28] *Paris Adult Theatre I* v. *Slaton*, 413 U.S. 49, 56 n.6 (1973); *State* v. *Smith*, 422 S.W.2d 50 (Mo. 1967); *United States* v. *Kennerley*, 209 F.119 (S.D.N.Y. 1913) (L. Hand, J.).

complete rejection of their use. If the expert testimony is focused upon a particular aspect of the test for obscenity, and if in that context it helps the jury to understand that part of the test, or apply that part of the test, or understand some aspect of the material at issue, then it becomes a very desirable addition to an obscenity case.

At the outset, it should be observed that, like any other testimony, expert testimony in an obscenity case must be legally relevant. This issue arises most often in the context of offered testimony as to the presence or absence of harm from exposure to obscene or pornographic materials. The validity of obscenity laws in general has been settled by *Paris Adult Theatre I* v. *Slaton,*[29] and even to the extent the issue may be reopened, either under state constitutions or the federal constitution, it is a question of law and not one of fact. The simple fact that there may be factual or scientific data used in the legal argument does not mean that the issue is appropriate for consideration by the trier of fact. Thus, testimony offered on behalf of the defense that scientific studies, or psychological opinion, or anything else show exposure to sexually explicit materials not to be harmful is immaterial. It does not tend to prove anything that is actually at issue in the case and thus should be excluded. It is the function of the trier of fact to determine whether or not the appropriate statute includes the particular conduct at issue, not whether or not the assumptions on which the statute is based are correct. Naturally, this applies equally to testimony presented on behalf of the prosecution. It is not the function of the prosecution to present evidence in *justification* of a criminal statute. Therefore, expert testimony offered by the prosecution to show that obscenity does cause moral decay, or criminal activity, is likewise not related to any determination involved in applying the statute to a particular book or movie, or to a particular defendant. It is, therefore, also immaterial and should be excluded.

The concept of the "dominant theme" of the material at issue is one that provides the potential for the appropriate use of expert testimony. In the original *Roth* test for obscenity, it was necessary that the determination of obscenity be based upon the "dominant theme of the material taken as a whole." [30] The words "dominant theme" do not appear in the current test for obscenity, but the work must still be "taken as a whole" in making determinations of appeal to the prurient interest and presence or absence of literary, artistic, political, or

[29] 413 U.S. 49 (1973).
[30] *Roth* v. *United States,* 354 U.S. 476, 489 (1957).

scientific value.[31] It does not seem as if the elimination of the words "dominant theme" has any major substantive significance—it is probably little more than the Court's eliminating what appears to be a redundancy. It is still an essential element of any determination of obscenity that the entire work be evaluated, and defining what the entire work is still involves a determination of intent and purpose.[32] Looked at in this way, it is still both relevant and important in an obscenity case to be able to identify the major purpose and theme of the material, and expert testimony may be of considerable value in this inquiry. It is true, of course, that the major theme or effect of a work depends in large part on the identity of the individual who is making the determination.[33] But there is still a function for the expert in pointing out themes, or connections, not readily ascertainable by a lay juror, but nonetheless of significance. "In accordance with the command that the work be considered 'as a whole,' experts may illustrate that particular passages are significantly related to other less sensational passages which place the former in a cast otherwise unapparent when considered in isolation." [34] This use of expert testimony might be explained by use of an example of an "underground" newspaper, such as was at issue in *Kois* v. *Wisconsin*.[35] The problem is the relationship, if any, of explicit sexual references, descriptions, drawings, and photographs to the underlying political theme of the publication. This relationship may very well not even occur to the members of the jury, but that does not mean that it did not or cannot exist either in the intent of the authors or publishers, or in the minds of the readers of the publication. Therefore, expert testimony would serve a valuable function by explaining this relationship. The expert might be a sociologist, or political scientist, or psychologist, and not necessarily an expert in literature. Perhaps the expert might be the publisher of a similar newspaper. But the important factor is that the expert would be able to explain to the jury, in terms of his or her particular knowledge, what the major theme of the publication was and how the various parts of the publication related to "the whole." This testimony could, of course, be contradicted by other testimony,

---

[31] *Miller* v. *California,* 413 U.S. 15, 24 (1973).

[32] *See generally* Chapter 5.3 *supra.*

[33] *See United States* v. *One Carton Positive Motion Picture Film Entitled "491,"* 247 F.Supp. 450, 467 (S.D.N.Y. 1965), *rev'd on other grounds,* 367 F.2d 889 (2d Cir. 1966).

[34] Stern, *Toward a Rationale for the Use of Expert Testimony in Obscenity Litigation,* 20 CASE W. RES. L. REV. 527, 547 (1969).

[35] 408 U.S. 229 (1972). Other cases are cited in the notes to Chapter 5.3 *supra.*

and in any event it need not be taken as true by the trier of fact, but it might very well assist in bringing to the jury's attention certain factors or interpretations not within the range of the average juror's experiences or knowledge, and thus fits squarely within the classic function of expert testimony.

Although it is technically possible to foresee expert testimony in explication of the concept of the "average man," [36] this seems of extremely limited utility. The jury ideally represents the average person and, if not, is presumably capable of at least discerning what the average person is like. This may, of course, be somewhat of a legal fiction, but it is a legal fiction that has endured in many other areas of law. While the "average person" is not the same as the "reasonable man" in tort law, or similar ideals in trust or patent law, they are all similar in the sense that we can reasonably expect such an individual to be within the ken of the members of the jury.[37] But it has been suggested that "the possibility does remain, however, that the fact-finder may be unaware of widespread psychological characteristics which, if brought to his attention, would modify somewhat his notion of the average man." [38] Thus, it would be "proper to allow a psychiatrist to testify to the effects of a film upon the viewer's unconscious." [39] But this seems to go in actuality to the existence or nonexistence of an appeal to the prurient interest, and not to the issue of who is the average person. If the two concepts can be separated, at least as to the applicability of expert testimony, then it is in the latter area, and not the former, that such testimony can have its greatest significance.

It is, therefore, appropriate to turn to an exploration of the use of expert testimony on the issue of the appeal of the material to the prurient interest. It seems as if the use of expert testimony in this context depends significantly on the construction to be given to the term "appeal to the prurient interest." [40] If that phrase connotes intent, then the availability of expert testimony in this area seems more closely aligned with that of expert testimony in the area of literary

---

[36] *See generally* Chapter 4 *supra.*

[37] *See State* v. *Jungclaus,* 176 Neb. 641, 126 N.W. 2d 858 (1964), holding that the term "average man" need not be further explained to the jury in the court's instructions. The implication, therefore, would also be that no expert assistance is necessary. *Cf. State* v. *Hudson County News Co.,* 41 N.J. 247, 263 n.9, 196 A.2d 225, 233 n.9 (1963).

[38] Stern, *supra* note 34, at 550.

[39] *Id.*

[40] *See generally* Chapter 5.1 *supra.*

value. In other words, if we are looking at the author's "real meaning," then experts in the analysis of this type of material, whether books, magazines, newspapers, or motion pictures, would be of greatest utility. But if the construction is such that the *effect* of the material is the determinative inquiry, then experts from psychology and psychiatry would be much more appropriate. They are the ones who could actually explain to the jury whether or not the material would have the stimulative effect on the average person that is the focus of the obscenity laws. Traditionally, expert testimony as to "appeal to the prurient interest" has been of the latter variety.[41] It is clear that the determination of appeal to the prurient interest cannot be based upon the jurors' own reactions to the material, in the sense of their own sexual stimulation or interest.[42] They must be making a determination of the effect of the material on others, and this is therefore an appropriate use of expert testimony. This type of factor "strongly suggest[s] the need for expert testimony by one who has studied various types of material." [43] The psychologist or psychiatrist can explain how material of the type in question does or does not cause sexual stimulation, or appeal to a "morbid or shameful" interest in sex. Since material that appeals to a normal, as opposed to a prurient, interest in sex may not be proscribed by the obscenity laws, the expert may also serve a valuable function in explaining the difference between the normal and the abnormal.

For expert testimony as to prurient interest to be of value, it is crucial that the expert speak of a "recipient group" which is legally appropriate for the case at hand. Thus, in the typical case, the expert testimony should not discuss the possible or probable effect on juveniles or those of "deviant" sexual interests,[44] but only on the average man. But if the case involves "deviant" materials, which are aimed at a probable recipient group with decidedly different sexual tendencies than the vast majority of the population, then the expert testimony must discuss and explain the sexual tendencies of this deviant group. In fact, it may very well be that expert testimony is *required* in a case

---

[41] *See, e.g., United States* v. *One Carton Positive Motion Picture Film Entitled "491,"* 247 F.Supp. 450 (S.D.N.Y. 1965), *rev'd on other grounds,* 367 F.2d 889 (2nd Cir. 1966); *State* v. *Onorato,* 3 Conn. Cir. 438, 216 A.2d 859 (1965); *Yudkin* v. *State,* 229 Md. 223, 182 A.2d 798 (1962); *State* v. *Jungclaus,* 176 Neb. 641, 126 N.W.2d 858 (1964).

[42] *See generally* Comment, *Expert Testimony in Obscenity Cases,* 18 HASTINGS L.J. 161, 170–174.

[43] *Id.* at 172.

[44] *Volanski* v. *United States,* 246 F.2d 842 (6th Cir. 1957).

involving such "deviant" materials.[45] Similarly, in a case involving distribution of obscene material to minors, under a statute appropriately drafted in accordance with *Ginsberg* v. *New York*,[46] an expert in child psychology or a related field might testify as to the effect this material would have on minors. But since minors and their reactions are more within the experiences and knowledge of the jury, expert testimony would not be required here, as it probably is with materials directed at deviant groups.

Expert testimony as to the appeal to prurient interest, involving as it does discussion of the effect of such material on the reader or viewer, can all too easily reduce itself to testimony as to whether obscene material in general has any harmful effects. If this happens, the testimony, whether offered by prosecution or defense, becomes worthless.[47] The testimony must be related to the particular material at issue. If this is done, then the expert testimony as to appeal to the prurient interest may have considerable value.

One of the most fruitful uses of expert testimony would be in the determination of contemporary community standards.[48] In the pre-*Miller* days of national community standards, such testimony would, of course, have been of even greater importance, since by definition the standard to be applied was beyond the knowledge and experiences of the average member of the jury. In fact, it was the concept of national community standards that led many courts to require affirmative expert testimony in obscenity cases,[49] for without testimony as to what the standards were, it would be impossible for a jury to determine whether or not the material at issue violated them. National community standards have since been rejected by the Supreme Court,[50] and an even more recent decision has clearly expressed the Court's view that the contemporary standards of a given community are within the knowledge of the members of the jury drawn from that community.[51] But there still remains a strong basis for the use of expert testimony on this issue.[52] In the wake of *Miller*, many states have enacted statutes requiring that the community

[45] The question is specifically left open by the Supreme Court in *Paris Adult Theatre I* v. *Slaton*, 413 U.S. 49, 56 n.6 (1973). *See generally* Chapter 4.3 *supra*.

[46] 390 U.S 629 (1968). *See generally* Chapter 4.5 *supra*.

[47] *See* text accompanying note 29 *supra*.

[48] *See generally* Chapter 6 *supra*.

[49] *See* cases cited in note 12 *supra*.

[50] *Miller* v. *California*, 413 U.S. 15 (1973).

[51] *Hamling* v. *United States*, 418 U.S. 87 (1974).

[52] This issue is discussed in more detail in Chapter 6.7 *supra*.

standards be statewide.[53] While it is highly probable that many jurors will be aware of statewide standards, the extent to which this is actually true in a given case depends both on the size and diversity of the state, and on the experiences of the particular juror. Thus, expert testimony as to the statewide standards may be of considerable assistance. Furthermore, community standards as to sexual materials may not necessarily be something that jurors have noticed or thought about, and it is conceivable that a juror's impressions about contemporary community standards can be modified by the appropriate use of expert testimony. Recent cases have not dealt with the issue, but earlier authority supports the admission of expert testimony as to contemporary community standards.[54] The difficulty in this area, however, lies in the identification of exactly what type of expertise is at issue. Given that one of the requirements of expert testimony is that the subject be "beyond the ken of the average layman," [55] it is easy to see why some have been skeptical about the utility of expert testimony as to community standards.[56] Its applicability may depend on the geographic contours of the community at issue as they relate to the community from which the jurors are actually drawn. Even if these two communities are congruent, it does not follow that the juror cannot be assisted or enlightened as to what the community standards are in terms of depiction or description of sexual activities. The natural inclination of many jurors would be to equate the community's standards with their own,[57] a phenomenon the courts should properly be trying to avoid. The presence of expert testimony may have the beneficial result of dissuading a juror from doing so.

A more fundamental problem with expert testimony on the issue of contemporary community standards is the general requirement that the expert be knowledgeable, skilled, or experienced in the particular field about which he or she is testifying.[58] There is no field or acknowledged area of expertise for contemporary community standards.

---

[53] *See, e.g.,* CONN. GEN. STAT. § 53a–193(a) (3) (Supp. 1975); 13 VT. STAT. § 2801 (6)(B) (Supp. 1975); N. CAR. GEN. STAT. § 14–1901.1 (b)(2) (Supp. 1975).

[54] *See, e.g., Kahm* v. *United States,* 300 F.2d 78 (5th Cir. 1962), *cert. denied,* 369 U.S. 859; *Alexander* v. *United States,* 271 F.2d 140 (8th Cir. 1959); *People* v. *Aday,* 226 Cal. App. 520, 38 Cal. Rptr. 199 (1964), *cert. denied,* 379 U.S. 931; *City of Chicago* v. *Kimmel,* 31 Ill.2d 202, 201 N.E.2d 386 (1964). *Contra, State* v. *Vollmar,* 389 S.W.2d 20 (Mo. 1965); *People* v. *Finkelstein,* 11 N.Y.2d 300, 229 N.Y.S. 2d 367, 183 N.E.2d 661 (1963).

[55] MCCORMICK ON EVIDENCE § 13 at 29 (2d ed. Cleary 1972).

[56] Stern, *supra* note 1, at 551–554.

[57] Kalven, *The Metaphysics of the Law of Obscenity,* 1960 SUP. CT. REV. 1, 38–39 (1960).

[58] MCCORMICK ON EVIDENCE § 13 at 30 (2d ed. Cleary 1972).

Much expert testimony in this area does not directly concern contemporary community standards, but rather involves "expert" statistical or sampling testimony about what a sample of the community actually believes.[59] This does not mean that there cannot be experts on contemporary community standards, however. While we have not traditionally acknowledged this as a discrete area of expertise, there are people in many fields who in fact have such expertise.[60] If, by virtue of training or experience, someone has substantial knowledge of the community's views regarding depiction or description of sexual activity, then such testimony should be admissible. Thus, perhaps more than in other areas, expert testimony about contemporary community standards depends for its utility on the particular qualifications of the expert. If it can be shown that the expert has both the training and the opportunity to evaluate contemporary community standards, then the testimony can be extremely useful.

Finally, we turn to expert testimony in the determination of serious literary, artistic, political, or scientific value. This has, of course, traditionally been the most common use of expert testimony, especially under previous formulations of the literary-value concept. Certainly, in the era of prosecutions of works such as *Ulysses, An American Tragedy,* and *Lady Chatterley's Lover,* testimony by literary experts was both necessary and frequent. Most obscenity trials during this era consisted primarily of the testimony of experts in literature and the arts. After *Roth,* however, the use of such testimony diminished. It again became very important in litigation under the *Memoirs* test, however, which required for a finding of obscenity that material be "utterly without redeeming social value." [61] The words of this standard were so absolute that virtually any arguable value for the material at issue was sufficient to prevent such a finding, and expert testimony as to an enormous range of possible literary, scientific, social, political, artistic, educational, and other value became prevalent.[62] This trend came to an abrupt halt with *Miller* v. *California,*[63] which specifically rejected the *Memoirs* test and in its place substituted the requirement that the material be without "serious liter-

[59] See the descriptions of such testimony in *Miller* v. *California,* 413 U.S. 15, 31 n.12 (1973). *Compare Hamling* v. *United States,* 418 U.S. 87, 108 n.10 (1974).

[60] This issue is discussed in more detail in Chapter 6.7 *supra.* The Supreme Court acknowledged in *Miller* that such expertise is possible. 413 U.S. at 31 n.12.

[61] *Memoirs* v. *Massachusetts,* 383 U.S. 413 (1966).

[62] For examples of the use of such testimony, see the cases cited in the notes to chapter 7.1 *supra.*

[63] 413 U.S. 15 (1973).

ary, artistic, political, or scientific value." [64] When this is combined with *Miller*'s addition of a "hard core" requirement,[65] the effect can be seen to be, and in fact has been, a diminution of the importance of experts in this area. As the material which is prosecuted becomes more explicit and more generally commercial pornography, expert testimony has tended less towards a determination of literary, artistic, political, or scientific value. But to the extent that the material at issue is something other than commercial pornography, expert testimony on the value of the material remains important. The new test requires that the value be "serious," which connotes an evaluation of intent as well as the relationship of the claimed value to the entire work. In this determination, experts on literature, or drama, or film, can be extremely helpful. Similarly, experts in government or political science or sociology can be helpful on the issue of political value, and scientific experts can be helpful if there is claimed scientific value. If it is argued that certain material has medical value, who better than a physician to describe and explain what that value would be? The most difficult kind of value to determine would be artistic. The mere fact that a work is well-photographed, or accompanied by good music, or the like, does not mean that the material may not be obscene. Thus, for expert testimony to be helpful here, it must not only explain the artistic qualities of the work, but must also explain how or why this artistic quality would be important to the anticipated recipients of the material.

16.2   Selection of the Expert

As the foregoing section has tried to make clear, selection of the expert is perhaps the most important factor in the use of such testimony in obscenity cases. Counsel should first determine the particular issues on which expert testimony is desired. A great mistake in this area is to pick the expert first and then try to conform the testimony to the issues to be presented at trial. It is far better to plan the use of expert testimony first, and then select the expert whose qualifications are most appropriate to this use. The attorney should decide at the outset on which of the aspects of the test for obscenity expert testimony will be presented. This will generally indicate the type of expert needed. If testimony is desired as to appeal to the prurient interest, then experts in the area of psychology and psychiatry would be most

[64] *See generally* Chapter 7.2 *supra.*
[65] *See* Chapter 5.4 *supra.*

appropriate. If testimony is desired as to contemporary community standards, then statisticians or public opinion analysts might be desired, or perhaps police officers, journalists, ministers, or others who are especially knowledgeable and experienced as to community views and beliefs. And if there is to be expert testimony as to literary, artistic, political, or scientific value, then the appropriate expert would be one from the particular field in which it is claimed that the material has value.

If possible, the expert's qualifications should relate in detail to the issues to be presented. A psychiatrist with training and experience in sexual deviance, or in sexual arousal, would be better on the issue of prurient interest than one without such particular expertise. Testimony as to contemporary community standards is better from one whose expertise relates to community acceptance of sexual matters, than from one who merely has a general expertise in community opinion.

One issue to be faced is whether to select an expert of local or national background and fame. Obviously, if the issue is contemporary community standards, then a local witness is a necessity in order that the testimony relate particularly to the community whose standards are at issue. But the decision is harder for other kinds of expert testimony. The jurors are likely to be impressed by experts with national reputations and credentials, but they may also relate more to an expert who comes from the same locality they do. This determination must be based on an evaluation of the jurors' views, and no generalizations are likely to be of assistance. It is, however, an issue that should be carefully considered.

Finally, counsel must anticipate the cross-examination when initially selecting the expert. Obviously, the expert's qualifications must be impeccable. It is best that the expert not have a history of testifying often on the same side in obscenity cases. Likewise, it may be best if he or she has not written or spoken on the advisability or necessity of obscenity laws, so that he or she cannot be attacked as testifying from a political or social view as to obscenity laws in general, rather than on the particular materials at hand.

16.3 Direct Examination

A few general observations about direct examination of the expert are perhaps in order here.[66] First, the major part of the direct

[66] For a thorough discussion of direct and cross-examination of experts in ob-

testimony may involve the expert's qualifications, an area which may be viewed with a great deal of skepticism. Special attention should be paid to having the witness describe in detail his or her education, training, experience, publications, and so forth. The aim should be not only to describe the qualifications, but to explain how they relate to the particular matter at hand. The establishment of the qualifications of the expert is most important for one who will be testifying as to contemporary community standards. It must not only be established that because of training and education he or she is a better analyst and perceiver of contemporary community standards than the average person, but also that the expert has had ample opportunity to observe the standards of the particular community at issue. If this is done, the testimony can be very persuasive.

The other major factor, and one that has been stressed throughout this chapter, is that the expert's testimony must be narrowly and specifically related to a particular aspect of the standards for obscenity. The expert should not be asked whether the work is obscene, or what the effects are of obscenity generally, but what in *this* material appeals to the prurient interest, and how, or what in *this* material has scientific value, and how it is beneficial. The expert need not prove the entire case. The testimony should always be in terms of the expert's particular qualifications, and should be restricted to that. The expert should not be allowed to stray into legal conclusion or areas outside of his field of expertise.[67] If expert testimony is to be of assistance, it is because the expert has some specialized knowledge, and to be most useful he should be allowed and encouraged to testify in terms of that knowledge.

A good direct examination of an expert in an obscenity case will anticipate the cross-examination, and thus ought to present in as favorable a light as possible any bias of the witness or other weakness that can be exploited on cross-examination.

16.4   Cross-Examination

No exhaustive discussion of cross-examination will be attempted here,[68] although a few special factors will be mentioned. One is the

---

scenity cases, with many informative examples from actual trial transcripts, see Rogge, *Obscenity Litigation*, 10 AM. JUR. TRIALS §§ 56–62 (1965).

[67] This also prevents the possibility that the witness will be subject to cross-examination in areas outside of his expertise. *Cf. State* v. *J-R Distributors, Inc.,* 82 Wash.2d 584, 512 P.2d 1049 (1973), *cert. denied,* 418 U.S. 949.

[68] *See* note 66 *supra*.

necessity of challenging, if at all possible, the expert's credentials as they relate to the subject of the testimony. A national name or an impressive educational and professional background may be effectively dealt with by showing, on cross-examination, that the expertise, however impressive, does not relate to the matter at hand.[69] The same can be done by attempting to show that the expert's experience with this type of material is limited.

It is also possible to show that the expert's views have a political or sociological bias. If an expert testifies that the material does not appeal to the prurient interest, it is helpful to be able to get him to say that in his opinion very little, if anything, appeals to the prurient interest. Or if the testimony is that the material does have that appeal, it can be "exposed" by showing that the expert also thinks that far "milder" material also appeals to the prurient interest. The purpose, of course, is to show that the expert's views are really views as to obscenity laws in general, and thus are either legally irrelevant or of little value.

The most important assistance to a good cross-examination is knowledge in advance of the particular expert to be called. Thus, any pretrial disclosure will help the cross-examiner (although, conversely, it will hurt as to his own witnesses) to study the expert's qualifications and research his or her publications, and thus be prepared for an effective cross-examination.

[69] A very effective example, in the context of a voir dire examination, can be found in Rogge, *supra* note 66, at 234–235.

17

Instructing the Jury

17.1 Substantive Standards for Instructions

Understanding the legal test for obscenity, the concept of scienter, and other such difficult legal formulations is no easy task for an attorney or judge. It is substantially more difficult for the juror, who has no legal training at all. Thus, the formulation of fair and informative jury instructions becomes a matter of critical importance.

The most important instructions are those on the issue of obscenity itself. The indictment will often be in the language of the governing statute, and therefore the defendant will often be charged with the sale, distribution, or exhibition of material that is not only obscene, but perhaps also immoral, vile, filthy, disgusting, lewd, lascivious, or indecent. It is important that the jury understand that these additional adjectives add nothing, as a matter of current law, to the charge, to the available defenses, or to the quantity or quality of proof required. If they find that the work is obscene, in accordance with the instructions as to the meaning of that term, then they need not consider whether the material can also be described by these other words. And if they find that the material is not obscene, then they must acquit even if they think the work is immoral or indecent or any of the other descriptions.[1]

The court should explain to the jury that in order for material to be legally obscene it must both come within the statutory coverage *and* meet the constitutional definition of obscenity. Thus, in a federal prosecution, the jury should be informed of the fact that the word obscene may include only those things which are included within the

---

[1] *See* E. DEVITT and C. BLACKMAR, FEDERAL JURY PRACTICE AND INSTRUCTIONS §14.03 (1970). *Cf. Flying Eagle Publications, Inc.* v. *United States*, 285 F.2d 307 (1st Cir. 1961).

Supreme Court's construction of the federal obscenity statutes.[2] In a state prosecution, the description of the kind of sexual conduct that is included within the coverage of the statute may come from the statute itself or from an authoritative construction by the state's highest court. In either event, the instructions should include these definitions or limiting constructions. They must also make clear, in either a state or federal prosecution, that this is only an initial test. Even if the material comes within the coverage of statute, it must still be tested in accordance with the constitutional parameters of obscenity as set forth in *Miller* v. *California.*[3] It is crucial that the jury fully understand that they must find that *all* of the tests be satisfied, that the material appeals to a prurient interest in sex, that it is patently offensive, *and* that it is lacking in serious literary, artistic, political, or scientific value. As the obscenity test is explained to the jury, they will be hit with a barrage of conjunctive and disjunctive phrases which cannot help but be confusing, and thus the importance of explaining the relationship of each element of the test cannot be overemphasized. There does not seem to be any particular need to include the "hard-core" concept in jury instructions, but it may be included if it is felt that it might be an aid to jury understanding.

Good instructions on the definition of obscenity will look upon the *Miller* test only as the starting point for a more detailed explanation of each of the terms and concepts which it embodies. Thus, the concept of prurient interest should be explained so that the jury understands the difference between material that appeals to a prurient interest in sex and material that merely deals with the subject of sex or sexual conduct.[4] They should be told that they must evaluate the work as a whole and cannot base a finding on isolated excerpts from the material.[5] If the material at issue is a motion picture, then the jury will in virtually every instance have seen it in its entirety, and thus a simple cautionary instruction to consider it as a whole will be sufficient. But if the material is a book, or a magazine, or a number of them, then the jury will probably have only briefly looked at them by the time they

[2] *See generally* Chapter 9 *supra.* The original source of the guidelines, which should be included verbatim in the instructions, is *Miller* v. *California,* 413 U.S. 15, 25 (1973). Various cases have incorporated these standards into the federal obscenity statutes. *See, e.g., United States* v. *12 200-Ft. Reels of Film,* 413 U.S. 123, 130 n.7 (1973).

[3] 413 U.S. 15, 24 (1973). Although the test is described as "basic guidelines for the trier of fact," the instructions should at some point include most of the actual words found in the *Miller* test, which can then be explained and elaborated upon.

[4] *See* Chapter 5.1 *supra.*

[5] *See* Chapter 5.3 *supra* and cases cited in note 51 thereof.

retire for their deliberations. In this case a number of alternatives are possible. The trial judge can tell the jurors that they must consider all of the material, and consider it as a whole, and leave it at that.[6] But this does not seem a strong enough instruction to counterbalance the jurors' natural inclination to focus only on the most offensive parts, especially since these will be the parts that have been emphasized and described during the course of the trial. The opposite extreme would be to require the jury to read the books in open court.[7] But this procedure seems unduly cumbersome, especially for lengthy or predominantly textual material. Given that a careful and comprehensive review of the materials is the ultimate goal, this goal is not likely to be achieved if the jurors feel like goldfish in a fishbowl while they are reading the material at issue. The most advantageous course seems to be to instruct the jury that they must actually read all of the material whose obscenity is to be decided, but let them do the reading as part of their deliberations in a more relaxed and private environment than the public courtroom.

It is important that the jury understand the concept of the average man. The instructions should make it clear that the jurors should not base their verdict on their own personal views as to the material at issue, since avoiding this effect is the primary purpose of both the "average person" and "contemporary community standards" aspects of the test for obscenity.[8] The instructions should also make an affirmative effort to explain that the effect on children or particularly susceptible adults is not the test and the effect on these groups should not be considered. It is not unusual that a jury's natural inclination would be to think in terms of children and "weak" adults when evaluating the material in an obscenity case, and the instructions should be designed to offset this likely predisposition. Of course, if the case is one involving materials designed for and distributed to members of "deviant" groups,[9]

---

[6] *See Alexander* v. *United States*, 271 F.2d 140 (8th Cir. 1959).

[7] *See United States* v. *West Coast News Co.*, 228 F. Supp. 171, 178 (W.D. Mich. 1964), *aff'd*, 357 F.2d 855 (6th Cir. 1966), *rev'd on other grounds sub nom. Aday* v. *United States*, 388 U.S. 447 (1967). It has even been suggested that all of the material be read *to* the jury. *See* Rogge, *Obscenity Litigation*, 10 AM. JUR. TRIALS §53 at 173 (1965).

[8] *See Hamling* v. *United States*, 418 U.S. 87 (1974); *Smith* v. *California*, 361 U.S. 147, 172 n.3 (1959) (Harlan, J., concurring in part and dissenting in part); E. DEVITT and C. BLACKMAR, FEDERAL JURY PRACTICE AND INSTRUCTIONS §41.10 at 522 (1970) ("Obscenity is not a matter of individual taste. The personal opinion of a juror as to the material here in question is not the proper basis for a determination whether or not the material is obscene.").

[9] *See* Chapter 4.3 *supra*.

or to minors,[10] then the instructions must explain that it is members of these groups whose prurient interest is relevant. If pandering is not part of the prosecution's case, then the jury should be instructed to disregard the advertising of the materials in question or the setting in which they are distributed, but if pandering is part of the theory of the prosecution, then the jury should be instructed as to just what pandering is and that it should be taken into account only if they feel the issue is a close one on the question of the obscenity vel non of the materials.[11]

Instructions as to contemporary community standards are of critical importance.[12] The court should explain the purpose of the community standards concept and relate it both to the prurient-interest test and to the patent offensiveness test. If the applicable state statute specifies the relevant community,[13] then the instructions must incorporate the appropriate geographic boundaries. If there is no such statutory compulsion, then the trial judge may either define the local community which he feels is applicable to the particular case, or not give any geographic contours of the community at all, and rely on the jurors' own individual perceptions of what the relevant community consists of. Although this latter procedure was specifically approved in *Hamling* v. *United States*,[14] on the grounds that delineation of a specific community is not a constitutional requirement, this certainly does not mean that specifying a particular community is impermissible. In fact, such a course will considerably minimize the degree of juror uncertainty, and make it easier for jury evaluation of community standards to be based on evidence of community standards actually presented at the trial. To the extent that the jurors' perceptions of the community may not coincide with the legally relevant community,[15] specification of that legally relevant community becomes increasingly important.

[10] *See* Chapter 4.5 *supra*. This assumes, of course, that the indictment is brought under a statute specifically directed to distribution of obscene materials to minors, as in *Ginsberg* v. *New York,* 390 U.S. 629 (1968).

[11] *See* Chapter 4.4 *supra*.

[12] *See generally* Chapter 6 *supra*.

[13] Some of these statutes are cited in Chapter 6, note 43 *supra*. This is a characteristic of a growing number of state statutes enacted or amended since *Miller*. A requirement for a geographically specific community may also be imposed by binding judicial authority as, for example, in *People* v. *Heller,* 33 N.Y.2d 314, 352 N.Y.S.2d 601, 307 N.E.2d 805 (1973) (entire State of New York must be used as the governing community in cases arising under New York obscenity statute).

[14] 418 U.S. 87 (1974).

[15] *See* Chapters 6.4 and 6.5 *supra*.

Instructions regarding the lack of serious literary, artistic, political, or scientific value should stress the First Amendment values
of protection of divergent or minority views. Thus, the jurors should
know that it is not whether or not they would find serious value in
any of the works at issue, but whether some significant portion of the
population would find this value.[16] The instructions on this element of
the test should also explain the meaning of the word "serious" in this
context and explain the relatively broad definition to be given to the
four enumerated categories in which serious value may be found. If
expert testimony is given as to this or any other element of obscenity,
then the jury should be instructed both as to expert testimony in general and as to the particular function of expert testimony in obscenity
cases. If only the defense employs expert testimony, the prosecution
is entitled to an instruction that there is no legal compulsion on the
prosecution to produce any expert testimony, although the jury may
of course consider the factual weight to be given to the presence or
absence of expert testimony on behalf of a particular party.

One of the most difficult instructions to formulate will be that
dealing with scienter.[17] The jury must be instructed that the defendant
must be shown to have had knowledge of the "character" of the materials, which means, at the least, that he knew the materials were
sexually explicit. It is unnecessary for the prosecution to show that the
defendant knew or thought the materials were legally obscene, and
this should also be part of the instructions.[18] The most difficult part
of scienter instructions is explaining proof of scienter. Thus, extensive instructions on the use of circumstantial evidence, accomplice
testimony, and the admissibility of prior similar acts on the issue of
intent[19] may all be required, depending upon the type of proof of scienter that is offered. Naturally, there must also be instructions as to the
elements of intent or willfulness for every element of the offense, not
only that of obscenity.

Naturally, there will also be instructions as to the other funda-

---

[16] *See* Chapter 7.2 *supra.*

[17] *See generally* Chapter 11.6 *supra.*

[18] In E. DEVITT and C. BLACKMAR, FEDERAL JURY PRACTICE AND INSTRUCTIONS
§41.17 at 525 (1970), there is a suggested instruction to the effect that a good-faith
belief that the materials were not obscene is a complete defense in an obscenity
prosecution. There seems to be little, if any, case law support for this proposition
and it goes considerably beyond the accepted definition of the scienter requirement.
The authors have since seemed to recognize its weaknesses. See *Id.,* 1974 Supp.
§41.17 at 341.

[19] *See, e.g., United States* v. *Deaton,* 381 F.2d 114 (2d Cir. 1967).

mentals of the case, such as burden of proof, credibility of witnesses, weight of evidence, and so forth, but these will not be significantly different in an obscenity case from other types of litigation. Therefore, these other types of instructions are not covered here, although they of course cannot be ignored at trial. As to those instructions which do not relate particularly to obscenity cases, forms for such instructions, as an aid to the material discussed in this section, will be found in Appendix A of this book. Naturally, these are not the only possible instructions, and they would of course have to be modified in accordance with the facts and governing statute of a particular case, but they do embody the current substantive law of obscenity as is discussed in the bulk of this treatise.

In light of the complexity of the instructions in an obscenity case, the court should seriously consider furnishing written instructions to the jury.[20] This practice should tend to lessen the likelihood of undue emphasis on only one aspect of the test for obscenity.

17.2 Requests for Instructions

The vast majority of substantive legal questions raised in an obscenity case arise in the context of instructions to the jury. In addition, the judge's instructions are, in most cases, the last thing the jury hears before they begin their deliberations. For these and other reasons, counsel should pay particular care to requests for jury instructions, and should, if possible, submit requests as to *all* desired instructions, with citations of authority accompanying each instruction. Counsel should not assume that the court will instruct on any particular matters, and requesting instructions as to all of the elements of the case, and any supported by the evidence, will best preserve appellate rights[21] as well as producing the fairest and most comprehensive instructions. Counsel will have the best chance of having his requested instructions given if those requests accurately state the law. If the requests are overly argumentative, verbose, or incorrect, then counsel runs the risk of not getting any instruction at all on the particular point, or getting one in

---

[20] *See United States* v. *Senak,* 477 F.2d 304 (7th Cir. 1973), *cert. denied,* 414 U.S. 856; *United States* v. *Johnson,* 466 F.2d 537 (8th Cir. 1972), *cert. denied,* 409 U.S. 1111.

[21] *Cf. United States* v. *DeCarlo,* 458 F.2d 358 (3rd Cir. 1972), *cert. denied,* 409 U.S. 843; *United States* v. *Wilford,* 493 F.2d 730 (3rd Cir. 1974); *United States* v. *Robinson,* 448 F.2d 715 (8th Cir. 1971), *cert. denied,* 405 U.S. 927.

a very different form than that requested.[22] The more reasonable the requests are, the better are the chances of having them given in the form suggested by counsel.

Of course, in a criminal case, the court must give instructions on the basic legal issues of the case even if they are not requested by counsel.[23] Thus, in an obscenity case, the court should always instruct as to the type of sexual conduct the portrayal of which is included in the statute,[24] the elements of the constitutional test for obscenity, the meaning of the most important concepts therein, such as "appeal to the prurient interest," "as a whole," "patently offensive," "average person," "contemporary community standards," and "serious literary, artistic, political, or scientific value," the other elements of the offense charged, and scienter. This is of course in addition to those issues of general criminal law which may be part of a required charge in the given jurisdiction, such as burden of proof, presumption of innocence, and so forth.

In a case arising out of facts taking place on or before June 23, 1973, the date of the Supreme Court's decision in *Miller* v. *California*,[25] defense counsel should request instructions based both on *Miller* and *Memoirs* v. *Massachusetts*,[26] since the defendant is entitled to whatever benefits can be derived from either test.[27] The two main differences between *Memoirs* and *Miller* are the geographic contours of community standards and the replacement of the "utterly without redeeming social value" test. Thus, in a pre-*Miller* case, material cannot be obscene unless it offends both local and national standards, and, in addition to lacking serious literary, artistic, political, or scientific value, is also utterly without redeeming social value.

Since many evidentiary and other rulings at trial may depend on the court's understanding of counsel's theory of the case, as many requested instructions as possible, with supporting authority, should be submitted in advance of the trial. Additions and modifications of the requests can be made later if the evidence so indicates.

[22] *See, e.g., United States* v. *American Radiator and Standard Sanitary Corp.*, 433 F.2d 174 (3rd Cir. 1970), *cert. denied*, 401 U.S. 948 (1971); *United States* v. *Billingsley*, 474 F.2d 63 (6th Cir. 1973), *cert. denied*, 414 U.S. 819.

[23] *See, e.g., Todorow* v. *United States*, 173 F.2d 439 (9th Cir. 1949), *cert. denied*, 337 U.S. 925; *Strauss* v. *United States*, 376 F.2d 316 (5th Cir. 1967).

[24] This applies whether the specifics come from the statute itself or from an authoritative judicial construction.

[25] 413 U.S. 15 (1973).

[26] 383 U.S. 486 (1966).

[27] *Hamling* v. *United States*, 418 U.S. 87 (1974); *United States* v. *Groner*, 494 F.2d 499 (5th Cir. 1974).

17.3 Objections to Instructions

Since many of the possible points of appeal in an obscenity case will involve substantive legal standards as finally expressed in instructions to the jury, it is crucial that counsel preserve any possible points of appeal as to claimed defects or deficiencies in the instructions.[28] This must be done by making timely objections to the instructions the court has decided to give, or to the failure to give certain instructions requested by counsel. It is advisable for the court to have a conference in chambers in a complex case such as an obscenity case, so that any objections involving major substantive points of law can be fully argued before the court makes its final decisions as to instructions. Counsel objecting to any ruling at that time should make sure that his objections are noted. But in any case the objections should be repeated, specifically and completely, after the instructions are given if such action is required in order to preserve appellate rights.[29]

[28] *See generally* E. DEVITT and C. BLACKMAR, FEDERAL JURY PRACTICE AND INSTRUCTIONS §§7.03 and 7.04 (1970 and 1974 Supp.).

[29] *See* FED. R. CRIM. P. 30; *Hamling* v. *United States,* 418 U.S .87 (1974) (failure of court, in obscenity case, to hear objections to instructions out of presence of jury violated Rule 30 and was error, but would not require reversal in absence of prejudice to defendant); *United States* v. *Wild,* 422 F.2d 34 (2d Cir. 1969), *cert. denied,* 402 U.S. 986 (1971) (failure to object to pandering instruction waives right to argue error on appeal).

APPENDIX A

Questions on Voir Dire Examination of Prospective Jurors

Following are some suggested questions, or lines of inquiry, for either the court or counsel in examining prospective jurors in an obscenity case. Some would be useful to both defense and prosecution, and some are more appropriate for questioning by one side or the other. Counsel should select only those that seem relevant to his theory of the case or theory of jury selection. Of course, affirmative answers to some of these questions may require more detailed probing. The questions suggested here relate only to obscenity litigation, and other questions should be added depending on the nature of the case.

1. Are you in any way in the business of producing or distributing motion pictures, or operating a motion picture theater? Is any member of your family or close friend in such a business, or do they have such an occupation? Are you, or any relative or close friend, involved in any other aspect of the entertainment business?

2. Are you in any way in the business of publishing, editing, manufacturing, or selling books, magazines, or newspapers? Is any member of your family or close friend in such a business or do they have such an occupation?

3. Are you, or any member of your family or close friend, employed by or connected with the police department or any other law enforcement agency? Are you, or any member of your family or close friend, employed by a government or government agency? If so, which ones? Are you or any such friends or relatives employed by the Post Office Department or the Customs Service?

4. Are you married? How many children do you have? Grandchildren? What are their ages?

5. What schools or colleges did you attend or are you attending? What degrees or diplomas have you received? What was your college major or specialization?

6. What is your occupation? Where are you employed? What is your title? What is your spouse's occupation, place of business, and title?

7. Where do you live? Do you rent or do you own your own home? How long have you lived there? Where have you lived in the past?

8. What clubs, organizations, or associations do you belong to? Have any of them taken a particular stand regarding obscenity or pornography or the obscenity laws? What is that position?

9. Are you or have you been a member of an organization whose purpose is to encourage more vigorous enforcement of the obscenity laws, or to eliminate objectionable books, magazines, motion pictures, or television programs?

10. Are you or have you been a member of an organization whose purpose is to advocate the elimination of obscenity laws, or to oppose the enforcement of them, or to oppose censorship in general?

11. Are you a member of a religious faith whose doctrines prohibit the seeing of certain movies or the reading of certain books depending on their treatment of sex?

12. Do you feel that there is too much sex in movies today? In books and magazines? On television?

13. Are there any adult bookstores in your neighborhood? Does that bother you? Does the idea of adult bookstores in general bother you? Have you ever been in one? How often? Did you buy anything?

14. Have you ever seen or read a so-called "adult" magazine or book? When? How often?

15. Is there a theater in your neighborhood that shows X-rated or adult movies? Does it bother you? Does it disturb you that people go to this theater or to any such theater? Have you ever been to an X-rated or adult movie? When? How often? Were you offended? How often do you attend any kind of movie?

16. Have you ever been to a play where some of the actors were completely nude? How often? Were you offended?

17. Have you ever seen a so-called "stag" movie? If so, how often?

18. Are you or would you be offended by portrayal of a sexual act in a motion picture? On the stage? In a book or magazine?

19. Are you offended by nudity in movies? In magazines?

20. Are you offended by the idea of premarital sex? Extramarital sex?

21. Does the idea of sexual acts other than sexual intercourse offend you?

22. Does the idea of oral sex offend you?

23. Does the idea of homosexuality offend you?

24. Does the idea of group sex offend you?

25. Does the idea of masturbation offend you?

26. Does the idea of interracial sex offend you?

27. Does the idea of sex between humans and animals offend you?

28. Are you offended by the thought that some people can be sexually stimulated by whipping, or beating, or other such acts?

29. Do you feel you could see a motion picture, or a magazine, which contained depictions of those things which offended you, and still look at it with an open mind? Do you feel that you could accept the idea that something which offends and disgusts you personally may not be obscene as a matter of law? Are you willing to base your judgment on the evidence you see and hear, and the instructions from the court, without regard for your personal tastes or opinions regarding the movie (book) (magazine) you will see?

30. Do you believe that adults should be able to see or read whatever they want, regardless of sexual content?

31. Do you have a personal opinion of people who deal in books or movies about sex? What is that opinion?

32. Do you believe that people are or can be hurt as a result of exposure to obscene materials? Do you believe that such materials are harmless? Are you willing to base your verdict on the legal definition of obscenity, and not on your views as to whether or not the material is harmful? Do you believe it is possible for something to be legally obscene?

33. Obscenity cases and obscenity law are frequently in the news. Have you read any of these news stories? How much do you know about obscenity law? Can you put aside all of that and decide this case solely on what you see and hear during the course of the trial?

34. Have you ever been personally involved with the obscenity laws, such as by making an official report or complaint about objectionable material, or being involved in some way in an obscenity trial, or having a friend or relative who was involved in an obscenity trial, or writing or speaking publicly about obscenity or the obscenity laws?

35. In the course of this trial, you are going to be required to see (read) a sexually explicit movie (book) (magazine) which is part of this case. On account of this, or the nature of this case, would any of you rather not act as a juror in this case? Is there any other reason any of you would prefer not to be a juror in this case?

36. The materials which are the subject of the indictment are alleged to be obscene. Do any of you now believe that these materials are obscene?

37. In order for material to be obscene, it must meet a number of tests as to which the court will instruct you. If it does not meet all of them it is not obscene. Do you feel you could find that material which offended both you and the community could still not be obscene as a matter of law?

38. Are you a member of a church or synagogue? How often do you attend services? How often do you attend meetings of other groups related in some way to your church or synagogue?

39. What is your view as to the role of the church in our society?

40. What is your view of the Bible?

41. Do you believe that people should be able to do whatever they want to do as long as it doesn't hurt other people?

42. Do you believe that consenting adults should be able to participate in whatever sexual acts they wish?

43. Do you believe that jurors should be concerned with whether certain laws are good laws or bad laws?

44. Do you believe that, except for having children in marriage, any interest in sex is bad?

45. Do you believe that all people have an interest in sex?

46. Do you feel that all interest in sex is good?

47. In your opinion, should laws against homosexuality be done away with?

48. Do you believe that people should be denied jobs because they are homosexuals?

49. Do you believe that homosexuals are sick people?

50. Do you believe that prostitution should be against the law?

51. Do you believe that sexual openness among teenagers should be encouraged? Discouraged?

52. Do you think young people know too much about sex these days? Too little?

53. Should parents discuss sex with their children? If so, at what age?

54. Do you feel that laws should promote the moral codes of our society?

55. Do you consider your views about sex to be about the same as most people's, more conservative, or more liberal?

56. Why do you feel that people go to movies or read books that show or describe explicit sexual conduct?

57. Are you embarrassed when you talk about sex?

Some Suggested Jury Instructions

[Only instructions dealing particularly with obscenity issues are included here. Obviously, instructions on other aspects of the case will also be needed.]

Obscenity

It is for you to determine whether or not the material you have seen is obscene. You must disregard any previous notions you may have had and apply the legal definition of obscenity. In order for this material to be legally obscene, all of the following must exist:

1. The average person, applying contemporary community standards, would find that the film (book) (magazine), taken as a whole, appeals to the prurient interest in sex.
2. The film (book) (magazine) depicts or describes sexual conduct in a patently offensive way.
3. The film (book) (magazine), taken as a whole, lacks serious literary, artistic, political, or scientific value.

I will explain the terms involved in this definition, but remember, if any of these tests is not met, the material is not obscene. [This basic definition should be repeated after the terms are defined.]

Prurient Interest

You must determine whether the material appeals to a prurient interest in sex, for unless it does it cannot be obscene. A prurient interest in sex is not the same as a candid, wholesome, or healthy interest in sex. Material does not appeal to the prurient interest just because it deals with sex, or shows nude bodies. Prurient interest is an unhealthy, unwholesome, morbid, degrading, and shameful interest in sex, a leering or longing interest. An appeal to prurient interest is an appeal to sexual desire, not an appeal to sexual interest. An interest in sex is normal, but if the material appeals to an abnormal interest in sex, it can appeal to the prurient interest.

Average Person

In determining whether or not the material appeals to a prurient interest in sex, you must determine whether the average person in the community would find that the material has such appeal. People have different views as to the propriety of certain material. What may be prurient to some is not prurient to others. What may be offensive to some might be entertaining or artistic to others. Obscenity is not, however, a matter of individual taste. Your personal opinion as a juror about this material is not a proper basis for determining whether or not the material is obscene or appeals to the prurient interest. You must judge how the average person in the community would view this material.

When I speak of the average person, I mean the average adult in the community. How juveniles would view this material, or what the effect on juveniles would be, is not part of your consideration. We know also that there are individuals in the community who are especially susceptible or especially sensitive to materials dealing with sex, and that there are also those who are unusually sophisticated as to sexual matters. But you are not to consider the views of these people, or the effects that this material would have on them. You are to consider the appeal of this material to the average person, the person with average sex instincts, in determining whether or not this material appeals to the prurient interest.

Taken as a Whole

In making your determination of whether or not the average person would find that this material appeals to the prurient interest, you must consider the material as a whole, in its entirety. The fact that one portion or scene of the material may have some appeal to the prurient interest is not sufficient. The appeal to the prurient interest must be the main and principal appeal of the material. The effect of isolated excerpts cannot be part of your consideration. In determining whether an appeal to the prurient interest is the main and principal appeal of the material, you should consider the intended effect on the intended and probable recipients of the material.

Contemporary Community Standards

Whether this material, taken as a whole, appeals to the prurient interest, and whether it portrays sexual conduct in a patently offensive way, must be measured in terms of the contemporary community standards of the state of X. You must determine whether or not this material violates those standards; in other words, whether it goes substantially beyond the limits of candor that the community deems acceptable in the description or depiction of sexual conduct. Again, this must be based on the material as a whole, and not on isolated excerpts.

Remember that the standards to be applied are contemporary community standards. Standards change over time, and you may find acceptable materials which were unacceptable in the past, or you may find unacceptable material which might be acceptable in the future.

Contemporary community standards are determined by what the community as a whole in fact finds acceptable. The community as a whole is society at large, and not particular people or particular groups. What some people think the community ought or ought not to accept is not important, nor is what you, as an individual juror, think is good or bad. It is what people in general, the community as a whole, accept that is determinative.

In determining what the contemporary community standards of the state of X are, you may consider your knowledge of what is acceptable in the community, as well as evidence in this case showing what appears in motion pictures, magazines, and other forms of communication, together with any expert testimony. [If there is expert testimony, a standard instruction regarding such testimony should be given.] Merely because something is available in the community does not mean that it is acceptable by the community, but you should remember that the community may find acceptable that which you, or even a majority of people, find personally distasteful.

[This instruction should be modified if a statewide definition of community is not used.]

Patently Offensive

In order to be obscene, the material must depict or describe sexual conduct in a patently offensive way, that is, it must do so in a way that offends the contemporary community standards of the state of X. Not all descriptions or depictions of sexual conduct are patently offensive. You must find that the description or depiction of sexual conduct goes substantially beyond customary limits of candor for it to be patently offensive.

Sexual Conduct

The patently offensive representation must be of sexual conduct for the material to be obscene. Mere nudity is not sexual conduct. Sexual conduct is defined as [insert here the appropriate statutory definition or authoritative judicial construction, in compliance with *Miller* v. *California*, 413 U.S 15 (1973)]. Only those materials which depict or describe patently offensive, hard-core sexual conduct are within the scope of the obscenity laws.

Literary, Artistic, Political or Scientific Value

In order for you to find that this material is obscene, you must also find that, taken as a whole, it lacks serious literary, artistic, political, or scientific value. If the material has such value, it is not obscene even if it appeals to the prurient interest in sex, and even if it depicts or describes sexual conduct in a patently offensive way. In judging whether the value is serious, you should consider the intent of the material. If it is a serious literary or artistic effort, or if it attempts to convey scientific information, or a political point of view, it cannot be obscene. But if the intent is to appeal to the prurient interest, then the mere insertion of other matter, irrelevant to the predominant theme of the material, will not prevent you from determining that the material is obscene. Remember that sex can be a legitimate subject for literature, art, scientific inquiry, or political argument, and such serious treatments of sex, even if appealing to the prurient interest and patently offensive, cannot be obscene.

Pandering

There has been evidence attempting to show that the defendant pandered to the prurient interest of the intended and probable recipients of the material. In other words, the promotion, publicity, and advertising of the material emphasized the sexually provocative aspects of the material in order to cater to the prurient interest of potential customers. If you find that this has been the case, you may consider such evidence in determining whether or not the material is obscene, but only if you otherwise consider the case a "close" case. If the material is definitely not obscene, by itself, no amount of pandering may make it so. Similarly, if the material is definitely obscene, pandering is not necessary to support this determination.

Deviant Groups

There has been evidence attempting to show that the intended and probable recipients of the material in question were members of a deviant sexual group, to wit: [insert definition from 1 American Handbook of Psychiatry 593–604 (Arieti ed. 1959)]. If you find that this was the case, then you are to determine whether the material appeals to the prurient interest in terms of the average member of that deviant group, and not the average person in the community.

Juveniles

The defendant has been charged under a statute making it a crime to distribute, sell, or exhibit to minors material which is obscene as to minors or is harmful to minors. Harmful to minors means obscene as to minors. If you find that the material has in fact been so distributed, sold, or exhibited, then, in your determination of whether the material is obscene, you are to consider the tests for obscenity in terms, not of the average person in the community, but of the average person of the age of the actual recipients. In other words, you are to judge whether the material taken as a whole appeals to the prurient interest of such minors, whether it depicts or describes sexual conduct which is patently offensive, or unsuitable, for such minors, and whether it is lacking in serious literary, artistic, scientific, or political value for such minors.

Scienter

The prosecution in this case must prove beyond a reasonable doubt that the defendant had *scienter,* or knowledge, of the materials at issue. It is not necessary that the defendant be shown to have actually seen or read the materials, but only that the defendant knew the nature and character of the materials. It does not matter that the defendant did not believe the materials were obscene. If the defendant knew the nature and character of the materials, that is, knew that they were sexually explicit and contained descriptions or depictions of sexual conduct, then the requirement of knowledge would be satisfied.

Comparable Materials

You have seen evidence of other materials similar to the ones at issue in this trial. But merely because other materials are available, or have not been prosecuted, does not mean that they represent contemporary community standards. Only if such materials are in fact accepted by the community at large are they relevant in determining the contemporary standards of the community.

Some Typical Forms

1. Indictment

[Indictments are generally drafted to track the language of the governing statute, and therefore no form is included. The indictment should specify the exact date and place of the offense, as well as the name or title of the particular materials alleged to be obscene.]

2. Motion to Dismiss

[Caption]

Motion to Dismiss Indictment

The defendant, upon the indictment herein, moves for an order dismissing the indictment upon the grounds that:

1. The indictment does not state facts sufficient to constitute an offense.

2. The indictment fails to sufficiently apprise the defendant of the charges against him, and does not adequately protect the defendant against double jeopardy.

3. The statute upon which the indictment is based is unconstitutional on its face in that it is an illegal restriction on the rights of free speech guaranteed under the First (and Fourteenth) Amendment to the United States Constitution.

4. The statute upon which the indictment is based is unconstitutional on its face in that it is unconstitutionally overbroad by prohibiting speech protected by the First (and Fourteenth) Amendment to the United States Constitution.

5. The statute upon which the indictment is based is unconstitutional on its face in that it is void for vagueness by not sufficiently giving notice of what acts are prohibited.

6. The statute upon which the indictment is based is unconstitutional on its face in that it does not describe with sufficient specificity the sexual conduct which may not be depicted or described.

7. The statute upon which the indictment is based is unconstitutional as applied to the alleged conduct of the defendant, which is protected from prosecution by the First (and Fourteenth) Amendment to the United States Constitution.

8. The book (magazine) (motion picture) which the defendant is charged with selling (distributing) (exhibiting) (transporting) is not obscene as a matter of law. [Attach affidavit incorporating by reference the materials at issue.]

9. This court is without jurisdiction over the alleged offense or over the defendant.

10. The indictment fails to allege that the defendant's alleged actions were done knowingly or willfully.

The defendant further says that the issues raised herein are capable of determination without a trial of the general issue and requests a hearing on this motion to dismiss prior to trial.

Signature

3. *Motion to Suppress Evidence*

[Caption]

Motion to Suppress Evidence

The defendant says that he is a person aggrieved by an unlawful search and seizure and moves that this court suppress the use against him, and return to him, any and all of the following evidence:

1. Any prints of the motion picture _____.

2. Any film clips, photographs, or reproductions taken directly or indirectly from the motion picture _____.

3. Any copies of books (magazines) entitled _____, _____, and _____, and any other books (magazines) seized from premises at _____ on or about _____.

The property was seized from the defendant's premises at_____ on or about _____.

The search and seizure of the aforesaid property was illegal and in violation of the First, Fourth, Fifth, and Fourteenth Amendments to the United States Constitution for the following reasons:

1. There was not probable cause for believing the existence of the grounds on which the warrant was issued.

2. The magistrate who issued the warrant did not see (view) (read) any of the materials seized.

3. The magistrate who issued the warrant did not conduct a searching focus on the issue of obscenity prior to issuing the warrant.

4. The warrant was issued on the basis of a conclusory affidavit not sufficiently descriptive of the materials to be seized.

5. The warrant did not specifically describe the materials to be seized.

6. The search and seizure was conducted without authority of a search warrant.

[Add any additional grounds not peculiar to obscenity litigation.]

[Attach affidavit describing the circumstances of the search and seizure.]

Signature

4. Motion for a Bill of Particulars

[Caption]

Motion for a Bill of Particulars

The defendant moves that the government be required to serve a bill of particulars, as follows:

1. Set forth with particularity the exact date, time, place, and nature of the alleged sale (distribution) (exhibition).

2. Set forth with particularity the purchaser or recipient of the materials alleged to have been sold (distributed).

3. Set forth the geographic community whose standards the material at issue is alleged to offend.

4. State whether the defendant is charged with selling (exhibiting) (distributing) the materials to members of deviant sexual groups, and, if so, describe such group(s) with particularity.

5. State whether the defendant is charged with pandering the material and, if so, state with particularity such alleged pandering.

6. State the ages of the juveniles to whom the defendant is charged with selling (distributing) (exhibiting) the material at issue.

Signature

5. Motion for Exculpatory Evidence

[Caption]

Motion for Exculpatory Evidence

The defendant moves that the prosecution be required to produce any and all evidence in its possession showing, indicating, or tending to show or indicate the innocence of the defendant, or relating to any defenses to this prosecution, including, without limitation, any information or opinions, received from experts or otherwise, that the book (magazine) (film) _____ is not obscene.

Signature

6. *Motion for Discovery and Inspection*

[May be used by prosecution or defense in criminal cases if jurisdiction permits reciprocal discovery. Also applicable to civil cases.]

[Caption]

Motion for Discovery and Inspection

The defendant moves for an order directing the production and permission to inspect and copy of the following:

1. Any motion picture (positives or negatives), still photographs (positives and negatives), press release, advertisement, poster, brochure or other material relating to the content or marketing of the motion picture entitled _____.

2. All contracts, documents, correspondence, memoranda, letters, purchase orders, invoices, shipping orders, routing slips, labels, or other documents or writings of a like kind relating to the sale, distribution, transportation, or exhibition of the motion picture entitled _____.

3. The names and reports of any experts who have seen the motion picture entitled _____.

[Add any additional requests that the nature of the case may require.]

Signature

7. *Motion for Pretrial Order (Standards Applied)*

[Caption]

Motion for a Pretrial Order

The defendant (prosecution) moves the court for an order designating, prior to trial, the definition of "community" which is to be used in determining the admissibility of evidence of contemporary community standards and in instructing the jury on contemporary community standards.

Signature

APPENDIX D

Statutes

18 U.S.C. § 1461. Mailing obscene or crime-inciting matter.

Every obscene, lewd, lascivious, indecent, filthy or vile article, matter, thing, device, or substance; and

Every article or thing designed, adapted, or intended for producing abortion, or for any indecent or immoral use; and

Every article, instrument, substance, drug, medicine, or thing which is advertised or described in a manner calculated to lead another to use or apply it for producing abortion, or for any indecent or immoral purpose; and

Every written or printed card, letter, circular, book, pamphlet, advertisement, or notice of any kind giving information, directly or indirectly, where, or how, or from whom, or by what means any of such mentioned matters, articles, or things may be obtained or made, or where or by whom any act or operation of any kind for the procuring or producing of abortion will be done or performed, or how or by what means abortion may be produced, whether sealed or unsealed; and

Every paper, writing, advertisement, or representation that any article, instrument, substance, drug, medicine, or thing may, or can, be used or applied for producing abortion, or for any indecent or immoral purpose; and

Every description calculated to induce or incite a person to so use or apply any such article, instrument, substance, drug, medicine, or thing—

Is declared to be nonmailable matter and shall not be conveyed in the mails or delivered from any post office or by any letter carrier.

Whoever knowingly uses the mails for the mailing, carriage in the mails, or delivery of anything declared by this section or section 3001(e) of title 39 to be nonmailable, or knowingly causes to be delivered by mail according to the direction thereon, or at the place at which it is directed to be delivered by the person to whom it is addressed, or knowingly takes any such thing from the mails for the purpose of circulating or disposing thereof, or of aiding in the circulation or disposition thereof, shall be fined not more than $5,000 or imprisoned not more than five years, or both, for the first such offense, and shall be fined not more than $10,000 or imprisoned not more than ten years, or both, for each such offense thereafter.

The term "indecent", as used in this section includes matter of a character tending to incite arson, murder, or assassination.

18 U.S.C. § 1462. Importation or transportation of obscene matters.

Whoever brings into the United States, or any place subject to the jurisdiction thereof, or knowingly uses any express company or other common carrier, for carriage in interstate or foreign commerce—

(a) any obscene, lewd, lascivious, or filthy book, pamphlet, picture, motion-picture film, paper, letter, writing, print, or other matter of indecent character; or

(b) any obscene, lewd, lascivious, or filthy phonograph recording, electrical transcription, or other article or thing capable of producing sound; or

(c) any drug, medicine, article, or thing designed, adapted, or intended for producing abortion, or for any indecent or immoral use; or any written or printed card, letter, circular, book, pamphlet, advertisement, or notice of any kind giving information, directly or indirectly, where, how, or of whom, or by what means any of such mentioned articles, matters, or things may be obtained or made; or

Whoever knowingly takes from such express company or other common carrier any matter or thing the carriage of which is herein made unlawful—

Shall be fined not more than $5,000 or imprisoned not more than five years, or both, for the first such offense and shall be fined not more than $10,000 or imprisoned not more than ten years, or both, for each such offense thereafter.

18 U.S.C. § 1463. Mailing indecent matter on wrappers or envelopes.

All matter otherwise mailable by law, upon the envelope or outside cover or wrapper of which, and all postal cards upon which, any delineations, epithets, terms, or language of an indecent, lewd, lascivious, or obscene character are written or printed or otherwise impressed or apparent, are nonmailable matter, and shall not be conveyed in the mails nor delivered from any post office nor by any letter carrier, and shall be withdrawn from the mails under such regulations as the Postal Service shall prescribe.

Whoever knowingly deposits for mailing or delivery, anything declared by this section to be nonmailable matter, or knowingly takes the same from the mails for the purpose of circulating or disposing of or aiding in the circulation or disposition of the same, shall be fined not more than $5,000 or imprisoned not more than five years, or both.

18 U.S.C. § 1464. Broadcasting obscene language.

Whoever utters any obscene, indecent, or profane language by means of radio communication shall be fined no more than $10,000 or imprisoned not more than two years, or both.

18 U.S.C. § 1465. Transportation of obscene matters for sale or distribution.

Whoever knowingly transports in interstate or foreign commerce for the purpose of sale or distribution any obscene, lewd, lascivious, or filthy book, pamphlet, picture, film, paper, letter, writing, print, silhouette, drawing, figure, image, cast, phonograph recording, electrical transcription or other article capable of producing sound or any other matter of indecent or immoral character, shall be fined not more than $5,000 or imprisoned not more than five years, or both.

The transportation as aforesaid of two or more copies of any publication or two or more of any article of the character described above, or a combined total of five such publications and articles, shall create a presumption that such publications or articles are intended for sale or distribution, but such presumption shall be rebuttable.

When any person is convicted of a violation of this Act, the court in its judgment of conviction may, in addition to the penalty prescribed, order the confiscation and disposal of such items described herein which were found in the possession or under the immediate control of such person at the time of his arrest.

19 U.S.C. § 1305. Immoral articles; prohibition of importation.

(a) All persons are prohibited from importing into the United States from any foreign country any book, pamphlet, paper, writing, advertisement, circular, print, picture, or drawing containing any matter advocating or urging treason or insurrection against the United States, or forcible resistance to any law of the United States, or containing any threat to take the life of or inflict bodily harm upon any person in the United States, or any obscene book, pamphlet, paper, writing, advertisement, circular, print, picture, drawing, or other representation, figure, or image on or of paper or other material, or any cast, instrument, or other article which is obscene or immoral, or any drug or medicine or any article whatever for causing unlawful abortion, or any lottery ticket, or any printed paper that may be used as a lottery ticket, or any advertisement of any lottery. No such articles whether imported separately or contained in packages with other goods entitled to entry, shall be admitted to entry; and all such articles and, unless it appears to the satisfaction of the appropriate customs officer that the obscene or other prohibited articles contained in the package were inclosed therein without the knowledge or consent of the importer, owner, agent, or consignee, the entire contents of the package in which such articles are contained, shall be subject to seizure and forfeiture as hereinafter provided: *Provided,* That the drugs hereinbefore mentioned, when imported in bulk and not put up for any of the purposes hereinbefore specified, are excepted from the operation of this subdivision: *Provided further,* That the Secretary of the Treasury may, in his discretion, admit the so-called classics or books of recognized and established literary or scientific merit, but may, in his discretion, admit such classics or books only when imported for noncommercial purposes.

Upon the appearance of any such book or matter at any customs office, the same shall be seized and held by the appropriate customs officer to await the judgment of the district court as hereinafter provided; and no protest shall be taken to the United States Customs Court from the decision of such customs officer. Upon the seizure of such book or matter such customs officer shall transmit information thereof to the district attorney of the district in which is situated the office at which such seizure has taken place, who shall institute proceedings in the district court for the forfeiture, confiscation, and destruction of the book or matter seized. Upon the adjudication that such book or matter thus seized is of the character the entry of which is by this section prohibited, it shall be ordered destroyed and shall be destroyed. Upon adjudication that such book or matter thus seized is not of the character the entry of which is by this section prohibited, it shall not be excluded from entry under the provisions of this section.

In any such proceeding any party in interest may upon demand have the facts at issue determined by a jury and any party may have an appeal or the right of review as in the case of ordinary actions or suits.

39 U.S.C. § 3001. Nonmailable matter.

(a) Matter the deposit of which in the mails is punishable under section 1302, 1341, 1342, 1461, 1463, 1714, 1715, 1716, 1717 or 1718 of title 18 is nonmailable.

(b) Except as provided in subsection (c) of this section, nonmailable matter which reaches the office of delivery, or which may be seized or detained for violation of law, shall be disposed of as the Postal Service shall direct.

(c)(1) Matter which—

(A) exceeds the size and weight limits prescribed for the particular class of mail; or

(B) is of a character perishable within the period required for transportation and delivery;

is nonmailable.

(2) Matter made nonmailable by this subsection which reaches the office of destination may be delivered in accordance with its address, if the party addressed furnishes the name and address of the sender.

(d) Matter otherwise legally acceptable in the mails which—

(1) is in the form of, and reasonably could be interpreted or construed as, a bill, invoice, or statement of account due; but

(2) constitutes, in fact, a solicitation for the order by the addressee of goods or services, or both;

is nonmailable matter, shall not be carried or delivered by mail, and shall be disposed of as the Postal Service directs, unless such matter bears on its face, in conspicuous and legible type in contrast by typography, layout, or color with other printing on its face, in accordance with regulations which the Postal Service shall prescribe—

(A) the following notice: "This is a solicitation for the

order of goods or services, or both, and not a bill, invoice, or statement of account due. You are under no obligation to make any payments on account of this offer unless you accept this offer."; or

(B) in lieu thereof, a notice to the same effect in words which the Postal Service may prescribe.

(e)(1) Any matter which is unsolicited by the addressee and which is designed, adapted, or intended for preventing conception (except unsolicited samples thereof mailed to a manufacturer thereof, a dealer therein, a licensed physician or surgeon, or a nurse, pharmacist, druggist, hospital, or clinic) is nonmailable matter, shall not be carried or delivered by mail, and shall be disposed of as the Postal Service directs.

(2) Any unsolicited advertisement of matter which is designed, adapted, or intended for preventing conception is nonmailable matter, shall not be carried or delivered by mail, and shall be disposed of as the Postal Service directs unless the advertisement—

(A) is mailed to a manufacturer of such matter, a dealer therein, a licensed physician or surgeon, or a nurse, pharmacist, druggist, hospital, or clinic; or

(B) accompanies in the same parcel any unsolicited sample excepted by paragraph (1) of this subsection.

An advertisement shall not be deemed to be unsolicited for the purposes of this paragraph if it is contained in a publication for which the addressee has paid or promised to pay a consideration or which he has otherwise indicated he desires to receive.

(f) Except as otherwise provided by law, proceedings concerning the mailability of matter under this chapter and chapters 71 and 83 of title 18 shall be conducted in accordance with chapters 5 and 7 of title 5.

(g) The district courts, together with the District Court of the Virgin Islands and the District Court of Guam, shall have jurisdiction, upon cause shown, to enjoin violations of section 1716 of title 18.

39 U.S.C. § 3006. Unlawful matter.

Upon evidence satisfactory to the Postal Service that a person is obtaining or attempting to obtain remittances of money or property of any kind through the mail for an obscene, lewd, lascivious, indecent, filthy, or vile thing or is depositing or causing to be deposited in the United States mail information as to where, how, or from whom such a thing may be obtained, the Postal Service may—

(1) direct any postmaster at an office at which mail arrives, addressed to such a person or to his representative, to return the mail to the sender marked "Unlawful"; and

(2) forbid the payment by a postmaster to such a person or his representative of any money order or postal note drawn to the order of either and provide for the return to the remitter of the sum named in the money order.

39 U.SC. § 3007. *Detention of mail for temporary periods.*

(a) In preparation for or during the pendency of proceedings under sections 3005 and 3006 of this title, the United States district court in the district in which the defendant receives his mail shall, upon application therefor by the Postal Service and upon a showing of probable cause to believe either section is being violated, enter a temporary restraining order and preliminary injunction pursuant to rule 65 of the Federal Rules of Civil Procedure directing the detention of the defendant's incoming mail by the postmaster pending the conclusion of the statutory proceedings and any appeal therefrom. The district court may provide in the order that the detained mail be open to examination by the defendant and such mail be delivered as is clearly not connected with the alleged unlawful activity. An action taken by a court hereunder does not affect or determine any fact at issue in the statutory proceedings.

(b) This section does not apply to mail addressed to publishers of newspapers and other periodical publications entitled to a periodical publication rate or to mail addressed to the agents of those publishers.

39 U.S.C. § 3008. *Prohibition of pandering advertisements.*

(a) Whoever for himself, or by his agents or assigns, mails or causes to be mailed any pandering advertisement which offers for sale matter which the addressee in his sole discretion believes to be erotically arousing or sexually provocative shall be subject to an order of the Postal Service to refrain from further mailings of such materials to designated addresses thereof.

(b) Upon receipt of notice from an addressee that he has received such mail matter, determined by the addressee in his sole discretion to be of the character described in subsection (a) of this section, the Postal Service shall issue an order, if requested by the addressee, to the sender thereof, directing the sender and his agents or assigns to refrain from further mailing to the named addressees.

(c) The order of the Postal Service shall expressly prohibit the sender and his agents or assigns from making any further mailings to the designated addresses, effective on the thirtieth calendar day after receipt of the order. The order shall also direct the sender and his agents or assigns to delete immediately the names of the designated addressees from all mailing lists owned or controlled by the sender or his agents or assigns and, further, shall prohibit the sender and his agents or assigns from the sale, rental, exchange, or other transaction involving mailing lists bearing the names of the designated addressees.

(d) Whenever the Postal Service believes that the sender or anyone acting on his behalf has violated or is violating the order given under this section, it shall serve upon the sender, by registered or certified mail, a complaint stating the reasons for its belief and request that any response thereto be filed in writing with the Postal Service within 15 days after the date of such service. If the Postal Service, after appropriate hearing if requested by the sender, and without a hearing if such a hearing is not requested, thereafter determines that the order given has been or is being violated, it is authorized to request the Attorney General to make application, and the Attorney General is authorized to make application, to a district court of the United States for an order directing compliance with such notice.

(e) Any district court of the United States within the jurisdiction of which any mail matter shall have been sent or received in violation of the order provided for by this section shall have jurisdiction, upon application by the Attorney General, to issue an order commanding compliance with such notice. Failure to observe such order may be punishable by the court as contempt thereof.

(f) Receipt of mail matter 30 days or more after the effective date of the order provided for by this section shall create a rebuttable presumption that such mail was sent after such effective date.

(g) Upon request of any addressee, the order of the Postal Service shall include the names of any of his minor children who have not attained their nineteenth birthday, and who reside with the addressee.

(h) The provisions of subchapter II of chapter 5, relating to administrative procedure, and chapter 7, relating to judicial review, of title 5, shall not apply to any provisions of this section.

(i) For purposes of this section—

(1) mail matter, directed to a specific address covered in the order of the Postal Service, without designation of a specific addressee thereon, shall be considered as addressed to the person named in the Postal Service's order; and

(2) the term "children" includes natural children, stepchildren, adopted children, and children who are wards of or in custody of the addressee or who are living with such addressee in a regular parent-child relationship.

39 U.S.C. § 3010. Mailing of sexually oriented advertisements.

(a) Any person who mails or causes to be mailed any sexually oriented advertisement shall place on the envelope or cover thereof his name and address as the sender thereof and such mark or notice as the Postal Service may prescribe.

(b) Any person, on his own behalf or on the behalf of any of his children who has not attained the age of 19 years and who resides with him or is under his care, custody, or supervision, may file with the Postal Service a statement, in such form and manner as the Postal Service may prescribe, that he desires to receive no sexually oriented advertisements through the mails. The Postal Service shall maintain and keep current, insofar as practicable, a list of the names and addresses of such persons and shall make the list (including portions thereof or changes therein) available to any person, upon such reasonable terms and conditions as it may prescribe, including the payment of such service charge as it determines to be necessary to defray the cost of compiling and maintaining the list and making it available as provided in this sentence. No person shall mail or cause to be mailed any sexually oriented advertisement to any individual whose name and address has been on the list for more than 30 days.

(c) No person shall sell, lease, lend, exchange, or license the use of, or, except for the purpose expressly authorized by this section, use any mailing list compiled in whole or in part from the list maintained by the Postal Service pursuant to this section.

(d) "Sexually oriented advertisement" means any advertisement that depicts, in actual or simulated form, or explicitly describes, in a predominantly sexual context, human genitalia, any act of natural or unnatural sexual intercourse, any act of sadism or masochism, or any other erotic subject directly related to the foregoing. Material otherwise within the definition of this subsection shall be deemed not to constitute a sexually oriented advertisement if it constitutes only a small and insignificant part of the whole of a single catalog, book, periodical, or other work the remainder of which is not primarily devoted to sexual matters.

39 U.S.C. § 3011. Judicial enforcement.

(a) Whenever the Postal Service believes that any person is mailing or causing to be mailed any sexually oriented advertisement in violation of section 3010 of this title, it may request the Attorney General to commence a civil action against such person in a district court of the United States. Upon a finding by the court of a violation of that section, the court may issue an order including one or more of the following provisions as the court deems just under the circumstances:

(1) a direction to the defendant to refrain from mailing any sexually oriented advertisement to a specific addressee, to any group of addressees, or to all persons;

(2) a direction to any postmaster to whom sexually oriented advertisements originating with such defendant are tendered for transmission through the mails to refuse to accept such advertisements for mailing; or

(3) a direction to any postmaster at the office at which registered or certified letters or other letters or mail arrive, addressed to the defendant or his representative, to return the registered or certified letters or other letters or mail to the sender appropriately marked as being in response to mail in violation of section 3010 of this title, after the defendant, or his representative, has been notified and given reasonable opportunity to examine such letters or mail and to obtain delivery of mail which is clearly not connected with activity alleged to be in violation of section 3010 of this title.

(b) The statement that remittances may be made to a person named in a sexually oriented advertisement is prima facie evidence that such named person is the principal, agent, or representative of the mailer for the receipt of remittances on his behalf. The court is not precluded from ascertaining the existence of the agency on the basis of any other evidence.

(c) In preparation for, or during the pendency of, a civil action under subsection (a) of this section, a district court of the United States, upon application therefor by the Attorney General and upon a showing of probable cause to believe the statute is being violated, may enter a temporary restraining order or preliminary injunction containing such terms as the court deems just, including, but not limited to, provisions enjoining the defendant from mailing any sexually oriented advertisement to any person or class of persons, directing any postmaster to refuse to accept such defendant's sexually oriented advertisements for mailing, and directing the detention of the defendant's incoming mail by any postmaster pending the conclusion of the judicial proceedings. Any action taken by a court under this subsection does not affect or determine any fact at issue in any other proceeding under this section.

(d) A civil action under this section may be brought in the judicial district in which the defendant resides, or has his principal place of business, or in any judicial district in which any sexually oriented advertisement mailed in violation of section 3010 has been delivered by mail according to the direction thereon.

(e) Nothing in this section or in section 3010 shall be construed as amending, preempting, limiting, modifying, or otherwise in any way affecting section 1461 or 1463 of title 18 or section 3006, 3007, or 3008 of this title.

Model Penal Code § 251.4. Obscenity.

(1) *Obscene Defined.* Material is obscene if, considered as a whole, its predominant appeal is to prurient interest, that is, a shameful or morbid interest, in nudity, sex or excretion, and if in addition it goes substantially beyond customary limits of candor in describing or representing such matters. Predominant appeal shall be judged with reference to ordinary adults unless it appears from the character of the material or the circumstances of its dissemination to be designed for children or other specially susceptible audience. Undeveloped photographs, molds, printing plates, and the like, shall be deemed obscene notwithstanding that processing or other acts may be required to make the obscenity patent or to disseminate it.

(2) *Offenses.* Subject to the affirmative defense provided in Subsection (3), a person commits a misdemeanor if he knowingly or recklessly:

(a) sells, delivers or provides, or offers or agrees to sell, deliver or provide, any obscene writing, picture, record or other representation or embodiment of the obscene; or

(b) presents or directs an obscene play, dance or performance, or participates in that portion thereof which makes it obscene; or

(c) publishes, exhibits or otherwise makes available any obscene material; or

(d) possesses any obscene material for purposes of sale or other commercial dissemination; or

(e) sells, advertises or otherwise commercially disseminates material, whether or not obscene, by representing or suggesting that it is obscene.

A person who disseminates or possesses obscene material in the course of his business is presumed to do so knowingly or recklessly.

(3) *Justifiable and Non-Commercial Private Dissemination.* It is an affirmative defense to prosecution under this Section that dissemination was restricted to:

(a) institutions or persons having scientific, educational, governmental or other similar justification for possessing obscene material; or

(b) non-commercial dissemination to personal associates of the actor.

(4) *Evidence; Adjudication of Obscenity.* In any prosecution under this Section evidence shall be admissible to show: ˙

(a) the character of the audience for which the material was designed or to which it was directed;

(b) what the predominant appeal of the material would be for ordinary adults or any special audience to which it was directed, and what effect, if any, it would probably have on conduct of such people;

(c) artistic, literary, scientific, educational or other merits of the material;

(d) the degree of public acceptance of the material in the United States;

(e) appeal to prurient interest, or absence thereof, in advertising or other promotion of the material; and

(f) the good repute of the author, creator, publisher or other person from whom the material originated.

Expert testimony and testimony of the author, creator, publisher or other person from whom the material originated, relating to factors entering into the determination of the issue of obscenity, shall be admissible. The Court shall dismiss a prosecution for obscenity if it is satisfied that the material is not obscene.

Major U.S. Supreme Court Obscenity Cases

Roth v. *United States*
354 U.S. 476 (1957)

MR. JUSTICE BRENNAN delivered the opinion of the Court.

The constitutionality of a criminal obscenity statute is the question in each of these cases. In *Roth,* the primary constitutional question is whether the federal obscenity statute[1] violates the provision of the First Amendment that "Congress shall make no law . . . abridging the freedom of speech, or of the press . . . ." In *Alberts,* the primary constitutional question is whether the obscenity provisions of the California Penal Code[2] invade the freedoms of speech and press as they may be incorporated in

[1] The federal obscenity statute provided, in pertinent part:
"Every obscene, lewd, lascivious, or filthy book, pamphlet, picture, paper, letter, writing, print, or other publication of an indecent character; and—

. . .
"Every written or printed card, letter, circular, book, pamphlet, advertisement, or notice of any kind giving information, directly or indirectly, where or how, or from whom, or by what means any of such mentioned matters, articles, or things may be obtained or made, . . . whether sealed or unsealed . . .

. . .
"Is declared to be nonmailable matter and shall not be conveyed in the mails or delivered from any post office or by any letter carrier.
"Whoever knowingly deposits for mailing or delivery, anything declared by this section to be nonmailable, or knowingly takes the same from the mails for the purpose of circulating or disposing thereof, or of aiding in the circulation or disposition thereof, shall be fined not more than $5,000 or imprisoned not more than five years, or both." 18 U.S.C. § 1461.
The 1955 amendment of this statute, 69 Stat. 183, is not applicable to this case.
[2] The California Penal Code provides, in pertinent part:
"Every person who wilfully and lewdly, either:

. . .
"3. Writes, composes, stereotypes, prints, publishes, sells, distributes, keeps for sale, or exhibits any obscene or indecent writing, paper, or book; or designs, copies, draws, engraves, paints, or otherwise prepares any obscene or indecent picture or print; or molds, cuts, casts, or otherwise makes any obscene or indecent figure; or,
"4. Writes, composes, or publishes any notice or advertisement of any such writing, paper, book, picture, print or figure; . . .

. . .
"6. . . . is guilty of a misdemeanor. . . ." West's Cal. Penal Code Ann., 1955, § 311.

the liberty protected from state action by the Due Process Clause of the Fourteenth Amendment.

Other constitutional questions are: whether these statutes violate due process,[3] because too vague to support conviction for crime; whether power to punish speech and press offensive to decency and morality is in the States alone, so that the federal obscenity statute violates the Ninth and Tenth Amendments (raised in *Roth*); and whether Congress, by enacting the federal obscenity statute, under the power delegated by Art. I, § 8, cl. 7, to establish post offices and post roads, pre-empted the regulation of the subject matter (raised in *Alberts*).

Roth conducted a business in New York in the publication and sale of books, photographs and magazines. He used circulars and advertising matter to solicit sales. He was convicted by a jury in the District Court for the Southern District of New York upon 4 counts of a 26-count indictment charging him with mailing obscene circulars and advertising, and an obscene book, in violation of the federal obscenity statute. His conviction was affirmed by the Court of Appeals for the Second Circuit.[4] We granted certiorari.[5]

Alberts conducted a mail-order business from Los Angeles. He was convicted by the Judge of the Municipal Court of the Beverly Hills Judicial District (having waived a jury trial) under a misdemeanor complaint which charged him with lewdly keeping for sale obscene and indecent books, and with writing, composing and publishing an obscene advertisement of them, in violation of the California Penal Code. The conviction was affirmed by the Appellate Department of the Superior Court of the State of California in and for the County of Los Angeles.[6] We noted probable jurisdiction.[7]

The dispositive question is whether obscenity is utterance within the area of protected speech and press.[8] Although this is the first time the question has been squarely presented to this Court, either under the First Amendment or under the Fourteenth Amendment, expressions found in numerous opinions indicate that this Court has always assumed that obscenity is not protected by the freedoms of speech and press. *Ex parte Jackson,* 96 U.S. 727, 736–737; *United States* v. *Chase,* 135 U.S. 255, 261; *Robertson* v. *Baldwin,* 165 U.S. 275, 281; *Public Clearing House* v. *Coyne,* 194 U.S. 497, 508; *Hoke* v. *United States,* 227 U.S. 308, 322; *Near* v. *Minnesota,* 283 U.S. 697, 716; *Chaplinsky* v. *New Hampshire,* 315 U.S. 568; 571–572; *Hannegan* v. *Esquire, Inc.,* 327 U.S. 146, 158;

---

[3] In *Roth,* reliance is placed on the Due Process Clause of the Fifth Amendment, and in *Alberts,* reliance is placed upon the Due Process Clause of the Fourteenth Amendment.

[4] 237 F. 2d 796.

[5] 352 U.S. 964. Petitioner's application for bail was granted by MR. JUSTICE HARLAN in his capacity as Circuit Justice for the Second Circuit. 1 L. Ed. 2d 34, 77 Sup. Ct. 17.

[6] 138 Cal. App. 2d Supp. 909, 292 P. 2d 90. This is the highest state appellate court available to the appellant. Cal. Const., Art. VI, § 5; see *Edwards* v. *California,* 314 U.S. 160.

[7] 352 U.S. 962.

[8] No issue is presented in either case concerning the obscenity of the material involved.

Winters v. *New York,* 333 U.S. 507, 510; *Beauharnais* v. *Illinois,* 343 U.S. 250, 266.[9]

The guaranties of freedom of expression [10] in effect in 10 of the 14 States which by 1792 had ratified the Constitution, gave no absolute protection for every utterance. Thirteen of the 14 States provided for the prosecution of libel,[11] and all of those States made either blasphemy or profanity, or both, statutory crimes.[12] As early as 1712, Massachusetts made it criminal to publish "any filthy, obscene, or profane song, pamphlet, libel or mock sermon" in imitation or mimicking of religious services. Acts and Laws of the Province of Mass. Bay, c. CV, § 8 (1712),

[9] See also the following cases in which convictions under obscenity statutes have been reviewed: *Grimm* v. *United States,* 156 U.S. 604; *Rosen* v. *United States,* 161 U.S. 29; *Swearingen* v. *United States,* 161 U.S. 446; *Andrews* v. *United States,* 162 U.S. 420; *Price* v. *United States,* 165 U.S. 311; *Dunlop* v. *United States,* 165 U.S. 486; *Bartell* v. *United States,* 227 U.S. 427; *United States* v. *Limehouse,* 285 U.S. 424.

[10] Del. Const., 1792, Art. I, § 5; Ga. Const., 1777, Art. LXI; Md. Const., 1776, Declaration of Rights, § 38; Mass. Const., 1780, Declaration of Rights, Art. XVI; N.H. Const., 1784, Art. I, § XXII; N.C. Const., 1776, Declaration of Rights, Art. XV; Pa. Const., 1776, Declaration of Rights, Art. XII; S.C. Const., 1778, Art. XLIII; Vt. Const., 1777, Declaration of Rights, Art. XIV; Va. Bill of Rights, 1776, § 12.

[11] Act to Secure the Freedom of the Press (1804), 1 Conn. Pub. Stat. Laws 355 (1808); Del. Const., 1792, Art. I, § 5; Ga. Penal Code, Eighth Div., § VIII (1817), Digest of the Laws of Ga. 364 (Prince 1822); Act of 1803, c. 54, II Md. Public General Laws 1096 (Poe 1888); *Commonwealth* v. *Kneeland,* 37 Mass. 206, 232 (1838); Act for the Punishment of Certain Crimes Not Capital (1791), N.H. Laws 1792, 253; Act Respecting Libels (1799), N.J. Rev. Laws 411 (1800); *People* v. *Croswell,* 3 Johns. (N.Y.) 337 (1804); Act of 1803, c. 632, 2 Laws of N.C. 999 (1821); Pa. Const., 1790, Art. IX, § 7; R.I. Code of Laws (1647), Proceedings of the First General Assembly and Code of Laws 44–45 (1647); R.I. Const., 1842, Art. I, § 20; Act of 1804, 1 Laws of Vt. 366 (Tolman 1808); *Commonwealth* v. *Morris,* 1 Brock. & Hol. (Va.) 176 (1811).

[12] Act for the Punishment of Divers Capital and Other Felonies, Acts and Laws of Conn. 66, 67 (1784); Act Against Drunkenness, Blasphemy, §§ 4, 5 (1737), 1 Laws of Del. 173, 174 (1797); Act to Regulate Taverns (1786), Digest of the Laws of Ga. 512, 513 (Prince 1822); Act of 1723, c. 16, § 1, Digest of the Laws of Md. 92 (Herty 1799); General Laws and Liberties of Mass. Bay, c. XVIII, § 3 (1646), Mass. Bay Colony Charters & Laws 58 (1814); Act of 1782, c. 8, Rev. Stat. of Mass. 741, § 15 (1836); Act of 1798, c. 33, §§ 1, 3, Rev. Stat. of Mass. 741, § 16 (1836); Act for the Punishment of Certain Crimes Not Capital (1791), N.H. Laws 1792, 252, 256; Act for the Punishment of Profane Cursing and Swearing (1791), N.H. Laws 1792, 258; Act for Suppressing Vice and Immorality, §§ VIII, IX (1798), N.J. Rev. Laws 329, 331 (1800); Act for Suppressing Immorality, § IV (1788), 2 Laws of N.Y. 257, 258 (Jones & Varick 1777–1789); *People* v. *Ruggles,* 8 Johns. (N.Y.) 290 (1811); Act . . . for the More Effectual Suppression of Vice and Immorality, § III (1741), 1 N.C. Laws 52 (Martin Rev. 1715–1790); Act to Prevent the Grievous Sins of Cursing and Swearing (1700), II Statutes at Large of Pa. 49 (1700–1712); Act for the Prevention of Vice and Immorality, § II (1794), 3 Laws of Pa. 177, 178 (1791–1802); Act to Reform the Penal Laws, §§ 33, 34 (1798), R.I. Laws 1798, 584, 595; Act for the More Effectual Suppressing of Blasphemy and Prophaneness (1703), Laws of S.C. 4 (Grimké 1790); Act, for the Punishment of Certain Capital, and Other High Crimes and Misdemeanors, § 20 (1797), 1 Laws of Vt. 332, 339 (Tolman 1808); Act, for the Punishment of Certain Inferior Crimes and Misdemeanors, § 20 (1797), 1 Laws of Vt. 352, 361 (Tolman 1808); Act for the Effectual Suppression of Vice, § 1 (1792), Acts of General Assembly of Va. 286 (1794).

Mass. Bay Colony Charters & Laws 399 (1814). Thus, profanity and obscenity were related offenses.

In light of this history, it is apparent that the unconditional phrasing of the First Amendment was not intended to protect every utterance. This phrasing did not prevent this Court from concluding that libelous utterances are not within the area of constitutionally protected speech. *Beauharnais* v. *Illinois,* 343 U.S. 250, 266. At the time of the adoption of the First Amendment, obscenity law was not as fully developed as libel law, but there is sufficiently contemporaneous evidence to show that obscenity, too, was outside the protection intended for speech and press.[13]

The protection given speech and press was fashioned to assure unfettered interchange of ideas for the bringing about of political and social changes desired by the people. This objective was made explicit as early as 1774 in a letter of the Continental Congress to the inhabitants of Quebec:

> "The last right we shall mention, regards the freedom of the press. The importance of this consists, besides the advancement of truth, science, morality, and arts in general, in its diffusion of liberal sentiments on the administration of Government, its ready communication of thoughts between subjects, and its consequential promotion of union among them, whereby oppressive officers are shamed or intimidated, into more honourable and just modes of conducting affairs." 1 Journals of the Continental Congress 108 (1774).

All ideas having even the slightest redeeming social importance—unorthodox ideas, controversial ideas, even ideas hateful to the prevailing climate of opinion—have the full protection of the guaranties, unless excludable because they encroach upon the limited area of more important interests.[14] But implicit in the history of the First Amendment is the rejection of obscenity as utterly without redeeming social importance. This rejection for that reason is mirrored in the universal judgment that obscenity should be restrained, reflected in the international agreement of over 50 nations,[15] in the obscenity laws of all the 48 States,[16] and in the 20

[13] Act Concerning Crimes and Punishments, § 69 (1821), Stat. Laws of Conn. 109(1824); *Knowles* v. *State,* 3 Day (Conn.) 103 (1808); Rev. Stat. of 1835, c. 130, § 10, Rev. Stat. of Mass. 740 (1836); *Commonwealth* v. *Holmes,* 17 Mass. 335 (1821); Rev. Stat. of 1842, c. 113, § 2, Rev. Stat. of N.H. 221 (1843); Act for Suppressing Vice and Immorality, § XII (1798), N.J. Rev. Laws 329, 331 (1800); *Commonwealth* v. *Sharpless,* 2. S. & R. (Pa.) 91 (1915).

[14] *E.g., United States* v. *Harriss,* 347 U.S. 612; *Breard* v. *Alexandria,* 341 U.S. 622; *Teamsters Union* v. *Hanke,* 339 U.S. 470; *Kovacs* v. *Cooper,* 336 U.S. 77; *Prince* v. *Massachusetts,* 321 U.S. 158; *Labor Board* v. *Virginia Elec. & Power Co.,* 314 U.S. 469; *Cox* v. *New Hampshire,* 312 U.S. 569; *Schenck* v. *United States,* 249 U.S. 47.

[15] Agreement for the Suppression of the Circulation of Obscene Publications, 37 Stat. 1511; Treaties in Force 209 (U.S. Dept. State, October 31, 1956).

[16] Hearings before Subcommittee to Investigate Juvenile Delinquency of the Senate Committee on the Judiciary, pursuant to S. Res. 62, 84th Cong., 1st Sess. 49–52 (May 24, 1955).

Although New Mexico has no general obscenity statute, it does have a statute giving to municipalities the power "to prohibit the sale or exhibiting of obscene or immoral publications, prints, pictures, or illustrations." N.M. Stat Ann., 1953, §§ 14–21–3, 14–21–12.

obscenity laws enacted by the Congress from 1842 to 1956.[17] This is the same judgment expressed by this Court in *Chaplinsky* v. *New Hampshire,* 315 U.S. 568, 571–572:

> ". . .There are certain well-defined and narrowly limited classes of speech, the prevention and punishment of which have never been thought to raise any Constitutional problem. *These include the lewd and obscene . . . . It has been well observed that such utterances are no essential part of any exposition of ideas, and are of such slight social value as a step to truth that any benefit that may be derived from them is clearly outweighed by the social interest in order and morality. . . .*" (Emphasis added.)

We hold that obscenity is not within the area of constitutionally protected speech or press.

It is strenuously urged that these obscenity statutes offend the constitutional guaranties because they punish incitation to impure sexual *thoughts,* not shown to be related to any overt antisocial conduct which is or may be incited in the persons stimulated to such *thoughts.* In *Roth,* the trial judge instructed the jury: "The words 'obscene, lewd and lascivious' as used in the law, signify that form of immorality which has relation to sexual impurity and has a tendency to excite lustful *thoughts.*" (Emphasis added.) In *Alberts,* the trial judge applied the test laid down in *People* v. *Wepplo,* 78 Cal. App. 2d Supp. 959, 178 P. 2d 853, namely, whether the material has "a substantial tendency to deprave or corrupt its readers by inciting lascivious *thoughts* or arousing lustful desires." (Emphasis added.) It is insisted that the constitutional guaranties are violated because convictions may be had without proof either that obscene material will perceptibly create a clear and present danger of antisocial conduct,[18] or will probably induce its recipients to such conduct.[19] But, in light of our holding that obscenity is not protected speech, the complete answer to this argument is in the holding of this Court in *Beauharnais* v. *Illinois, supra,* at 266:

> "Libelous utterances not being within the area of constitutionally protected speech, it is unnecessary, either for us or for the State courts, to consider the issues behind the phrase 'clear and present danger.' Certainly no one would contend that obscene speech, for example, may be punished only upon a showing of such circumstances. Libel, as we have seen, is in the same class."

[17] 5 Stat. 548, 566; 11 Stat. 168; 13 Stat. 504, 507; 17 Stat. 302; 17 Stat. 598; 19 Stat. 90; 25 Stat. 187, 188; 25 Stat. 496; 26 Stat. 567, 614–615; 29 Stat. 512; 33 Stat. 705; 35 Stat. 1129, 1138, 41 Stat. 1060 46 Stat. 688; 48 Stat. 1091, 1100; 62 Stat. 768; 64 Stat. 194; 64 Stat. 451; 69 Stat. 183; 70 Stat. 699.

[18] *Schenck* v. *United States,* 249 U.S. 47. This approach is typified by the opinion of Judge Bok (written prior to this Court's opinion in *Dennis* v. *United States,* 341 U.S. 494) in *Commonwealth* v. *Gordon,* 66 Pa. D. & C. 101, aff'd *sub nom. Commonwealth* v. *Feigenbaum,* 166 Pa. Super, 120, 70 A, 2d 389.

[19] *Dennis* v. *United States,* 341 U.S. 494. This approach is typified by the concurring opinion of Judge Frank in the *Roth* case, 237 F. 2d, at 801. See also Lockhart & McClure, Literature, The Law of Obscenity, and the Constitution, 38 Minn. L. Rev. 295 (1954).

However, sex and obscenity are not synonymous. Obscene material is material which deals with sex in a manner appealing to prurient interest.[20] The portrayal of sex, *e.g.,* in art, literature and scientific works,[21] is not itself sufficient reason to deny material the constitutional protection of freedom of speech and press. Sex, a great and mysterious motive force in human life, has indisputably been a subject of absorbing interest to mankind through the ages; it is one of the vital problems of human interest and public concern. As to all such problems, this Court said in *Thornhill* v. *Alabama,* 310 U.S. 88, 101–102:

> "The freedom of speech and of the press guaranteed by the Constitution embraces at the least the liberty to discuss publicly and truthfully *all matters of public concern* without previous restraint or fear of subsequent punishment. The exigencies of the colonial period and the efforts to secure freedom from oppressive administration developed a broadened conception of these liberties as adequate to supply the public need for *information and education with respect to the significant issues of the times. . . .* Freedom of discussion, if it would fulfill its historic function in this nation, must embrace *all issues about which information is needed or appropriate to enable the members of society to cope with the exigencies of their period."* (Emphasis added.)

The fundamental freedoms of speech and press have contributed greatly to the development and well-being of our free society and are indispensable to its continued growth.[22] Ceaseless vigilance is the watchword to prevent their erosion by Congress or by the States. The door barring federal and state intrusion into this area cannot be left ajar; it must be kept tightly closed and opened only the slightest crack necessary to prevent encroachment upon more important interests.[23] It is therefore vital that the standards for judging obscenity safeguard the protection of freedom of

---

[20] *I.e.,* material having a tendency to excite lustful thoughts. WEBSTER'S NEW INTERNATIONAL DICTIONARY (unabridged, 2d ed., 1949) defines *prurient,* in pertinent part, as follows:

". . . Itching; longing; uneasy with desire or longing; of persons, having itching, morbid, or lascivious longings; of desire, curiosity, or propensity, lewd. . . ."

Pruriency is defined, in pertinent part, as follows:

". . . Quality of being prurient; lascivious desire or thought. . . ."

See also *Mutual Film Corp.* v. *Industrial Comm'n,* 236 U.S. 230, 242, where this Court said as to motion pictures: ". . . They take their attraction from the general interest, eager and wholesome it may be, in their subjects, but a *prurient interest may be excited and appealed to. . . ."* (Emphasis added.)

We perceive no significant difference between the meaning of obscenity developed in the case law and the definition of the A. L. I., Model Penal Code, § 207.10 (2) (Tent. Draft No. 6, 1957), viz.:

". . . A thing is obscene if, considered as a whole, its predominant appeal is to prurient interest, i.e., a shameful or morbid interest in nudity, sex, or excretion, and if it goes substantially beyond customary limits of candor in description or representation of such matters. . . ." See Comment, *id.,* at 10, and the discussion at page 29 *et seq.*

[21] See, *e.g., United States* v. *Dennett,* 39 F. 2d 564.

[22] Madison's Report on the Virginia Resolutions, 4 Elliot's Debates 571.

[23] See note 14, *supra.*

speech and press for material which does not treat sex in a manner appealing to prurient interest.

The early leading standard of obscenity allowed material to be judged merely by the effect of an isolated excerpt upon particularly susceptible persons. *Regina* v. *Hicklin,* [1868] L. R. 3 Q. B. 360.[24] Some American courts adopted this standard [25] but later decisions have rejected it and substituted this test: whether to the average person, applying contemporary community standards, the dominant theme of the material taken as a whole appeals to prurient interest.[26] The *Hicklin* test, judging obscenity by the effect of isolated passages upon the most susceptible persons, might well encompass material legitimately treating with sex, and so it must be rejected as unconstitutionally restrictive of the freedoms of speech and press. On the other hand, the substituted standard provides safeguards adequate to withstand the charge of constitutional infirmity.

Both trial courts below sufficiently followed the proper standard. Both courts used the proper definition of obscenity. In addition, in the *Alberts* case, in ruling on a motion to dismiss, the trial judge indicated that, as the trier of facts, he was judging each item as a whole as it would affect the normal person,[27] and in *Roth,* the trial judge instructed the jury as follows:

> ". . . The test is not whether it would arouse sexual desires or sexual impure thoughts in those comprising a particular segment of the community, the young, the immature or the highly prudish or would leave another segment, the scientific or highly educated or the so-called worldly-wise and sophisticated indifferent and unmoved. . . .

> "The test in each case is the effect of the book, picture or publication considered as a whole, not upon any particular class, but upon all those whom it is likely to reach. In other words, you determine its impact upon the average person in the community. The books, pictures and circulars must be judged as a whole, in their entire context, and you are not to consider detached or separate portions in reaching a conclusion. You judge the circulars, pictures and publications

---

[24] But see the instructions given to the jury by Mr. Justice Stable in *Regina* v. *Martin Secker Warburg,* [1954] 2 All Eng. 683 (C.C.C.).

[25] *United States* v. *Kennerley,* 209 F. 119; *MacFadden* v. *United States,* 165 F. 51; *United States* v. *Bennett,* 24 Fed. Cas. 1093; *United States* v. *Clarke,* 38 F. 500; *Commonwealth* v. *Buckley,* 200 Mass. 346, 86 N.E. 910.

[26] *E.g., Walker* v. *Popenoe,* 80 U.S. App. D.C. 129, 149 F. 2d 511; *Parmelee* v. *United States,* 72 App. D.C. 203, 113 F. 2d 729; *United States* v. *Levine,* 83 F. 2d 156; *United States* v. *Dennett,* 39 F. 2d 564; *Kahn* v. *Feist, Inc.,* 70 F. Supp. 450, aff'd, 165 F. 2d 188; *United States* v. *One Book Called "Ulysses,"* 5 F. Supp. 182, aff'd, 72 F.2d 705; *American Civil Liberties Union* v. *Chicago,* 3 Ill. 2d 334, 121 NE 2d 585; *Commonwealth* v. *Isenstadt,* 318 Mass. 543, 62 N.E. 2d. 840; *Missouri* v. *Becker,* 364 Mo. 1079, 272 S.W. 2d 283; *Adams Theatre Co.* v. *Keenan,* 12 N.J. 267, 96 A. 2d 519; *Bantam Books, Inc.* v. *Melko,* 25 N.J. Super. 292, 96 A. 2d 47; *Commonwealth* v. *Gordon,* 66 Pa. D. & C. 101, aff'd, *sub nom. Commonwealth* v. *Feigenbaum,* 166 Pa. Super. 120, 70 A. 2d 389; cf. *Roth* v. *Goldman,* 172 F. 2d 788, 794–795 (concurrence).

[27] In *Alberts,* the contention that the trial judge did not read the materials in their entirety is not before us because not fairly comprised within the questions presented. U.S. Sup. Ct. Rules, 15 (1)(c)(1).

which have been put in evidence by present-day standards of the community. You may ask yourselves does it offend the common conscience of the community by present-day standards.

. . .

"In this case, ladies and gentlemen of the jury, you and you alone are the exclusive judges of what the common conscience of the community is, and in determining that conscience you are to consider the community as a whole, young and old, educated and uneducated, the religious and the irreligious—men, women and children."

It is argued that the statutes do not provide reasonably ascertainable standards of guilt and therefore violate the constitutional requirements of due process. *Winters* v. *New York,* 333 U.S. 507. The federal obscenity statute makes punishable the mailing of material that is "obscene, lewd, lascivious, or filthy . . . or other publication of an indecent character." [28] The California statute makes punishable, *inter alia,* the keeping for sale or advertising material that is "obscene or indecent." The thrust of the argument is that these words are not sufficiently precise because they do not mean the same thing to all people, all the time, everywhere.

Many decisions have recognized that these terms of obscenity statutes are not precise.[29] This Court, however, has consistently held that lack of precision is not itself offensive to the requirements of due process. ". . . [T]he Constitution does not require impossible standards"; all that is required is that the language "conveys sufficiently definite warning as to the proscribed conduct when measured by common understanding and practices. . . ." *United States* v. *Petrillo,* 332 U.S. 1, 7–8. These words, applied according to the proper standard for judging obscenity, already discussed, give adequate warning of the conduct proscribed and mark ". . . boundaries sufficiently distinct for judges and juries fairly to administer the law . . . . That there may be marginal cases in which it is difficult to determine the side of the line on which a particular fact situation falls is no sufficient reason to hold the language too ambiguous to define a criminal offense. . . ." *Id.,* at 7. See also *United States* v. *Harriss,* 347 U.S. 612, 624, n. 15; *Boyce Motor Lines, Inc.* v. *United States,* 342 U.S. 337, 340; *United States* v. *Ragen,* 314 U.S. 513, 523–524; *United States* v. *Wurzbach,* 280 U.S. 396; *Hygrade Provision Co.* v. *Sherman,* 266 U.S. 497; *Fox* v. *Washington,* 236 U.S. 273; *Nash* v. *United States,* 229 U.S. 373.[30]

---

[28] This Court, as early as 1896, said of the federal obscenity statute:
". . . Every one who uses the mails of the United States for carrying papers or publications must take notice of what, in this enlightened age, is meant by decency, purity, and chastity in social life, and what must be deemed obscene, lewd, and lascivious." *Rosen* v. *United States,* 161 U.S. 29, 42.

[29] *E.g., Roth* v. *Goldman,* 172 F. 2d 788, 789; *Parmelee* v. *United States,* 72 App. D. C. 203, 204, 113 F 2d 729, 730; *United States* v. *4200 Copies International Journal,* 134 F. Supp. 490, 493; *United States* v. *One Unbound Volume,* 128 F. Supp. 280, 281.

[30] It is argued that because juries may reach different conclusions as to the same material, the statutes must be held to be insufficiently precise to satisfy due process requirements. But, it is common experience that different juries may reach different

In summary, then, we hold that these statutes, applied according to the proper standard for judging obscenity, do not offend constitutional safeguards against convictions based upon protected material, or fail to give men in acting adequate notice of what is prohibited.

Roth's argument that the federal obscenity statute unconstitutionally encroaches upon the powers reserved by the Ninth and Tenth Amendments to the States and to the people to punish speech and press where offensive to decency and morality is hinged upon his contention that obscenity is expression not excepted from the sweep of the provision of the First Amendment that *"Congress* shall make *no law* . . . abridging the freedom of speech, or of the press. . . ."* (Emphasis added.) That argument falls in light of our holding that obscenity is not expression protected by the First Amendment.[31] We therefore hold that the federal obscenity statute punishing the use of the mails for obscene material is a proper exercise of the postal power delegated to Congress by Art. I, § 8, cl. 7.[32] In *United Public Workers* v. *Mitchell,* 330 U.S. 75, 95–96, this Court said:

> ". . . The powers granted by the Constitution to the Federal Government are subtracted from the totality of sovereignty originally in the states and the people. Therefore, when objection is made that the exercise of a federal power infringes upon rights reserved by the Ninth and Tenth Amendments, the inquiry must be directed toward the granted power under which the action of the Union was taken. If granted power is found, necessarily the objection of invasion of those rights, reserved by the Ninth and Tenth Amendments, must fail. . . ."

Alberts argues that because his was a mail-order business, the California statute is repugnant to Art. I, § 8, cl. 7, under which the Congress allegedly pre-empted the regulatory field by enacting the federal obscenity statute punishing the mailing or advertising by mail of obscene material. The federal statute deals only with actual mailing; it does not eliminate the power of the state to punish "keeping for sale" or "advertising" obscene material. The state statute in no way imposes a burden or interferes with the federal postal functions. ". . . The decided cases which indi-

---

results under any criminal statute. That is one of the consequences we accept under our jury system. Cf. *Dunlop* v. *United States,* 165 U.S. 486, 499–500.

[31] For the same reason, we reject, in this case, the argument that there is greater latitude for state action under the word "liberty" under the Fourteenth Amendment than is allowed to Congress by the language of the First Amendment.

[32] In *Public Clearing House* v. *Coyne,* 194 U.S. 497, 506–508, this Court said:

"The constitutional principles underlying the administration of the Post Office Department were discussed in the opinion of the court in *Ex parte Jackson,* 96 U.S. 727, in which we held that the power vested in Congress to establish post offices and post roads embraced the regulation of the entire postal system of the country; that Congress might designate what might be carried in the mails and what excluded. . . . It may . . . refuse to include in its mails such printed matter or merchandise as may seem objectionable to it upon the ground of public policy . . . . For more than thirty years not only has the transmission of obscene matter been prohibited, but it has been made a crime, punishable by fine or imprisonment, for a person to deposit such matter in the mails. The constitutionality of this law we believe has never been attacked. . . ."

cate the limits of state regulatory power in relation to the federal mail service involve situations where state regulation involved a direct, physical interference with federal activities under the postal power or some direct, immediate burden on the performance of the postal functions. . . ." *Railway Mail Assn.* v. *Corsi,* 326 U.S. 88, 96.

The judgments are

Affirmed.

[Opinions of Warren, C. J., and Harlan, J., Douglas, J., and Black, J., are omitted.]

Miller v. *California*
413 U.S. 15 (1973)

Mr. Chief Justice Burger delivered the opinion of the Court.

This is one of a group of "obscenity-pornography" cases being reviewed by the Court in a re-examination of standards enunciated in earlier cases involving what Mr. Justice Harlan called "the intractable obscenity problem." *Interstate Circuit, Inc.* v. *Dallas,* 390 U.S. 676, 704 (1968) (concurring and dissenting).

Appellant conducted a mass mailing campaign to advertise the sale of illustrated books, euphemistically called "adult" material. After a jury trial, he was convicted of violating California Penal Code § 311.2(a), a misdemeanor, by knowingly distributing obscene matter,[1] and the Appel-

---

[1] At the time of the commission of the alleged offense, which was prior to June 25, 1969, §§ 311.2(a) and 311 of the California Penal Code read in relevant part:

"§ 311.2 Sending or bringing into state for sale or distribution; printing, exhibiting, distributing or possessing within state

"(a) Every person who knowingly: sends or causes to be sent, or brings or causes to be brought, into this state for sale or distribution, or in this state prepares, publishes, prints, exhibits, distributes, or offers to distribute, or has in his possession with intent to distribute or to exhibit or offer to distribute, any obscene matter is guilty of a misdemeanor. . . ."

"§ 311. Definitions

"As used in this chapter:

"(a) 'Obscene' means that to the average person, applying contemporary standards, the predominant appeal of the matter, taken as a whole, is to prurient interest, i.e., a shameful or morbid interest in nudity, sex, or excretion, which goes substantially beyond customary limits of candor in description or representation of such matters and is matter which is utterly without redeeming social importance.

"(b) 'Matter' means any book, magazine, newspaper, or other printed or written material or any picture, drawing, photograph, motion picture, or other pictorial representation or any statue or other figure, or any recording, transcription or mechanical, chemical or electrical reproduction or any other articles, equipment, machines or materials.

"(c) 'Person' means any individual, partnership, firm, association, corporation, or other legal entity.

"(d) 'Distribute' means to transfer possession of, whether with or without consideration.

late Department, Superior Court of California, County or Orange, summarily affirmed the judgment without opinion. Appellant's conviction was specifically based on his conduct in causing five unsolicited advertising brochures to be sent through the mail in an envelope addressed to a restaurant in Newport Beach, California. The envelope was opened by the manager of the restaurant and his mother. They had not requested the brochures; they complained to the police.

The brochures advertise four books entitled "Intercourse," "Man-Woman," "Sex Orgies Illustrated," and "An Illustrated History of Pornography," and a film entitled "Marital Intercourse." While the brochures contain some descriptive printed material, primarily they consist of pictures and drawings very explicitly depicting men and women in groups of two or more engaging in a variety of sexual activities, with genitals often prominently displayed.

I

This case involves the application of a State's criminal obscenity statute to a situation in which sexually explicit materials have been thrust by aggressive sales action upon unwilling recipients who had in no way indicated any desire to receive such materials. This Court has recognized that the States have a legitimate interest in prohibiting dissemination or exhibition of obscene material [2] when the mode of dissemination carries with it a

---

"(e) 'Knowingly' means having knowledge that the matter is obscene."

Section 311 (c) of the California Penal Code, *supra,* was amended on June 25, 1969, to read as follows:

"(e) 'Knowingly' means being aware of the character of the matter."

Cal. Amended Stats. 1969, c 249 § 1, p. 598. Despite appellant's contentions to the contrary, the record indicates that the new § 311 (c) was not applied *ex post facto* to his case, but only the old § 311 (e) as construed by state decisions prior to the commission of the alleged offense. See *People* v. *Pinkus,* 256 Cal. App. 2d 941, 948–950, 63 Cal. Rptr. 680, 685–686 (App. Dept., Superior Ct., Los Angeles, 1967); *People* v. *Campise,* 242 Cal. App. 2d 905, 914, 51 Cal. Rptr. 815, 821 (App. Dept., Superior Ct., San Diego, 1966). Cf. *Bouie* v. *City of Columbia,* 378 U.S. 347 (1964). Nor did § 311.2, *supra,* as applied, create any "direct, immediate burden on the performance of the postal functions," or infringe on congressional commerce powers under Art. I, § 8, cl. 3. *Roth* v. *United States,* 354 U.S. 476, 494 (1957), quoting *Railway Mail Assn.* v. *Corsi,* 326 U.S. 88, 96 (1945). See also *Mishkin* v. *New York,* 383 U.S. 502, 506 (1966); *Smith* v. *California,* 361 U.S. 147, 150–152 (1959).

[2] This Court has defined "obscene material" as "material which deals with sex in a manner appealing to prurient interest," *Roth* v. *United States, supra,* at 487, but the *Roth* definition does not reflect the precise meaning of "obscene" as traditionally used in the English language. Derived from the Latin *obscaenus, ob,* to, plus *caenum,* filth, "obscene" is defined in the Webster's Third New International Dictionary (Unabridged 1969) as "1a: disgusting to the senses . . . b: grossly repugnant to the generally accepted notions of what is appropriate . . . 2: offensive or revolting as countering or violating some ideal or principle." The Oxford English Dictionary (1933 ed.) gives a similar definition, "[o]ffensive to the senses, or to taste or refinement; disgusting, repulsive, filthy, foul, abominable, loathsome."

The material we are discussing in this case is more accurately defined as "pornography" or "pornographic material." "Pornography" derives from the Greek (*pornè,* harlot, and *graphos,* writing). The word now means "1: a description of prostitutes or prostitution 2: a depiction (as in writing or painting) of licentiousness or lewdness: a portrayal of erotic behavior designed to cause sexual excitement." Webster's

significant danger of offending the sensibilities of unwilling recipients or of exposure to juveniles. *Stanley* v. *Georgia,* 394 U.S. 557, 567 (1969); *Ginsberg* v. *New York,* 390 U.S. 629, 637–643 (1968); *Interstate Circuit, Inc.* v. *Dallas, supra,* at 690; *Redrup* v. *New York,* 386 U.S. 767, 769 (1967); *Jacobellis* v. *Ohio,* 378 U.S. 184, 195 (1964). See *Rabe* v. *Washington,* 405 U.S. 313, 317 (1972) (BURGER, C. J., concurring); *United States* v. *Reidel,* 402 U.S. 351, 360–362 (1971) (opinion of MARSHALL, J.); *Joseph Burstyn, Inc.* v. *Wilson,* 343 U.S. 495, 502 (1952); *Breard* v. *Alexandria,* 341 U.S. 622, 644–645 (1951); *Kovacs* v. *Cooper,* 336 U.S. 77, 88–89 (1949); *Prince* v. *Massachusetts,* 321 U.S. 158, 169–170 (1944). Cf. *Butler* v. *Michigan,* 352 U.S. 380, 382–383 (1957); *Public Utilities Comm'n* v. *Pollak,* 343 U.S. 451, 464–465 (1952). It is in this context that we are called on to define the standards which must be used to identify obscene material that a State may regulate without infringing on the First Amendment as applicable to the States through the Fourteenth Amendment.

The dissent of MR. JUSTICE BRENNAN reviews the background of the obscenity problem, but since the Court now undertakes to formulate standards more concrete than those in the past, it is useful for us to focus on two of the landmark cases in the somewhat tortured history of the Court's obscenity decisions. In *Roth* v. *United States,* 354 U.S. 476 (1957), the Court sustained a conviction under a federal statute punishing the mailing of "obscene, lewd, lascivious or filthy . . ." materials. The key to that holding was the Court's rejection of the claim that obscene materials were protected by the First Amendment. Five Justices joined in the opinion stating:

> "All ideas having even the slightest redeeming social importance —unorthodox ideas, controversial ideas, even ideas hateful to the prevailing climate of opinion—have the full protection of the [First Amendment] guaranties, unless excludable because they encroach upon the limited area of more important interests. But implicit in the history of the First Amendment is the rejection of obscenity as utterly without redeeming social importance. . . . This is the same judgment expressed by this Court in *Chaplinsky* v. *New Hampshire,* 315 U.S. 568, 571–72:
>
> " '. . . There are certain well-defined and narrowly limited classes of speech, the prevention and punishment of which have never been thought to raise any Constitutional problem. *These include the lewd and obscene . . . . It has been well observed that such utterances are no essential part of any exposition of ideas, and are of such slight social value as a step to truth that any benefit that may be derived*

Third New International Dictionary, *supra.* Pornographic material which is obscene forms a sub-group of all "obscene" expression, but not the whole, at least as the word "obscene" is now used in our language. We note, therefore, that the words "obscene material," as used in this case, have a specific judicial meaning which derives from the *Roth* case, *i.e.,* obscene material "which deals with sex." *Roth, supra,* at 487. See also ALI Model Penal Code § 251.4 (1) "Obscene Defined." (Official Draft 1962.)

from them is clearly outweighed by the social interest in order and morality. . . .' [Emphasis by Court in *Roth* opinion.]
"We hold that obscenity is not within the area of constitutionally protected speech or press." 354 U.S., at 484–485 (footnotes omitted).

Nine years later, in *Memoirs* v. *Massachusetts,* 383 U.S. 413 (1966), the Court veered sharply away from the *Roth* concept and, with only three Justices in the plurality opinion, articulated a new test of obscenity. The plurality held that under the *Roth* definition

"as elaborated in subsequent cases, three elements must coalesce: it must be established that (a) the dominant theme of the material taken as a whole appeals to a prurient interest in sex; (b) the material is patently offensive because it affronts contemporary community standards relating to the description or representation of sexual matters; and (c) the material is utterly without redeeming social value." *Id.,* at 418.

The sharpness of the break with *Roth,* represented by the third element of the *Memoirs* test and emphasized by MR. JUSTICE WHITE'S dissent, *id.,* at 460–462, was further underscored when the *Memoirs* plurality went on to state:

"The Supreme Judicial Court erred in holding that a book need not be 'unqualifiedly worthless before it can be deemed obscene.' A book cannot be proscribed unless it is found to be *utterly* without redeeming social value." *Id.,* at 419 (emphasis in original).

While *Roth* presumed "obscenity" to be "utterly without redeeming social importance," *Memoirs* required that to prove obscenity it must be affirmatively established that the material is *"utterly* without redeeming social value." Thus, even as they repeated the words of *Roth,* the *Memoirs* plurality produced a drastically altered test that called on the proscecution to prove a negative, *i.e.,* that the material was *"utterly* without redeeming social value"—a burden virtually impossible to discharge under our criminal standards of proof. Such considerations caused Mr. Justice Harlan to wonder if the *"utterly* without redeeming social value" test had any meaning at all. See *Memoirs* v. *Massachusetts, id.,* at 459 (Harlan, J., dissenting). See also *id.,* at 461 (WHITE, J., dissenting); *United States* v. *Groner,* 479 F.2d 577, 579–581 (CA5 1973).

Apart from the initial formulation in the *Roth* case, no majority of the Court has at any given time been able to agree on a standard to determine what constitutes obscene, pornographic material subject to regulation under the States' police power. See *e. g., Redrup* v. *New York,* 386 U.S., at 770–771. We have seen "a variety of views among the members of the Court unmatched in any other course of constitutional adjudication." *Interstate Circuit, Inc.* v. *Dallas,* 390 U.S., at 704–705 (Harlan, J., concurring and dissenting) (footnote omitted).[3] This is not remarkable, for in the area of freedom of speech and press the courts must always remain

[3] In the absence of a majority view, this Court was compelled to embark on the practice of summarily reversing convictions for the dissemination of materials that at least five members of the Court, applying their separate tests, found to be protected

sensitive to any infringement on genuinely serious literary, artistic, political, or scientific expression. This is an area in which there are few eternal verities.

The case we now review was tried on the theory that the California Penal Code § 311 approximately incorporates the three-stage *Memoirs* test, *supra.* But now the *Memoirs* test has been abandoned as unworkable by its author,[4] and no Member of the Court today supports the *Memoirs* formulation.

II

This much has been categorically settled by the Court, that obscene material is unprotected by the First Amendment. *Kois* v. *Wisconsin,* 408 U.S. 229 (1972); *United States* v. *Reidel,* 402 U.S., at 354; *Roth* v. *United States, supra,* at 485.[5] "The First and Fourteenth Amendments have never been treated as absolutes [footnote omitted]." *Breard* v. *Alexandria,* 341 U.S., at 642, and cases cited. See *Times Film Corp.* v. *Chicago,* 365 U.S. 43, 47–50 (1961); *Joseph Burstyn, Inc.* v. *Wilson,* 343 U.S., at 502. We acknowledge, however, the inherent dangers of undertaking to regulate any form of expression. State statutes designed to regulate obscene materials must be carefully limited. See *Interstate Circuit, Inc.* v. *Dallas, supra,* at 682–685. As a result, we now confine the permissible scope of such regulation to works which depict or describe sexual conduct. That conduct must be specifically defined by the applicable state law, as written or authoritatively construed.[6] A state offense must also be limited to works which, taken as a whole, appeal to the prurient interest in sex,

---

by the First Amendment. *Redrup* v. *New York,* 386 U.S. 767 (1967). Thirty-one cases have been decided in this manner. Beyond the necessity of circumstances, however, no justification has ever been offered in support of the *Redrup* "policy." See *Walker* v. *Ohio,* 398 U.S. 434–435 (1970) (dissenting opinions of BURGER, C. J., and Harlan, J.). The *Redrup* procedure has cast us in the role of an unreviewable board of censorship for the 50 States, subjectively judging each piece of material brought before us.

[4] See the dissenting opinion of MR. JUSTICE BRENNAN in *Paris Adult Theatre I* v. *Slaton, post,* p. 73.

[5] As Mr. Chief Justice Warren stated, dissenting, in *Jacobellis* v. *Ohio,* 378 U.S. 184, 200 (1964):

"For all the sound and fury that the *Roth* test has generated, it has not been proved unsound, and I believe that we should try to live with it—at least until a more satisfactory definition is evolved. No government—be it federal, state, or local —should be forced to choose between repressing all material, including that within the realm of decency, and allowing unrestrained license to publish any material, no matter how vile. There must be a rule of reason in this as in other areas of the law, and we have attempted in the *Roth* case to provide such a rule."

[6] See, *e.g.,* Oregon Laws 1971, c. 743, Art. 29, §§ 255–262, and Hawaii Penal Code, Tit. 37, §§ 1210–1216, 1972 Hawaii Session Laws, Act 9, c. 12, pt. II, pp. 126–129, as examples of state laws directed at depiction of defined physical conduct, as opposed to expression. Other state formulations could be equally valid in this respect. In giving the Oregon and Hawaii statutes as examples, we do not wish to be understood as approving of them in all other respects nor as establishing their limits as the extent of state power.

We do not hold, as MR. JUSTICE BRENNAN intimates, that all States other than Oregon must now enact new obscenity statutes. Other existing state statutes, as construed heretofore or hereafter, may well be adequate. See *United States* v. *12 200-ft. Reels of Film, post,* at 130 n. 7.

which portray sexual conduct in a patently offensive way, and which, taken as a whole, do not have serious literary, artistic, political, or scientific value.

The basic guidelines for the trier of fact must be: (a) whether "the average person, applying contemporary community standards" would find that the work, taken as a whole, appeals to the prurient interest, *Kois* v. *Wisconsin, supra,* at 230, quoting *Roth* v. *United States, supra,* at 489; (b) whether the work depicts or describes, in a patently offensive way, sexual conduct specifically defined by the applicable state law; and (c) whether the work, taken as a whole, lacks serious literary, artistic, political, or scientific value. We do not adopt as a constitutional standard the *"utterly* without redeeming social value" test of *Memoirs* v. *Massachusetts,* 383 U.S., at 419; that concept has never commanded the adherence of more than three Justices at one time.[7] See *supra,* at 21. If a state law that regulates obscene material is thus limited, as written or construed, the First Amendment values applicable to the States through the Fourteenth Amendment are adequately protected by the ultimate power of appellate courts to conduct an independent review of constitutional claims when necessary. See *Kois* v. *Wisconsin, supra,* at 232; *Memoirs* v. *Massachusetts, supra,* at 459–460 (Harlan, J., dissenting); *Jacobellis* v. *Ohio,* 378 U.S., at 204 (Harlan, J., dissenting); *New York Times Co.* v. *Sullivan,* 376 U.S. 254, 284–285 (1964); *Roth* v. *United States, supra,* at 497–498 (Harlan, J., concurring and dissenting).

We emphasize that it is not our function to propose regulatory schemes for the States. That must await their concrete legislative efforts. It is possible, however, to give a few plain examples of what a state statute could define for regulation under part (b) of the standard announced in this opinion, *supra:*

(a) Patently offensive representations or descriptions of ultimate sexual acts, normal or perverted, actual or simulated.

(b) Patently offensive representations or descriptions of masturbation, excretory functions, and lewd exhibition of the genitals.

Sex and nudity may not be exploited without limit by films or pictures exhibited or sold in places of public accommodation any more than live sex and nudity can be exhibited or sold without limit in such public places.[8] At a minimum, prurient, patently offensive depiction or descrip-

---

[7] "A quotation from Voltaire in the flyleaf of a book will not constitutionally redeem an otherwise obscene publication . . . ." *Kois* v. *Wisconsin,* 408 U.S. 229, 231 (1972). See *Memoirs* v. *Massachusetts,* 383 U.S. 413, 461 (1966) (WHITE, J., dissenting). We also reject, as a constitutional standard, the ambiguous concept of "social importance." See *id.,* at 462 (WHITE, J., dissenting).

[8] Although we are not presented here with the problem of regulating lewd public conduct itself, the States have greater power to regulate nonverbal, physical conduct than to supress depictions or descriptions of the same behavior. In *United States* v. *O'Brien,* 391 U.S. 367, 377 (1968), a case not dealing with obscenity, the Court held a State regulation of conduct which itself embodied both speech and nonspeech elements to be "sufficiently justified if . . . it furthers an important or substantial governmental interest; if the governmental interest is unrelated to the suppression of free expression; and if the incidental restriction on alleged First Amendment freedoms is no greater than is essential to the furtherance of that interest." See *California* v. *LaRue,* 409 U.S. 109, 117–118 (1972).

tion of sexual conduct must have serious literary, artistic, political, or scientific value to merit First Amendment protection. See *Kois* v. *Wisconsin, supra,* at 230–232; *Roth* v. *United States, supra,* at 487; *Thornhill* v. *Alabama,* 310 U.S. 88, 101–102 (1940). For example, medical books for the education of physicians and related personnel necessarily use graphic illustrations and descriptions of human anatomy. In resolving the inevitably sensitive question of fact anl law, we must continue to rely on the jury system, accompanied by the safeguards that judges, rules of evidence, presumption of innocence, and other protective features provide, as we do with rape, murder, and a host of other offenses against society and its individual members.[9]

Mr. Justice Brennan, author of the opinions of the Court, or the plurality opinions, in *Roth* v. *United States, supra; Jacobellis* v. *Ohio, supra; Ginzburg* v. *United States,* 383 U.S. 463 (1966); *Mishkin* v. *New York,* 383 U.S. 502 (1966); and *Memoirs* v. *Massachusetts, supra,* has abandoned his former position and now maintains that no formulation of this Court, the Congress, or the States can adequately distinguish obscene material unprotected by the First Amendment from protected expression, *Paris Adult Theatre I* v. *Slaton, post,* p. 73 (Brennan, J., dissenting). Paradoxically, Mr. Justice Brennan indicates that suppression of unprotected obscene material is permissible to avoid exposure to unconsenting adults, as in this case, and to juveniles, although he gives no indication of how the division between protected and nonprotected materials may be drawn with greater precision for these purposes than for regulation of commercial exposure to consenting adults only. Nor does he indicate where in the Constitution he finds the authority to distinguish between a willing "adult" one month past the state law age of majority and a willing "juvenile" one month younger.

Under the holdings announced today, no one will be subject to prosecution for the sale or exposure of obscene materials unless these materials depict or describe patently offensive "hard core" sexual conduct specifically defined by the regulating state law, as written or construed. We are satisfied that these specific prerequisites will provide fair notice to a dealer in such materials that his public and commercial activities may bring prosecution. See *Roth* v. *United States, supra,* at 491–492. Cf. *Ginsberg* v. *New York,* 390 U.S., at 643.[10] If the inability to define regulated materials

[9] The mere fact juries may reach different conclusions as to the same material does not mean that constitutional rights are abridged. As this Court observed in *Roth* v. *United States,* 354 U.S., at 492 n. 30, "it is common experience that different juries may reach different results under any criminal statute. That is one of the consequences we accept under our jury system. Cf. *Dunlop* v. *United States,* 165 U.S. 486, 499–500."

[10] As Mr. Justice Brennan stated for the Court in *Roth* v. *United States, supra,* at 491–492:

"Many decisions have recognized that these terms of obscenity statutes are not precise. [Footnote omitted.] This Court, however, has consistently held that lack of precision is not itself offensive to the requirements of due process. '. . . [T]he Constitution does not require impossible standards'; all that is required is that the language 'conveys sufficiently definite warning as to the proscribed conduct when measured by common understanding and practices. . . .' *United States* v. *Petrillo,* 332 U.S. 1, 7–8. These words, applied according to the proper standard for judging

with ultimate, god-like precision altogether removes the power of the States or the Congress to regulate, then "hard core" pornography may be exposed without limit to the juvenile, the passerby, and the consenting adult alike, as, indeed, MR. JUSTICE DOUGLAS contends. As to MR. JUSTICE DOUGLAS' position, see *United States* v. *Thirty-seven Photographs,* 402 U.S. 363, 379–380 (1971) (Black, J., joined by DOUGLAS, J., dissenting); *Ginzburg* v. *United States, supra,* at 476, 491–492 Black, J., and DOUGLAS, J., dissenting); *Jacobellis* v. *Ohio, supra,* at 196 (Black, J., joined by DOUGLAS, J., concurring); *Roth, supra,* at 508–514 (DOUGLAS, J., dissenting). In this belief, however, MR. JUSTICE DOUGLAS now stands alone.

MR. JUSTICE BRENNAN also emphasizes "institutional stress" in justification of his change of view. Noting that "[t]he number of obscenity cases on our docket gives ample testimony to the burden that has been placed upon this Court," he quite rightly remarks that the examination of contested materials "is hardly a source of edification to the members of this Court." *Paris Adult Theatre I* v. *Slaton, post,* at 92, 93. He also notes, and we agree, that "uncertainty of the standards creates a continuing source of tension between state and federal courts . . . ." "The problem is . . . that one cannot say with certainty that material is obscene until at least five members of this Court, applying inevitably obscure standards, have pronounced it so." *Id.,* at 92, 93.

It is certainly true that the absence, since *Roth,* of a single majority view of this Court as to proper standards for testing obscenity has placed a strain on both state and federal courts. But today, for the first time since *Roth* was decided in 1957, a majority of this Court has agreed on concrete guidelines to isolate "hard core" pornography from expression protected by the First Amendment. Now we may abandon the casual practice of *Redrup* v. *New York,* 386 U.S. 767 (1967), and attempt to provide positive guidance to federal and state courts alike.

This may not be an easy road, free from difficulty. But no amount of "fatigue" should lead us to adopt a convenient "institutional" rationale— an absolutist, "anything goes" view of the First Amendment—because it will lighten our burdens.[11] Such an abnegation of judicial supervision in this field would be inconsistent with our duty to uphold the constitutional guarantees." *Jacobellis* v. *Ohio, supra,* at 187–188 (opinion of BRENNAN, J.). Nor should we remedy "tension between state and federal courts" by arbitrarily depriving the States of a power reserved to them under the

---

obscenity, already discussed, give adequate warning of the conduct proscribed and mark '. . . boundaries sufficiently distinct for judges and juries fairly to administer the law . . . . That there may be marginal cases in which it is difficult to determine the side of the line on which a particular fact situation falls is no sufficient reason to hold the language too ambiguous to define a criminal offense. . . .' *Id.,* at 7. See also *United States* v. *Harriss,* 347 U.S. 612, 624, n. 15; Boyce *Motor Lines, Inc.* v. *United States,* 342 U.S. 337, 340; *United States* v. *Ragen,* 314 U.S. 513, 523–524; *United States* v. *Wurzbach,* 280 U.S. 396; *Hygrade Provision Co.* v. *Sherman,* 266 U.S. 497; *Fox* v. *Washington,* 236 U.S. 273; *Nash* v. *United States,* 229 U.S. 373."

[11] We must note, in addition, that any assumption concerning the relative burdens of the past and the probable burden under the standards now adopted is pure speculation.

Constitution, a power which they have enjoyed and exercised continuously from before the adoption of the First Amendment to this day. See *Roth* v. *United States, supra,* at 482–485. "Our duty admits of no 'substitute for facing up to the tough individual problems of constitutional judgment involved in every obscenity case.' [*Roth* v. *United States, supra,* at 498]; see *Manual Enterprises, Inc.* v. *Day,* 370 U.S. 478, 488 (opinion of Harlan, J.) [footnote omitted]." *Jacobellis* v. *Ohio, supra,* at 188 (opinion of BRENNAN, J.).

III

Under a National Constitution, fundamental First Amendment limitations on the powers of the States do not vary from community to community, but this does not mean that there are, or should or can be, fixed, uniform national standards of precisely what appeals to the "prurient interest" or is "patently offensive." These are essentially questions of fact, and our Nation is simply too big and too diverse for this Court to reasonably expect that such standards could be articulated for all 50 States in a single formulation, even assuming the prerequisite consensus exists. When triers of fact are asked to decide whether "the average person, applying contemporary community standards" would consider certain materials "prurient," it would be unrealistic to require that the answer be based on some abstract formulation. The adversary system, with lay jurors as the usual ultimate factfinders in criminal prosecutions, has historically permitted triers of fact to draw on the standards of their community, guided always by limiting instructions on the law. To require a State to structure obscenity proceedings around evidence of a *national* "community standard" would be an exercise in futility.

As noted before, this case was tried on the theory that the California obscenity statute sought to incorporate the tripartite test of *Memoirs*. This, a "national" standard of First Amendment protection enumerated by a plurality of this Court, was correctly regarded at the time of trial as limiting state prosecution under the controlling case law. The jury, however, was explicitly instructed that, in determining whether the "dominant theme of the material as a whole . . . appeals to the prurient interest" and in determining whether the material "goes substantially beyond customary limits of candor and affronts contemporary community standards of decency," it was to apply "contemporary community standards of the State of California."

During the trial, both the prosecution and the defense assumed that the relevant "community standards" in making the factual determination of obscenity were those of the State of California, not some hypothetical standard of the entire United States of America. Defense counsel at trial never objected to the testimony of the State's expert on community standards [12] or to the instructions of the trial judge on "statewide" stand-

---

[12] The record simply does not support appellant's contention, belatedly raised on appeal, that the State's expert was unqualified to give evidence on California "community standards." The expert, a police officer with many years of specialization in obscenity offenses, had conducted an extensive statewide survey and had given expert evidence on 26 occasions in the year prior to this trial. Allowing such expert testi-

ards. On appeal to the Appellate Department, Superior Court of California, County of Orange, appellant for the first time contended that application of state, rather than national, standards violated the First and Fourteenth Amendments.

We conclude that neither the State's alleged failure to offer evidence of "national standards," nor the trial court's charge that the jury consider state community standards, were constitutional errors. Nothing in the First Amendment requires that a jury must consider hypothetical and unascertainable "national standards" when attempting to determine whether certain materials are obscene as a matter of fact, Mr. Chief Justice Warren pointedly commented in his dissent in *Jacobellis* v. *Ohio, supra,* at 200:

> "It is my belief that when the Court said in *Roth* that obscenity is to be defined by reference to 'community standards,' it meant community standards—not a national standard, as is sometimes argued. I believe that there is no provable 'national standard' . . . . At all events, this Court has not been able to enunciate one, and it would be unreasonable to expect local courts to divine one."

It is neither realistic nor constitutionally sound to read the First Amendment as requiring that the people of Maine or Mississippi accept public depiction of conduct found tolerable in Las Vegas, or New York City.[13] See *Hoyt* v. *Minnesota,* 399 U.S. 524–525 (1970) (BLACKMUN, J., dissenting); *Walker* v. *Ohio,* 398 U.S. 434 (1970) (BURGER, C. J., dissenting); *id.,* at 434–435 (Harlan, J., dissenting); *Cain* v. *Kentucky,* 397 U.S. 319 (1970) (BURGER, C. J., dissenting); *id.,* at 319–320 (Harlan, J., dissenting); *United States* v. *Groner,* 479 F. 2d, at 581–583; O'Meara &

---

mony was certainly not constitutional error. Cf. *United States* v. *Augenblick,* 393 U.S. 348, 356 (1969).

[13] In *Jacobellis* v. *Ohio,* 378 U.S. 184 (1964), two Justices argued that application of "local" community standards would run the risk of preventing dissemination of materials in some places because sellers would be unwilling to risk criminal conviction by testing variations in standards from place to place. *Id.,* at 193–195 (opinion of BRENNAN, J., joined by Goldberg, J.). The use of "national" standards, however, necessarily implies that materials found tolerable in some places but not under the "national" criteria, will nevertheless be unavailable where they are acceptable. Thus, in terms of danger to free expression, the potential for suppression seems at least as great in the application of a single nationwide standard as in allowing distribution in accordance with local tastes, a point which Mr. Justice Harlan often emphasized. See *Roth* v. *United States,* 354 U.S., at 506.

Appellant also argues that adherence to a "national standard" is necessary "in order to avoid unconscionable burdens on the free flow of interstate commerce." As noted *supra,* at 18 n. 1, the application of domestic state police powers in this case did not intrude on any congressional powers under Art. I, § 8, cl. 3, for there is no indication that appellant's materials were ever distributed interstate. Appellant's argument would appear without substance in any event. Obscene material may be validly regulated by a State in the exercise of its traditional local power to protect the general welfare of its population despite some possible incidental effect on the flow of such materials across state lines. See, *e.g., Head* v. *New Mexico Board,* 374 U.S. 424 (1963); *Huron Portland Cement Co.* v. *Detroit,* 362 U.S. 440 (1960); *Breard* v. *Alexandria,* 341 U.S. 622 (1951); *H. P. Hood & Sons* v. *Du Mond,* 336 U.S. 525 (1949); *Southern Pacific Co.* v. *Arizona,* 325 U.S. 761 (1945); *Baldwin* v. *G. A. F. Seelig, Inc.,* 294 U.S. 511 (1935); *Sligh* v. *Kirkwood,* 237 U.S. 52 (1915).

Shaffer, Obscenity in The Supreme Court: A Note on *Jacobellis* v. *Ohio,* 40 Notre Dame Law. 1, 6–7 (1964). See also *Memoirs* v. *Massachusetts,* 383 U.S., at 458 (Harlan, J., dissenting); *Jacobellis* v. *Ohio, supra,* at 203–204 (Harlan, J., dissenting); *Roth* v. *United States, supra,* at 505–506 (Harlan, J., concurring and dissenting). People in different States vary in their tastes and attitudes, and this diversity is not to be strangled by the absolutism of imposed uniformity. As the Court made clear in *Mishkin* v. *New York,* 383 U.S., at 508–509, the primary concern with requiring a jury to apply the standard of "the average person, applying contemporary community standards" is to be certain that, so far as material is not aimed at a deviant group, it will be judged by its impact on an average person, rather than a particularly susceptible or sensitive person—or indeed a totally insensitive one. See *Roth* v. *United States, supra,* at 489. Cf. the now discredited test in *Regina* v. *Hicklin,* [1868] L. R. 3 Q. B. 360. We hold that the requirement that the jury evaluate the materials with reference to "contemporary standards of the State of California" serves this protective purpose and is constitutionally adequate.[14]

IV

The dissenting Justices sound the alarm of repression. But, in our view, to equate the free and robust exchange of ideas and political debate with commercial exploitation of obscene material demeans the grand conception of the First Amendment and its high purposes in the historic struggle for freedom. It is a "misuse of the great guarantees of free speech and free press . . . ." *Breard* v. *Alexandria,* 341 U.S., at 645. The First Amendment protects works which, taken as a whole, have serious literary, artistic, political, or scientific value, regardless of whether the government or a majority of the people approve of the ideas these works represent. "The protection given speech and press was fashioned to assure unfettered interchange of *ideas* for the bringing about of political and social changes desired by the people." *Roth* v. *United States, supra,* at 484 (emphasis added). See *Kois* v. *Wisconsin,* 408 U.S., at 230–232; *Thornhill* v. *Alabama,* 310 U.S., at 101–102. But the public portrayal of hard-core sexual

---

[14] Appellant's jurisdictional statement contends that he was subjected to "double jeopardy" because a Los Angeles County trial judge dismissed, before trial, a prior prosecution based on the same brochures, but apparently alleging exposures at a different time in a different setting. Appellant argues that once material has been found not to be obscene in one proceeding, the State is "collaterally estopped" from ever alleging it to be obscene in a different proceeding. It is not clear from the record that appellant properly raised this issue, better regarded as a question of procedural due process than a "double jeopardy" claim, in the state courts below. Appellant failed to address any portion of his brief on the merits to this issue, and appellee contends that the question was waived under California law because it was improperly pleaded at trial. Nor is it totally clear from the record before us what collateral effect the pretrial dismissal might have under state law. The dismissal was based, at least in part, on a failure of the prosecution to present affirmative evidence required by state law, evidence which was apparently presented in this case. Appellant's contention, therefore, is best left to the California courts for further consideration on remand. The issue is not, in any event, a proper subject for appeal. See *Mishkin* v. *New York,* 383 U.S. 502, 512–514 (1966).

conduct for its own sake, and for the ensuing commercial gain, is a different matter.[15]

There is no evidence, empirical or historical, that the stern 19th century American censorship of public distribution and display of material relating to sex, see *Roth* v. *United States, supra,* at 482–485, in any way limited or affected expression of serious literary, artistic, political, or scientific ideas. On the contrary, it is beyond any question that the era following Thomas Jefferson to Theodore Roosevelt was an "extraordinarily vigorous period," not just in economics and politics, but in *belles lettres* and in "the outlying fields of social and political philosophies." [16] We do not see the harsh hand of censorship of ideas—good or bad, sound or unsound—and "repression" of political liberty lurking in every state regulation of commercial exploitation of human interest in sex.

MR. JUSTICE BRENNAN finds "it is hard to see how state-ordered regimentation of our minds can ever be forestalled." *Paris Adult Theatre I* v. *Slaton, post,* at 110 (BRENNAN, J., dissenting). These doleful anticipations assume that courts cannot distinguish commerce in ideas, protected by the First Amendment, from commercial exploitation of obscene material. Moreover, state regulation of hard-core pornography so as to make it unavailable to nonadults, a regulation which MR. JUSTICE BRENNAN finds constitutionally permissible, has all the elements of "censorship" for adults; indeed even more rigid enforcement techniques may be called for with such dichotomy of regulation. See *Interstate Circuit, Inc.* v. *Dallas,* 390 U.S., at 690.[17] One can concede that the "sexual revolution" of recent years may have had useful byproducts in striking layers of prudery from a subject long irrationally kept from needed ventilation. But it does not follow that no regulation of patently offensive "hard core" materials is needed or permissible; civilized people do not allow unregulated access to heroin because it is a derivative of medicinal morphine.

In sum, we (a) reaffirm the *Roth* holding that obscene material is not

[15] In the apt words of Mr. Chief Justice Warren, appellant in this case was "plainly engaged in the commercial exploitation of the morbid and shameful craving for materials with prurient effect. I believe that the State and Federal Governments can constitutionally punish such conduct. That is all that these cases present to us, and that is all we need to decide." *Roth* v. *United States, supra,* at 496 (concurring opinion).

[16] See 2 V. Parrington, Main Currents in American Thought *ix et seq.* (1930). As to the latter part of the 19th century, Parrington observed "A new age had come and other dreams—the age and the dreams of a middle-class sovereignty . . . . From the crude and vast romanticisms of that vigorous sovereignty emerged eventually a spirit of realistic criticism, seeking to evaluate the worth of this new America, and discover if possible other philosophies to take the place of those which had gone down in the fierce battles of the Civil War." *Id.,* at 474. Cf. 2 S. Morison, H. Commager & W. Leuchtenburg, The Growth of the American Republic 197–233 (6th ed. 1969); Paths of American Thought 123–166, 203–290 (A. Schlesinger & M. White ed. 1963) (articles of Fleming, Lerner, Morton & Lucia White, E. Rostow, Samuelson, Kazin, Hofstadter); and H. Wish, Society and Thought in Modern America 337–386 (1952).

[17] "[W]e have indicated . . . that because of its strong and abiding interest in youth, a State may regulate the dissemination to juveniles of, and their access to, material objectionable as to them, but which a States clearly could not regulate as to adults. *Ginsberg* v. *New York,* . . . [390 U.S. 629 (1968)]." *Interstate Circuit, Inc.* v. *Dallas,* 390 U.S. 676, 690 (1968) (footnote omitted).

protected by the First Amendment; (b) hold that such material can be regulated by the States, subject to the specific safeguards enunciated above, without a showing that the material is "*utterly* without redeeming social value"; and (c) hold that obscenity is to be determined by applying "contemporary community standards," see *Kois* v. *Wisconsin, supra,* at 230, and *Roth* v. *United States, supra,* at 489, not "national standards." The judgment of the Appellate Department of the Superior Court, Orange County, California, is vacated and the case remanded to that court for further proceedings not inconsistent with the First Amendment standards established by this opinion. See *United States* v. *12 200-ft. Reels of Film, post,* at 130 n. 7.

Vacated and remanded.

[Opinions of Douglas, J., Brennan, J., Stewart, J., and Marshall, J., are omitted.]

Paris Adult Theatre I v. *Slaton*
413 U.S. 49 (1973)

MR. CHIEF JUSTICE BURGER delivered the opinion of the Court.

Petitioners are two Atlanta, Georgia, movie theaters and their owners and managers, operating in the style of "adult" theaters. On December 28, 1970, respondents, the local state district attorney and the solicitor for the local state trial court, filed civil complaints in that court alleging that petitioners were exhibiting to the public for paid admission two allegedly obscene films, contrary to Georgia Code Ann. § 26–2101.[1] The two films

---

[1] This is a civil proceeding. Georgia Code Ann. § 26–2101 defines a criminal offense, but the exhibition of materials found to be "obscene" as defined by that statute may be enjoined in a civil proceeding under Georgia case law. *1024 Peachtree Corp.* v. *Slaton,* 228 Ga. 102, 184 S.E. 2d 144 (1971); *Walter* v. *Slaton,* 227 Ga. 676, 182 S.E. 2d 464 (1971); *Evans Theatre Corp.* v. *Slaton,* 227 Ga. 377, 180 S.E. 2d 712 (1971). See *infra,* at 54. Georgia Code Ann. § 26–2101 reads in relevant part:

"Distributing obscene materials.

"(a) A person commits the offense of distributing obscene materials when he sells, lends, rents, leases, gives, advertises, publishes, exhibits or otherwise disseminates to any person any obscene material of any description, knowing the obscene nature thereof, or who offers to do so, or who possesses such material with the intent so to do . . . .

"(b) Material is obscene if considered as a whole, applying community standards, its predominant appeal is to prurient interest, that is, a shameful or morbid interest in nudity, sex or excretion, and utterly without redeeming social value and if, in addition, it goes substantially beyond customary limits of candor in describing or representing such matters. . . .

. . .

"(d) A person convicted of distributing obscene material shall for the first offense be punished as for a misdemeanor, and for any subsequent offense shall be punished

in question, "Magic Mirror" and "It All Comes Out in the End," depict sexual conduct characterized by the Georgia Supreme Court as "hard core pornography" leaving "little to the imagination."

Respondents' complaints, made on behalf of the State of Georgia, demanded that the two films be declared obscene and that petitioners be enjoined from exhibiting the films. The exhibition of the films was not enjoined, but a temporary injunction was granted *ex parte* by the local trial court, restraining petitioners from destroying the films or removing them from the jurisdiction. Petitioners were further ordered to have one print each of the films in court on January 13, 1971, together with the proper viewing equipment.

On January 13, 1971, 15 days after the proceedings began, the films were produced by petitioners at a jury-waived trial. Certain photographs, also produced at trial, were stipulated to portray the single entrance to both Paris Adult Theatre I and Paris Adult Theatre II as it appeared at the time of the complaints. These photographs show a conventional, inoffensive theater entrance, without any pictures, but with signs indicating that the theaters exhibit "Atlanta's Finest Mature Feature Films." On the door itself is a sign saying: "Adult Theatre—You must be 21 and able to prove it. If viewing the nude body offends you, Please Do Not Enter."

The two films were exhibited to the trial court. The only other state evidence was testimony by criminal investigators that they had paid admission to see the films and that nothing on the outside of the theater indicated the full nature of what was shown. In particular, nothing indicated that the films depicted—as they did—scenes of simulated fellatio, cunnilingus, and group sex intercourse. There was no evidence presented that minors had ever entered the theaters. Nor was there evidence presented that petitioners had a systematic policy of barring minors, apart from posting signs at the entrance. On April 12, 1971, the trial judge dismissed respondents' complaints. He assumed "that obscenity is established," but stated:

> "It appears to the Court that the display of these films in a commercial theatre, when surrounded by requisite notice to the public of their nature and by reasonable protection against the exposure of these films to minors, is constitutionally permissible."

On appeal, the Georgia Supreme Court unanimously reversed. It assumed that the adult theaters in question barred minors and gave a full warning to the general public of the nature of the films shown, but held that the films were without protection under the First Amendment. Citing the opinion of this Court in *United States* v. *Reidel,* 402 U.S. 351 (1971), the Georgia court stated that "the sale and delivery of obscene material to willing adults is not protected under the first amendment." The Georgia court also held *Stanley* v. *Georgia,* 394 U.S. 557 (1969), to be

---

by imprisonment for not less than one nor more than five years, or by a fine not to exceed $5,000, or both."

The constitutionality of Georgia Code Ann. § 26–2101 was upheld against First Amendment and due process challenges in *Gable* v. *Jenkins,* 309 F. Supp. 998 (ND Ga. 1969), aff'd *per curiam,* 397 U.S. 592 (1970).

inapposite since it did not deal with "the commercial distribution of pornography, but with the right of Stanley to possess, in the privacy of his home, pornographic films." 228 Ga. 343, 345, 185 S.E. 2d 768, 769 (1971). After viewing the films, the Georgia Supreme Court held that their exhibition should have been enjoined, stating:

> "The films in this case leave little to the imagination. It is plain what they purport to depict, that is, conduct of the most salacious character. We hold that these films are also hard core pornography, and the showing of such films should have been enjoined since their exhibition is not protected by the first amendment." *Id.,* at 347, 185 S.E. 2d, at 770.

I

It should be clear from the outset that we do not undertake to tell the States what they must do, but rather to define the area in which they may chart their own course in dealing with obscene material. This Court has consistently held that obscene material is not protected by the First Amendment as a limitation on the state police power by virtue of the Fourteenth Amendment. *Miller* v. *California, ante,* at 23–25; *Kois* v. *Wisconsin,* 408 U.S. 229, 230 (1972); *United States* v. *Reidel, supra,* at 354; *Roth* v. *United States,* 354 U.S. 476, 485 (1957).

Georgia case law permits a civil injunction of the exhibition of obscene materials. See *1024 Peachtree Corp.* v. *Slaton,* 228 Ga. 102, 184 S.E. 2d 144 (1971); *Walter* v. *Slaton,* 227 Ga. 676, 182 S.E. 2d 464 (1971); *Evans Theatre Corp.* v. *Slaton,* 227 Ga. 377, 180 S.E. 2d 712 (1971). While this procedure is civil in nature, and does not directly involve the state criminal statute proscribing exhibition of obscene material,[2] the Georgia case law permitting civil injunction does adopt the definition of "obscene materials" used by the criminal statute.[3] Today, in *Miller* v. *California, supra,* we have sought to clarify the constitutional definition of obscene material subject to regulation by the States, and we vacate and remand this case for reconsideration in light of *Miller.*

This is not to be read as disapproval of the Georgia civil procedure employed in this case, assuming the use of a constitutionally acceptable standard for determining what is unprotected by the First Amendment. On

---

[2] See Georgia Code Ann. § 26–2101, set out *supra,* at 51 n. 1.

[3] In *Walter* v. *Slaton,* 227 Ga. 676, 182 S.E. 2d 464 (1971), the Georgia Supreme Court described the cases before it as follows:
"Each case was commenced as a civil action by the District Attorney of the Superior Court of Fulton County jointly with the Solicitor of the Criminal Court of Fulton County. In each case the plaintiffs alleged that the defendants named therein were conducting a business of exhibiting motion picture films to members of the public; that they were in control and possession of the described motion picture film which they were exhibiting to the public on a fee basis; that said film 'constitutes a flagrant violation of Ga. Code § 26–2101 in that the sole and dominant theme of the motion picture film . . . considered as a whole, and applying contemporary standards, appeals to the prurient interest in sex and nudity, and that said motion picture film is utterly and absolutely without any redeeming social value whatsoever and transgresses beyond the customary limits of candor in describing and discussing sexual matters.' " *Id.,* at 676–677, 182 S.E. 2d, at 465.

the contrary, such a procedure provides an exhibitor or purveyor of materials the best possible notice, prior to any criminal indictments, as to whether the materials are unprotected by the First Amendment and subject to state regulation.[4] See *Kingsley Books, Inc. v. Brown,* 354 U.S. 436, 441–444 (1957). Here, Georgia imposed no restraint on the exhibition of the films involved in this case until after a full adversary proceeding and a final judicial determination by the Georgia Supreme Court that the materials were constitutionally unprotected.[5] Thus the standards of *Blount* v. *Rizzi,* 400 U.S. 410, 417 (1971); *Teitel Film Corp.* v. *Cusack,* 390 U.S. 139, 141–142 (1968); *Freedman* v. *Maryland,* 380 U.S. 51, 58–59 (1965), and *Kingsley Books, Inc.* v. *Brown, supra,* at 443–445, were met. Cf. *United States* v. *Thirty-seven Photographs,* 402 U.S. 363, 367–369 (1971) (opinion of WHITE, J.).

Nor was it error to fail to require "expert" affirmative evidence that the materials were obscene when the materials themselves were actually placed in evidence. *United States* v. *Groner,* 479 F.2d 577, 579–586 (CA5 1973); *id.,* at 586–588 (Ainsworth, J., concurring); *id.,* at 588–589 (Clark, J., concurring); *United States* v. *Wild,* 422 F. 2d 34, 35–36 (CA2 1969), cert. denied, 402 U.S. 986 (1971); *Kahm* v. *United States,* 300 F. 2d 78, 84 (CA5), cert. denied, 369 U.S. 859 (1962); *State* v. *Amato,* 49 Wis. 2d 638, 645, 183 N.W. 2d 29, 32 (1971), cert. denied *sub nom. Amato* v. *Wisconsin,* 404 U.S. 1063 (1972). See *Smith* v. *California,* 361 U.S. 147, 172 (1959) (Harlan, J., concurring and dissenting); *United States* v. *Brown,* 328 F. Supp. 196, 199 (ED Va. 1971). The films, obviously, are the best evidence of what they represent.[6] "In the cases in which this Court has decided obscenity questions since *Roth,* it has regarded the materials as sufficient in themselves for the determination of the question." *Ginzburg* v. *United States,* 383 U.S. 463, 465 (1966).

---

[4] This procedure would have even more merit if the exhibitor or purveyor could also test the issue of obscenity in a similar civil action, prior to any exposure to criminal penalty. We are not here presented with the problem of whether a holding that materials were not obscene could be circumvented in a later proceeding by evidence of pandering. See *Memoirs* v. *Massachusetts* 383 U.S. 413, 458 n. 3 (1966) (Harlan, J., dissenting); *Ginzburg* v. *United States,* 383 U.S. 463, 496 (1966) (Harlan, J., dissenting).

[5] At the specific request of petitioners' counsel, the copies of the films produced for the trial court were placed in the "administrative custody" of that court pending the outcome of this litigation.

[6] This is not a subject that lends itself to the traditional use of expert testimony. Such testimony is usually admitted for the purpose of explaining to lay jurors what they otherwise could not understand. Cf. 2 J. Wigmore, Evidence §§ 556, 559 (3d ed. 1940). No such assistance is needed by jurors in obscenity cases; indeed the "expert witness" practices employed in these cases have often made a mockery out of the otherwise sound concept of expert testimony. See *United States* v. *Groner,* 479 F. 2d 577, 585–586 (CA5 1973); *id.,* at 587–588 (Ainsworth, J., concurring). "Simply stated, hard core pornography . . . can and does speak for itself." *United States* v. *Wild,* 422 F. 2d 34, 36 (CA2 1970), cert. denied, 402 U.S. 986 (1971). We reserve judgment, however, on the extreme case, not presented here, where contested materials are directed at such a bizarre deviant group that the experience of the trier of fact would be plainly inadequate to judge whether the material appeals to the prurient interest. See *Mishkin* v. *New York,* 383 U.S. 502, 508–510 (1966); *United States* v. *Klaw,* 350 F. 2d 155, 167–168 (CA2 1965).

II

We categorically disapprove the theory, apparently adopted by the trial judge, that obscene, pornographic films acquire constitutional immunity from state regulation simply because they are exhibited for consenting adults only. This holding was properly rejected by the Georgia Supreme Court. Although we have often pointedly recognized the high importance of the state interest in regulating the exposure of obscene materials to juveniles and unconsenting adults, see *Miller* v. *California, ante,* at 18–20; *Stanley* v. *Georgia,* 394 U.S., at 567; *Redrup* v. *New York,* 386 U.S. 767, 769 (1967), this Court has never declared these to be the only legitimate state interests permitting regulation of obscene material. The States have a long-recognized legitimate interest in regulating the use of obscene material in local commerce and in all places of public accommodation, as long as these regulations do not run afoul of specific constitutional prohibitions. See *United States* v. *Thirty-seven Photographs, supra,* at 376–377 (opinion of WHITE, J.); *United States* v. *Reidel,* 402 U.S., at 354–356. Cf. *United States* v. *Thirty-seven Photographs, supra,* at 378 (STEWART, J., concurring). "In an unbroken series of cases extending over a long stretch of this Court's history, it has been accepted as a postulate that 'the primary requirements of decency may be enforced against obscene publications.' [*Near* v. *Minnesota,* 283 U.S. 697, 716 (1931)]." *Kingsley Books, Inc.* v. *Brown, supra,* at 440.

In particular, we hold that there are legitimate state interests at stake in stemming the tide of commercialized obscenity, even assuming it is feasible to enforce effective safeguards against exposure to juveniles and to passersby.[7] Rights and interests "other than those of the advocates are involved." *Breard* v. *Alexandria,* 341 U.S. 622, 642 (1951). These include the interest of the public in the quality of life and the total community environment, the tone of commerce in the great city centers, and, possibly, the public safety itself. The Hill-Link Minority Report of the Commission on Obscenity and Pornography indicates that there is at least an arguable correlation between obscene material and crime.[8] Quite apart

---

[7] It is conceivable that an 'adult" theater can—if it really insists—prevent the exposure of its obscene wares to juveniles. An "adult" bookstore, dealing in obscene books, magazines, and pictures, cannot realistically make this claim. The Hill-Link Minority Report of the Commission on Obscenity and Pornography emphasizes evidence (the Abelson National Survey of Youth and Adults) that, although most pornography may be bought by elders, "the heavy users and most highly exposed people to pornography are adolescent females (among women) and adolescent and young adult males (among men)." The Report of the Commission on Obscenity and Pornography 401 (1970). The legitimate interest in preventing exposure of juveniles to obscene material cannot be fully served by simply barring juveniles from the immediate physical premises of "adult" bookstores, when there is a flourishing "outside business" in these materials.

[8] The Report of the Commission on Obscenity and Pornography 390–412 (1970). For a discussion of earlier studies indicating "a division of thought [among behavioral scientists] on the correlation between obscenity and socially deleterious behavior," *Memoirs* v. *Massachusetts, supra,* at 451, and references to expert opinions that obscene material may induce crime and antisocial conduct, see *id.,* at 451–453 (Clark, J., dissenting). Mr. Justice Clark emphasized:
"While erotic stimulation caused by pornography may be legally insignificant in itself, there are medical experts who believe that such stimulation frequently mani-

from sex crimes, however, there remains one problem of large proportions aptly described by Professor Bickel:

> "It concerns the tone of the society, the mode, or to use terms that have perhaps greater currency, the style and quality of life, now and in the future. A man may be entitled to read an obscene book in his room, or expose himself indecently there . . . . We should protect his privacy. But if he demands a right to obtain the books and pictures he wants in the market, and to foregather in public places—discreet, if you will, but accessible to all—with others who share his tastes, *then to grant him his right is to affect the world about the rest of us, and to impinge on other privacies.* Even supposing that each of us can, if he wishes, effectively avert the eye and stop the ear (which, in truth, we cannot), what is commonly read and seen and heard and done intrudes upon us all, want it or not." 22 The Public Interest 25–26 (Winter 1971).[9] (Emphasis added.)

As Mr. Chief Justice Warren stated, there is a "right of the Nation and of the States to maintain a decent society . . . ," *Jacobellis* v. *Ohio,* 378 U.S. 184, 199 (1964) (dissenting opinion).[10] See *Memoirs* v. *Massachusetts,* 383 U.S. 413, 457 (1966) (Harlan, J., dissenting); *Beauharnais* v. *Illinois,* 343 U.S. 250, 256–257 (1952); *Kovacs* v. *Cooper,* 336 U.S. 77, 86–88 (1949).

But, it is argued, there are no scientific data which conclusively demonstrate that exposure to obscene material adversely affects men and women or their society. It is urged on behalf of the petitioners that, absent such a demonstration, any kind of state regulation is "impermissible." We reject this argument. It is not for us to resolve empirical uncertainties underlying state legislation, save in the exceptional case where that legislation plainly

---

fests itself in criminal sexual behavior or other antisocial conduct. For example, Dr. George W. Henry of Cornell University has expressed the opinion that obscenity, with its exaggerated and morbid emphasis on sex, particularly abnormal and perverted practices, and its unrealistic presentation of sexual behavior and attitudes, may induce antisocial conduct by the average person. A number of sociologists think that this material may have adverse effects upon individual mental health, with potentially disruptive consequences for the community.

. . .

"Congress and the legislatures of every State have enacted measures to restrict the distribution of erotic and pornographic material, justifying these controls by reference to evidence that antisocial behavior may result in part from reading obscenity." *Id.,* at 452–453 (footnotes omitted).

[9] See also Berns, Pornography vs. Democracy: The Case for Censorship, in 22 The Public Interest 3 (Winter 1971); van den Haag, in Censorship: For & Against 156–157 (H. Hart ed. 1971).

[10] "In this and other cases in this area of the law, which are coming to us in ever-increasing numbers, we are faced with the resolution of rights basic both to individuals and to society as a whole. Specifically, we are called upon to reconcile the right of the Nation and of the States to maintain a decent society and, on the other hand, the right of individuals to express themselves freely in accordance with the guarantees of the First and Fourteenth Amendments." *Jacobellis* v. *Ohio, supra,* at 199 (Warren, C. J., dissenting).

impinges upon rights protected by the Constitution itself.[11] MR. JUSTICE BRENNAN, speaking for the Court in *Ginsberg* v. *New York,* 390 U.S. 629, 642–643 (1968), said: "We do not demand of legislatures 'scientifically certain criteria of legislation.' *Noble State Bank* v. *Haskell,* 219 U.S. 104, 110." Although there is no conclusive proof of a connection between antisocial behavior and obscene material, the legislature of Georgia could quite reasonably determine that such a connection does or might exist. In deciding *Roth,* this Court implicitly accepted that a legislature could legitimately act on such a conclusion to protect *"the social interest in order and morality." Roth* v. *United States,* 354 U.S., at 485, quoting *Chaplinsky* v. *New Hampshire,* 315 U.S. 568, 572 (1942) (emphasis added in *Roth).*[12]

From the beginning of civilized societies, legislators and judges have acted on various unprovable assumptions. Such assumptions underlie much lawful state regulation of commercial and business affairs. See *Ferguson* v. *Skrupa,* 372 U.S. 726, 730 (1963); *Breard* v. *Alexandria,* 341 U.S., at 632–633, 641–645; *Lincoln Federal Labor Union* v. *Northwestern Iron & Metal Co.,* 335 U.S. 525, 536–537 (1949). The same is true of the federal securities and antitrust laws and a host of federal regulations. See *SEC* v. *Capital Gains Research Bureau, Inc.,* 375 U.S. 180, 186–195 (1963); *American Power & Light Co.* v. *SEC,* 329 U.S. 90, 99–103 (1946); *North American Co.* v. *SEC,* 327 U.S. 686, 705–707 (1946), and cases cited. See also *Brooks* v. *United States,* 267 U.S. 432, 436–437 (1925), and *Hoke* v. *United States,* 227 U.S. 308, 322 (1913). On the basis of these assumptions both Congress and state legislatures have, for example, drastically restricted associational rights by adopting antitrust laws, and have strictly regulated public expression by issuers of and dealers in securities, profit sharing "coupons," and "trading stamps," commanding what they must and must not publish and announce. See *Sugar Institute, Inc.* v. *United States,* 297 U.S. 553, 597–602 (1936); *Merrick* v. *N. W. Halsey & Co.,* 242 U.S. 568, 584–589 (1917); *Caldwell* v. *Sioux Falls Stock Yards Co.,* 242 U.S. 559, 567–568 (1917); *Hall* v. *Geiger-Jones Co.,* 242 U.S. 539, 548–552 (1917); *Tanner* v. *Little,* 240 U.S. 369, 383–386 (1916); *Rast* v. *Van Deman & Lewis Co.,* 240 U.S. 342, 363–368 (1916). Understandably those who entertain an absolutist view of the First Amendment find it uncomfortable to explain why rights of association, speech, and press should be severely restrained in the marketplace of goods and money, but not in the marketplace of pornography.

Likewise, when legislatures and administrators act to protect the physi-

---

[11] Mr. Justice Holmes stated in another context, that:
"[T]he proper course is to recognize that a state legislature can do whatever it sees fit to do unless it is restrained by some express prohibition in the Constitution of the United States or of the State, and that Courts should be careful not to extend such prohibitions beyond their obvious meaning by reading into them conceptions of public policy that the particular Court may happen to entertain." *Tyson & Brother* v. *Banton,* 273 U.S. 418, 446 (1927) (dissenting opinion joined by Brandeis, J.).

[12] *"It has been well observed that such* [lewd and obscene] *utterances are no essential part of any exposition of ideas, and are of such slight social value as a step to truth that any benefit that may be derived from them is clearly outweighed by the social interest in order and morality." Roth* v. *United States* 354 U.S. 476, 485 (1957), quoting *Chaplinsky* v. *New Hampshire,* 315 U.S. 568, 572 (1942) (emphasis added in *Roth).*

cal environment from pollution and to preserve our resources of forests, streams, and parks, they must act on such imponderables as the impact of a new highway near or through an existing park or wilderness area. See *Citizens to Preserve Overton Park* v. *Volpe,* 401 U.S. 402, 417–420 (1971). Thus, § 18(a) of the Federal-Aid Highway Act of 1968, 23 U.S.C. § 138, and the Department of Transportation Act of 1966, as amended, 82 Stat. 824, 49 U.S.C. § 1653(f), have been described by Mr. Justice Black as "a solemn determination of the highest law-making body of this Nation that the beauty and health-giving facilities of our parks are not to be taken away for public roads without hearings, factfindings, and policy determinations under the supervision of a Cabinet officer . . . ." *Citizens to Preserve Overton Park, supra,* at 421 (separate opinion joined by BRENNAN, J.). The fact that a congressional directive reflects unprovable assumptions about what is good for the people, including imponderable aesthetic assumptions, is not a sufficient reason to find that statute unconstitutional.

If we accept the unprovable assumption that a complete education requires the reading of certain books, see *Board of Education* v. *Allen,* 392 U.S. 236, 245 (1968), and *Johnson* v. *New York State Education Dept.,* 449 F. 2d 871, 882–883 (CA2 1971) (dissenting opinion), vacated and remanded to consider mootness, 409 U.S. 75 (1972), *id.,* at 76–77 (MARSHALL, J., concurring), and the well nigh universal belief that good books, plays, and art lift the spirit, improve the mind, enrich the human personality, and develop character, can we then say that a state legislature may not act on the corollary assumption that commerce in obscene books, or public exhibitions focused on obscene conduct, have a tendency to exert a corrupting and debasing impact leading to antisocial behavior? "Many of these effects may be intangible and indistinct, but they are nonetheless real." *American Power & Light Co.* v. *SEC, supra,* at 103. Mr. Justice Cardozo said that all laws in Western civilization are "guided by a robust common sense . . . ." *Steward Machine Co.* v. *Davis,* 301 U.S. 548, 590 (1937). The sum of experience, including that of the past two decades, affords an ample basis for legislatures to conclude that a sensitive, key relationship of human existence, central to family life, community welfare, and the development of human personality, can be debased and distorted by crass commercial exploitation of sex. Nothing in the Constitution prohibits a State from reaching such a conclusion and acting on it legislatively simply because there is no conclusive evidence or empirical data.

It is argued that individual "free will" must govern, even in activities beyond the protection of the First Amendment and other constitutional guarantees of privacy, and that government cannot legitimately impede an individual's desire to see or acquire obscene plays, movies, and books. We do indeed base our society on certain assumptions that people have the capacity for free choice. Most exercises of individual free choice—those in politics, religion, and expression of ideas—are explicitly protected by the Constitution. Totally unlimited play for free will, however, is not allowed in our or any other society. We have just noted, for example, that neither the First Amendment nor "free will" precludes States from having "blue sky" laws to regulate what sellers of securities may write or publish about their wares. See *supra,* at 61–62. Such laws are to protect the weak, the uninformed, the unsuspecting, and the gullible from the exercise of their own volition. Nor do modern societies leave disposal of garbage and sewage up to the individual "free will," but impose regulation to protect both public health and the appearance of public places. States are told by some that they must await a "laissez-faire" market solution to the obscenity-pornography problem, paradoxically "by people who have never otherwise had a kind word to say for laissez-faire," particularly in solving urban, commercial, and environmental pollution problems. See I. Kristol, On the Democratic Idea in America 37 (1972).

The States, of course, may follow such a "laissez-faire" policy and drop all controls on commercialized obscenity, if that is what they prefer, just as they can ignore consumer protection in the marketplace, but nothing in the Constitution *compels* the States to do so with regard to matters falling within state jurisdiction. See *United States* v. *Reidel,* 402 U.S., at 357; *Memoirs* v. *Massachusetts,* 383 U.S., at 462 (WHITE, J., dissenting). "We do not sit as a super-legislature to determine the wisdom, need, and propriety of laws that touch economic problems, business affairs, or social conditions." *Griswold* v. *Connecticut,* 381 U.S. 479, 482 (1965). See *Ferguson* v. *Skrupa,* 372 U.S., at 731; *Day-Brite Lighting, Inc.* v. *Missouri,* 342 U.S. 421, 423 (1952).

It is asserted, however, that standards for evaluating state commercial regulations are inapposite in the present context, as state regulation of access by consenting adults to obscene material violates the constitutionally protected right to privacy enjoyed by petitioners' customers. Even assuming that petitioners have vicarious standing to assert potential customers' rights, it is unavailing to compare a theater open to the public for a fee, with the private home of *Stanley* v. *Georgia,* 394 U.S., at 568, and the marital bedroom of *Griswold* v. *Connecticut, supra,* at 485–486. This Court, has, on numerous occasions, refused to hold that commercial ventures such as a motion-picture house are "private" for the purpose of civil rights litigation and civil rights statutes. See *Sullivan* v. *Little Hunting Park, Inc.,* 396 U.S. 229, 236 (1969); *Daniel* v. *Paul,* 395 U.S. 298, 305–308 (1969); *Blow* v. *North Carolina,* 379 U.S. 684, 685–686 (1965); *Hamm* v. *Rock Hill,* 379 U.S. 306, 307–308 (1964); *Heart of Atlanta Motel, Inc.* v. *United States,* 379 U.S. 241, 247, 260–261 (1964). The Civil Rights Act of 1964 specifically defines motion-picture houses and theaters as places of "public accommodation" covered by the Act as operations affecting commerce. 78 Stat. 243, 42 U.S.C. §§2000a (b)(3), (c).

Our prior decisions recognizing a right to privacy guaranteed by the Fourteenth Amendment included "only personal rights that can be deemed 'fundamental' or 'implicit in the concept of ordered liberty.' *Palko* v. *Connecticut,* 302 U.S. 319, 325 (1937)." *Roe* v. *Wade,* 410 U.S. 113, 152 (1973). This privacy right encompasses and protects the personal intimacies of the home, the family, marriage, motherhood, procreation, and child rearing. Cf. *Eisenstadt* v. *Baird,* 405 U.S. 438, 453–454 (1972); *id.,* at 460, 463–465 (WHITE, J., concurring); *Stanley* v. *Georgia, supra,* at 568; *Loving* v. *Virginia,* 388 U.S. 1, 12 (1967); *Griswold* v. *Connecticut, supra,* at 486; *Prince* v. *Massachusetts,* 321 U.S. 158, 166 (1944); *Skinner* v. *Oklahoma,* 316 U.S. 535, 541 (1942); *Pierce* v. *Society of Sisters,* 268 U.S. 510, 535 (1925); *Meyer* v. *Nebraska,* 262 U.S. 390, 399 (1923). Nothing, however, in this Court's decisions intimates that there is any "fundamental" privacy right "implicit in the concept of ordered liberty" to watch obscene movies in places of public accommodation.

If obscene material unprotected by the First Amendment in itself carried with it a "penumbra" of constitutionally protected privacy, this Court would not have found it necessary to decide *Stanley* on the narrow basis of the "privacy of the home," which was hardly more than a reaffirmation that "a man's home is his castle." Cf. *Stanley* v. *Georgia, supra,* at 564.[13] Moreover, we have declined to equate the privacy of the home relied on in *Stanley* with a "zone" of "privacy" that follows a distributor or a consumer of obscene materials wherever he goes. See *United States* v. *Orito, post,* at 141–143; *United States* v. *12 200-ft. Reels of Film, post,* at 126–129; *United States* v. *Thirty-seven Photographs,* 402 U.S., at 376–377 (opinion of WHITE, J.); *United States* v. *Reidel, supra,* at 355. The idea of a "privacy" right and a place of public accommodation are, in this context, mutually exclusive. Conduct or depictions of conduct that the state police power can prohibit on a public street do not become automatically protected by the Constitution merely because the conduct is moved to a bar or a "live" theater stage, any more than a "live" performance of a man and woman locked in a sexual embrace at high noon in Times Square is protected by the Constitution because they simultaneously engage in a valid political dialogue.

It is also argued that the State has no legitimate interest in "control [of] the moral content of a person's thoughts," *Stanley* v. *Georgia, supra,* at 565, and we need not quarrel with this. But we reject the claim that the State of Georgia is here attempting to control the minds or thoughts of those who patronize theaters. Preventing unlimited display or distribution of obscene material, which by definition lacks any serious literary, artistic, political, or scientific value as communication, *Miller* v. *California, ante,* at 24, 34, is distinct from a control of reason and the intellect. Cf. *Kois* v. *Wisconsin,* 408 U.S. 229 (1972); *Roth* v. *United States, supra,* at 485–487; *Thornhill* v. *Alabama,* 310 U.S. 88, 101–102 (1940); Finnis, "Reason and Passion"; The Constitutional Dialectic of Free Speech and Obscenity, 116 U. Pa. L.Rev. 222, 229–230, 241–243 (1967). Where communication of ideas, protected by the First Amendment, is not involved, or the particular privacy of the home protected by *Stanley,* or any of the other "areas or zones" of constitutionally protected privacy, the mere fact that, as a consequence, some human "utterances" or "thoughts"

---

[13] The protection afforded by *Stanley* v. *Georgia,* 394 U.S. 557 (1969), is restricted to a place, the home. In contrast, the constitutionally protected privacy of family, marriage, motherhood, procreation, and child rearing is not just concerned with a particular place, but with a protected intimate relationship. Such protected privacy extends to the doctor's office, the hospital, the hotel room, or as otherwise required to safeguard the right to intimacy involved. Cf. *Roe* v. *Wade,* 410 U.S. 113, 152–154 (1973); *Griswold* v. *Connecticut,* 381 U.S. 479, 485–486 (1965). Obviously, there is no necessary or legitimate expectation of privacy which would extend to marital intercourse on a street corner or a theater stage.

may be incidentally affected does not bar the State from acting to protect legitimate state interests. Cf. *Roth* v. *United States, supra,* at 483, 485–487; *Beauharnais* v. *Illinois,* 343 U.S., at 256–257. The fantasies of a drug addict are his own and beyond the reach of government, but government regulation of drug sales is not prohibited by the Constitution. Cf. *United States* v. *Reidel, supra,* at 359–360 (Harlan, J., concurring).

Finally, petitioners argue that conduct which directly involves "consenting adults" only has, for that sole reason, a special claim to constitutional protection. Our Constitution establishes a broad range of conditions on the exercise of power by the States, but for us to say that our Constitution incorporates the proposition that conduct involving consenting adults only is always beyond state regulation,[14] is a step we are unable to take.[15] Commercial exploitation of depictions, descriptions, or exhibitions of obscene conduct on commercial premises open to the adult public falls within a State's broad power to regulate commerce and protect the public environment. The issue in this context goes beyond whether someone, or even the majority, considers the conduct depicted as "wrong" or "sinful." The States have the power to make a morally neutral judgment that public exhibition of obscene material, or commerce in such material, has a tendency to injure the community as a whole, to endanger the public safety, or to jeopardize, in Mr. Chief Justice Warren's words, the States' "right . . . to maintain a decent society." *Jacobellis* v. *Ohio,* 378 U.S., at 199 (dissenting opinion).

To summarize, we have today reaffirmed the basic holding of *Roth* v. *United States, supra,* that obscene material has no protection under the First Amendment. See *Miller* v. *California, supra,* and *Kaplan* v. *California, post,* p. 115. We have directed our holdings, not at thoughts or speech, but at depiction and description of specifically defined sexual conduct that States may regulate within limits designed to prevent infringement of First Amendment rights. We have also reaffirmed the holdings of *United States* v. *Reidel, supra,* and *United States* v. *Thirty-seven Photographs, supra,* that commerce in obscene material is unprotected by any

---

[14] Cf. J. Mill, On Liberty 13 (1955 ed.).

[15] The state statute books are replete with constitutionally unchallenged laws against prostitution, suicide, voluntary self-mutilation, brutalizing "bare fist" prize fights, and duels, although these crimes may only directly involve "consenting adults." Statutes making bigamy a crime surely cut into an individual's freedom to associate, but few today seriously claim such statutes violate the First Amendment or any other constitutional provision. See *Davis* v. *Beason,* 133 U.S. 333, 344–345 (1890). Consider also the language of this Court in *McLaughlin* v. *Florida,* 379 U.S. 184, 196 (1964), as to adultery; *Southern Surety Co.* v. *Oklahoma,* 241 U.S. 582, 586 (1916), as to fornication; *Hoke* v. *United States,* 227 U.S. 308, 320–322 (1913), and *Caminetti* v. *United States,* 242 U.S. 470, 484–487, 491–492 (1917), as to "white slavery"; *Murphy* v. *California,* 225 U.S. 623, 629 (1912), as to billiard halls; and the *Lottery Case,* 188 U. S. 321, 355–356 (1903), as to gambling. See also the summary of state statutes prohibiting bearbaiting, cockfighting, and other brutalizing animal "sports," in Stevens, Fighting and Baiting, in Animals and Their Legal Rights 112–127 (Leavitt ed. 1970). As Professor Irving Kristol has observed: "Bearbaiting and cockfighting are prohibited only in part out of compassion for the suffering animals; the main reason they were abolished was because it was felt that they debased and brutalized the citizenry who flocked to witness such spectacles." On the Democratic Idea in America 33 (1972).

constitutional doctrine of privacy. *United States* v. *Orito, post,* at
141–143; *United States* v. *12 200-ft. Reels of Film, post,* at 126–129. In
this case we hold that the States have a legitimate interest in regulating
commerce in obscene material and in regulating exhibition of obscene
material in places of public accommodation, including so-called "adult"
theaters from which minors are excluded. In light of these holdings, nothing precludes the State of Georgia from the regulation of the allegedly
obscene material exhibited in Paris Adult Theatre I or II, provided that
the applicable Georgia law, as written or authoritatively interpreted by the
Georgia courts, meets the First Amendment standards set forth in *Miller*
v. *California, ante,* at 23–25. The judgment is vacated and the case
remanded to the Georgia Supreme Court for further proceedings not
inconsistent with this opinion and *Miller* v. *California, supra.* See *United
States* v. *12 200-ft. Reels of Film, post,* at 130 n. 7.

Vacated and remanded.

[Opinions of Douglas, J., Brennan, J., Stewart, J., and Marshall, J., are
omitted.]

Heller v. *New York*
413 U.S. 483 (1973)

MR. CHIEF JUSTICE BURGER delivered the opinion of the Court.

We granted certiorari in this case to determine whether a judicial officer
authorized to issue warrants, who has viewed a film and finds it to be
obscene, can issue a constitutionally valid warrant for the film's seizure as
evidence in a prosecution against the exhibitor, without first conducting an
adversary hearing on the issue of probable obscenity.

Petitioner was manager of a commercial movie theater in the Greenwich
Village area of New York City. On July 29, 1969, a film called "Blue
Movie" was exhibited there. The film depicts a nude couple engaged in
ultimate sexual acts. Three police officers saw part of the film. Apparently
on the basis of their observations, an assistant district attorney of New
York County requested a judge of the New York Criminal Court to see a
performance. On July 31, 1969, the judge, accompanied by a police
inspector, purchased a ticket and saw the entire film. There were about
100 other persons in the audience. Neither the judge nor the police
inspector recalled any signs restricting admission to adults.[1]

At the end of the film, the judge, without any discussions with the
police inspector, signed a search warrant for the seizure of the film and
three "John Doe" warrants for the arrest of the theater manager, the
projectionist, and the ticket taker, respectively. No one at the theater was

---

[1] The prosecution presented no evidence that juveniles were actually present in the
theater.

notified or consulted prior to the issuance of the warrants. The judge signed the warrants because "it was, and is my opinion that that film is obscene, and was obscene as I saw it then under the definition of obscene, that is [in] . . . section 235.00 of the Penal Law." Exhibition of an obscene film violates New York Penal Law § 235.05.[2]

The warrants were immediately executed by police officers. Three reels, composing a single copy of the film, were seized. Petitioner, the theater manager, was arrested, as were the projectionist and the ticket taker.[3] No pretrial motion was made for the return of the film or for its suppression as evidence. Nor did petitioner make a pretrial claim that seizure of the film prevented its exhibition by use of another copy, and the record does not conclusively indicate whether such a copy was available. On September 16, 1969, 47 days after his arrest and the seizure of the movie, petitioner came to trial, a jury having been waived, before three judges of the New York City Criminal Court.

At trial, the prosecution's case rested almost solely on testimony concerning the arrests and the seizure of the film, together with the introduction into evidence of the seized film itself. The film was exhibited to the trial judges. The defense offered three "expert" witnesses: an author, a professor of sociology, and a newspaper writer. These witnesses testified that the film had social, literary, and artistic importance in illustrating "a growing and important point of view about sexual behavior" as well as providing observations "about the political and social situation in this country today. . . ." Petitioner testified that the theater's employees were instructed not to admit persons who appeared to be under 18 years of age, unless they "had identification" that they were 18. Petitioner also testified that there was a sign at the box office stating that "no one under 17

---

[2] New York Penal Law § 235.05 reads in relevant part:
"A person is guilty of obscenity when, knowing its content and character, he:
"1. Promotes, or possesses with intent to promote, any obscene material; or
"2. Produces, presents or directs an obscene performance or participates in a portion thereof which is obscene or which contributes to its obscenity.
"Obscenity is a class A misdemeanor."
The terms used in § 235.05 are defined by New York Penal Law § 235.00, which reads in relevant part:
"The following definitions are applicable to sections 235.05, 235.10 and 235.15:
"1. 'Obscene.' Any material or performance is 'obscene' if (a) considered as a whole, its predominant appeal is to prurient, shameful or morbid interest in nudity, sex, excretion, sadism or masochism, and (b) it goes substantially beyond customary limits of candor in describing or representing such matters, and (c) it is utterly without redeeming social value. Predominant appeal shall be judged with reference to ordinary adults unless it appears from the character of the material or the circumstances of its dissemination to be designed for children or other specially susceptible audience.
"2. 'Material' means anything tangible which is capable of being used or adapted to arouse interest, whether through the medium of reading, observation, sound or in any other manner.
"3. 'Performance' means any play, motion picture, dance or other exhibition performed before an audience.
"4. 'Promote' means to manufacture, issue, sell, give, provide, lend, mail, deliver, transfer, transmute, publish, distribute, circulate, disseminate, present, exhibit or advertise, or to offer or agree to do the same."
[3] The cases against the ticket taker and projectionist were dismissed on the motion of the prosecutor.

[would be] admitted." Both at the end of the prosecution's case and his own case, petitioner moved to dismiss the indictment on the ground that the seizure of the film, without a prior adversary hearing, violated the Fourteenth Amendment.

At the close of trial on September 17, 1969, petitioner was found guilty by all three judges of violating New York Penal Law § 235.05. On appeal, both the Supreme Court of the State of New York, Appellate Term, and the Court of Appeals of the State of New York viewed the film and affirmed petitioner's conviction. The Court of Appeals, relying on this Court's opinion in *Lee Art Theatre* v. *Virginia*, 392 U.S. 636, 637 (1968), held that an adversary hearing was not required prior to seizure of the film, and that the judicial determination which occurred prior to seizure in this case was constitutionally sufficient. In so holding, the Court of Appeals explicitly disapproved, as going "beyond any requirement imposed on State courts by the Supreme Court," *Astro Cinema Corp.* v. *Mackell*, 422 F. 2d 293 (CA2 1970), and *Bethview Amusement Corp.* v. *Cahn*, 416 F. 2d 410 (CA2 1969), cert. denied, 397 U.S. 920 (1970), cases requiring an adversary hearing prior to any seizure of movie film. 29 N.Y. 2d 319, 323, 277 N.E. 2d 651, 653 (1971).

We affirm this holding of the Court of Appeals of the State of New York. This Court has never held, or even implied, that there is an absolute First or Fourteenth Amendment right to a prior adversary hearing applicable to all cases where allegedly obscene material is seized. See *Times Film Corp.* v. *Chicago*, 365 U.S. 43 (1961); *Kingsley Books, Inc.* v. *Brown*, 354 U.S. 436, 440–442 (1957). In particular, there is no such absolute right where allegedly obscene material is seized, pursuant to a warrant, to preserve the material as evidence in a criminal prosecution. In *Lee Art Theatre* v. *Virginia*, *supra*, the Court went so far as to suggest that it was an open question whether a judge need "have viewed the motion picture before issuing the warrant." [4] Here the judge viewed the entire film and, indeed, witnessed the alleged criminal act. It is not contested that the judge was a "neutral, detached magistrate," that he had a full opportunity for independent judicial determination of probable cause prior to issuing the warrant, and that he was able to "focus searchingly on the question of obscenity." See *Marcus* v. *Search Warrant*, 367 U.S. 717, 731–733 (1961). Cf. *Coolidge* v. *New Hampshire*, 403 U.S. 443, 449–453 (1971); *Giordenello* v. *United States*, 357 U.S. 480, 485–486 (1958); *Johnson* v. *United States*, 333 U.S. 10, 14–15 (1948).

In *United States* v. *Thirty-seven Photographs*, 402 U.S. 363 (1971), and *Freedman* v. *Maryland*, 380 U.S. 51 (1965), we held that " 'because

---

[4] "It is true that a judge may read a copy of a book in courtroom or chambers but not as easily arrange to see a motion picture there. However, we need not decide in this case whether the justice of the peace should have viewed the motion picture before issuing the warrant. The procedure under which the warrant issued solely upon the conclusory assertions of the police officer without any inquiry by the justice of the peace into the factual basis for the officer's conclusions was not a procedure 'designed to focus searchingly on the question of obscenity.' [*Marcus* v. *Search Warrant*, 367 U.S. 717], at 732, and therefore fell short of constitutional requirements demanding necessary sensitivity to freedom of expression. See *Freedman* v. *Maryland*, 380 U.S. 51, 58–59." 392 U.S., at 637.

only a judicial determination in an adversary proceeding ensures the necessary sensitivity to freedom of expression, only a procedure requiring a judicial determination suffices to impose a valid *final restraint*.' " 402 U.S., at 367, quoting 380 U.S., at 58 (emphasis added). Those cases involved, respectively, seizure of imported materials by federal customs agents and state administrative licensing of motion pictures, both civil procedures directed at absolute suppression of the materials themselves. Even in those cases, we did not require that the adversary proceeding must take place prior to *initial* seizure. Rather, it was held that a judicial determination must occur "promptly so that administrative delay does not in itself become a form of censorship." [5] *United States* v. *Thirty-seven Photographs, supra,* at 367; *Freedman* v. *Maryland, supra,* at 57–59. See *Blount* v. *Rizzi,* 400 U.S. 410, 419–421 (1971); *Teitel Film Corp.* v. *Cusack,* 390 U.S. 139, 141–142 (1968); *Bantam Books, Inc.* v. *Sullivan,* 372 U.S. 58, 70–71 (1963).

In this case, of course, the film was not subjected to any form of "final restraint," in the sense of being enjoined from exhibition or threatened with destruction. A copy of the film was temporarily detained in order to *preserve it as evidence.* There has been no showing that the seizure of a copy of the film precluded its continued exhibition. Nor, in this case, did temporary restraint in itself "become a form of censorship," even making the doubtful assumption that no other copies of the film existed. Cf. *United States* v. *Thirty-seven Photographs, supra,* at 367; *Freedman* v. *Maryland, supra,* at 57–59. A judicial determination of obscenity, following a fully adversary trial, occurred within 48 days of the temporary seizure. Petitioner made no pretrial motions seeking return of the film or challenging its seizure, nor did he request expedited judicial consideration of the obscenity issue, so it is entirely possible that a prompt judicial determination of the obscenity issue in an adversary proceeding could have been obtained if petitioner had desired.[6] Although we have refrained from establishing rigid, specific time deadlines in proceedings involving seizure of allegedly obscene material, we have definitely excluded from any consideration of "promptness" those delays caused by the choice of the defendant. See *United States* v. *Thirty-seven Photographs, supra,* at 373–374. In this case, the barrier to a prompt judicial determination of the obscenity issue in an adversary proceeding was not the State, but petitioner's decision to waive pretrial motions and reserve the obscenity issue for trial. Cf. *Kingsley Books, Inc.* v. *Brown,* 354 U.S., at 439.

---

[5] We further hold "(1) there must be assurance, 'by statute or authoritative judicial construction, that the censor will, within a specified brief period, either issue a license or go to court to restrain showing the film'; (2) '[a]ny restraint imposed in advance of a final judicial determination on the merits must similarly be limited to preservation of the status quo for the shortest fixed period compatible with sound judicial resolution'; and (3) 'the procedure must also assure a prompt final judicial decision' to minimize the impact of possibly erroneous administrative action. [*Freedman* v. *Maryland,* 380 U.S.], at 58–59." United *States* v. *Thirty-seven Photographs,* 402 U.S., at 367.

[6] The State of New York has represented that it stands ready to grant "immediate" adversary hearings on pretrial motions challenging seizures of material arguably protected by the First Amendment. No such motion was made by petitioner.

Petitioner's reliance on the Court's decisions in *A Quantity of Books* v. *Kansas,* 378 U.S. 205 (1964), and *Marcus* v. *Search Warrant,* 367 U.S. 717 (1961), is misplaced. Those cases concerned the seizure of large quantities of books for the sole purpose of their destruction,[7] and this Court held that, in those circumstances, a prior judicial determination of obscenity in an adversary proceeding was required to avoid "danger of abridgment of the right of the public in a free society to unobstructed circulation of nonobscene books." *A Quantity of Books* v. *Kansas, supra,* at 213. We do not disturb this holding. Courts will scrutinize any large-scale seizure of books, films, or other materials presumptively protected under the First Amendment to be certain that the requirements of *A Quantity of Books* and *Marcus* are fully met. " 'Any system of prior restraints of expression comes to this Court bearing a heavy presumption against its constitutional validity.' " *New York Times Co.* v. *United States,* 403 U.S. 713, 714 (1971); quoting *Bantam Books, Inc.* v. *Sullivan,* 372 U.S., at 70; *Organization for a Better Austin* v. *Keefe,* 402 U.S. 415, 419 (1971); *Carroll* v. *Princess Anne,* 393 U.S. 175, 181 (1968). See *Near* v. *Minnesota,* 283 U.S. 697 (1931).

But seizing films to destroy them or to block their distribution or exhibition is a very different matter from seizing a single copy of a film for the *bona fide* purpose of preserving it as evidence in a criminal proceeding, particularly where, as here, there is no showing or pretrial claim that the seizure of the copy prevented continuing exhibition of the film.[8] If such a seizure is pursuant to a warrant, issued after a determination of probable cause by a neutral magistrate, and, following the seizure, a prompt[9] judicial determination of the obscenity issue in an adversary proceeding is available at the request of any interested party, the seizure is constitution-

[7] In particular, *Marcus* involved seizure by police officers acting pursuant to a general warrant of 11,000 copies of 280 publications. 367 U.S., at 723. Unlike this case, there was no independent judicial determination of obscenity by a neutral, detached magistrate, nor were the seizures made to preserve evidence for a criminal prosecution. *Id.,* at 732. The sole purpose was to seize the articles as contraband and to cause them "to be publicly destroyed, by burning or otherwise." *Id.,* at 721 n. 6. In *A Quantity of Books* v. *Kansas,* 378 U.S. 205 (1964), 1,715 copies of 31 publications were seized by a county sheriff, also without any prior judicial determination of obscenity and, again, for the sole purpose of destroying the publications as contraband. *Id.,* at 206–209.

[8] In *Mishkin* v. *New York,* 383 U.S. 502 (1966), this Court refused to review the legality of a seizure of books challenged under *A Quantity of Books, supra,* primarily because the record did not reveal the number of books seized as evidence under the warrant or "whether the books seized . . . were on the threshold of dissemination." *Id.,* at 513. If *A Quantity of Books* applied to *all* seizures of obscene material, there would have been no need for the Court to abstain from review in *Mishkin,* since the parties had conceded that there was no prior adversary hearing. This is not to say that multiple copies of a single film may be seized as purely cumulative evidence, or that a State may circumvent *Marcus* or *A Quantity of Books* by incorporating, as an element of a criminal offense, the number of copies of the obscene materials involved.

[9] By "prompt," we mean the shortest period "compatible with sound judicial resolution." See *United States* v. *Thirty-seven Photographs,* 402 U.S., at 367; *Blount* v. *Rizzi,* 400 U.S. 410, 417 (1971); *Freedman* v. *Maryland,* 380 U.S. 51, at 58–59 (1965).

ally permissible. In addition, on a showing to the trial court that other copies of the film are not available to the exhibitor, the court should permit the seized film to be copied so that showing can be continued pending a judicial determination of the obscenity issue in an adversary proceeding.[10] Otherwise, the film must be returned.[11]

With such safeguards, we do not perceive that an adversary hearing *prior* to a seizure by lawful warrant would materially increase First Amendment protection. Cf. *Carroll* v. *Princess Anne, supra,* at 183–184. The necessity for a prior judicial determination of probable cause will protect against gross abuses, while the availability of a prompt judicial determination in an adversary proceeding following the seizure assures that difficult marginal cases will be fully considered in light of First Amendment guarantees, with only a minimal interference with public circulation pending litigation. The procedure used by New York in this case provides such First Amendment safeguards, while also serving the public interests in full and fair prosecution for obscenity offenses. Counsel for New York has argued that movie films tend to "disappear" if adversary hearings are afforded prior to seizure. We take judicial notice that such films may be compact, readily transported for exhibition in other jurisdictions, easily destructible, and particularly susceptible to alteration by cutting and splicing critical parts of film.

Petitioner also challenged his conviction on substantive, as opposed to procedural, ground arguing that he was convicted under standards of obscenity both overbroad and unconstitutionally vague. In addition, petitioner argues that films shown only to consenting adults in private have a particular claim to constitutional protection. In *Miller* v. *California, ante,* p. 15, and *Paris Adult Theatre I* v. *Slaton, ante,* p. 49, decided June 21, 1973, we dealt with these substantive issues. A majority of this Court has now approved guidelines for the lawful state regulation of obscene material. The judgment of the Court of Appeals of the State of New York is therefore vacated and this case remanded for the sole purpose of affording the New York courts an opportunity to reconsider these substantive issues in light of *Miller* and *Paris Adult Theatre I.* See *United States* v. *12 200-ft. Reels of Film, ante,* at 130 n .7.

Vacated and remanded.

[Opinions of Douglas, J., Brennan, J., Stewart, J., and Marshall, J., are omitted.]

---

[10] At oral argument, counsel for petitioner agreed that a prompt opportunity to obtain a copy from the seized film at "an independent lab under circumstances that would assure that there was no tampering with the film" with the original returned within "24 hours" would "satisfy" his "First Amendment position." Tr. of Oral Arg. 28. Petitioner never requested such a copy below.

[11] Failure to permit copying of seized material adversely affects First Amendment interests; prompt copying of seized material should be permitted. If copying is denied, return of the seized material should be required. On the other hand, violations of Fourth Amendment standards would require that the seized material be excluded from evidence. See *Roaden* v. *Kentucky, post,* p. 496; *Lee Art Theater* v. *Virginia,* 392 U.S., at 637. Cf. *Mapp* v. *Ohio,* 367 U.S. 643 (1961).

Roaden v. *Kentucky*
413 U.S. 496 (1973)

MR. CHIEF JUSTICE BURGER delivered the opinion of the Court.

The question presented in this case is whether the seizure of allegedly obscene material, contemporaneous with and as an incident to an arrest for the public exhibition of such material in a commercial theater may be accomplished without a warrant.

On September 29, 1970, the sheriff of Pulaski County, Kentucky, accompanied by the district prosecutor, purchased tickets to a local drive-in theater. There the sheriff observed, in its entirety, a film called "Cindy and Donna" and concluded that it was obscene and that its exhibition was in violation of a state statute. A substantial part of the film was also observed by a deputy sheriff from a vantage point on the road outside the theater. Since the petitioner conceded the obscenity of the film at trial, that issue is not before us for decision.[1]

The sheriff, at the conclusion of the film, proceeded to the projection booth, where he arrested petitioner, the manager of the theater, on the charge of exhibiting an obscene film to the public contrary to Ky. Rev. Stat. § 436.101 (1973).[2] Concurrent with the arrest, the sheriff seized one

---

[1] Petitioner's lawyer made the following statement to the trial jury during the closing arguments:

"I would be good enough to tell you at the outset that, in behalf of Mr. Roaden, I am not going to get up here and defend the film observed yesterday nor the revolting scenes in it or try to argue or persuade you that those scene[s] were not obscene." App. 37.

[2] Kentucky Revised Statutes § 436.101 (1973), reads in relevant part as follows: "Obscene matter, distribution, penalties, destruction.

"(1) As used in this section:

"(a) 'Distribute' means to transfer possession of, whether with or without consideration.

"(b) 'Matter' means any book, magazine, newspaper, or other printed or written material or any picture, drawing, photograph, motion picture, or other pictorial representation or any statue or other figure, or any recording, transcription or mechanical, chemical or electrical reproduction or any other articles, equipment, machines or materials.

"(c) 'Obscene' means that to the average person, applying contemporary standards, the predominant appeal of the matter, taken as a whole, is to prurient interest, a shameful or morbid interest in nudity, sex, or excretion, which goes substantially beyond customary limits of candor in description or representation of such matters.

"(d) 'Person' means any individual, partnership, firm, asociation, corporation, or other legal entity.

"(2) Any person who, having knowledge of the obscenity thereof, sends or causes to be sent, or brings or causes to be brought, into this state for sale or distribution, or in this state prepares, publishes, prints, exhibits, distributes, or offers to distribute, or has in his possesion with intent to distribute or to exhibit or offer to distribute, any obscene matter is punishable by fine of not more than $1,000 plus five dollars ($5.00) for each additional unit of material coming within the provisions of this chapter, which is involved in the offense, not to exceed ten thousand dollars ($10,000), or by imprisonment in the county jail for not more than six (6) months plus one (1) day for each additional unit of material coming within the provisions of this chapter, and which is involved in the offense, such basic maxmium and additional days not to exceed 360 days in the county jail, or by both such fine and imprisonment. If such person has previously been convicted of a violation of this

copy of the film for use as evidence. It is uncontested: (a) that the sheriff had no warrant when he made the arrest and seizure, (b) that there had been no prior determination by a judicial officer on the question of obscenity, and (c) that the arrest was based solely on the sheriff's observing the exhibition of the film.

On September 30, 1970, the day following the arrest of petitioner and the seizure of the film, the Grand Jury of Pulaski County heard testimony concerning the scenes and content of the film and returned an indictment charging petitioner with exhibiting an obscene film in violation of Ky. Rev. Stat. § 436.101. On October 3, 1970, petitioner entered a plea of not guilty in the Pulaski Circuit Court, and the case was set for trial. On October 12, 1970, petitioner filed a motion to suppress the film as evidence and to dismiss the indictment. The motion was predicated upon the ground that the film was "improperly, unlawfully and illegally seized, contrary to . . . the laws of the land." Four days later, on October 16, 1970, the Pulaski Circuit Court heard argument at an adversary hearing on petitioner's motion. The motion was denied.

Petitioner's trial began on October 20, 1970. The arresting sheriff and one of his deputies were the only witnesses for the prosecution. The sheriff testified that the film displayed nudity and "intimate love scenes." The sheriff further testified that, upon viewing the film, he determined that it was obscene and that its exhibition violated state law. He therefore arrested petitioner. Together with the testimony of the sheriff, the film itself was introduced in evidence. Petitioner's motion to suppress the film was renewed, and again overruled. The sheriff's deputy took the stand and testified that he had viewed the final 30 minutes of the film from a vantage point on a public road outside the theater. Following this testimony, the jury was permitted to see the film.

Petitioner testified in his own behalf. He stated that, to his knowledge, no juveniles had been admitted to see the film, and that he had received no complaints about the film until it was seized by the sheriff. At the close

---

subsection, he is punishable by fine of not more than $2,000 plus five dollars ($5.00) for each additional unit of material coming within the provisions of this chapter, which is involved in the offense, not to exceed $25,000, or by imprisonment in the county jail for not more than one (1) year, or by both such fine and such imprisonment. If a person has been twice convicted of a violation of this section, a violation of this subsection is punishable by imprisonment in the state penitentiary not exceeding five (5) years.

. . .

"(8) The jury, or the court, if a jury trial is waived, shall render a general verdict, and shall also render a special verdict as to whether the matter named in the charge is obscene. The special verdict or findings on the issue of obscenity may be: 'We find the . . . (title or description of matter) to be obscene,' 'We find the . . . (title or description of matter) not to be obscene,' as they may find each item is or is not obscene.

"(9) Upon the conviction of the accused, the court may, when the conviction becomes final, order any matter or advertisemest, in respect whereof the accused stands convicted, and which remains in the possession or under the control of the attorney general, commonwealth's attorney, county attorney, city attorney or their authorized assistants, or any law enforcement agency, to be destroyed, and the court may cause to be destroyed any such material in its possession or under its control."

of his testimony, the jury found petitioner guilty as charged. The jury rendered both a general verdict of guilty and a special verdict that the film was obscene, as provided by Ky. Rev. Stat. § 436.101 (8).

On appeal, the Court of Appeals of Kentucky affirmed petitioner's conviction. The Court of Appeals first emphasized that "[i]t was conceded by [petitioner's] counsel in closing argument to the jury that the film is obscene. No issue is presented on appeal as to the obscenity of the material." 473 S.W. 2d 814, 815 (1971). The Court of Appeals then held that the film was properly seized incident to a lawful arrest, distinguishing the holdings of this Court in *A Quantity of Books* v. *Kansas,* 378 U.S. 205 (1964), and *Marcus* v. *Search Warrant,* 367 U.S. 717 (1961), on the ground that those decisions related to seizure of allegedly obscene materials "for destruction or suppression, not to seizures incident to an arrest for possessing, selling, or exhibiting a specific item." 473 S.W. 2d, at 815. It also distinguished *Lee Art Theatre* v. *Virginia,* 392 U.S. 636 (1968), on the grounds that there film "had been seized pursuant to a [defective] search warrant, not incident to an arrest." 473 S.W. 2d, at 816. The Court of Appeals relied on a decision of a federal three-judge court in *Hosey* v. *City of Jackson,* 309 F. Supp. 527 (SD Miss. 1970), which concluded that:

> "[S]eizure of an allegedly obscene film as an incident to lawful arrests for a crime committed in the presence of the arresting officers, i.e., the public showing of such film, does not exceed constitutional bounds in the absence of a prior judicial hearing on the question of its obscenity." *Id.,* at 533.

The Court of Appeals specifically declined to follow a decision by another federal three-judge court in *Ledesma* v. *Perez,* 304 F. Supp. 662 (ED La. 1969), which held unconstitutional the seizure of allegedly obscene material incident to an arrest, but without a warrant or a prior adversary hearing.[3]

I

The Fourth Amendment proscription against "unreasonable . . . seizures," applicable to the States through the Fourteenth Amendment, must not be read in a vacuum. A seizure reasonable as to one type of material in one setting may be unreasonable in a different setting or with respect to another kind of material. Cf. *Coolidge* v. *New Hampshire,* 403 U.S. 443, 471–472 (1971); *id.,* at 509–510 (Black, J., concurring and dissenting); *id.,* at 512–513 (WHITE, J., concurring and dissenting). The question to be resolved is whether the seizure of the film without a warrant was unreasonable under Fourth Amendment standards and, if so, whether the film was therefore inadmissible at the trial. The seizure of instruments of a

---

[3] We vacated the judgment in *Hosey* v. *City of Jackson,* 309 F. Supp. 527 (SD Miss. 1970), on the grounds of the Court's policy of noninterference in state prosecution; we did not reach the merits. *Hosey* v. *City of Jackson,* 401 U.S. 987 (1971). We also vacated the judgment in *Ledesma* v. *Perez,* 304 F. Supp. 662 (ED La. 1969), again on the grounds of noninterference with state criminal proceedings prior to adjudications by state courts. *Perez* v. *Ledesma,* 401 U.S. 82 (1971).

crime, such as a pistol or a knife, or "contraband or stolen goods or objects dangerous in themselves," *id.,* at 472, are to be distinguished from quantities of books and movie films when a court appraises the reasonableness of the seizure under Fourth or Fourteenth Amendment standards.

Marcus v. *Search Warrant, supra,* held that a warrant for the seizure of allegedly obscene books could not be issued on the conclusory opinion of a police officer that the books sought to be seized were obscene. Such a warrant lacked the safeguards demanded "to assure nonobscene material the constitutional protection to which it is entitled. . . . [T]he warrants issued on the strength of the conclusory assertions of a single police officer, without any scrutiny by the judge of any materials considered by the complainant to be obscene." 367 U.S., at 731–732. There had been "no step in the procedure before seizure designed to focus searchingly on the question of obscenity." *Id.,* at 732.

The sense of this holding was reaffirmed in *A Quantity of Books* v. *Kansas, supra,* where the Court found unconstitutional a "massive seizure" of books from a commercial bookstore for the purpose of destroying the books as contraband. The result was premised on the lack of an adversary hearing prior to seizure, and the Court did not find it necessary to reach the claim that the seizure violated Fourth Amendment standards. 378 U.S., at 210 n. 2. However, the Court emphasized:

> "It is no answer to say that obscene books are contraband, and that consequently the standards governing searches and seizures of allegedly obscene books should not differ from those applied with respect to narcotics, gambling paraphernalia and other contraband. We rejected that proposition in *Marcus.*" *Id.,* at 211–212.

Lee Art Theatre v. *Virginia, supra,* was to the same effect with regard to seizure of a film from a commercial theater regularly open to the public. There a warrant for the seizure of the film was issued on the basis of a police officer's affidavit giving the titles of the film and asserting in conclusory fashion that he had personally viewed the films and considered them obscene. The films were seized pursuant to the warrant and introduced into evidence in a criminal case against the exhibitor. Conviction ensued. On review, the Court held that "[t]he admission of the films in evidence requires reversal of petitioner's conviction" because

> "[t]he procedure under which the warrant issued solely upon the conclusory assertions of the police officer without any inquiry by the justice of the peace into the factual basis for the officer's conclusions was not a procedure 'designed to focus searchingly on the question of obscenity,' *id.,* [*Marcus* v. *Search Warrant, supra*] at 732, and therefore fell short of constitutional requirements demanding necessary sensitivity to freedom of expression." 392 U.S., at 637.

No mention was made in the brief *per curiam Lee Art Theatre* opinion as to whether or not the seizure was incident to an arrest. The Court relied on *Marcus* and *A Quantity of Books.*

The common thread of *Marcus, A Quantity of Books,* and *Lee Art Theatre* is to be found in the nature of the materials seized and the setting in which they were taken. See *Stanford* v. *Texas,* 379 U.S. 476, 486 (1965).[4] In each case the material seized fell arguably within First Amendment protection, and the taking brought to an abrupt halt an orderly and presumptively legitimate distribution or exhibition. Seizing a film then being exhibited to the general public presents essentially the same restraint on expression as the seizure of all the books in a bookstore. Such precipitate action by a police officer, without the authority of a constitutionally sufficient warrant, is plainly a form of prior restraint and is, in those circumstances, unreasonable under Fourth Amendment standards. The seizure is unreasonable, not simply because it would have been easy to secure a warrant, but rather because prior restraint of the right of expression, whether by books or films, calls for a higher hurdle in the evaluation of reasonableness. The setting of the bookstore or the commercial theater, each presumptively under the protection of the First Amendment, invokes such Fourth Amendment warrant requirements because we examine what is "unreasonable" in the light of the values of freedom of expression.[5] As we stated in *Stanford* v. *Texas, supra:*

> "In short, . . . the constitutional requirement that warrants must particularly describe the 'things to be seized' is to be accorded the most scrupulous exactitude when the 'things' are books, and the basis for their seizure is the ideas which they contain. See *Marcus* v. *Search Warrant,* 367 U.S. 717; *A Quantity of Books* v. *Kansas,* 378 U.S. 205. No less a standard could be faithful to First Amendment freedoms. The constitutional impossibility of leaving the protection of those freedoms to the whim of the officers charged with executing the warrant is dramatically underscored by what the officers saw fit to seize under the warrant in this case." 379 U.S., at 485 (footnotes omitted).

Moreover, ordinary human experience should teach that the seizure of a movie film from a commercial theater with regularly scheduled performances, where a film is being played and replayed to paid audiences, presents a very different situation from that in which contraband is changing hands or where a robbery or assault is being perpetrated. In the latter settings, the probable cause for an arrest might justify the seizure of weapons, or other evidence or instruments of crime, without a warrant. Cf. *Chimel* v. *California,* 395 U.S. 752, 764 (1969); *id.,* at 773–774 (WHITE, J., dissenting); *Preston* v. *United States,* 376 U.S. 364, 367 (1964). Where there are exigent circumstances in which police action literally must be "now or never" to preserve the evidence of the crime, it is reasonable to permit action without prior judicial evaluation.[6] See *Cham-*

---

[4] In *Stanford* v. *Texas, supra,* we acknowledged the difference between books and weapons, narcotics, or cases of whiskey.

[5] This does not mean an adversary proceeding is needed before seizure, since a warrant may be issued *ex parte. Heller* v. *New York, ante,* p. 483.

[6] Counsel for Kentucky, together with counsel for New York in *Heller* v. *New York, ante,* at 493, and counsel for California as *amicus curiae* in *Heller,* have emphasized that allegedly obscene films are particularly difficult evidence to preserve unless kept in custody. We again take judicial notice that films may be compact, may be easy to destroy or to remove to another jurisdiction, and may be subject to

bers v. *Maroney,* 399 U.S. 42, 47–51 (1970). Cf. *Carroll* v. *United States,* 267 U.S. 132 (1925). The facts surrounding the "massive seizures" of books in *Marcus* and *A Quantity of Books,* or the seizure of the film in *Lee Art Theatre,* presented no such "now or never" circumstances.

II

The film seized in this case was being exhibited at a commercial theater showing regularly scheduled performances to the general public. The seizure proceeded solely on a police officer's conclusions that the film was obscene; there was no warrant. Nothing prior to seizure afforded a magistrate an opportunity to "focus searchingly on the question of obscenity." See *Heller* v. *New York, ante,* at 488–489; *Marcus* v. *Search Warrant,* 367 U.S., at 732. If, as *Marcus* and *Lee Art Theatre* held, a warrant for seizing allegedly obscene material may not issue on the mere conclusory allegations of an officer, *a fortiori,* the officer may not make such a seizure with no warrant at all. "The use by government of the power of search and seizure as an adjunct to a system for the suppression of objectionable publications is not new. . . . The Bill of Rights was fashioned against the background of knowledge that unrestricted power of search and seizure could also be an instrument for stifling liberty of expression." *Marcus* v. *Search Warrant, supra,* at 724, 729. In this case, as in *Lee Art Theatre,* the admission of the film in evidence requires reversal of petitioner's conviction. 392 U.S., at 637.

The judgment of the Court of Appeals of Kentucky is reversed and this case remanded for further proceedings not inconsistent with this opinion.

Reversed and remanded.

[Opinions of Douglas, J., Brennan, J., Stewart, J., and Marshall, J., are omitted.]

———————

Hamling v. *United States*
418 U.S. 87 (1974)

MR. JUSTICE REHNQUIST delivered the opinion of the Court.

On March 5, 1971, a grand jury in the United States District Court for the Southern District of California indicted petitioners William L. Hamling, Earl Kemp, Shirley R. Wright, David L. Thomas, Reed Enterprises, Inc., and Library Service, Inc., on 21 counts of an indictment charging use of the mails to carry an obscene book, The Illustrated Presidential

---

pretrial alterations by cutting out scenes and resplicing reels. See *ibid.* But, as the *Heller* case demonstrates, where films are scheduled for exhibition in a commercial theater open to the public, procuring a warrant based on a prior judicial determination of probable cause of obscenity need not risk loss of the evidence.

Report of the Commission on Obscenity and Pornography, and an obscene advertisement, which gave information as to where, how, and from whom and by what means the Illustrated Report might be obtained, and of conspiracy to commit the above offenses, in violation of 18 U.S.C. §§ 2, 371, and 1461.[1] Prior to trial, petitioners moved to dismiss the indictment on the grounds that it failed to inform them of the charges, and that the grand jury had insufficient evidence before it to return an indictment and was improperly instructed on the law. Petitioners also challenged the petit jury panel and moved to strike the venire on the ground that there had been an unconstitutional exclusion of all persons under 25 years of age. The District Court denied all of these motions.

Following a jury trial, petitioners were convicted on 12 counts of mailing and conspiring to mail the obscene advertisement.[2] On appeal, the United States Court of Appeals for the Ninth Circuit affirmed. 481 F. 2d 307 (1973). The jury was unable to reach a verdict with regard to the counts of the indictment which charged the mailing of the allegedly obscene Illustrated Report.[3] The advertisement found obscene is a single sheet brochure mailed to approximately 55,000 persons in various parts of the United States; one side of the brochure contains a collage of photographs from the Illustrated Report; the other side gives certain information and an order blank from which the Illustrated Report could be ordered.

The Court of Appeals accurately described the photographs in the brochure as follows:

> "The folder opens to a full page splash of pictures portraying heterosexual and homosexual intercourse, sodomy and a variety of deviate sexual acts. Specifically, a group picture of nine persons, one male engaged in masturbation, a female masturbating two males, two couples engaged in intercourse in reverse fashion while one female participant engages in fellatio of a male; a second group picture of six persons, two males masturbating, two fellatrices practicing the act, each bearing a clear depiction of ejaculated seminal fluid on their faces; two persons with the female engaged in the act of fellatio and the male in female masturbation by hand; two separate pictures of males engaged in cunnilinction; a film strip of six frames depicting lesbian love scenes including a cunnilinguist in action and female

---

[1] The indictment is reproduced in full at App. 14–31.

[2] Each petitioner was convicted on counts 1–5 and 7–13 of the indictment. App. 9. Petitioner Hamling was sentenced to imprisonment for one year on the conspiracy count, and consecutive to that, concurrent terms of three years each on the 11 substantive counts, and he was fined $32,000. Petitioner Kemp was sentenced to imprisonment for one year and one day on the conspiracy count, and consecutive to that, concurrent terms of two years each on the 11 substantive counts. Petitioners Wright and Thomas received suspended sentences of one and one-half years, and were placed on probation for five years. Petitioners Reed Enterprises, Inc., and Library Services, Inc., were fined $43,000 and $12,000, respectively.

[3] Those counts on which the jury was unable to reach a verdict and upon which a mistrial was declared were counts 15, 16, 17, 19, and 21. App. 10. After presentation of the Government's case, the District Court dismissed four of the substantive counts (6, 14, 18, and 20) for lack of proof. App. 7; Brief for United States 6 n. 4. The obscenity *vel non* of the Illustrated Report was thus not at issue in the Court of Appeals nor is it at issue in this Court.

masturbation with another's hand and a vibrator, and two frames, one depicting a woman mouthing the penis of a horse, and a second poising the same for entrance into her vagina." 481 F. 2d, at 316–317.[4]

The reverse side of the brochure contains a facsimile of the Illustrated Report's cover, and an order form for the Illustrated Report. It also contains the following language:

"THANKS A LOT, MR. PRESIDENT. A monumental work of research and investigation has now become a giant of a book. All the facts, all the statistics, presented in the best possible fomat . . . and . . . completely illustrated in black and white and full color. Every facet of the most controversial public report ever issued is covered in detail.

"The book is a MUST for the research shelves of every library, public or private, seriously concerned with full intellectual freedom and adult selection. "Millions of dollars in public funds were expended to determine the PRECISE TRUTH about eroticism in the United States today, yet every possible attempt to suppress this information was made from the very highest levels.

"Even the President dismissed the facts, out of hand. The attempt to suppress this volume is an inexcusable insult directed at every adult in this country. Each individual MUST be allowed to make his own decision; the facts are inescapable. Many adults, MANY OF THEM, will do just that after reading the REPORT. In a truly free society, a book like this wouldn't even be necessary."

The Court of Appeals indicated that the actual report of the Commission on Obscenity and Pornography is an official Government document printed by the United States Government Printing Office. The major difference between the Illustrated Report, charged to be obscene in the indictment, and the actual report is that the Illustrated Report contained illustrations, which the publishers of the Illustrated Report said were included " 'as examples of the type of subject matter discussed and the type of material shown to persons who were part of the research projects engaged in for the Commission as basis for their *Report.*' " 481 F. 2d, at 315.

The facts adduced at trial showed that postal patrons in various parts of the country received the brochure advertising the Illustrated Report. The mailings these persons received consisted of an outer envelope, an inner return envelope addressed to Library Service, Inc., at a post office box in San Diego, California, and the brochure itself, which also identified Library Service, Inc., at the same address, as the party responsible for the

[4] The only printed words appearing on the interfold of pictures are:
"In the Katzman Studies (1970) for the Commission (see page 180), some 90 photographs were rated on five-point scales for 'obscene' and 'sexually stimulating' by the control group. Group activity scenes of the type here illustrated could have been part of the 90. Both these group sex pictures are from the Danish magazine Porno Club No. 3, supposedly this was filmed at a 'live show' night club in Copenhagen. There are many similar clubs."

mailing. The outer envelopes bore a postmark that indicated they were mailed from North Hollywood, California, on or about January 12, 1971, and that the postage was affixed to the envelopes by a Pitney-Bowes meter number.

The mailing of these brochures was accomplished by petitioners through the use of other businesses. Approximately 55,000–58,000 of these brochures were placed in envelopes, and postage was affixed to them by one Richard and one Venita Harte, who operate the Academy Addressing and Mailing Service. The brochures and the Pitney-Bowes meter number, with which they affixed the postage, were supplied to them by one Bernard Lieberman of Regent House, Inc., of North Hollywood, California, who, on January 11, 1971, had paid the United States Postal Service to set $3,300 worth of postage on the meter number. Regent House was billed $541.15 by the Hartes for their services. Regent House in turn charged its services and costs for the postage and the Hartes' mailing service to Reed Enterprises, Inc., which paid the bill on January 19, 1971, with a check signed by petitioner Hamling.

Those individuals responding to the brochure would be sent copies of the Illustrated Report, which would be mailed with postage affixed by a second Pitney-Bowes meter number which was installed at Library Service, Inc., at the direction of an employee of Pitney-Bowes. The rental agreement for this meter was signed for Library Service by petitioner David Thomas, whom that employee identified as the person with whom he had dealt on the matter.

The evidence indicated that the individual petitioners were officers in the corporate petitioners, and also indicated that they were involved with selling the Illustrated Report, which entailed mailing out the advertising brochure. Petitioner Hamling, as president of Reed Enterprises, Inc., signed the check on the corporation's behalf in payment to Regent House for the mailing of the advertisement. Petitioner Kemp was the editor of the Illustrated Report, and was vice president of Library Service, Inc., and Greenleaf Classics, Inc., which is the publisher of the Illustrated Report.[5] He signed the application on behalf of Library Service, Inc., for the post office box in San Diego, which was the same post office box on the return envelope sent with the advertisement and on the advertisement itself. Petitioner Thomas signed the rental agreement for the latter postage meter which was used in affixing postage for sending copies of the Illustrated Report, and which Thomas directed to be installed at Library Service.

Petitioner Wright was the secretary of Reed Enterprises, Inc., and Greenleaf Classics, Inc. Wright assisted the postal superintendent in obtaining Kemp's signature on the application for the post office box in San Diego. Wright also received a memorandum from London Press, Inc.,

---

[5] Greenleaf Classics, Inc., was also indicted, but was acquitted on the counts involving the brochure, including the conspiracy count. As mentioned above, the jury was unable to reach a verdict on the counts involving the Illustrated Report. See n. 3, *supra*.

the printer of the Illustrated Report, addressed to her as representative of Reed Enterprises, Inc., confirming the shipment of 28,537 copies of the Illustrated Report. Various other corporate documents tended to show the individual petitioners' involvement with the corporate petitioners. Both the Government and the petitioners introduced testimony from various expert witnesses concerning the obscenity *vel non* of both the Illustrated Report and the brochure.

In affirming the convictions of these petitioners for the distribution of the obscene brochure, the Court of Appeals rejected various contentions made by the petitioners. The Court of Appeals also rejected petitioners' petition for rehearing and suggestion for rehearing en banc. We granted certiorari, 414 U.S. 1143 (1974), and now affirm the judgment of the Court of Appeals.

I

These petitioners were convicted by a jury on December 23, 1971. App. 9. The Court of Appeals affirmed their convictions in an opinion filed on June 7, 1973. The Court of Appeals originally denied rehearing and suggestion for rehearing en banc on July 9, 1973. That order was withdrawn by the Court of Appeals to be reconsidered in light of this Court's decisions, announced June 21, 1973, in *Miller* v. *California,* 413 U.S. 15, and related cases,[6] and was submitted to the en banc court, by order dated August 20, 1973.[7] On August 22, 1973, the Court of Appeals entered an order denying the petition for rehearing and the suggestion for rehearing en banc.

The principal question presented by this case is what rules of law shall govern obscenity convictions that occurred prior to the date on which this Court's decision in *Miller* v. *California, supra,* and its companion cases were handed down, but which had not at that point become final. Petitioners mount a series of challenges to their convictions based upon the so-called *Memoirs* test for the proscription of obscenity. (*Memoirs* v. *Massachusetts,* 383 U.S. 413 (1966).) They also attack the judgments as failing to comply with the standards enunciated in the *Miller* cases, and conclude by challenging other procedural and evidentiary rulings of the District Court.

[6] *Paris Adult Theatre I* v. *Slaton,* 413 U.S. 49 (1973); *Kaplan* v. *California,* 413 U.S. 115 (1973); *United States* v. *12 200-ft. Reels of Film,* 413 U.S. 123 (1973); *United States* v. *Orito,* 413 U.S. 139 (1973).

[7] Upon withdrawing the original order denying rehearing for reconsideration in light of *Miller* v. *California, supra,* and the related cases, the Court of Appeals stated (Pet. for Cert. App. 39–40):

"We heretofore determined that the evidence was abundantly sufficient to meet, and the District Court's jury instructions in full compliance with, the essential elements of the *Roth-Memoirs* test. *United States* v. *One Reel of Film,* et al., —— F. 2d —— (1st Cir. July 16, 1973, No. 73–1181) at pages 5 and 7 of the slip opinion, in considering the same problem, succinctly states:

" '*A fortiori* the more relaxed standards announced by the Supreme Court were met.
" '[W]e see no possible reason to remand, especially as the Supreme Court has just addressed itself to the construction and adequacy of the federal statute involved. See *United States* v. *12 200-Ft. Reels of Super 8mm. Film, supra,* 41 U.S. L. W. at 4963, n. 7.' "

Questions as to the constitutionality of 18 U.S.C. § 1461,[8] the primary statute under which petitioners were convicted, were not strangers to this Court prior to the *Miller* decision. In *Roth* v. *United States,* 354 U.S. 476 (1957), the Court held that this statute did not offend the free speech and free press guarantees of the First Amendment, and that it did not deny the due process guaranteed by the Fifth Amendment because it was "too vague to support conviction for crime." *Id.,* at 480. That holding was reaffirmed in *United States* v. *Reidel,* 402 U.S. 351 (1971). See also *Manual Enterprises, Inc.* v. *Day,* 370 U.S. 478 (1962); *Ginzburg* v. *United States,* 383 U.S. 463 (1966). Prior to *Miller,* therefore, this Court had held that 18 U.S.C. § 1461, "applied according to the proper standard for judging obscenity, do[es] not offend constitutional safeguards against convictions based upon protected material, or fail to give men in acting adequate notice of what is prohibited." *Roth* v. *United States, supra,* at 492.

These petitioners were tried and convicted under the definition of obscenity originally announced by the Court in *Roth* v. *United States, supra,* and significantly refined by the plurality opinion in *Memoirs* v. *Massachusetts, supra.* The *Memoirs* plurality held that under the *Roth* definition

> "as elaborated in subsequent cases, three elements must coalesce: it must be established that (a) the dominant theme of the material taken as a whole appeals to a prurient interest in sex; (b) the material is patently offensive because it affronts contemporary community standards relating to the description or representation of sexual matters; and (c) the material is utterly without redeeming social value." *Id.,* at 418.

Petitioners make no contention that the instructions given by the District Court in this case were inconsistent with the test of the *Memoirs* plurality. They argue instead that the obscenity *vel non* of the brochure has

[8] Title 18 U.S.C. § 1461 provides in pertinent part:
"Every obscene, lewd, lascivious, indecent, filthy or vile article, matter, thing, device, or substance; and—
. . .
"Every written or printed card, letter, circular, book, pamphlet, advertisement, or notice of any kind giving information, directly or indirectly, where, or how, or from whom, or by what means any of such mentioned matters, articles, or things may be obtained or made . . . .
. . .
"Is declared to be nonmailable matter and shall not be conveyed in the mails or delivered from any post office or by any letter carrier.
"Whoever knowingly uses the mails for the mailing, carriage in the mails, or delivery of anything declared by this section or section 3001 (e) of Title 39 to be nonmailable, or knowingly causes to be delivered by mail according to the direction thereon, or at the place at which it is directed to be delivered by the person to whom it is addressed, or knowingly takes any such thing from the mails for the purpose of circulating or disposing thereof, or of aiding in the circulation or disposition thereof, shall be fined not more than $5,000 or imprisoned not more than five years, or both, for the first such offense, and shall be fined not more than $10,000 or imprisoned not more than ten years, or both, for each such offense thereafter. . . ."

not been established under the *Memoirs* test. The Court of Appeals ruled against petitioners on this score, concluding that the jury's finding that the brochure was obscene under the *Memoirs* plurality test was correct. Petitioners argue at length that their expert witnesses established that the brochure did not appeal to a prurient interest in sex, that it was not patently offensive, and that it had social value. Examining the record below, we find that the jury could constitutionally find the brochure obscene under the *Memoirs* test. Expert testimony is not necessary to enable the jury to judge the obscenity of material which, as here, has been placed into evidence. See *Paris Adult Theatre I* v. *Slaton,* 413 U.S. 49, 56 (1973); *Kaplan* v. *California,* 413 U.S. 115, 120–121 (1973); *Ginzburg* v. *United States, supra,* at 465. In this case, both the Government and the petitioners introduced testimony through expert witnesses concerning the alleged obscenity of the brochure. The jury was not bound to accept the opinion of any expert in weighing the evidence of obscenity, and we conclude that its determination that the brochure was obscene was supported by the evidence and consistent with the *Memoirs* formulation of obscenity.

Petitioners nevertheless contend that since the jury was unable to reach a verdict on the counts charging the obscenity *vel non* of the Illustrated Report itself, that report must be presumed to be nonobscene, and therefore protected by the First Amendment. From this premise they contend that since the brochure fairly advertised the Illustrated Report, the brochure must also be nonobscene. The Court of Appeals rejected this contention, noting that "[t]he premise is false. The jury made no finding on the charged obscenity of the Report." 481 F. 2d, at 315. The jury in this case did not *acquit* the petitioners of the charges relating to the distribution of the allegedly obscene Illustrated Report. It instead was unable to reach a verdict on the counts charging the distribution of the Illustrated Report, and accordingly, the District Court declared a mistrial as to those counts. App. 9–10. It has, of course, long been the rule that consistency in verdicts or judgments of conviction is not required. *United States* v. *Dotterweich,* 320 U.S. 277, 279 (1943); *Dunn* v. *United States,* 284 U.S. 390, 393 (1932). "The mere fact juries may reach different conclusions as to the same material does not mean that constitutional rights are abridged. As this Court observed in *Roth* v. *United States,* 354 U.S., at 492 n. 30, 'it is common experience that different juries may reach different results under any criminal statute. That is one of the consequences we accept under our jury system. Cf. *Dunlop* v. *United States,* 165 U.S. 486, 499–500.' " *Miller* v. *California,* 413 U.S., at 26 n. 9. The brochure in this case stands by itself, and must accordingly be judged. It is not, as petitioners suggest, inseparable from the Illustrated Report, and it cannot be seriously contended that an obscene advertisement could not be prepared for some type of nonobscene material. If consistency in jury verdicts as to the obscenity *vel non* of identical materials is not constitutionally required, *Miller* v. *California, supra,* the same is true *a fortiori* of verdicts as to separate materials, regardless of their similarities.

Our *Miller* decisions dealing with the constitutional aspects of obscenity prosecutions were announced after the petitioners had been found guilty by a jury, and their judgment of conviction affirmed by a panel of the Court of Appeals. Our prior decisions establish a general rule that a change in the law occurring after a relevant event in a case will be given effect while the case is on direct review. *United States* v. *Schooner Peggy,* 1 Cranch 103 (1801); *Linkletter* v. *Walker,* 381 U.S. 618, 627 (1965); *Bradley* v. *School Board of Richmond,* 416 U.S. 696, 711 (1974). Since the judgment in this case has not become final, we examine the judgment against petitioners in the light of the principles laid down in the *Miller* cases. While the language of 18 U.S.C. § 1461 has remained the same throughout this litigation, the statute defines an offense in terms of "obscenity," and this Court's decisions, at least since *Roth* v. *United States, supra,* indicate that there are constitutional limitations which must be borne in mind in defining that statutory term. Thus any constitutional principle enunciated in *Miller* which would serve to benefit petitioners must be applied in their case.

Recognizing that the *Memoirs* plurality test had represented a sharp break with the test of obscenity as announced in *Roth* v. *United States, supra,* our decision in *Miller* v. *California* reformulated the test for the determination of obscenity *vel non:*

> "The basic guidelines for the trier of fact must be: (a) whether 'the average person, applying contemporary community standards' would find that the work, taken as a whole, appeals to the prurient interest . . . ; (b) whether the work depicts or describes, in a patently offensive way, sexual conduct specifically defined by the applicable state law; and (c) whether the work, taken as a whole, lacks serious literary, artistic, political, or scientific value." 413 U.S., at 24.

The Court of Appeals held on rehearing that the *Miller* cases generally prescribed a more relaxed standard of review under the Federal Constitution for obscenity convictions, and that therefore petitioners could derive no benefit from the principles enunciated in those cases. See n. 7, *supra.* Petitioners concede that this observation may be true in many particulars, but that in at least two it is not. They contend that the *Miller* treatment of the concept of "national standards" necessarily invalidates the District Court's charge to the jury in their case relating to the standard by which the question of obscenity was to be judged, and they further contend that the general language of 18 U.S.C. § 1461 is, in the light of the holding in the *Miller* cases, unconstitutionally vague.

A

The trial court instructed the jury that it was to judge the obscenity *vel non* of the brochure by reference to "what is reasonably accepted according to the contemporary standards of the community as a whole. . . . Contemporary community standards means the standards generally held throughout this country concerning sex and matters pertaining to sex. This phrase means, as it has been aptly stated, the average conscience of the time, and the present critical point in the compromise between candor and shame, at which the community may have arrived here and now." App. 241. Petitioners describe this as an instruction embodying the principle of "national standards" which, although it may have been proper under the law as it existed when they were tried, cannot be sustained under the law as laid down in *Miller,* where the Court stated:

> "Nothing in the First Amendment requires that a jury must consider hypothetical and unascertainable 'national standards' when attempting to determine whether certain materials are obscene as a matter of fact." 413 U.S., at 31–32.

Paradoxically, however, petitioners also contend that in order to avoid serious constitutional questions the standards in federal obscenity prosecutions *must* be national ones, relying on *Manual Enterprises, Inc.* v. *Day,* 370 U.S., at 488 (opinion of Harlan, J.), and *United States* v. *Palladino,* 490 F. 2d 499 (CA1 1974). Petitioners assert that our decisions in the two federal obscenity cases decided with *Miller*[9] indicate that this Court has not definitively decided whether the Constitution requires the use of nationwide standards in federal obscenity prosecutions.

We think that both of these contentions evidence a misunderstanding of our *Miller* holdings. *Miller* rejected the view that the First and Fourteenth Amendments require that the proscription of obscenity be based on uniform nationwide standards of what is obscene, describing such standards as "hypothetical and unascertainable," 413 U.S., at 31. But in so doing the Court did not require as a constitutional matter the substitution of some smaller geographical area into the same sort of formula; the test was stated in terms of the understanding of "the average person, applying contemporary community standards." *Id.,* at 24. When this approach is coupled with the reaffirmation in *Paris Adult Theatre I* v. *Slaton,* 413 U.S., at 56, of the rule that the prosecution need not as a matter of constitutional law produce "expert" witnesses to testify as to the obscenity of the materials, the import of the quoted language from *Miller* becomes clear. A juror is entitled to draw on his own knowledge of the views of the average person in the community or vicinage from which he comes for making the required determination, just as he is entitled to draw on his knowledge of the propensities of a "reasonable" person in other areas of the law. *Stone* v. *New York, C. & St. L. R. Co.,* 344 U.S. 407, 409 (1953); *Schulz* v. *Pennsylvania R. Co.,* 350 U.S 523, 525–526 (1956). Our holding in *Miller* that California could constitutionally proscribe obscenity in terms of a "statewide" standard did not mean that any such precise geographic area is required as a matter of constitutional law.

Our analysis in *Miller* of the difficulty in formulating uniform national standards of obscenity, and our emphasis on the ability of the juror to ascertain the sense of the "average person, applying contemporary community standards" without the benefit of expert evidence, clearly indicates that 18 U.S.C. §1461 is not to be interpreted as requiring proof of the uniform national standards which were criticized in *Miller.* In *United*

---

[9] *United States* v. *Orito,* 413 U.S. 139 (1973); *United States* v. *12 200-ft. Reels of Film,* 413 U.S. 123 (1973).

States v. *12 200-ft. Reels of Film,* 413 U.S. 123 (1973), a federal obscenity case decided with *Miller,* we said:

> "We have today arrived at standards for testing the constitutionality of state legislation regulating obscenity. See *Miller* v. *California, ante,* at 23–25. These standards are applicable to federal legislation." *Id.,* at 129–130.

Included in the pages referred to in *Miller* is the standard of "the average person, applying contemporary community standards." In view of our holding in *12 200-ft Reels of Film,* we hold that 18 USC. § 1461 incorporates this test in defining obscenity.

The result of the *Miller* cases, therefore, as a matter of constitutional law and federal statutory construction, is to permit a juror sitting in obscenity cases to draw on knowledge of the community or vicinage from which he comes in deciding what conclusion "the average person, applying contemporary community standards" would reach in a given case. Since this case was tried in the Southern District of California, and presumably jurors from throughout that judicial district were available to serve on the panel which tried petitioners, it would be the standards of that "community" upon which the jurors would draw. But this is not to say that a District Court would not be at liberty to admit evidence of standards existing in some place outside of this particular district, if it felt such evidence would assist the jurors in the resolution of the issues which they were to decide.

Our Brother BRENNAN suggests in dissent that in holding that a federal obscenity case may be tried on local community standards, we do violence both to congressional prerogative and to the Constitution. Both of these arguments are foreclosed by our decision last Term in *United States* v. *12 200-ft. Reels of Film, supra,* that the *Miller* standards, including the "contemporary community standards" formulation, applied to federal legislation. The fact that distributors of allegedly obscene materials may be subjected to varying community standards in the various federal judicial districts into which they transmit the materials does not render a federal statute unconstitutional because of the failure of application of uniform national standards of obscenity. Those same distributors may be subjected to such varying degrees of criminal liability in prosecutions by the States for violations of state obscenity statutes; we see no constitutional impediment to a similar rule for federal prosecutions. In *Miller* v. *California,* 413 U.S., at 32, we cited with approval Mr. Chief Justice Warren's statement that:

> "[W]hen the Court said in *Roth* that obscenity is to be defined by reference to 'community standards,' it meant community standards— not a national standard, as is sometimes argued. I believe that there is no provable 'national standard,' and perhaps there should be none. At all events, this Court has not been able to enunciate one, and it would be unreasonable to expect local courts to divine one. It is said

that such a 'community' approach may well result in material being proscribed as obscene in one community but not in another, and, in all probability, that is true. But communities throughout the Nation are in fact diverse, and it must be remembered that, in cases such as this one, the Court is confronted with the task of reconciling conflicting rights of the diverse communities within our society and of individuals." *Jacobellis* v. *Ohio,* 378 U.S. 184, 200–201 (1964) (dissenting opinion).

Judging the instruction given by the District Court in this case by these principles, there is no doubt that its occasional references to the community standards of the "nation as a whole" delineated a wider geographical area than would be warranted by *Miller, 12 200-ft. Reels of Film,* and our construction of § 1461 herein, *supra,* at 105. Whether petitioners were materially prejudiced by those references is a different question. Certainly the giving of such an instruction does not render their convictions void as a matter of constitutional law. This Court has emphasized on more than one occasion that a principal concern in requiring that a judgment be made on the basis of "contemporary community standards" is to assure that the material is judged neither on the basis of each juror's personal opinion, nor by its effect on a particularly sensitive or insensitive person or group. *Miller* v. *California, supra,* at 33; *Mishkin* v. *New York,* 383 U.S. 502, 508–509 (1966); *Roth* v. *United States,* 354 U.S., at 489. The District Court's instruction in this case, including its reference to the standards of the "nation as a whole," undoubtedly accomplished this purpose.

We have frequently held that jury instructions are to be judged as a whole, rather than by picking isolated phrases from them. *Boyd* v. *United States,* 271 U.S. 104, 107 (1926). In the unusual posture of this case, in which petitioners agree that the challenged instruction was proper at the time it was given by the District Court, but now seek to claim the benefit of a change in the law which casts doubt on the correctness of portions of it, we hold that reversal is required only where there is a probability that the excision of the references to the "nation as a whole" in the instruction dealing with community standards would have materially affected the deliberations of the jury. Cf. *Namet* v. *United States,* 373 U.S. 179, 190–191 (1963); *Lopez* v. *United States,* 373 U.S. 427, 436 (1963). Our examination of the record convinces us that such a probability does not exist in this case.

Our Brother BRENNAN takes us to task for reaching this conclusion, insisting that the District Court's instructions and its exclusion of the testimony of a witness, Miss Carlsen, who had assertedly conducted a survey of standards in the San Diego area require that petitioners be accorded a new trial. As we have noted, *infra,* at 124–125, the District Court has wide discretion in its determination to admit and exclude evidence, and this is particularly true in the case of expert testimony. *Stillwell Mfg. Co.* v. *Phelps,* 130 U.S. 520, 527 (1889); *Barnes* v. *Smith,* 305 F. 2d 226,

232 (CA 10 1962); 2 J. Wigmore, Evidence § 561 (3d ed. 1940).[10] But even assuming that the District Court may have erred in excluding the witness' testimony in light of the *Miller* cases, we think arguments made by petitioners' counsel and urging the admission of the survey re-emphasize the confusing and often gossamer distinctions between "national" standards and other types of standards. Petitioners' counsel, in urging the District Court to admit the survey, stated:

> "We have already had experts who have testified and expect to bring in others who have testified both for the prosecution and the defense that the material that they found was similar in all cities. . . ." Tr. 3931.
> "This witness can testify about experiences she had in one particular city. Whether this is or not a typical city is for the jury to decide." Tr. 3932.
> "Now this supports the national survey. It is not something that stands alone. The findings here are consistent with the national survey and as part of the overall picture, taking into account, of course, that this is something that has taken place after the national survey, which was about two years ago, that Dr. Abelson performed." Tr. 3934–3935.

The District Court permitted Dr. Wilson, one of the four expert witnesses who testified on behalf of petitioners, to testify as to materials he found available in San Diego, as a result of having spent several days there. Tr. 3575. He was then asked by petitioners' counsel whether this material was "similar to or different than" the material found in other cities where he had also visited adult bookstores. The witness responded that he thought "essentially the same kinds of material are found throughout the United States." Tr. 3577. These statements, in colloquies between counsel and Dr. Wilson, only serve to confirm our conclusion that while there may have been an error in the District Court's references to the "community standards of the nation as a whole" in its instructions, and in its stated reasons for excluding the testimony of Miss Carlsen, these errors do not require reversal under the standard previously enunciated.[11]

---

[10] The stated basis for the District Court's exclusion of the testimony of Miss Carlsen was that her survey was not framed in terms of "national" standards, but it is not at all clear that the District Court would have admitted her testimony had it been so framed. "[A] specific objection *sustained* . . . is sufficient, though naming an untenable ground, if some other tenable one existed." 1 J. Wigmore, Evidence § 18, p. 32 (3d ed. 1940), citing *Kansas City S. R. Co.* v. *Jones,* 241 U.S. 181 (1916). Miss Carlsen was a student at San Diego State University who worked part time at F. W. Woolworth, doing composition layouts of newspaper advertising for the company's store in Fashion Valley. She had undertaken a "Special Studies" course with her journalism professor, Mr. Haberstroh, who was also offered by petitioners as an expert witness at the trial. Miss Carlsen had circulated through the San Diego area and asked various persons at random whether they thought "adults should be able to buy and view this book and material." Tr. 3926.

[11] The sequence of events in this case is quite different from that in *Saunders* v. *Shaw,* 244 U.S. 317 (1917), upon which our Brother BRENNAN relies. There the Supreme Court of Louisiana directed the entry of judgment against an intervening defendant who had prevailed in the trial court, on the basis of testimony adduced merely as an offer of proof by the plaintiff, and to which the intervening defendant

B

Petitioners next argue that prior to our decision in *Miller,* 18 U.S.C. § 1461 did not contain in its language, nor had it been construed to apply to, the specific types of sexual conduct referred to in *Miller,* and therefore the section was unconstitutionally vague as applied to them in the prosecution of these cases. Such an argument, however, not only neglects this Court's decisions prior to *Miller* rejecting vagueness challenges to the federal statute, but also fundamentally misconceives the thrust of our decision in the *Miller* cases.

In *Roth* v. *United States,* 354 U.S., at 491, we upheld the constitutionality of 18 U.S.C. § 1461 against a contention that it did "not provide reasonably ascertainable standards of guilt and therefore violate[s] the constitutional requirements of due process." In noting that the federal obscenity statute made punishable the mailing of material that is "obscene, lewd, lascivious, or filthy . . . [and of] other publication[s] of an indecent character," the Court stated in *Roth:*

> "Many decisions have recognized that these terms of obscenity statutes are not precise. This Court, however, has consistently held that lack of precision is not itself offensive to the requirements of due process. '. . . [T]he Constitution does not require impossible standards'; all that is required is that the language 'conveys sufficiently definite warning as to the proscribed conduct when measured by common understanding and practices. . . .' *United States* v. *Petrillo,* 332 U.S. 1, 7–8. These words, applied according to the proper standard for judging obscenity, already discussed, give adequate warning of the conduct proscribed and mark '. . . boundaries sufficiently distinct for judges and juries fairly to administer the law. . . . That there may be marginal cases in which it is difficult to determine the side of the line on which a particular fact situation falls is no sufficient reason to hold the language too ambiguous to define a criminal offense. . . .' *Id.,* at 7." 354 U.S., at 491–492 (footnote omitted).

Other decisions dealing with the pre-*Miller* constitutionality or interpretation of 18 U.S.C. § 1461 in other contexts have not retreated from the language of *Roth.* See, *e.g., United States* v. *Reidel,* 402 U.S. 351 (1971); *Ginzburg* v. *United States,* 383 U.S. 463 (1966); *Manual Enterprises, Inc.* v. *Day,* 370 U.S. 478 (1962). And as made clear by the opinion of Mr. Justice Harlan in *Manual Enterprises,* the language of 18

---

had therefore had no occasion to respond. Since the trial court had ruled that the issue to which plaintiff's proof was addressed was irrelevant, this Court reversed the Supreme Court of Louisiana in order that the intervening defendant might have an opportunity to controvert the plaintiff's proof. Here petitioners were given full latitude in rebutting every factual issue dealt with in the Government's case, and no claim is made that the jury was permitted to rely on evidence introduced merely by way of offer of proof which was not subject to cross-examination or to contradiction by countervailing evidence offered by the petitioners. The present case seems to us much closer to *Ginzburg* v. *United States,* 383 U.S. 463 (1966), than to *Saunders.*

U.S.C. § 1461 had been, prior to the date of our decision in *Miller,* authoritatively construed in a manner consistent with *Miller:*

> "The words of section 1461, 'obscene, lewd, lascivious, indecent, filthy or vile,' connote something that is portrayed in a manner so offensive as to make it unacceptable under current community *mores.* While in common usage the words have different shades of meaning, the statute since its inception has always been taken as aimed at obnoxiously debasing portrayals of sex. Although the statute condemns such material irrespective of the *effect* it may have upon those into whose hands it falls, the early case of *United States* v. *Bennett,* 24 Fed. Cas. 1093 (No. 14571), put a limiting gloss upon the statutory language: the statute reaches only indecent material which, as now expressed in *Roth* v. *United States, supra,* at 489, 'taken as a whole appeals to prurient interest.' " 370 U.S., at 482–484 (footnotes omitted) (emphasis in original).

At no point does *Miller* or any of the other obscenity decisions decided last Term intimate that the constitutionality of pre-*Miller* convictions under statutes such as 18 U.S.C. § 1461 was to be cast in doubt. Indeed, the contrary is readily apparent from the opinions in those cases. We made clear in *Miller,* 413 U.S., at 24 n. 6, that our decision was not intended to hold all state statutes inadequate, and we clearly recognized that existing statutes "as construed heretofore or hereafter, may well be adequate." That recognition is emphasized in our opinion in *United States* v. *12 200-ft. Reels of Film,* 413 U.S. 123 (1973). That case had come to this Court on appeal from the District Court's dismissal of the Government's forfeiture action under 19 U.S.C. § 1305(a), which statute the District Court had found unconstitutional. In vacating the District Court's constitutional decision and remanding the case to the District Court for a determination of the obscenity *vel non* of the materials there involved, we stated:

> "We further note that, while we must leave to state courts the construction of state legislation, we do have a duty to authoritatively construe federal statutes where 'a serious doubt of constitutionality is raised' and ' "a construction of the statute is fairly possible by which the question may be avoided." ' *United States* v. *Thirty-seven Photographs,* 402 U.S. 363, 369 (1971) (opinion of WHITE, J.), quoting from *Crowell* v. *Benson,* 285 U.S. 22, 62 (1932). If and when such a 'serious doubt' is raised as to the vagueness of the words 'obscene,' 'lewd,' 'lascivious,' 'filthy,' 'indecent,' or 'immoral' as used to describe regulated material in 19 U.S.C. § 1305(a) and 18 U.S.C. § 1462, see *United States* v. *Orito,* [413 U.S.,] at 140 n. 1, we are prepared to construe such terms as limiting regulated material to patently offensive representations or descriptions of that specific 'hard core' sexual conduct given as examples in *Miller* v. *California,* [413 U.S.,] at 25. See *United States* v. *Thirty-seven Photographs, supra,* at 369–374 (opinion of WHITE, J.). Of course, Congress could always define other specific 'hard core' conduct." 413 U.S., at 130 n. 7.

Miller undertook to set forth examples of the types of material which a statute might proscribe as portraying sexual conduct in a patently offensive way, 413 U.S., at 25–26, and went on to say that no one could be prosecuted for the "sale or exposure of obscene materials unless these materials depict or describe patently offensive 'hard core' sexual conduct specifically defined by the regulating state law, as written or construed." *Id.*, at 27. As noted above, we indicated in *United States* v. *12 200-ft. Reels of Film, supra,* at 130 n. 7, that we were prepared to construe the generic terms in 18 U.S.C. § 1462 to be limited to the sort of "patently offensive representations or descriptions of that specific 'hard core' sexual conduct given as examples in *Miller* v. *California."* We now so construe the companion provision in 18 U.S.C. § 1461, the substantive statute under which this prosecution was brought. As so construed, we do not believe that petitioners' attack on the statute as unconstitutionally vague can be sustained.

Miller, in describing the type of material which might be constitutionally proscribed, 413 U.S., at 25, was speaking in terms of substantive constitutional law of the First and Fourteenth Amendments. See *Jenkins* v. *Georgia, post,* at 160–161. While the particular descriptions there contained were not intended to be exhaustive, they clearly indicate that there is a limit beyond which neither legislative draftsmen nor juries may go in concluding that particular material is "patently offensive" within the meaning of the obscenity test set forth in the *Miller* cases. And while the Court in *Miller* did refer to "specific prerequisites" which "will provide fair notice to a dealer in such materials," 413 U.S., at 27, the Court immediately thereafter quoted the language of the Court in *Roth* v. *United States,* 354 U.S., at 491–492, concluding with these words:

> " 'That there may be marginal cases in which it is difficult to determine the side of the line on which a particular fact situation falls is no sufficient reason to hold the language too ambiguous to define a criminal offense. . . .' " 413 U.S., at 28 n. 10.

The *Miller* cases, important as they were in enunciating a constitutional test for obscenity to which a majority of the Court subscribed for the first time in a number of years, were intended neither as legislative drafting handbooks nor as manuals of jury instructions. Title 18 U.S.C. § 1461 had been held invulnerable to a challenge on the ground of unconstitutional vagueness in *Roth;* the language of *Roth* was repeated in *Miller,* along with a description of the types of material which could constitutionally be proscribed and the adjuration that such statutory proscriptions be made explicit either by their own language or by judicial construction; and *United States* v. *12 200-ft. Reels of Film, supra,* made clear our willingness to construe federal statutes dealing with obscenity to be limited to material such as that described in *Miller.* It is plain from the Court of Appeals' description of the brochure involved here that it is a form of hard-core pornography well within the types of permissibly proscribed depictions described in *Miller,* and which we now hold § 1461 to cover. Whatever complaint the distributor of material which presented a more difficult question of obscenity *vel non* might have as to the lack of a previous limiting construction of 18 U.S.C. § 1461, these petitioners have none. See *Dennis* v. *United States,* 341 U.S. 494, 511–515 (1951) (opinion of Vinson, C. J.).

Nor do we find merit in petitioners' contention that cases such as *Bouie* v. *City of Columbia,* 378 U.S. 347 (1964), require reversal of their convictions. The Court in *Bouie* held that since the crime for which the petitioners there stood convicted was "not enumerated in the statute" at the time of their conduct, their conviction could not be sustained. *Id.,* at 363. The Court noted that "a deprivation of the right of fair warning can result not only from vague statutory language but also from an unforeseeable and retroactive judicial expansion of narrow and precise statutory language." *Id.,* at 352. But the enumeration of specific categories of material in *Miller* which might be found obscene did not purport to make criminal, for the purpose of 18 U.S.C. § 1461, conduct which had not previously been thought criminal. That requirement instead added a "clarifying gloss" to the prior construction and therefore made the meaning of the .federal statute involved here "more definite" in its application to federal obscenity prosecutions. *Bouie* v. *City of Columbia, supra,* at 353. Judged by both the judicial construction of § 1461 prior to *Miller,* and by the construction of that section which we adopt today in the light of *Miller,* petitioners' claims of vagueness and lack of fair notice as to the proscription of the material which they were distributing must fail.

C

Petitioners' final *Miller*-based contention is that our rejection of the third part of the *Memoirs* test and our revision of that test in *Miller* indicates that 18 U.S.C. § 1461 was at the time of their convictions unconstitutionally vague for the additional reason that it provided insufficient guidance to them as to the proper test of "social value." But our opinion in *Miller* plainly indicates that we rejected the *Memoirs* "social value" formulation, not because it was so vague as to deprive criminal defendants of adequate notice, but instead because it represented a departure from the definition of obscenity in *Roth,* and because in calling on the prosecution to "prove a negative," it imposed a "[prosecutorial] burden virtually impossible to discharge" and which was not constitutionally required. 413 U.S., at 22. Since *Miller* permits the imposition of a lesser burden on the prosecution in this phase of the proof of obscenity than did *Memoirs,* and since the jury convicted these petitioners on the basis of an instruction concedely [sic] based on the *Memoirs* test, petitioners derive no benefit from the revision of that test in *Miller.*

II

Petitioners attack the sufficiency of the indictment under which they were charged for two reasons: first, that it charged them only in the statutory language of 18 U.S.C. § 1461, which they contend was unconstitutionally vague as applied to them; and, second, that the indictment failed to give them adequate notice of the charges against them. As noted above, however, at the time of petitioners' convictions, *Roth* v. *United States* had held that the language of § 1461 was not "too vague to support conviction for crime." 354 U.S., at 480. See *United States* v. *Reidel,* 402 U.S., at 354.

Our prior cases indicate that an indictment is sufficient if it, first, contains the elements of the offense charged and fairly informs a defendant of the charge against which he must defend, and, second, enables him to plead an acquittal or conviction in bar of future prosecutions for the same offense. *Hagner* v. *United States,* 285 U.S. 427 (1932); *United States* v. *Debrow,* 346 U.S. 374 (1953). It is generally sufficient that an indictment set forth the offense in the words of the statute itself, as long as "those words of themselves fully, directly, and expressly, without any uncertainty or ambiguity, set forth all the elements necessary to constitute the offence intended to be punished." *United States* v. *Carll,* 105 U.S. 611, 612 (1882). "Undoubtedly the language of the statute may be used in the general description of an offence, but it must be accompanied with such a statement of the facts and circumstances as will inform the accused of the specific offence, coming under the general description, with which he is charged." *United States* v. *Hess,* 124 U.S. 483, 487 (1888).

Russell v. *United States,* 369 U.S. 749 (1962), relied upon by petitioners, does not require a finding that the indictment here is insufficient. In *Russell,* the indictment recited the proscription of 2 U.S.C. § 192, and charged that the defendants had refused to answer questions that "were pertinent to the question then under inquiry" by a committee of Congress. In holding that the indictment was insufficient because it did not state the subject which was under inquiry, this Court stated:

> "[T]he very core of criminality under 2 U.S.C. § 192 is pertinency to the subject under inquiry of the questions which the defendant refused to answer. What the subject actually was, therefore, is central to every prosecution under the statute. Where guilt depends so crucially upon such *a specific identification of fact,* our cases have uniformly held that an indictment must do more than simply repeat the language of the criminal statute." 369 U.S., at 764 (emphasis added).

The definition of obscenity, however, is not a question of fact, but one of law; the word "obscene," as used in 18 U.S.C. § 1461, is not merely a generic or descriptive term, but a legal term of art. See *Roth* v. *United States,* 354 U.S., at 487–488; *Manual Enterprises, Inc.* v. *Day,* 370 U.S., at 482–487 (opinion of Harlan, J.); *United States* v. *Thevis,* 484 F. 2d 1149, 1152 (CA5 1973), cert. pending, No. 73–1075; *United States* v. *Luros,* 243 F. Supp. 160, 167 (ND Iowa), cert. denied, 382 U.S. 956 (1965). The legal definition of obscenity does not change with each indictment; it is a term sufficiently definite in legal meaning to give a defendant notice of the charge against him. *Roth* v. *United States, supra,* at 491–492; *Manual Enterprises, Inc.* v. *Day, supra,* at 482–487 (opinion of Harlan, J.). Since the various component parts of the constitutional definition of obscenity need not be alleged in the indictment in order to establish its sufficiency, the indictment in this case was sufficient to adequately inform petitioners of the charges against them.[12]

Petitioners also contend that in order for them to be convicted under 18 U.S.C. § 1461 for the crime of mailing obscene materials, the Government must prove that they knew the materials mailed were obscene. That statute provides in pertinent part that "[w]hoever knowingly uses the mails for the mailing . . . of anything declared by this section . . . to be nonmailable . . ." is guilty of the proscribed offense. Consistent with the statute, the District Court instructed the jury, *inter alia,* that in order to prove specific intent on the part of these petitioners, the Government had to demonstrate that petitioners "knew the envelopes and packages containing the subject materials were mailed or placed . . . in Interstate Commerce, and . . . that they had knowledge of the character of the materials." App. 236. The District Court further instructed that the "[petitioners'] belief as to the obscenity or non-obscenity of the material is irrelevant." *Ibid.*

Petitioners contend that this instruction was improper and that proof of scienter in obscenity prosecutions requires, "at the very least, proof both of knowledge of the contents of the material and awareness of the obscene character of the material." Brief for Petitioner Kemp 31–32. In support of this contention, petitioners urge, as they must, that we overrule our prior decision in *Rosen* v. *United States,* 161 U.S. 29 (1896). We decline that invitation, and hold that the District Court in this case properly instructed the jury on the question of scienter.

In *Rosen* v. *United States, supra,* this Court was faced with the question of whether, under a forerunner statute to the present 18 U.S.C. § 1461, see Rev. Stat. § 3893, 19 Stat. 90, c. 186, a charge of mailing obscene material must be supported by evidence that a defendant "knew or believed that such [material] could be properly or justly characterized as obscene . . . ." 161 U.S., at 41. The Court rejected this contention, stating:

> "The statute is not to be so interpreted. The inquiry under the statute is whether the paper charged to have been obscene, lewd, and lascivious was in fact of that character, and if it was of that character and was deposited in the mail by one who knew or had notice at the time of its contents, the offence is complete, although the defendant himself did not regard the paper as one that the statute forbade to be carried in the mails. Congress did not intend that the question as to

[12] Petitioners' further contention that our remand to the District Court in *United States* v. *Orito,* 413 U.S. 139 (1973), for reconsideration of the sufficiency of the indictment in light of *Miller* and *United States* v. *12 200-ft. Reels of Film,* indicates that the sufficiency of their indictment is in question misses the mark. In *Orito,* we reviewed a District Court judgment which had dismissed an indictment under 18 U.S.C. § 1462 and held the statute unconstitutional. In upholding the statute and vacating the judgment of the District Court, we remanded the case for reconsideration of the indictment in light of *Miller* and *12 200-ft. Reels,* which had, of course, enunciated new standards for state and federal obscenity prosecutions, and for reconsideration in light of our opinion reversing the District Court's holding that the statute was unconstitutional. Here of course, the District Court and the Court of Appeals have already upheld both the sufficiency of the indictment and the constitutionality of 18 U.S.C. § 1461, and we agree with their rulings.

the character of the paper should depend upon the opinion or belief of the person who, with knowledge or notice of its contents, assumed the responsibility of putting it in the mails of the United States. The evils that Congress sought to remedy would continue and increase in volume if the belief of the accused as to what was obscene, lewd, and lascivious was recognized as the test for determining whether the statute has been violated." *Id.,* at 41–42.

Our subsequent cases have not retreated from this general rule, either as a matter of statutory or constitutional interpretation, nor have they purported to hold that the prosecution must prove a defendant's knowledge of the legal status of the materials he distributes.

In *Smith* v. *California,* 361 U.S. 147 (1959), this Court was faced with a challenge to the constitutionality of a Los Angeles ordinance which had been construed by the state courts as making the proprietor of a bookstore absolutely liable criminally for the mere possession in his store of a book later judicially determined to be obscene, even though he had no knowledge of the contents of the book. The Court held that the ordinance could not constitutionally eliminate altogether a scienter requirement, and that, in order to be constitutionally applied to a book distributor, it must be shown that he had "knowledge of the contents of the book." *Id.,* at 153. The Court further noted that "[w]e need not and most definitely do not pass today on what sort of mental element is requisite to a constitutionally permissible prosecution of a bookseller for carrying an obscene book in stock." *Id.,* at 154.

Smith does not support petitioners' claim in this case, since it dealt with an ordinance which totally dispensed with any proof of scienter on the part of the distributor of obscene material. Nor did the Court's decision in *Manual Enterprises, Inc.* v. *Day, supra,* also relied upon by petitioners, suggest otherwise. There Mr. Justice Harlan's opinion, recognizing that scienter was required for a criminal prosecution under 18 U.S.C. §1461, rejected the Government's contention that such a requirement was unnecessary in an administrative determination by the Post Office Department that certain materials were nonmailable under that section. That opinion concluded that the obscene advertising proscription of the federal statute was not applicable in such an administrative determination unless the publisher of the materials knew that at least some of his advertisers were offering to sell obscene material. Such proof was deemed lacking and therefore the publishers could not be administratively prohibited from mailing the publications.[13]

Significantly, a substantially similar claim to the instant one was rejected by this Court in *Mishkin* v. *New York,* 383 U.S. 502 (1966). In examining a New York statute, the Court there noted that the New York Court of Appeals had "authoritatively interpreted" the statutory provision to

[13] MR. JUSTICE BRENNAN joined by MR. CHIEF JUSTICE WARREN and MR. JUSTICE DOUGLAS, concluded that 18 U.S.C. § 1461 does not authorize the Postmaster General to employ any administrative process of his own to close the mails to matter which, in his view, falls within the ban of that section. *Manual Enterprises, Inc.* v. *Day,* 370 U.S. 478, 495–519 (1962) (separate opinion).

require the "vital element of scienter" and that it had defined the required mental element as follows:

> " 'A reading of the [New York] statute . . . as a whole clearly indicates that only those who are in some manner aware of the *character* of the material they attempt to distribute should be punished. It is not innocent but *calculated purveyance* of filth which is exorcised...' " *Id.*, at 510 (emphasis in original), quoting from *People* v. *Finkelstein*, 9 N.Y. 2d 342, 344–345, 174 N.E. 2d 470, 471 (1961).

The Court emphasized that this construction of the New York statute "foreclosed" the defendant's challenge to the statute based on *Smith* v. *California, supra,* and stated:

> "The Constitution requires proof of scienter to avoid the hazard of self-censorship of constitutionally protected material and to compensate for the ambiguities inherent in the definition of obscenity. The New York definition of the scienter required by [the New York statute] amply serves those ends, and therefore fully meets the demands of the Constitution. Cf. *Roth* v. *United States,* 354 U.S., at 495–496 (WARREN, C. J., concurring)." 383 U.S., at 511.

The *Mishkin* holding was reaffirmed in *Ginsberg* v. *New York,* 390 U.S. 629 (1968). There the Court was again faced with the sufficiency of the scienter requirement of another New York statute, which proscribed the "knowing" distribution of obscene materials to minors. "Knowingly" was defined in the statute as "knowledge" of, or "reason to know" of the character and content of the material. Citing *Mishkin,* and the New York Court of Appeals' construction of the other similar statutory language, the Court rejected the challenge to the scienter provision.

We think the "knowingly" language of 18 U.S.C. § 1461, and the instructions given by the District Court in this case satisfied the constitutional requirements of scienter. It is constitutionally sufficient that the prosecution show that a defendant had knowledge of the contents of the materials he distributed, and that he knew the character and nature of the materials. To require proof of a defendant's knowledge of the legal status of the materials would permit the defendant to avoid prosecution by simply claiming that he had not brushed up on the law. Such a formulation of the scienter requirement is required neither by the language of 18 U.S.C. § 1461 nor by the Constitution.

> "Whenever the law draws a line there will be cases very near each other on opposite sides. The precise course of the line may be uncertain, but no one can come near it without knowing that he does so, if he thinks, and if he does so it is familiar to the criminal law to make him take the risk." *United States* v. *Wurzbach,* 280 U.S. 396, 399 (1930).

Petitioners also make a broad attack on the sufficiency of the evidence. The general rule of application is that "[t]he verdict of a jury must be sustained if there is substantial evidence, taking the view most favorable to the Government, to support it." *Glasser* v. *United States,* 315 U.S. 60, 80 (1942). The primary responsibility for reviewing the sufficiency of the evidence to support a criminal conviction rests with the Court of Appeals, which in this case held that the Government had satisfied its burden. We agree. Based on the evidence before it, the jury was entitled to conclude that the individual petitioners, as corporate officials directly concerned with the activities of their organizations, were aware of the mail solicitation scheme, and of the contents of the brochure. The evidence is likewise sufficient to establish the existence of a conspiracy to mail the obscene brochure. The existence of an agreement may be shown by circumstances indicating that criminal defendants acted in concert to achieve a common goal. See, *e.g., Blumenthal* v. *United States,* 332 U.S. 539, 556–558 (1947).

III

We turn now to petitioners' attack on certain evidentiary rulings of the District Court. Petitioners have very much the laboring oar in showing that such rulings constitute reversible error, since "in judicial trials, the whole tendency is to leave rulings as to the illuminating relevance of testimony largely to the discretion of the trial court that hears the evidence." *NLRB* v. *Donnelly Co.,* 330 U.S. 219, 236 (1947); *Michelson* v. *United States,* 335 U.S. 469, 480 (1948); *Salem* v. *United States Lines Co.,* 370 U.S. 31, 35 (1962).

Petitioners offered in evidence at trial three categories of allegedly comparable materials argued to be relevant to community standards: (1) materials which had received second-class mailing privileges; (2) materials which had previously been the subject of litigation and had been found to be "constitutionally protected"; and (3) materials openly available on the newsstands. The District Court, after examining the materials, refused to admit them into evidence on the grounds that "they tend to confuse the jury" and "would serve no probative value in comparison to the amount of confusion and deluge of material that could result therefrom." App. 158. The Court of Appeals concluded that the District Court was correct in rejecting the proffered evidence, stating that any abuse of discretion in refusing to admit the materials themselves had been "cured by the District Court's offer to entertain expert testimony with respect to the elements to be shown for the advice of the jury." 481 F. 2d, at 320. Here the District Court permitted four expert witnesses called by petitioners to testify extensively concerning the relevant community standards.

The defendant in an obscenity prosecution, just as a defendant in any other prosecution, is entitled to an opportunity to adduce relevant, competent evidence bearing on the issues to be tried. But the availability of similar materials on the newsstands of the community does not automatically make them admissible as tending to prove the nonobscenity of the materials which the defendant is charged with circulating. As stated by the Court of Appeals, the mere fact that materials similar to the brochure at issue here "are for sale and purchased at book stores around the country does not make them witnesses of virtue." *Ibid.* Or, as put by the Court of Appeals in *United States* v. *Manarite,* 448 F. 2d 583 (CA2 1971):

> "Mere availability of similar material by itself means nothing more than that other persons are engaged in similar activities." *Id.,* at 593.

Nor do we think the District Court erred in refusing petitioners' offer of a magazine which had received a second-class mailing privilege.[14] While federal law, see former 39 U.S.C. § 4354 (1964 ed.); 39 CFR Pt. 132 (1973), may lay down certain standards for the issuance of a second-class mailing permit, this Court has held that these standards give postal inspectors no power of censorship. *Hannegan* v. *Esquire, Inc.,* 327 U.S. 146 (1946). The mere fact that a publication has acquired a second-class mailing privilege does not therefore create any presumption that it is not obscene.

Finally, we do not think the District Court abused its discretion in refusing to admit certain allegedly comparable materials, a film and two magazines,[15] which had been found to be nonobscene by this Court. See *Pinkus* v. *Pitchess,* 429 F. 2d 416 (CA9), aff'd *sub nom. California* v. *Pinkus,* 400 U.S. 922 (1970); *Burgin* v. *South Carolina,* 404 U.S. 806 (1971), rev'g 255 S.C. 237, 178 S.E. 2d 325 (1970). A judicial determination that particular matters are not obscene does not necessarily make them relevant to the determination of the obscenity of other materials, much less mandate their admission into evidence.

Much of the material offered by petitioners was not of demonstrated relevance to the issues in this case. Such of it that may have been clearly relevant was subject to the District Court's observation that it would tend to create more confusion than enlightenment in the minds of the jury, and to the court's expressed willingness to permit the same material to be treated in the testimony of expert witnesses. The District Court retains considerable latitude even with admittedly relevant evidence in rejecting that which is cumulative, and in requiring that which is to be brought to the jury's attention to be done so in a manner least likely to confuse that body. We agree with the Court of Appeals that the District Court's discretion was not abused.[16]

Petitioners' second contention is that the District Court erred in instructing the jury as to the determination of the prurient appeal of the brochure. At the trial, the Government introduced, over petitioners' objection, testimony from an expert witness that the material in the Illustrated Report appealed to the prurient interest of various deviant sexual groups.[17]

---

[14] The magazine offered was entitled Nude Living, No. 63. The foundation alleged for its admissibility was that it had received a second-class mailing privilege. App. 212–213.

[15] Brief for Petitioner Kemp 69.

[16] Other proffered materials, alleged to be comparable, included numerous magazines and films, and also the survey (see n. 10, *supra*) conducted by the student at San Diego State University of the reactions of people in the San Diego area to the Illustrated Report and the brochure. Brief for Petitioner Kemp 64–71.

[17] Petitioners also contend that this evidence was at variance with the Government's answer to their Bill of Particulars. Brief for Petitioner Hamling 49–50. The Court of Appeals assumed, without deciding, that such evidence did constitute a var-

The testimony concerning the brochure was that it appealed to a prurient interest in general, and not specifically to some deviant group. Petitioners concede, however, that each of the pictures said to appeal to deviant groups did in fact appear in the brochure.[18] The District Court accordingly instructed the jury that in deciding whether the predominant appeal of the Illustrated Report and the brochure was to a prurient interest in sex, it could consider whether some portions of those materials appealed to a prurient interest of a specifically defined deviant group as well as whether they appealed to the prurient interest of the average person. App. 239–241. The Court of Appeals found no error in the instruction, since it was "manifest that the District Court considered that some of the portrayals in the Brochure might be found to have a prurient appeal" to a deviant group. 481 F. 2d, at 321.

Petitioners contend that the District Court's instruction was improper because it allowed the jury to measure the brochure by its appeal to the prurient interest not only of the average person but also of a clearly defined deviant group. Our decision in *Mishkin* v. *New York,* 383 U.S. 502 (1966), clearly indicates that in measuring the prurient appeal of allegedly obscene materials, *i.e.,* whether the "dominant theme of the material taken as a whole appeals to a prurient interest in sex," consideration may be given to the prurient appeal of the material to clearly defined deviant sexual groups. Petitioners appear to argue that if some of the material appeals to the prurient interest of sexual deviants while other parts appeal to the prurient interest of the average person, a general finding that the material appeals to a prurient interest in sex is somehow precluded. But we stated in *Mishkin* v. *New York:*

> "Where the material is designed for and primarily disseminated to a clearly defined deviant sexual group, rather than the public at large, the prurient-appeal requirement of the *Roth* test is satisfied if the dominant theme of the material taken as a whole appeals to the prurient interest in sex of the members of that group. The reference to the 'average' or 'normal' person in *Roth,* 354 U.S., at 489–490, does not foreclose this holding. . . . We adjust the prurient-appeal requirement to social realities by permitting the appeal of this type of material to be assessed in terms of the sexual interests of its intended and probable recipient group; and since our holding requires that the recipient group be defined with more specificity than in terms of sexually immature persons, it also avoids the inadequacy of the most-susceptible-person facet of the [*Regina* v.] *Hicklin* [[1868] L. R. 3 Q. B. 360] test." 383 U.S., at 508–509 (footnotes omitted).

The District Court's instruction was consistent with this statement in *Mishkin.* The jury was instructed that it must find that the materials as a whole appealed generally to a prurient interest in sex. In making that determination, the jury was properly instructed that it should measure the

iance, but concluded that "such variance was in no wise a surprise or prejudice to the defendants as their own expert opinion testimony interwove and covered the same field completely." 481 F. 2d, at 322. We agree with the Court of Appeals.

[18] Brief for Petitioner Hamling 49–50.

prurient appeal of the materials as to all groups. Such an instruction was also consistent with our recent decision in the *Miller* cases. We stated in *Miller:*

> "As the Court made clear in *Mishkin* v. *New York,* 383 U.S., at 508–509, the primary concern with requiring a jury to apply the standard of 'the average person, applying contemporary community standards' is to be certain that, *so far as material is not aimed at a deviant group,* it will be judged by its impact on an average person, rather than a particularly susceptible or sensitive person—or indeed a totally insensitive one." 413 U.S., at 33 (emphasis added).

Finally, we similarly think petitioners' challenge to the pandering instruction given by the District Court is without merit. The District Court instructed the jurors that they must apply the three-part test of the plurality opinion in *Memoirs* v. *Massachusetts,* 383 U.S., at 418, and then indicated that the jury could, in applying that test, if it found the case to be close, also consider whether the materials had been pandered, by looking to their "[m]anner of distribution, circumstances of production, sale, . . . advertising . . . . [and] editorial intent . . . ." App. 245. This instruction was given with respect to both the Illustrated Report and the brochure which advertised it, both of which were at issue in the trial.

Petitioners contend that the instruction was improper on the facts adduced below and that it caused them to be "convicted" of pandering. Pandering was not charged in the indictment of the petitioners, but it is not, of course, an element of the offense of mailing obscene matter under 18 U.S.C. § 1461. The District Court's instruction was clearly consistent with our decision in *Ginzburg* v. *United States,* 383 U.S. 463 (1966), which held that evidence of pandering could be relevant in the determination of the obscenity of the materials at issue, as long as the proper constitutional definition of obscenity is applied. Nor does the enactment by Congress of 39 U.S.C. § 3008, enabling the Postal Service to cease forwarding pandering advertisements at the request of an addressee, authorize, as contended by petitioners, the pandering of obscene advertisements. That statute simply gives a postal recipient the means to insulate himself from advertisements which offer for sale matter "which the addressee in his sole discretion believes to be erotically arousing or sexually provocative," by instructing the Post Office to order the sender to refrain from mailing any further advertisements to him. See *Rowan* v. *U.S. Post Office Dept.,* 397 U.S. 728 (1970). The statute does not purport to authorize the mailing of legally obscene pandering advertisements, which continues to be proscribed by 18 U.S.C. § 1461. See 39 U.S.C. § 3011 (e).

IV

Petitioners' final contentions are directed at alleged procedural irregularities said to have occurred during the course of the trial.

They first contend that the District Court committed reversible error by denying their request to make additional objections to the court's instructions to the jury out of the presence of the jury. Prior to closing arguments and instructions to the jury the parties had made a record with respect to the instructions which the Court indicated it would give. After argument and instructions, but before the jury had retired, petitioners' counsel approached the bench and requested that the jury be excused in order that he might present further objections to the charge. The court declined to excuse the jury, saying:

> "You have made all the objections suitable that I can think of. I want to send this Jury out. If you want to make a statement, make a statement." App. 257.

Petitioners contend that the court's refusal to excuse the jury violated the provisions of Fed. Rule Crim. Proc. 30, and requires reversal. Rule 30 provides:

> "At the close of the evidence or at such earlier time during the trial as the court reasonably directs, any party may file written requests that the court instruct the jury on the law as set forth in the requests. At the same time copies of such requests shall be furnished to adverse parties. The court shall inform counsel of its proposed action upon the requests prior to their arguments to the jury, but the court shall instruct the jury after the arguments are completed. No party may assign as error any portion of the charge or omission therefrom unless he objects thereto before the jury retires to consider its verdict, stating distinctly the matter to which he objects and the grounds of his objection. *Opportunity shall be given to make the objection out of the hearing of the jury and, on request of any party, out of the presence of the jury.*" (Emphasis added.)

Nothing in Rule 30 transfers from the district court to counsel the function of deciding at what point in the trial, consistent with established practice, counsel shall be given the opportunity required by Rule 30 to make a record on the instructions given by the court. But when counsel at the close of the court's instruction to the jury indicates that he wishes to make objections of a kind which could not previously have been brought to the court's attention, he runs the risk of waiving a claim of error under the fourth sentence of the Rule unless the court indicates that it will permit such objections to be made after the jury retires. Since the court here asked counsel for comments, and did not indicate that it would permit objections which could not have been previously formulated to be made after the jury retired, we agree with the Court of Appeals that the District Court erred in refusing to permit such objections to be made out of the presence of the jury. We also agree with the Court of Appeals' conclusion that such procedural error does not mandate reversal.

The courts of appeals have taken varying approaches to the question of when a failure to comply with the provisions of Rule 30 constitutes reversible error.[19] Some appear to have applied a general rule that such a violation is not reversible error unless the defendant demonstrates that he has been prejudiced. *United States* v. *Hall,* 200 F. 2d 957 (CA2 1953); *United States* v. *Titus,* 221 F. 2d 571 (CA2), cert. denied, 350 U.S. 832 (1955); *United States* v. *Fernandez,* 456 F. 2d 638 (CA2 1972); *Hodges* v. *United States,* 243 F. 2d 281 (CA5 1957); *Sultan* v. *United States,* 249 F. 2d 385 (CA5 1957). Others appear to have adopted a rule whereby a violation is not reversible error where it affirmatively appears that the defendant was not prejudiced. *United States* v. *Schartner,* 426 F. 2d 470 (CA3 1970); *Lovely* v. *United States,* 169 F. 2d 386 (CA4 1948). At least one Court of Appeals appears to take the position that the failure to comply with Rule 30 is automatic grounds for reversal, regardless of attenuating circumstances. *Hall* v. *United States,* 378 F. 2d 349 (CA10 1967).

The Court of Appeals in this case felt that the rule announced by the Third Circuit in *United States* v. *Schartner, supra,* was the appropriate one for application where Rule 30 has not been complied with. The court in *Schartner* held that a District Court's failure to comply with the "out of the presence of the jury" requirement of Rule 30, upon proper request by a party, constitutes reversible error "unless it be demonstrable on an examination of the whole record that the denial of the right did not prejudice" the defendant's case. 426 F. 2d, at 480. Applying that rule, the Court of Appeals here concluded that there was no prejudice to any of the petitioners as a result of the District Court's failure to comply with Rule 30.

The language in Rule 30 at issue here was added to that rule by a 1966 amendment; prior to that time the rule had only provided that a party should be given the opportunity to make the objection out of the *hearing* of the jury. The significance of the change was not elaborated by the Advisory Committee in its note accompanying the rule, which merely mentioned the change. Courts examining the rule have found that it is principally designed to avoid the subtle psychological pressures upon the jurors which would arise if they were to view and hear defense counsel in a posture of apparent antagonism toward the judge. *Lovely* v. *United States, supra,* at 391; *Hodges* v. *United States, supra,* at 283–284; *United*

---

[19] Federal Rule Civ. Proc. 51 states that "[o]pportunity shall be given to make the objection out of the hearing of the jury." Though the "out-of-the-presence-of-the-jury" language is not contained in that rule, the Advisory Committee's note attending Fed. Rule Crim. Proc. 30 states that it is to "correspond to Rule 51 of the Federal Rules of Civil Procedure . . . . It seemed appropriate that on a point such as instructions to juries there should be no difference in procedure between civil and criminal cases." The Government argues that in considering whether failure to comply with Fed. Rule Crim. Proc. 30 requires reversal, the appropriate test should be similar to the general standard of consideration where there is a failure to comply with Fed. Rule Civ. Proc. 51, *i.e.,* reversal is required "if there is reasonable basis for concluding that the colloquy had in the presence of the jury as a result of the judge's ignoring or denying a proper request was prejudicial." *Swain* v. *Boeing Airplane Co.,* 337 F. 2d 940, 943 (CA2 1964), cert. denied, 380 U.S. 951 (1965). This approach was used by a panel of the Court of Appeals for the Second Circuit in a case involving failure to comply with Fed. Rule Crim. Proc. 30. *United States* v. *Fernandez,* 456 F. 2d 638 (1972).

States v. *Schartner, supra,* at 479. While that goal might be served in many cases by a sufficiently low-tone bench conference, the ultimate way to assure the goal is to comply with the rule.

Petitioners urge that we adopt a strict approach and declare that any noncompliance with the rule requires reversal. We think such an approach would be unduly mechanical, and would be inconsistent with interpretation *in pari materia* of Rule 30 and other relevant provisions of the Federal Rules of Criminal Procedure, since Rule 52(a) specifically provides that "[a]ny error, defect, irregularity or variance which does not affect substantial rights shall be disregarded." This provision suggests the soundness of an approach similar to that of the Court of Appeals here and the various other Courts of Appeals, *supra,* which have in some manner examined the prejudice to the defendant in deciding whether reversal is required where there is a failure to comply with Rule 30.

We conclude that the Court of Appeals did not err in refusing to reverse petitioners' convictions for the failure to comply with the provisions of Rule 30. The Court of Appeals felt that it should apply the somewhat stricter test of the *Schartner* case, *supra;* the court felt that "the rule of *Fernandez,* [456 F. 2d 638, CA2,] places a burden upon a defendant in a criminal case that he may not be able to carry." 481 F. 2d, at 324. Applying the *Schartner* test, the Court of Appeals determined that there was no prejudice to petitioners from the failure to hold the instruction-objection session out of the presence of the jury. Our independent examination of that bench conference convinces us that the holding of the Court of Appeals was correct. The bench conference was one of many at the trial and there is no indication in the record that the discussion was heard by the jury. The colloquy between petitioners' counsel and the court concerned purely legal issues, App. 257–265, and the District Court had prior to that point indicated its rulings with respect to the instructions requested by counsel. We express no view, of course, as to whether a court of appeals may follow the apparently more lenient standard of requiring the defendant to demonstrate that he was prejudiced. See *United States* v. *Fernandez,* 456 F. 2d, at 643–644.

Petitioners' second procedural contention is that the trial jury was improperly constituted because an allegedly cognizable class of citizens, "young adults," which petitioners define as those between the ages of 18 and 24 years, were systematically excluded.[20] Petitioners therefore argue that the District Court abused its discretion in refusing to grant a continuance until a new jury, which would have presumably contained a greater ratio of young persons, was drawn.

At the time of petitioners' indictment and trial, the jury-selection plan of the Southern District of California, adopted pursuant to 28 U.S.C. §§ 1863(b)(2), 1863(b)(4), 82 Stat. 55, provided for the periodic emptying and refilling of the master jury wheel from voter registration lists. At that point, it had been slightly less than four years since the jury

---

[20] In connection with their motion to strike the venire, petitioners introduced evidence which they contended established that "young persons were a cognizable group and that they were more tolerant than older persons in matters pertaining to the depiction of sexually explicit material." Brief for Petitioner Hamling 88.

wheel in the District had last been filled. Petitioners' argument is that because the jury wheel had last been filled in 1968, the youngest potential juror for their trial was at least 24 years old. The petitioner called as a witness the Clerk of the Southern District of California, who testified that within one month the master wheel would be refilled with the persons who then appeared on the voters' registration list and that the master list would then contain the names of persons 21 years of age and over. Tr. 94–98. A 1972 amendment to 28 U.S.C. § 1863 (b)(4) (1970 ed., Supp. II) provided that the periodic emptying and refilling of the master wheel should occur at specified intervals, "not [to] exceed four years." Pub.L.No. 92–269, § 2, 86 Stat. 117. The District Court denied petitioners' motion to strike the venire, but stated that the evidence presented indicated that "it is time to change the jury master wheel." Tr. 93. The petitioners then moved for a continuance of approximately one month, so that their jury would be drawn from a master wheel that included persons 21 years of age or over. Tr. 95–98. The District Court denied the motion.

The Court of Appeals assumed, without deciding, that the young do constitute a cognizable group or class, but concluded that petitioners had "failed to show, let alone establish, a purposeful systematic exclusion of the members of that class whose names, but for such systematic exclusion would otherwise be selected for the master jury wheel," and therefore that the District Court's refusal to grant a continuance was not an abuse of discretion. 481 F. 2d, at 314. We agree with the Court of Appeals.

Petitioners do not cite case authority for the proposition that the young are an identifiable group entitled to a group-based protection under our prior cases, see *Hernandez* v. *Texas,* 347 U.S. 475, 479–480 (1954); claims of exclusion of the young from juries have met with little success in the federal courts.[21] Assuming, as did the Court of Appeals, that the young are such a group, we do not believe that there is evidence in this case sufficient to make out a prima facie case of discrimination which would in turn place the burden on the Government to overcome it. The master wheel under the Southern District of California plan, as under plans in other judicial districts, is periodically emptied and then refilled with names from the available voter lists. Persons added to the voter lists subsequent to one filling of the jury wheel are therefore not added to the wheel until the next refilling. But some play in the joints of the jury-selection process is necessary in order to accommodate the practical problems of judicial administration. Congress could reasonably adopt procedures which, while designed to assure that "an impartial jury [is] drawn from a cross-section of the community," *Thiel* v. *Southern Pacific Co.,* 328 U.S. 217, 220 (1946); *Smith* v. *Texas,* 311 U.S. 128, 130 (1940), at the same time take into account practical problems in judicial administration. Unless we were to require the daily refilling of the jury wheel, Congress may necessarily conclude that some periodic delay in updating the wheel is

---

[21] See, *e.g., United States* v. *Butera,* 420 F. 2d 564 (CA1 1970); *United States* v. *Camara,* 451 F. 2d 1122 (CA1 1971); *United States* v. *Gooding,* 473 F. 2d 425 (CA5 1973); *United States* v. *Kuhn,* 441 F. 2d 179 (CA5 1971); *United States* v. *Gast,* 457 F. 2d 141 (CA7), cert. denied, 406 U.S. 969 (1972).

reasonable to permit the orderly administration of justice.[22] Invariably of course, as time goes on, the jury wheel will be more and more out of date, especially near the end of the statutorily prescribed time period for updating the wheel. But if the jury wheel is not discriminatory when completely updated at the time of each refilling, a prohibited "purposeful discrimination" does not arise near the end of the period simply because the young and other persons have belatedly become eligible for jury service by becoming registered voters. *Whitus* v. *Georgia,* 385 U.S. 545, 551 (1967); see *Avery* v. *Georgia,* 345 U.S. 559 (1953); *Alexander* v. *Louisiana,* 405 U.S. 625 (1972). Since petitioners failed to establish a discriminatory exclusion of the young from their jury, the District Court properly exercised its discretion in refusing to grant petitioners' motion for a continuance.

Petitioners' third procedural contention is that the District Court erred in refusing to ask certain questions on *voir dire* concerning possible religious and other biases of the jurors.[23] Specifically, petitioners requested the court to ask questions as to whether the jurors' educational, political, and religious beliefs might affect their views on the question of obscenity. App. 78–81. The Court of Appeals concluded that the District Court's examination on the *voir dire* of the prospective jurors "was full, complete and . . . fair to the [petitioners] as contemplated by Rule 24 (a), Federal Rules of Criminal Procedure," 481 F. 2d, at 314. Noting that petitioners had requested the submission of numerous questions to the petit panel, the Court of Appeals stated:

> "The District Court asked many of the questions as submitted, many in altered and consolidated form, and declined to ask many others which were cumulative and argumentative. The handling of those questions not asked was clearly within the range of the District Court's discretion in the matter and no clear abuse of the discretion nor prejudice to the [petitioners] has been shown." *Ibid.*

We agree with the Court of Appeals. Federal Rules Crim. Proc. 24 (a) permits a district court to conduct the *voir dire* examination, making such use of questions submitted by the parties as it deems proper. The District Court here asked questions similar to many of those submitted by petitioners, and its examination was clearly sufficient to test the qualifications and

---

[22] Various delays in refilling jury wheels have been upheld by the federal courts. *E.g., United States* v. *Pentado,* 463 F. 2d 355 (CA5 1972) (three years); *United States* v. *Gooding, supra* (three years, four months); *United States* v. *Kuhn, supra* (five years).

[23] Petitioners also contend that certain actions of the Government's attorney before the grand jury prejudiced that body against them. The Court of Appeals, in rejecting this contention, stated:

"The record before us is totally lacking of any evidence or showing of any kind that any member of the Grand Jury was biased or prejudiced in any degree against any of the [petitioners], except only a supposition as to how the members may have reacted upon a view of the Brochure and Report. The presumption of regularity which attaches to Grand Jury proceedings still abides. . . . [T]he assignment has no merit." 481 F. 2d, at 313 (citations omitted).

We agree with the Court of Appeals.

competency of the prospective jurors. Petitioners' reliance on this Court's decisions in *Aldridge* v. *United States,* 283 U.S. 308 (1931), and *Ham* v. *South Carolina,* 409 U.S. 524 (1973), is misplaced. Those cases held that in certain situations a judge must inquire into possible racial prejudices of the jurors in order to satisfy the demands of due process. But in *Ham* v. *South Carolina, supra,* we also rejected a claim that the trial judge had erred in refusing to ask the jurors about potential bias against beards, noting our inability "to constitutionally distinguish possible prejudice against beards from a host of other possible similar prejudices . . . ." *Id.,* at 528. Here, as in *Ham,* the trial judge made a general inquiry into the jurors' general views concerning obscenity. Failure to ask specific questions as to the possible effect of educational, political, and religious biases did "not reach the level of a constitutional violation," *ibid.,* nor was it error requiring the exercise of our supervisory authority over the administration of justice in the federal courts. We hold that the District Court acted within its discretion in refusing to ask the questions.

The judgment of the Court of Appeals for the Ninth Circuit in this case is

Affirmed.

[Opinions of Douglas, J., Brennan, J., Stewart, J., and Marshall, J., are omitted.]

Jenkins v. *Georgia*
418 U.S. 153 (1974)

MR. JUSTICE REHNQUIST delivered the opinion of the Court.

Appellant was convicted in Georgia of the crime of distributing obscene material. His conviction, in March 1972, was for showing the film "Carnal Knowledge" in a movie theater in Albany, Georgia. The jury that found appellant guilty was instructed on obscenity pursuant to the Georgia statute, which defines obscene material in language similar to that of the definition of obscenity set forth in this Court's plurality opinion in *Memoirs* v. *Massachusetts,* 383 U.S. 413, 418 (1966):

> "Material is obscene if considered as a whole, applying community standards, its predominant appeal is to prurient interest, that is, a shameful or morbid interest in nudity, sex or excretion, and utterly without redeeming social value and if, in addition, it goes substantially beyond customary limits of candor in describing or representing such matters." Ga. Code Ann. § 26–2101 (b) (1972).[1]

---

[1] Section 26–2101 is entitled "Distributing obscene materials." Subsection (a) of § 26–2101 provides in relevant part: "A person commits the offense of distributing obscene materials when he . . . exhibits or otherwise disseminates to any person any obscene material of any description, knowing the obscene nature thereof . . . ."

We hold today in *Hamling* v. *United States, ante,* p. 87, that defendants convicted prior to the announcement of our *Miller* decisions but whose convictions were on direct appeal at that time should receive any benefit available to them from those decisions. We conclude here that the film "Carnal Knowledge" is not obscene under the constitutional standards announced in *Miller* v. *California,* 413 U.S. 15 (1973), and that the First and Fourteenth Amendments therefore require that the judgment of the Supreme Court of Georgia affirming appellant's conviction be reversed.

Appellant was the manager of the theater in which "Carnal Knowledge" was being shown. While he was exhibiting the film on January 13, 1972, local law enforcement officers seized it pursuant to a search warrant. Appellant was later charged by accusation, Ga. Code Ann. § 27–704 (1972), with the offense of distributing obscene material.[2] After his trial in the Superior Court of Dougherty County, the jury, having seen the film and heard testimony, returned a general verdict of guilty on March 23, 1972.[3] Appellant was fined $750 and sentenced to 12 months' probation. He appealed to the Supreme Court of Georgia, which by a divided vote affirmed the judgment of conviction on July 2, 1973. That court stated that the definition of obscenity contained in the Georgia statute was "considerably more restrictive" than the new test set forth in the recent case of *Miller* v. *California, supra,* and that the First Amendment does not protect the commercial exhibition of "hard core" pornography. The dissenting Justices, in addition to other disagreements with the court, thought that "Carnal Knowledge" was entitled to the protection of the First and Fourteenth Amendments. Appellant then appealed to this Court and we noted probable jurisdiction, 414 U.S. 1090 (1973).

We agree with the Supreme Court of Georgia's implicit ruling that the Constitution does not require that juries be instructed in state obscenity

---

Subsection (c) of § 26–2101 provides that "[material], not otherwise obscene, may be obscene under this section if the distribution thereof . . . is a commercial exploitation of erotica solely for the sake of their prurient appeal." Subsection (d) provides that a first offense under the section shall be punished as a misdemeanor and that any subsequent offense shall be punished by one to five years' imprisonment and/or a fine not to exceed $5,000.

[2] The accusation, App. 8, charged appellant "with the offense of Distributing Obscene Material" for knowingly exhibiting a motion picture to the general public which contained conduct showing "(a) an act of sexual intercourse, (b) a lewd exposure of the sexual organs, (c) a lewd appearance in a state of partial or complete nudity, (d) a lewd caress or indecent fondling of another person" contrary to the laws of Georgia. The latter-quoted language appears in Ga. Code Ann. § 26–2011, entitled "Public indecency," which makes performance of any of the listed acts in a public place a misdemeanor. Under Ga. Code Ann. § 26–2105, it is a crime to exhibit a motion picture portraying acts which would constitute "public indecency" under § 26–2011 if performed in a public place. Appellant's arrest warrant specified § 26–2105 as the statute he was charged with violating. In view of our holding today, we need not reach appellant's contention that he was denied due process because the warrant specified only § 26–2105, while the jury was allowed to convict under § 26–2101. However, we note that appellant's demurrer to the accusation demonstrates his awareness that he was being charged with the § 26–2101 offense, App. 9, and that he requested numerous instructions on obscenity, *id.,* at 47–49.

[3] Appellant's trial jury was alternatively instructed under subsections (a) and (c) of § 26–2101 (pandering), see n. 1, *supra,* and under § 26–2105, see n. 2, *supra.*

cases to apply the standards of a hypothetical statewide community. *Miller* approved the use of such instructions; it did not mandate their use. What *Miller* makes clear is that state juries need not be instructed to apply "national standards." We also agree with the Supreme Court of Georgia's implicit approval of the trial court's instructions directing jurors to apply "community standards" without specifying what "community." *Miller* held that it was constitutionally permissible to permit juries to rely on the understanding of the community from which they came as to contemporary community standards, and the States have considerable latitude in framing statutes under this element of the *Miller* decision. A state may choose to define an obscenity offense in terms of "contemporary community standards" as defined in *Miller* without further specification, as was done here, or it may choose to define the standards in more precise geographic terms, as was done by California in *Miller*.

We now turn to the question of whether appellant's exhibition of the film was protected by the First and Fourteenth Amendments, a question which appellee asserts is not properly before us because appellant did not raise it on his state appeal. But whether or not appellant argued this constitutional issue below, it is clear that the Supreme Court of Georgia reached and decided it. That is sufficient under our practice. *Raley* v. *Ohio,* 360 U.S. 423, 436 (1959). We also note that the trial court instructed the jury on charges other than the distribution charge.[4] However, the jury returned a general verdict and appellee does not suggest that appellant's conviction can be sustained on these alternative grounds. Cf. *Stromberg* v. *California,* 283 U.S. 359, 367–368 (1931).

There is little to be found in the record about the film "Carnal Knowledge" other than the film itself.[5] However, appellant has supplied a variety of information and critical commentary, the authenticity of which appellee does not dispute. The film appeared on many "Ten Best" lists for 1971, the year in which it was released. Many but not all of the reviews were favorable. We believe that the following passage from a review which appeared in the Saturday Review is a reasonably accurate description of the film:

> "[It is basically a story] of two young college men, roommates and lifelong friends forever preoccupied with their sex lives. Both are first met as virgins. Nicholson is the more knowledgeable and attractive of the two; speaking colloquially, he is a burgeoning bastard. Art Garfunkel is his friend, the nice but troubled guy straight out of those early Feiffer cartoons, but *real*. He falls in love with the lovely Susan (Candice Bergen) and unknowingly shares her with his college buddy. As the 'safer' one of the two, he is selected by Susan for marriage.
>
> "The time changes. Both men are in their thirties, pursuing suc-

---

[4] See n. 3, *supra*.

[5] Appellant testified that the film was "critically acclaimed as one of the ten best pictures of 1971 and Ann Margret has received an Academy Award nomination for her performance in the picture." He further testified that "Carnal Knowledge" had played in 29 towns in Georgia and that it was booked in 50 or 60 more theaters for spring and summer showing. App. 24.

cessful careers in New York. Nicholson has been running through an average of a dozen women a year but has never managed to meet the right one, the one with the full bosom, the good legs, the properly rounded bottom. More than that, each and every one is a threat to his malehood and peace of mind, until at last, in a bar, he finds Ann-Margret, an aging bachelor girl with striking cleavage and, quite obviously, something of a past. 'Why don't we shack up?' she suggests. They do and a horrendous relationship ensues, complicated mainly by her paranoidal desire to marry. Meanwhile, what of Garfunkel? The sparks have gone out of his marriage, the sex has lost its savor, and Garfunkel tries once more. And later, even more foolishly, again." [6]

Appellee contends essentially that under *Miller* the obscenity *vel non* of the film "Carnal Knowledge" was a question for the jury, and that the jury having resolved the question against appellant, and there being some evidence to support its findings, the judgment of conviction should be affirmed. We turn to the language of *Miller* to evaluate appellee's contention.

Miller states that the questions of what appeals to the "prurient interest" and what is "patently offensive" under the obscenity test which it formulates are "essentially questions of fact." 413 U.S., at 30. "When triers of fact are asked to decide whether 'the average person, applying contemporary community standards' would consider certain materials 'prurient' it would be unrealistic to require that the answer be based on some abstract formulation. . . . To require a State to structure obscenity proceedings around evidence of a *national* 'community standard' would be an exercise in futility." *Ibid.* We held in *Paris Adult Theatre I* v. *Slaton,* 413 U.S. 49 (1973), decided on the same day, that expert testimony as to obscenity is not necessary when the films at issue are themselves placed in evidence. *Id.,* at 56.

But all of this does not lead us to agree with the Supreme Court of Georgia's apparent conclusion that the jury's verdict against appellant virtually precluded all further appellate review of appellant's assertion that his exhibition of the film was protected by the First and Fourteenth Amendments. Even though questions of appeal to the "prurient interest" or of patent offensiveness are "essentially questions of fact," it would be a serious misreading of *Miller* to conclude that juries have unbridled discretion in determining what is "patently offensive." Not only did we there say that "the First Amendment values applicable to the States through the Fourteenth Amendment are adequately protected by the ultimate power of appellate courts to conduct an independent review of constitutional claims when necessary," 413 U.S., at 25, but we made it plain that under that holding "no one will be subject to prosecution for the sale or exposure of obscene materials unless these materials depict or describe patently offensive 'hard core' sexual conduct. . . ." *Id.,* at 27.

We also took pains in *Miller* to "give a few plain examples of what a

---

[6] Review of "Carnal Knowledge" by Hollis Alpert, Saturday Review, July 3, 1971, p. 18.

state statute could define for regulation under part (b) of the standard announced," that is, the requirement of patent offensiveness. *Id.,* at 25. These examples included "representations or descriptions of ultimate sexual acts, normal or perverted, actual or simulated," and "representations or descriptions of masturbation, excretory functions, and lewd exhibition of the genitals." *Ibid.* While this did not purport to be an exhaustive catalog of what juries might find patently offensive, it was certainly intended to fix substantive constitutional limitations, deriving from the First Amendment, on the type of material subject to such a determination. It would be wholly at odds with this aspect of *Miller* to uphold an obscenity conviction based upon a defendant's depiction of a woman with a bare midriff, even though a properly charged jury unanimously agreed on a verdict of guilty.

Our own viewing of the film satisfies us that "Carnal Knowledge" could not be found under the *Miller* standards to depict sexual conduct in a patently offensive way. Nothing in the movie falls within either of the two examples given in *Miller* of material which may constitutionally be found to meet the "patently offensive" element of those standards, nor is there anything sufficiently similar to such material to justify similar treatment. While the subject matter of the picture is, in a broader sense, sex, and there are scenes in which sexual conduct including "ultimate sexual acts" is to be understood to be taking place, the camera does not focus on the bodies of the actors at such times. There is no exhibition whatever of the actors' genitals, lewd or otherwise, during these scenes. There are occasional scenes of nudity, but nudity alone is not enough to make material legally obscene under the *Miller* standards.

Appellant's showing of the film "Carnal Knowledge" is simply not the "public portrayal of hard core sexual conduct for its own sake, and for the ensuing commercial gain" which we said was punishable in *Miller. Id.,* at 35. We hold that the film could not, as a matter of constitutional law, be found to depict sexual conduct in a patently offensive way, and that it is therefore not outside the protection of the First and Fourteenth Amendments because it is obscene. No other basis appearing in the record upon which the judgment of conviction can be sustained, we reverse the judgment of the Supreme Court of Georgia.

Reversed.

[Opinions of Douglas, J., Brennan, J., Stewart, J., and Marshall, J., are omitted.]

Ginsberg v. *New York*
390 U.S. 629 (1968)

MR. JUSTICE BRENNAN delivered the opinion of the Court.

This case presents the question of the constitutionality on its face of a New York criminal obscenity statute which prohibits the sale to minors under 17 years of age of material defined to be obscene on the basis of its appeal to them whether or not it would be obscene to adults.

Appellant and his wife operate "Sam's Stationery and Luncheonette" in Bellmore, Long Island. They have a lunch counter, and, among other things, also sell magazines including some so-called "girlie" magazines. Appellant was prosecuted under two informations, each in two counts, which charged that he personally sold a 16-year-old boy two "girlie" magazines on each of two dates in October 1965, in violation of § 484-h of the New York Penal Law. He was tried before a judge without a jury in Nassau County District Court and was found guilty on both counts.[1] The judge found (1) that the magazines contained pictures which depicted female "nudity" in a manner defined in subsection 1(b), that is "the showing of . . . female . . . buttocks with less than a full opaque covering, or the showing of the female breast with less than a fully opaque covering of any portion thereof below the top of the nipple . . . ," and (2) that the pictures were "harmful to minors" in that they had, within the meaning of subsection 1(f) "that quality of . . . representation . . . of nudity . . . [which] . . . (i) predominantly appeals to the prurient, shameful or morbid interest of minors, and (ii) is patently offensive to prevailing standards in the adult community as a whole with respect to what is suitable material for minors, and (iii) is utterly without redeeming social importance for minors." He held that both sales to the 16-year-old boy

---

[1] Appellant makes no attack upon § 484–h as applied. We therefore have no occasion to consider the sufficiency of the evidence, or such issues as burden of proof, whether expert evidence is either required or permissible, or any other questions which might be pertinent to the application of the statute. Appellant does argue that because the trial judge included a finding that two of the magazines "contained verbal descriptions and narrative accounts of sexual excitement and sexual conduct," an offense not charged in the informations, the conviction must be set aside under *Cole* v. *Arkansas,* 333 U.S. 196. But this case was tried and the appellant was found guilty only on the charges of selling magazines containing pictures depicting female nudity. It is therefore not a case where defendant was tried and convicted of a violation of one offense when he was charged with a distinctly and substantially different offense.

The full text of § 484–h is attached as Appendix A. It was enacted in L. 1965, c. 327, to replace an earlier version held invalid by the New York Court of Appeals in *People* v. *Kahan,* 15 N.Y. 2d 311, 206 N.E. 2d 333, and *People* v. *Bookcase, Inc.,* 14 N.Y. 2d 409, 201 N.E. 2d 14. Section 484–h in turn was replaced by L. 1967, c. 791, now §§ 235.20–235.22 of the Penal Law. The major changes under the 1967 law added a provision that the one charged with a violation "is presumed to [sell] with knowledge of the character and content of the material sold . . . ," and the provision that "it is an affirmative defense that: (a) The defendant had reasonable cause to believe that the minor involved was seventeen years old or more; and (b) Such minor exhibited to the defendant a draft card, driver's license, birth certificate or other official or apparently official document purporting to establish that such minor was seventeen years old or more." Neither addition is involved in this case. We intimate no view whatever upon the constitutional validity of the presumption. See in general *Smith* v. *California,* 361 U.S. 147; *Speiser* v. *Randall,* 357 U.S. 513; 41 N.Y. U. L. Rev. 791 (1966); 30 Albany L. Rev. 133 (1966).

The 1967 law also repealed outright § 484–i which had been enacted one week after § 484–h. L. 1965, c. 327. It forbade sales to minors under the age of 18. The New York Court of Appeals sustained its validity against a challenge that it was void for vagueness. *People* v. *Tannenbaum,* 18 N.Y. 2d 268, 220 N.E. 2d 783. For an analysis of § 484–i and a comparison with § 484–h see 33 Brooklyn L. Rev. 329 (1967).

therefore constituted the violation under § 484–h of "knowingly to sell . . .
to a minor" under 17 of "(a) any picture . . . which depicts nudity . . .
and which is harmful to minors," and "(b) any . . . magazine . . . which
contains . . . [such pictures] . . . and which, taken as a whole, is harmful
to minors." The conviction was affirmed without opinion by the Appellate
Term, Second Department, of the Supreme Court. Appellant was denied
leave to appeal to the New York Court of Appeals and then appealed to
this Court. We noted probable jurisdiction. 388 U.S. 904. We affirm.[2]

I.

The "girlie" picture magazines involved in the sales here are not
obscene for adults, *Redrup* v. *New York,* 386 U.S. 767.[3] But § 484–h

[2] The case is not moot. The appellant might have been sentenced to one year's
imprisonment, or a $500 fine or both. N.Y. Penal Law § 1937. The trial judge how-
ever exercised authority under N.Y. Penal Law § 2188 and on May 17, 1966, suspended sentence on all counts. Under § 470–a of the New York Code of Criminal
Procedure, the judge could thereafter recall appellant and impose sentence only
within one year, or before May 17, 1967. The judge did not do so. Although *St.
Pierre* v. *United States,* 319 U.S. 41, held that a criminal case had become moot
when the petitioner finished serving his sentence before direct review in this Court,
St. Pierre also recognized that the case would not have been moot had "petitioner
shown that under either state or federal law further penalties or disabilities can be
imposed on him as result of the judgment which has now been satisfied." *Id.,* at 43.
The State of New York concedes in its brief in this Court addressed to mootness
"that certain disabilities do flow from the conviction." The brief states that among
these is "the possibility of ineligibility for licensing under state and municipal license
laws regulating various lawful occupations . . . ." Since the argument, the parties
advised the Court that, although this is the first time appellant has been convicted of
any crime, this conviction might result in the revocation of the license required by
municipal law as a prerequisite to engaging in the luncheonette business he carries
on in Bellmore, New York. Bellmore is an "unincorporated village" within the Town
of Hempstead, Long Island, 1967 N.Y.S. Leg. Man. 1154. The town has a licensing
ordinance which provides that the "Commissioner of Buildings . . . may suspend or
revoke any license issued, in his discretion, for . . . (e) conviction of any crime."
LL 21, Town of Hempstead, eff. December 1, 1966, § 8.1 (e). In these circumstances the case is not moot since the conviction may entail collateral consequences
sufficient to bring the case within the *St. Pierre* exception. See *Fiswick* v. *United
States,* 329 U.S. 211, 220–222. We were not able to reach that conclusion in *Tannenbaum* v. *New York,* 388 U.S. 439, or *Jacobs* v. *New York,* 388 U.S. 431, in
which the appeals were dismissed as moot. In *Tannenbaum* there was no contention
that the convictions under the now repealed § 484–i entailed any collateral consequences. In *Jacobs* the appeal was dismissed on motion of the State which alleged,
inter alia, that New York law did not impose "any further penalty upon conviction
of the misdemeanor here in issue." Appellant did not there show, or contend, that
his license might be revoked for "conviction of any crime"; he asserted only that the
conviction might be the basis of a suspension under a provision of the Administrative Code of the City of New York requiring the Department of Licenses to assure
that motion picture theatres are not conducted in a manner offensive to "public
morals."

[3] One of the magazines was an issue of the magazine "Sir." We held in *Gent* v.
Arkansas, decided with *Redrup* v. *New York,* 386 U.S. 767, 769, that an Arkansas
statute which did not reflect a specific and limited state concern for juveniles was
unconstitutional insofar as it was applied to suppress distribution of another issue of
that magazine. Other cases which turned on findings of nonobscenity of this type of
magazine include: *Central Magazine Sales, Ltd.* v. *United States,* 389 U.S. 50;
Conner v. *City of Hammond,* 389 U.S. 48; *Potomac News Co.* v. *United States,* 389
U.S. 47; *Mazes* v. *Ohio,* 388 U.S. 453; *A Quantity of Books* v. *Kansas,* 388 U.S.

does not bar the appellant from stocking the magazines and selling them to persons 17 years of age or older, and therefore the conviction is not invalid under our decision in *Butler* v. *Michigan,* 352 U.S. 380.

Obscenity is not within the area of protected speech or press. *Roth* v. *United States,* 354 U.S. 476, 485. The three-pronged test of subsection 1(f) for judging the obscenity of material sold to minors under 17 is a variable from the formulation for determining obscenity under *Roth* stated in the plurality opinion in *Memoirs* v. *Massachusetts,* 383 U.S. 413, 418. Appellant's primary attack upon § 484–h is leveled at the power of the State to adapt this *Memoirs* formulation to define the material's obscenity on the basis of its appeal to minors, and thus exclude material so defined from the area of protected expression. He makes no argument that the magazines are not "harmful to minors" within the definition in subsection 1(f). Thus "[n]o issue is presented . . . concerning the obscenity of the material involved." *Roth, supra,* at 481, n. 8.

The New York Court of Appeals "upheld the Legislature's power to employ variable concepts of obscenity" [4] in a case in which the same challenge to state power to enact such a law was also addressed to § 484–h. *Bookcase, Inc.* v. *Broderick,* 18 N.Y. 2d 71, 218 N.E. 2d 668, appeal dismissed for want of a properly presented federal question, *sub nom. Bookcase, Inc.* v. *Leary,* 385 U.S. 12. In sustaining state power to enact the law, the Court of Appeals said, *Bookcase, Inc.* v. *Broderick,* at 75, 218 N.E. 2d at 671:

> "[M]aterial which is protected for distribution to adults is not necessarily constitutionally protected from restriction upon its dissemination to children. In other words, the concept of obscenity or of unprotected matter may vary according to the group to whom the questionable material is directed or from whom it is quarantined. Because of the State's exigent interest in preventing distribution to children of objectionable material, it can exercise its power to protect the health, safety, welfare and morals of its community by barring the distribution to children of books recognized to be suitable for adults."

Appellant's attack is not that New York was without power to draw the line at age 17. Rather, his contention is the broad proposition that the scope of the constitutional freedom of expression secured to a citizen to

---

452; *Books, Inc.* v. *United States,* 388 U.S. 449; *Aday* v. *United States,* 388 U.S. 447; *Avansino* v. *New York,* 388 U.S. 446; *Sheperd* v. *New York,* 388 U.S. 444; *Friedman* v. *New York,* 388 U.S. 441; *Keney* v. *New York,* 388 U.S. 440; see also *Rosenbloom* v. *Virginia,* 388 U.S. 450; *Sunshine Book Co.* v. *Summerfield,* 355 U.S. 372.

[4] *People* v. *Tannenbaum,* 18 N.Y. 2d 268, 270, 220 N.E. 2d 783, 785, dismissed as moot, 388 U.S. 439. The concept of variable obscenity is developed in Lockhart & McClure, Censorship of Obscenity: The Developing Constitutional Standards, 45 Minn. L. Rev. 5 (1960). At 85 the authors state:

"Variable obscenity . . . furnishes a useful analytical tool for dealing with the problem of denying adolescents access to material aimed at a primary audience of sexually mature adults. For variable obscenity focuses attention upon the make-up of primary and peripheral audiences in varying circumstances, and provides a reasonably satisfactory means for delineating the obscene in each circumstance."

read or see material concerned with sex cannot be made to depend upon whether the citizen is an adult or a minor. He accordingly insists that the denial to minors under 17 of access to material condemned by § 484–h, insofar as that material is not obscene for persons 17 years of age or older, constitutes an unconstitutional deprivation of protected liberty.

We have no occasion in this case to consider the impact of the guarantees of freedom of expression upon the totality of the relationship of the minor and the State, cf. *In re Gault,* 387 U.S. 1, 13. It is enough for the purposes of this case that we inquire whether it was constitutionally impermissible for New York, insofar as § 484–h does so, to accord minors under 17 a more restricted right than that assured to adults to judge and determine for themselves what sex material they may read or see. We conclude that we cannot say that the statute invades the area of freedom of expression constitutionally secured to minors.[5]

Appellant argues that there is an invasion of protected rights under § 484–h constitutionally indistinguishable from the invasions under the Nebraska statute forbidding children to study German, which was struck down in *Meyer* v. *Nebraska,* 262 U.S. 390; the Oregon statute interfering with children's attendance at private and parochial schools, which was struck down in *Pierce* v. *Society of Sisters,* 268 U.S. 510; and the statute compelling children against their religious scruples to give the flag salute, which was struck down in *West Virginia State Board of Education* v. *Barnette,* 319 U.S. 624. We reject that argument. We do not regard New York's regulation in defining obscenity on the basis of its appeal to minors under 17 as involving an invasion of such minors' constitutionally protected freedoms. Rather § 484–h simply adjusts the definition of obscenity "to social realities by permitting the appeal of this type of material to be assessed in terms of the sexual interests . . ." of such minors. *Mishkin* v. *New York,* 383 U.S. 502, 509; *Bookcase, Inc.* v. *Broderick, supra,* at 75, 218 N.E. 2d, at 671. That the State has power to make that adjustment seems clear, for we have recognized that even where there is an invasion of protected freedoms "the power of the state to control the conduct of children reaches beyond the scope of its authority over adults . . . ."

---

[5] Suggestions that legislatures might give attention to laws dealing specifically with safeguarding children against pornographic material have been made by many judges and commentators. See, *e.g., Jacobellis* v. *Ohio,* 378 U.S. 184, 195 (opinion of JUSTICES BRENNAN and GOLDBERG); id., at 201 (dissenting opinion of THE CHIEF JUSTICE); *Ginzburg* v. *United States,* 383 U.S. 463, 498, n. 1 (dissenting opinion of MR. JUSTICE STEWART); *Interstate Circuit, Inc.* v. *City of Dallas,* 366 F. 2d 590, 593; *In re Louisiana News Co.,* 187 F. Supp. 241; 247; *United States* v. *Levine,* 83 F. 2d 156; *United States* v. *Dennett,* 39 F. 2d 564; R. Kuh, Foolish Figleaves? 258–260 (1967); Emerson, Toward a General Theory of the First Amendment, 72 Yale L. J. 877, 939 (1963); Gerber, A Suggested Solution to the Riddle of Obscenity, 112 U. Pa. L. Rev. 834, 848 (1964); Henkin, Morals and the Constitution: The Sin of Obscenity, 63 Col. L. Rev. 391, 413, n. 68 (1963); Kalven, The Metaphysics of the Law of Obscenity, 1960 Sup. Ct. Rev. 1, 7; Magrath, The Obscenity Cases: Grapes of Roth, 1966 Sup. Ct. Rev. 7, 75.

The obscenity laws of 35 other States include provisions referring to minors. The laws are listed in Appendix B to this opinion. None is a precise counterpart of New York's § 484–h and we imply no view whatever on questions of their constitutionality.

Prince v. *Massachusetts,* 321 U.S. 158, 170.[6] In *Prince* we sustained the conviction of the guardian of a nine-year-old girl, both members of the sect of Jehovah's Witnesses, for violating the Massachusetts Child Labor Law by permitting the girl to sell the sect's religious tracts on the streets of Boston.

The well-being of its children is of course a subject within the State's constitutional power to regulate, and, in our view, two interests justify the limitations in § 484–h upon the availability of sex material to minors under 17, at least if it was rational for the legislature to find that the minors' exposure to such material might be harmful. First of all, constitutional interpretation has consistently recognized that the parents' claim to authority in their own household to direct the rearing of their children is basic in the structure of our society. "It is cardinal with us that the custody, care and nurture of the child reside first in the parents, whose primary function and freedom include preparation for obligations the state can neither supply nor hinder." *Prince* v. *Massachusetts, supra,* at 166. The legislature could properly conclude that parents and others, teachers for example, who have this primary responsibility for children's well-being are entitled to the support of laws designed to aid discharge of that responsibility. Indeed, subsection 1(f)(ii) of § 484–h expressly recognizes the parental role in assessing sex-related material harmful to minors according "to prevailing standards in the adult community as a whole with respect to what is suitable material for minors." Moreover, the prohibition against sales to minors does not bar parents who so desire from purchasing the magazines for their children.[7]

[6] Many commentators, including many committed to the proposition that "[n]o general restriction on expression in terms of 'obscenity' can . . . be reconciled with the first amendment," recognize that "the power of the state to control the conduct of children reaches beyond the scope of its authority over adults," and accordingly acknowledge a supervening state interest in the regulation of literature sold to children, Emerson, Toward a General Theory of the First Amendment, 72 Yale L. J. 877, 938, 939 (1963):

"Different factors come into play, also, where the interest at stake is the effect of erotic expression upon children. The world of children is not strictly part of the adult realm of free expression. The factor of immaturity, and perhaps other considerations, impose different rules. Without attempting here to formulate the principles relevant to freedom of expression for children, it suffices to say that regulations of communication addressed to them need not conform to the requirements of the first amendment in the same way as those applicable to adults."

See also Gerber, *supra,* at 848; Kalven, *supra,* at 7; Magrath, *supra,* at 75. *Prince* v. *Massachusetts* is urged to be constitutional authority for such regulation. See. *e.g.,* Kuh, *supra,* at 258–260; Comment, Exclusion of Children from Violent Movies, 67 Col. L. Rev. 1149, 1159–1160 (1967); Note, Constitutional Problems in Obscenity Legislation Protecting Children, 54 Geo. L. J. 1379 (1966).

[7] One commentator who argues that obscenity legislation might be constitutionally defective as an imposition of a single standard of public morality would give effect to the parental role and accept laws relating only to minors. Henkin, Morals and the Constitution: The Sin of Obscenity, 63 Col. L. Rev. 391, 413, n. 68 (1963):

"One must consider also how much difference it makes if laws are designed to protect ony the morals of a child. While many of the constitutional arguments against morals legislation apply equally to legislation protecting the morals of children, one can well distinguish laws which do not impose a morality on children, but which support the right of parents to deal with the morals of their children as they see fit."

The State also has an independent interest in the well-being of its youth. The New York Court of Appeals squarely bottomed its decision on that interest in *Bookcase, Inc.* v. *Broderick, supra,* at 75, 218 N.E. 2d, at 671. Judge Fuld, now Chief Judge Fuld, also emphasized its significance in the earlier case of *People* v. *Kahan,* 15 N.Y. 2d 311, 206 N.E. 2d 333, which had struck down the first version of § 484–h on grounds of vagueness. In his concurring opinion, *id.,* at 312, 206 N.E. 2d, at 334, he said:

> "While the supervision of children's reading may best be left to their parents, the knowledge that parental control or guidance cannot always be provided and society's transcendent interest in protecting the welfare of children justify reasonable regulation of the sale of material to them. It is, therefore, altogether fitting and proper for a state to include in a statute designed to regulate the sale of pornography to children special standards, broader than those embodied in legislation aimed at controlling dissemination of such material to adults."

In *Prince* v. *Massachusetts, supra,* at 165, this Court, too, recognized that the State has an interest "to protect the welfare of children" and to see that they are "safeguarded from abuses" which might prevent their "growth into free and independent well-developed men and citizens." The only question remaining, therefore, is whether the New York Legislature might rationally conclude, as it has, that exposure to the materials proscribed by § 484–h constitutes such an "abuse."

Section 484–e of the law states a legislative finding that the material condemned by § 484–h is "a basic factor in impairing the ethical and moral development of our youth and a clear and present danger to the people of the state." It is very doubtful that this finding expresses an accepted scientific fact.[8] But obscenity is not protected expression and may be suppressed without a showing of the circumstances which lie behind the phrase "clear and present danger" in its application to protected speech. *Roth* v. *United States, supra,* at 486–487.[9] To sustain state power to exclude material defined as obscenity by § 484–h requires only that we be able to say that it was not irrational for the legislature to find that exposure to material condemned by the statute is harmful to minors. In *Meyer* v. *Nebraska, supra,* at 400, we were able to say that children's knowledge of the German language "cannot reasonably be regarded as harmful." That cannot be said by us of minors' reading and seeing sex material. To be sure, there is no lack of "studies" which purport to demonstrate that

---

See also Elias, Sex Publications and Moral Corruption: The Supreme Court Dilemma, 9 Wm. & Mary L. Rev. 302, 320–321 (1967).

[8] Compare *Memoirs* v. *Massachusetts,* 383 U.S., at 424 (opinion of DOUGLAS, J.) with *id.,* at 441 (opinion of Clark, J.). See Kuh, *supra,* pp. 18–19; Gaylin, Book Review, 77 Yale L. J. 579, 591–595 (1968); Magrath, *supra,* at 52.

[9] Our conclusion in *Roth,* at 486–487, that the clear and present danger test was irrelevant to the determination of obscenity made it unnecessary in that case to consider the debate among the authorities whether exposure to pornography caused antisocial consequences. See also *Mishkin* v. *New York, supra; Ginzburg* v. *United States, supra; Memoirs* v. *Massachusetts, supra.*

obscenity is or is not "a basic factor in impairing the ethical and moral development of . . . youth and a clear and present danger to the people of the state." But the growing consensus of commentators is that "while these studies all agree that a causal link has not been demonstrated, they are equally agreed that a causal link has not been disproved either." [10] We do not demand of legislatures "scientifically certain criteria of legislation." *Noble State Bank* v. *Haskell,* 219 U.S. 104, 110. We therefore cannot say that § 484–h, in defining the obscenity of material on the basis of its appeal to minors under 17, has no rational relation to the objective of safeguarding such minors from harm.

II.

Appellant challenges subsections (f) and (g) of § 484–h as in any event void for vagueness. The attack on subsection (f) is that the definition of obscenity "harmful to minors" is so vague that an honest distributor of publications cannot know when he might be held to have violated § 484–h. But the New York Court of Appeals construed this definition to be "virtually identical to the Supreme Court's most recent statement of the elements of obscenity. [*Memoirs* v. *Massachusetts,* 383 U.S. 413, 418]," *Bookcase, Inc.* v. *Broderick, supra,* at 76, 218 N.E. 2d, at 672. The definition therefore gives "men in acting adequate notice of what is prohibited" and does not offend the requirements of due process. *Roth* v.

---

[10] Magrath, *supra,* at 52. See, *e.g., id.,* at 49–56; Dibble, Obscenity: A State Quarantine to Protect Children, 39 So. Cal. L. Rev. 345 (1966); Wall, Obscenity and Youth: The Problem and a Possible Solution, Crim. L. Bull., Vol. 1, No. 8, pp. 28, 30 (1965); Note, 55 Cal. L. Rev. 926, 934 (1967); Comment, 34 Ford. L. Rev. 692, 694 (1966). See also J. Paul & M. Schwartz, Federal Censorship: Obscenity in the Mail, 191–192; Blakey, Book Review, 41 Notre Dame Law. 1055, 1060, n. 46 (1966); Green, Obscenity, Censorship, and Juvenile Delinquency, 14 U. Toronto L. Rev. 229, 249 (1962); Lockhart & McClure, Literature, The Law of Obscenity, and the Constitution, 38 Minn. L. Rev. 295, 373–385 (1954); Note, 52 Ky. L. J. 429, 447 (1964). But despite the vigor of the ongoing controversy whether obscene material will perceptibly create a danger of antisocial conduct, or will probably induce its recipients to such conduct, a medical practitioner recently suggested that the possibility of harmful effects to youth cannot be dismissed as frivolous. Dr. Gaylin of the Columbia University Psychoanalytic Clinic, reporting on the views of some psychiatrists in 77 Yale L. J., at 592–593, said:

"It is in the period of growth [of youth] when these patterns of behavior are laid down, when environmental stimuli of all sorts must be integrated into a workable sense of self, when sensuality is being defined and fears elaborated, when pleasure confronts security and impulse encounters control—it is in this period, undramatically and with time, that legalized pornography may conceivably be damaging."

Dr. Gaylin emphasizes that a child might not be as well prepared as an adult to make an intelligent choice as to the material he chooses to read:

"[P]sychiatrists . . . made a distinction between the reading of pornography, as unlikely to be per se harmful, and the permitting of the reading of pornography, which was conceived as potentially destructive. The child is protected in his reading of pornography by the knowledge that it is pornographic, *i.e.,* disapproved. It is outside of parental standards and not a part of his identification processes. To openly permit implies parental approval and even suggests seductive encouragement. If this is so of parental approval, it is equally so of societal approval—another potent influence on the developing ego." *Id.,* at 594.

United States, supra, at 492; see also *Winters* v. *New York,* 333 U.S. 507, 520.

As is required by *Smith* v. *California,* 361 U.S. 147, § 484–h prohibits only those sales made "knowingly." The challenge to the *scienter* requirement of subsection (g) centers on the definition of "knowingly" insofar as it includes "reason to know" or "a belief or ground for belief which warrants further inspection or inquiry of both: (i) the character and content of any material described herein which is reasonably susceptible of examination by the defendant, and (ii) the age of the minor, provided however, that an honest mistake shall constitute an excuse from liability hereunder if the defendant made a reasonable bona fide attempt to ascertain the true age of such minor."

As to (i), § 484–h was passed after the New York Court of Appeals decided *People* v. *Finkelstein,* 9 N.Y. 2d 342, 174 N.E. 2d 470, which read the requirement of *scienter* into New York's general obscenity statute, § 1141 of the Penal Law. The constitutional requirement of *scienter,* in the sense of knowledge of the contents of material, rests on the necessity "to avoid the hazard of self-censorship of constitutionally protected material and to compensate for the ambiguities inherent in the definition of obscenity," *Mishkin* v. *New York, supra,* at 511. The Court of Appeals in *Finkelstein* interpreted § 1141 to require "the vital element of scienter" and defined that requirement in these terms: "A reading of the statute [§ 1141] as a whole clearly indicates that only those who are *in some manner aware of the character of the material* they attempt to distribute should be punished. It is not innocent but *calculated* purveyance of filth which is exorcised . . . ." 9 N.Y. 2d, at 344–345, 174 N.E. 2d, at 471. (Emphasis supplied.) In *Mishkin* v. *New York, supra,* at 510–511, we held that a challenge to the validity of § 1141 founded on *Smith* v. *California, supra,* was foreclosed in light of this construction. When § 484–h was before the New York Legislature its attention was directed to *People* v. *Finkelstein,* as defining the nature of *scienter* required to sustain the statute. 1965 N.Y.S. Leg. Ann. 54–56. We may therefore infer that the reference in provision (i) to knowledge of "the *character* and content of any material described herein" incorporates the gloss given the term "character" in *People* v. *Finkelstein.* In that circumstance *Mishkin* requires rejection of appellant's challenge to provision (i) and makes it unnecessary for us to define further today "what sort of mental element is requisite to a constitutionally permissible prosecution," *Smith* v. *California, supra,* at 154.

Appellant also attacks provision (ii) as impermissibly vague. This attack however is leveled only at the proviso according the defendant a defense of "honest mistake" as to the age of the minor. Appellant argues that "the statute does not tell the bookseller what effort he must make before he can be excused." The argument is wholly without merit. The proviso states expressly that the defendant must be acquitted on the ground of "honest mistake" if the defendant proves that he made "a reasonable bona fide attempt to ascertain the true age of such minor." Cf. 1967 Penal Law § 235.22(2), n. 1, *supra.*

Affirmed.

APPENDIX A TO OPINION OF THE COURT.

New York Penal Law § 484–h as enacted by L. 1965, c. 327, provides:

§ 484–h. Exposing minors to harmful materials

1. Definitions. As used in this section:

(a) "Minor" means any person under the age of seventeen years.

(b) "Nudity" means the showing of the human male or female genitals, pubic area or buttocks with less than a full opaque covering, or the showing of the female breast with less than a fully opaque covering of any portion thereof below the top of the nipple, or the depiction of covered male genitals in a discernibly turgid state.

(c) "Sexual conduct" means acts of masturbation, homosexuality, sexual intercourse, or physical contact with a person's clothed or unclothed genitals, pubic area, buttocks or, if such person be a female, breast.

(d) "Sexual excitement" means the condition of human male or female genitals when in a state of sexual stimulation or arousal.

(e) "Sado-masochistic abuse" means flagellation or torture by or upon a person clad in undergarments, a mask or bizarre costume, or the condition of being fettered, bound or otherwise physically restrained on the part of one so clothed.

(f) "Harmful to minors" means that quality of any description or representation, in whatever form, of nudity, sexual conduct, sexual excitement, or sado-masochistic abuse, when it:

(i) predominantly appeals to the prurient, shameful or morbid interest of minors, and

(ii) is patently offensive to prevailing standards in the adult community as a whole with respect to what is suitable material for minors, and

(iii) is utterly without redeeming social importance for minors.

(g) "Knowingly" means having general knowledge of, or reason to know, or a belief or ground for belief which warrants further inspection or inquiry of both:

(i) the character and content of any material described herein which is reasonably susceptible of examination by the defendant, and

(ii) the age of the minor, provided however, that an honest mistake shall constitute an excuse from liability hereunder if the defendant made a reasonable bona fide attempt to ascertain the true age of such minor.

2. It shall be unlawful for any person knowingly to sell or loan for monetary consideration to a minor:

(a) any picture, photograph, drawing, sculpture, motion picture film, or similar visual representation or image of a person or portion of the human body which depicts nudity, sexual conduct or sado-masochistic abuse and which is harmful to minors, or

(b) any book, pamphlet, magazine, printed matter however reproduced, or sound recording which contains any matter enumerated in paragraph (a) of subdivision two hereof, or explicit and detailed verbal
descriptions or narrative accounts of sexual excitement, sexual conduct or
sado-masochistic abuse and which, taken as a whole, is harmful to minors.

3. It shall be unlawful for any person knowingly to exhibit for a monetary consideration to a minor or knowingly to sell to a minor an admission
ticket or pass or knowingly to admit a minor for a monetary consideration
to premises whereon there is exhibited, a motion picture, show or other
presentation which, in whole or in part, depicts nudity, sexual conduct or
sado-masochistic abuse and which is harmful to minors.

4. A violation of any provision hereof shall constitute a misdemeanor.

[Appendix B to the Court's opinion is omitted. Opinions of Harlan, J.,
Stewart, J., Douglas, J., Black, J., and Fortas, J., are omitted.]

Ginzburg v. *United States*
383 U.S. 463 (1966)

MR. JUSTICE BRENNAN delivered the opinion of the Court.

A judge sitting without a jury in the District Court for the Eastern District of Pennsylvania [1] convicted petitioner Ginzburg and three corporations controlled by him upon all 28 counts of an indictment charging violation of the federal obscenity statute, 18 U.S.C. § 1461 (1964 ed.).[2] 224
F. Supp. 129. Each count alleged that a resident of the Eastern District
received mailed matter, either one of three publications challenged as
obscene, or advertising telling how and where the publications might be
obtained. The Court of Appeals for the Third Circuit affirmed, 338 F. 2d
12. We granted certiorari, 380 U.S. 961. We affirm. Since petitioners do
not argue that the trial judge misconceived or failed to apply the standards

[1] No challenge was or is made to venue under 18 U.S.C. § 1461 (1964 ed.).

[2] The federal obscenity statute, 18 U.S.C. § 1461, provides in pertinent part:
"Every obscene, lewd, lascivious, indecent, filthy or vile article, matter, thing,
device, or substance; and—
. . .

"Every written or printed card, letter, circular, book, pamphlet, advertisement, or
notice of any kind giving information, directly or indirectly, where, or how, or from
whom, or by what means any of such mentioned matters . . . may be obtained . . .
. . .

"Is declared to be nonmailable matter and shall not be conveyed in the mails or
delivered from any post office or by any letter carrier.
"Whoever knowingly uses the mails for the mailing, carriage in the mails, or
delivery of anything declared by this section to be nonmailable . . . shall be fined
not more than $5,000 or imprisoned not more than five years, or both, for the first
such offense . . . ."

we first enunciated in *Roth* v. *United States,* 354 U.S. 476,[3] the only serious question is whether those standards were correctly applied.[4]

In the cases in which this Court has decided obscenity questions since *Roth,* it has regarded the materials as sufficient in themselves for the determination of the question. In the present case, however, the prosecution charged the offense in the context of the circumstances of production, sale, and publicity and assumed that, standing alone, the publications themselves might not be obscene. We agree that the question of obscenity may include consideration of the setting in which the publications were presented as an aid to determining the question of obscenity, and assume without deciding that the prosecution could not have succeeded otherwise. As in *Mishkin* v. *New York, post,* p. 502, and as did the courts below, 224 F. Supp., at 134, 338 F. 2d, at 14–15, we view the publications against a background of commercial exploitation of erotica solely for the sake of their prurient appeal.[5] The record in that regard amply supports the decision of the trial judge that the mailing of all three publications offended the statute.[6]

The three publications were EROS, a hard-cover magazine of expensive format; Liaison, a bi-weekly newsletter; and *The Housewife's Handbook on Selective Promiscuity* (hereinafter the *Handbook*), a short book. The issue of EROS specified in the indictment, Vol. I, No. 4, contains 15 articles and photo-essays on the subject of love, sex, and sexual relations. The specified issue of Liaison, Vol. 1, No. 1, contains a prefatory "Letter from the Editors" announcing its dedication to "keeping sex an art and preventing it from becoming a science." The remainder of the issue consists of digests of two articles concerning sex and sexual relations which had earlier appeared in professional journals and a report of an interview with a psychotherapist who favors the broadest license in sexual relationships. As

---

[3] We are not, however, to be understood as approving all aspects of the trial judge's exegesis of *Roth,* for example his remarks that "the community as a whole is the proper consideration. In this community, our society, we have children of all ages, psychotics, feeble-minded and other susceptible elements. Just as they cannot set the pace for the average adult reader's taste, they cannot be overlooked as part of the community." 224 F. Supp., at 137. Compare *Butler* v. *Michigan,* 352 U.S. 380.

[4] The Government stipulated at trial that the circulars advertising the publications were not themselves obscene; therefore the convictions on the counts for mailing the advertising stand only if the mailing of the publications offended the statute.

[5] Our affirmance of the convictions for mailing EROS and Liaison is based upon their characteristics as a whole, including their editorial formats, and not upon particular articles contained, described, or excerpted in them. Thus we do not decide whether particular articles, for example, in EROS, although identified by the trial judge as offensive, should be condemned as obscene whatever their setting. Similarly, we accept the Government's concession, note 13, *infra,* that the prosecution rested upon the manner in which the petitioners sold the *Handbook;* thus our affirmance implies no agreement with the trial judge's characterizations of the book outside that setting.

[6] It is suggested in dissent that petitioners were unaware that the record being established could be used in support of such an approach, and that petitioners should be afforded the opportunity of a new trial. However, the trial transcript clearly reveals that in several points the Government announced its theory that made the mode of distribution relevant to the determination of obscenity, and the trial court admitted evidence, otherwise irrelevant, toward that end.

the trial judge noted, "[w]hile the treatment is largely superficial, it is presented entirely without restraint of any kind. According to defendants' own expert, it is entirely without literary merit." 224 F. Supp., at 314. The *Handbook* purports to be a sexual autobiography detailing with complete candor the author's sexual experiences from age 3 to age 36. The text includes, and prefatory and concluding sections of the book elaborate, her views on such subjects as sex education of children, laws regulating private consensual adult sexual practices, and the equality of women in sexual relationships. It was claimed at trial that women would find the book valuable, for example as a marriage manual or as an aid to the sex education of their children.

Besides testimony as to the merit of the material, there was abundant evidence to show that each of the accused publications was originated or sold as stock in trade of the sordid business of pandering—"the business of purveying textual or graphic matter openly advertised to appeal to the erotic interest of their customers." [7] EROS early sought mailing privileges from the postmasters of Intercourse and Blue Ball, Pennsylvania. The trial court found the obvious, that these hamlets were chosen only for the value their names would have in furthering petitioners' efforts to sell their publications on the basis of salacious appeal; [8] the facilities of the post offices were inadequate to handle the anticipated volume of mail, and the privileges were denied. Mailing privileges were then obtained from the postmaster of Middlesex, New Jersey. EROS and Liaison thereafter mailed several million circulars soliciting subscriptions from that post office; over 5,500 copies of the *Handbook* were mailed.

The "leer of the sensualist" also permeates the advertising for the three publications. The circulars sent for EROS and Liaison stressed the sexual candor of the respective publications, and openly boasted that the publishers would take full advantage of what they regarded as an unrestricted

[7] *Roth* v. *United States, supra,* 354 U.S., at 495–496 (WARREN, C. J., concurring).

[8] Evidence relating to petitioners' efforts to secure mailing privileges from these post offices was, contrary to the suggestion of MR. JUSTICE HARLAN in dissent, introduced for the purpose of supporting such a finding. Scienter had been stipulated prior to trial. The Government's position was revealed in the following colloquy, which occurred when it sought to introduce a letter to the postmasters of Blue Ball, Pennsylvania:

"The COURT. Who signed the letter?

"Mr. CREAMER. It is signed by Frank R. Brady, Associate Publisher of Mr. Ginzburg. It is on Eros Magazine, Incorporated's stationery.

"The COURT. And your objection is——

"Mr. SHAPIRO. It is in no way relevant to the particular issue or publication upon which the defendant has been indicted and in my view, even if there was an identification with respect to a particular issue, it would be of doubtful relevance in that event.

"The COURT. Anything else to say?

"Mr. CREAMER. If Your Honor pleases, there is a statement in this letter indicating that it would be advantageous to this publication to have it disseminated through Blue Ball, Pennsylvania, post office. I think this clearly goes to intent, as to what the purpose of publishing these magazines was. At least, it clearly establishes one of the reasons why they were disseminating this material.

"The COURT. Admitted."

license allowed by law in the expression of sex and sexual matters.[9] The advertising for the *Handbook,* apparently mailed from New York, consisted almost entirely of a reproduction of the introduction of the book, written by one Dr. Albert Ellis. Although he alludes to the book's informational value and its putative therapeutic usefulness, his remarks are preoccupied with the book's sexual imagery. The solicitation was indiscriminate, not limited to those, such as physicians or psychiatrists, who might independently discern the book's therapeutic worth.[10] Inserted in each advertisement was a slip labeled "GUARANTEE" and reading, "Documentary Books, Inc. unconditionally guarantees full refund of the price of THE HOUSEWIFE'S HANDBOOK ON SELECTIVE PROMIS-CUITY if the book fails to reach you because of U.S. Post Office censorship interference." Similar slips appeared in the advertising for EROS and Liaison; they highlighted the gloss petitioners put on the publications, eliminating any doubt what the purchaser was being asked to buy.[11]

This evidence, in our view, was relevant in determining the ultimate question of obscenity and, in the context of this record, serves to resolve all ambiguity and doubt. The deliberate representation of petitioners' publications as erotically arousing, for example, stimulated the reader to accept them as prurient; he looks for titillation, not for saving intellectual

[9] Thus, one EROS advertisement claimed:
"Eros is a child of its times. . . . [It] is the result of recent court decisions that have realistically interpreted America's obscenity laws and that have given to this country a new breadth of freedom of expression. . . . EROS takes full advantage of this new freedom of expression. It is *the* magazine of sexual candor."
In another, more lavish spread:
"EROS is a new quarterly devoted to the subjects of Love and Sex. In the few short weeks since its birth, EROS has established itself as the rave of the American intellectual community—and the rage of prudes everywhere! And it's no wonder: EROS handles the subjects of Love and Sex with complete candor. The publication of this magazine—which is frankly and avowedly concerned with erotica—has been enabled by recent court decisions ruling that a literary piece or painting, though explicitly sexual in content, has a right to be published if it is a genuine work of art.
"EROS is a genuine work of art. . . ."
An undisclosed number of advertisements for Liaison were mailed. The outer envelopes of these ads ask, "Are you among the chosen few". The first line of the advertisement eliminates the ambiguity: "Are you a member of the sexual elite?" It continues:
"That is, are you among the few happy and enlightened individuals who believe that a man and woman can make love without feeling pangs of conscience? Can you read about love and sex and discuss them without blushing and stammering?
"If so, you ought to know about an important new periodical called *Liaison.*
. . .
"In short, *Liaison* is Cupid's Chronicle. . . .
"Though *Liaison* handles the subjects of love and sex with complete candor, I wish to make it clear that it is not a scandal sheet and it is not written for the man in the street. *Liaison* is aimed at intelligent, educated adults who can accept love and sex as part of life.
". . . I'll venture to say that after you've read your first biweekly issue, *Liaison* will be your most eagerly awaited piece of mail."
[10] Note 13, *infra.*
[11] There is much additional evidence supporting the conclusion of petitioners' pandering. One of petitioners' former writers for Liaison, for example, testified about the editorial goals and practices of that publication.

content. Similarly, such representation would tend to force public confrontation with the potentially offensive aspects of the work; the brazenness of such an appeal heightens the offensiveness of the publications to those who are offended by such material. And the circumstances of presentation and dissemination of material are equally relevant to determining whether social importance claimed for material in the courtroom was, in the circumstances, pretense or reality—whether it was the basis upon which it was traded in the marketplace or a spurious claim for litigation purposes. Where the purveyor's sole emphasis is on the sexually provocative aspects of his publications, that fact may be decisive in the determination of obscenity. Certainly in a prosecution which, as here, does not necessarily imply suppression of the materials involved, the fact that they originate or are used as a subject of pandering is relevant to the application of the *Roth* test.

A proposition argued as to EROS, for example, is that the trial judge improperly found the magazine to be obscene as a whole, since he concluded that only four of the 15 articles predominantly appealed to prurient interest and substantially exceeded community standards of candor, while the other articles were admittedly nonoffensive. But the trial judge found that "[t]he deliberate and studied arrangement of EROS is editorialized for the purpose of appealing predominantly to prurient interest and to insulate through the inclusion of nonoffensive material." 224 F. Supp., at 131. However erroneous such a conclusion might be if unsupported by the evidence of pandering, the record here supports it. EROS was created, represented and sold solely as a claimed instrument of the sexual stimulation it would bring. Like the other publications, its pervasive treatment of sex and sexual matters rendered it available to exploitation by those who would make a business of pandering to "the widespread weakness for titillation by pornography." [12] Petitioners' own expert agreed, correctly we think, that "[if]f the object [of a work] is material gain for the creator through an appeal to the sexual curiosity and appetite," the work is pornographic. In other words, by animating sensual detail to give the publication a salacious cast, petitioners reinforced what is conceded by the Government to be an otherwise debatable conclusion.

A similar analysis applies to the judgment regarding the *Handbook*. The bulk of the proofs directed to social importance concerned this publication. Before selling publication rights to petitioners, its author had printed it privately; she sent circulars to persons whose names appeared on membership lists of medical and psychiatric associations, asserting its value as an adjunct to therapy. Over 12,000 sales resulted from this solicitation, and a number of witnesses testified that they found the work useful in their professional practice. The Government does not seriously contest the claim that the book has worth in such a controlled, or even neutral environment. Petitioners, however, did not sell the book to such a limited audience, or focus their claims for it on its supposed therapeutic or educational value; rather, they deliberately emphasized the sexually provocative aspects of the work, in order to catch the salaciously disposed. They pro-

[12] Schwartz, Morals Offenses and the Model Penal Code, 63 Col. L. Rev. 669, 677 (1963).

claimed its obscenity; and we cannot conclude that the court below erred in taking their own evaluation at its face value and declaring the book as a whole obscene despite the other evidence.[13]

The decision in *United States* v. *Rebhuhn,* 109 F. 2d 512, is persuasive authority for our conclusion.[14] This was a prosecution under the predecessor to § 1461, brought in the context of pandering of publications assumed useful to scholars and members of learned professions. The books involved were written by authors proved in many instances to have been men of scientific standing, as anthropologists or psychiatrists. The Court of Appeals for the Second Circuit therefore assumed that many of the books were entitled to the protection of the First Amendment, and "could lawfully have passed through the mails, if directed to those who would be likely to use them for the purposes for which they were written. . . ." 109 F. 2d, at 514. But the evidence, as here, was that the defendants had not disseminated them for their "proper use, but . . . woefully misused them, and it was that misuse which constituted the gravamen of the crime." *Id.,* at 515. Speaking for the Court in affirming the conviction, Judge Learned Hand said:

> ". . . [T]he works themselves had a place, though a limited one, in anthropology and in psychotherapy. They might also have been lawfully sold to laymen who wished seriously to study the sexual practices of savage or barbarous peoples, or sexual aberrations; in other words, most of them were not obscene per se. In several decisions we have held that the statute does not in all circumstances forbid the dissemination of such publications . . . . However, in the case at bar, the prosecution succeeded . . . when it showed that the defendants had indiscriminately flooded the mails with advertisements, plainly designed merely to catch the prurient, though under the guise of distributing works of scientific or literary merit. We do not mean that the distributor of such works is charged with a duty to insure that they shall reach only proper hands, nor need we say what care he must use, for these defendants exceeded any possible limit; the circulars were no more than appeals to the salaciously disposed, and no [fact fiinder] could have failed to pierce the fragile screen, set up to cover that purpose." 109 F. 2d, at 514–515.

[13] The Government drew a distinction between the author's and petitioners' solicitation. At the sentencing proceeding the United States Attorney stated:

". . . [the author] was distributing . . . only to physicians; he never had widespread, indiscriminate distribution of the Handbook and, consequently, the Post Office Department did not interfere. . . . If Mr. Ginzburg had distributed and sold and advertised these books solely to . . . physicians . . . we, of course, would not be here this morning with regard to The Housewife's Handbook . . . ."

[14] The Proposed Official Draft of the ALI Model Penal Code likewise recognizes the question of pandering as relevant to the obscenity issue, § 251.4(4); Tentative Draft No. 6 (May 6, 1957), pp. 1–3, 13–17, 45–46, 53; Schwartz, *supra*, n. 12; see Craig, Suppressed Books, 195–206 (1963). Compare *Grove Press, Inc.* v. *Christenberry,* 175 F. Supp. 488, 496–497 (D. C. S. D. N. Y. 1959), aff'd 276 F. 2d 433 (C. A. 2d Cir. 1960); *United States* v. *One Book Entitled Ulysses,* 72 F. 2d 705, 707 (C. A. 2d Cir. 1934), affirming 5 F. Supp. 182 (C. S. D. N. Y. 1933). See also The Trial of Lady Chatterly—Regina v. Penguin Books, Ltd. (Rolph, ed. 1961).

We perceive no threat to First Amendment guarantees in thus holding that in close cases evidence of pandering may be probative with respect to the nature of the material in question and thus satisfy the *Roth* test.[15] No weight is ascribed to the fact that petitioners have profited from the sale of publications which we have assumed but do not hold cannot themselves be adjudged obscene in the abstract; to sanction consideration of this fact might indeed induce self-censorship, and offend the frequently stated principle that commercial activity, in itself, is no justification for narrowing the protection of expression secured by the First Amendment.[16] Rather, the fact that each of these publications was created or exploited entirely on the basis of its appeal to prurient interests [17] strengthens the conclusion that the transactions here were sales of illicit merchandise, not sales of constitutionally protected matter.[18] A conviction for mailing obscene publications, but explained in part by the presence of this element, does not necessarily suppress the materials in question, nor chill their proper distribution for a proper use. Nor should it inhibit the enterprise of others seeking through serious endeavor to advance human knowledge or understanding in science, literature, or art. All that will have been determined is that questionable publications are obscene in a context which brands them as obscene as that term is defined in *Roth*—a use inconsistent with any claim to the shelter of the First Amendment.[19] "The nature of the materials is, of course, relevant as an attribute of the defendant's conduct, but the materials are thus placed in context from which they draw color and character. A wholly different result might be reached in a different setting." *Roth* v. *United States*, 354 U.S., at 495 (WARREN, C. J., concurring).

[15] Our conclusion is consistent with the statutory scheme. Although § 1461, in referring to "obscene . . . matter" may appear to deal with the qualities of material in the abstract, it is settled that the mode of distribution may be a significant part in the determination of the obscenity of the material involved. *United States* v. *Rebhuhn, supra.* Because the statute creates a criminal remedy cf. *Manual Enterprises* v. *Day*, 370 U.S. 478, 495 (opinion of BRENNAN, J.), it eadily admits such an interpretation, compare *United States* v. *31 Photographs, etc.*, 156 F. Supp. 350 (D. C. S. D. N. Y. 1957).

[16] See *New York Times* v. *Sullivan*, 376 U.S. 254, 265–266; *Smith* v. *California*, 361 U.S. 147, 150.

[17] See *Valentine* v. *Chrestensen*, 316 U.S. 52, where the Court viewed handbills purporting to contain protected expression as merely commercial advertising. Compare that decision with *Jamison* v. *Texas*, 318 U.S. 413, and *Murdock* v. *Pennsylvania*, 319 U.S. 105, where speech having the characteristics of advertising was held to be an integral part of religious discussions and hence protected. Material sold solely to produce sexual arousal, like commercial advertising, does not escape regulation because it has been dressed up as speech, or in other contexts might be recognized as speech.

[18] Compare *Breard* v. *Alexandria*, 341 U.S. 622, with *Martin* v. *Struthers*, 319 U.S. 141. Cf. *Kovacs* v. *Cooper*, 336 U.S. 77; *Giboney* v. *Empire Storage Co.*, 336 U.S. 490; *Cox* v. *Louisiana*, 379 U.S. 536, 559.

[19] One who advertises and sells a work on the basis of its prurient appeal is not threatened by the perhaps inherent residual vagueness of the *Roth* test, cf. *Dombrowski* v. *Pfister*, 380 U.S. 479, 486–487, 491–492; such behavior is central to the objectives of criminal obscenity laws. ALI Model Penal Code, Tentative Draft No. 6 (May 6, 1957), pp. 1–3, 13–17; Comments to the Proposed Official Draft § 251.4, *supra;* Schwartz, Morals Offenses and the Model Penal Code, 63 Col. L. Rev. 669, 677–681 (1963); Paul & Schwartz, Federal Censorship—Obscenity in the Mail, 212–219 (1961); see *Mishkin* v. *New York, post*, p. 502, at 507, n. 5.

It is important to stress that this analysis simply elaborates the test by which the obscenity vel non of the material must be judged. Where an exploitation of interests in titillation by pornography is shown with respect to material lending itself to such exploitation through pervasive treatment or description of sexual matters, such evidence may support the determination that the material is obscene even though in other contexts the material would escape such condemnation.

Petitioners raise several procedural objections, principally directed to the findings which accompanied the trial court's memorandum opinion, Fed. Rules Crim. Proc. 23. Even on the assumption that petitioners' objections are well taken, we perceive no error affecting their substantial rights.

Affirmed

[Opinions of Douglas, J., Black, J., Harlan, J., and Stewart, J., are omitted.]

Mishkin v. *New York*
383 U.S. 502 (1966)

MR. JUSTICE BRENNAN delivered the opinion of the Court.

This case, like *Ginzburg* v. *United States, ante,* p. 463, also decided today, involves convictions under a criminal obscenity statute. A panel of three judges of the Court of Special Sessions of the City of New York found appellant guilty of violating § 1141 of the New York Penal Law [1] by hiring others to prepare obscene books, publishing obscene books, and

[1] Section 1141 of the Penal Law, in pertinent part, reads as follows:

"1. A person who . . . has in his possession with intent to sell, lend, distribute . . . any obscene, lewd, lascivious, filthy, indecent, sadistic, masochistic or disgusting book . . . or who . . . prints, utters, publishes, or in any manner manufactures, or prepares any such book . . . or who

"2. In any manner, hires, employs, uses or permits any person to do or assist in doing any act or thing mentioned in this section, or any of them,

"Is guilty of a misdemeanor . . . .

. . . .

"4. The possession by any person of six or more identical or similar articles coming within the provisions of subdivision one of this section is presumptive evidence of a violation of this section.

"5. The publication for sale of any book, magazine or pamphlet designed, composed or illustrated as a whole to appeal to and commercially exploit prurient interest by combining covers, pictures, drawings, illustrations, caricatures, cartoons, words, stories and advertisements or any combination or combinations thereof devoted to the description, portrayal or deliberate suggestion of illicit sex, including adultery, prostitution, fornication, sexual crime and sexual perversion or to the exploitation of sex and nudity by the presentation of nude or partially nude female figures, posed, photographed or otherwise presented in a manner calculated to provoke or incite prurient interest, or any combination or combinations thereof, shall be a violation of this section."

possessing obscene books with intent to sell them.[2] 26 Misc. 2d 152, 207 N.Y.S. 2d 390 (1960). He was sentenced to prison terms aggregating three years and ordered to pay $12,000 in fines for these crimes.[3] The Appellate Division, First Department, affirmed those convictions. 17 App. Div. 2d 243, 234 N.Y.S. 2d 342 (1962). The Court of Appeals affirmed without opinion. 15 N.Y. 2d 671, 204 N.E. 2d 209 (1964), remittitur amended, 15 N.Y. 2d 724, 205 N.E. 2d 201 (1965). We noted probable jurisdiction. 380 U.S. 960. We affirm.

Appellant was not prosecuted for anything he said or believed, but for what he did, for his dominant role in several enterprises engaged in producing and selling allegedly obscene books. Fifty books are involved in this case. They portray sexuality in many guises. Some depict relatively normal heterosexual relations, but more depict such deviations as sado-masochism, fetishism, and homosexuality. Many have covers with drawings of scantily clad women being whipped, beaten, tortured, or abused. Many, if not most, are photo-offsets of typewritten books written and illustrated by authors and artists according to detailed instructions given by the appellant. Typical of appellant's instructions was that related by one author who testified that appellant insisted that the books be "full of sex scenes and lesbian scenes . . . . [T]he sex had to be very strong, it had to be rough, it had to be clearly spelled out. . . . I had to write sex very bluntly, make the sex scenes very strong. . . . [T]he sex scenes had to be unusual sex scenes between men and women, and women and women, and men and men. . . . [H]e wanted scenes in which women were making love with women. . . . [H]e wanted sex scenes . . in which there were lesbian scenes. He didn't call it lesbian, but he described women making love to women and men . . . making love to men, and there were spankings and scenes—sex in an abnormal and irregular fashion." Another

---

[2] The information charged 159 counts of violating § 1141; in each instance a single count named a single book, although often the same book was the basis of three counts, each alleging one of the three types of § 1141 offenses. Of these, 11 counts were dismissed on motion of the prosecutor at the outset of the trial and verdicts of acquittal were entered on seven counts at the end of trial. The remaining § 1141 counts on which appellant was convicted are listed in the Appendix to this opinion.

Appellant was also convicted on 33 counts charging violations of § 330 of the General Business Law for failing to print the publisher's and printer's names and addresses on the books. The Appellate Division reversed the convictions under these counts, and the Court of Appeals affirmed. The State has not sought review of that decision in this Court.

[3] The trial court divided the counts into five groups for purposes of sentencing. One group consisted of the possession counts concerning books seized from a basement storeroom in a warehouse; a second group of possession counts concerned books seized from appellant's retail bookstore, Publishers' Outlet; the third consisted of the publishing counts; the fourth consisted of the counts charging him with hiring others to prepare the books, and the fifth consisted of the counts charging violations of the General Business Law. Sentences of one year and a $3,000 fine were imposed on one count of each of the first four groups; the prison sentences on the first three were made consecutive and that on the count in the fourth group was made concurrent with that in the third group. A $500 fine was imposed on one count in the fifth group. Sentence was suspended on the convictions on all other counts. The suspension of sentence does not render moot the claims as to invalidity of the convictions on those counts.

author testified that appellant instructed him "to deal very graphically with
. . . the darkening of the flesh under flagellation. . . ." Artists testified in
similar vein as to appellant's instructions regarding illustrations and covers
for the books.

All the books are cheaply prepared paperbound "pulps" with imprinted
sales prices that are several thousand percent above costs. All but three
were printed by a photo-offset printer who was paid 40¢ or 15¢ per copy,
depending on whether it was a "thick" or "thin" book. The printer was
instructed by appellant not to use appellant's name as publisher but to
print some fictitious name on each book, to "make up any name and
address." Appellant stored books on the printer's premises and paid part
of the printer's rent for the storage space. The printer filled orders for the
books, at appellant's direction, delivering them to appellant's retail store,
Publishers' Outlet, and, on occasion, shipping books to other places.
Appellant paid the authors, artists, and printer cash for their services,
usually at his bookstore.

I.

Appellant attacks § 1141 as invalid on its face, contending that it
exceeds First Amendment limitations by proscribing publications that are
merely sadistic or masochistic, that the terms "sadistic" and "masochistic"
are impermissibly vague, and that the term "obscene" is also impermissibly vague. We need not decide the merits of the first two contentions, for
the New York courts held in this case that the terms "sadistic" and
"masochistic," as well as the other adjectives used in § 1141 to describe
proscribed books, are "synonymous with 'obscene.' " 26 Misc. 2d, at 154,
207 N.Y.S. 2d, at 393. The contention that the term "obscene" is also
impermissibly vague fails under our holding in *Roth* v. *United States,* 354
U.S. 476, 491–492. Indeed, the definition of "obscene" adopted by the
New York courts in interpreting § 1141 delimits a narrower class of conduct than that delimited under the *Roth* definition, *People* v. *Richmond
County News, Inc.,* 9 N.Y. 2d 578, 586–587, 175 N.E. 2d 681, 685–686
(1961),[4] and thus § 1141, like the statutes in *Roth,* provides reasonably
ascertainable standards of guilt.[5]

[4] "It [obscene material covered by § 1141] focuses predominantly upon what is
sexually morbid, grossly perverse and bizarre, without any artistic or scientific purpose or justification. Recognizable 'by the insult it offers, invariably, to sex, and to
the human spirit' (D. H. Lawrence, Pornography and Obscenity [1930], p. 12), it is
to be differentiated from the bawdy and the ribald. Depicting dirt for dirt's sake, the
obscene is the vile, rather than the coarse, the blow to sense, not merely to sensibil-
ity. It smacks, at times, of fantasy and unreality, of sexual perversion and sickness
and represents, according to one thoughtful scholar, 'a debauchery of the sexual faculty.' (Murray, Literature and Censorship, 14 Books on Trial 393, 394; see, also,
Lockhart and McClure, Censorship of Obscenity: The Developing Constitutional
Standards, 45 Minn. L. Rev. 5, 65.)" 9 N.Y. 2d, at 587, 175 N.E. 2d, at 686.
See also *People* v. *Fritch,* 13 N.Y. 2d 119, 123, 192 N.E. 2d 713, 716 (1963):
"In addition to the foregoing tests imposed by the decisions of the [United States]
Supreme Court, this court interpreted section 1141 of the Penal Law in *People* v.
Richmond County News . . . as applicable only to material which may properly be
termed 'hard-core pornography.' "
[5] The stringent scienter requirement of § 1141, as interpreted in *People* v. *Finkel-*

Appellant also objects that § 1141 is invalid as applied, *first,* because the books he was convicted of publishing, hiring others to prepare, and possessing for sale are not obscene, and *second,* because the proof of scienter is inadequate.

1. *The Nature of the Material.*—The First Amendment prohibits criminal prosecution for the publication and dissemination of allegedly obscene books that do not satisfy the *Roth* definition of obscenity. States are free to adopt other definitions of obscenity only to the extent that those adopted stay within the bounds set by the constitutional criteria of the *Roth* definition, which restrict the regulation of the publication and sale of books to that traditionally and universally tolerated in our society.

The New York courts have interpreted obscenity in § 1141 to cover only so-called "hard-core pornography," see *People* v. *Richmond County News, Inc.,* 9 N.Y. 2d 578, 586–587, 175 N.E. 2d 681, 685–686 (1961), quoted in note 4, *supra.* Since that definition of obscenity is more stringent than the *Roth* definition, the judgment that the constitutional criteria are satisfied is implicit in the application of § 1141 below. Indeed, appellant's sole contention regarding the nature of the material is that some of the books involved in this prosecution,[6] those depicting various deviant sexual practices, such as flagellation, fetishism, and lesbianism, do not satisfy the prurient-appeal requirement because they do not appeal to a prurient interest of the "average person" in sex, that "instead of stimulating the erotic, they disgust and sicken." We reject this argument as being founded on an unrealistic interpretation of the prurient-appeal requirement.

Where the material is designed for and primarily disseminated to a clearly defined deviant sexual group, rather than the public at large, the prurient-appeal requirement of the *Roth* test is satisfied if the dominant theme of the material taken as a whole appeals to the prurient interest in sex of the members of that group. The reference to the "average" or "normal" person in *Roth,* 354 U.S., at 489–490, does not foreclose this holding.[7] In regard to the prurient-appeal requirement, the concept of the

---

stein, 9 N.Y. 2d 342, 345, 174 N.E. 2d 470, 472 (1961), also eviscerates much of appellant's vagueness claim. See, *infra,* pp. 510–512. See generally, *Boyce Motor Lines, Inc.* v. *United States,* 342 U.S. 337, 342; *American Communications Assn.* v. *Douds,* 339 U.S. 382, 412–413; *Screws* v. *United States,* 325 U.S. 91, 101–104 (opinion of MR. JUSTICE DOUGLAS); *United States* v. *Ragen,* 314 U.S. 513, 524; *Gorin* v. *United States,* 312 U.S. 19, 27–28; *Hygrade Provision Co.* v. *Sherman,* 266 U.S. 497, 501–503; *Omacchevarria* v. *Idaho,* 246 U.S. 343, 348.

[6] It could not be plausibly maintained that all of the appellant's books, including those dominated by descriptions of relatively normal heterosexual relationships, are devoid of the requisite prurient appeal.

[7] See *Manual Enterprises, Inc.* v. *Day,* 370 U.S. 478, 482 (opinion of HARLAN, J.); Lockhart and McClure, Censorship of Obscenity: The Developing Constitutional Standards, 45 Minn. L. Rev. 5, 72–73 (1960).

It is true that some of the material in *Alberts* v. *California,* decided with *Roth,* resembled the deviant material involved here. But no issue involving the obscenity of the material was before us in either case. 354 U.S., at 481, n. 8. The basic question for decision there was whether the publication and sale of obscenity, however defined, could be criminally punished in light of First Amendment guarantees. Our discussion of definition was not intended to develop all the nuances of a definition required by the constitutional guarantees.

"average" or "normal" person was employed in *Roth* to serve the essentially negative purpose of expressing our rejection of that aspect of the *Hicklin* test, *Regina* v. *Hicklin,* [1868] L. R. 3 Q. B. 360, that made the impact on the most susceptible person determinative. We adjust the prurient-appeal requirement to social realities by permitting the appeal of this type of material to be assessed in terms of the sexual interests of its intended and probable recipient group; and since our holding requires that the recipient group be defined with more specificity than in terms of sexually immature persons,[8] it also avoids the inadequacy of the most-susceptible-person facet of the *Hicklin* test.

No substantial claim is made that the books depicting sexually deviant practices are devoid of prurient appeal to sexually deviant groups. The evidence fully establishes that these books were specifically conceived and marketed for such groups. Appellant instructed his authors and artists to prepare the books expressly to induce their purchase by persons who would probably be sexually stimulated by them. It was for this reason that appellant "wanted an emphasis on beatings and fetishism and clothing—irregular clothing, and that sort of thing, and again sex scenes between women; always sex scenes had to be very strong." And to be certain that authors fulfilled his purpose, appellant furnished them with such source materials as Caprio, Variations in Sexual Behavior, and Krafft-Ebing, Psychopathia Sexualis. Not only was there proof of the books' prurient appeal, compare *United States* v. *Klaw,* 350 F. 2d 155 (C. A. 2d Cir. 1965), but the proof was compelling; in addition appellant's own evaluation of his material confirms such a finding. See *Ginzburg* v. *United States, ante,* p. 463.

2. *Scienter.*—In *People* v. *Finkelstein,* 9 N.Y. 2d 342, 344–345, 174 N. E. 2d 470, 471 (1961), the New York Court of Appeals authoritatively interpreted § 1141 to require the "vital element of scienter," and it defined the required mental element in these terms:

"A reading of the statute [§ 1141] as a whole clearly indicates that only those who are in some manner aware of the *character* of the material they attempt to distribute should be punished. It is not innocent but *calculated purveyance* of filth which is exorcised . . . ."[9] (Emphasis added.)

Appellant's challenge to the validity of § 1141 founded on *Smith* v. *California,* 361 U.S. 147, is thus foreclosed,[10] and this construction of § 1141

[8] See generally, 1 American Handbook of Psychiatry 593–604 (Arieti ed. 1959), for a description of the pertinent types of deviant sexual groups.

[9] For a similar scienter requirement see Model Penal Code § 251.4 (2); Commentary, Model Penal Code (Tentative Draft No. 6, 1957), 14, 49–51; cf. Schwartz, Morals Offenses and the Model Penal Code, 63 Col. L. Rev. 669, 677 (1963).

We do not read Judge Froessel's parenthetical reference to knowledge of the contents of the books in his opinion in *People* v. *Finkelstein,* 11 N.Y. 2d 300, 304, 183 N.E. 2d 661, 663 (1962), as a modification of this definition of scienter. Cf. *People* v. *Fritch,* 13 N.Y. 2d 119, 126, 192 N.E. 2d 713, 717–718 (1963).

[10] The scienter requirement set out in the text would seem to be, as a matter of state law, as applicable to publishers as it is to booksellers, both types of activities are encompassed within subdivision 1 of § 1141. Moreover, there is no need for us to speculate as to whether this scienter requirement is also present in subdivision 2

makes it unnecessary for us to define today "what sort of mental element is requisite to a constitutionally permissible prosecution." *Id.,* at 154. The Constitution requires proof of scienter to avoid the hazard of self-censorship of constitutionally protected material and to compensate for the ambiguities inherent in the definition of obscenity. The New York definition of the scienter required by § 1141 amply serves those ends, and therefore fully meets the demands of the Constitution,[11] Cf. *Roth* v. *United States,* 354 U.S., at 495–496 (WARREN, C. J., concurring).

Appellant's principal argument is that there was insufficient proof of scienter. This argument is without merit. The evidence of scienter in this record consists, in part, of appellant's instructions to his artists and writers; his efforts to disguise his role in the enterprise that published and sold the books; the transparency of the character of the material in question, highlighted by the titles, covers, and illustrations; the massive number of obscene books appellant published, hired others to prepare, and possessed for sale; the repetitive quality of the sequences and formats of the books; and the exorbitant prices marked on the books. This evidence amply shows that appellant was "aware of the character of the material" and that his activity was "not innocent but calculated purveyance of filth."

II.

Appellant claims that all but one of the books were improperly admitted in evidence because they were fruits of illegal searches and seizures. This claim is not capable in itself of being brought here by appeal, but only by a petition for a writ of certiorari under 28 U.S.C. § 1257 (3) (1964 ed.) as specifically setting up a federal constitutional right.[12] Nevertheless, since appellant challenged the constitutionality of § 1141 in this prosecution, and the New York courts sustained the statute, the case is properly here on appeal, and our unrestricted notation of probable jurisdiction justified appellant's briefing of the search and seizure issue. *Flournoy* v. *Weiner,* 321 U.S. 253, 263; *Prudential Ins. Co.* v. *Cheek,* 259 U.S. 530, 547. The nonappealable issue is treated, however, as if contained in a petition for a writ of certiorari, see 28 U.S.C. § 2103 (1964 ed.), and the unrestricted notation of probable jurisdiction of the appeal is to be

---

of § 1141 (making it a crime to hire others to prepare obscene books), for appellant's convictions for that offense involved books for the publication of which he was also convicted.

No constitutional claim was asserted below or in this Court as to the possible duplicative character of the hiring and publishing counts.

[11] The first appeal in *Finkelstein* defining the scienter required by § 1141 was decided after this case was tried, but before the Appellate Division and Court of Appeals affirmed these convictions. We therefore conclude that the state appellate courts were satisfied that the § 1141 scienter requirement was correctly applied at trial.

The § 1141 counts did not allege appellant's knowledge of the character of the books, but appellant has not argued, below or here, that this omission renders the information constitutionally inadequate.

[12] Unlike the claim here, the challenges decided in the appeals in *Marcus* v. *Search Warrant,* 367 U.S. 717, and *A Quantity of Copies of Books* v. *Kansas,* 378 U.S. 205, implicated the constitutional validity of statutory schemes establishing procedures for seizing the books.

understood as a grant of the writ on that issue. The issue thus remains within our certiorari jurisdiction, and we may, for good reason, even at this stage, decline to decide the merits of the issue, much as we would dismiss a writ of certiorari as improvidently granted. We think that this is a case for such an exercise of our discretion.

The far-reaching and important questions tendered by this claim are not presented by the record with sufficient clarity to require or justify their decision. Appellant's standing to assert the claim in regard to all the seizures is not entirely clear; there is no finding on the extent or nature of his interest in two book stores, the Main Stem Book Shop and Midget Book Shop, in which some of the books were seized. The State seeks to justify the basement storeroom seizure, in part, on the basis of the consent of the printer-accomplice; but there were no findings as to the authority of the printer over the access to the storeroom, or as to the voluntariness of his alleged consent. It is also maintained that the seizure in the storeroom was made on the authority of a search warrant; yet neither the affidavit upon which the warrant issued nor the warrant itself is in the record. Finally, while the search and seizure issue has a First Amendment aspect because of the alleged massive quality of the seizures, see *A Quantity of Copies of Books* v. *Kansas,* 378 U.S. 205, 206 (opinion of BRENNAN, J.); *Marcus* v. *Search Warrant,* 367 U.S. 717, the record in this regard is inadequate. There is neither evidence nor findings as to how many of the total available copies of the books in the various bookstores were seized and it is impossible to determine whether the books seized in the basement storeroom were on the threshold of dissemination. Indeed, this First Amendment aspect apparently was not presented or considered by the state courts, nor was it raised in appellant's jurisdictional statement; it appeared for the first time in his brief on the merits.

In light of these circumstances, which were not fully apprehended at the time we took the case, we decline to reach the merits of the search and seizure claim; insofar as notation of probable jurisdiction may be regarded as a grant of the certiorari writ on the search and seizure issue, that writ is dismissed as improvidently granted. "Examination of a case on the merits . . .may bring into 'proper focus' a consideration which . . . later indicates that the grant was improvident." *The Monrosa* v. *Carbon Black,* 359 U.S. 180, 184.

Affirmed.

APPENDIX TO OPINION OF THE COURT
THE CONVICTIONS BEING REVIEWED

Exhibit No.	Title of Book	Possession	§ 1141 Counts Naming the Book	
			Pub-lishing	Hiring Others
1	Chances Go Around	1	63	111
2	Impact	2	64	112
3	Female Sultan	3	65	113
4	Satin Satellite	4		

Exhibit No.	Title of Book	§ 1141 Counts Naming the Book		
		Possession	Publishing	Hiring Others
5	Her Highness	5	67	115
6	Mistress of Leather	6	68	116
7	Educating Edna	7	69	117
8	Strange Passions	8	70	118
9	The Whipping Chorus Girls	9	71	119
10	Order Of The Day and Bound Maritally	10	72	120
11	Dance With the Dominant Whip	11	73	121
12	Cult Of The Spankers	12	74	122
13	Confessions	13	75	123
14 & 46	The Hours Of Torture	14 & 40	76	124
15 & 47	Bound In Rubber	15 & 41	77	125
16 & 48	Arduous Figure Training at Bondhaven	16 & 42	78	126
17 & 49	Return Visit To Fetterland	17 & 43	79	127
18	Fearful Ordeal in Restraintland	18	80	128
19 & 50	Women In Distress	19 & 44	81	129
20 & 54	Pleasure Parade No. 1	20 & 48	82	130
21 & 57	Screaming Flesh	21 & 51	86	134
22 & 58	Fury	22 & 52		
23	So Firm So Fully Packed	23	87	135
24	I'll Try Anything Twice	24		
25 & 59	Masque	25 & 53		
26	Catanis	26		
27	The Violated Wrestler	27	89	137
28	Betrayal	28		
29	Swish Bottom	29	90	138
30	Raw Dames	30	91	139
31	The Strap Returns	31	92	140
32	Dangerous Years	32	93	141
43	Columns of Agony	37	95	144
44	The Tainted Pleasure	38	96	145
45	Intense Desire	39	97	146
51	Pleasure Parade No. 4	45	85	133
52	Pleasure Parade No. 3	46	84	132
53	Pleasure Parade No. 2	47	83	131
55	Sorority Girls Stringent Initiation	49	98	147
56	Terror At The Bizarre Museum	50	99	148
60	Temptation	57		
61	Peggy's Distress On Planet Venus	58	101	150
62	Ways of Discipline	59	102	151
63	Mrs. Tyrant's Finishing School	60	103	152
64	Perilous Assignment	61	104	153
68	Bondage Correspondence		107	156
69	Woman Impelled		106	155
70	Eye Witness		108	157
71	Stud Broad		109	158
72	Queen Bee		110	159

[Opinions of Black, J, Douglas, J., and Stewart, J., are omitted.]

Smith v. California
361 U.S. 147 (1959)

MR. JUSTICE BRENNAN delivered the opinion of the Court.

Appellant, the proprietor of a bookstore, was convicted in a California Municipal Court under a Los Angeles City ordinance which makes it unlawful "for any person to have in his possession any obscene or indecent writing, [or] book . . . [i]n any place of business where . . . books . . . are sold or kept for sale." [1] The offense was defined by the Municipal Court, and by the Appellate Department of the Superior Court,[2] which affirmed the Municipal Court judgment imposing a jail sentence on appellant, as consisting solely of the possession, in the appellant's bookstore, of a certain book found upon judicial investigation to be obscene. The definition included no element of scienter—knowledge by appellant of the contents of the book—and thus the ordinance was construed as imposing a "strict" or "absolute" criminal liability.[3] The appellant made timely objection below that if the ordinance were so construed it would be in conflict with the Constitution of the United States. This contention, together with other contentions based on the Constitution,[4] was rejected, and the case comes here on appeal. 28 U.S.C. 1257 (2); 358 U.S. 926.

[1] The ordinance is § 41.01.1 of the Municipal Code of the City of Los Angeles. It provides:
"INDECENT WRITINGS, ETC.—POSSESSION PROHIBITED:
"It shall be unlawful for any person to have in his possession any obscene or indecent writing, book, pamphlet, picture, photograph, drawing, figure, motion picture film, phonograph recording, wire recording or transcription of any kind in any of the following places:
"1. In any school, school-grounds, public park or playground or in any public place, grounds, street or way within 300 yards of any school, park or playground;
"2. In any place of business where ice cream, soft drinks, candy, food, school supplies, magazines, books, pamphlets, papers, pictures or postcards are sold or kept for sale;
"3. In any toilet or restroom open to the public;
"4. In any poolroom or billiard parlor, or in any place where alcoholic liquor is sold or offered for sale to the public;
"5. In any place where phonograph records, photographs, motion pictures, or transcriptions of any kind are made, used, maintained, sold or exhibited."
[2] In this sort of proceeding, "the highest court of a State in which a decision could be had." 28 U.S.C. § 1257. Cal. Const., Art. VI, §§ 4, 4b, 5. See *Edwards* v. *California*, 314 U.S. 160, 171.
[3] See Hall, General Principals of Criminal Law, p. 280. The Appellate Department's opinion is at 161 Cal. App. 2d Supp. 860, 327 P. 2d 636. The ordinance's elimination of scienter was, in fact, a reason assigned by that court for upholding it as permissible supplementary municipal legislation against the contention that the field was occupied by California Penal Code § 311, a state-wide obscenity statute which requires scienter.
[4] These other contentions, which are made again here, are that evidence of a nature constitutionally required to be allowed to be given for the defense as to the obscene character of a book was not permitted to be introduced; that a constitutionally impermissible standard of obscenity was applied by the trier of the facts; and that the book was not in fact obscene. In the light of our determination as to the constitutional permissibility of a strict liability law under the circumstances presented by this case, we need not pass on these questions. For the purposes of discussion, we shall asume without deciding that the book was correctly adjudged below to be obscene.

Almost 30 years ago, Chief Justice Hughes declared for this Court: "It is no longer open to doubt that the liberty of the press, and of speech, is within the liberty safeguarded by the due process clause of the Fourteenth Amendment from invasion by state action. It was found impossible to conclude that this essential personal liberty of the citizen was left unprotected by the general guaranty of fundamental rights of person and property. . . ." *Near* v. *Minnesota,* 283 U.S. 697, 707. It is too familiar for citation that such has been the doctrine of this Court, in respect of these freedoms, ever since. And it also requires no elaboration that the free publication and dissemination of books and other forms of the printed word furnish very familiar applications of these constitutionally protected freedoms. It is of course no matter that the dissemination takes place under commercial auspices. See *Joseph Burstyn, Inc.* v. *Wilson,* 343 U.S. 495; *Grosjean* v. *American Press Co.,* 297 U.S. 233. Certainly a retail bookseller plays a most significant role in the process of the distribution of books.

California here imposed a strict or absolute criminal responsibility on appellant not to have obscene books in his shop. "The existence of a *mens rea* is the rule of, rather than the exception to, the principles of Anglo-American criminal jurisprudence." *Dennis* v. *United States,* 341 U.S. 494, 500.[5] Still, it is doubtless competent for the States to create strict criminal liabilities by defining criminal offenses without any element of scienter—though even where no freedom-of-expression question is involved, there is precedent in this Court that this power is not without limitations. See *Lambert* v. *California,* 355 U.S. 225. But the question here is as to the validity of this ordinance's elimination of the scienter requirement—an elimination which may tend to work a substantial restriction on the freedom of speech and of the press. Our decisions furnish examples of legal devices and doctrines, in most applications consistent with the Constitution, which cannot be applied in settings where they have the collateral effect of inhibiting the freedom of expression, by making the individual the more reluctant to exercise it. The States generally may regulate the allocation of the burden of proof in their courts, and it is a common procedural device to impose on a taxpayer the burden of proving his entitlement to exemptions from taxation, but where we conceived that this device was being applied in a manner tending to cause even a self-imposed restriction of free expression, we struck down its application. *Speiser* v. *Randall,* 357 U.S. 513. See *Near* v. *Minnesota, supra,* at 712–713. It has been stated here that the usual doctrines as to the separability of constitutional and unconstitutional applications of statutes may not apply where their effect is to leave standing a statute patently capable of many unconstitutional applications, threatening those who validly exercise their rights of free expression with the expense and inconvenience of criminal prosecution. *Thornhill* v. *Alabama,* 310 U.S. 88, 97–98. Cf. *Staub* v. *City of Baxley,* 355 U.S. 313.[6] And this Court has intimated that stricter standards of permissible statutory vagueness may be applied to a statute having a potentially inhibiting effect on speech; a man may the less be required to act at his peril here, because the free dissemination of ideas may be the

[5] See also Williams, Criminal Law—The General Part, p. 238 *et seq.*
[6] See Note, 61 Harv. L. Rev. 1208.

loser. *Winters* v. *New York,* 333 U.S. 507, 509–510, 517–518. Very much to the point here, where the question is the elimination of the mental element in an offense, is this Court's holding in *Wieman* v. *Updegraff,* 344 U.S. 183. There an oath as to past freedom from membership in subversive organizations, exacted by a State as a qualification for public employment, was held to violate the Constitution in that it made no distinction between members who had, and those who had not, known of the organization's character. The Court said of the elimination of scienter in this context: "To thus inhibit individual freedom of movement is to stifle the flow of democratic expression and controversy at one of its chief sources." *Id.,* at 191.

These principles guide us to our decision here. We have held that obscene speech and writings are not protected by the constitutional guarantees of freedom of speech and the press. *Roth* v. *United States* ,354 U.S. 476.[7] The ordinance here in question, to be sure, only imposes criminal sanctions on a bookseller if in fact there is to be found in his shop an obscene book. But our holding in *Roth* does not recognize any state power to restrict the dissemination of books which are not obscene; and we think this ordinance's strict liability feature would tend seriously to have that effect, by penalizing booksellers, even though they had not the slightest notice of the character of the books they sold. The appellee and the court below analogize this strict liability penal ordinance to familiar forms of penal statutes which dispense with any element of knowledge on the part of the person charged, food and drug legislation being a principal example. We find the analogy instructive in our examination of the question before us. The usual rationale for such statutes is that the public interest in the purity of its food is so great as to warrant the imposition of the highest standard of care on distributors—in fact an absolute standard which will not hear the distributor's plea as to the amount of care he has used. Cf. *United States* v. *Balint,* 258 U.S. 250, 252–253, 254. His ignorance of the character of the food is irrelevant. There is no specific constitutional inhibition against making the distributors of food the strictest censors of their merchandise, but the constitutional guarantees of the freedom of speech and of the press stand in the way of imposing a similar requirement on the bookseller. By dispensing with any requirement of knowledge of the contents of the book on the part of the seller, the ordinance tends to impose a severe limitation on the public's access to constitutionally protected matter. For if the bookseller is criminally liable without knowledge of the contents, and the ordinance fulfills its purpose,[8] he will tend to restrict the books he sells to those he has inspected; and thus the State will have imposed a restriction upon the distribution of constitutionally protected as well as obscene literature. It has been well observed of a statute construed as dispensing with any requirement of scienter that:

[7] In the *Roth* opinion there was also decided *Alberts* v. *California,* which dealt with the power of the States in this area.

[8] The effectiveness of absolute criminal liability laws in promoting caution has been subjected to criticism. See Hall, General Principles of Criminal Law, pp. 300–301. See generally Williams, Criminal Law—The General Part, pp. 267–274; Sayre, Public Welfare Offenses, 33 Col. L. Rev. 55; Mueller, On Common Law Mens Rea, 42 Minn. L. Rev. 1043; *Morissette* v. *United States,* 342 U.S. 246.

"Every bookseller would be placed under an obligation to make himself aware of the contents of every book in his shop. It would be altogether unreasonable to demand so near an approach to omniscience." [9] *The King v. Ewart,* 25 N.Z.L.R. 709, 729 (C.A.). And the bookseller's burden would become the public's burden, for by restricting him the public's access to reading matter would be restricted. If the contents of bookshops and periodical stands were restricted to material of which their proprietors had made an inspection, they might be depleted indeed. The bookseller's limitation in the amount of reading material with which he could familiarize himself, and his timidity in the face of his absolute criminal liability, thus would tend to restrict the public's access to forms of the printed word which the State could not constitutionally suppress directly. The bookseller's self-censorship, compelled by the State, would be a censorship affecting the whole public, hardly less virulent for being privately administered. Through it, the distribution of all books, both obscene and not obscene, would be impeded.

It is argued that unless the scienter requirement is dispensed with, regulation of the distribution of obscene material will be ineffective, as booksellers will falsely disclaim knowledge of their books' contents or falsely deny reason to suspect their obscenity. We might observe that it has been some time now since the law viewed itself as impotent to explore the actual state of a man's mind. See Pound, The Role of the Will in Law, 68 Harv. L. Rev. 1. Cf. *American Communications Assn.* v. *Douds,* 339 U.S. 382, 411. Eyewitness testimony of a bookseller's perusal of a book hardly need be a necessary element in proving his awareness of its contents. The circumstances may warrant the inference that he was aware of what a book contained, despite his denial.

We need not and most definitely do not pass today on what sort of mental element is requisite to a constitutionally permissible prosecution of a bookseller for carrying an obscene book in stock; whether honest mistake as to whether its contents in fact constituted obscenity need be an excuse; whether there might be circumstances under which the State constitutionally might require that a bookseller investigate further, or might put on him the burden of explaining why he did not, and what such circumstances might be. Doubtless any form of criminal obscenity statute applicable to a bookseller will induce some tendency to self-censorship and have some inhibitory effect on the dissemination of material not obscene, but we consider today only one which goes to the extent of eliminating all mental elements from the crime.

We have said: "The fundamental freedoms of speech and press have contributed greatly to the development and well-being of our free society and are indispensable to its continued growth. Ceaseless vigilance is the

---

[9] Common-law prosecutions for the dissemination of obscene matter strictly adhered to the requirement of scienter. See the discussion in *Attorney General* v. *Simpson,* 93 Irish L. T. 33, 37, 38 (Dist. Ct.). Cf. Obscene Publications Act, 1959, 7 & 8 Eliz. 2, c. 66, § 2 (5); American Law Institute Model Penal Code § 207.10 (7) (Tentative Draft No. 6, May 1957), and Comments, pp. 49–51.

The general California obscenity statute, Penal Code § 311, requires scienter, see note 3, and was of course sustained by us in *Roth* v. *United States, supra.* See note 7.

watchword to prevent their erosion by Congress or by the States. The door barring federal and state intrusion into this area cannot be left ajar; it must be kept tightly closed and opened only the slightest crack necessary to prevent encroachment upon more important interests." *Roth* v. *United States, supra,* at 488.[10] This ordinance opens that door too far. The existence of the State's power to prevent the distribution of obscene matter does not mean that there can be no constitutional barrier to any form of practical exercise of that power. Cf. *Dean Milk Co.* v. *City of Madison,* 340 U.S. 349. It is plain to us that the ordinance in question, though aimed at obscene matter, has such a tendency to inhibit constitutionally protected expression that it cannot stand under the Constitution.

Reversed.

[Opinions of Frankfurter, J., Douglas, J., Black, J., and Harlan, J., are omitted.]

---

[10] We emphasized in *Roth*, at p. 484, that there is a "limited area" where such other interests prevail, and we listed representative decisions in note 14 at that page.

Table of Cases Cited

Topical Index